Fertile Crossroads

New Directions in Anthropological Archaeology

Series Editor: Thomas E. Levy, University of California, San Diego

Editorial Board
Guillermo Algaze University of California, San Diego
Geoffrey E. Braswell University of California, San Diego
Paul S. Goldstein University of California, San Diego
Joyce Marcus University of Michigan
Charles Stanish Institute for the Advanced Study of Culture and the Environment, University of South Florida

This series focuses on new theory driven approaches to anthropological archaeology around the world. Scholars who contribute to the series come from diverse theoretical backgrounds that encompass the full range of theory—from processual to post-processual approaches. An underlying unifying theme is the exploration of how both natural and/or cultural environments influence the evolution, growth and collapse of human societies. To achieve these goals, contributions also highlight the application of new approaches in data acquisition, curation, analyses and dissemination.

Published:

Assembling the Village in Medieval Bambuk
An Archaeology of Interaction at Diouboye, Senegal
Cameron Gokee

Comparative Perspectives on Past Colonisation, Maritime Interaction and Cultural Integration
Edited by Lene Melheim, H.kon Glørstad and Zanette Tsigaridas Glørstad

Framing Archaeology in the Near East
The Application of Social Theory to Fieldwork
Edited by Ianir Milevski and Thomas E. Levy

Mediterranean Resilience
Collapse and Adaptation in Antique Maritime Societies
Edited by Assaf Yasur-Landau, Gil Gambash and Thomas E. Levy

Peripheral Concerns
Urban Development in the Bronze Age Southern Levant
Susan Cohen

Preserving Cultural Heritage in the Digital Age
Sending Out an S.O.S.
Edited by Nicola Lercari, Willeke Wendrich, Benjamin W. Porter, Margie M. Burton, and Thomas E. Levy

Profane Landscapes, Sacred Spaces
Edited by Miroslav Bárta and Jiř. Janák

Searching for Structure in Pottery Analysis
Applying Multiple Scales and Instruments to Production
Edited by Alan F. Greene and Charles W. Hartley

Seaways to Complexity
A Study of Sociopolitical Organisation Along the Coast of Northwestern Scandinavia in the Late Neolithic and Early Bronze Age
Knut Ivar Austvoll

Fertile Crossroads

Elites and Exchange in the Southern Levant's Early Iron Age

Sarah Malena

SHEFFIELD UK   BRISTOL CT

Published by Equinox Publishing Ltd.
UK: Office 415, The Workstation, 15 Paternoster Row, Sheffield, South Yorkshire S1 2BX
USA: ISD, 70 Enterprise Drive, Bristol, CT 06010

www.equinoxpub.com

First published 2025

© Sarah Malena 2025

All rights reserved. No part of this publication may be reproduced or transmitted in any form or by any means, electronic or mechanical, including photocopying, recording or any information storage or retrieval system, without prior permission in writing from the publishers.

British Library Cataloguing-in-Publication Data

A catalogue record for this book is available from the British Library.

ISBN-13 978 1 80050 474 5 (hardback)
         978 1 80050 475 2 (ePDF)
         978 1 80050 541 4 (ePub)

Library of Congress Cataloging-in-Publication Data

Names: Malena, Sarah, author.
Title: Fertile crossroads : elites and exchange in the Southern Levant's early Iron Age / Sarah Malena.
Description: Bristol, CT : Equinox Publishing Ltd., 2025. | Series: New directions in anthropological archaeology / series editor, Thomas E. Levy, University of California, San Diego | Includes bibliographical references and index. | Summary: "Fertile Crossroads examines how, despite the lack of large-scale institutional support throughout the ancient world, small-scale leaders persisted in long-distance interactions and established the foundations for Iron Age polities"-- Provided by publisher.
Identifiers: LCCN 2023056636 (print) | LCCN 2023056637 (ebook) | ISBN 9781800504745 (hardback) | ISBN 9781800504752 (pdf) | ISBN 9781800505414 (epub)
Subjects: LCSH: Iron age--Middle East. | Elite (Social sciences)--Middle East. | Exchange--Middle East--History. | Middle East--Commerce--History.
Classification: LCC GN780.32.M4 M35 2024 (print) | LCC GN780.32.M4 (ebook) | DDC 939.4/02--dc23/eng/20240323
LC record available at https://lccn.loc.gov/2023056636
LC ebook record available at https://lccn.loc.gov/2023056637

Printed and bound by CPI Group (UK) Ltd, Croydon, CR0 4YY
Typeset by S.J.I. Services, New Delhi, India

This work is dedicated to my mother, Audrey, who provided an exceptional model and whose compassion and encouragement knew no limits.

Contents

	Acknowledgments	ix
	List of Abbreviations	xi
	List of Figures and Tables	xiii
1	Introduction	1
2	Interactions with the Philistines in 1 & 2 Samuel	25
3	Solomon's Interactions and Economic Policies	66
4	The Special Case of Jerusalem – A Discussion	120
5	Epigraphic Evidence Relating to Exchange	135
6	Nonlocal Ceramics in the Iron I–IIA Transition	153
7	Synthesis and Conclusions	193
	Bibliography	210
	Index of Subjects	240
	Index Locorum	254

Acknowledgments

Many thanks to Tom Levy, editor of this series, along with Janet Joyce and other members of Equinox Publishing, for enthusiastically accepting this work for publication and guiding it to completion. I'd like to acknowledge Bloomsbury Press as well, who gave permission for me to reproduce my chapter 'Influential Inscriptions' from the volume *Scribes and Scribalism*, edited by Mark Leuchter (2020). Mark also offered advice and encouragement, as did Seth Sanders, as I was working on the inscriptions portion of this study. Participants in various conference sessions, from regional to international meetings, also influenced important refinements of my arguments. Comments from anonymous readers on this manuscript and related writing provided additional supportive and helpful feedback that has improved this work considerably. The inevitable presence of errors or imperfections are, of course, my own contribution.

Faculty and friends from the graduate programs in History and Judaic Studies at the University of California, San Diego deserve special acknowledgment and appreciation. The foundation for this book is my doctoral dissertation, which was co-supervised by Tom Levy and Bill Propp. Their influence as teachers and mentors is evident throughout this work. Perhaps most importantly though, both Bill and Tom, from distinct perspectives, challenged me to find alternative paths through well-trodden territory. This encouragement proved critical, as it enabled creative problem solving that led me to alternative approaches to thinking about interactions in this period. Other committee members included David Noel Freedman (ז״ל), Richard Elliott Friedman, David Goodblatt (ז״ל), and Patrick Patterson. The collective wisdom of these scholars was an invaluable resource, and their individual approaches each contributed important perspectives that bettered my analysis. The History and Judaic Studies programs provided financial support for travel, research, and writing, for which I remain grateful. In addition, the camaraderie and lively intellectual exchange with my fellow graduate students at UCSD and excavation staff and volunteers in the Faynan were intensely enriching. In sum, the interdisciplinary environment that facilitated textual study, historical debates, and fieldwork absolutely shaped the way I conceive of doing my work. Guidance from this faculty and support from these communities persist despite years gone by.

It is with great appreciation that I also acknowledge colleagues at my current institution, St. Mary's College of Maryland, especially my fellow faculty in the History department and those in other departments who devoted precious time to read portions of my work while I was developing some of the ideas. The college has been generous with funding requests, course releases, and other resources that have helped this book reach completion, and I am very grateful for that support. This project relied heavily on cooperative and patient library staff, especially Brenda Rogers and Kat Ryner, who ably tracked down and managed my many requests. For that they also deserve special thanks.

While the foregoing support for this work was essential to its creation and completion as a scholarly product, my friends and family deserve mention for their personal support and patience. The St. Mary's Pizza Crew reliably provides the best nourishment (for stomach and soul) and warmest community – thank you for welcoming me and my family into your fold, and for making sure work was not my only occupation. Friends from Wells Road similarly provided the finest sustenance and company during earlier stages of this work. I have deep gratitude for my dear friend and sharp colleague Shawna Dolansky, who is an unwavering support and excellent influence, for reminding me that my ideas should be heard by others. Finally, thank you to my closest family – my dad, Daryl, my boys, Nathan and Evan, and Don – who have endured with very few complaints while I spent many hours writing and revising this work. Their love and optimism buoy me always.

List of Abbreviations

AB	Anchor Bible
ABD	*Anchor Bible Dictionary*, David Noel Freedman, ed.
AJA	*American Journal of Archaeology*
AOAT	Alter Orient und Altes Testament
BA	*Biblical Archaeologist*
BAAL	*Bulletin d'Archéologie et d'Architecture Libanaises*
BAR	*Biblical Archaeology Review*
BASOR	*Bulletin of the American Schools of Oriental Research*
BDB	*Hebrew and English Lexicon of the Old Testament*, Brown, Driver, and Briggs
BHS	Biblia Hebraica Stuttgartensia
BJPES	*Bulletin of the Jewish Palestine Exploration Society*
BJS	Brown Judaic Studies Series
BoR	Cypro-Phoenician Black-on-Red pottery
BR	*Bible Review*
BZAW	Beihefte zur Zeitschrift für die alttestamentliche Wissenschaft
CA	*Current Anthropology*
CBR	*Currents in Biblical Research*
CBQ	*Catholic Biblical Quarterly*
CHANE	Culture and History of the Ancient Near East
DH	Deuteronomistic History
Dtr	Deuteronomistic Historian(s) (or editors/redactors)
E&L	*Egypt and the Levant*
EA	El Amarna Correspondence
ELRAP	Edom Lowlands Regional Archaeological Project
ErIsr	*Eretz-Israel*
FAT	Forschungen zum Alten Testament
HALOT	*The Hebrew and Aramaic Lexicon of the Old Testament*, Koehler and Baumgartner
HSM	Harvard Semitic Monographs
HTR	*The Harvard Theological Review*
IEJ	Israel Exploration Journal
JANES	Journal for Ancient Near Eastern Studies
JAOS	Journal of the American Oriental Society
JAS	Journal of Archaeological Science
JBL	Journal of Biblical Literature
JEA	Journal of Egyptian Archaeology
JESHO	Journal of the Economic and Social History of the Orient
JHS	Journal of Hebrew Scriptures

JJAR	Jerusalem Journal of Archaeology
JMA	Journal of Mediterranean Archaeology
JNES	Journal of Near Eastern Studies
JPOS	Journal of the Palestine Oriental Society
JQR	Jewish Quarterly Review
JSOT	Journal for the Study of the Old Testament
JSOTSup	Journal for the Study of the Old Testament Supplemental Series
JSS	Journal of Semitic Studies
KEN	Khirbat en-Nahas
Kh.	Khirbet/Khirbat
LBA	Late Bronze Age
LC	Low Chronology
LXX	Septuagint
MT	Masoretic Text
NEA	Near Eastern Archaeology
NEAEHL	*The New Encyclopedia of Archaeological Excavations in the Holy Land*, Ephraim Stern, ed.
OBO	Orbis biblicus et orientalis
OJA	Oxford Journal of Archaeology
OLA	Orientalia lovaniensia analecta
PEQ	Palestine Exploration Quarterly
PN	Personal Name
PNAS	Proceedings of the National Academy of Sciences
QPW	Qurayyah Painted Ware
RINAP	The Royal Inscriptions of the Neo-Assyrian Period
SAHL	Studies in the Archaeology and History of the Levant
SAOC	Studies in Ancient Oriental Civilization
SBLDS	Society of Biblical Literature Dissertation Series
SHAJ	Studies in the History and Archaeology of Jordan
SHANE	Studies in the History of the Ancient Near East
SHCANE	Studies in the History and Culture of the Ancient Near East
SJOT	Scandinavian Journal of the Old Testament
SWBA	Social World of Biblical Antiquity
T.	Tel/l
TA	Tel Aviv
TIP	Third Intermediate Period (Egypt)
TSSI	Textbook of Syrian Semitic Inscriptions
UF	Ugarit-Forschungen
VT	Vetus Testamentum
VTSup	Supplements to Vetus Testamentum
ZAW	Zeitschrift für die alttestamentliche Wissenschaft
ZDPV	Zeitschrift des deutschen Palästina-Vereins

List of Figures and Tables

Figures

1.1:	Traditional chronology of Israel's first kings, based on the biblical texts.	8
2.1:	Overview of sites related to the Ark Narrative and Eben-ezer conflict.	28
2.2:	Possible routes related to the Ark Narrative and Eben-ezer conflict. Routes based on reconstructions in Dorsey, *The Roads and Highways of Ancient Israel* (Baltimore: Johns Hopkins University Press, 1991). Map: Google Earth, © 2020.	29
2.3:	Potential routes related to Michmash Pass and known areas of metallurgical activity. Map: Google Earth, © 2020.	37
2.4:	Potential interaction zones and routes related to Saul's interactions. Map: Google Earth, © 2020.	40
2.5:	Overview of sites related to David's interactions. Map: Google Earth, © 2020.	42
2.6:	Overview of interactions with Philistines, and key sites in the region. Map: Google Earth, © 2020.	54
3.1:	Places related to interregional interactions in 1 Kings 3–11. Map: Google Earth, © 2020.	70
3.2:	Map of administrative districts. Borders based on Rainey and Notley, *The Sacred Bridge* (Jerusalem: Carta, 2006), 175. Map: Google Earth, © 2020.	96
3.3:	Solomon's fortifications, as described in 1 Kings 9:15–18. Map: Google Earth, © 2020.	102
5.1:	Find locations of late 11th–10th century BCE inscriptions. Map: Google Earth, © 2020.	138
6.1:	Lands of origin of ceramic imports. Map: Google Earth, © 2020.	157
6.2:	QPW full range of distribution. Map: Google Earth, © 2020.	162
6.3:	QPW in southern Levantine sites. Map: Google Earth, © 2020.	164
6.4:	BoR samples of southern Levant and Cypriot origins. Map: Google Earth, © 2020.	167
6.5:	Full distribution map of Cypriot wares (map symbols: white circle = WP ware; dark red circle = Bichrome; bright red = BoR). Map: Google Earth, © 2020.	169
6.6:	Cypriot imports, northern distribution. Map: Google Earth, © 2020 (Map symbols: white circle = WP ware; dark red circle = Bichrome; bright red = BoR).	171
6.7:	Cypriot imports, southern distribution. Map: Google Earth, © 2020 (Map symbols: white circle = WP ware; dark red circle = Bichrome; bright red = BoR).	173

| 6.8: | Origins of Aegean wares and their distribution in the Levant. Map: Google Earth, © 2020. | 175 |
| 6.9: | Aegean imports in southern Levantine sites. Map: Google Earth, © 2020. | 176 |

Tables

1.1:	Chronological framework.	7
5.1:	Southern Levantine inscriptions from the Iron I–IIA transition.	137
6.1:	Find locations of Qurayyah Painted Ware.	163
6.2:	Distances from Qurayyah.	163
6.3:	Sites with Cypriot imports.	168
6.4:	Cypriot imports near rivers.	170
6.5:	Aegean Imports.	177

Introduction

My initial venture into the study of early Iron Age interactions developed out of a curiosity about the biblical claims of King Solomon's vast trade operations. Even though much of the ancient presentations of Solomon were unmistakably the stuff of legend, I was intrigued about what prompted such traditions. From the annalistic accounts of his reign in Kings, to the veiled authorial figure in Qohelet, to the luxurious and sensual imagery in the Song of Songs, there was something essential between trade and an idea of Solomon. But as recently as the beginning of our current century, the evidence of long-distance trade in the approximate time of the biblical king's reign, the 10th century BCE, was virtually non-existent. Very occasional discoveries were known, but they were anomalies. The conventional wisdom about long-distance interactions asserted that following the collapse of the Late Bronze Age trade systems, Iron Age peoples were severed from the transportation and exchange networks that once connected the Aegean, Anatolian, Mesopotamian, Levantine, Egyptian, and Arabian worlds. According to that understanding, and the available evidence, far-reaching trade enterprises would not emerge again until the Phoenicians and the Greeks colonized the Mediterranean in the 9th and 8th centuries. Such a reconstruction proposed that there was a historically 'dark' period of relative isolation for the initial two to three centuries of the Iron Age. As a result, an investigation of trade appeared misplaced and anachronistic.

Despite an epistemologically bleak situation, I remained interested in the notion of long-distance relations during the early Iron Age. The suddenness proposed for the end and new beginnings of trade relations did not fit well with the Mediterranean's cultural traditions of the period, as a time of movement and change (i.e., migration traditions like the Trojan War or the Exodus), or with an intuitive understanding that societal changes take time. Rather than focus on trade and commerce, I turned my attention to the study of interactions and exchange during the early Iron Age as the basis of my doctoral dissertation, which is the foundation for this book. In that research, I found exchange apparent in material culture, such as luxury goods and prestige items, as well as more mundane objects, and in less obvious places, such as scribal activity and emulation habits. The evidence I found coordinated with conflict zones near roads and highways that were critical for the movement of traded goods, as well as with areas with important resources, and I argued that local elites, many of whom we cannot identify by name, must have been in competition over smaller-scale interactions of the period. The completion of my dissertation coincided with a critical development in this topic, a veritable boom in archaeological discoveries related to interregional interactions in the Iron I to IIA transition period, roughly the late 11th to early 9th centuries BCE. Today, evidence of interregional exchange is not only available but abundant, and this present volume seeks to test my proposals, which anticipated the positive evidence of exchange, with our newly acquired knowledge about the era. I feel confident that the basic arguments not only hold up but are confirmed and strengthened by the evidence that is available to us today.

Understanding the Southern Levant's Ancient Past

The southern Levant's transition from the Iron I to the Iron IIA periods has been one of the more contentious subjects among historians and archaeologists who study this region. The primary reasons for this scholarly debate stem from interconnected issues related to how we know what we know. Despite the flood of new evidence and scholarly exchange about the period, there are still very few epigraphic sources; archaeology-based chronologies continue to undergo thorough reevaluation; and the most extensive written source describing the period remains the Hebrew Bible, a complex source with widely varying interpretations regarding its historical value. Additionally, reconstructions from these different types of evidence (i.e., epigraphic, literary, and archaeological) often do not agree. The discrepancy between these resources is most pronounced in the depiction of early polities and their economic interactions. Thus, this work must begin with an orientation to the nature of the evidence, the debates, and the disciplines and theoretical models that have set the tone for investigations.

Ancient Israel and its neighboring regions, discussed here as the eastern Mediterranean and southern Levant, have long captured the interest of scholars and explorers. Those investigators have rarely been satisfied with using the biblical text as their sole resource. Thus, the region has been thoroughly examined by geographers, historians, ethnographers, archaeologists, and others. These ventures formed the basis of historical and archaeological research into the region, commonly discussed as the Holy Land in earlier scholarship. As our disciplinary knowledge and methods have grown, so has their sophistication and specialization, which means that the project I outline below requires engagement across various disciplines in order to address our available evidence and previous proposals. Each type of evidence will be dealt with according to the standards of the appropriate disciplines.[1] And while this project is, above all, historical and archaeological in its orientation and goals, it also engages with the work of literary scholars, epigraphers, anthropologists, geographers, and regional specialists.[2] With each of these fields come respective analytical methods and scholarly debates that have influenced my approach. The starting point, partial setting, and a large portion of evidence for this project are biblical. Thus, an influential field for this work is biblical criticism, especially historical biblical criticism, which seeks to understand the biblical writings according to the historical and cultural circumstances that were most influential in their creation.

Biblical Histories and Biblical Criticism

Critiques of the traditional approach to biblical scholarship (and by extension biblical archaeology) started gaining ground in the 1970s. J. Van Seters's *Abraham in History and Tradition* and T. Thompson's *The Historicity of the Patriarchal Narratives* call into question the conventional stance that the Bible's patriarchal stories were related to the historical and archaeological periods that they describe.[3] Once the patriarchal narratives were successfully questioned, critiques of the exodus and settlement narratives followed. By the 1990s, reevaluation of the historicity of the early monarchy (in biblical terms the careers of Saul, David, and Solomon) became the focus. Within this context, a core of scholars more aggressively challenged the position that the biblical texts could provide evidence for any historical inquiry.[4] This group, and others who followed in these views, became known as biblical minimalists.

The impact of these critiques cannot be overstated for those who use a historical critical approach when examining the Deuteronomistic History (DH), the main collection of biblical material that will be of concern in Chapters Two and Three. The DH is made up of the biblical books Deuteronomy, Joshua, Judges, 1 and 2 Samuel, and 1 and 2 Kings, and was compiled and composed just before and after the Neo-Babylonian conquest of Judah and Jerusalem in the 6th century BCE.[5] Basic principles of working with the DH are the idea that the ancient compliers drew from extensive source material and that source criticism can identify phases of composition in the texts. Another important attribute of this collection is that a governing principle in its composition and structure is, fundamentally, historical. The minimalist challenge called more attention to the fact that the DH filters its history through the biases of its period of compilation and the concerns of its authors. In other words, it may say much more about the 6th century than any other periods it describes.[6] An inevitable consequence of this shift in scholarly thought has been a marginalization of thinking historically about earlier periods of the Iron Age. Historians are faced with an existential question: if the DH cannot provide source material about earlier periods, such as the 11th and 10th centuries, and extrabiblical, historical sources are few, how can one do history?

Although some critics intended to do away with histories of ancient Israel altogether, the more lasting result of the minimalist challenge has strengthened and diversified historical approaches to biblical scholarship and to the region. In general, the debates forced the reevaluation of methods and assumptions (both modern and ancient). New perspectives stimulated scholarship, as alternatives to the traditional historical reconstructions competed with defenders of more conventional histories.[7] Notably, many scholars sought support for their approaches in the theoretical foundations of historians in other specialties and scholars in closely related fields. Relevant for the topics under examination here is the renewed attention to memory studies and its application to the material in the Deuteronomistic History (DH).[8] While the present study is not grounded in the theory of collective memory, one inevitably encounters the DH's relationship to memory creation in its efforts to curate a history. Frequent reminders, such as 'to this day' (e.g., 1 Kgs 8:8), mention of monuments or ruins (e.g., 1 Sam 7:12–17), social practices (e.g., 1 Kgs 3:2), and folk sayings (e.g., 1 Sam 18:7), are as critical to our understanding of the narrative's composition as the written or annalistic sources (e.g., 1 Kgs 11:41) that source-critical scholarship traditionally focuses on. The examination in Chapters Two and Three proceeds with the premises that the text has the potential to be informative about various periods – logically more often about later eras – and that all possibilities should be scrutinized. It is in the spirit of more critical and creative inquiry that I attempt to examine the biblical history of the late 11th and 10th centuries.

The Contentious 10th Century

For decades, biblical Israel's 10th century seemed to be synonymous with Israel's historical and archaeological past. Y. Yadin's declarations that he had found physical evidence of Solomon's building projects in the archaeological remains of Hazor, Megiddo, and Gezer (1 Kings 9:15) were at the heart of this consensus view until I. Finkelstein proposed a radical shift in his understanding of the stratigraphy at major sites in the region.[9] The proposal sparked intense debate and reevaluation, not only of 'Solomonic' levels and architecture but also of the entire stratigraphy of excavations whose chronologies were based on parallels to material culture at influential sites, most critically Megiddo, which in effect called into question all of Israel's archaeological chronologies. The consequences have reached far beyond Israel's excavations. Sites and chronologies throughout the Levant and into the eastern Mediterranean are also being revisited as a result.

For the chronology of the southern Levant, scholars have traditionally relied on stratigraphy, pottery seriation, and other parallels (e.g., architectural styles) to establish relative chronologies. Links to historical and narrative texts, frequently those of the DH, were commonly invoked to assign absolute dates to archaeological strata and significant features. Today's archaeologists have added radiocarbon dating to their chronometric techniques. In theory, using multiple methods should provide more confidence in arriving at results; however, Finkelstein's challenge for the 10th century caused a debate and reevaluation of all approaches.

The debates are able to be so extensive because the agreed-upon chronological anchors for the region's earlier stages of the Iron Age are separated by 400 years.[10] Egypt's administrative presence, which began in the Late Bronze Age and continued into the Iron I, is well-attested. At a number of sites, there are good associations between Egypt's 20th Dynasty and key archaeological strata, setting one anchor in the mid-12th century. The earliest, undisputed anchor for the Iron II is at the end of the 8th century, when Assyrian destruction layers and occupation are evident across the landscape. In between these periods, there are good candidates for additional anchors that *could* have identifiable, archaeological correlates – Shoshenq's campaign in the late 10th century or 9th century activity by the Omrides and Arameans – but evidence thought to be related to these events has also been disputed.

During this 400-year span, there was little direct, external influence on the region, which contributed in part to relatively stable ceramic traditions, across centuries where historians and historical archaeologists anticipated great change based primarily on the biblical history, assuming, for example, that such dynamic events as the advent of the Davidic monarchy or the establishment of the northern kingdom of Israel would be evident in material culture. What has been remembered in biblical tradition as a period of radical political and cultural change did not produce as dramatic an effect on archaeological remains, at least as they are now interpreted by more cautious researchers.[11] Finkelstein's challenge targeted this span's lack of external chronological anchors, affecting our understanding of the 11th, 10th, and 9th centuries, where change in material culture is more subtle and region-specific.

Finkelstein turned his attention to problems he had observed in various Iron I and early Iron II sites and proposed an across-the-board shift in absolute chronology, lowering dates of strata by a century across the region. The most controversial result of this Low Chronology (LC) was the reassignment of so-called 'Solomonic' architecture and urban remains to the 9th century, leaving to the 10th century no monumental constructions or urban settlements. The biblical history of a great Davidic and Solomonic state, it was determined, could not be reconciled with this new scheme.[12] The initial challenge was published in 1996 and has been revised frequently since then.[13] The main foundations of his arguments over the years have been Philistine pottery, parallels to Omride sites, radiocarbon debates, and assigning destruction layers to historical campaigns. A number of the supporting claims have shifted considerably as a result of responses to his arguments, but the overall critique and the spirit of radical reassessment have had a lasting effect.[14]

More recently, Finkelstein's work has ventured into historical reconstruction, focusing on the biblical histories of Saul, the Benjaminite territory, and the northern kingdom.[15] Attention to these aspects of the Iron I–IIA histories is important due to the biblical bias against rivals to the Davidic line and centralized worship in Jerusalem, but Finkelstein's approach to biblical material is inconsistent with his critiques of other scholars. In his book, *The Forgotten Kingdom*, Finkelstein's willingness to rely on biblical sources describing the north (e.g., "even vague memories" are trustworthy resources for the historian) contradicts his assessments of other scholars' methods, of other portions of the biblical narratives, and of the same biblical passages for other historical applications.[16] Finkelstein's introduction to his book lays bare what is at the heart of the bias: the traditional attention to Jerusalem, Judah, and the Davidic history have shortchanged the place of the north in historical reconstructions.[17] The critique is warranted and continues to be relevant, but Finkelstein's inconsistency ventures into problematic historical method and threatens to undermine his larger research agenda.

Shifting Perspective: The Transition from Iron I to Iron II

What was most important about Finkelstein's 1996 proposal was the impetus it provided to separate archaeological chronologies and interpretations from the biblical narratives. Finkelstein was right that there were critical, logical problems in the system that required a ruthless reassessment of assumptions and foundations.[18] His challenge has pushed archaeologists and historians to scrutinize their views of the entire region, with a positive effect. Among the most important changes have been the modifications made to the conventional dates for the Iron IIA period (1000–925), which were derived from assumptions based on the biblical United Monarchy. Radiocarbon dating has both tempered the more extreme aspects of Finkelstein's proposed LC, and contributed to a correction of the traditional view. A. Mazar's response, a Modified Conventional Chronology (MCC), attempts to divorce the periodization from the problematic biblical chronology. According to this system, the Iron IIA runs from ca. 980–ca. 830.[19]

Since radiocarbon dating has not been able to settle the debates within this period, Z. Herzog and L. Singer-Avitz have focused on ceramic analysis, proposing subdivisions of the Iron IIA based on their comparisons of assemblages in the south and the north.[20] Reference to early Iron IIA and late Iron IIA has become standard, following their arguments, and others have suggested additional subdivisions based on ceramic analyses of more recent excavations and continued discussion of regional variations.[21] Therefore, the old standard of ceramic analysis, with contributing information from radiocarbon dating, provides structure to the re-conceptualization of the end of the Iron I and divisions within the Iron IIA periods.

The intense scrutiny resulting from the chronology debates has turned attention to the transitions between periods, especially between the Iron I and IIA.[22] Rather than take for granted the biblical storyline of David's sweeping conquests and Solomon's organization, critical reevaluation has intensified on questions of the emergence of the region's polities, kingdoms known from later Iron Age records (biblical and extrabiblical). It is becoming clearer that the transition was not as swift nor as simple as traditional histories portrayed it. Following the biblical narrative, the shift was once thought to have resulted from David's campaigns across the land, ca. 1000 BCE. Careful evaluation of sites throughout the region shows that a transition between the Iron I and II took various forms. At some sites, there is evidence of violent destruction that marks the end of Iron I material culture (e.g., at Tell Qasile X, Yoqneam XVII, Tell Keisan 9, Megiddo VIA, Tel Hadar V, and Khirbet Qeiyafa).[23] Seemingly in contradiction, other sites, most notably Khirbat en-Nahas and Timna, show evidence of local growth and industry during the transition, suggesting a different type of change. Still other sites, however, do not have evidence of a punctuated shift to the Iron IIA (e.g., Tyre, Tell Abu Hawam, Tel Reḥov). At these sites, there may be a blend of late Iron I and early Iron II ceramic assemblages.

Without a dramatic event to separate the two phases, it can be difficult to fix a date for the transition. Where there was continuity of settlement, there is less evidence of the transition. Residents who lived in more peaceful locations cleaned and reused their spaces, rather than covering over and rebuilding above debris layers where there had been destruction. This process minimized the amount of remains for archaeologists to find, potentially skewing chronologies because only the later phases are more visible.[24] More recent excavations have succeeded in revealing more nuance in the ceramic repertoire, which is also calling attention to variations in periodization based on regional diversity – not simply between 'Israelite' and 'Philistine,' but a more discrete geographic difference that does not yet have an agreed-upon terminology.[25] The result has the potential to have a profound impact on our archaeological and historical understanding. There was both punctuated and gradual change between the Iron I and II periods, and there was considerable variation both between and within broader geographic regions (e.g., Shephelah, highland, coast, etc.). The changes began as early as the late 11th century and stretched across the 10th century. For those familiar with the biblical and traditional histories of the region, this reconstruction is a contradiction of the 'United Monarchy.' What it also reveals, however, is a diversity that is exciting for our understanding of how cultural and political identities developed in what must be considered an important formative time for the southern Levant.

Chronology in This Study

Because the various studies presented in this book stem from fully distinct types of evidence, a chronological scheme based strictly on either archaeological or textual evidence is impractical. Therefore, the discussions are oriented according to the very general scheme presented in Table 1.1.[26] This framework incorporates not just the 10th century, but also material related to the late 11th century and early 9th century. The span aligns well with the possibilities for an Iron I–IIA transition throughout the region, which also acknowledges that changes in long-distance interactions would not have been sudden or limited to the 10th century. A longer time frame allows for a better understanding of how interregional interactions developed in a distinctly Iron Age context. A consequence of a generous chronological scope is that if certain contexts are determined to be later or earlier than currently understood (e.g., revisions to the absolute dating of inscriptions or imports[27]), the analysis can be reevaluated in respect to the adjacent periods while also remaining relevant to our understanding of how long-distance interactions related to Iron Age power structures.

Table 1.1: Chronological framework.

Archaeological Phase	Absolute Dates
End of Iron I	Late 11th–early 10th centuries BCE
Iron I–IIA transition	Beginning in the late 11th/early 10th centuries BCE, ending in the second half of the 10th century BCE
Early Iron IIA	Second half of the 10th century BCE
Late Iron IIA	Most of the 9th century BCE

The chronological heart of this project is, nevertheless, the 10th century BCE, in part because of its reputed interregional trade in the biblical histories.[28] This period is also of interest, however, because, even without the biblical bias, the 10th century was a time of transformation and intensification. Archaeological periodization situates the shift from the Iron Age I to the Iron II in the middle of the century because of transitions evident in material culture.[29] Settlement patterns also reveal that this era experienced significant change in organization.[30] Egypt renewed campaigns into the Levant towards the end of the century, and Levantine polities caught the interest of the expanding Neo-Assyrian state soon after, by the mid-9th century. This study attempts to show that these contacts were preceded by interaction from local to interregional levels for some time. The relevant evidence requires that the limits for this study be extended from the late 11th to the end of the 10th and, in some cases, beginning of the 9th centuries.

Biblical Chronology and the 10th Century

The biblical figures most important for this study, Saul, David, and Solomon, cannot be assigned precise regnal years or life spans. Traditional reckoning results in the rough timeline represented in Figure 1.1. We can be sure that historical figures would not conform to such convenient schemes. The biblical historians, the exilic redactor of the DH especially, modified (or created) timelines of the early monarchs to fit greater historiographic needs.[31] The 40-year reigns of David and Solomon are universally accepted by critical scholars as symbolic. Forty years characterizes one generation, and while each individual is remembered to be personally flawed, each man's reign is symbolic of critical advancements in the people's relationship to the deity and, by extension, their stability in the region: David receives YHWH's promise of an eternal dynasty, and Solomon (although provoking an amendment to the Davidic covenant) honors the deity with a monumental temple and the dedication of a permanent earthly residence.[32] The generation-length reigns are a way of communicating stability, completeness, and otherwise positive things for the people and land during these eras. The years should not be used to estimate historical reigns for these figures.

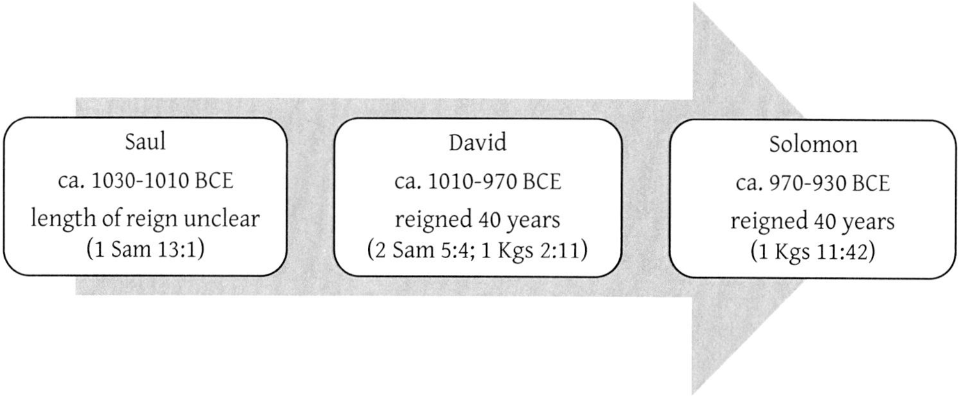

Saul	David	Solomon
ca. 1030–1010 BCE	ca. 1010–970 BCE	ca. 970–930 BCE
length of reign unclear	reigned 40 years	reigned 40 years
(1 Sam 13:1)	(2 Sam 5:4; 1 Kgs 2:11)	(1 Kgs 11:42)

Figure 1.1: Traditional chronology of Israel's first kings, based on the biblical texts.

In a chronology-centric scholarly climate, however, some understanding of the biblical chronology must be established before the present discussion can move forward. My treatment of the biblical texts includes 1 Samuel 4 through 1 Kings 11. Precise dates cannot be recovered from this history, but we can piece together a rough idea of the chronological relationships among the figures based on the text's presentation.[33]

- Samuel's career seems to be significantly earlier than Saul's and David's, and his role in each figure's story is critical, which makes it reasonable that Samuel's career overlapped with both Saul and David, as the narrative describes.
- Saul, David, and Solomon were of successive generations (although see next two points).
- While David and Solomon are said to have died of natural causes and not prematurely, Saul died on the battlefield. David's lamentation (2 Sam 1:17–27) implies that Saul was *not* in the twilight of his career at the time.
- Although the biblical account suggests the three figures labeled Israel's first 'kings' never reigned at the same time, it seems likely that Saul and David contended for leadership beyond the history's presentation, overlapping during a significant portion of their careers. Solomon and David, if David was very elderly at the time of his death, may have served as co-regents. As we will see, evidence suggests that there were various elite parties in the region potentially vying for leadership, and we should understand these three rulers in light of regional competition.
- David and Solomon's reigns should not be assumed to have lasted 40 years each.[34]
- Finally, the standard anchor for estimating the chronologies of these figures is 1 Kings 14:25, which states that Shishaq went up to Jerusalem in the fifth year of Rehoboam. That event is typically situated ca. 925 BCE.[35]

Based on this information, it is reasonable, from a critical standpoint, that the time allotted for Solomon and David should be shortened, both as a correction for the symbolic 40 years and due to the reasonable likelihood that these figures' careers overlapped to some extent. The implications of shifting this chronology are significant in relation to traditional views of biblical archaeology. Even a generous 25 to 30 years each for David and Solomon changes Saul into a 10th century figure. Saul's timeline shifts from the late 11th to the early 10th century. David would be positioned in the early to mid-10th century, and

Solomon in the mid-10th century to ca. 930 BCE. This estimate, albeit vague and hypothetical, seems more likely than the traditional timeline.

Correlating the biblical figures directly with extrabiblical evidence is expressly *not* a goal of this study, but since the DH is an important resource, and extrabiblical material is also essential, some comparison is inevitable. In my understanding, the transition to monarchy that is remembered and traced out through the figures of Saul, his children, David, and Solomon took place throughout much of the 10th century. As it happens, the transition between the Iron I and IIA periods appears to coincide with this process. I do not, however, consider the biblical history's account of this sociopolitical change to be an explanation of the changes detected 'on the ground' through settlement patterns and material culture. Rather, as I express at the beginning of this introduction, this era was a period of various transformations and the final stages of greater changes that began with the demise of the Late Bronze Age political and economic systems and the decline of Egypt's New Kingdom. The transition period culminated in new identities, boundaries, and power relationships. Just as the extrabiblical evidence informs our historical reconstruction of the period, the biblical narratives too may provide informative insights into, and alternative perspectives of, the changes that were taking place.

Additional Contentious Issues

Aside from the historicity and chronological debates, the areas of contention with the greatest impact on studying intercultural exchange are related to social complexity. Long-distance trade is typically associated with state-level societies, but what the historicity and archaeology debates have brought to light is that we cannot assume that the sociopolitical entities of the region in the period prior to the 9th century looked like the later Iron Age polities, or that societies fit nicely into Service's traditional, evolutionary framework of change from tribe to chiefdom to state.[36] Instead, we have seen unexpected developments, like the remains of large-scale industry, but no sign of a capital city that organized it or evidence of scribal activity without palaces. I suggest that we can account for these seeming anomalies by recognizing that there were small-scale elites who operated according to notions of complex statehood even though they did not have the means to be state builders in a material or traditional sense. They fit in between traditional leadership definitions, drawing popular power from ethnic and community ties while modeling themselves on the memories of power left behind from a previous age.[37] As a result, the archaeological setting might appear simplistic, but a local leader's *modus operandi* might include collecting exotic vessels, employing a scribe, or exploiting a resource on a grand scale. Thus, it is possible to see long-distance exchange among leaders and not see the expected evidence of a state-level society.

The scholarly debates have also forced the reevaluation of notions of ethnicity and identity. Not all are germane to this study, but questions of this sort are unavoidable when looking at the exchange, acquisition, and display of nonlocal materials. It is fairly widely accepted that the entities 'Israel' of the Merneptah stele, of Saul's supporters, of the Tel Dan stele, or of the Deuteronomist's day were each distinct. One can no longer reconstruct a large, homogenous kingdom of Israel in the 10th century, as was common in previous histories. Instead, we have to assume a more diverse population (in ethnicity and class), which also means a more complex picture of identities.[38] For many of these communities, we are without their own accounts of who they were and what distinct values they held regarding their place in the region, social stratification, and relationships to foreign culture or interactions with other groups.[39] This study strives to reduce assumptions based on later Iron Age presentations of regional identities (that is, based on biblical or Neo-Assyrian texts), and, when later views must be relied on, I aim to make the relationship to the historical sources apparent.

The various critiques of texts, archaeological materials, and interpretations of chronology, social complexity, and identity create a challenge for describing the times, places, and peoples that are at issue in this project. Some remaining clarification and definition are in order. In earlier studies, the region under examination would be referred to as 'ancient Israel' or the 'land/s of the Bible.' Now that scholarly interest extends beyond the biblical point of view, and now that it is clear that there was much more diversity than previously imagined, neither term adequately describes the geography and groups under discussion. Instead, I frequently rely on the (admittedly imperfect) convention of the 'southern Levant,' meaning the southern half of the eastern Mediterranean coast along with adjacent, populated zones inland. This descriptor avoids the later Iron Age biblical labels and is applicable regardless of differences in chronology, social complexity, ethnicity, or the type of evidence under examination. Where more narrow and appropriate titles are available, I make use of them.

Finally, despite these changes in how we conceptualize and discuss the region and its inhabitants, this project also relies heavily on the sub-disciplines of historical and cultural geography in biblical studies and Levantine archaeology. In addition to traditional approaches, more recent examinations focus on relationships between space and power.[40] Others that rely on archaeological survey, geomorphological study, and settlement patterns in addition to biblical and historical records have allowed for the reconstruction of Iron Age roads throughout the region.[41] These studies also inform my reconstructions of the logistics and impact of interaction.

Approaches to the Study of Trade, Exchange, and Interaction

The dominant investigations and debates regarding trade in the southern Levant have a long history, rooted in European and American exploration of the Levant in the second half of the 19th century. The traditional approach to questions of interregional trade in the southern Levant started with biblical texts. Earlier researchers relied heavily on the Bible's accounts and essentially paraphrased the narratives in their reconstructions.[42] Even with a relatively critical approach according to the scholar's own time and with the assistance of extrabiblical evidence from archaeology and other cultures, this early scholarship today appears naïve and embarrassingly uncritical of the biblical text. The second half of the 20th century saw improved methods and standards in biblical criticism, biblical archaeology, historical geography and ancient Near Eastern studies. These changes were influenced in part by a greater awareness of the ancient world through new discovery but also by a greater engagement with theoretical approaches from other fields, such as economic, sociological, and anthropological contributions, which lent more sophistication and complexity to reconstructions of trade and cultural interactions in the past. Despite these changes, the underlying assumptions in this scholarship still relied too heavily on the biblical narrative to meet today's standards.[43]

More recently, interpretive models from other disciplines are proving effective in expanding our examinations of how cultures interact.[44] Scholarship is responding to a larger critique of the heavy influence of 'Western' bias. Approaches stemming from movements in feminist, postmodernist, and postcolonial studies call our attention to new questions and new perspectives. The boundaries between humanistic and social sciences are fading in some approaches, but in others, stricter divides remain. This is particularly apparent in highly specialized, technical aspects of archaeological research (e.g., chemical source analyses, radiocarbon dating). Nevertheless, the results of these specialized projects tend to be disseminated with interpretation through the final publication of excavation reports, with an increasing interest in researchers to address various audiences within and outside of the academy. While the biblical texts remain influential in historical reconstructions of the past, these newer perspectives and investigative strategies are helping us open up paths for new discussions of some well-trodden intellectual roads.

To get to the new interpretations, we have to examine the notions that shaped prior investigations and that continue to be influential. To start, we have to address the most fundamental of the concepts, diffusion. It is at the core of all discussions of trade and exchange. It was a very popular explanation in the first half of the 20th century to account for common cultural traits across distances.[45] The principle appears logical, that similarities in culture are primarily the result of materials and ideas being shared from one group to another, but it is too obvious and general to pass muster in today's scholarship. More importantly, underlying biases about the relationship between presumably innovative cultures versus those who merely received new ideas or technologies expose the flaws in this line of reasoning. Reactions against overused, vague, and problematic diffusion explanations impacted the study of intercultural exchange, resulting in decreased interest until new analytical frameworks emerged in the second half of the 20th century.

Because of the material nature of trade, the ideas of Karl Marx and Friedrich Engels underlie most trade and exchange research. These thinkers' influence intensified in the mid-20th century due to renewed interest in Marxist theory among Western scholars. The trend redirected attention to issues such as class, inequality, labor, exploitation, and their effects on social change. G. Mendenhall's peasant revolt theory was the most popular expression of this wave for the study of ancient Israel.[46] This particular application did not achieve lasting acceptance in its own right, but its influence did, and Marxist themes such as economic difference are now common throughout biblical research. In this study, the concept of inequality in class and power is important, especially in the face of arguments about a relatively classless early Israelite society.[47] In contrast, I will argue that there was a significant distinction in class and social standing for those who participated in regional and long-distance exchange, and that their competition to dominate exchange activities contributed to changes in the social and political landscape.

Max Weber's blend of sociology, economic history, and study of religion and society presents an alternative understanding of social and economic difference. Although originally published in German in the interwar years, his work was not translated to English until the 1950s, and biblical scholars did not engage with his ideas fully and directly until the last decades of the 20th century, when various social scientific approaches became popular in biblical studies.[48] Among Weber's work, discussions of patrimonial structure and patronage in society relate best to questions of interaction. L. Stager's research on the archaeology of family uses Weber's principles to interpret archaeological changes from the Late Bronze to the Iron Age, as does his argument about the nature of the Solomonic kingdom, which relies on Weber's patrimonial structure.[49] Stager's students J. D. Schloen and R. Simkins have also used Weberian interpretations.[50] In their works, social inequalities and the exchange systems tied to them are formalized and stabilized through kinship language and structures. In this way, negative effects of inequality and exchange are mitigated by notions of familial bonds.

The influence of historian F. Braudel and the Annales School is also in the background of interaction studies today, including the present work.[51] Braudel's broad-based approach revolutionized academic investigations not only in history but also in the social sciences. His shift of emphasis away from the prominent historical individual or single moment to larger factors as contributors to change over time (and over longer periods of time) melded especially well with anthropological approaches. The Annales influence is important in my discussion here in a number of ways. I will consider various factors in investigating how interaction affected the region, but more importantly, I look beyond the named figures in the texts and maintain that there were many influential actors in the region. Only a small number of them are known to us by name, but many others are apparent to us through the physical evidence of cultural exchange. These figures, I argue, wielded a great amount of power in the region.

Karl Polanyi's research rekindled interest in trade studies, specifically, among economists, historians, and anthropologists. Although his arguments about the nature of ancient economies have been much criticized, the work of Polanyi and his students brought the subject of trade back into scholarly debate and created a model for interdisciplinary and comparative methods.[52] Sabloff and Lamberg-Karlovsky's volume *Ancient Civilization and Trade* showcases various scholars' employment of the interdisciplinary approach that Polanyi fostered.[53] Although his theories have been acknowledged in passing in various studies, Polanyi's approach has only recently been systematically applied to the biblical material, by R. Nam.[54]

Emerging from methodological debates among archaeologists more specifically, C. Renfrew and R. McCormick Adams each pushed for more attention to trade and exchange from their colleagues in the 1970s, arguing for the importance of exchange in understanding social change.[55] Their works have been among the most influential in ancient Near Eastern studies. K. V. Flannery's work on Olmec trade is also considered a successful archaeological study and model for exploring the importance of trade in social change.[56] Despite some popularity following these studies, trade as a focus in archaeological research declined again with the rise of postprocessual approaches. By translating, so to speak, the study of trade into terms that are more compatible with theoretical and philosophical perspectives in current archaeological approaches, A. Bauer and A. S. Agbe-Davies have attempted to revive the subject in their work.[57]

One the most popular analytical models for interaction studies has been Wallerstein's 'World System Analysis.'[58] It has been successfully applied to studies of the ancient Near East, in historical contexts and less literate periods.[59] The model's core-periphery dynamic is attractive for the southern Levant because the region was, more often than not, at the periphery of significant core powers. However, the model is not the best tool for this study. One fairly obvious problem is that the ancient Near East did not have a clear core power following the Late Bronze Age collapse and the decline of Egypt's New Kingdom. Despite the biblical history's claim to Israel's dominance in the 10th century, extrabiblical evidence does not support the identification of any dominant polity for some time. In fact, power relationships and historical identities are uncertain for many of the players until the 9th century.

We also face a challenge in relying on World System Analysis for the Late Bronze Age, in setting the scene for this period. An important critique of the world system model is that it overvalues or overemphasizes the influence of the core and fails to recognize change or innovation at the periphery.[60] This tendency is evident among some scholars, who are reluctant to ascribe developments in social complexity during the earlier centuries of the southern Levant's Iron Age to local populations, preferring to give credit to the New Kingdom legacy or to early influence from Assyria instead.[61] Evaluating the smaller-scale, regional relationships (e.g., among coast, hill country, and desert or between key sites) within the southern Levant is critical in this period, when long-distance exchange was so dramatically curtailed and power structures on the scale of a world system not yet formalized.

Relevant Models for This Study

In response to the limitations of World System Analysis and earlier theories, scholars have proposed and expanded on alternative models for researching exchange. Three in particular better fit the conditions in the southern Levant in the early Iron Age: peer polity interaction, interaction spheres, and salient identities.

Peer Polity Interaction

Renfrew's 'peer polity interaction' model offers one alternative to World System Analysis.[62] He devised the model in an attempt to avoid limitations of the world system with its core-periphery dominance, and to meld theories that focused on either internal or external agents of change. The model considers interactions of various kinds, such as trade, warfare, emulation, imitation, and information exchange. By looking broadly at interaction types, the model includes material/tangible culture (e.g., ceramics, architecture) as well as symbolic elements (e.g., language, ideology). It is designed for conditions where there are numerous small, autonomous units that share much of the same culture.[63] Because of their similarities and proximity, these polities do not operate in isolation, but rather interact regularly. The interaction and intense competition among the peer units tend to cause a shift in the power relationships, and one unit often will dominate the others, forming a state or, at its greatest extent, an empire.

In his explication of the theory and the possible benefits of its application, Renfrew anticipated much of what has been debated recently for the southern Levant:

> ...the intermediate-scale interactions between local but independent communities... are perhaps the most informative and certainly the most neglected. For it is at this level that those uniformities emerge which sometimes seem to have a significant role in determining the future pattern of development. The significant unit is thus seen, in this perspective, to be the larger community beyond the polity level, comprised of loosely related, yet politically independent, interacting groups. It is here, for instance, that the processes of ethnic formation must in many cases operate, and here too that the foundations for the later emergence of nation state are laid.[64]

The peer polity interaction model addresses the individual, autonomous communities and their relations with similar units in an interaction network (ranging from local to interregional). Renfrew notes that changes that result from peer interaction impact both sociopolitical organization and identity formation. This model is attractive for application to the southern Levant because of the peer relationships (or at least the absence of one dominant core unit) of the interacting communities, the allowance for different types of interaction, and because of the changes that such interaction tends to bring, namely identity formation and social complexity, two things that changed considerably in the southern Levant in the years between Egyptian and Neo-Assyrian dominance.

Interaction Spheres

J. Caldwell's 'Hopewell interaction spheres' model, which he developed to explain patterns he observed in prehistoric North American sites, also influences my analysis.[65] This model predates Wallerstein's but was not applied outside of North American archaeology until alternatives to world systems were being sought out. Caldwell uses the term 'interaction sphere' to explain shared cultural traits that he observed in communities that were otherwise independent and distinct. The model explains the cultural continuity in a specific aspect of society (e.g., elite burial practices and luxury goods), and proposes that autonomous sites were linked through exchange relations.[66] The model also relates exchange activities to changes in social complexity. As the connections between communities grow, social bonds develop beyond the local levels, and eventually the smaller communities become linked in a larger structure. These changes shift the relationships and social organization both within an individual community and among autonomous sites in the exchange network.

N. Yoffee and G. Stein have each applied the interaction sphere model to prehistoric Mesopotamian culture.[67] Yoffee stresses the importance of the interaction sphere as a more useful model than world systems in cases where the geography of interaction is limited, and he emphasizes the importance of the interaction sphere in the self-identification process that necessarily occurs as autonomous groups encounter each other, and as their encounters spur changes in social organization in each of the autonomous groups.[68] Similar to the peer polity model, this approach suits the southern Levant in terms of geographic scale and the social organization of small, independent societies. The interaction sphere concept, however, allows for more variation and flexibility.

G. Stein has revisited the model to investigate the Ubaid cultural horizon more specifically. The approach does not require that subjects fit into the core-periphery hierarchy or any other preconceived power relationships. In addition, the interaction sphere approach avoids overlooking local variation and innovation. In the Ubaid case, Stein explains, researchers' attention to Ubaid culture has been disproportionate to the archaeological evidence, in which local cultural variation predominates, with different degrees of adoption of Ubaid traits. Thus, publications suggest much more homogeneity (or Ubaid dominance in core-periphery terms) than the evidence supports.[69] In Stein's formulation, the interaction sphere model, combined with identity theory, allows for the examination of both the shared culture of the interaction sphere and the participants' local, preexisting cultures without automatically creating a research bias of one over the other.

Interaction Spheres and Salient Identities

E. Schortman and P. Urban have proposed yet another focus (not a model per se) for interaction studies.[70] Their approach also allows for flexibility in the interacting partners' relationships (e.g., dominant or peer relations) and gives more emphasis to the role of social identities in exchange activities than the interaction sphere model does alone. Their research emphasizes the concept of 'salient identities', that is, 'an affiliation or set of affiliations which are used more commonly than others and whose members, as a result, share a strong feeling of common purpose and support.'[71] Such affiliations should result in recoverable material remains, and thus be particularly useful for archaeological research.[72] When the affiliations can be identified and connected to patterned behavior, changes in time and space, then their approach has the potential to explain social change.[73] Schortman focuses on elites and describes a chain reaction that links identity and interaction activities. Local elites who are able to gain access to nonlocal goods create the demand for interregional interaction. The interaction supports the development of a salient identity among the participants that then solidifies the elites' role in the exchange network.[74] This reconstruction predicts local and regional sociopolitical change. The development of an elite group of exchange partners separates the elites from other members of their own communities (local change) and, despite their shared interests with their elite community, also creates competition and even warfare within the exchange network (regional to interregional change).[75]

The three approaches have considerable overlap and are not mutually exclusive. All provide structures for assessing interactions that are described in narrative form or are apparent in material evidence. Each model has a slightly different emphasis that will be useful for the distinct evidence types and for considering different consequences of interaction. Peer polity interaction has the potential to highlight regional political change with its focus on competition and emulation. The interaction spheres model provides a framework for making sense of the nonlocal and specialized artifacts that begin to appear across the region, even where there is considerable variation from site to site. Finally, the identity formation approaches (Schortman and Urban's salient identities and Stein's local and *oikumene* identities) supply a foundation for examining how interaction influences the less tangible ideological changes in these populations. Normally pairing or combining models might prove hazardous, but I propose that these frameworks are in fact complementary and can be applied together.[76] With the diverse and seemingly incompatible bodies of evidence that are available for the study of the Iron I–IIA, the nuances among these models allow for their application across the different types of evidence. Further, their respective emphases align well with what is most accessible in the varied data, from heroic characters in biblical narratives to ostraca and painted sherds, while still taking into account broader societal impact.

The Organization of This Study

Before applying these interpretive frameworks, it is necessary to work through the available evidence. The period of focus for this study corresponds to the century or two prior to substantial, contemporary historical documentation of the Iron Age. With the exception of a handful of Egyptian writings, most notably Shoshenq I's Karnak relief and the semi-historical(?) Report of Wenamun, no contemporary sources refer to the region. Contemporary evidence comes instead from a small number of very brief inscriptions and archaeological remains. The paucity of evidence is contrasted by the vivid depictions in the biblical writings, describing kingdoms, imperial behavior, and international trade. Despite the discrepancies, this study relies on all three types of evidence: biblical, contemporary historical/epigraphic, and archaeological. Each demands a different set of evaluative tools and scholarly literature, and so will be treated separately. Only after the different types of evidence are reviewed independently will they be combined with the theoretical frameworks discussed above.

The Hebrew Bible's DH, specifically 1 and 2 Samuel and the beginning of 1 Kings, provides the most information of the biblical material on interregional exchange in the 11th and 10th centuries.[77] The present concern receives much attention in the DH in general because of the history's theological argument that interacting with other groups endangered Israel's fidelity to YHWH. Despite interaction being a frequent concern in the history, some episodes are more useful than others for historical investigation. I have selected two areas of focus that are the most fruitful: relations with the Philistines and Solomon's interactions. My approach to these topics is guided by historical biblical criticism, which takes into consideration cultural contexts that we know from ancient Near Eastern history and archaeology.

The books of 1 and 2 Samuel follow the careers of three leaders of the Israelite community: Samuel, Saul, and David. Each of these men's story tells of relations with neighboring peoples, such as Ammonites, Moabites, and Arameans, but relations with the Philistines receive the most attention and are a constant concern in the narratives, despite the composite nature of the history. In Chapter Two, I focus on the tales of interactions between the early Israelite community and these coastal neighbors. For each of the episodes that detail relations with the Philistines, I judge the narrative's suitability for historical use and then combine the best of that evidence to explore the nature and importance of the interactions. What I find is that there is a pattern to the interactions, and that they intensified as the history moves from Samuel's era to David's. Keeping in mind the constraint of the narrative's perspectives (that is, a later historical and political bias), the interactions grew and escalated based on competitive interactions. In short, Philistine leaders attempted to control roads and key passages that connected the Philistine heartland to major highways to the north, east, and southeast. This control gave Philistia power to manipulate traffic and provided access to resources. The Philistine movements not only provoked hostile interaction from the hill country, led by Saul, but also fueled competition for control of the routes and passages. Eventually, David's mixture of warfare, banditry, alliance, and diplomacy won him control of the hill country passages, control of a larger consolidated territory, and dominance in regional leadership.

Chapter Three turns to Solomon's interactions, both inter- and intra-regional. As in Chapter Two, I evaluate the usefulness of the narrative portions that describe exchange in Solomon's day. Because Solomon's reign came to be remembered as the climax of early monarchic state formation, the history attracted elaboration at various points in the Bible's composition and revision. Regarding his long-distance activities, typically the grandest claims are the least reliable; however, claims to interactions with Phoenicia and Egypt are more likely to have had some correlation to historical relations, at least in terms of the regions' engagement with the southern Levantine hill country. Some descriptions of Solomon's domestic policies also appear to be grounded in 10th century events.

Based on the policies that are depicted, the territory that Solomon attempted to unify was diverse in its economic offerings. His district organization exploited agricultural or natural resources in some cases; in others, the districts correspond to transportation corridors, revealing an effort to control traffic in the region. From both views of Solomon's activities, domestic and interregional, there is evidence of involvement in long-distance exchange that was moving through the southern Levant.

The next chapter represents a meeting point between the world of biblical narrative examined in Chapters Two and Three and the examination of material evidence in Chapters Five and Six. Chapter Four addresses the role of Jerusalem in interregional interactions, based on biblical and extrabiblical (historical and archaeological) evidence. The case of Jerusalem demands special attention because of the contrast between the centrality of the city in the biblical worldview and the very limited material evidence that can be dated to the early Iron Age. Recent excavations have had a large impact on how both bodies of evidence are evaluated. Based on Jerusalem's role in the Late Bronze Age, newer archaeological evidence from the city, and a critical view of the biblical history (established in Chapters Two and Three), I determine that Iron I–IIA Jerusalem was a significant site in the southern hill country and was not isolated from long-distance exchange networks. Even though the precise details about leadership of the early Iron Age city remain elusive, the location maintained some importance during these years.

Chapter Five turns to contemporary historical and epigraphic evidence. While examples of longer writings exist (e.g., the Gezer tablet and the Khirbet Qeiyafa inscription), typical epigraphic material in the southern Levant consists of simply a name or name formula on an object. Needless to say, these sources are not substantial enough to provide explicit testimony of trade relations. They are, however, informative in other ways. In this chapter, I review the collection of inscriptions from the southern Levant that have been dated to this period and compare them to contemporary evidence from the neighboring regions of Egypt and Byblos. From this evidence, I argue that although the southern Levant's inscriptions do not describe trade or exchange, they are a product of interregional interaction. Writing was a specialized activity and was most likely the privilege of elite members of communities. The local leaders that possessed inscribed objects were engaged in other privileged activities such as the acquisition of nonlocal goods – in other words, long-distance trade.

Archaeological remains have long been relied on for evidence of exchange relations among cultures. On the simplest level, the discovery of a nonlocal item at a site is proof of exchange across distance, and with the ability to detect an artifact's place of origin through scientific testing, such items provide concrete evidence to researchers. The subsequent analysis of how and why goods were transported remains complex, but the knowledge that a foreign object changed hands is a firm starting place. In Chapter Six, nonlocal ceramics from the Aegean, Cyprus, and northwest Arabia provide the physical evidence of long-distance exchange. The geographic distributions of these artifacts reveal different exchange networks and clarify which sites and areas were able to participate in the growing exchange activities.

Chapter Seven brings all the evidence presented in these separate cases into one conversation. By adding the discrete studies of Chapters Two through Six together, we can see that interactions were in fact lively and increasing in the transition to the early Iron II period. Each type of evidence speaks to a considerable number of interactions, and together the activities involve all areas of the southern Levant. Some areas witnessed more intensity than others, which is revealed through regional summaries of the combined evidence. In addition to this comprehensive view of the material, I review the theoretical models presented above in order to evaluate the significance of the interactions. The interaction spheres approach provides an interpretive structure for understanding the seemingly sporadic appearance of imported and luxury goods, as well as the contexts related to elite participation in interregional relations, and the impact of these activities. Focusing on elite identity helps us examine how elites maintained their connection to local communities while fostering new identities tied to interregional relations. Peer polity interaction assumes a broader vantage point and supplies a framework for characterizing the different types of interactions and their impact on southern Levantine societies. The result of these activities had a profound effect in the region. Interactions increased contact among areas that were otherwise distinct. At the same time, we can detect a rise in status for those who were in positions to control resources and strategic locations. An elite leadership community grew from those holding positions of power, and they interacted through cooperative and competitive relations. The sum of these relations was the development of diverse bases of power whose respective spheres of influence we now recognize as small polities. In other words, interregional exchange and the elites who participated in it gave rise to the earliest expressions of the Levant's Iron Age kingdoms.

Notes

1 This conviction is challenging in the context of ever-increasing specialization that is also necessary in scholarship; however, some problems require a multidisciplinary strategy. In the introduction to her work on prehistoric/pre-Hellenic Greece, Margalit Finkelberg urges, "The culmination of any historical enquiry is the point where the results of several disciplines coincide… We have to consider every scrap of information that can throw light on human prehistory, for the simple reason that it is only such a multidisciplinary approach that can give us a wider perspective of the past and guarantee real progress in the field" (*Greeks and Pre-Greeks: Aegean Prehistory and Greek Heroic Tradition* [Cambridge: Cambridge University Press, 2005], 8–9).
2 The work of W. F. Albright, and his blend of ancient history, philology, archaeology, ancient Near Eastern cultural studies, and critical view of the biblical text, influenced the development of American biblical scholarship. Although many of Albright's arguments are problematic according to today's scrutiny, his multidisciplinary method revolutionized how scholars investigate and understand ancient Israel and its neighbors. My approach comes out of that scholarly heritage and strives to work in the spirit of Albright's multidisciplinary method. It is not, however, simply Albrightian, as I hope to demonstrate below.
3 Thomas L. Thompson, *The Historicity of the Patriarchal Narratives: The Quest for the Historical Abraham* (BZAW 133; Berlin; New York: Walter de Gruyter, 1974); John Van Seters, *Abraham in History and Tradition* (New Haven: Yale University Press, 1975).
4 Niels Peter Lemche, *The Israelites in History and Tradition* (London; Louisville: Westminster John Knox Press, 1998); Keith W. Whitelam, *The Invention of Ancient Israel: The Silencing of Palestinian History* (New York: Routledge, 1996); Philip R. Davies, *In Search of "Ancient Israel"* (JSOTSup 148; Sheffield: JSOT Press, 1992).
5 See Chapters Two and Three for a more detailed discussion of my understanding of the Deuteronomistic History. In short, I largely follow the double redaction theory proposed by Frank Moore Cross.
6 Ian Douglas Wilson, *Kingship and Memory in Ancient Judah* (New York: Oxford University Press, 2017), 58. Although as I discuss, especially in Chapter Three, the same is true for the source materials the compilers used.
7 For an overview of the influence on the discipline, see Megan Bishop Moore and Brad E. Kelle, *Biblical History and Israel's Past: The Changing Study of the Bible and History* (Grand Rapids: Eerdmans, 2011), 37–42; for more detailed treatment, see Megan Bishop Moore, *Philosophy and Practice in Writing a History of Ancient Israel* (New York: T&T Clark, 2006).

8. Daniel Pioske, *David's Jerusalem: Between Memory and History* (New York; London: Taylor & Francis, 2015); idem, *Memory in a Time of Prose: Studies in Epistemology, Hebrew Scribalism, and the Biblical Past* (Oxford; New York: Oxford University Press, 2018); Wilson, *Kingship and Memory in Ancient Judah*.
9. Israel Finkelstein, "The Archaeology of the United Monarchy: An Alternative View," *Levant* 28, no. 1 (1996): 177–87; see also, more recently, idem, "A Great United Monarchy? Archaeological and Historical Perspectives," in *One God - One Cult - One Nation: Archaeological and Biblical Perspectives*, ed. Reinhard G. Kratz and Hermann Spieckermann (BZAW 405; Berlin; New York: Walter de Gruyter, 2010), 3–28. For a review of the debates and how the biblical text has been (mis-)used, see William M. Schniedewind, "Excavating the Text of 1 Kings 9: In Search of the Gates of Solomon," in *Historical Biblical Archaeology and the Future: The New Pragmatism*, ed. Thomas E. Levy (London; Oakville: Equinox Publishing, 2010), 241–49.
10. Amihai Mazar, "The Debate over the Chronology of the Iron Age in the Southern Levant: Its History, the Current Situation and a Suggested Resolution," in *The Bible and Radiocarbon Dating: Archaeology, Text and Science*, ed. Thomas E. Levy and Thomas Higham (London; Oakville: Equinox Publishing, 2005), 17.
11. In light of the minimalist critique, it is less common for archaeologists to link excavation results to biblical figures. This trend did not, however, deter Eilat Mazar in discussing her excavations in Jerusalem (see Chapter Four), or the excavators of Khirbet Qeiyafa in their interpretations; see most recently, Yosef Garfinkel, Saar Ganor, and Michael G. Hasel, *In the Footsteps of King David: Revelations from an Ancient Biblical City* (London: Thames & Hudson, 2018).
12. David W. Jamieson-Drake's work has been highly influential in the assumptions about the necessary elements of statehood (*Scribes and Schools in Monarchic Judah: A Socio-Archeological Approach* [SWBA 9; JSOTSup 109; Sheffield: Almond Press, 1991]).
13. Finkelstein, "The Archaeology of the United Monarchy." For updates devoted to his proposal, see idem, "A Low Chronology Update: Archaeology, History and Bible," in *The Bible and Radiocarbon Dating: Archaeology, Text and Science*, ed. Thomas E. Levy and Thomas Higham (London; Oakville: Equinox Publishing, 2005), 31–42; idem, "A Great United Monarchy?"; Israel Finkelstein and Eli Piasetzky, "The Iron Age Chronology Debate: Is the Gap Narrowing?" *NEA* 74, no. 1 (2011): 50–54. Finkelstein has also published numerous iterations of his system as refutations or endorsements to the publication of excavation results, radiocarbon results, and key finds that appear to have an impact on the debates.
14. Raz Kletter provides one of the sharpest evaluations of Finkelstein's overall method in "Chronology and United Monarchy: A Methodological Review," *ZDPV* 120 (2004): 13–54; see also Daniel A. Frese and David Noel Freedman, "Samaria I as a Chronological Anchor of Finkelstein's Low Chronology: An Appraisal," *ErIsr* 25; Ephraim Stern Volume, ed. Jospeh Aviram (Jerusalem: The Israel Exploration Society, 2009), 36* – 44*; Daniel A. Frese and Thomas E. Levy, "Four Pillars of the Iron Age Low Chronology," in *Historical Biblical Archaeology and the Future: The New Pragmatism*, ed. Thomas E. Levy (London; Oakville: Equinox Publishing, 2010), 187–202.
15. The publications are numerous. Among the most recent are Israel Finkelstein, "Northern Royal Traditions in the Bible and the Ideology of a 'United Monarchy' Ruled from Samaria," in *Stones, Tablets, and Scrolls: Periods of the Formation of the Bible*, ed. Peter Dubovský and Federico Giuntoli (Tübingen: Mohr Siebeck, 2020), 113–26; idem, "Saul and Highlands of Benjamin Update: The Role of Jerusalem," in *Saul, Benjamin and the Emergence of Monarchy in Israel: Biblical and Archaeological Perspectives*, ed. Joachim J. Krause, Omer Sergi, and Kristin Weingart (Atlanta: Society of Biblical Literature, 2020), 33–56; idem, "First Israel, Core Israel, United (Northern) Israel," *NEA* 82, no. 1 (2019): 8–15.
16. Israel Finkelstein, *The Forgotten Kingdom: The Archaeology and History of Northern Israel* (Ancient Near Eastern Monographs 5; Atlanta: Society of Biblical Literature, 2013), 5.
17. Ibid., 1–5.
18. Finkelstein, "The Archaeology of the United Monarchy," 178.
19. Amihai Mazar, "The Iron Age Chronology Debate: Is the Gap Narrowing? Another Viewpoint," *NEA* 74, no. 2 (2011): 105–11.
20. Ze'ev Herzog and Lily Singer-Avitz, "Redefining the Centre: The Emergence of State in Judah," *TA* 31 (2004): 209–44; idem, "Sub-Dividing the Iron Age IIA in Northern Israel: A Suggested Solution to the Chronological Debate," *TA* 33 (2006): 163–95.
21. The absolute dates for the transition between these phases continue to be debated and refined. See Finkelstein and Piasetzky, "Is the Gap Narrowing?"; Mazar, "Is the Gap Narrowing?"; Hayah Katz and Avraham Faust, "The Chronology of the Iron Age IIA in Judah in Light of Tel 'Eton Tomb C3 and Other Assemblages," *BASOR* 371 (2014): 103–27; Zachary Thomas, Kyle H. Keimer, and Yosef Garfinkel, "The Early Iron Age IIA Ceramic Assemblage from Khirbet al-Ra'i," *Jerusalem Journal of Archaeology* 1 (2021): 375–449.

22 The intensity of research into clarifying this transition is evident in many publications; most recently, the inaugural volume (2021) of the *Jerusalem Journal of Archaeology* is dedicated to papers from a 2019 conference titled "State Formation Processes in the 10th Century BCE Levant" devoted to research into clarifying the transition period and sociopolitical change of the time.

23 Radiocarbon dating of these destruction levels situates the transition in the late 11th to early 10th century; see Amihai Mazar and Christopher Bronk Ramsey, "14C Dates and the Iron Age Chronology of Israel: A Response," *Radiocarbon* 50, no. 2 (2008): 176, 178, fig. 4; idem, "A Response to Finkelstein and Piasetzky's Criticism and 'New Perspective,'" *Radiocarbon* 52, no. 4 (2010): 1685–86.

24 Katz and Faust, "The Chronology of the Iron Age IIA in Judah," 104. Katz and Faust argue that the chronology debate in general has contributed to what amounts to a late 10th century avoidance among researchers. They explain that, out of caution, many Iron IIA ceramic assemblages have been assigned absolute dates corresponding to the end of the period, and that those that cannot be dated that late are dated very early. They observe, "[t]his leaves much of the Iron IIA without any assemblages. While this is not an impossible situation and could have resulted from a number of factors, it is still strange and, in our opinion, a distorted picture, which is worth examining" (ibid., 104–105).

25 These issues are far from settled, however; for an example of the debates involved in understanding more discrete regional variation see, Avraham Faust, "Between the Highland Polity and Philistia: The United Monarchy and the Resettlement of the Shephelah in the Iron Age IIA, with a Special Focus on Tel ʿEton and Khirbet Qeiyafa," *BASOR* 383 (2020): 115–36; Gunnar Lehmann and Hermann Michael Niemann, "When Did the Shephelah Become Judahite?" *TA* 41, no. 1 (2014): 77–94.

26 This framework is derived from the Modified Conventional Chronology proposed by Ahimai Mazar, augmented by the subdivisions discussed above. Regional variation is not represented in this basic scheme but is taken into account where appropriate. See Mazar, "Is the Gap Narrowing?"; Finkelstein and Piasetzky, "Is the Gap Narrowing?"; Herzog and Singer-Avitz, "Sub-Dividing the Iron Age IIA in Northern Israel"; idem, "Redefining the Centre: The Emergence of State in Judah"; Katz and Faust, "The Chronology of the Iron Age IIA in Judah"; see also additional refinement based on more recent Megiddo evidence in Assaf Kleiman et al., "The Date and Origin of Black-on-Red Ware: The View from Megiddo," *American Journal of Archaeology* 123, no. 4 (2019): 531–55. A 'Middle Iron IIA' has recently been proposed for southern sites; see Thomas, Keimer, and Garfinkel, "The Early Iron Age IIA Ceramic Assemblage from Khirbet al-Raʿi." This chronological framework situates the entire Iron IIA from ca. 1000–ca. 830 or later.

27 See, for example, Kleiman et al., "The Date and Origin of Black-on-Red Ware"; Benjamin Sass and Israel Finkelstein, "The Swan-Song of Proto-Canaanite in the Ninth Century BCE in Light of an Alphabetic Inscription from Megiddo," *Semitica et Classica* 9 (2016): 19–42.

28 For the most part, reference to absolute chronology will follow the Modified Conventional Chronology (MCC) introduced by Amihai Mazar ("The Debate over the Chronology").

29 Finkelstein and Piasetzky, "Is the Gap Narrowing?"; Mazar, "Is the Gap Narrowing?"

30 For a recent review of settlement patterns (although I am not in full agreement with the accompanying reconstructions), see Avraham Faust, "The 'United Monarchy' on the Ground: the Disruptive Character of the Iron Age I–II Transition and the Nature of Political Transformations," *JJAR* 1 (2021): 15–67.

31 David Miano, *Shadow on the Steps: Time Measurement in Ancient Israel* (Atlanta: Society of Biblical Literature, 2010), 57, 117, 209–214. Miano notes that even Saul's enigmatic 2-year reign can be accounted for, a necessity in order to fit the 480-year timeframe from the Exodus to the beginning of Solomon's temple construction.

32 Similar considerations, although presented as a negative image, must have been at work in the treatment (i.e., redaction) of Saul's history, which lays the foundation for his successors. For the 'negatives,' as in the opposite of favorable as well as in a photographic sense, see Gregory Mobley, "Glimpses of the Heroic Saul," in *Saul in Story and Tradition*, ed. Marsha C. White and Carl S. Ehrlich (FAT 47; Tübingen: Mohr Siebeck, 2006), 80–87.

33 Baruch Halpern presents a detailed examination of the many chronological factors in the text related to David's reign (*David's Secret Demons: Messiah, Murderer, Traitor, King* [Grand Rapids: Eerdmans, 2001], 229–242).

34 Based on the careers of the Judahite kings, an average reign was just shy of 20 years.

35 This study will assume this date as a rough chronological marker for the event, and views this as the biblical memory of Shoshenq I's campaign that is depicted on the Bubastite portal at Karnak. Shoshenq and Shishaq are discussed in Chapters Three through Seven.

36 In contrast to more traditional applications (Elman Service, *Primitive Social Organization*, 2nd ed. [New York: Random House, 1971]; John S. Holladay, Jr., "The Kingdoms of Israel and Judah: Political and Economic

Centralization in the Iron IIA–B [ca. 1000–750 BCE]," in *The Archaeology of Society in the Holy Land*, ed. Thomas E. Levy; 2nd ed. [London: Leicester University Press, 1998], 368–98) or the minimalist-friendly interpretation of Jamieson-Drake (see Chapter Five). The discussion about the poor fit of the traditional models to the southern Levant picked up steam around the turn of the century and is ongoing; see Oystein S. LaBianca and Randall W. Younker, "The Kingdoms of Ammon, Moab and Edom: The Archaeology of Society in Late Bronze/Iron Age Transjordan (ca. 1400–500 BCE)," in *The Archaeology of Society in the Holy Land*, ed. Thomas E. Levy; 2nd ed. (London: Leicester University Press, 1998), 399–415; Daniel M. Master, "State Formation Theory and the Kingdom of Ancient Israel," *JNES* 60, no. 2 (2001): 117–31; Alexander H. Joffe, "The Rise of Secondary States in the Iron Age Levant," *JESHO* 45, no. 4 (2002): 425–67; Thomas E. Levy, Erez Ben-Yosef, and Mohammad Najjar, "The Iron Age Edomite Lowlands Regional Archaeological Project: Research, Design, and Methodology," in *New Insights into the Iron Age Archaeology of Edom, Southern Jordan: Surveys, Excavations and Research from the University of California, San Diego & Department of Antiquities of Jordan, Edom Lowlands Regional Archaeology Project (ELRAP)*, ed. Thomas E. Levy et al. (Monumenta Archaeologica 35; Los Angeles: The Cotsen Institute of Archaeology Press, 2014), 2–8; Bruce E. Routledge, *Moab in the Iron Age: Hegemony, Polity, Archaeology* (Philadelphia: University of Pennsylvania Press, 2004), 117–119. See, more recently, Erez Ben-Yosef, "Rethinking the Social Complexity of Early Iron Age Nomads," *JJAR* 1 (2021): 155–79; Alexander H. Joffe, "Defining the State," in *Enemies and Friends of the State: Ancient Prophecy in Context*, ed. Christopher A. Rollston (Winona Lake: Eisenbrauns, 2018): 3–24; Benjamin W. Porter, *Complex Communities: The Archaeology of Early Iron Age West-Central Jordan.* (Tucson: University of Arizona Press, 2013); Bruce E. Routledge, "Is There an Iron Age Levant?" *Revista Del Instituto de Historia Antigua Oriental* 18 (2017), 49–76; Zachary Thomas, "On the Archaeology of the 10th Century BCE Israel and the Idea of the 'State,'" *PEQ* 153, no. 3 (2021): 244–57.

37 We see examples of this tension in leadership models from other periods as well, for example in the Levantine rulers during the Amarna period, who were situated between local and imperial power (Nadav Na'aman, "The Contribution of the Amarna Letters to the Debate on Jerusalem's Political Position in the Tenth Century B.C.E.," *BASOR* 304 [1996]: 20–21) and later Iron Age rulers of Edom (Neil G. Smith, Mohammad Najjar, and Thomas E. Levy, "New Perspectives on the Iron Age Edom Steppe and Highlands: Khirbat Al-Malayqtah, Khirbat Al-Kur, Khirbat Al-Iraq Shmaliya, and Tawilan," in *New Insights into the Iron Age Archaeology of Edom, Southern Jordan: Surveys, Excavations and Research from the University of California, San Diego & Department of Antiquities of Jordan, Edom Lowlands Regional Archaeology Project [ELRAP]*, ed. Thomas E. Levy et al. [Monumenta Archaeologica 35; Los Angeles: The Cotsen Institute of Archaeology Press, 2014], 287–90). Marian Feldman has made a complementary argument based on art historical methods and evidence that early Iron Age elites were informed by legacies of LBA power; see *Communities of Style: Portable Luxury Arts, Identity, and Collective Memory in the Iron Age Levant* (Chicago; London: University of Chicago Press, 2014).

38 For a recent overview of the issues, see Aren M. Maeir, "On Defining Israel: Or, Let's Do the *Kulturkreislehre* Again!," *Hebrew Bible and Ancient Israel* 10, no. 2 (2021): 106–48. See also related discussions in idem, "Philistine and Israelite Identities: Some Comparative Thoughts," *Die Welt Des Orients* 49, no. 2 (2019): 151–60; Aren M. Maeir and Itzhaq Shai, "Reassessing the Character of the Judahite Kingdom: Archaeological Evidence for Non-Centralized, Kinship-Based Components," in *From Sha'ar Hagolan to Shaaraim: Essays in Honor of Prof. Yosef Garfinkel*, ed. Saar Ganor et al. (Jerusalem: Israel Exploration Society, 2016), 323–40. Maier's discussions are in contrast to arguments based in Avraham Faust's research, represented in various publications but laid out in length in the influential volume *Israel's Ethnogenesis: Settlement, Interaction, Expansion and Resistance* (London: Equinox Publishing, 2008). For an earlier survey of the issues, see James C. Miller, "Ethnicity and the Hebrew Bible: Problems and Prospects," *CBR* 6, no. 2 (2008): 170–213; and the influential works of Fredrik Barth, *Ethnic Groups and Boundaries: The Social Organization of Culture Difference* (Boston: Little, Brown, 1969); and Geoff Emberling, "Ethnicity in Complex Societies: Archaeological Perspectives," *Journal of Archaeological Research* 5, no. 4 (1997): 295–344.

39 The examination of this aspect of interactions – that is, of perceptions of traders and consumers by each other and how such perceptions influence exchange – is very important but also very difficult to do with limited contemporary historical sources. For an exploration regarding exchange in the eastern Mediterranean in the early Iron Age, see Susan Sherratt, "Greeks and Phoenicians: Perceptions of Trade and Traders in the Early First Millennium BC," in *Social Archaeologies of Trade and Exchange: Exploring Relationships among People, Places, and Things*, ed. Alexander A. Bauer and Anna S. Agbe-Davies (Walnut Creek: Left Coast Press, 2010), 119–42.

40 Stephen C. Russell, *Space, Land, Territory, and the Study of the Bible* (Leiden: Brill, 2017); idem, *The King and the Land: A Geography of Royal Power in the Biblical World* (Oxford: Oxford University Press, 2016).

41 David A. Dorsey, *The Roads and Highways of Ancient Israel* (Baltimore: Johns Hopkins University Press, 1991); Anson F. Rainey and R. Steven Notley, *The Sacred Bridge: Carta's Atlas of the Biblical World* (Jerusalem: Carta, 2006); Erez Ben-Yosef, "Technology and Social Process Oscillations in Iron Age Copper Production and Power in Southern Jordan," Ph.D. diss. (University of California, San Diego, 2010), 66–126; Erez Ben-Yosef, Mohammad Najjar, and Thomas E. Levy, "Local Iron Age Trade Routes in Northern Edom: From the Faynan Copper Ore District to the Highlands," in *New Insights into the Iron Age Archaeology of Edom, Southern Jordan: Surveys, Excavations and Research from the University of California, San Diego & Department of Antiquities of Jordan, Edom Lowlands Regional Archaeology Project (ELRAP)*, ed. Thomas E. Levy et al. (Monumenta Archaeologica 35; Los Angeles: The Cotsen Institute of Archaeology Press, 2014), 493–575.

42 John Bright, *A History of Israel*, 4th ed. (Philadelphia: Westminster Press, 2000); William Foxwell Albright, *Archaeology and the Religion of Israel*, 5th ed. (Baltimore: Johns Hopkins Press, 1968); idem, "New Light on the Early History of Phoenician Colonization," *BASOR* 83 (1941): 14–22; Benjamin Mazar, "The Aramean Empire and Its Relations with Israel," *BA* 25, no. 4 (1962): 98–120.

43 Moshe Elat, *Economic Relations in the Lands of the Bible (ca. 1000-539 B.C.E.)* (Jerusalem: Bialik Institute, 1977); idem, "Trade in the Period of the Monarchy," in *The World History of the Jewish People, Volume IV, part II: The Age of Monarchies: Culture and Society*, ed. Abraham Malamat (Jerusalem: Massada Press, 1979), 174–86; idem, "The Monarchy and the Development of Trade in Ancient Israel," in *State and Temple Economy in the Ancient Near East: Proceedings of the International Conference*, ed. Edward Lipiński (Leuven: Departement Oriëntalistiek, 1979), 527–46; Morris Silver, *Prophets and Markets: The Political Economy of Ancient Israel* (Boston; Hingham: Kluwer-Nijhoff, 1983); Andrew Sherratt and Susan Sherratt, "The Growth of the Mediterranean Economy in the Early First Millennium BC," *World Archaeology* 24, no. 3 (1993): 361–78; Holladay, "The Kingdoms of Israel and Judah"; Lowell K. Handy, ed., *The Age of Solomon: Scholarship at the Turn of the Millennium* (SHCANE 11; Leiden; New York: Brill, 1997); Lawrence E. Stager and Philip J. King, *Life in Biblical Israel* (Louisville: Westminster John Knox Press, 2001), 183–185, 189–195.

44 E.g., entanglement theory and network analysis provide intriguing intellectual frameworks for thinking about cultural interactions.

45 Alexander A. Bauer and Anna S. Agbe-Davies, "Trade and Interaction in Archaeology," in *Social Archaeologies of Trade and Exchange: Exploring Relationships among People, Places, and Things*, ed. Alexander A. Bauer and Anna S. Agbe-Davies (Walnut Creek: Left Coast Press, 2010), 29–34.

46 George E. Mendenhall, *The Tenth Generation: The Origins of the Biblical Tradition* (Baltimore: Johns Hopkins University Press, 1973). This explanation was continued by Norman K. Gottwald in *The Tribes of Yahweh: A Sociology of the Religion of Liberated Israel, 1250-1050 B.C.E.* (Maryknoll: Orbis Books, 1979).

47 See Chapter Five.

48 Max Weber, *Ancient Judaism*, trans. Hans H. Gerth and Don Martindale (Glencoe: Free Press, 1952); idem, *The Protestant Ethic and the Spirit of Capitalism*, trans. Talcott Parsons (New York: Scribner, 1958); idem, *Economy and Society: An Outline of Interpretive Sociology*, ed. Guenther Roth and Claus Wittich; trans. Ephraim Fischoff (New York: Bedminster Press, 1968).

49 Lawrence E. Stager, "The Archaeology of the Family in Ancient Israel," *BASOR* 260 (1985): 1–35; idem, "The Patrimonial Kingdom of Solomon," in *Symbiosis, Symbolism, and the Power of the Past: Canaan, Ancient Israel, and Their Neighbors from the Late Bronze Age through Roman Palaestina*, ed. William G. Dever and Seymour Gitin (Winona Lake: Eisenbrauns, 2003), 63–74.

50 J. David Schloen, "Caravans, Kenites, and Casus Belli: Enmity and Alliance in the Song of Deborah," *CBQ* 55, no. 1 (1993): 18–38; idem, *The House of the Father as Fact and Symbol: Patrimonialism in Ugarit and the Ancient Near East* (SAHL 2; Winona Lake: Eisenbrauns, 2001); Ronald A. Simkins, "Patronage and the Political Economy of Monarchic Israel," *Semeia* 87 (1999): 123–44; idem, "Family in the Political Economy of Monarchic Judah," *The Bible and Critical Theory* 1, no. 1 (2004): 1–17.

51 Fernand Braudel, *The Mediterranean and the Mediterranean World in the Age of Philip II*, trans. S. Reynolds, 2 vols. (Berkeley: University of California Press, 1995).

52 Robert B. Revere, "'No Man's Coast': Ports of Trade in the Eastern Mediterranean," in *Trade and Market in the Early Empires: Economies in History and Theory*, ed. Karl Polanyi, Conrad M. Arensberg, and Harry W. Pearson (Glencoe: Free Press, 1957), 38–63; Karl Polanyi, *The Great Transformation* (Boston: Beacon Press, 1962); idem, *Primitive, Archaic, and Modern Economies; Essays of Karl Polanyi*, ed. George Dalton (Boston: Beacon Press, 1971).

53 Jeremy A Sabloff and C. C Lamberg-Karlovsky, eds. *Ancient Civilization and Trade* (Albuquerque: University of New Mexico Press, 1975).

54 Roger S. Nam, *Portrayals of Economic Exchange* (Leiden; Boston: Brill, 2012).

55 Robert McCormick Adams, "Anthropological Perspectives on Ancient Trade," *CA* 15, no. 3 (1974): 239–58; Colin Renfrew, *The Emergence of Civilisation: The Cyclades and the Aegean in the Third Millennium B.C.* (London: Methuen, 1972); idem, "Trade as Action at a Distance: Questions of Integration and Communication," in *Ancient Civilization and Trade*, ed. Jeremy A. Sabloff and C. C. Lamberg-Karlovsky (Albuquerque: University of New Mexico Press, 1975), 3–59.

56 Kent V. Flannery, "The Olmec and the Valley of Oaxaca: A Model for Inter-Regional Interaction in Formative Times," in *Dumbarton Oaks Conference on the Olmec*, ed. Elizabeth Benson (Washington, D.C.: Dumbarton Oaks, 1968), 79–110.

57 Alexander A. Bauer and Anna S. Agbe-Davies, "Rethinking Trade as a Social Activity: An Introduction," in *Social Archaeologies of Trade and Exchange: Exploring Relationships among People, Places, and Things*, ed. Alexander A. Bauer and Anna S. Agbe-Davies (Walnut Creek: Left Coast Press, 2010), 13–28.

58 Immanuel Wallerstein, *The Modern World System: Capitalist Agriculture and the Origins of the European World-Economy in the Sixteenth Century* (New York: Academic Press, 1974).

59 Guillermo Algaze, *The Uruk World System: The Dynamics of Expansion of Early Mesopotamian Civilization* (Chicago: University of Chicago Press, 1993); Sherratt and Sherratt, "The Growth of the Mediterranean Economy in the Early First Millennium BC."

60 Gil J. Stein, "From Passive Periphery to Active Agents: Emerging Perspectives in the Archaeology of Interregional Interaction," *American Anthropologist* 104, no. 3 (2002): 903–16; idem, "Rethinking World Systems: Power, Distance, and Diasporas in The Dynamics of Inter-Regional Interaction," in *World Systems Theory in Practice: Leadership, Production, and Exchange*, ed. P. Nick Kardulias (Lanham: Rowman and Littlefield, 1999), 153–77.

61 For example, Finkelstein, "A Great United Monarchy?," 7. This position is mostly apparent in minimalist-oriented interpretations.

62 Colin Renfrew, "Introduction: Peer Polity Interaction and Socio-Political Change," in *Peer Polity Interaction and Socio-Political Change*, ed. Colin Renfrew and John F. Cherry (Cambridge; New York: Cambridge University Press, 1986), 1–18.

63 Renfrew notes the challenge that the smaller units are often lumped into one archaeological culture because of their similarities (ibid., 2).

64 Ibid., 7.

65 Joseph Caldwell's explanation of this model is concise and somewhat abstract. Stuart Struever's application of it exhibits its potential (Joseph R. Caldwell, "Interaction Spheres in Prehistory," in *Hopewellian Studies*, ed. Joseph R. Caldwell and Robert L. Hall [Illinois State Museum Scientific Papers 12; Springfield: Illinois State Museum, 1964], 134–43; Stuart Struever, "The Hopewell Interaction Sphere in Riverine – Western Great Lakes Culture History," in *Hopewellian Studies*, ed. Joseph R. Caldwell and Robert L. Hall [Illinois State Museum Scientific Papers 12; Springfield: Illinois State Museum, 1964], 85–106).

66 In the Hopewell interaction sphere, the shared cultural traits were not simply explained through the distribution of an imported material or type of artifact, but trade networks were an important part of the interaction system.

67 Norman Yoffee, "Mesopotamian Interaction Spheres," in *Early Stages in the Evolution of Mesopotamian Civilization: Soviet Excavations in Northern Iraq*, ed. Norman Yoffee and Jeffrey J. Clark (Tucson: University of Arizona Press, 1994), 257–70; Gil J. Stein, "Local Identities and Interaction Spheres: Modeling Regional Variation in the Ubaid Horizon," in *Beyond the Ubaid: Transformation and Integration in the Late Prehistoric Societies of the Middle East*, ed. Robert A. Carter and Graham Philip (SAOC 63; Chicago: Oriental Institute of the University of Chicago, 2010), 23–44.

68 Yoffee, "Mesopotamian Interaction Spheres," 268.

69 Stein, "Local Identities and Interaction Spheres," 32–33.

70 Edward M. Schortman and Patricia A. Urban, "Modeling Interregional Interaction in Prehistory," *Advances in Archaeological Method and Theory* 11 (1987): 37–95; Edward M. Schortman, "Interregional Interaction in Prehistory: The Need for a New Perspective," *American Antiquity* 54, no. 1 (1989): 52–65. These works pre-date Stein's but do not figure into his use of identity theory.

71 Schortman, "Interregional Interaction in Prehistory," 54.

72 Ibid., 57. Schortman suggests four categories: technological, social, ideological, and proxemic (proper use of space), the last three of which would be used among participants in interaction.

73 Ibid., 57–59.

74 Ibid., 59.

75 Ibid., 60–61.

76 Indeed, both Renfrew's and Schortman and Urban's work reference Caldwell's as similar or influential.
77 The Deuteronomistic History (DH) takes precedence here because of its proximity to the period. The Chronicler's history also recounts Israel's 11th–10th centuries; however it is a later composition, written during the Persian period. Although the Chronicler did make use of older sources, and in some cases sources independent from the DH, there is significant repetition between the two histories because of Chronicles' heavy reliance on the Deuteronomistic work. Where the differences are of historical significance for this study, they are addressed. Of the poetic sources and wisdom literature that also purport to be related to the Davidic and Solomonic periods, none can be counted on for historical reliability for the 11th–10th centuries.

2 Interactions with the Philistines in 1 & 2 Samuel

This chapter is the first of two that examine select reports of interaction in the biblical history. The first study is of relations with the Philistines of 1 and 2 Samuel, which are traditionally understood to correspond to the late 11th and early 10th centuries BCE. Chapter Two examines accounts of interactions in Solomon's history (1 Kings 3–11), which the Deuteronomistic History (DH) presents as a continuation of the 1 and 2 Samuel material. Combined, these histories present the DH's account of Israel's transition from a collection of tribal societies linked by a common ancestry and culture to a singular, centralized state based in Jerusalem. I argue in both Chapters Two and Three that regional and interregional interactions were critical in the DH's version of these developments. The most dramatic and obvious impact is expressed in political change, but, by the end of the Solomon Narrative, we can identify more implicit reference to cultural change as well.

Although the cast of characters and regional polities is extensive across the Samuel stories, this first examination focuses on relations with the Philistines, relations that span the careers of Samuel, Saul, and David. Comprehensive analysis of any one of these figures' careers would result in a full volume, so this chapter is strictly limited to the most intensive interactions, according to the biblical narrative. Because each of the interactions examined below presents its own analytical challenges, discussions of source criticism and historical and archaeological contexts are specific to each episode. It is also important to note that, in light of the fact that we have no extrabiblical confirmation of the figures in the narrative, my discussion engages with the biblical material in the world it imagines, a presumed historical context of the late 11th and 10th centuries, while also acknowledging the importance of later centuries in the text's development. Another critical issue to address before looking at the episodes in detail is the fact that the biblical narrative frequently speaks indiscriminately of the 'Philistines' as a homogeneous and unified people. We can be quite sure that any historical reality was much more complex, but where the text fails to provide more discrete identifying information, I follow the narrative's lead and resist imposing more detail where it isn't supplied; I take the same approach for the use of 'Israelite' as a general identifier.[1] These passages simply cannot be used to understand early Iron Age identity and diversity.[2] My historical questions pertain more to the potential for interactions in the region, rather than being a test of historicity for the main characters. Based on events described in the biblical history, which incorporate several originally independent narratives, I conclude that reported interactions between Israelites and Philistines were connected to interregional exchange, and that the interactions were increasingly motivated by competition for control of the routes in and near the hill country. These interactions eventually led to shifts in leadership and territorial control.

Focus on the Philistines

There are several reasons for the intense attention given to the Philistines in the Samuel narratives. Generally speaking, the Philistines were the most conspicuous neighbor of the earliest core population of Israelites/hill-country residents. Philistine culture, in its earliest form, was a transplant from the Aegean, and Philistine settlements urbanized earlier than other Iron Age groups in the southern Levant.[3] These two factors (i.e., urbanization and nonlocal culture) would have made Philistine communities exceptionally different from other, contemporary southern Levantine cultures, especially the inland populations of the Iron I and early Iron IIA. Judging from the biblical narratives, Philistine conspicuousness influenced interactions with their neighbors and impacted the way these relations were remembered and eventually recorded.

In addition to these cultural factors, the geographic relationship between Philistine and early Israelite settlements ensured interaction. Both were bordered on their opposite sides by geographic boundaries: the Mediterranean to Philistia's west, and the Jordan Valley to Israel's east. Between them was the Shephelah, a territory that both populations desired, as it was good for human occupation and for supporting crops and livestock. Despite some obvious differences in culture, Philistines and Israelites had several challenges in common, such as growing populations, identity formation and redefinition, and changing social and state complexity. Their shared problems did not typically lead to camaraderie.[4] Instead, they competed for resources and, as I argue here, control of routes used for commerce.

Of the non-Israelite groups mentioned in the text, the Philistines are the most apparent in archaeological and extrabiblical materials, due, in large part, to their distinctiveness and punctuated arrival in the southern Levant.[5] As a result, there has been a relative confidence in identifying Philistine culture (although not without complications), and research has produced a large body of scholarship.[6] This is especially evident when compared to regions east of the Jordan or to the north, where transitions and differences in material culture are subtler at this time. In contrast, Philistine culture and Philistines' interactions in the region appear more accessible to modern scholars, which has resulted in an intense interest in the interaction activities of this cultural and political group.

Evidence and Approach

The biblical depiction of interactions includes the Eben-ezer battle(s) and the ark's travels (1 Samuel 4–7); Saul's interactions with Philistines, especially at the Michmash Pass (1 Samuel 13–14) and the Jezreel Valley (1 Samuel 28–31); and David's interactions with Philistines (1 Samuel 17–2 Samuel 8; 2 Samuel 21, 23). A critical historical analysis of these texts necessarily relies on source criticism and scholarship of the Deuteronomistic History. Martin Noth was the first to argue that the common elements running from Deuteronomy through 2 Kings signal a distinct unit within the Hebrew Bible, which has come to be known as the Deuteronomistic History (DH).[7] Since Noth, there have been various lines of argument regarding the potential author(s) and reconstructions of the work's composition, but nearly all agree that the history is a compilation of older stories and sources assembled into one large work late in the Judean monarchy or during the exile.[8] My understanding of this work generally follows Frank Moore Cross's theory of a double redaction of the DH.[9] This theory holds that the main history was constructed during Josiah's reign by an author/redactor, the Deuteronomistic Historian (Dtr). That history was revised during the exile to explain the destruction of Jerusalem and the fate of the Davidic kingdom.[10] From a historical perspective, if the bulk of the history was based on pre-exilic traditions and sources, we may have access to older accounts describing early Iron Age regional interactions and emerging states, but each account must be scrutinized to determine its usefulness for historical inquiry.

The depictions of interactions with the Philistines stem from a wide range of the history's sources, from what are arguably the oldest prose portions of the Bible to the Dtr's own contributions, and potentially to even later additions.[11] Relying on any portion of 1 and 2 Samuel for historical purposes is a contentious affair. The DH represents a number of different historical periods, potentially ranging from cultural memories of the 11th–10th centuries BCE to editorial work and supplementation in the 6th century BCE. In general, it is possible that any episode in the narrative might convey more about a later author's time than about the events being described. In addition to these chronological and source critical issues and the Dtr's particular biases (e.g., a specific theology favoring centralization in Jerusalem and pro-Davidic traditions), there is no extrabiblical evidence of the individuals whose stories drive the history. In order to proceed, however, this study allows for the existence of historical versions of the main events and characters, mainly Samuel (and the ark), Saul, and David. For each episode, I attempt to identify the material best suited for historical discussion, acknowledge potential weaknesses, and, when necessary, introduce extrabiblical, supporting evidence from geographic and archaeological research, to build a reasonable historical assessment and reconstruction.

Prelude to Monarchy: Eben-ezer and the Ark's Travels

The first interactions in Samuel involve conflict between Philistines and Israelites at Eben-ezer, a location in the northern Shephelah between Shiloh, Aphek, and Mizpah.[12] The material in 1 Samuel 4–7 describes hostilities between generic 'Philistines' and 'Israel' over some time. According to the story, the Philistines initially gained the upper hand with the capture of the ark (4:2), but later, the two groups battled again, resulting in Israel's victory and the reclamation of territory (7:10–14). This portion of the text is the most difficult of the Samuel episodes in terms of our historical aims, and very little that is related in the narrative can be applied to specific historical reconstruction. The material is important, however, in relation to the interactions that follow, involving Saul and David. We will see that the geography that is described in 1 Samuel 4–7 suggests an influential pattern of interactions between Philistines and their highland neighbors.

Close examination reveals that the episode is a composite of multiple sources.[13] The bulk of the action appears within the source known as the Ark Narrative (1 Sam 4:1b–7:1).[14] Appended to the end of the Ark Narrative is additional material describing Samuel's involvement in a conflict with Philistines (1 Sam 7:2–14). The verses that describe this conflict most directly (and with the least amount of theological and literary elaboration) are 1 Samuel 4:1–2; 7:7, 10–14.

Despite some detail in these verses, there are still problems in terms of reconstructing the events. It is unclear if there was one battle or more at Eben-ezer. To take the text at face value, the region of Eben-ezer saw repeated clashes between the two groups, but the narrative leaves us with questions about how much time passed and additional conflict occurred before the matter was settled. If there was only one battle, then the narrative disagrees with itself. The most glaring discrepancies are whether Israelites (7:11) or Philistines (4:10) won the battle, and whether or not Samuel was involved. The account in 1 Samuel 7 appears to correct the embarrassing details of the Israelites' defeat and the ark's capture, and does so in Deuteronomistic fashion. A third understanding lies in a combination of these possibilities, that there was an extended period of conflict in the region of Eben-ezer, resulting in a number of traditions about the area. While this option does not settle the narrative and source-critical problems, it is likely to be closer to the historical situation of the late 11th and early 10th centuries.

The Interactions

It is generally agreed that any historical basis to the Eben-ezer accounts should be sought in the narrative's geography rather than in details about characters or the dramatic elements (Figure 2.1).[15]

Figure 2.1: Overview of sites related to the Ark Narrative and Eben-ezer conflict.

Fortunately, the narrative reveals much in its geographic details. There are two main areas of interaction in the narrative. The action within the Ark Narrative focuses on a southern approach to Benjamin. The Eben-ezer battle descriptions locate the action around routes that approached Benjamin from the north. I suggest that the contests for dominance in the region were related to the value of the routes that passed between the coastal territories and the Benjaminite hill country, precisely those described in the Eben-ezer accounts and the ark's movements (Figure 2.2).

Figure 2.2: Possible routes related to the Ark Narrative and Eben-ezer conflict. Routes based on reconstructions in Dorsey, *The Roads and Highways of Ancient Israel* (Baltimore: Johns Hopkins University Press, 1991). Map: Google Earth, © 2020.

Northern Routes

The events of the Eben-ezer conflict that frame the Ark Narrative (1 Sam 4:1–2 and 7:2–14) draw our attention to the northern region of Philistine and Israelite territories. According to 1 Samuel 4:1, the Philistine troops prepared at Aphek. Although the Philistine heartland lay further south, the town of Aphek played an important role in Philistine interactions in this episode, as well as later in the history. The site's location, situated at the source of the Yarkon River, was integral in exchange activities. Since the river was difficult to cross, all coastal land traffic, including, and most importantly, travel on the international coast highway, the Via Maris, was naturally diverted from the coast to the source of the river – that is, to Aphek.[16] Whoever controlled the town gained power from the inevitability that travelers had to pass through this location. Indeed, its importance is confirmed in historical and archaeological evidence across many eras.[17]

A Philistine operation at Aphek provided advantages beyond control of the coastal route. Substantial Philistine remains, along with evidence of intercultural interaction, have been discovered at the mouth of the Yarkon, at the port city Tell Qasile, suggesting that Philistines may have been exploiting the trade opportunities at the port.[18] I propose that, in addition to the typically assumed coastal and maritime trade, Philistine interest extended to the east. With a secure handle on coastal routes through port cities and control of the Via Maris at Aphek, Philistines may have focused on another of Aphek's advantages, which was as a nexus of several routes that connected to the hill country, the Jordan Valley, and eastern highways. If Philistines were interested in expanding their use or control of routes toward the east, Aphek was a logical point of departure. The combination of these factors suggests a deliberate strategy to participate in, or even dominate, regional and interregional traffic from a base at Aphek.

The Israelite towns associated with the Eben-ezer battle(s), Shiloh and Mizpah especially, also occupied strategic locations.[19] Both were situated along the main highway of the hill country, the Ridge Road, which connected highland settlements from Hebron to Shechem, with extensions to other key regions (south to the Beersheba Valley and north to the Jezreel Valley and Beth-Shean). A cursory survey shows that many sites along this road were populated during this period.[20] If these areas were allied or united, the Ridge Road would have been critical in connecting them. Whether Israel moved into battle from Shiloh or Mizpah (or another location on the Ridge Road, Bethel perhaps?), the traditions suggest that Israel made strategic use of this route in defensive and political activities.[21]

Having explored the geography related to both groups, a question presents itself: what was the source of provocation between Aphek and the Ridge Road? I contend it was the roads that passed through the hills. According to D. Dorsey, about a dozen roads connected the Ridge Road and the coast, with at least four passing directly through Aphek and about that many more passing near the site. Similarly, about a dozen routes led east from the Ridge Road, to the Jordan Valley.[22] The southernmost of Dorsey's Samaria roads show the potential for a full route from Aphek through the hill country to the east.[23] From Aphek, one could travel to Shiloh via a fork in the road at Khirbet Tibna. Passing by that fork and heading south on the same road from Aphek led one to Jericho via Bethel, which happens to sit between Shiloh and Mizpah on the Ridge Road.[24] It would be illogical to propose that Philistine success in a campaign east of Aphek, or, conversely, Israelite success west of the Ridge Road (especially in the span between Shiloh and Mizpah), was not related to these highways. The region between the Philistine and Israelite bases contained some of the most important crossings through the hill country, important enough to warrant armed conflict.

Southern Routes

The ark's journey after its capture, particularly its path back into Israelite hands as described in 1 Samuel 5:6–7:2, follows a southern alternative to the routes implied in the Eben-ezer material. The ark passed from Ashdod to Gath and Ekron, then through

Beth-Shemesh to Kiriath-jearim. In other words, in leaving Philistia, it followed the Soreq Valley, one of three major valley roads that connected the hill country to the west throughout the biblical period.[25] Each of the ark's layovers corresponds to towns located at strategic positions, which allowed for participation in, as well as monitoring of, the traffic through the region. In theory, the ark could represent anything (e.g., people, traffic, goods) that moved along the same route, and, if we look beyond the narrative's theological concerns, we see an exchange corridor mapped out by the ark's movements.

The ark's point of departure, Ashdod, sat on the international coastal highway, where traffic flowing in local and interregional channels mingled. The intermediate sites of Gath, Ekron, Beth-shemesh, and Kiriath-jearim were at the frontlines of the shifting territories of Philistines, Canaanites (and their descendants), and Israelites in the 11th and 10th centuries, and in border tensions between Philistia and Judah throughout the Iron Age. Eventually, the ark returned to Israelite territory by passing into the highlands and back to the ridge settlements.[26]

Similar to the Eben-ezer accounts of interactions, the area of interest or contention is the intermediate zone, here represented by the ark's passage from Gath and Ekron to Beth-shemesh and Kiriath-jearim.[27] Both Beth-shemesh and Kiriath-jearim mediated passage between different geographic, ethnic, and political zones. Beth-shemesh features in discussions of borders and security in the biblical history, and excavations at the site have discovered unusual finds such as an iron smithy, a 10th century inscription, and luxury goods.[28] Kiriath-jearim also sat at a hub of activity, as a gateway between the hill country and lowlands. In biblical tradition, that translated to the boundary between Canaanite and non-Canaanite, and between tribal allotments.[29] Looking at the story from this perspective, the ark represents cultural exchange along the passage from the coast through the Shephelah and back into the hill country.

An Exchange of Goods

The Ark Narrative is, at its core, a tale of exchange. The nature of the story – overwhelmingly theological and mythic (including etiologies and allusions to Israel's classic myth/epic, the Exodus) – precludes a historical analysis of the details, but it is useful to entertain the economic implications of the story.[30] The ark passed into Philistine hands with Israel's defeat at Eben-ezer. This type of exchange is well-known in the ancient world – religious objects, typically constructed of high value materials, were regularly carried off by victors. This act symbolized a supernatural victory that accompanied the earthly one. In addition to the political, ideological, and psychological messages that the acquisition conveyed, the taking of the ark was an economic victory, both in the taking of booty but also in the potential tribute that the victor could impose if the Philistines were able to assert dominance further.

According to the Ark Narrative, however, the Philistines were not able to maintain the upper hand. They returned the ark with value added: gifts of gold and cattle from the Philistine leaders. Theologically, the gold objects and cattle serve as an offering to YHWH. According to P. K. McCarter, they function as 'decontamination' as well as 'compensation' for the Philistine lords/people.[31] They are presented to the deity along with the whole sacrifice of the cows in a religious ritual. As in the Exodus tale, YHWH is recognized as the ultimate power by both the actors in the story and by its audience. However, the gifts also serve as political and economic tools. The objects would have held both ritual and intrinsic value in their very material, and thus function as tribute from the Philistine lords to YHWH/Israel.[32] Due to the nature of the story, it is difficult to deem these details historical, but the overall power struggle and exchange of religious and luxury goods between Philistia and Israel are appropriate for an early Iron Age setting. It should not, therefore, be surprising that Israel's history asserts that the outcome of the Eben-ezer conflicts resulted in both political and economic victories in relation to Philistia.

Preliminary Conclusions

The Ark Narrative's climax traces the ark back into Israel's hands with a gift of tribute from the beleaguered Philistines. Even though there can be little confidence in this as a depiction of a precise historical event of the 11th–10th centuries, a general sense of the political dynamic and geography suggested in the text can be considered plausible for the period. This conclusion relies to some extent on the antiquity of the Ark Narrative itself, but even if we are reasonably skeptical about drawing historical conclusions from a mythic tale, anthropological approaches suggest a similar political landscape for this period.[33] The Eben-ezer accounts and current historiography depict decentralized religious and political circumstances and a tense relationship between Philistines and Israelites. The biblical tale lacks a singular leader, and there does not appear to be 'national' unity. From Shiloh to the battlefield, to Beth-shemesh, to Kiriath-jearim, and back to Samuel at Mizpah, there is little to suggest that these locations and various peoples were under one authority. This image is in accord with more recent models (to be discussed below) depicting decentralization that continued into the 10th century and possibly later, in contrast to depictions of centralization under Saul and David. What unifies the narrative's elements, aside from the ark as the focal point, are the highway networks that linked the events and characters, as well as the interactions that were inevitable from the use of these routes. Whether at Eben-ezer or along the ark's journey, there were tense negotiations along the roads that guarded passage between the Philistine coast and the central hill country. As a result of such tension, we might expect cooperation or consolidation in regional leadership (of either the Philistine towns or the hill country) for the defense of routes and borders. In the episodes that follow, we do indeed see these types of developments. Interaction and conflict along these same routes are factors in the rise of the regional leaders Saul and David, and in the consolidation of territories that would become the core of an early monarchic polity.

Saul

Saul's career in the biblical narrative is inseparable from interactions with the Philistines. It begins and ends with them. Saul's commission stems from a crisis of Philistine oppression (1 Sam 9:16), and his life ends on the battlefield, defeated by a Philistine coalition (1 Samuel 31). Although Saul interacted with other allies and foes, dealings with the Philistines dominate his history – second only to the rivalry with David – and provide important depictions of his interregional activities that may have the potential to be useful for historical analysis.[34] Two critical events will be the focus here: the battle at the Michmash Pass and the battle in the Jezreel Valley.

Battle at the Michmash Pass

Drawn in by the presence of a Philistine outpost (מצב/נציב) between Michmash and Geba/Gibeah, Saul, Jonathan, and the Israelites battled for the pass and expelled the Philistines from the Benjaminite hill country (1 Sam 13:2–14:23). This episode has a complex composition, and there are multiple layers. Some scholars reconstruct an older history (now largely lost due to the prioritization of a pro-Davidic history) that documented Saul's career and supplied material such as the Michmash battle event to later historians.[35] Complicating analysis of its origins and redaction are many corruptions in the manuscript traditions. Fortunately, we do not have to know each turn of the compositional history to evaluate the event itself. A simpler analysis will suffice.

The narrative presents more than one account of the same battle.[36] One is briefly reported in 13:2-6; that same event is presented as a dramatic narrative in 14:1-23. Between these two is additional material related to the event or deemed relevant by redactor(s). This material includes Saul's sacrifice at Gilgal (13:7b-15a), Philistine activities in the vicinity of the pass (13:17-18), and the Philistine metallurgical services on which Israelites relied (13:19-21).

Matters of Translation and Interpretation

The Location

Several related place names are associated with this event: Gibeath-ha-Elohim (from the first mention of the Philistine post in 1 Sam 10:5), Gibeah, and Geba. The similar names pose a problem for historical reconstruction. Are we to understand that there were two or more places, similarly named, that were important in the event? Or are the three names, variations from the same root, גבע, meaning 'hill,' all referring to one site? Even though גבע-based names were common designations for prominent hill-top sites, I follow the arguments of Miller and Arnold, that all three versions of the place name, particularly in relation to this episode, refer to one site, today's Jaba, that overlooks the pass.[37] Their solution, compelling in and of itself, also solves difficulties otherwise perceived in the episode. If Geba and Gibeah were two different places, the narrative appears confused and disjointed, not to mention implausible.[38] Instead, if we understand both Gibeah and Geba as references to the site directly opposite the pass from Michmash (modern Mukhmas), the narrative plays out with less difficulty, and the dynamic between Jonathan and the Saulides on the one hand, and the Philistine outpost and supporting troops on the other, can be more easily explained.

The Philistine Presence

The point of irritation that provoked the fighting was the Philistine מצב/נציב, first introduced in the narrative in 1 Samuel 10:5.[39] The מצב/נציב is not mentioned again until 1 Samuel 13–14, where it is the focus of the dramatic action. The use of both נציב and מצב, like the variations in the location name Geba/Gibeah, suggests that at least two sources contributed to the present text. נציב occurs early in the episode (1 Sam 13:3-4), and מצב

dominates from 1 Samuel 13:23 on.[40] Typically, for these instances, the nouns are translated as 'garrison,' implying a well-staffed, well-fortified military installation under the command of a central authority. Alternatively, the words might be translated as 'prefect,' suggesting an officer of some kind, implying an overseer of a Philistine occupation of the hill country.[41] Neither translation is fully satisfying, nor matches well the assumptions of the narrative. An armed garrison would be unlikely to fall to one man and his armor-bearer. The idea of a 'prefect,' a single officer 'assassinated' by Jonathan, is plausible, but often this interpretation is accompanied by the notion of a widespread Philistine occupation of the hill country, which is not required by the narrative.[42] Instead, translating the term more literally as a 'station,' 'installation,' or '(out)post' conveys the most necessary meaning and does not impose more than we know onto the translation and the episode. There is no unnecessary ambiguity in this choice – the resulting sense is that a Philistine installation (a person, guard staff, and/or structure) watched over the pass, and the threat to the station precipitated a full-scale battle.

Despite the corruption and confusion in Saul's history generally, many scholars hold that an event at the Michmash Pass has historical grounding. The proposed event was an attack by Jonathan on a Philistine post (as commander, Saul receives general credit in 13:4) that resulted in regional conflict. The account was recorded in more than one source, and the geographic dynamics are probable not only for the place but also for the time. Additionally, if one holds to the theory that Saul's battle against Nahash of Ammon *followed* the Michmash battle historically, contrary to its current place in the narrative in 1 Samuel 11, then there is a strong case for understanding this event as a critical moment in transforming Saul's career.[43] Saul would have been established first as a local leader designated through an elite lineage (1 Sam 9:1), whose military successes led to his engagement in affairs beyond his familial territory (e.g., in Jabesh-Gilead, toward Philistia and the south, and in Jezreel). In time, Saul became a regional leader with impressive military victories in addition to his worthy family status, thus explaining how Saul ben Kish of Benjamin became known as Israel's first king.

Regional Hegemony

Discussion of this episode has been couched in a broader understanding that Saul's rise stemmed from his leadership in an Israelite uprising against more powerful Philistine overlords.[44] This notion is influenced by the broader view of the DH.[45] The groundwork is laid in the book of Judges, where the narrator works in broad strokes, speaking of 'Israel's' oppression under the 'Philistines,' but, if we read carefully, interaction between Israelites and Philistines is not geographically widespread. For example, the geography of Samson's story, in Judges 13–16, does not reach much further east than the fringes of Philistine territory. When we turn to the book of Samuel, the Philistines are indeed the most frequent interaction partner, but their presence in the narrative is limited to specific battles. The narrative leading up to the Michmash Pass incident clouds the issue. Samuel's career summary, in typical Judges fashion, states that the Philistines were banished from Israel for all of Samuel's days (1 Sam 7:13), but Samuel is sent to Saul in 1 Samuel 9:16 because Saul will be called to deliver Israel from the Philistines. This kind of inconsistency is typical of a composite narrative, and of the Dtr's tendency to tweak the backdrop and invoke the image of an oppressive foreign hand upon Israel that reinvigorates divine intervention.

This broad, exaggerated characterization persists in modern historical reconstruction. It is not uncommon to read that the Philistines had, in the time of Samuel and Saul, occupied or oppressed Israel (generally), or that the battle at Eben-ezer was a successful liberation (though short-lived, to accommodate the Saul stories). The dramatic hyperbole of the narrative should not cloud the history of these interactions. In fact, when it comes to the hill country in the time of Saul, there is no *specific* evidence in the text, or in the archaeological record, of widespread overlordship by Philistines. To support this kind of theory, we would need evidence of administrative centers, within the hill country, comparable to Egypt's colonization in the Late Bronze/early Iron Age or to Assyria's program later in the Iron Age. The archaeological evidence suggests the opposite.[46] Without better evidence for Philistine hegemony, we must look for another explanation for Saul's interactions at the Michmash Pass. According to the narrative for this episode, there were Philistines in the area, but limited to the outpost (before Jonathan's attack), and we are not told why they were there. This understanding of a limited Philistine presence is the basis for the present discussion.

Interactions at the Pass

One way to approach analysis of this interaction is to ask: what were the Philistines seeking or defending in the central hill country? The simplest answer is the pass itself. The wadi between Michmash and Geba/Gibeah was the focus of military campaigns at various points in the region's history, and this instance falls in with that tendency.[47] It was a strategic crossroads connected to the Ridge Road and routes like those related to the Eben-ezer episode. From these routes and the central hills, this pass provided the main descent into the Jordan Valley. Instead of imagining this post as an extension of a Philistine occupation policy, which would be better carried out through administrative centers in towns or cities, or as a defense for Philistine residents nearby, of which there is no evidence, this installation is better explained as related to the crossroads.

The next logical question is: why would Philistines install a post at a remote location, at least in relation to their main settlement? The outpost can be explained in light of the highway networks. Just as in the Eben-ezer event, Philistines had good access to the international coastal routes, but to access the routes in the eastern Jordan Valley, they had to pass through the central hill country. Secured transportation through the Michmash Pass meant an open door to additional trade connections and eastern highways. A post at the pass may also have provided a source of revenue as a safe layover for travelers, or in the way of tolls (which could easily be seen by locals as a source of oppression). If the post was guarding transportation, we have an alternative interpretation for the Philistine 'razzias' that went out along the Ophrah road, the Beth-Horon road, and into the desert valley (13:17–18), precisely the directions we would expect for movement to or from the pass. What were 'raiding parties' to the Israelites might have been 'monitors' to the Philistines.

Previously, it was difficult to imagine what commercial interests might have motivated the Philistines to seek control of the Michmash Pass, but due to excavations over the last 15 years, it is now fully plausible, even very likely, that they were engaged in metallurgical trade involving the east and west sides of the Jordan Valley.[48] Excavations in the Faynan region (biblical Punon) of the Jordanian desert and Timna in the southern Arabah demonstrate that intense, local copper smelting was active from the 11th to 9th centuries BCE, and that, during this time, there was a long-distance trade network that reached far beyond the Arabah.[49] Further north, the earliest known iron smelting in the ancient Near East is now attested at Tell Hammeh on Jordan's Zarqa River (near Tell Deir 'Alla and Tell es-Sa'idiyeh), which functioned from the late 10th to the mid-8th centuries. In addition, other iron production activity has been identified in the region from the Iron IIA, at Beth-Shemesh, Tell eṣ-Ṣafi/Gath, Tel Reḥov, Megiddo, and Hazor.[50] The discoveries at Tell eṣ-Ṣafi, which date to the early Iron IIA, are the only known evidence of Philistine metallurgy, which happens to be reported in the addendum to the account(s) of battle at the pass (13:19–21, see below).[51] Most sites show evidence of both iron and copper processing.[52] The remains at Tell Hammeh and Beth-Shemesh indicate that the metallurgists were not novices merely learning or experimenting. Rather, they were advanced in their craft and used standardized practices, suggesting that the technology had been developed prior to the end of the 10th century and was shared across some geographic distance.[53]

In light of these discoveries, there is much more to say about the value of the Michmash Pass. Workshops like the ones at Beth-Shemesh and Tell eṣ-Ṣafi acquired raw materials either from recycled objects or from metal in the form of ingots or billets that were initially processed near the copper and iron sources. The nearest raw material resources in the region that were exploited at this time were east of the Jordan: iron to the north, and copper to the south (Figure 2.3). The production sites of Tell Hammeh, Khirbat en-Nahas, and Timna were used only for metal production. There were no domestic sites (excluding workers' quarters) associated with the smelting activities to suggest a resident, consumer population that was served by the industrial operations, which means that the products were distributed outside their immediate locations for additional processing and consumption, presumably to smithies like the ones at Tell eṣ-Ṣafi and Beth-Shemesh.[54] The Michmash Pass was the most convenient passage from Philistia, the Shephelah, and a significant portion of the hill country (especially in relation to Benjamin) to the Jordanian and Arabah Valley metal sources. When we add to this picture the value of worked metal in general – derived from the elaborate process necessary to acquire ore (itself a rarity), transform it to workable metal (requiring command of resources and location for smelting, as well as a high level of technological specialization and expertise), and transform it once again into final products (yet another set of specialized skills) – control of the Michmash Pass impacted what had the potential to be the most lucrative, locally based trade operation in the region.

Two asides in the biblical story suggest potential connections to this interpretation. According to 1 Samuel 13:19–21, Israelites relied on Philistine metalsmiths because 'there was no metalsmith to be found in all the land of Israel.' And in 1 Samuel 14:21, some 'Hebrews' who were previously 'with' the Philistines joined Saul and his forces in the battle. Admittedly, both notes pose some historical problems. The metallurgy note was once independent from the battle narrative. Its original form appears to have been a record of prices for tool maintenance. When it was incorporated into the narrative, it became an explanation of why only Saul and Jonathan were armed (13:19b, 22).[55] The passage itself does not explicitly claim that metallurgy was related to the outpost, and it is not possible to prove that the biblical material has a *direct* relationship to the archaeological evidence.

Figure 2.3: Potential routes related to Michmash Pass and known areas of metallurgical activity. Map: Google Earth, © 2020.

The second note, 1 Samuel 14:21, seems to conflict with much of the biblical (as well as scholarly) presentation of the relationship between Israelites and Philistines. It states that some Israelites were cooperative with Philistines. In the context of an oppressive Philistine force (as the Bible claims), interpreters must go to some lengths to explain why there would be any cooperation from Israelites.[56] It is more likely that, just as a potential Philistine presence may have existed only in select locations and on a limited scale, there was inevitably intercultural cooperation in particular circumstances. In the case of the Michmash Pass, the cooperative effort may have been related to the pass as an important stage in transportation and trade networks. As the narrative reads now, however, the emphasis is on the Israelites' shift in allegiance to Saul. This detail probably stems from an earlier narrative (i.e., the History of Saul's Rise) that argued for Saul's success in uniting and leading the Israelites. Despite the greater narrative's assertions to the contrary, both passages acknowledge that Philistines and Israelites interacted cooperatively.

If this material does indeed shed light on the Michmash Pass episode, it adds important nuance to our understanding of Philistine-Israelite relations. The possibility that the Israelites relied on the Philistines for metallurgical services is compelling. Biblical evidence leads us to believe that Israelites were not traditionally metalsmiths.[57] This information may be historically accurate but probably not for the reason the text gives, that the Philistines forbade it. The reasons Israelites may have turned to others for smithing services were more likely due to cultural, kinship, demographic, and environmental factors.[58] A cultural or social distance from metalsmiths explains why Israelites would 'go down' for tool maintenance (1 Sam 13:20). The likely descent from the hill country would have been to the lowland, probably the Shephelah (encompassing both Beth-Shemesh and Tell eṣ-Ṣafi), or to the Jordan Valley. It is also logical that there would be Israelites involved in the trade that passed through the hill country; in other words, it is difficult to imagine that they would have been isolated from such activity. This likelihood may explain why 1 Samuel 14:21 recollects cooperation between some 'Hebrews' and the Philistines before the battle at the pass. Some Israelites were engaged in the exchange activities that occurred at the pass. In this scenario, we can account for both cooperative (commerce) and hostile (objection to foreigners, to foreign gain from exploiting the area, to a toll at the pass) interactions. If the trade was lucrative, the pass would have been an attractive acquisition for control by local leaders (i.e., Saul and Jonathan). Saul and Jonathan's victory to take over the pass may have been popular among the area's residents for both economic and ethnic reasons, thus propelling Saul to a greater leadership position.

Battle in the Jezreel Valley

Saul's encounter with the Philistines in the Jezreel Valley moves the narrative focus to the northern reaches of both Philistine and Israelite territories (assuming the focus on hill-country Israelites). In the structure of the present narrative, there is a long build-up to this conflict, with notices of the troops' movements in 1 Samuel 28:4 and 29:1, before the battle is addressed in 1 Samuel 31. The events are described two more times in the DH: partially recounted in narrative form in 2 Samuel 1:1–10 and remembered in David's lament in 2 Samuel 1:19–27. Despite more than one telling of the encounter, there is little attention focused on the event itself. Only a few verses (1 Sam 28:4; 29:1; 31:1–7) describe the Jezreel Valley conflict, and these must be adjusted slightly to reconstruct a logical historical account (1 Sam 29:1; 28:4; 31:1–7).[59] A tentative reconstruction of the event follows these lines: based on a provocation or strategy not revealed in the narrative, the Philistines organized at Aphek, while the Israelites assembled in the valley, near the Jezreel Spring (29:1). As battle neared, the Philistines camped at Shunem across the valley from the Israelites, who were camped near the base of Mount Gilboa (28:4). Battle ensued, and Saul, his sons, and many troops died. The Israelites fled the area, and the Philistines took over the Jezreel territory (31:1–3, 6–7).

Examination of the material reveals several stages of composition and redaction, some of which can be reconstructed.[60] An older, cohesive narrative has been obscured by the history of David's rise, which, not surprisingly, steers the events in the interest of David's image, at the expense of the details of the exchange with Philistia.[61] The shuffling that occurred within 1 Samuel 28–31 illustrates the liberty that was taken with Saul's history. There should be no doubt that more information about this battle was compromised in similar ways, or simply eliminated as Saul's record was devalued. Nevertheless, an account, albeit brief, remains: the progression of troop movement toward the Jezreel Valley, followed by battle and Saul's death at Gilboa, is generally accepted to be the basic sequence of events of Saul's final days.

Interactions in the Jezreel

The precise reason for the Jezreel conflict is not evident from the text alone. As in the previous episodes, the Philistines are typically portrayed as aggressors who were taking over Israelite territory. In the same vein, I contend that attention to the routes and exchange habits of the region reveals a better explanation: hostilities at Mount Gilboa may have stemmed from competition in the Jezreel Valley, at least in part for commercial purposes (Figure 2.4).

The Jezreel Valley provided the best east-west crossing in the region with a naturally formed passage that cut through the central mountain range. The valley's importance is indicated by the prominent and long-occupied sites in the region (e.g., Megiddo) and by records of political conflict (e.g., Shoshenq's campaign). Its broad western opening allowed traffic from a large stretch of the coastal highway to turn eastward. From the west, the highway moved along the Jezreel Valley to its eastern extent, which was the purported location of Saul's battle with the Philistines. From here, the highway followed the Harod River Valley to the Beth-Shean region, and from there to several fords across the Jordan River.[62] The meeting point of the Jezreel and Harod Valleys was also an important location for a number of north-south crossings through the mountain ranges that connected Canaan and Israel with the Beqaʿ Valley to the north.[63] The confluence of routes explains the appearance of sites like Shunem and Jezreel, each sitting at the base of a prominent hill in the valley (Moreh and Gilboa, respectively). These locations made the sites desirable as watch posts over this highway and as strategic positions for defense or battle across the valley. Commercial and political activity around the valley and its major crossroads is a predictable extension of these geographic factors.

Figure 2.4: Potential interaction zones and routes related to Saul's interactions. Map: Google Earth, © 2020.

Saul's final military engagement fits well into this scenario. Although there is no archaeological confirmation of Philistines in the eastern Jezreel Valley (no small detail for historical evaluation!), research now shows that commerce was established (or renewed/continued) along this key route early in the Iron Age.[64] Based on textual evidence, D. Schloen's proposal of a commercial *casus belli* during Deborah's era establishes a case for competition in this territory prior to an Israelite monarchy and explains how commercial traffic could have increased during the decentralization processes after the end of the Late Bronze Age.[65] In the broad context of the region's social organization and political cycles, the transition leading to historical kingdoms is a pivot period wherein decentralization waned and the competition for new power centers grew.[66] If Saul was vying for strength in the region, the Jezreel was extremely valuable territory. Economic benefits would undoubtedly come to any regional contender who could win control of the pass, and the reputation of such a figure would have spread into other regions whose agents used the crossing. If the interactions examined thus far reflect an early Iron Age historical situation, Philistine interest in reaching the Jordan Valley is reflected in battles at Eben-ezer and the Michmash Pass, and if so, Israelite action in these conflicts may have thwarted Philistine efforts to cross the Jordan through the central hills. This dynamic may have led some Philistines (or allies to Philistines or other opponents remembered as 'Philistines')[67] to look toward the Jezreel Valley to achieve the same goals. Running parallel to the Philistine territory, however, would have been Saul's growing influence.[68] Although a northern conflict seems less likely, being some distance from the centers of both parties, the Jezreel Valley provided access to important routes to the east and was undoubtedly the battlefield in efforts among regional leaders seeking to control commerce and transportation.[69]

Preliminary Conclusions

After reviewing the first phases of Israelite-Philistine interactions in Samuel, we find a distinct pattern of hostilities at strategic east-west passages. These episodes have traditionally been used as evidence of Philistine aggression and hegemony in the region, where Israelites are typically portrayed as defenders of their hill-country territories, but the usual aggression-defense argument is flawed. The battles occurred at passes, not at key cities that could be used to administer over a subjected population. The traditional explanation neither illuminates the reasons why Philistines would have ventured eastward, nor delves into the complexity of the small-scale political development that was soon to create larger-scale changes to the region's social and political makeup.

In contrast, turning attention to a common element in the stories, that is, activity at key passes and routes, does lead us to a plausible explanation for the conflicts and for the pattern of interactions. The text contends that Philistines were active east of their main territory, progressing farther east in each tale. The best candidates for their interest were the copper and iron industries that were accessed across the Jordan (especially from the perspective of central highland sources).[70] The routes and interregional connections that facilitated metallurgical trade would have included other exchange as well. In this light, it was most likely commercial interests that motivated Philistines to cross the growing Israelite territory to reach routes and resources east of the Jordan Valley. According to this interpretation, the biblical accounts explain that Philistines attempted to do this through the Shephelah and hill country but were stopped by Israelite opposition in the battles of Eben-ezer and the Michmash Pass. The Jezreel battle may have developed as a result of the other two conflicts if Philistines sought an alternative route to the Jordan Valley after a more direct route through the hill country (i.e., the Michmash Pass) proved too dangerous or costly to pursue. Saul's potential motivations are slightly harder to reconstruct. His actions can be described as defensive, but the battle at Jezreel suggests a different tack. It is likely that Saul sought control of the key crossings at Michmash and Jezreel to increase his political power and economic position. While he was reportedly successful in the first exchange, which probably led to an increased following among the hill-country population, he overextended in his attempt to control a northern, alternative east-west passage.

David

The accounts of David's interactions with the Philistines include antagonistic and cooperative relationships. David's early reputation came at the Philistines' expense, but he is also remembered as having formed a close alliance with Achish of Gath. If there are historical underpinnings to these stories, it is notable that complex regional interactions led to David's influence over a small region adjacent to both Saul's and Achish's domains, to which he later added territory from the southern hill country and lowlands, Jebus/Jerusalem, and eventually Saul's Benjamin (see Figure 2.5). This consolidation effort was the largest yet according to biblical depiction. Analysis of the areas of interaction described in the text indicate that such an expansion aimed at influencing exchange activities between the Mediterranean and the Jordan Valley.

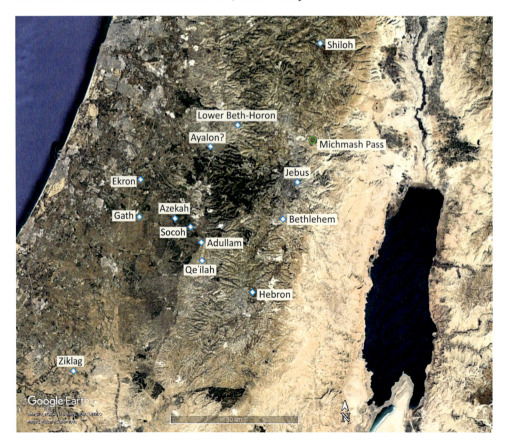

Figure 2.5: Overview of sites related to David's interactions. Map: Google Earth, © 2020.

Sources and Historical Challenges

Close attention to the biblical narrative reveals that ancient authors had a variety of sources to draw from in writing about David's life, including heroic folk legend and oral traditions, community histories and cultural memories, and possibly royal or administrative records. This variety alone makes analysis complex; the added weight given to David as the founder of a royal dynasty favored by YHWH increases the literary and historical issues.[71] David's story is largely apologetic, necessitating skepticism of its claims and historical worth. Despite this challenge, many scholars recognize that there are older, historically informative sources preserved in the DH, even allowing for the possibility that some sources may have originated close to, if not during, the 10th century, but determining (and finding consensus on) which portions of the text reflect those sources remains contentious.

Scholarly literature on David's history and its sources is vast. The most influential avenues of research for this study are the source criticism of the history of David, as well as evaluation of the literary and historical character of the texts. The foundation for such studies was laid by Leonhard Rost in 1926 when he argued for a 'History of David's Rise' source that recorded how David came to power.[72] This source, now typically understood to run from around 1 Samuel 16 through some portion of 2 Samuel 5, underlies almost all of the interactions examined below. It was not, however, the product of one historian. Its creation, like many of the larger units within the DH, was based on yet additional sources.[73] The discussion that follows will address the various source-critical, historical, and literary issues as they arise in the stories of interactions with Philistines. David's affairs are organized into three sections: David in Saul's court, David and his men, and David as Philistine ally.

In Saul's Court

Wherever we choose to locate the start of David's career, we cannot separate his rise to power from his service in Saul's court. Despite the way the DH now reads – that YHWH and Samuel kicked off David's career with the anointing of the young shepherd boy who happened to become Saul's court musician (1 Sam 16) – the more plausible historical reconstruction is that David, with a reputation as a heroic man of war (גבור חיל ואיש מלחמה; 1 Sam 16:18), gained a following among fellow soldiers while in Saul's army. David's early days are presented in legendary form in 1 Samuel 17 and 18, with his underdog victory over the Philistine warrior (later identified as Goliath) and his ability to supply the outlandish bride price for Michal (1 Sam 18:20–27).[74] Regardless of the historicity of these events, it is likely that David's performance in battle against Philistines contributed to his rise to power.

The folk saying first quoted in 1 Samuel 18:7, 'Saul has killed his thousands; David, his tens of thousands,' may be the oldest or best evidence of the successes that came to both men.[75] Although the saying does not identify the unfortunate enemies, the majority of evidence suggests it was the Philistines who suffered as a result of this pairing. The sum of the material on David's earliest days, 1 Samuel 16–18, provides little concrete and reliable evidence for the purposes of writing history today, but a few things can be drawn out of it. David's career was built on his success as a warrior, possibly originating from before he joined Saul's forces (1 Sam 16:18). While with Saul, David was highly successful in conflicts with the Philistines (at the battle introduced in 1 Sam 17:1 and celebrated in 1 Sam 18:7), and was closely linked to the next generation of leadership (through Jonathan and Michal, 1 Sam 18–20). David's success created the opportunity for a shift from leading Saul's army to rivaling Saul's authority (1 Samuel 18ff).

David and His Men

Much of the evidence regarding interactions with the Philistines comes from stories of 'David and his men.' The material is presented in the form of short battle accounts and brief notes of heroic deeds:

1 Sam 23:1–13	Qeʻilah incident
2 Sam 5:17–21, 22–25	Two accounts of Philistines at the Rephaim Valley
2 Sam 8:1	Philistines and Metheg-haʾammah[76]
2 Sam 21:15–22	Tales of David's men
2 Sam 23:8–12, 18–23	David's warrior-heroes
2 Sam 23:13–17	Philistines at the Rephaim Valley and Bethlehem outpost

Most of the material is not fully integrated into the main narrative. On the one hand, the sources are easily separated from the greater Samuel narrative, but on the other, there is little context associated with the accounts. The most vexing problem for historical applications is the absence of chronological contexts for these events. There are, however, clues in these sources, and working through them does result in important evidence regarding David's early days.[77]

Sorting out a chronological orientation for these episodes is critical for examining the nature of interactions with Philistia. I propose that most of these episodes occurred before Saul's death, when David had become well-known as a warrior and charismatic leader but had not yet secured control of a territory. If David's activities with his men were indeed contemporary to the episodes where Saul engaged the Philistines, then we already have some understanding of why the parties were in conflict. The Philistines were involved in an effort to connect with eastern trade. David's activities in the south, and in relation to Saul's, indicate that David was also vying for participation in the exchange network.

There is significant overlap across the 'David and his men' material, indicating some redundancy as well as closeness (variously in geography, chronology, or literary form) between the episodes. The associations are not close enough to be dismissed simply as mere repetitions (they are too distinct in content); instead, they corroborate the encounters to a certain extent. Highlighting the relationships among these texts also builds a case for historical reconstruction. Most of these events can be placed earlier in David's career, when he, along with a band of fellow warrior-heroes, made names for themselves in battles against Philistines.

The Qeʻilah incident is the longest unit in this collection of evidence (1 Sam 23:1–13).[78] In this episode, David and his men defeated the Philistines who were attacking the town of Qeʻilah. News of David's success, however, revealed his location to Saul, who then took up pursuit, causing David and his men to flee the town. The narrative follows a formula that is repeated in other battle accounts where David and his men are fighting the Philistines (2 Sam 5:17–25): the Philistines attack; David requests guidance from YHWH, who assures David will be victorious; and in the end, David saves the people. The Qeʻilah incident adheres to the formula in verses 1–5, but then the narrative continues with additional content about David's conflict with Saul.

The story's reliance on the oracle formula might reveal an older source at the heart of this account. This example, along with the two in 2 Samuel 5:17–25, may preserve traditional tales of David's successes, somewhat like the folk saying of David and Saul's many victories (1 Sam 18:7). Its apologetic nature, along with apparent elaboration on the initial Qeʿilah report, however, leads to questions about the extent of the author's dramatic license in crafting the episode. That David would have been engaged in a battle against a group of Philistines for Qeʿilah, and that Saul was following David's movements, are not problematic, although David's motives may not have been to 'save' the town, as the narrative claims. A strikingly similar event of a raid at Qiltu (biblical Qeʿilah) during the Amarna period (14th century BCE) was recorded in letters from Shuwardata of Gath and ʿAbdi-Ḫeba of Jerusalem.[79] The attack on the town by a band of ʿApiru resulted in a significant regional conflict followed by the installation of Egyptian forces in Jerusalem. The parallels suggest that Qeʿilah was in fact a strategic location in between Philistia and the southern hill country, making it a source of competition among regional leaders (see additional discussion below). Keeping in mind the later exchange with Achish of Gath (who, we must assume, was the Philistine leader most invested in Qeʿilah), where David received land in return for his service (1 Sam 27:5–6), this episode appears to remember an earlier period of contention as David carved out his own territory, before he and the leadership in Gath came to an agreement.

The stories in 2 Samuel 5:17–21, 22–25 follow the same oracle formula as the Qeʿilah episode, making it likely that they came from a common source or story type about David and his men. The stories' current location obscures the original context. There is a distinct difference in the source material between verses 17–25 and what precedes them. As the narrative reads now, it appears that David fought the Philistines after he had captured Jerusalem, but this association comes from the placement of verses 17–25. They, along with verses 11–16, were added to the end of the 'History of David's Rise' source, which appears to conclude at 2 Samuel 5:10.[80] Because the oracle stories follow this material, they are traditionally understood to be chronologically later than David's move to Jerusalem. Details in the stories, however, indicate an earlier point in David's career. His communication method with YHWH, for example, implies a time prior to David's role as a recognized leader of the people. There is no hint of a court structure that should have been in place if the episodes were from David's Jerusalem period.[81]

Comparison of these stories to others in David's history narrows the chronological window further, to the period when David was no longer loyal to Saul and not yet allied with Gath. The significant details are in the geographic references to the 'stronghold' (at Adullam) and the Philistine camp(s) in the Rephaim Valley. According to 1 Samuel 22:1–2, David used a stronghold at Adullam as a base of operations following his break with Saul and before he became increasingly empowered, initially in Hebron and later in Jerusalem. In the context of the redacted text of 2 Samuel 5, Jerusalem, with a stronghold in the City of David (2 Sam 5:9), is understood to be David's base in 2 Samuel 5:17. When removed from the context of 2 Samuel 5:6–16, however, the stronghold's location loses its Jerusalem referent. In this case, we should understand Adullam rather than the City of David as the location of this particular base.

The other common geographic element is the Rephaim Valley, named as the staging ground for the Philistine forces in 2 Samuel 5:18, 22 and in 2 Samuel 23:13.[82] The first two references come from the oracle stories. The third is from the story of David's three warriors who retrieved water for him from Bethlehem (2 Sam 23:13–17). We have already established that the 2 Samuel 5:17–25 episodes are out of their chronological position, which frees them from a period after Jebus was taken. In addition, David's use of the (Adullam) stronghold (mentioned in two of the three Rephaim Valley conflicts) must have been limited to a period between David's service to Saul and his alliance with Gath, his subsequent move to Hebron, or his move to Jerusalem.

Thus, it stands to reason that these stories should be situated in that same chronological window when David was independent but not fully empowered in his own right.[83] In addition, the Rephaim Valley stories do not reveal any tension regarding David's allegiance to Philistine leadership. Had the Rephaim Valley events occurred after David's cooperation with Achish, we might expect an explanation of just how David's relationship with Gath's leader had soured. While shifts in the region's relations are to be expected, the absence of an explanation of why David would have been fighting his (former) ally is out of character compared to the detail we have at other points in the history. The proposal that the Rephaim Valley events occurred before David aligned with Philistia is the best solution.

The episode in 2 Samuel 23:1–17 requires some additional analysis, as it mentions a Philistine outpost near Bethlehem. The short tale describes David's men's heroic venture to retrieve water for him from a cistern guarded by Philistine troops. The cistern and outpost are not mentioned in any other tradition concerning Bethlehem, outside the parallel in 1 Chronicles 11:15–19. For the present purposes, the well or cistern is of little concern, but the historicity of the Bethlehem outpost is important. It would demonstrate further penetration by Philistines toward the Jordan Valley and create a more complex picture of David's relationship to this portion of the hill country.

Arguments about the episode's composition have placed it across the chronological spectrum, from the oldest of the Samuel material to the latest of the biblical texts.[84] There is little evidence by which to judge the episode, but there is some indication of the editorial and transmission history that it experienced. The episode must have found its way to its present location because of an association between the officers known as 'the Three' and the three warriors who accompany David in the story. The men in this tale should not be identified with the named men in the surrounding text. The association suggests that the title 'Three' may have inspired a story about three warriors with David, which works against a claim for historicity. At the same time, there is awkwardness in the narrative from verse 13 to 14 to 15, suggesting a piecemeal composition or editorial work. If verse 14 is removed, there is a better narrative: 13, 15–17. The formula in verse 14 of subject + אז + location reveals a later clarification connecting this episode to a previous historical situation. It is notable that verse 14 does not harmonize *within* the biblical narrative. The notes in verse 14 connect a cultural memory of a Philistine presence in Bethlehem some time ago to the editor's audience. That verse 14 may be separate from the episode is not necessarily an argument for a historical Philistine outpost, but it does speak to an independent tradition of one.

The remaining material consists of brief notes remembering David and his men in the appendices to Samuel. In addition to the typical problems that accompany transmission and redaction, significant corruption occurred in 2 Samuel 21 and 23, affecting the names of figures and places.[85] Nonetheless, there are strong arguments in favor of the antiquity of the material. Among these arguments are the uniqueness of the content and the possibility that there are independent sources represented in these portions of the text.

Geography plays a role once again. Battle descriptions correspond roughly to the locations of Saul's conflicts with the Philistines; that is, they appear to be in the Shephelah, between Benjamin and the eastern Philistine zone (guarded by Gath). It is quite likely that these battles too would have occurred earlier rather than later in David's career, and that David and his men would have been fighting for or with Saul. One in particular warrants detailed discussion. The location פס־דמים/א is the battleground in both the David and Goliath tale (1 Sam 17:1) and in the tradition of Eleazar ben Dodo (1 Chron 11:12–14 // 2 Sam 23:9–10).[86] The coincidences of this unusual location name and the defeat of a great Philistine warrior by an Israelite hero indicate that the two versions recount the same event; however, the closer parallels to the 1 Samuel 17 story appear in the tales of David and his men in 2 Samuel 21. If the David tale in 1 Samuel 17 was simply appropriated from the hero story known to us through 2 Samuel 21:15–22, why or how did פס־דמים, known otherwise only from the account in 1 Chronicles 11:13 (presumably also originally in 2 Sam 23:9), enter the picture? Rather than contend that elements of unrelated tales were consolidated into the (David) version in 1 Samuel 17, perhaps the parallels indicate that the events were related chronologically. The stories of close combat between Philistine and Israelite warrior-heroes stemmed from the time when David and his men were in Saul's service.

Lastly, David's roster of warriors in 2 Samuel 23 is mostly Judahite men, one third from the environs of Bethlehem. The particular collection of men suggests it reflects an earlier stage in David's career, when he was a rising warrior with kin and local connections rather than a king with an army drawn from a broader population base.[87] It is possible and likely that, due to the nature of the appendices (compiled from unrelated sources), and the shuffled condition of the material, one or another item would be from later in David's career, but the majority of the content points to an earlier stage, when David built a power base from his activities in the hill country south of Benjamin and in the Shephelah.

Despite having been dispersed throughout the history of David, the tales of his activities with his band of warriors took place prior to David's alliance with Achish. During this period, David was making a name and establishing himself as a key player in the area east of Philistia and south of Saul's territory. Now we can evaluate the relationship between this geography and regional interaction. David's base coincided with routes to the east that the Philistines may have been using in an effort to skirt Saul's domain.

Interactions against the Philistines

If my analysis above is correct, once Saul had expanded his influence throughout Benjamin, Philistines with an interest in reaching the Jordan Valley had to exploit alternate routes. One solution was to head north, which resulted in the battle in the Jezreel Valley (1 Sam 31). Another solution was to skirt the southern border of Saul's territory. In the biblical narrative, David's encounters against the Philistines are concentrated along routes in this southern region.

The most direct southern alternative for the Philistines to reach the Jordan Valley would have been to travel from Gath along the Elah Valley toward Bethlehem, then to Jerusalem, and then to the river crossing.[88] The biblical narrative describes conflict at several points on this route. Once independent from Saul, David based his operations at the stronghold of Adullam, which provided easy access to traffic on a variety of roads, including the route to Transjordan via Bethlehem. Some battles involved the Rephaim Valley near Bethlehem and Jerusalem. In this same territory was the crossroad with the Ridge Road that passed Hebron, Bethlehem, and Jerusalem on its way north into Saul's territory. Like its northern counterpart at Michmash, a Philistine outpost at Bethlehem protected traffic at a key juncture with the Ridge Road, the last main crossroads before the descent to the Jordan Valley.

David's concentration on Adullam and his taking of Qeʿilah strengthen the case that he was competing for involvement in or control of this corridor. Adullam and Qeʿilah were located just south of the Gath-Bethlehem route, accessed by a road descending from Adullam to Socoh.[89] Adullam's position, just off several routes, provided quick access for monitoring traffic. Qeʿilah sat at the intersection of two critical roads. One paralleled the coast highway and the main Ridge Road. It connected key cities, like Lower Beth-Horon and Ayalon, to Beersheba.[90] The other route that passed through Qeʿilah connected the coast with the Judahite portion of the main Ridge Road. This highway passed from Tel Mor through Gath before meeting the inland highway at Beth-zur, which was situated between Bethlehem and Hebron.[91] Qeʿilah lay just over ten miles from Gath on this road and about five miles from Socoh along another, where Saul and David are said to have fought the Philistines (1 Sam 17:1). At the edge and meeting point of three territories (i.e., Achish's, Saul's, and David's), the battle for Qeʿilah would have been a consequential event for regional interactions and had the potential to put David on the map as a serious contender in the region.

David's move on Qeʿilah is justified in the biblical narrative as a liberation or salvation from Philistines; 1 Samuel 23:5 ends with: 'David saved (וישׁע) Qeʿilah's residents.' In addition to alluding to a Davidic legacy, the text's assertion here implies that residents of Qeʿilah were oppressed by Philistine overlords, or that they identified with David and his men as kin or rightful leaders. These assumptions cannot be maintained uncritically, and the narrative even concedes that David's actions were not well received by Qeʿilah's residents (1 Sam 23:7–13). A historical David's motivations were probably not so noble. The narrative provides an alternative view in 1 Samuel 22:7–13, in which Saul criticizes David by calling him a 'highwayman' who cannot enrich his followers with land and fields.[92] It is difficult to know the source of this critique – Saul's words are certainly an ancient author's invention and do heighten the tension in the story – but it may better reflect a historical reality than readers would at first assume. The narrative depicts David taking advantage of a decentralized political landscape in the south to accumulate a territory through conquest and create a name for himself among the region's leaders.

The Qeʿilah battle demonstrates what types of military and economic gains were at stake. In this scenario, the Philistines had an interest in fighting for Qeʿilah because it guarded a significant road to Gath from the hill country (which was a source of raiding parties like David's!). David's acquisition could not have gone unnoticed by them. Furthermore, if 1 Samuel 23:7–13 preserves historical information, Qeʿilah had some kind of agreement with Saul. David's victory meant increased independence and power for Saul's rival, instead of being the marginalized nuisance in the Negev that Saul might have settled for. As a result, Saul mobilized to regain Qeʿilah from David. Whichever leader claimed the territory would also gain control of the direct route between the southern highland and the Philistine coast, exchange with the Jordan Valley, as well as control of traffic between Benjamin and Beersheba's highway. David's conquest meant that Achish and Saul would face a significant obstacle on the main roads leading to their territories.

In sum, even though we cannot connect the dots directly from one conflict to another, David's hostile interactions with the Philistines corresponds to routes that would have allowed alternate passage between Philistia and the Jordan Valley and would have impacted routes connecting Philistia and Saul's territory to the south. Alternatives were necessary for the Philistines due to Saul's increased control of the Benjaminite hill country. For some time, David operated from an independent base at Adullam, but his involvement in this territory escalated with the capture of Qeʻilah. At this point, David's role must have shifted from a local leader of a band of men in the wilderness to a regional contender.

David's Alliance with Achish

The DH records two attempts by David to approach Achish, the king of Gath. According to the redacted text, David had a narrow escape from the king in 1 Samuel 21:11–15, before allying with him in 1 Samuel 27–29 against their common opponent, Saul. We are not told why David approached Achish in the first episode, except that he was fleeing Saul. David abandoned this attempt when Achish's servants noted his leadership status and recited the folk saying celebrating David's prowess. In response, David feigned madness to distract from the threat he might pose. In 1 Samuel 27, David sought out Achish, but this time, David approached with his household, his men, and a proposal. He offered his service in exchange for a sanctioned residence in Philistine territory, and Achish granted him Ziklag. David then remained in Achish's service until Saul's Jezreel battle, from which David was (conveniently) excused. The narrative does not record any further communication between David and Achish after the preparations for the march to Jezreel.

The Achish-David episodes appear to come from two sources. One contributed the shorter episode in 1 Samuel 21:11–15.[93] This episode is brief and appears to interrupt a longer narrative regarding the priests of Nob. A different (older?) source is responsible for 1 Samuel 27:1–28:2 and 29:1–11, which was unified prior to the editorial insertion of the En-Dor episode in 1 Samuel 28:3–25.[94] The longer source is more elaborate in character development, and portions of it exhibit phrases distinctive of the Dtr (likely due to the Dtr's editorial work).[95] Despite their different lengths, they have in common some basic elements. Both versions:

a) report that David sought refuge in Philistia;
b) reiterate the folk saying of Saul and David's heroics;
c) put the folk saying in the mouths of Philistine leaders' support staff (Achish's servants in 21:12; Philistine commanders in 29:3);
d) show off David's clever deception before the king; and
e) ultimately result in the safe escape/dismissal of David.

This basic pattern may be the most problematic issue for arguments in favor of a historical David-Achish partnership.[96] The Hebrew Bible contains a number of iterations of this formula, which is likely a sub-group of a larger flight motif that is very familiar through tales such as Abraham and Sarah before the Philistine king Abimelech of Gerar (Genesis 20); Isaac and Rebeccah before Abimelech of Gerar (Genesis 26); David before Achish (1 Sam 21:11–15); David before Achish (1 Sam 27–29); David before Abimelech (or Ahimelech?[97]) (Psalm 34:1); and Shimei's slaves' flight to Achish of Gath (1 Kings 2:39–46; although this episode does not adhere as well to the pattern, it appears to be related to it).[98]

It is an impossible task to determine either the origins of this narrative formula or which of the biblical variations might have served as a template for the others. The more important questions are: what are implications of the use of this formula for the history of relations between David and the Philistines? Is the pattern simply a formula into which a legendary David was inserted, or did a historic interaction with Philistia easily lend itself to narrative expression through this motif? Of the biblical versions, the patriarchs are the easiest to dismiss as a product of the folk-tale formula, due to the anachronism of a Philistine king in what is supposed to have transpired before the migrations at the end of the Late Bronze Age. For David, the problem is more difficult, and it would be too rash – and unfair to ancient authors – to dismiss any possibility of interaction based on the use of a popular motif to recount that past.

Modern historical concerns were not shared by the biblical authors. In all of the texts where David interacts with Achish, literary and apologetic efforts outshine historical claims. This habit is evident in the two episodes where David flees to Gath. In 1 Samuel 21:11–15, Achish's men are provided the opportunity to reiterate the folk saying that was apparently well-known in later times, suggesting that David's reputation was far-reaching 'back in the day.' David is given the opportunity to demonstrate his cunning mind and escape a potentially dangerous situation.[99] In the second meeting, David also comes across in a positive light, already powerful, established, and, yet again, clever. Motives for these episodes are in line with other elements of the 'David's Rise' saga. As readers, we are sympathetic for the righteous man who must flee the mad and jealous king; David's craftiness allows him to navigate the tense arrangement so that he continues to build his reputation among his own people, while staying in good graces with Achish and thus protected, while also waiting out Saul's self-destruction. Such is the literary David.

A historical David cannot easily be extracted from these episodes, but the text's concern for the relationship between David and Achish requires that we examine it further. To begin, it appears that we have two versions of the same event. Does a contrasting doublet indicate a revision to David's history, where 1 Samuel 21:11–15 fixes his embarrassing resume as a mercenary against highlanders? It is possible. The apology present throughout 1 Samuel 27–31 reveals similar attempts to explain away a past alliance with Gath and David's role in Saul's demise. It appears that no one was comfortable with the idea that David fought in league with the Philistines, potentially in battle against Saul and the Israelites. It is this reasoning that has led many scholars to propose that, yes, there was a historical alliance between David and Gath. The persistence of the apology cannot conclusively prove that the alliance is historical, but it does urge a close examination.

Fortunately, we can turn to additional research to assess the events. Excavations have demonstrated conclusively that Tell eṣ-Ṣafi, identified with biblical Gath, played an important role in the region during the 10th century; this element of the stories correlates well with the extrabiblical evidence.[100] The basic premise, that a figure like David could have had dealings with Gath's leadership, is not itself implausible, but arguments questioning the historicity of the figure King Achish pose one challenge to the reliability of the relationship. The name Achish is known from extrabiblical evidence, but that Achish is mentioned in a Philistine inscription and Assyrian records, which describe a king of Ekron (not Gath) in the 7th (not 10th) century. The Ekron inscription, which also proved Tel Miqne was in fact the remains of Ekron, provided evidence to support what many scholars had long suspected, that the name of Ekron's king, called Ikausu in Assyrian, was the same name as biblical Achish; both names are West Semitic forms of Ἀχαιος, 'Achaean,' meaning 'Greek.'

This name, along with Ashdod's 8th century king Yamani, attests to an Aegean-affirming self-identification among Iron Age Philistine kings.[101] In evaluating the inscription, J. Naveh suggests that Ekron's Achish and other non-Semitic names in 7th century records attest to 'a national awakening' in Philistia, emphasizing 'their kinship with the Greeks on Cyprus.'[102] From this context, Naveh argues that the name Achish in 1 Samuel and 1 Kings 2:39–40 is likely a 'reflection' of the 7th century Ekronite king onto David's Gittite ally.[103] Naveh concludes that the biblical author supplied details known from his own period in order to illustrate the 10th century history.

While Naveh's argument is sound, and we see this tendency in many narratives, biblical or otherwise, the appellation Achaean/Achish/'Greek' for the leaders of Philistine communities may have been important in more than one period as a demonstration of identity or affiliation. Recent discoveries from Tell eṣ-Ṣafi/Gath may provide corroborating support. Excavators argue that a sherd containing a 10th century alphabetic inscription should be read as two personal names of Aegean origin.[104] If they are correct, this inscription testifies to Aegean-oriented ethnic identification in Gath, as well as participation in elite-driven scribal culture. In addition, a sherd from a rare Argolid bowl has also been recovered from the site, which demonstrates that contacts with the Aegean (direct or indirect) were important to Gath's residents – most likely to its elites.[105] The project's principal investigator, A. Maeir, has identified other possible indications of cultural closeness, such as hearth and house styles.[106]

Comparative archaeological data may indicate that Gath maintained cultural distinction within the southern Levant during this period. Faust and Lev-Tov argue that Gath exhibited cultural distinction compared to other Philistine cities in the 10th century (evidenced in the number of pig bones at various sites over time).[107] The researchers suggest that the reason lies in Gath's position as the largest Philistine city on the eastern extent of the coastal territory and its 'regular contact with the Israelites.'[108] These claims are not without controversy, as debates continue about how best to understand ancient identities based on archaeological research, and how presumptive we may be about cultural homogeneity or diversity.[109] What is not in dispute, however, is Gath's exceptional example according to various criteria during this era. If Gath's role in the region's interactions was enhanced through cultural distinctiveness or through exhibitions of Aegean cultural attributes, this explanation could also encompass Gath's Argolid pottery example and the Aegean names on the inscribed sherd. The 'awakening' of a Philistine-Aegean identity that Naveh argues for in the 8th and 7th centuries would have been fueled by increased contact with Greek trade and Philistine economic resurgence, but it may also have been inspired by cultural memory of earlier Philistine leaders who asserted their Aegean identities.[110] This is not to say that we can label the DH's Davidic-era Achish or his activities as historical, but it may be plausible that an Aegean/Achaean name was also meaningful in 10th century Gath, and thus not necessarily anachronistic.

The Samuel narrative's depictions of David and Achish's interactions, when judged by literary qualities alone, may not at first appear to have historical credence. With the extra-biblical material, however, the *setting* that is assumed by the narratives appears not only to be reasonable for the time period, but even likely. Where the narrative, archaeology, and other extrabiblical sources are most in line is in Gath's role as a significant city, possibly a leader in interactions with non-Philistines, and in Gath's character as ethnically and culturally distinct from its Shephelah and highland contemporaries. An alliance between David and Gath is plausible and can be explored further.

Interactions in Alliance with the Philistines

The details have been clouded by the ancient historians' apologies, but, at some point, David and Achish appear to have made a deal. In contrast to the canonized story, wherein David seeks refuge from Saul's jealous wrath, the alliance likely arose from a common desire to be rid of the obstacles to both Achish's and David's goals. The narrative's slant aside, David and Achish probably began their relationship as rivals and later joined their efforts to weaken Saul's control of the roads through Benjamin.[111]

Recall that Saul succeeded in denying Philistines passage through the Benjamin hill country. In response, the Philistines turned to alternate passages to the east. The most direct option was via Gath and the Elah Valley to Bethlehem and on to the Jordan. This passage skirted along the southern extent of Saul's territory, but David and his men – as a part of Saul's army or as independent agents – made this route difficult as well, and battled near Gath, Socoh, the Rephaim Valley, and Bethlehem. As David strengthened his base, he demonstrated that he could take Qeʻilah and build a territory of his own, based first in Adullam and later in Hebron. His dominance effectively blocked Philistine access south of Saul's territory (with the notable exception of Jerusalem, whose participation is unknown).[112] The combination of Saul and David's efforts shut down Philistine access to the east from the Benjaminite hills to the Negev.

The impetus of the negotiations may have been any number of things: a rift between David and Saul, as the biblical narrative argues, David's reputation, or a choice on the part of Gath preferring one ally or territory over another. We will not know for certain, but consequences of the proposed alliance can be teased out of the regional dynamic. When David allied with Gath, both parties would have experienced significant benefits.

The economic consequences would have been immediate. To begin, Philistines could have gained access east through David's territory, with protection offered by his men, and David could collect tolls. In exchange, through a cooperative agreement with Gath, David gained access to coastal trade, which was increasing between the Aegean and southern Levant.[113] David also expanded his holdings through the condition that he be granted his own town, Ziklag (1 Sam 27:5–6).[114] The site's precise location is unknown, but being within Gath's domain and proximate to David's activities implies that Ziklag was south of Gath and west of the southern hills. The acquisition of a site in this region extended David's influence along a broader west-east stretch, from Ziklag to Carmel and En-gedi.[115] This span would have forced all inland trade moving north from the Negev or Arabah through David's territory. The pact also detracted from Saul's previous gains. If Saul had negotiated relationships in the Shephelah, those connections may have been hurt by David's involvement in the exchange networks in neighboring areas.

Politically, David and at least some of the Philistines were able to work together against Saul. Saul's territory was expanding, but the David-Achish alliance allowed for a coordinated effort to divide Saul's attention across more than one front. The challenge is apparent in 1 Samuel 23:27–28, when Saul abandoned his pursuit of David to respond to another Philistine threat. Saul's growing base had already impacted exchange routes through Benjamin. It is logical that traffic through Jezreel would have been attractive for additional expansion. David's alliance with Gath, however, had consequences for this larger exchange network. With a firm grasp of the territory south of Saul, David had the potential to make a deal involving Philistine trade in the hill country. We can imagine that David's role – if he was not in the battle at Jezreel – was to maintain a threat in the south during the northern campaign. In return for his assistance, the Philistines may have helped David take over the

Benjaminite territory, and the two parties could then have cooperated in trade between the Mediterranean and the Jordan and Arabah Valleys.[116]

Chapter Conclusions and Implications

At the close of this initial step in the investigation, the biblical evidence tips in favor of interregional exchange activity involving Philistia and the hill country during the end of the 11th and first half of the 10th century. The biblical material, though complicated from a historical perspective, remembers exchange between these southern Levantine neighbors. Virtually all interactions involving the Philistines correspond to key roads and exchange networks in and around the emerging Israelite territory (Figure 2.6). This statement is true across the different stages of political organization and different types of sources, from myth, to military history, to the apologetic, whether pro-Saul, pro-David, or pro-Deuteronomistic theology. In addition, the extrabiblical material, though limited, is supportive of the conclusion that encounters with the Philistines were related to regional interaction networks.

Having identified key geographic areas, I can address a secondary, and more consequential, research question, which is: what were the impacts of these activities? The biblical accounts in Samuel attest to regional competition for control of trade-related locations, which then prompted consolidation efforts on the part of the region's leaders. The most successful, in this body of evidence, proved to be the Philistine princes/kings, Saul in his rule over Benjamin, and David, who succeeded not only in solidifying control over a southern territory based out of Hebron, but who also went on to join this territory with his conquest of Jebus/Jerusalem and Benjamin.

In the prelude to monarchy, the action of the Eben-ezer battle(s) and the ark's travels follow highway networks and trade routes that linked Philistia and the central highlands. Two zones receive the focus: 1) the region between northern Philistia (including Aphek) and the Ridge Road (between Shiloh and Mizpah); and 2) the Soreq Valley highway that ran through the border zone between eastern Philistia (i.e., Ekron and Gath) and the Benjamin hill country (via Beth-Shemesh and Kiriath-jearim). Exchange interests as motivation for the conflict are implicit in the focus on the region between Philistia and the hill country, especially in light of the key routes that ran through the area. Exchange is explicit in the transfer of goods that occurs in the Ark Narrative.

During Saul's tenure, the most direct evidence of exchange comes from the circumstances surrounding the Michmash Pass battle. Some Philistines were engaged in affairs that necessitated a manned outpost, which involved some 'Hebrews,' and which in some way related to metallurgical services that Israelites had been using. Drawing on extrabiblical evidence, I argue that Philistine interest in metallurgical trade across the Jordan was the impetus for Philistine activities in the Benjamin hill country and later in the Jezreel Valley. While the text emphasizes the Deuteronomistic explanation of Saul's role as a liberator of Israel from foreign oppression, the geography of his conflicts with the Philistines suggests that he was tightening control over routes that led from Philistia (or the west generally) to the Jordan Valley. Once successful at the Michmash Pass and along the borders of Philistia, Saul expanded his efforts to the north by engaging a Philistine coalition at Jezreel. This campaign was his most ambitious, and it demonstrates that his motivations were not simply to defend his constituents or the more idealistic 'all Israel' of biblical depiction, but to maintain his hold on access to the Jordan Valley against the Philistines.

Figure 2.6: Overview of interactions with Philistines, and key sites in the region. Map: Google Earth, © 2020.

David's interactions stand in strong contrast to Saul's, but in the end, they were both motivated by the desire to control access through the highlands. In David's case, his flexibility in allegiance proved a successful approach, as he eventually dominated more territory, including, at a minimum, Judah, non-Israelite Jerusalem, and the Benjamin hills. According to the text, David's interactions with Philistia were carried out through both military conflict and strategic alliance. The most explicit exchange came in the form of land, but, like his contemporaries, the geography of David's activities indicates that he was maneuvering to control key routes through the highland regions.

David's sphere of influence grew with each stage of his career, with each expansion adding to his control of trade networks. David's work with Saul secured his familiarity with the Shephelah border and the southern border of Benjamin, shoring up some of the most direct east-west routes between Philistia and the Jordan Valley. When David moved away from Saul's leadership, he gained purportedly unclaimed territory in the south (at least in the biblical recollection). During his renegade days, David and his band of men increased his influence, expanding it to all edges of Judah's hills, which secured a role in traffic related to Negev routes. In addition, David acquired territory through his own activities and his deal with Philistia – some of which is explicitly described in the text, some of which we have to infer (e.g., gaining control of Benjamin). By the time of Saul's death, David appears to have solidified his place as a leader of the south, as an ally of Philistia, and as possessing enough power and resources to assume leadership of Benjamin and take Jerusalem. This consolidation of territory meant exclusive control over east-west traffic from the Benjaminite hills to southern Judah, with potential shared participation in Philistine efforts from the southern coast and desert traffic north to the Jezreel Valley.

The combined evidence of interactions indicates there was an escalation in the region. From the description of the Eben-ezer conflict to David's consolidation of power, control of routes and influence over certain regions fell into fewer hands. In 1 Samuel 4–7, there is little to suggest that Philistine leadership, Shephelah villages, or highland residents asserted regular control of the contested territories outside of their village, town, or city borders. As Saul's career progressed, he expanded his influence – through success against the Philistines – from a zone of several towns and key locations (e.g., the Michmash Pass) in the heart of Benjamin, to the west, where he engaged in battles against the Philistines in the Shephelah borderland and along valley routes. The culmination of David's efforts shows that he was able to build a base south of Benjamin, including the hill country and lowland to the west, and then move to incorporate both Jerusalem and Saulide territory. His success essentially guaranteed his involvement in, if not control over, southern traffic between the Mediterranean coast, the southern Jordan Valley, and the Arabah. Perhaps the greatest consequence of these interactions was that the intense competition for trade routes that fueled the hostilities between the Philistines, Saul, and David led to the creation of the first multi-tribal polity described in the DH.

Notes

1 Frequently in this chapter, I emphasize the imprecision of the label 'Philistines' by opting not to use the definite article in English, even if it might appear in the biblical text. The DH often fails to convey where Philistine opponents were from, whether they were made up of a coalition, or what their numbers were. The difference between 'the Philistines' (implying a wholeness or totality) versus 'Philistines' (implying uncertainty about more precise identities) is meaningful for the present discussion. My aim in using less definite language is to check the tendency to assume that the interactions involved a monolithic Philistine force. We should likewise view critically the text's assumption or assertion that Israel was unified or uniform during this era.

2 Research connecting archaeology with ethnicity and identity more closely examines diversity within larger labels such as Philistine or Israelite, dynamics between Philistine populations and their neighbors, as well as similarities and expressions of their differences between groups. For another recent discussion of the relations between Philistines in this era, with special attention to the biblical accounts, see

Ido Koch, "On Philistines and Early Israelite Kings: Memories and Perceptions," in *Saul, Benjamin, and the Emergence of Monarchy in Israel: Biblical and Archaeological Perspectives*, ed. Joachim J. Krause, Omer Sergi, and Kristin Weingart (Atlanta: SBL Press, 2020), 7–32.The detailed excavation of Tell eṣ-Ṣafi/Gath is providing more nuance to our knowledge of various phases of Philistine culture, and principal investigator Aren M. Maeir addresses the problem of identity and diversity in a number of recent publications (Maeir, "On Defining Israel"; idem, "A 'Repertoire of Otherness'? Identities in Early Iron Age Philistia," in *Proceedings of the 5th "Broadening Horizons" Conference [Udine 5-8 June 2017]: Volume 1. From the Prehistory of Upper Mesopotamia to the Bronze and Iron Age Societies of the Levant*, ed. M. Iamoni [West & East, Monografie 2; Trieste: University of Trieste, 2020], 161–70; idem, "Philistine and Israelite Identities"; Maeir and Shai, "Reassessing the Character of the Judahite Kingdom." Although there have been critiques more recently, including by Maeir (and others, see below), ethnicity and identity studies have been important in improving the influence of the biblical bias in research; Bryan Jack Stone, "The Philistines and Acculturation: Culture Change and Ethnic Continuity in the Iron Age," *BASOR* 298 (1995): 7–32; Faust, *Israel's Ethnogenesis*, 111–156; Avraham Faust and Justin Lev-Tov, "The Constitution of Philistine Identity: Ethnic Dynamics in Twelfth to Tenth Century Philistia," *OJA* 30, no. 1 (2011): 13–31. For discussions of the Late Bronze Age to Iron I transition, see Elizabeth Bloch-Smith and Beth Alpert Nakhai, "A Landscape Comes to Life: The Iron Age I," *NEA* 62, no. 2 (1999): 62–92, 101–27; Ann E. Killebrew, *Biblical Peoples and Ethnicity: An Archaeological Study of Egyptians, Canaanites, Philistines, and Early Israel, 1300-1100 B.C.E.* (Atlanta: Society of Biblical Literature, 2005).

3   Assaf Yasur-Landau provides a comprehensive discussion of the Philistine migration to the Levant in his book *The Philistines and Aegean Migration at the End of the Late Bronze Age* (Cambridge: Cambridge University Press, 2014); see also David Ben-Shlomo, "Pottery and Terracottas in Philistia during the Early Iron Age: Aspects of Change and Continuity" in *Change, Continuity, and Connectivity: North-Eastern Mediterranean at the Turn of the Bronze Age and in the Early Iron Age*, ed. Łukasz Niesiołowski-Spanò and Marek Węcowski (Weisbaden: Harrassowitz Verlag, 2018), 141–57.

4   Whether the Israelites were a product of a migration (as biblical traditions maintain) or descendants of Canaanites, they developed an identity based on a history of migration, expressed through the traditions of the patriarchs, exodus, exile, and return. In this sense, Israelites and Philistines had parallel stories, both having migrated (or maintained stories of migration) in the Late Bronze to Iron Age transition.

5   Not surprisingly, there is a longer process of migration than historical and literary sources let on, but it is also clear that there was a dramatic 'surge' in Philistine settlement following the first indications (Aren M. Maeir, "The Tell Eṣ-Ṣâfi/Gath Archaeological Project: Overview," *NEA* 80, no. 4 [2017]: 212–31). Susan Sherratt (followed by Alexander Bauer) has argued for a commercial component to the introduction of Sea Peoples/Philistine culture in the Levant (Susan Sherratt, "'Sea Peoples' and the Economic Structure of the Late Second Millennium in the Eastern Mediterranean," in *Mediterranean Peoples in Transition: Thirteenth to Early Tenth Centuries BCE*, ed. Seymour Gitin, Amihai Mazar, and Ephraim Stern [Jerusalem: Israel Exploration Society, 1998], 292–313; Alexander A. Bauer, "Cities of the Sea: Maritime Trade and the Origin of Philistine Settlement in the Early Iron Age Southern Levant," *OJA* 17, no. 2 [1998]: 149–68). Their works are useful explorations of economic factors in the early Iron I changes, but note also the challenge by Tristan Barako ("The Philistine Settlement as Mercantile Phenomenon?," *AJA* 104, no. 3 [2000]: 513–30).

6   The recent publications detailing the results of excavation of Tell eṣ-Ṣafi/Gath and Ashkelon have greatly increased our knowledge; in addition to references already mentioned, see the special issues of *Near Eastern Archaeology* focused on Tell eṣ-Ṣafi/Gath (*NEA* 80, no. 4 [2017]; *NEA* 81, no. 1 [2018]); Aren M. Maeir, ed., *Tell Es-Safi/Gath: The 1996-2005 Seasons*, 2 vols. (Ägypten Und Altes Testament 69; Wiesbaden: Harrassowitz, 2012); for Ashkelon, see most recently Lawrence E. Stager, Daniel M. Master, and Adam J. Aja, eds., *Ashkelon 7: The Iron Age I.* (University Park: Eisenbrauns, 2020). See also Ann E. Killebrew and Gunnar Lehmann, eds., *The Philistines and Other "Sea Peoples" in Text and Archaeology* (Archaeology and Biblical Studies 15; Atlanta: Society of Biblical Literature, 2013); Eliezer D. Oren, ed., *The Sea Peoples and Their World: A Reassessment* (Philadelphia: University of Pennsylvania Press, 2013).

7   Martin Noth, *The Deuteronomistic History*, trans. David J. A. Clines (JSOTSup 15; Sheffield: JSOT Press, 1981).

8   Approaches after Noth tend to fall into two groups, following either Frank Moore Cross's double redaction theory or Rudolf Smend's (supplemented by Walter Dietrich and Timo Veijola) multiple redaction theory that the initial history (DtrG) was succeeded by nomistic redaction (DtrN) and prophetic redaction (DtrP). See Frank Moore Cross, *Canaanite Myth and Hebrew Epic: Essays in the History of the Religion of Israel* (Cambridge: Harvard University Press, 1973), 274–289.; Rudolf Smend, "The Law and the Nations: A

Contribution to Deuteronomistic Tradition History," in *Reconsidering Israel and Judah: Recent Studies on the Deuteronomistic History*, trans. P. T. Daniels; ed. Gary N. Knoppers and J. Gordon McConville (Winona Lake: Eisenbrauns, 2000), 494–509; see also Albert De Pury, Thomas Römer, and Jean-Daniel Macchi, eds., *Israel Constructs Its History: Deuteronomistic Historiography in Recent Research* (JSOTSup 306; Sheffield: Sheffield Academic Press, 2000).

9 Cross, *Canaanite Myth and Hebrew Epic*, 274–289. See also Richard Elliott Friedman, *The Exile and Biblical Narrative: The Formation of the Deuteronomistic and Priestly Works* (HSM 22; Chico: Scholars Press, 1981).

10 Cross referred to the author of the Josianic edition as Dtr[1] and the exilic redaction as Dtr[2]. The distinction between the two editions does not play a large part in the analysis in the present chapter. For this reason, I will simply refer to the Dtr, which will indicate either author/redactor/edition of the DH.

11 For discussion of interactions with the Philistines closer to the main period of biblical composition in the 7th and 6th centuries, see Avraham Faust and Ehud Weiss, "Judah, Philistia, and the Mediterranean World: Reconstructing the Economic System of the Seventh Century B.C.E.," *BASOR* 338 (2005): 71–92. Regarding the early Iron Age, Faust argues that the earliest stages of interaction with Philistines were so influential that they laid the groundwork for attitudes about Israelite interaction with foreigners in general (Faust, *Israel's Ethnogenesis*, 63).

12 The precise location of Eben-ezer is unknown. 'Izbet Ṣarṭah has been put forward as a good candidate (Rainey and Notley, *The Sacred Bridge*, 144), but seeking out archaeological remains of a town or village may be misguided. The narrative does not point to such a site. The etiology in 1 Samuel 7:12 references a very vague location, 'between Mizpah and Shen/Jeshanah.' There is no hint of an occupied settlement in Samuel's day or later, and no mention of inhabitants or the conquest of a town. It is more likely that Eben-ezer was a battleground, an open field or valley.

13 The historical and literary components to this episode are many. At play are older sources (the Ark Narrative and the histories of Saul's and Samuel's careers), a possible pre-Deuteronomistic composition, the process of integration into the larger structure of the DH, as well as the massaging that was necessary to create a cohesive overall narrative. Behind the literary works and cultural memory traditions are what could be called religio-political tensions and histories of the transition from tribal and chieftain leadership to monarchs, tensions between prophets and kings, and religio-political centers: Shiloh, Mizpah, Kiriath-Jearim, and, implicitly, Jerusalem.

14 Leonhard Rost is credited with the foundational work on the Ark Narrative (*The Succession to the Throne of David*, trans. M. D. Rutter and D. M. Gunn [Sheffield, England: Almond Press, 1982]). For subsequent studies, see Joseph Blenkinsopp, "Kiriath-Jearim and the Ark," *JBL* 88, no. 2 (1969): 143–56; Antony F. Campbell, *The Ark Narrative (1 Sam 4–6, 2 Sam 6): A Form-Critical and Traditio-Historical Study* (SBLDS 16; Missoula: Scholars Press, 1975); idem, "Yahweh and the Ark: A Case Study in Narrative," *JBL* 98, no. 1 (1979): 31–43; P. Kyle McCarter, *I Samuel: A New Translation* (AB 8; Garden City: Doubleday, 1980); Marsha C. White, "'History of Saul's Rise': Saulide Propaganda in 1 Samuel 1–14," in *"A Wise and Discerning Mind": Essays in Honor of Burke O. Long*, ed. Saul M. Olyan and Robert C. Culley (BJS 325; Providence: Brown University, 2000), 271–92; idem, "Searching for Saul," *BR* 17, no. 2 (2001): 22–29, 52–53; Patrick D. Miller Jr. and J. J. M. Roberts, *The Hand of the Lord: A Reassessment of the "Ark Narrative" of 1 Samuel* (Atlanta: Society of Biblical Literature, 2008).

15 Rainey and Notley, *The Sacred Bridge*, 143–44. This is the consensus even among those who are more critical in historicity debates. Finkelstein says it explicitly ("The Philistines in the Bible," *JSOT* 27, no. 2 [2002]: 154–155; see also Israel Finkelstein and Neil Asher Silberman, *The Bible Unearthed: Archaeology's New Vision of Ancient Israel and the Origin of Its Sacred Texts* [New York: Free Press, 2001], 134) as do James Maxwell Miller and John Haralson Hayes (*A History of Ancient Israel and Judah*, 2nd ed. [Louisville: Westminster John Knox Press, 2006], 128). Lester L. Grabbe suggests that if there had been conflict in the Shephelah, Israelites would have initiated raids on dominant Philistines ("From Merneptah to Sheshonq: If We Had Only the Bible...," in *Israel in Transition, From Late Bronze II to Iron IIA (c. 1250-850 BCE): Volume 2: The Texts*, ed. Lester L. Grabbe [The Library of Hebrew Bible/Old Testament Studies 521; London: Continuum International Publishing Group, 2011], 98–99). Mario Liverani implies a basic historical accuracy in his depiction of Philistine treatment of the Shephelah and Hill Country (*Israel's History and the History of Israel* [London; Oakville: Equinox Publishing, 2005], 69–71).

16 Dorsey, *Roads and Highways*, 57–61.

17 The site's occupation begins in the Early Bronze I and continued into the Islamic period. Major fortifications, other monumental architecture, and diplomatic correspondence are just some of the discoveries that attest to Aphek's strategic location. The Egyptian 'Governor's Residence' from the New Kingdom is

highly suggestive of the city's administrative importance just prior to the period described in the biblical narrative. See Moshe Kochavi, "The History and Archeology of Aphek-Antipatris: A Biblical City in the Sharon Plain," BA 44, no. 2 (1981): 75–86; Mosheh Kokhavi and Miriam Tadmor, *Aphek in Canaan: The Egyptian Governor's Residence and Its Finds* (Jerusalem: Israel Museum, 1990).

18 Amihai Mazar, *Excavations at Tell Qasile* (Qedem 12, 20; Jerusalem: Institute of Archaeology, Hebrew University of Jerusalem, 1980).

19 While the strategic aspects of their locations apply regardless of chronology, neither site's history/archaeology aligns neatly with the biblical material describing this period. Excavations indicate that Shiloh's occupation ended near the Ark Narrative's timeframe, at which time occupation at Mizpah was in its early stages. It has been frequently repeated that Shiloh's destruction came at the hands of the Philistines and is depicted in this episode, but the text does not claim the Philistines reached or attacked the site, and archaeological evidence does not reveal who, in fact, destroyed it (R. A. Pearce, "Shiloh and Jer. Vii 12, 14 & 15," VT 23, no. 1 [1973]: 105–8; Israel Finkelstein et al., "Excavations at Shiloh 1981–1984: Preliminary Report," TA 12, no. 2 [1985]: 123–80; Donald G. Schley, *Shiloh: A Biblical City in Tradition and History* [JSOTSup; Sheffield: JSOT Press, 1989], 196). Mizpah's importance spans several periods within the biblical history, so we are faced with the fact that later events may have influenced the story. Tell en-Naṣbeh, argued to be biblical Mizpah, has yielded material culture typical for the hill country, as well as locally-made Philistine bichrome pottery and possible Cypro-Phoenician imports. The site does have evidence of occupation after the Iron I (with evidence of collard rim jars, Philistine pottery, silos, wine presses, and a kiln) and was fortified in the early 9th century; see Jeffrey Zorn, "An Inner and Outer Gate Complex at Tell En-Nasbeh," BASOR 307 (1997): 53; idem, "New Insights from Old Wine Presses," PEQ 130 (1998): 154–61; idem, "The Dating of an Early Iron Age Kiln from Tell Al-Nasbah," Levant 30 (1998): 199–202; idem, "A Note on the Date of the 'Great Wall' of Tell En-Naṣbeh: A Rejoinder," TA 26 (1999): 146–50.

20 Dorsey refers to this route as ancient Israel's 'National Highway' due to its importance throughout the Iron Age (*Roads and Highways*, 117–19).

21 The Israelites' base at the start of the conflict in 1 Samuel 4:1 is unclear. The episode begins with the Israelites marching out to engage the Philistines. The present text implies that they marched from Shiloh, but this association is the result of redaction. The starting place is not explicitly stated in the text.

22 Dorsey, *Roads and Highways*, 163–80. Two routes in Dorsey's Judah group (J1 and J2) cross into this territory as well (ibid., 181–85).

23 Ibid., 170–171.

24 Ibid., 134, 170–71. With this in mind, it is curious that Bethel does not appear in this narrative (Anson F. Rainey, "Looking for Bethel: An Exercise in Historical Geography," in *Confronting the Past: Archaeological and Historical Essays on Ancient Israel in Honor of William G. Dever*, ed. Seymour Gitin, J. Edward Wright, and J. P. Dessel [Winona Lake: Eisenbrauns, 2006], 269–73; Victor H. Matthews, "Back to Bethel: Geographical Reiteration in Biblical Narrative," JBL 128 [2009]: 149–65).

25 To the north is the Ayalon Valley road and to the south the Elah Valley road. Each of these valley routes was guarded by a major city in/near the Shephelah border zone: the Ayalon by Gezer, the Soreq by Ekron, and the Elah by Gath (Dorsey, *Roads and Highways*, 181–91).

26 Either to Mizpah with Samuel, as described in 1 Samuel 7, or, if the Ark Narrative's original conclusion is indeed now located in 2 Samuel 6, to Jerusalem.

27 The passage through both Philistine border towns raises some questions. Why should the ark pass through both Gath and Ekron before heading east? Was there a critical reason that both cities were included in the story, but other major Philistine cities were not? Judging by the route alone, Gath seems to be the surprise in the story, since there was a more direct route from Ashdod to Ekron to the Ayalon Valley road. In the late Iron I–early Iron IIA, however, Ashdod and Gath were the major Philistine cities; Ekron was not yet as important (Aren M. Maeir, "The Tell Es-Safi/Gath Archaeological Project 1996–2010: Introduction, Overview and Synopsis of Results," in *Tell Es-Safi/Gath: The 1996–2005 Seasons*, ed. Aren. M. Maeir, 2 vols. [Ägypten und Altes Testament 69; Wiesbaden: Harrassowitz, 2012], 39–40). The mention of the three cities may reflect concerns from two different authors, one earlier (closer to when Ashdod and Gath were predominant) and one later (when Ekron was the main eastern city).

28 Beth-shemesh features prominently in narratives about the emerging Israelite/Judahite territory and state. It is named in boundary delineations (Josh 15:10; 19:22), even though it was not taken from its inhabitants according to Judges 1:33. It was a Levitical city according to Joshua 21:16. During the monarchic period, it had an administrative role for Solomon according to 1 Kings 4:9, and was the site of a border war between Amaziah and Jehoash (2 Kgs 14:1–12). Excavations at the site suggest ethnic complexity

and some turbulent times (Shlomo Bunimovitz, Zvi Lederman, and Dale W. Manor, "The Archaeology of Border Communities: Renewed Excavations at Tel Beth-Shemesh, Part 1: The Iron Age," NEA 72, no. 3 [2009]: 114–42). McCarter argues that the text is commenting on Beth-shemesh's inability to provide a proper priest from among its residents, raising some questions about the ancient author's possible concerns about the city's ethnic composition (McCarter, I Samuel, 131).

29 Blenkinsopp characterizes Kiriath-jearim as a 'nodal point', where the territories of Benjamin, Judah, and Dan's initial allotment met ("Kiriath-Jearim and the Ark," 148).

30 Etiology and other traditional mythic/epic elements in the story dictate that the literary nature of this exchange is far more recoverable than any historical events. The allusions to the Exodus tale (e.g., the Philistine priests' similarities to the Egyptian priests, plagues forcing the release of the ark/people, gold objects given with the ark's/people's departure) have obscured any history that might have been behind a tribute exchange between Philistia and Israel in this early period. No doubt various political exchanges occurred between the two, but this episode's details cannot provide specific historical evidence.

31 McCarter, I Samuel, 133.

32 Ibid.

33 E.g., Faust, Israel's Ethnogenesis, 111–156; Faust and Lev-Tov, "Constitution of Philistine Identity."

34 That is, within the context of the biases of the ancient authors. Saul's story cannot easily be removed from the larger narrative concern of the history of Israelite monarchic institutions, of which there are multiple points of view. For discussion of this context and source analysis of 1 Samuel, see Baruch Halpern, The Constitution of the Monarchy in Israel (HSM 25; Chico: Scholars Press, 1981).

35 Marsha White refers to it as the 'History of Saul's Rise' paralleling the proposed 'History of David's Rise' source ("History of Saul's Rise"). See also J. Maxwell Miller, "Saul's Rise to Power: Some Observations Concerning 1 Sam 9:1–10:16; 10:26–11:15 and 13.2–14:46," CBQ 36 (1974): 157–74; Patrick M. Arnold, Gibeah: The Search for a Biblical City (JSOTSup 79; Sheffield: JSOT Press, 1990); Diana V. Edelman, King Saul in the Historiography of Judah (JSOTSup 121; Sheffield: Sheffield Academic Press, 1991); idem, "Saul Ben Kish in History and Tradition," in The Origins of Ancient Israelite States, ed. Volkmar Fritz and Philip R. Davies (JSOTSup 228; Sheffield: Sheffield Academic, 1996), 142–59; White, "Searching for Saul"; idem, "Saul and Jonathan in 1 Samuel 1 and 14," in Saul in Story and Tradition, ed. Marsha C. White and Carl S. Ehrlich (FAT 47; Tübingen: Mohr Siebeck, 2006), 119–38. Recently, Israel Finkelstein has weighed in on the pre-Deuteronomistic historical traditions; for an overview of his arguments, see "Saul and Highlands of Benjamin Update."

36 This is a fairly accepted argument, but there are alternative readings. McCarter, for example, interprets the text as an old, cohesive but textually corrupt, narrative, with only one significant interpolation (1 Sam 13:7b–15a). His reading is that Jonathan attacked a Philistine prefect (1 Sam 13:2, followed by additional background information) that then prompted a full-scale battle, in which Jonathan was again the hero (1 Sam 14:1–23; see I Samuel, 224–42). However, the narrative's progression in chapter 14 is particularly strange if the events of 1 Samuel 13:2-6 came before. Why was Jonathan's attack a surprise if he had already 'assassinated' the Philistine prefect? Are the intervening 'background' materials explicitly or convincingly connected? In addition, McCarter appears reluctant to address source critical issues that suggest themselves from variations in the terms נציב and מצב and the place name changes between Geba and Gibeah. These literary and source-critical elements appear to rule out the cohesion that he sees in the story.

37 Miller's discussion begins with the reasoning that has been used to support the identification of Tell el-Ful with Gibeah. The identification, provided first by Robinson and later argued by Albright, influenced the conclusion that Jaba must be a separate site, namely Geba. Miller then reviews all references to the various forms of the name and determines that variations of גבע all refer to Jaba except for Gibeath-Kiriath-Jearim and the name and place Gibeon (identified with modern el-Jib; J. Maxwell Miller, "Geba/Gibeah of Benjamin," VT 25, no. 2 [1975]: 145–66). Arnold's arguments build from Miller's, adding a review of the problems in the archaeology of Tell el-Ful and the region's landscape (Arnold, Gibeah). Their arguments have not become the consensus, and the debate continues, for example in publications by William Schniedewind ("The Search for Gibeah: Notes on the Historical Geography of Central Benjamin," in "I Will Speak the Riddles of Ancient Times": Archaeological and Historical Studies in Honor of Amihai Mazar on the Occasion of His Sixtieth Birthday, ed. Aren M. Maeir and Pierre de Miroschedji (Winona Lake: Eisenbrauns, 2006], 711–22) and Israel Finkelstein ("Tell El-Ful Revisited: The Assyrian and Hellenistic Periods [with a New Identification]," PEQ 143, no. 2 [2011]: 106–18).

38 The effort to maintain that Gibeah and Geba are separate sites results in several emendations (one often causing the need for the next) and problematic archaeological reconstructions (summarized in Miller, "Geba/Gibeah of Benjamin"; Arnold, *Gibeah*; Finkelstein, "Tell El-Ful Revisited"). The most problematic textual issue is in imagining that Saul observed the pass and battle from a more distant location, especially if one holds to the identification of Tell el-Ful as Gibeah. In addition, it distorts the history in the narrative by increasing the Philistine presence, which in turn reinforces an exaggerated view of Philistine domination, a view that likely influenced the argument for multiple locations in the first place. See, for example, Rainey and Notley, *The Sacred Bridge*, 145–146.

39 The MT is plural in this one example, an exception to the rest of the instances in the episode in 1 Samuel 13–14 and in contrast to textual variants. Edelman supplies the simplest explanation, that the plural resulted from a metathesis of the י and ב (Edelman, *King Saul*, 55, note 3).

40 Miller explains the alteration as the result of two parallel stories rather than an appropriation of one into another ("Saul's Rise to Power," 162).

41 Many standard translations (King James and New King James Versions, Jewish Publication Society [1917], and New Revised Standard Version) choose 'garrison' throughout the episode. The newer Jewish Publication Society TANAKH translation (1985; 1999) distinguishes between the two nouns, translating נציב as 'prefect' (1 Sam 10:5; 13:3–4) and מצב as 'garrison' (1 Sam 13:23; 14:1, 4) or 'outpost' (14:6, 11). The 'garrison' translation is preferred among some scholars: Itamar Singer, "Egyptians, Canaanites, and Philistines in the Period of the Emergence of Israel," in *From Nomadism to Monarchy: Archaeological and Historical Aspects of Early Israel*, ed. Israel Finkelstein and Nadav Na'aman (Jerusalem: Israel Exploration Society, 1994), 282–338; Halpern, *David's Secret Demons*, e.g., 150–153. McCarter tends toward 'outpost' but does use 'garrison' in 14:15 (*I Samuel*, 232–242). Rainey and Notley entertain various possibilities: 'representative,' 'commissioner,' 'garrison,' and 'officer' (*The Sacred Bridge*, 145–146).

42 McCarter's translation and interpretation are an example; see *I Samuel*, 224–42.

43 Miller, "Saul's Rise to Power," 172–174.

44 E.g., McCarter, *I Samuel*, 241–242; Singer, "Egyptians, Canaanites, and Philistines," 322–25; Rainey and Notley, *The Sacred Bridge*, 145–146; Faust, *Israel's Ethnogenesis*, 143–146.

45 It has probably also been influenced by trends in scholarship that have favored revolution as a stage in the path to state formation for Israel. The 'peasant revolt' model for the emergence of Israel, first put forward by Mendenhall and followed by Gottwald in the 1970s, argues for a revolt against elite Canaanite overlords by oppressed peasants (i.e., future Israelites; see Mendenhall, *The Tenth Generation*; Gottwald, *The Tribes of Yahweh*). This theory addresses the period prior to the advent of kingship, but the proposal (despite having lost support among most scholars) plays into the underdog characterization that is built into the DH's framework and the modern understanding that the Philistines were more sophisticated in their social and technological development.

46 Faust argues for a deliberate and successful cultural avoidance between Philistia and the hill county (*Israel's Ethnogenesis*, 191–220).

47 Arnold, *Gibeah*, 110–22.

48 For recent discussions of the Iron I–II metallurgical evidence of bronze and iron technologies, see Yulia Gottlieb, "Judah of Iron vs. Israel of Copper: The Metalworking Development in the Land of Israel and Its Historical Implications," in *Mining for Ancient Copper: Essays in Memory of Beno Rothenberg*, ed. Erez Ben-Yosef (Tel Aviv University Sonia and Marco Nadler Institute of Archaeology Monograph Series 37; Tel Aviv: Tel Aviv University, Sonia and Marco Nadler Institute of Archaeology, 2018), 435–54; Naama Yahalom-Mack and Adi Eliyahu-Behar, "The Transition from Bronze to Iron in Canaan: Chronology, Technology, and Context," *Radiocarbon* 57, no. 2 (2015): 285–305. It is becoming increasingly common to see the copper trade invoked in archaeological discussions of this period; see recently, Erez Ben-Yosef and Omer Sergi, "The Destruction of Gath by Hazael and the Arabah Copper Industry: A Reassessment," in *Tell it in Gath: Studies in the History and Archaeology of Israel, Essays in Honor of Aren M. Maeir on the Occasion of his Sixtieth Birthday*, ed. I. Shai et al. (Münster: Zaphon, 2018), 461–480; Israel Finkelstein and Benjamin Sass, "The Exceptional Concentration of Inscriptions at Iron IIA Gath and Rehob and the Nature of the Alphabet in the Ninth Century BCE," in *Oral et écrit dans l'Antiquité orientale: les processus de rédaction et d'édition*, ed. T. Römer et al. (Leuven: Peeters, 2021) 127–173. Amihai Mazar, "The Beth Shean Valley and its Vicinity in the 10th Century BCE," *Jerusalem Journal of Archaeology* 1 (2021): 241–271.

49 Thomas E. Levy et al., eds., *New Insights into the Iron Age Archaeology of Edom, Southern Jordan: Surveys, Excavations, and Research from the University of California, San Diego & Department of Antiquities of Jordan, Edom Lowlands Regional Archaeology Project (ELRAP)*, 2 vols. (Monumenta Archaeologica 35; Los Angeles: The

Cotsen Institute of Archaeology Press, 2014); Erez Ben-Yosef, "The Central Timna Valley Project: Research Design and Preliminary Results," in *Mining for Ancient Copper: Essays in Memory of Beno Rothenberg*, ed. Erez Ben-Yosef (Tel Aviv University Sonia and Marco Nadler Institute of Archaeology Monograph Series 37; Tel Aviv: Tel Aviv University, Sonia and Marco Nadler Institute of Archaeology, 2018). See also Chapter Six.

50 H. Alexander Veldhuijzen and Thilo Rehren, "Slags and the City: Early Iron Production at Tell Hammeh, Jordan and Tel Beth-Shemesh, Israel," in *Metals and Mines – Studies in Archaeometallurgy* (London: Archetype, British Museum, 2007), 189–201; Yahalom-Mack and Eliyahu-Behar, "The Transition from Bronze to Iron in Canaan."

51 Adi Eliyahu-Behar et al., "Iron and Bronze Production in Iron Age IIA Philistia: New Evidence from Tell Es-Safi/Gath, Israel," *Journal of Archaeological Science* 39 (2012): 255–67.

52 Eliyahu-Behar et al., "Iron and Bronze Production in Iron Age IIA Philistia," 262–266. Yahalom-Mack and Eliyahu-Behar, "The Transition from Bronze to Iron in Canaan"; Gottlieb, "Judah of Iron vs. Israel of Copper."

53 The relationship between the smithy at Beth-Shemesh and the primary processing at Tell Hammeh continues to be investigated. A close relationship in technology is clear from the distinctive style and consistent size of tuyères that were discovered at both sites, but provenance testing of objects from Beth-Shemesh did not identify Tell Hammeh as a source. See Veldhuijzen and Rehren, "Slags and the City," 199; Eleanor Blakelock et al., "Slag Inclusions in Iron Objects and the Quest for Provenance: An Experiment and a Case Study," *Journal of Archaeological Science* 36 (2009): 1745–57.

54 Thomas E. Levy, "Pastoral Nomads and Iron Age Metal Production in Ancient Edom," in *Nomads, Tribes, and the State in the Ancient Near East, Cross-Disciplinary Perspectives* (Oriental Institute Seminars 5; Chicago: Oriental Institute of the University of Chicago, 2009), 147–77; Veldhuijzen and Rehren, "Slags and the City."

55 The cost of maintaining tools is not, on the surface, relevant to who did or did not have weapons at the time. Therefore, the pricing details reveal a previous purpose for the source material. An alternative explanation for the exception of Jonathan and Saul's weaponry, however, is found in their elite status. Saul's patriline in 1 Samuel 9:1 is qualified by the phrase חיל גבור. The title signals more than either 'warrior' or 'wealth' and should be understood to convey that Saul's family was elevated in this community. Saul's possession of weapons is yet another marker of this status.

56 One way to do so is to argue that Israelites were forced into service by the Philistines, but this explanation only dismisses the content of the verse.

57 Two biblical traditions suggest a cultural distinction. The ancestor of metalsmiths is Tubal-cain, descendant of Cain, according to the genealogy in Genesis 4:22. Cain's other descendants are also linked to itinerant groups (Gen 4:17–22). Solomon's artisan for the temple's bronze work was Hiram, son of a Naphtali woman and Tyrian smith, according to 1 Kings 7:13–47.

58 Metallurgists tended to move seasonally in order to coordinate smelting and processing with complimentary activities (e.g., seasonal pruning and harvesting dovetailed with the smelting season at Tell Hammeh) and service to consumers, whose settlements may not have been densely concentrated enough to allow for the permanent residency of the metallurgists (Veldhuijzen and Rehren, "Slags and the City"; see also M. J. Rowlands, "The Archaeological Interpretation of Prehistoric Metalworking," *World Archaeology* 3, no. 2 [1971]: 210–224, esp. 219–220).

59 If read in the current biblical order, the Philistines were prepared for imminent battle at Shunem (1 Sam 28:4) and then illogically mustered at Aphek (1 Sam 29:1) before defeating Saul and Israel at Mt. Gilboa (1 Sam 31). The confusion is settled if the En-Dor episode of 1 Samuel 28, along with its necessary setting within sight of the Philistine troops, had been relocated by an ancient author/redactor from a more likely location just preceding the battle account in 1 Samuel 31, as many commentators have suggested. The shift juxtaposes Saul's treatment of the Amalekites (recalled through the scolding from Samuel's ghost) with David's revenge on the Amalekites for the Ziklag raid (McCarter, *I Samuel*, 422–23).

60 Edelman suggests that David's lament may have been the source and inspiration for a prose account of the battle at Jezreel, and traces parallels between them ("Saul Ben Kish," 151–52). This argument would leave us with one source and its growth into other accounts. Such a relationship has been demonstrated with other biblical poems (i.e., the Song of the Sea and the Song of Deborah; see Cross, *Canaanite Myth and Hebrew Epic*, 123–144; Baruch Halpern, *The First Historians: The Hebrew Bible and History* [San Francisco: Harper and Row, 1988], 76–103), but it seems likely in this case that historical memory, along with the lament, contributed to the biblical history that we have now.

61 There is one additional account of the battle in 1 Chronicles 10:1-12. According to McCarter, in some places, it appears to be closer to an original version of the events (*I Samuel*, 439-44).

62 Yohanan Aharoni, *The Land of the Bible: A Historical Geography* (Philadelphia: Westminster Press, 1967), 21-22, 258; Dorsey, *Roads and Highways*, 103-16.

63 Dorsey, *Roads and Highways*, 93-102.

64 For discussion of archaeological indications of trade, see Chapter Six.

65 Schloen, "Caravans, Kenites, and Casus Belli," 18-38.

66 For a review of urbanization during this period, see Faust, *Israel's Ethnogenesis*, 113-119.

67 Omer Sergi suggests later southern authors imagined Saul's opponent to be Philistines because the authors were unfamiliar with the Jezreel Valley, and the Philistines were fitting as the 'archenemy of the kingdom of Judah' ("Saul, David, and the Formation of the Israelite Monarchy: Revisiting the Historical and Literary Context of 1 Samuel 9 – 2 Samuel 5," in *Saul, Benjamin, and the Emergence of Monarchy in Israel: Biblical and Archaeological Perspectives*, ed. Joachim J. Krause, Omer Sergi, and Kristin Weingart [Atlanta: SBL Press, 2020] 57-91; 72).

68 Influence rather than direct rule is more likely for Saul's reach at the time, contra to Finkelstein's arguments that Saul ruled up to the Jezreel valley ("Saul and Highlands of Benjamin Update").

69 A recent application of archaeomagnetic dating for many destruction layers in the southern Levant provides important support that there was conflict in this region in the late 10th century, namely at the sites of Horvat Tevet, Tel Reḥov, and Beth-Shean (Yoav Vaknin et al., "Reconstructing Biblical Military Campaigns Using Geomagnetic Field Data," *Proceedings of the National Academy of Sciences* 119, no. 44 [2022]: e2209117119). The study supports the fact that this area, critical for exchange, was a point of contention, and we may reason that the motivation for controlling the valley was exchange related. It is important to keep in mind however, that this analysis does not supply new information regarding who was involved in the conflict.

70 Trade interests have been proposed as a reason for Philistine activity in the hill country, but previously this argument could only be made in general and hypothetical terms. For example, Edelman proposes that trade to the east motivated Saul's expansion and interregional affairs but does not reconstruct what that trade would have been ("Saul Ben Kish," 157-58). Archaeological discoveries are completely changing our analysis of the Iron I-IIA setting, and it is now much clearer that there were very active exchange networks in this period. For more discussion of the material evidence, see especially Chapter Six.

71 The DH's depiction is governed by the notion of the Davidic covenant. Modern scholarly attention to the importance of David and this covenant begins with Gerhard Von Rad ("Die Deuteronomistische Geschichtstheologie in Den Königsbüchern," in *Gesammelte Studien Zum Alten Testament*, ed. Gerhard von Rad [Theologische Bücherei 8; München: Chr. Kaiser, 1958]). Detailed attention to 2 Samuel 7 is provided by Dennis J. McCarthy ("II Samuel 7 and the Structure of the Deuteronomistic History," *JBL* 84, no. 2 [1965]: 131-38); Cross (*Canaanite Myth and Hebrew Epic*, 241-264); P. Kyle McCarter (*II Samuel: A New Translation with Introduction, Notes, and Commentary* [AB 9; Garden City: Doubleday, 1984], 209-231, esp. 217-220); and William M. Schniedewind (*Society and the Promise to David: The Reception History of 2 Samuel 7:1-17* [New York: Oxford University Press, 1999]). Attention to the processes and concerns of the ancient historiographers, with special attention to David's career, is explored by Halpern (*David's Secret Demons*, esp. 107-141). More recently, Daniel Pioske has focused on memory in the shaping of the histories of David (*David's Jerusalem*) and Mahri Leonard-Fleckman considers northern Levantine and Assyrian sources as parallels for the developments in early Iron Age Judah (*The House of David: Between Political Formation and Literary Revision* [Minneapolis: Fortress Press, 2016]).

72 Rost, *The Succession to the Throne of David*. Another substantial source, the Court History of David or Succession Narrative (consisting of 2 Sam 9-20 and 1 Kgs 1-2), is essentially devoid of David's interactions with the Philistines. Since this source is considered to account for Solomon's succession to David, and Solomon's history does not record major interactions with Philistia, this silence in the text should not be surprising.

73 See ibid.; McCarter, *I Samuel*, 27-30; Robert P. Gordon, "David's Rise and Saul's Demise: Narrative Analogy in 1 Samuel 24-26," *Tyndale Bulletin* 31 (1980): 31, 37-64, esp. 38. Baruch Halpern distinguishes between A and B sources within this work to account for parallels and contradictions in the narrative (*The Constitution of the Monarchy in Israel*, 149-174; idem, *David's Secret Demons*).

74 David's career fighting the Philistines begins with the well-known David and Goliath story (1 Sam 17). It has long been observed that the name 'Goliath' is suspiciously rare in the episode and was most likely appropriated from a hero story of one of David's men, which happens to be preserved in 2 Samuel 21:19

(a portion of the tradition is also remembered in 1 Sam 21:9-10). In addition to the insertion of Goliath's name, the story has been extensively modified and elaborated over time. Generally, there is little reason to doubt that early in David's career he fought the Philistines in the Shephelah, but that is as far as we can comfortably go for historical purposes based on the evidence from this story. See McCarter, *I Samuel*, 284-309; Halpern, *David's Secret Demons*, 275-276. Of note for this episode, though, are debates concerning the depiction of the Philistine's armor, and whether the account can be situated in a historical context (of the action or the author's time). Azzan Yadin has proposed there was a later, Aegean influence on the story ("Goliath's Armor and Israelite Collective Memory," *VT* 54, no. 3 [2004]: 373-95; see also Finkelstein, "The Philistines in the Bible," 142-148). In contrast, Jeffery R. Zorn argues that the depiction of Goliath's armor is *not* inconsistent with the period or cultural situation described in the story ("Reconsidering Goliath: An Iron Age I Philistine Chariot Warrior," *BASOR* 360 [2010]: 1-22).

75 Presumably, this chant was not intended to compare the two or demonstrate David's surpassing of Saul, but employed parallelism to extol the military success of Israel's best warriors (McCarter, *I Samuel*, 312). In hindsight, however, story-tellers exploited the unavoidable association of David's ascent in leadership and fame. The sentiment is recounted in narrative form in 1 Samuel 18:30: as often as the Philistine commanders went into battle against Israel, David outperformed all of Saul's men and became famous. While the poetic phrase does not shed light on any particular battle in David's career, it does suggest a long tradition of conflict (presumably involving the Philistines) and David's path toward leadership based on his military accomplishments.

76 The note in 2 Samuel 8:1 appears to provide unique information, but no one has satisfactorily deciphered the critical phrase מתג האמה. Halpern suggests the phrase refers to a thing rather than a place (*David's Secret Demons*, 144-45); McCarter reviews some of the geographic possibilities and opts for a more general 'common land' based on the LXX (*II Samuel*, 242-47).

77 For a detailed treatment of the many chronological clues in the text, see Halpern, *David's Secret Demons*, 229-242.

78 Despite its apparent narrative cohesion, there are problematic elements in the story. Its beginning, 'And they told David…' (1 Sam 23:1), references informants that are no longer identified. In addition, it is not explained why the Philistines who were attacking the town would have brought with them livestock (1 Sam 23:5). Were the Philistines residents of the area? Did David raid inhabitants of Qeʿilah (including Philistines)?

79 E.g., EA 279-280; see Nadav Naʾaman, "David's Sojourn in Keilah in Light of the Amarna Letters," *VT* 60 (2010): 87-97; Anson F. Rainey, "Possible Involvement of Tell Eṣ-Ṣâfî (Tel Ẓafit) in the Amarna Correspondence," in *Tell Es-Safi/Gath: The 1996-2005 Seasons*, ed. Aren M. Maeir, 2 vols. (Ägypten und Altes Testament 69; Wiesbaden: Harrassowitz, 2012), 133-40. See also the arguments of Finkelstein regarding parallels between Saul's history and the Amarna texts, notably, "The Last Labayu: King Saul and the Expansion of the First North Israelite Territorial Entity," in *Essays on Ancient Israel and Its Near Eastern Context: A Tribute to Nadav Naʾaman*, ed. Yairah Amit (Winona Lake: Eisenbrauns, 2006), 171-87.

80 McCarter, *II Samuel*, 157-60.

81 The shift is most easily explained away as a difference in source material; however, there are additional distinctions. After his move to Jerusalem, David is depicted as king in his court, interacting with those outside of his palace through envoys, his general(s), or other messengers (e.g., 2 Sam 10), not as a renegade hero leading his band of men.

82 Despite the fact that the valley name appears to indicate a precise location, the actual place is not known, and the repetition of the name might signal a battle-story formula (as does the oracle formula discussed above). If there was one location by this name, consensus has situated it to the southwest of Jerusalem. The influence of the literary context surrounding 2 Samuel 5:17-25, however, should not be the main reason for locating the valley near Jerusalem. Another possibility is suggested by the name Rapha, part of a title which may have been given to Philistine warriors; 'votaries of Rapha' is McCarter's translation of the different formulae based on הרפה + ילד (*II Samuel*, 447-51). He builds from the arguments of Willesen and L'Heureux (F. Willesen, "The Philistine Corps of the Scimitar from Gath," *JSS* 3 [1958]: 327-35; Conrad L'Heureux, "The Ugaritic and Biblical Rephaim," *HTR* 67, no. 3 [1974]: 265-74; idem, "The Yelîdê Hārāpāʾ: A Cultic Association of Warriors," *BASOR* 221 [1976]: 83-85) ; cf. 2 Samuel 21:16, 18, 20, 22. The warriors' title may be the reason for the name applied to the battles' locations, regardless of each battle's precise geography. Nevertheless, each of these possibilities points to the potential for the episodes to have stemmed from the same period. The stories may refer to a particular time when battles happened at this location or against these enemies, or related battles may have been linked by the compiler with a 'Rephaim Valley' formula.

83 See Halpern, *David's Secret Demons*, 23.
84 Cross-cultural parallels to the motif of soldiers' response to a leader's thirst call into question the origin and historicity of the episode (Eleanor Hull, "David and the Well of Bethlehem: An Irish Parallel," *Folklore* 44, no. 2 [1933]: 214–18; McCarter, *II Samuel*, 495; Robert Gnuse, "Spilt Water – Tales of David [2 Sam 23,13-17] and Alexander [Arrian, Anabasis of Alexander 6.26.1-3]," *SJOT* 12, no. 2 [1998]: 233–48). Halpern takes the episode to be the oldest version of David's opportunity to take Saul's life, where 1 Samuel 26 retains the motif of retrieving water from a dangerous encounter (1 Sam 26:12), but 1 Samuel 24 replaces it with the less flattering image of Saul relieving himself (*David's Secret Demons*, 265–66, 274–76). Halpern's claim does not address the absence of the Bethlehem element in the 1 Samuel versions, but he does suppose that since the main army was in the Rephaim Valley (2 Sam 23:13), it is logical that the Philistine army set up a post in nearby Bethlehem. On the other end of the spectrum, Gnuse argues that the strongest parallels to the water-fetching tale are with Arrian's *Anabasis of Alexander* and, in the end, determines that the Hellenistic sources for the *Anabasis* influenced a late addition to the appendices of Samuel ("Spilt Water"). Gnuse is convincing in demonstrating that the *Anabasis* account and the David story are closer parallels than other tales of the same type, but he does not demonstrate conclusively why the biblical version must have relied on the Hellenistic one.
85 See discussion in Halpern, *David's Secret Demons*, 150–152.
86 The place name in 2 Samuel 23 appears to have been lost due to haplography; 1 Chronicles 11:13 preserves the original reading (McCarter, *II Samuel*, 490). For discussion of the complex connections among the related stories, see Halpern, *David's Secret Demons*, 148–149.
87 McCarter, *II Samuel*, 500–501; Halpern, *David's Secret Demons*, 65–67, 274–276.
88 Dorsey, *Roads and Highways*, 189–91, 204–6.
89 Dorsey's route J10 (ibid., 191–92).
90 Ibid., 151–54. Although the biblical text does not reveal if David's activities involved the Beersheba Valley with its lucrative exchange route (see Chapter Six for discussion of this area in relation to archaeological research), his control of these key locations suggests that he was at least able to intercept traffic from the Beersheba routes that was moving north to the hill country and Shephelah. His affairs in the south certainly imply interest. It also remains unclear how such involvement affected relations with Philistia, and whether a role in relation to the Beersheba Valley influenced his eventual alliance with Gath. For one reconstruction of David in the Beersheba Valley, see Diana V. Edelman, "Tel Masos, Geshur, and David," *JNES* 47, no. 4 (1988): 253–58.
91 Dorsey's route J11 (*Roads and Highways*, 192).
92 'As a highwayman' is McCarter's translation of the MT's לארב, the *lectio difficilior* reading over LXX's εις εχθρον, 'as an enemy' (Hebrew *לאיב resulting from confusion between ר and י ; McCarter, *I Samuel*, 360–62).This characterization voiced by Saul has gained ground as modern scholarship has distanced itself from the pro-David rhetoric of the narrative; for example, see Halpern, *David's Secret Demons*, esp. 23, 344, 479–480.
93 The Samuel A source (Halpern, *David's Secret Demons*, 20, 263–66).
94 The Samuel B source (ibid., 20–25, 263–266). Richard Elliott Friedman includes this version in the extended J source that runs from Genesis 2 through the Court History (*The Hidden Book in the Bible* [San Francisco: Harper Collins, 1998]).
95 The most obvious indicator is the phrase 'to this day' regarding Ziklag in 1 Samuel 27:6, but the Deuteronomistic character is also evident in the dialogue scenes (e.g., 27:5; 29:6-10) and in the record keeping that appears for David's household, the number of his men, the length of his service, etc.
96 Joseph Naveh briefly notes this pattern in his analysis of the name Achish from the Ekron inscription ("Achish-Ikausu in the Light of the Ekron Dedication," *BASOR* 310 [1998]: 36).
97 In some LXX and Vulgate mss, which Naveh explains as a similar borrowing from the 8th century king Ahimilki of Ashdod ("Achish-Ikausu," 36).
98 The flight to Egypt variation is yet another important sub-group (e.g., the patriarchs to Egypt; Solomon's adversaries to Egypt).
99 Madness plays a role twice in David's relations to a suzerain, first in 1 Samuel 16, when the young David is able to ease Saul's madness with his musical ability, and then in this episode 1 Samuel 21, when David escapes Achish.
100 Archaeological excavations are revealing a very important center at Tell eṣ-Ṣafi, identified with biblical Gath; see Maeir, *Tell Es-Safi/Gath*; and special issues of *Near Eastern Archaeology* dedicated to the project (*NEA* 80.4 [2017] and *NEA* 81.1 [2018]). Additional details are presented below and in Chapters Five and Six.

101 Naveh, "Achish-Ikausu."
102 Ibid., 36.
103 Finkelstein relies on Naveh's argument in his own claim for a late date to these stories ("The Philistines in the Bible," 133–136).
104 Aren M. Maeir et al., "A Late Iron Age I/Early Iron Age II Old Canaanite Inscription from Tell Es-Sâfi/Gath, Israel: Palaeography, Dating, and Historical-Cultural Significance," *BASOR* 351 (2008): 39–71. The inscription is discussed in more detail in Chapter Five.
105 Aren M. Maeir, Alexander Fantalkin, and Alexander Zuckerman, "The Earliest Greek Import in the Iron Age Levant," *Ancient West & East* 8 (2009): 57–80; and see discussion in Chapter Six.
106 Maeir, "The Tell Es-Safi/Gath Archaeological Project 1996–2010," 40–43.
107 Lev-Tov emphasizes that these results are based on a small quantity of remains; see Faust and Lev-Tov, "Constitution of Philistine Identity," 18–21, 26, note 11; Justin Lev-Tov, "A Preliminary Report on the Late Bronze and Iron Age Faunal Assemblages from Tell Es-Safi/Gath," in *Tell Es-Safi/Gath: The 1996-2005 Seasons*, ed. Aren M. Maeir, 2 vols. (Ägypten und Altes Testament 69; Wiesbaden: Harrassowitz, 2012), 589–612.
108 Faust and Lev-Tov, "Constitution of Philistine Identity," 26, note 11.
109 Maeir's strong cautions about overreaching based on this evidence are aimed especially at Faust's arguments about identity, namely related to pork consumption, the four-room house, and laws regarding menstruation (Maeir, "On Defining Israel").
110 There are several approaches that contribute to this proposal. Halpern argues that there is a pattern of archaizing apparent in the 8th and 7th centuries in line with this conclusion ("Sybil, or the Two Nations? Archaism, Kinship, Alienation, and the Elite Redefinition of Traditional Culture in Judah in the 8th–7th Centuries B.C.E.," in *The Study of the Ancient Near East in the Twenty-First Century: The William Foxwell Albright Centennial Conference*, ed. Jerrold S. Cooper and Glenn M. Schwartz [Winona Lake: Eisenbrauns, 1996], 291–338). Halpern later connects his earlier argument directly to the Achish debate (*David's Secret Demons*, 287). At the same time, commercial activities brought the Aegean and southern Levant into close contact, and Philistia came to dominate areas of the regional economy, which must have contributed to notions akin to 'national/ethnic pride' (Jane C. Waldbaum and Jodi Magness, "The Chronology of Early Greek Pottery: New Evidence from Seventh-Century B. C. Destruction Levels in Israel," *American Journal of Archaeology* 101, no. 1 [1997]: 23–40; Faust and Weiss, "Judah, Philistia, and the Mediterranean World").
111 The best reconstruction is probably of a precarious triangle of contemporary powers, wherein David, maybe the region's wild card, built toward a larger goal of taking the hill country through strategic shifts in his alliances.
112 The role of Jebus/Jerusalem in the region's interactions is explored in Chapter Four.
113 See Chapter Six.
114 The location of Ziklag remains uncertain. Recently, Jeffrey Blakely has revisited the problem and argued in favor of Tell esh-Shari'ah/Tel Sera', which is often cited as a candidate ("The Location of Medieval/Pre-Modern and Biblical Ziklag," *PEQ* 139, no. 1 [2007]: 21–26). Others include Tell el-Hesi, Tel Masos, Tell es-Seba', Tel Haror, Tel Halif, and Tel Zayit.
115 There is a conspicuous silence regarding the Beersheba Valley and Philistine activity south of Gath, which we might expect to be a part of the interactions. Excavations along this route provide plenty of evidence of interactions (see Chapter Six). Did Gath's dominance in the 10th century include the southern network? Or was the source material (and David's interactions) narrow enough that there is simply no record of it? Questions like these inhibit a more conclusive discussion of that particular region based on the biblical material alone.
116 Halpern shows that many beneficial consequences came to David due to the alliance with Gath, from commercial gains to assistance in eliminating other claimants to Israel's leadership. He suggests that it is likely that David was actually in the Jezreel battle, but his involvement was concealed to enhance his political image (*David's Secret Demons*, 79–81, 280–316).

3 Solomon's Interactions and Economic Policies

The Deuteronomistic History (DH) depicts Solomon's reign as a critical time in Israel's development. According to the beginning of 1 Kings, Solomon secured succession and inherited the territory that David conquered, which reportedly consisted of all the Israelite tribal allotments, as well as vassal territories to the north and east. In contrast to the narrative events in Samuel, Solomon's history dwells in administrative strategies rather than battlefield victories. This shift in narrative focus suggests two things about the purpose of the text: 1) that authors/editors crafted Solomon's story to be distinct from the preceding events and history; and 2) that authors/editors viewed the expansion of Israel's economy and status as among the most important accomplishments of Solomon's career. Such a history would seem to be of critical importance to an investigation of trade and exchange. Indeed, as the DH is our oldest and most extensive report of these activities, it has traditionally served as an authoritative guide for historical reconstructions of the 10th century BCE.[1] The text's continued role in that capacity is only compelling if it passes today's historical scrutiny, but, as we have seen in the previous chapter, the DH is problematic as a historical source.

As I discussed in the introduction, the second half of the 20th century saw a sea change in scholarly confidence regarding biblical history. Scholars applied intense scrutiny to the accounts of Solomon's reign, beginning in the 1980s. Criticism emerged following several decades of positivism based on epigraphic and archaeological discoveries that appeared to confirm biblical texts. The quintessential example for the Solomonic era was Y. Yadin's claim that he had discovered confirmation of Solomon's fortification projects that are described in 1 Kings 9:15.[2] Broad acceptance and enthusiasm about this connection dominated discussions of Israel's early monarchy, but it is also true that critical readers had noted potential problems in the Solomon Narrative for some time.

The critical scales tipped dramatically in the 1990s and early 2000s, when the weight of critique from literary, historical, and archaeological research combined to force a reevaluation of historical and archaeological anchors, such as those regarding Solomon's fortifications based on Yadin's arguments. The ensuing debates led to skepticism concerning not only traditional treatment of Solomon's reign, but also reliance on biblical texts for historical research and 'biblical archaeology' as an enterprise.[3] The debate was often summed up as 'minimalist' versus 'maximalist,' but over time, the gulf between opposing arguments has narrowed.[4] There is not yet a full consensus, but the scholarly tone has changed. Today, new approaches offer more nuance to the arguments from various disciplines. Most notably for an examination of Solomon's history is that awareness and critique of the biblical biases regarding Jerusalem and a Davidic dynasty play a larger role in scholarly analysis.

For the present discussion of interactions in Solomon's narrative, the use of source-critical and historical methods will bring us to the conclusion that it is possible to discern distinct historical and compositional phases in the accounts of Solomon's trade activities. For example, regarding interregional affairs, which concern the bulk of this chapter, we will see that some partnerships between the southern Levant and neighboring regions may be reasonably dated to the 10th century through historical and archaeological means, even though the narrative depictions of Solomon's activity were composed centuries later. Regarding domestic affairs, the discussion of which occupies the latter portion of this chapter, the narrative's authors associate notable changes in Israelite life with Solomon's career. Although the accounts may be exaggerated, there is reason to believe that Solomon at least *attempted* to use Israel's human resources to maximize the geographic and natural potential around him, to improve his state's economic standing. Most importantly, we observe – from the most explicit discussion to the most implicit assumptions in the sources – a pervasiveness of interregional interaction and concern for Solomon's use of resources in all levels of the narrative, which suggests fundamental relationships between the notion of a Solomonic era, long-distance exchange, and tensions between kin-based organization and elites at the head of the state. Crucially, we also find strong evidence that contradicts the image of a united Israel that the DH puts forward. Between veiled critiques and defensive overcompensation, it becomes apparent that Solomon had many more rivals 'within' Israel than we are supposed to believe. Ultimately, this critical evaluation supports a reconstruction of peer-polity competition among small-scale southern Levantine leaders during this time of transition between Iron I and IIA, which is depicted in the biblical history as the shift to a monarchy based in an urban, administrative Jerusalem.

This brief survey of scholarly foundations and challenges makes apparent that questions about a historical Solomon or the 10th century necessarily rely on more than historical-critical methods. Textual, source, and literary criticism inform how a historian deals with the source material, especially in terms of narrative cohesion and consistency, which are significant when developing a complex view of the material. The Solomon Narrative grew from many sources, which had various circumstances underlying their composition. Although the ancient historian(s) strove to create a unified work, we do not have to be observant of those same goals and can concentrate on the historical material more than (but not independent from) the literary efforts. It is also critical to note that a relative confidence about the literary structure and formation processes, so to speak, that led to the narrative's creation does not necessarily pave the way for historical reliability. Nevertheless, we must understand the text's genesis and growth prior to addressing historical questions.

Literary criticism has had a significant impact on the study of the Solomon Narrative. During the most heated years of the '10th century debate,' it offered a productive study of the material that could be isolated from historical uncertainty. One could evaluate not only the sources, patterns, and literary aspects of Solomon's narrative, but also the creation of Solomon the legend in later editions, texts, and traditions.[5] Likewise, social-scientific analysis has added perspectives that also do not need to be as closely tied to specific historical moments, but which may hold true for larger trends in social, cultural, and political change. More recently, studies that combine disciplinary approaches offer more nuanced proposals about the relationships between historical figures/places/events and the people who strove to construct their stories. Among these efforts, attention to cultural geography, memory studies, and gender studies has been particularly influential on the present examination.[6]

A Solomonic Era

Some important clarifications are necessary before proceeding. Although piecing together a historical Solomon is *not* the aim of this chapter, any discussion of the DH's depiction of the period must begin with an assumption about the figure's very existence. It is undeniable that the Solomon Narrative is inconsistent in content and historical reliability, but it is also necessary to concede that the work contains sufficient evidence – material which is diverse in origin and in presentation of events – to posit that the period represented as Solomon's reign in the DH was indeed a turning point in interregional exchange and remembered as such by the ancient authors. To arrive at such a conclusion, one must lay bare the unreliable elements of the narrative. Although depictions of Solomon's career became more fanciful as the narrative and stories developed over time, we should not wholly discount events from this history *a priori* when reconstructing the interaction of this period. As for the 10th century monarch, I will allow for the notion of a historical Solomon who governed over a territory centered on Jerusalem. At the same time, I will argue that Solomon *did not* dominate an empire or command the respect of the world's leaders, as depicted in the MT, but that he did very likely compete with rivals and participate in exchange relations in the region.

What we discover through close examination of the history is that even though we often cannot substantiate precise claims about Solomon and the details of his career, the text contains a claim about a Solomonic *era* that deserves our attention. The DH's history of Solomon remembers critical changes that took place after tribal or kin-based organization gave way to state systems, and before the Neo-Assyrian Empire influenced how local Levantine kingdoms conducted their affairs. I rely on the concept of a 'Solomonic era' to describe this time and Israelite/Judean authors' ideas about it. Those authors and the sources they relied on, including cultural memories, imagined Solomon to be at the head of all affairs involving Israelite lands in the early days of local monarchy. For example, regardless of who was historically responsible, Jerusalem's transition to an urban capital and the consolidation of a region's economic resources to a more centralized management system became, in Judean cultural memory, Solomon's endeavors and hallmarks of his reign. My investigation suggests there were many more participants involved in 10th century developments, but because of the Jerusalem and Davidic biases in the biblical accounts and the lack of contemporary historical sources, we are limited to the figure of Solomon as the exemplar for mid-10th century leadership. Instead of reconstructing the career of a historical Solomon based on what we determine to be 10th century affairs, we should think of a 'Solomonic era,' a concept that captures what the biblical sources record, as well as what was lost (i.e., other figures in the 10th century) as the ancient authors and processes of cultural memory attributed more and more events to the figure of Solomon.

Characteristics of the Solomon Narrative

The Solomon Narrative (1 Kgs 3–11) recounts the king's deeds and interactions. This unit is distinct from both the Succession Narrative (ending in 1 Kgs 2) and the history of the separate kingdoms of Israel and Judah (beginning in 1 Kgs 12).[7] The Deuteronomistic Historian (Dtr) wove together these historical narratives in such a way as to blur the beginnings and endings of distinct narratives and periods, so that themes of Solomon's history are present in the narrative before and after 1 Kings 3–11. For example, the groundwork for Solomon's legitimacy, achievements, and challenges is laid in the Succession Narrative, and the northern kingdom's distinct trajectory is the proverbial elephant in the room in the Solomon Narrative. The Dtr's history of Solomon has two goals: one is to highlight his accomplishments; the other is to assert an important claim that his polytheism was his greatest misstep (cast as apostasy from the Deuteronomistic perspective), which set in motion the fracturing of his territory into two independent kingdoms.[8] Notably, within this framework, commerce and interactions play critical roles. From building up the physical infrastructure to establishing an international reputation, the history asserts that Solomon's reign relied on exchange; thus, it demands detailed treatment and suggests that the ancient author(s) perceived that interactions were critical both to the growth of the kingdom and to the rift between the north and the south.

Scholars' positions on the authorship and editing of the Solomon Narrative are not uniform, but the following three points form the basis for the current discussion. First, the Dtr compiled this unit using sources regarding Solomon's reign (potentially ranging in type from royal records to legends about the king).[9] Second, in addition to sources, the narrative contains editorial introductions, summary, and commentary by the Dtr. And third, the narrative is arranged according to thematic concerns, at the expense of chronological accuracy.[10]

A number of issues pertaining to the literary aspect of the work continue to be debated. Although most recognize that there is a distinct textual unit devoted to Solomon's life and career, scholars' opinions vary regarding the degree of uniformity in the Solomon Narrative; that is, it has been variously described as a chaotic hodge-podge of disparate sources as well as a carefully crafted, cautionary tale. And while there is general agreement that older sources underlie the Deuteronomistic narrative, scholars differ regarding the nature, extent, and date of those sources, and whether they or the resulting narrative were intended to be historical or legendary works, moral instruction, or any combination of these purposes. There is also debate about the degree to which the Dtr altered, arranged, or contributed to a previously existing narrative on Solomon's reign and, similarly, the extent of subsequent editing or corruption after the DH was compiled/composed.[11]

Long-Distance Exchange in the Solomon Narrative

The quintessential Solomon takes shape in 1 Kings 3:4–15, with Solomon's dream revelation at Gibeon. The deity rewards the new monarch's humility and selflessness with the promise of a 'wise and discerning mind' as well as 'riches and glory' beyond compare with any other king (1 Kgs 3:12–13). This introduction to Solomon's reign situates the coming prosperity within a pious context and credits YHWH as the source of Solomon's good fortune, but it also declares a very earthly comparison with all previous and future examples of successful leadership (3:12) and with all contemporary examples of glory and prosperity (3:13).[12] The narrative directs its audience to think big and consider Solomon in a larger context of ancient Near Eastern kingship, a critical aspect of which was participation and competition in 'international' affairs (Figure 3.1).

70   FERTILE CROSSROADS

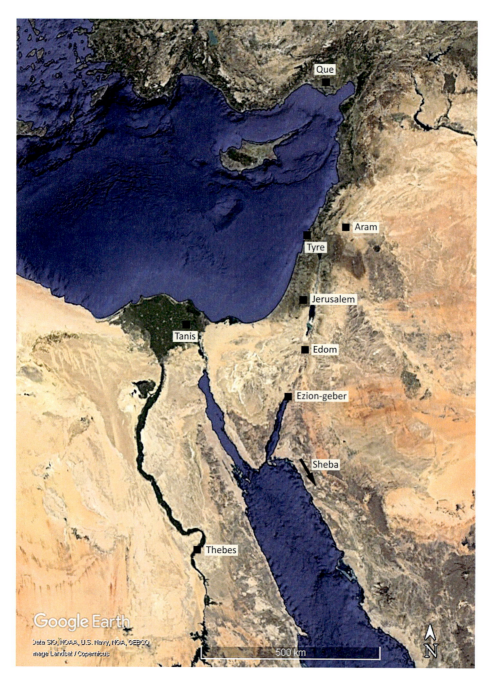

Figure 3.1: Places related to interregional interactions in 1 Kings 3–11. Map: Google Earth, © 2020.

Interregional interaction shows up in nearly all parts of the Solomon Narrative. Discussion of these relations begins in the first verse of the unit (1 Kgs 3:1) and continues nearly to the last (1 Kgs 11:40). Distinct concentrations appear in 1 Kings 4–5 and 9–10, and there are few portions of the narrative that are not related in some way to exchange.[13]

What we detect in the text is a wealth of sources available to the Dtr that recount Solomon's trade activities.[14] The narrative presents the material in several ways: in general statements of wealth and success; in lists or annals; and through Solomon's diplomatic interaction. In the grandest depictions, the more legendary Solomon dominates world affairs, but in the close examination below, we find that there is, in portions of the narrative, a more realistic depiction of interaction with contemporary leaders, involving activities such as diplomatic marriages and exchange in metals.

Exchange Involving Egypt

A casual reading of the Solomon Narrative results in the general impression that Solomon's diplomatic and exchange relations with Egypt were good toward the beginning of his reign but deteriorated toward the end. This depiction is a result of the Dtr's narrative structure. The historian situated seemingly positive interactions earlier in the narrative and reserved the less favorable for later. The arrangement masks what the historical record might have been. When viewed independently from the narrative scheme, the reports of relations with Egypt are varied, and the details uncertain. On the one hand, they claim that Solomon was allied through marriage to a pharaoh (1 Kgs 3:1; 7:8) who conquered Gezer and gave the city to Solomon (1 Kgs 9:16). On the other hand, certain passages convey that there was antagonism with Egypt: an unnamed pharaoh allied with Solomon's non-Israelite rivals (1 Kgs 11:14–25), and Shishaq harbored Jeroboam when he challenged Solomon (1 Kgs 11:40).[15] A third category exists where there is no explicit connection to Egyptian royalty: Solomon engaged in horse and chariot trade involving Egypt (1 Kgs 10:28–29).

The variety in these accounts is best explained as stemming from multiple sources, as many as four: 1) one based on Solomon's trade in elite goods (horses and chariots); 2) one based on a marriage alliance between Solomon and an Egyptian king; 3) one based on antagonism between a pharaoh and Jerusalem (under David and Solomon); and 4) one based on an alliance between Shishaq and Jeroboam against Solomon. None appears to be pure creation of the Dtr, though the Dtr added to and connected the pieces. The challenge to a historian comes in determining if the sources all describe separate and historic relations. The situation is made more difficult when only one of the references to an Egyptian leader includes a proper name and identifies an individual known from extrabiblical sources (i.e., Shishaq, Egypt's Shoshenq I, in 1 Kgs 11:40).[16] All other instances refer only to 'Pharaoh' (פרעה) and/or 'Egypt's King' (מלך מצרים). As a result, we cannot be certain of how many pharaohs ruled (or were envisioned to have ruled) over the course of Solomon's reign. Based on the biblical sources, we would reason that the answer could be as few as one, Shishaq/Shoshenq I, if the relationship between Egypt and Jerusalem was particularly volatile, or as many as three if sources numbered 2, 3, and 4 above each refer to a different monarch.

The effort to connect details in the Solomon Narrative with historical figures and events has produced many debates. There is not conclusive evidence to settle the issues completely, but we can narrow down the possibilities to what is more and less likely in relations between Egypt and the southern Levant. We know that Egyptian power was not as absolute or far reaching during the 10th century as it had been during the New Kingdom. This change impacted political and economic matters. As I explore in Chapter Five, the Report of Wenamun captures the moment well, especially from the perspective of Egyptian elites. Egypt could no longer dominate trade in the southeastern Mediterranean, and the symbols of Egyptian authority carried no weight. During the New Kingdom, an Egyptian king would have been in the position of higher authority in a relationship with a southern Levantine ruler, but the Egyptian state of the 11th and 10th centuries was quite different. Even with Shoshenq's successes in asserting more complete control along the Nile and resuming campaigns to the southern Levant, we do not have evidence of a sustained dominance over Egypt's neighbors. More than a century of a weakened Egypt allowed for the possibility of inconsistent relations with Jerusalem during the 10th century, especially from the point of view of observers in the southern Levant.

Horse Trade with Egypt

Some of the most extraordinary statements of Solomon's international trade come toward the close of the Solomon Narrative. In 1 Kings 10, we learn of Solomon's wealth and renown, maritime and Arabian trade, and his array of cavalry and chariotry (1 Kgs 10:26–29). The text details the trade in horses and chariots, stating: 'The source of Solomon's horses was (from) *mṣrym* (מצרים) and (from) *qwh* (קוה), and the king's traders took from *qwh* at a (fixed) price. A chariot from *mṣrym* was 600 silver and a horse 150, and thus they exported to all Hittite kings and all Aramean kings' (1 Kgs 10:28–29).[17] The most straightforward reading of the two place names in the passage is Egypt (*miṣrayim*) and Que. Que is easily identified as the small kingdom of Hiyawa in southeast Anatolia, known from Late Bronze and Iron Age inscriptions.[18] In the Hebrew Bible, the place name *mṣrym* always refers to Egypt. The reading is unproblematic except for the fact that some interpreters find Egypt out of place in what are otherwise eastern Anatolian and northern Levantine geographic references. The proposal of an additional Anatolian kingdom, Muṣri, has been refuted, leaving 'Egypt' as the most probable reading.[19]

Although horses and chariotry were an important part of Egyptian royal iconography from the founding of the New Kingdom onward, there is no extrabiblical evidence of 10th century trade in horses via Egypt. The most likely explanation for how Solomon came to be credited with this enterprise is that ancient historiographers took inspiration from their own day and crafted an anachronistic account.[20] Late 8th and early 7th century Neo-Assyrian records shed light on the importance of horses and chariotry in elite culture and for the operations of the empire.[21] S. Dalley's analysis of these records demonstrates that Neo-Assyrian rulers preferred *kusaya*, that is Kushite, horses and harnessing equipment for their chariotry, and that the horses and goods were associated with Egypt, which is referred to as *muṣri* in the Assyrian texts.[22] Some exchange was the result of tribute, as was the case in Osorkon IV's payment to Sargon II. In other cases, it was trade. Dalley argues that access to the *kusaya* horse trade was the motivating factor behind Assyrian interest in controlling Gaza as a trading post.[23] The exchange may have gone beyond horses and equipment. Dalley goes on to argue that Nubians entered the Assyrian ranks as equestrian experts, and that diplomatic and artistic exchange flowed between Assyria and the Nubian court.[24]

The importance of horses in elite Nubian culture is well-attested throughout the Iron Age, most famously from Piankhi/Piye, the Nubian pharaoh of the early 25th Dynasty who ruled as a contemporary to Tiglath-Pileser III, Shalmaneser V, and Sargon II. The value is unmistakable in Piankhi's lengthy victory inscription from Gebel Barkal, where he makes note of horses frequently in the campaign and details his disapproval of the poor treatment of royal horses in Hermopolis.[25] It is also demonstrated in physical remains from his reign. Four horses accompanied Piankhi in burial, a practice that was repeated by other 25th Dynasty kings.[26]

This burial tradition was not new at Piankhi's time. Excavations of earlier elite burials in Tombos and Hillat el-Arab (near the Third Cataract) attest to a long-established practice among Nubian elites, going back at least as early as the mid-10th century.[27] The Tombos burial included an interred horse and an iron bridle piece (which appears to be the earliest evidence of worked iron in Nubia), along with heirloom goods.[28] Excavators argue that the blend of Egyptian and Nubian culture (both in material goods and burial practices) reveals a complex statement of power as Nubia began to thrive under local rule following the decentralization of Egypt toward the end of the 20th Dynasty. The 10th century discoveries are certainly exciting contributions to our understanding of emerging Iron Age states and elite culture, especially among those who were at the peripheries of imperial Egypt. At present, however, we do not have evidence to connect the Nubian elites evident in the Tombos burial to the contemporary southern Levantine elites.[29] Based on this analysis, we should view the depiction in 1 Kings 10:28–29 as a reasonable reflection of an international horse trade, but during the 8th and 7th centuries, rather than the 10th.[30]

Egypt and Solomon's Adversaries

At the end of the Solomon Narrative, the DH reports that Egypt harbored two rivals to Solomon (11:14–40): Hadad, a member of an Edomite royal family (מזרע המלך הוא באדום), and Jeroboam, an Israelite elite (גבור חיל) and official (עבד) in Solomon's administration who oversaw the labor (סבל) in *Bet Yosef* and would go on to rule the northern kingdom after Solomon's death. Incidentally, the narrative also discusses a third rival, Rezon, an Aramean ruling from Damascus, who was reportedly involved in regional tensions but is not explicitly tied to Egypt. Putting aside the theological framework that the Dtr used to shape this section, the overarching sense of these reports is that there was considerable instability in the leadership of emerging Levantine polities, and across the greater southeastern Mediterranean. This general picture should not be surprising, since historical examples of regional rivalries and Egyptian involvement in Levantine politics are plentiful in Late Bronze and Iron Age records, but many textual and historical issues hinder our ability to rely on this material.

Textual problems abound in this portion of the Solomon Narrative. In looking solely at the MT, we find inconsistencies, such as in the spelling of Hadad, in references to the deity, and problems in narrative flow (e.g., 11:25). There is scribal difficulty evident in the confusion between the letters *dalet* (ד) and *resh* (ר). This last issue is not uncommon, but its consequences exacerbate historical problems, since these letters are the only difference in the place names Edom (אדם) and Aram (ארם), the home territories of two of the three rivals.[31] Additionally, differences between the MT and LXX raise questions about older Hebrew variants and compositional/redaction history.[32] Textual problems do not necessarily correspond to whether a text might be more or less reliable historically. The awkwardness is likely a sign of a blending or adding of sources, but difficult texts tend to invite scribal interference over time, to correct errors and smooth narrative clumsiness. In this case, the material concerning each of the rivals likely came from distinct sources, but they have been arranged to suit the Dtr's scheme for the conclusion of Solomon's story.

There are also literary characteristics that cannot be overlooked in a historical evaluation. The rivals pericope exhibits common storytelling tropes in the figures' actions and dialogue that serve to heighten the tension as Solomon appears to lose hold of his kingdom.[33] In the stories of Hadad and Jeroboam, it is easy enough to see the pattern of a heroic figure who flees a threat, is harbored abroad, and who returns later in life to challenge the more powerful order. In the Hebrew Bible, this motif is frequently expressed as a flight to Egypt, as in the best-known cases of Abraham, Joseph, and Moses. This sort of folkloristic element serves as the foundation for D. Edelman's argument that the figures form a 'trio of 'bad guy' characters,' who as a literary unit intensify the consequence determined for Solomon's theological transgressions.

The various textual and literary features of this episode complicate any consideration of this material for historical inquiry. The problems do not automatically disqualify the passages, but one must proceed with extreme caution. There is a general consensus that most of the material in 1 Kings 11:14–40 is not an original composition of the Dtr but derived from various sources. For those who *do* find kernels of historical information here regarding interactions with Egypt, the focus has been on names, lineages, and locations. Despite classic storytelling tropes in Hadad's story (including the prominent but unnamed 'Pharaoh, king of Egypt'), the text supplies details about his Egyptian wife and son. The son's name, Genubath, is Egyptian, but the author's ability to supply an Egyptian name does not automatically verify Hadad's historicity.[34] His wife's description is more intriguing. The text states that Hadad found favor with Pharaoh, and that the king gave him a woman to marry, a sister of his (i.e., the king's) wife. The text clarifies: אחות תחפנים הגבירה 'the sister of *tahpenes*, the *gebirah*' (1 Kgs 11:19). There is considerable debate about the verse and the name/term תחפנים, but the DH's sense is clear enough; it claims that Hadad married an elite Egyptian woman.[35] As for Jeroboam, the Dtr lays the foundation here for his important role in the next phase of Israelite history, but the detail in 1 Kings 11:40, that Egypt's king Shishaq harbored Jeroboam, a rival to the king in Jerusalem, is of obvious interest here.

As is the case for any references regarding Solomon's affairs, the material is unverifiable based on our available extrabiblical evidence. The earliest monumental Iron Age inscriptions from the southern Levant date to the 9th century.[36] Egyptian records show some involvement in the southern Levant, as we will see below and in subsequent chapters, but they do not correlate directly to the stories in 1 Kings 11. In light of these limitations, we must consider general circumstances of interregional interactions. In 'Israel, Edom and Egypt in the 10th Century B.C.E.,' Na'aman argues that competition for trade routes lay behind the account(s) of Solomon's adversaries.[37] He proposes that Solomon's trade activity threatened Egypt and other states' profits from interactions, arguing that the adversaries in the text expose a region-wide effort against Solomon's trade and economic success. Na'aman's views have changed since this article, but the general idea underlying his 1992 claim is important.[38] When relatively strong, Egypt was in a good position to manipulate trade involving many routes – along the Mediterranean, through the Negev, and along the Red Sea coast – and it appears that routes and commerce were a target of Shoshenq I's campaign. It is fully within the realm of possibility, based on historical examples prior to and after the 10th century, that Egypt would get involved in southern Levantine rivalries, as we will explore in subsequent chapters.[39] Elites of the southern Levant and Egypt played off the alliances and antagonisms in the region to advance their status and economic interests.

What we must also acknowledge, however, is that such tensions existed at the height of the Neo-Assyrian advance in the 8th century and during subsequent struggles for power in the 7th century, in other words, at precisely the time when many of the writings that came to be part of the DH were coming into being.[40] It is difficult to imagine that accounts of Solomon's rivals would not have been influenced by the later Iron Age circumstances. Scholars must continue to debate whether Solomon-era rivals were reinterpreted in light of those later concerns or were invented to give depth to the 8th–7th century events.[41] For now, it is wise to remain agnostic regarding the details of 1 Kings 11:14–40 for historical reconstructions, but it is reasonable to say that the 'international' dynamic portrayed in the episode is not out of character for the period or region. Whether or not the depiction stemmed from historical documentation or the memory of 10th century tensions, or from the fact that such relations were frequently the status quo and relatable to a later audience, cannot at present be determined.

Diplomatic Marriage and Egypt

The Solomon Narrative opens with a clear statement of cooperation between Egypt and Jerusalem: 'Solomon became related by marriage to the pharaoh, the king of Egypt; he married the pharaoh's daughter, and he brought her to the City of David...' (1 Kgs 3:1). This marriage alliance surfaces several times in the narrative (1 Kgs 7:8; 9:16, 24; 11:1), and, despite the fact that we learn almost nothing about the Egyptian princess as an individual, the union is significant in Solomon's history and is depicted as consequential for aspects of his kingdom and rule. According to the DH, Solomon's Egyptian father-in-law granted him territory, namely Gezer, which the Pharaoh had conquered and cleansed of Canaanites (1 Kgs 9:16), and Solomon's Egyptian wife received dedicated quarters in the newly constructed royal precinct in Jerusalem, perhaps implying a prominent role in the Solomonic state. Despite the potential importance of this information, the narrative leaves much unsaid, including the names of the Egyptian royals. The information is succinct, even curtailed, so that there is no narrative elaboration about the marriage and what such an arrangement might have meant to residents of Jerusalem in the 10th century. Examination of this account requires more than one line of inquiry concerning diplomatic marriage: one into biblical views, especially of the DH and its sources, and another into ancient Near Eastern historical sources, especially Egyptian.

Diplomatic marriage already had a long history in the ancient Near East by the time we reach the early Iron Age, and it continued well into the age of empires that developed in the mid-1st millennium BCE.[42] Consequently, we should not be surprised to see that there were accounts of such marriage arrangements in the biblical history. The DH famously claims international/intercultural marriages for David, for example with Geshurite Maacah (2 Sam 3:3), and for Ahab with the Phoenician Jezebel (1 Kgs 16:31). Rehoboam, being the son of Ammonite Naamah (1 Kgs 14:21), was presumably the product of a diplomatic marriage. And there are less prominent accounts of the practice among other figures.[43] Notably, in 1 Kings 11:19, as I introduced above, the DH reports a marriage between an Egyptian royal, the sister of תחפנים (typically rendered as the name 'Tahpenes' in English), the גבירה (a Hebrew term for 'queen/queen mother/chief wife') of an unnamed Pharaoh, and Hadad, a Levantine rival to David and Solomon. According to the LXX, the pharaoh Sousakim (Shoshenq I/biblical Shishaq) gave Jeroboam a bride named Ano, who was considered 'great among the king's daughters' and is described as the elder sister of Sousakim's wife Θεκεμείνας (the Greek version of תחפנים).[44] Although these last examples come with a host of textual and source-critical problems, they reveal a persistent notion that elites of the mid-late 10th century engaged in strategic marriages that crossed cultural and territorial boundaries.

It is also difficult to evaluate Solomon's Egyptian marriage alliance without addressing the infamous 'many foreign wives' prominently discussed toward the end of the Solomon Narrative (1 Kgs 11:1–6). For readers only casually acquainted with the biblical story, these marriages are among the more familiar elements of the DH's version of Solomon's career. Not only are they sensational and a prominent element as Solomon's story concludes, but the DH anchors the explanation of a divided kingdom and Solomon's 'fall' to his participation in his foreign wives' religious practices. The DH also includes Solomon's shrines to his wives' gods among the places and practices that Josiah suppressed in his reforms just prior to the end of the Judahite kingdom (2 Kgs 23:13–14). Conversely, the notion of Solomon's love for the exotic proved an indelible image that was not always considered problematic. Over many centuries, Solomonic legend grew, so that he was not only a king who participated in a number of marriage alliances but also the epitome of sensual experience, as characterized in the Song of Songs.[45] The differing interpretations over time remind us that the DH's negative portrayal of exogamy is not representative of all periods, and is, in fact, particular to the later periods of the monarchic era.

Despite the overwhelming notion of corruption by foreign wives, which the DH imparts, a source-critical examination of 1 Kings 3–11 shows that examples related to the Pharaoh's daughter are discussed matter-of-factly and seemingly without moral judgement. The basic material is brief, and the marriage is mentioned only a handful of times:

1 Kings 3:1	Solomon became son-in-law to Pharaoh, King of Egypt, he took Pharaoh's daughter (in marriage), and he brought her to the City of David until he completed construction of his house, *bet*-YHWH, and Jerusalem's (outer?) walls.
1 Kings 7:8	(Solomon's) house, where he would reside, in another court, was of this same work, and he made a house like this hall for Pharaoh's daughter, whom he took (in marriage).
1 Kings 9:16	[*Following notice of Solomon's constructions*] Pharaoh, King of Egypt, had gone up and captured Gezer, destroyed it by fire, and killed all of the Canaanites who lived in the city, and he gave it as a dowry to his daughter, Solomon's wife.
1 Kings 9:24	So Pharaoh's daughter went up from the City of David to her house that Solomon had built for her; then he built the Millo.
1 Kings 11:1	King Solomon loved many foreign women (along with Pharaoh's daughter) Moabite, Ammonite, Edomite, Sidonian, Hittite.

The exception to the trend here is 1 Kings 11:1, which is followed by a characteristically Deuteronomistic passage proclaiming the fate of Solomon's realm (vv. 2–13). The verse departs from the others in two important ways: 1) it discusses various foreign wives, not just the Egyptian royal; and 2) it is not associated with Solomon's construction of Jerusalem's new city center.[46] Leaving 1 Kings 11:1 aside, the references to the marriage alliance function as a thread running from the 'beginning' of Solomon's reign (that is, according to the Dtr's presentation) to the culmination of his building program. Given the treatment of the other marriages in 1 Kings 11:1-13, the Pharaoh's daughter passages and structure appear to be older than the Dtr, who relied on this material when shaping the Solomon history.[47] We can then view the comment, 'along with Pharaoh's daughter,' in 11:1 as a later addition (either by the Dtr or an even later editor) that ties together disparate traditions about diplomatic marriage and Jerusalem-area shrines associated with Solomon.[48]

Having established the likelihood that the 'Pharaoh's daughter' material was a source used by the Dtr, we must still determine what it contributes to the DH and whether it can be useful in our own inquiry. It is important to note that the narrative overall does not seem concerned with the Pharaoh's daughter as an individual person or as a literary character.[49] Instead, the focus is on Solomon's relationship to Egypt and Egypt's influence on Solomon and his kingdom. The connections in the text between the princess and locations (i.e., Solomon's palace, her palace, YHWH's temple, Gezer) may reflect the idea that an elite relationship between royal families was consequential, perhaps in a way that was evident to later generations – that is, through Egyptian style in art and architecture.[50]

It is notable that in the individual passages, the marriage to an Egyptian princess appears to have been a sign of prestige rather than reason for condemnation.[51] It is also notable that by the Dtr's day (late 7th–early 6th centuries), admiration for foreign influence and interactions had become highly problematic. Such activities could not be viewed separately from the devastation wrought by the Neo-Assyrian and Neo-Babylonian empires. Ancient authors like the Dtr viewed foreignness as a threat to proper Israelite theology and political autonomy, and Egyptian ambition in particular could not be disassociated from the power struggles of the later Iron Age and the demise of the Judahite kingdom. In contrast, ruling elites had for centuries invested in marriage alliances to establish political legitimacy and reliable relations with peers. They expressed their participation through shared cultural attributes such as the built environment, personal adornment, and imported goods for banqueting. The account of Solomon's purported marriage to an Egyptian princess seems to reflect this politically-oriented context that embraced elite, intercultural interactions, most likely prior to the height of the Assyrian empire and its threat to southern Levantine states.

The historicity of the marriage is quite another matter and is generally considered dubious. Aside from the obvious difficulty that there is no corroborating evidence outside of the Hebrew Bible, the usual objection is that it was unheard of for Egyptian kings to marry their daughters to non-Egyptians. The most important evidence for this argument is a letter in the Amarna correspondence (EA 4). The greeting of the letter is not extant, but it is likely a continuation of correspondence about the marriage of the Babylonian king Kadashman-Enlil's daughter to Amenhotep III, one of the most prestigious kings of Egypt's 18th Dynasty (mid-14th century BCE). The Babylonian, disappointed in the Egyptian's refusal to send a bride from his court, restates his peer's assertion: 'From of old a daughter of the king of Egypt has never been given to anyone.'[52] In contrast, Kadashman-Enlil's sister and daughter were among Amenhotep III's wives through diplomatic marriages.[53] The explicit nature of the document has retained its persuasive punch millennia later and has been offered as the definitive evidence against the claim that Solomon married an Egyptian princess.

The letter is unambiguous and indeed compelling, but scholars typically fail to discuss the span of four centuries between the Amarna correspondence and the 21st–22nd Dynasty rulers; incidentally, this is roughly the same chronological distance between Solomon's era and the composition of the DH. This distance does not rule out the possibility that Egypt's rulers would have adhered to the same prohibition, but it is important to acknowledge that the political and cultural contexts are distinct.[54] Egypt was decentralized by the end of the 20th Dynasty. In much of the 11th and 10th centuries, a king ruled from the eastern Delta (Lower Egypt), while an official in Thebes (Upper Egypt) who held two important titles, High Priest of Amun and military commander, oversaw the south.[55] Many northern rulers were descended from the Libyan elites who rose to prominence toward the end of the New Kingdom and who were deeply connected to New Kingdom power structures.[56] These rulers relied on both Egyptian and Libyan symbols of their power. They emulated New Kingdom pharaonic models and collected traditional Egyptian titles, but also retained characteristics of their Libyan identities. Notably, these included an emphasis on kinship relationships and titles such as 'Chief of the Meshwesh,' which distinguished leaders such as Shoshenq I as the most prominent individual in the Delta and highlighted his Libyan and pastoral-nomadic cultural background.[57]

Marriage alliances were a strategic tool in negotiating distinct sources of power along the Nile during the 11th and 10th centuries.[58] Unions that involved royals from the north and priestly families in the south had the potential to blend the most powerful lineages and produce an heir to both the Delta kingship and the Theban priestly line. The founder of the 22nd Dynasty, Shoshenq I, anchored himself to the southern power base through his children. His son Iuput was positioned as High Priest of Amun, and his daughter, Tashepenbast, was married to the Third Prophet of Amun, Djedthutefankh, who came from an elite, well connected, and well-decorated Theban family.[59] This alliance, along with strategic appointments of Libyan officials to other positions in Thebes, shifted the relationship between Upper and Lower Egypt. Rather than work in partnership with the High Priest of Amun, Shoshenq subsumed the southern power base. Although this evidence does not support the biblical claims of marriages between Egyptian and Levantine elites, it does introduce more complexity to other issues that are relevant, including the use of marriage as a political tool among elites in the broader, eastern Mediterranean context, and the dynamic among rival elites who had competing claims to power. These issues come into focus again later in this chapter.

To return to the biblical claim of Solomon's marriage alliance with Egypt, any scholar who chooses to entertain the idea must also grapple with the difficulty that the biblical Pharaoh is unnamed. Scholars seeking to identify Solomon's father-in-law with a historical figure have considered Siamun and Shoshenq I to be the best candidates.[60] The case for Siamun, the second-to-last pharaoh of the 21st Dynasty (ruled ca. 978–959), was popular among scholars in the second half of the 20th century. Siamun's Tanis relief records his domination of an enemy that may have been of Aegean ethnicity, which some scholars connect to the Philistines and a battle at Gezer (reconstructed from 1 Kgs 9:16).[61] S. Yeivin, relying on J. Goldwasser's interpretation of the Siamun relief and the biblical history, proposed that Solomon's alliance with Egypt came about through a complex power play. In this reconstruction, Solomon attempted to break an Egyptian-Byblian trade monopoly by partnering with Hiram/Phoenicia (see 1 Kgs 5:1–12 and analysis below), a move that provoked a military and diplomatic response from Siamun.[62] F. M. Cross proposed a different reconstruction but similarly focused on interregional political tensions. Building on the arguments of A. Malamat and B. Mazar, Cross argued that Siamun took Gezer in a campaign to annex Philistia for Egypt and that Solomon, in an effort to avoid war with Egypt, made a deal to acquire Gezer but allow Egyptian control of Philistine cities.[63] By today's standards, these proposals are too dependent on the biblical narrative, and their relevance is compromised further by the absence of recent understandings of archaeological contexts. Their exploratory thinking, however, continues to hold value. Both proposals considered the underlying economic and diplomatic needs of the contemporary leaders and strove to account for the cooperative as well as antagonistic relations depicted in the Solomon Narrative.

The other candidate favored by scholars is Shoshenq I (ruled ca. 945–924), whose involvement in the Levant is well-documented and frequently debated.[64] His reign is also notable because of its impact on understanding 10th century chronology in the southeastern Mediterranean.[65] Shoshenq's rise to power shows off his political acumen and family connections. He was prominent in elite circles, having served under his pharaonic predecessor Psusennes II and as the heir to the title Chief of the Meshwesh.[66] As we have already examined, Shoshenq dominated the Theban power base through family appointments and strategic marriage arrangements. Shoshenq's efforts ended roughly a century of decentralized rule (although decentralization eventually returned), and he was the first king to conduct a large-scale campaign into the southern Levant after the New Kingdom's decline, a feat he documented on the Bubastite portal at Karnak.[67] In addition, he commissioned a victory stele that was found at Megiddo. Although debate regarding the campaign is lively, geographic analysis of the locations on the Bubastite portal suggests that Shoshenq was not simply emulating the Levantine campaigns of his New Kingdom predecessors (or mimicking their campaign inscriptions). Rather, he appears to have been targeting sites that represented emerging leadership, as well as areas with strong economic potential, such as lucrative metallurgical resources and key locations on the commercial routes of the Arabah and Jordan Valleys.[68]

Shoshenq's potential participation in a marriage alliance, with a goal of using it for political or economic gain, might seem to fit his *modus operandi*, but evidence he engaged in these strategies beyond Egypt is lacking outside of the biblical sources noted above. Documentation of Shoshenq's involvement in Levantine affairs suggests efforts to (re)establish Egyptian contacts and control, especially in economic matters (e.g., donation of a statue to Byblos and his campaign to the southern Levant), but there is no substantial evidence that the king was able to sustain involvement in the Levant, whether through military action or through diplomatic means such as marriage.

Before concluding this discussion of potential interactions with Egypt, it is important to note, as I do elsewhere, that scholars are drawn to the most prestigious rulers and best-known figures when attempting to flesh out what is recorded in the biblical history.[69] The available evidence from the likes of Siamun or Shoshenq I provide an accessible starting place for inquiry, but it is wise to assume that we know the identities of *only a handful* of the 'movers and shakers' of the time. Many lesser known and anonymous-to-us figures undoubtedly played important roles in the 11th–9th centuries. Could it be that Egyptian or Levantine-Egyptian elites whose identities are unknown today exerted influence in the southern Levant in the generations following the collapse of the New Kingdom's empire? Could a descendant of an Egyptian elite family, perhaps even a distant member of an Egyptian royal, have married into a Jerusalemite dynasty in the 10th century and become the 'historical kernel' for the 'Pharaoh's daughter' tradition?[70] Limitations in documentation and other evidence should not prohibit questions about early Iron Age exchange relationships, of which diplomatic marriage is but one form, even if our ability to respond to these questions with definitive answers is not currently possible.

A final example illustrates that there were various participants involved in exchange and interactions between the southern Levant and Egypt. Elites from the Third Intermediate Period (TIP) left behind indications of exchange, especially in the form of luxury goods. Although excavated in the 1940s, the late 11th century BCE burial of Wendjebauendjed, Psusennes I's general and overseer of the temple of Khonsu in Tanis, has recently made scholarly headlines.[71] He was buried in the same chamber (NRT III) as Psusennes I, as well as other TIP kings and high officials. New analysis has determined that a number of the bronze shabti figurines from Wendjebauendjed's tomb were made of Arabah copper.[72] His burial goods also included luxury items such as fine metal vessels, one of which is extremely similar to the inscribed bowl from the Kefar Veradim burial deposit.[73] Wendjebauendjed's titles, burial location, and tomb offerings demonstrate not only that he was well-positioned in the 21st Dynasty power network, but also that his membership in the most elite circles of his day provided access to the most prestigious luxuries. Although there is no direct, historical link between Wendjebauendjed and Levantine diplomacy, this example helps to broaden our understanding of potential participants in the elite ranks, and exchange systems of the early Iron Age. Long-distance relations and exchange were not limited to kings and princesses.

Taken as a whole, an examination of Solomon's relations with Egypt leads to important conclusions about exchange in the 10th century BCE and the DH's presentation of the events. First, it is logical to be skeptical of the accounts of interactions with Egypt that are relayed in the DH. In light of the influences we can discern from the 8th through 6th centuries, when many aspects of the narrative were taking shape, it is difficult to feel confident about a 10th century Solomon from what later writers built as a foundation or justification for events closer to their own day. At the same time, critical examination of the marriage to a Pharaoh's daughter brings to light nuances about elite culture in the 21st and 22nd Dynasties, even if the biblical claim cannot be supported. Investigation of Solomon's trade in horses cannot be verified, but our search for information similarly introduces established elites in 10th century Nubia. The adversaries account (1 Kgs 11:14–40) remains problematic, but in its general sense, it may confirm that the 10th century was not an exception to Iron Age relations between these eastern Mediterranean neighbors. Egypt was involved in the southern Levant's political and economic affairs. Direct control under Shoshenq may have failed, but elite Egyptians were undoubtedly consumers of Levantine copper and participants in an elite culture that was shared across boundaries. If there was a special relationship between Egypt and Jerusalem, we cannot substantiate it outside of the biblical claims, but more important than a confirmation of the reported events are the facts gained from this inquiry: we are getting a much more vivid picture of emerging elites in the 10th century, and this era's elites were less isolated than is often imagined.

Exchange Involving Phoenicia

The DH describes, in detail, interactions between Solomon and Hiram, a contemporary king of Tyre, but not all the accounts are in agreement about the terms and results of their interactions. The narrative's reports focus on two major enterprises: a maritime partnership for Red Sea trade (1 Kgs 9:26–28; 10:11–12, 22), and an exchange agreement regarding building materials, agricultural goods, and border territory between the kingdoms of Jerusalem and Tyre, about which there appear to be two accounts (1 Kgs 5:15–25; 9:10–14).

Although in one account, there is tension between the monarchs (1 Kgs 9:13), most of the narrative is devoted to Solomon's diplomatic successes and economic gains as a result of the partnership (e.g., 1 Kgs 10:22).

Like the majority of the accounts in the Solomon Narrative, extrabiblical evidence from the 10th century does not pertain specifically to the relations with Phoenicia just described. Historical and archaeological evidence suggests that in the early Iron Age, there were maritime operations all along the eastern Mediterranean coast. Strategically situated cities with good harbors functioned as ports, connecting the sea with inland commerce and communities. Although some of the most powerful Late Bronze Age coastal cities were destroyed or abandoned between the 13th and 11th centuries, many smaller sites (compared to the larger Late Bronze Age cities) survived and filled the void in the Iron I.[74] In some of these centers, the cities were continuously inhabited without significant population or leadership disruptions. Epigraphic evidence from Byblos confirms that elites were actively asserting themselves in both local and interregional arenas as early as the 10th century, but written evidence from southern Phoenician elites remains elusive.[75] Archaeological evidence, however, supports the image of a commercially successful enterprise headquartered in Tyre from the 10th to the 8th centuries.[76] Our knowledge of who contributed to the growth of this city-state is hindered by the lack of written sources. Only the biblical history and Josephus' 1st century CE account provide information about a 10th century Tyrian king Hiram.[77] Complicating matters further is our knowledge of a later Hiram, king of Tyre, known from Assyrian records. This king ruled in the 730s and is frequently mentioned in royal and administrative documents that detail the Neo-Assyrian efforts to maximize control of Tyre's resources and commercial enterprise. Whether or not the 8th century Hiram was an inspiration for Solomon's contemporary continues to be a matter of debate. Ultimately, extrabiblical evidence provides some context for evaluating the depictions in the Solomon Narrative in relation to the 10th century, but, as with much of Solomon's history, the latter half of the 8th century appears to have been very influential on the way the ancient historians depicted Solomon's relations with Tyre.

Treaty, Constructions, and Northern Land

The DH claims that relations with Tyre were established prior to Solomon's reign. According to 2 Samuel 5:11, Hiram initiated a diplomatic relationship with David following the seizure of Jerusalem, and according to 1 Kings 5:15, the relationship was renewed once Solomon secured his position. In both cases, the DH reports that Hiram supplied building materials to the monarchs for construction projects in Jerusalem. While the DH extends only one verse to the agreement with David (perhaps only as a foundation for what will follow), the narrative indulges in recounting the alliance with Solomon. The depiction is carried out in two main exchanges: one prior to the temple construction (1 Kgs 5:15–25) and one after (1 Kgs 9:10–14). The two episodes record different perspectives on the arrangement and should be considered as coming from two distinct sources.

The first of these two is the most detailed (1 Kgs 5:15–25). Information on the agreement is conveyed through dialogue and narration. In their amicable exchange, Solomon and Hiram establish a treaty and reciprocate gifts: Hiram will provide Phoenician materials and artisans for Solomon's gift of food provisions to Hiram's house. The dialogue follows conventional language and form for ancient treaties, through which the leaders assert the nature of their peaceful relations and agree to an exchange of goods and gifts. Despite this form, the dialogue cannot be assumed to be a historical record of a 10th century treaty.[78] The text is idealized and Deuteronomized. The Dtr made use of a preexisting dialogue as a foundation, into which he inserted his theological messages. Hiram and Solomon's words, after the Dtr's editing, reiterate the historical conditions allowing Solomon, rather than David, to be the temple builder (1 Kgs 5:17–19); the dialogue bolsters the images of both Solomon and YHWH (1 Kgs 5:21). Even if we remove the Deuteronomistic elements from the episode, it is not likely that the text is a 10th century product. It is *too good* of an example of royal relations. Rather than a successful preservation of 10th century correspondence, the dialogue may have been influenced by the use of 'model letters' for scribal education, possibly from the 8th century.[79] Such letters would have been based on historical figures and potentially also historic relations, but they would reflect the social or political reality of the period of the scribal school more than the era of the subjects of the writings.

The second report (1 Kgs 9:10–14) consists of a brief summary of the Tyre-Jerusalem arrangement, which includes a gift/payment to Hiram consisting of Galilean cities rather than food provisions.[80] This version conveys that the partnership was not mutually satisfying. According to the narrative, Hiram was displeased with Solomon's gift but completed the exchange by paying 120 talents of gold. The history credits Hiram with naming the territory Cabul, presumably derived from the root כבל meaning 'hobbled' or 'fettered', expressing Hiram's sense of loss, burden, or indebtedness in taking on this territory. This reaction was intentionally crafted to minimize what Solomon appears to have lost in the exchange.[81] Contrary to Hiram's view, the land should have had significant cultural and economic value. If we follow the DH's depiction of Israelite geography, Cabul consisted of northern Israelite cities, which made up a portion of the tribal territory of Asher (Josh 19:24–31).[82] In addition to the insult of selling off Asher's traditional allotment, the text implies that Solomon turned over control of a region that was a direct link to Mediterranean exchange, which involved not only trade with Cyprus and Levantine coastal cities but also links to interests further east, including the Aegean and rich sources of silver.

The reminder that Cabul was still the name of the region 'until this day' (1 Kgs 9:13) demonstrates the Dtr's endorsement of this account. Despite the characteristic phrase, this version is less Deuteronomistic than the previous exchange. In this case, the Dtr included, rather than created, this account of Solomon's less amicable exchange with Hiram. Thus, the idea that Solomon gave up Israelite territory to Tyre appears to be a pre-Dtr view of the king. Although a precise date for this report cannot be determined, the less-flattering view of Solomon might point to certain historical situations being more probable than others. If the report relates to a historical Solomon, the depiction might stem from the period shortly after the establishment of a northern state, especially if hard feelings toward Davidides or Jerusalem influenced the account. In such a scenario, David's successors seem to have taken the heat for not challenging the growth of an expansive Tyrian state. Hiram's insult is yet another clue, and may point to 8th or 7th century influence, when the land was destroyed by the Assyrians and not rebuilt for imperial purposes.[83] The contrast between a productive south and a devastated north suits the Assyrian period, and, in this case, the text obscures the historical reason for the land's diminished value and the imperial force that caused its ruin.

When looking at both depictions, there are significant agreements and divergences. The two have in common that Solomon had an exchange agreement with Hiram for the supply of building materials, and that Solomon used land – either as a trade commodity or as a source for payment in agricultural goods – to secure Jerusalem's side of the agreement.[84] The contention between the two accounts suggests that there was a common historical situation that gave rise to stories of Solomon's dealings with Hiram, but from this common point, the accounts developed differently because of the additional historical circumstances of each source.[85] It is also apparent, however, that the Dtr's sources were not composed in the mid-10th century. As a result, we are left with a large window of time that might have influenced historical memory and written sources, from soon after Solomon's death to as late as the mid-7th century (or prior to the Dtr). If either is to be used for historical inquiry, it is best to set aside the more apologetic view and focus on the more critical account (1 Kgs 9:10–14), albeit with significant consideration for the historical circumstances that may have shaped it.

Maritime Trade

Later in the history, we learn of a maritime partnership between Solomon and Hiram, described in three parts: a) 1 Kings 9:26–28; b) 1 Kings 10:11–12; and c) 1 Kings 10:22. These reports are intertwined with the Queen of Sheba episode (1 Kgs 10:1–10, 13) and other illustrations of Solomon's wealth and success (10:14–15, 16–21, 23–27). The theme of maritime trade runs as a thread within a larger unit (1 Kgs 9:26–10:29) that illustrates Solomon's wealth from trade and tribute.

The three reports stem from more than one source, and at least two have been elaborated upon by the Dtr. The first, 1 Kings 9:26–28, can be read as a complete account: Solomon constructed a fleet at Ezion-geber and, with Hiram and his Phoenician seafarers' assistance, imported gold from Ophir. The second account assumes knowledge of a seafaring venture involving Hiram's fleet (but not explicitly linked to Ezion-geber), goods from Ophir, and the import of precious stones and *almug*-wood. This section concludes with the characteristic comment 'until this day' at the end of 10:12. The third account, 1 Kings 10:22, elaborates on the exotic nature of the imports. This verse notes that Solomon's fleet was made up of Tarshish ships, which imported luxury goods once every three years. There can be no doubt that the historian(s) intended to convey Solomon's success and largess through the trade partnership with the Phoenicians, commonly renowned for their maritime and exchange expertise.

Some aspects of these reports appear so extravagant that they easily draw suspicion. The terms Ophir (א[ו]פיר) and *almug*-wood (עצי אלמגים; 1 Kgs 10:11–12), Tarshish ships (אני תרשיש), ivory (שנהבים), and the enigmatic (קפים ותכיים; 1 Kgs 10:22) imply trade over great distances involving the Red Sea, the Mediterranean, and even southeast Asia.

The problematic phrase קפים ותכיים, traditionally translated as 'apes and peacocks,' appears only in 1 Kings 10:22 and in the parallel 2 Chronicles 9:21. Two explanations have the potential to account for this phrase. The traditional 'apes and peacocks' reading suggests that exotic animals were imported to Jerusalem from as far away as the Indian subcontinent. Like the animals, these non-Semitic words most likely became known to Hebrew speakers only during the exile or Persian periods (particularly the case for תכיים, 'peacock').[86] As a consequence, 1 Kings 10:22 would have to be considered a late supplement to the account of Solomon's commerce. Lipiński's alternative translation 'knives and razors,' however, results in a more logical and era-appropriate report.[87] That is, metal utensils, 'knives and razors,' would be appropriate among the shipment described in 1 Kings 10:22, and as we examine below and in subsequent chapters, Phoenician commercial interest in metals was critical in early Iron Age exchange. With this alternative translation, we may have a more logical meaning for the Iron Age Levant, but the new meaning does not narrow the description to Solomon's time or attest to his direct involvement in maritime exchange.

The *almug*-wood is the most unusual product described in 1 Kings 10:11–12, and, ideally, should provide information regarding the provenance of the text. Unfortunately, the material and the source of the word remain obscure.[88] Without knowing the identity of the material, the most significant information in the text becomes the Dtr's comment on it. He testifies that 'no such *almug*-wood has since been imported or seen until this day' (1 Kgs 10:12). The statement is not typical for the Dtr's 'until this day' formula. This occurrence explains an event or status that had ceased some time before the historian's day, instead of one still in existence. The best explanation for this comment is that the Dtr relied on an older (perhaps considerably older) source that testified to the import and use of this unusual material. It appears that one could no longer simply 'see for oneself' a remaining example in the Dtr's time; if one could, would not the historian have kept to his usual formula? What the Dtr seems certain of is that no one else had imported or seen so much of the material since Solomon, and that the Dtr's source provided the necessary evidence of its existence.

The narrative emphasizes Ophir as the destination for the fleet (1 Kgs 9:28; 10:11).[89] Unlike some of the exotica in these passages, this location is attested outside of the Solomon Narrative. Gold from Ophir, apparently known for its rare quality, appears in various biblical passages (e.g., Isaiah 13:12), as well as on an ostracon discovered at Tell Qasile.[90] What we do not know is where exactly Ophir was, and how long peoples of the Levant were interacting with it.[91] The context set by 1 Kings 9:26–28 leads us to believe that it was reached by the Red Sea. Researchers have put forward candidates in eastern Africa/Nubia, Arabia, and even as far abroad as India.[92] Much of the confusion in weighing the different proposals for an identification likely stems from the possibility that goods from all these far-away locations may have funneled through the famed Ophir, and recipients in the eastern Mediterranean world may not have known the lands of origin of each commodity. Current evidence and the cultural setting of the southern Levant narrows the possibilities to Nubia or Arabia as the most likely home to Ophir. Both are known as gold sources through historical, archaeological, and geological research, and both eastern Africa and Arabia were associated with trade in precious stones (either as sources or as intermediary steps in such exchange). Considering the influence of Egypt's 25th Dynasty in the affairs of the southern Levant and the importance of 8th century contexts in other parts of the Solomon Narrative, we might suspect a connection with Nubia. At the same time, the notice of goods from Ophir in 1 Kings 10:11 suggests an association with either an Arabian locale or Arabian traders. Without certain knowledge of Ophir's location, however, we cannot assess how long it was used as a source for precious commodities. The biblical material indicates only that the idea of Ophir gold and goods held social currency for the texts' authors and audiences. Although archaeology has verified that trade in exotic goods existed in the 10th century, and in theory they may have been related to what became known as Ophir, the biblical author's frame of reference does not appear to be a product of this earlier period. It is most likely that the Dtr's source imagined or revised Solomon's maritime trade through a later lens.

Similarly, the characterization of the fleet as being comprised of 'Tarshish ships' (1 Kgs 10:22) signaled something familiar for the history's audience. The term 'Tarshish' in other biblical passages is typically associated with Tyre/Phoenicia and Mediterranean trade, especially in silver, and most scholars identify the biblical term with ancient Tartessos in Spain.[93] The term is also very much at home in texts associated with periods of more intense literary composition, such as Isaiah 23 (late 8th–early 7th centuries) or Ezekiel 27 (6th century). These associations give away the source's historical context. The Tarshish characterization was a useful reference for conveying the idea that Solomon's ships were capable of bringing back the sizeable cargo from a great distance (see also 1 Kgs 22:49, and discussion below), just like ships known in the source's day for hauling Phoenician treasure from the western Mediterranean. Whether the imagery was meant to be figurative, to convey the scale of the operation, or more literal, as a historical account of Solomon's relationship to Phoenician seafaring, our understanding must be that this part of the history was based in later notions of maritime trade.

The last element in the maritime accounts that contributes to a discussion of the Dtr's sources is the shipbuilding and seafaring port 'Ezion-geber near Eloth' (1 Kgs 9:26). The northern end of today's Gulf of Eilat/Aqaba, where 1 Kings 9:26 points us, would have been a good location for trade headquarters. It provided access to the Red Sea and was situated at a convergence of land routes from the gulf coastlines and into the Levant via the Wadi Arabah and the Darb el-Ghazza. In addition, there were comparable activities in the area at other periods. The DH demonstrates that, at least to the Dtr, or in his time, there was significant interest in the area. The locations Ezion-geber and Eloth/Elath turn up several times in the DH, particularly during the divided monarchy.[94] According to the history, Judahite kings made claims to the area at two other times in the Iron Age: Jehoshaphat attempted (unsuccessfully) a trade venture from Ezion-geber (1 Kgs 22:49), and Azariah restored Elath to Judah (2 Kgs 14:22). The region came into and was taken from Jerusalem/Judahite control more than once. The other states vying for control of the area were most likely Israel and Aram.[95] Israel under the Omrides dominated much of the region, including Judah and Edom, making them good candidates for running operations from the port. Control shifted to Aram, probably under Hazael, in the 9th century. Later Rezin 'reclaimed' the port and drove out Judahites in the 8th century (2 Kgs 16:6).[96] After this notice, the DH is silent regarding Elath and Ezion-geber, even though the region continued as an important trade gateway and later fell into Assyrian hands. The DH fails to mention this turn of events, despite its significant concern for the location.

The Dtr's hand is evident in each of these Ezion-geber or Eloth/Elath accounts, exposing some piqued interest and potential bias that would affect the history.[97] Complicating matters more is the fact that archaeological research has not identified a 10th century candidate for Solomon's port. Tell el-Kheleifeh, thought by many to be the biblical Ezion-geber, dates to the later part of the monarchic era.[98] If these archaeological assessments are accurate, and Solomon had a port for Red Sea activity, Tell el-Kheleifeh's identification as Ezion-geber in 1 Kings 9:26 is anachronistic and would not predate the 8th century. In addition, the clarification of Ezion-geber's location (if not also the name itself or the entire verse) may have been added by the Dtr: 'The king Solomon built ships at Ezion-geber, *which is near Eloth on the Red Sea shore, in the land of Edom*' (1 Kgs 9:26). The explanation is necessary only if Ezion-geber was no longer in Judahite hands, which suggests that later periods heavily influenced this report in the history.

The DH, in light of the loss of this region from Judah's holdings, asserts a historical claim to the site. With Solomon established as the founder of a port at Ezion-geber/Elath, the history gives Jerusalem precedence over Samaria, Aram, Edom, and Assyria, all of whom controlled the region around the Gulf of Eilat at some point in the Iron Age. Like other aspirations evident in the DH, the Dtr was hopeful for another change of hands, whereby Josiah would reclaim Ezion-geber/Elath for Judah, thus restoring the land to Solomon's Deuteronomistic precedent (whether historical or not). This account provides the literary foundation for later actions or aspirations.

But what of Solomon's day? Did ancient historians (i.e., the Dtr and/or his sources) invent a history of Solomonic maritime trade? Recent research has established that imported luxury goods made their way to the southern Levant from far off lands, and there is indirect evidence that some goods came via maritime trade involving the Red Sea. The most notable example is the discovery of cinnamon residue in 11th and 10th century Phoenician flasks found at Tel Dor, Tel Qasile, and Kinneret.[99] This cinnamon originated in south/southeast Asia, was transported down the line through various peoples and ports before reaching the Levant, where it was then used to flavor/scent a liquid such as wine or oil. That liquid commodity was traded both in the southern Levant and potentially to the full reach of the Phoenician trade network in the Mediterranean. At present, some of the best arguments regarding how the spice reached the Levant point to maritime trade from India via the Red Sea.[100] This is not to say that the new discoveries support claims about Solomon's activities in 1 Kings 10, but the findings have completely changed our historical and archaeological frames of reference for the 10th century. As A. Gilboa and D. Namdar describe, various independent, early Iron Age 'entrepreneurs' participated in what became a long-reaching trade network.[101] In these years, prior to Neo-Assyrian control of routes and commerce, such a network functioned without centralized control, and undoubtedly spurred regional competition among elites.

Perhaps the best explanation of how Solomon came to be credited with such grandiose commercial achievements involving the Phoenicians and the Red Sea was as a representative in the cultural memory of local elites who were involved in portions of the early Iron Age trade networks. Some notion of interactions and competition among Levantine leaders may have existed, but detailed memory of it was not retained. Instead, historians, especially of the 8th and later centuries, supplied details relevant to Judah's interactions in these periods.[102] In the end, it is likely that a 10th century Judahite ruler might have engaged in some kind of exchange that involved Phoenicia, considering Tyre's growth and the increasing archaeological evidence of long-distance exchange, but the biblical evidence cannot be our sole source on the matter. It has been heavily influenced by authors during the later centuries of the Iron Age and represents the biases and circumstances of those years. If there is something to take away from the Solomon Narrative's account of relations with Hiram/Phoenicia, however, perhaps it is that access to trade and regional resources played a critical role in the relations among independent rulers.

Exchange Involving Arabia

The story of Solomon's involvement in exchange with Arabian monarchs may be the most memorable element of his long-distance interactions, and this is undoubtedly due to the appearance of the Queen of Sheba in the episode (1 Kgs 10:1–15). The account of Arabian exchange is intertwined with the reports of Solomon's maritime ventures and summaries of his wealth through tribute and trade. Although the history states that 'all of the Arabian kings' took part, not one monarch is named, and the only geographic detail is the reference to the famous queen's territory. Biblical Sheba, likely ancient Saba, was located in the southwestern corner of the Arabian Peninsula, today's Yemen, and was well-known in ancient times as the source of frankincense, myrrh, and other luxury goods.[103] According to the biblical story, the queen came to Jerusalem to test Solomon's wisdom and brought with her a great retinue, including camels bearing precious goods for Solomon. The report of Solomon's imports from Ophir (1 Kgs 10:11) directly follows the visit and is itself followed by an account that Solomon returned the queen's generosity with his own gifts (1 Kgs 10:13). On the heels of the episode with the queen, there is also notice that Solomon received tribute and trade goods from Arabian kings (1 Kgs 10:14–15). The Arabia sequence, which is intertwined with the reports of maritime trade, implies that the queen's visit secured safe passage for Solomon's and Hiram's ships through Arabian territories and connected Solomon to caravan trade in the Arabian Peninsula.

Determining the historicity of this account is complicated by the mixture of seemingly historical records with legendary material about Solomon's fame, and, as usual, by the lack of corroborating extrabiblical sources. Some of the questionable characteristics include vagueness on the one hand (e.g., no Arabian monarchs are named) and too detailed dialogue on the other (e.g., 1 Kgs 10:6–9), as well as grand depictions of material goods. The account also shows elements of editing and supplementation that compromise historical integrity.

The queen's visit (1 Kgs 10:1–10, 13) appears to interject into a discussion of Solomon's maritime trade partnership with Hiram (1 Kgs 9:26–28; 10:11–12). The combined narratives form part of a larger compendium of Solomon's trading, wealth, and other successes that ends with the description of horse and chariot trading in 1 Kings 10:29. The queen pericope, which may be a later composition, enhances the narrative so that Solomon's trading activity expands into an elaborate network involving monarchs from Phoenicia to Arabia and beyond. In addition, the queen's visit furthers the image of widespread recognition of YHWH's greatness and Solomon's success.[104] Due to the legendary character and ideological bias, there is general scholarly agreement that the account is not historically reliable for 10th century activities.

The remaining material on Arabia is brief or vague. The history states that 'all the kings of Arabia' traded with Solomon (1 Kgs 10:14–15). This report comes from the narrative that now surrounds the queen material. In this arrangement, the Arabian kings are among the many monarchs, merchants, and governors who participated in exchange with Solomon. Upon close examination, the verses appear to be a late supplement, and the report cannot be relied on for historical reconstruction.[105] It has, however, promoted investigation into whether Arabian kingdoms and interregional trade with them existed in the 10th century.

The most substantial archaeological evidence currently pertains to the region closest to Judah and the DH's interests. Research into Arabia's early Iron Age has grown in recent years, with new results regarding important northwest Arabian sites such as Qurayyah and Tayma. New excavations are confirming that these sites, which bear the hallmarks of complex settlements, were intensively involved in long-distance trade connections throughout the early Iron Age.[106] Tayma is well known through later historical sources, but Qurayyah's early Iron Age identity in still unknown.[107] Painted pottery from the site, however, is closely connected to the copper production in southern Israel and Jordan that was at its height in the 11th to 9th centuries.[108] That pottery, Qurayyah Painted Ware (QPW), has not been found in Jerusalem excavations, but there is reason to believe that Jerusalem's interaction sphere overlapped with the southern exchange networks that facilitated the distribution of QPW and Arabah copper. Excavation of one of the most prominent sites in this network, Khirbat en-Nahas, has produced evidence of both QPW and black burnished juglets, which originated in the Jerusalem area and have been found in E. Mazar's Ophel excavations.[109] While there is no direct evidence linking Solomon to these archaeological discoveries, cultural memory of a relationship between Jerusalem and southern trade in the early Iron Age, which involved northwestern Arabia, may have been incorporated into Solomon's history.

Epigraphic material leads us to another layer in the history's development. Neo-Assyrian royal inscriptions from the reigns of Tiglath-Pileser III (mid-8th century) to Ashurbanipal (mid-7th century) conspicuously record information about seven north Arabian queens. E. Bennett's recent analysis highlights the distinctions Assyrian scribes and artists made in their depiction of these monarchs.[110] The Arabian women, described as šarratu (the feminine form of šarram 'ruler'), are clearly the ruling elite, in some cases negotiating gifts or tribute, in other cases engaging in battle against the Assyrians throughout the western and southern portions of the empire. The parallels to the Bible's Arabian queen are striking and cannot be easily dismissed. The geographic label 'Sheba,' however, directs our attention to southern Arabia. This region is not as well understood archaeologically as the north but is known through Iron Age inscriptions. Arabian goods appear in Assyrian records during the reign of Tukulti-Ninurta II (890–884 BCE), which suggests that trade operations must have been established for some time, but records of individual monarchs do not appear until the 8th century.[111] G. Hatke argues that the social and political transitions from the Late Bronze to the early Iron Age were similar in south Arabia to what we know from the southern Levant. 'Ethnic states' emerged in the transition years, and by the 8th century, rulers were boasting of their accomplishments in vernacular scripts.[112] Saba was the most prominent of the south Arabian states in the 8th and 7th centuries, and its rulers left their own inscriptions and are recorded in Neo-Assyrian evidence.[113] For example, Sennacherib lists precious stones and aromatics that Saba's king Karib-il provided as a gift.[114] The combined historical evidence is overwhelming confirmation of Arabia's critical role in long-distance trade that brought precious goods from afar (i.e., east and south Africa, southwest Arabia, and southeast Asia) to the Levant, Mediterranean, and Mesopotamia, but the evidence that most resembles the Solomon Narrative's depiction of Arabian elites and exchange aligns best with 8th–6th century contexts.

The tensions and connections among the biblical account, Assyrian and Arabian inscriptions, and archaeology highlight the complexity in how Solomon's history may have come into being. We have compelling evidence that Arabian trade networks, north and south, played an integral part of early Iron Age spice trade, and that northwest Arabia contributed heavily to the copper network that bordered or involved what became Judahite territory. In other words, by the 10th century, Arabian trade was an important aspect of southern Levantine culture and the economies of the emerging states. The details of this earlier exchange and the elites that sought to control it were not documented in epigraphic and narrative accounts of that age (or the records no longer exist or have not been found), but it stands to reason that cultural memory retained notions of leaders who were connected to far away worlds and displayed conspicuous goods as proof of their status. By the time of the composition of Solomon's history, the author(s) took inspiration from more recent and notable examples, to supplement the memories of a Solomonic era.

Exchange Involving Metals and Metallurgy

Silver, gold, and copper/bronze feature prominently in descriptions of Solomon's constructions and in the records of tribute and riches that came to Solomon from around the world. For these reports to have stemmed from 10th century activities, there would have to have been significant interregional trade. Although copper was available in the southern Levant, gold, silver, and other materials (such as tin to make bronze) needed to be imported from lands beyond. Just as in the previous examples, recent research indicates that trade in some of these metals was in fact taking place during this period, but there is currently no direct evidence linking trade in metals or metallurgical activities to Solomon or a 10th century Jerusalemite ruler.

Copper/Bronze

A substantial portion of the Solomon Narrative touts the monarch's ability to equip his new constructions with ornate copper/bronze furnishings and adornment (1 Kgs 7:13–47).[115] In contrast to silver and gold, copper was locally sourced and produced in the southern Levant in the early Iron Age. Like the discussion of iron in the previous chapter, and silver below, research over the last two decades has completely changed our understanding of copper production in the southern Levant, including in which periods the resources were exploited and the reach of exchange.

The Arabah Valley, south of the Dead Sea, was a critical source of copper in the early Iron Age. The regions of Timna in the southwest and the Faynan in the northeast were both extensively exploited from the 11th to 9th centuries. The Timna operations began in the Late Bronze Age and supplied copper to New Kingdom Egypt, but metallurgical activities continued after Egypt had withdrawn from the Levant.[116] The Faynan activity originated as a local enterprise in the early Iron Age and was most active in the 11th to 9th centuries. The two Arabah production centers operated concurrently, and their remains exhibit shared metallurgical technologies. While investigations into both regions have produced ample evidence of mining and production activity, no documentary or epigraphic evidence exists to identify who was in charge of the metallurgical operations once Egypt had abandoned its efforts. Excavators from both projects argue for a local, centralized political body.[117]

Research and analysis of metals throughout the eastern Mediterranean has confirmed that products from the Arabah metal industry were transported to coastal sites, to Egypt, and to the Aegean. The Third Intermediate Period official, Wendjebauendjed, discussed above, was buried with shabti figurines that were made from Arabah copper.[118] We also now know that the copper reached at least as far as the Aegean, as it has been identified in Greek tripods from Olympia and Delphi.[119] And, as I discuss below, Arabah copper was used to debase silver when that metal supply was scarce in the these transition years.[120] In addition to adding to our knowledge of how critical the Arabah copper trade was for both the southern Levantine and eastern Mediterranean economies in the early Iron Age, each of these examples testifies to the importance of specialized metalwork in the lives of elites.

The DH's discussion of the copper/bronze work contains an additional, critical detail. In contrast to the purportedly vast amounts of imported goods in the narrative, the summary of the bronze vessels is followed by a specific clarification in 1 Kings 7:46: 'In the Jordan Valley, the king cast them in clay/earth molds between Succoth and Zarethan.'[121]

Much of Solomon's status in the narrative comes from his worldliness, his ability to bring the best goods, artisans, and knowledge of the world to Jerusalem, but in this case, the Dtr notes that the metallurgical work took place in the Jordan Valley at Succoth and Zarethan. Ancient audiences would have understood this to be the region of the Zarqa River, biblical Jabbok. In addition to being of strategic importance for water resources, defense, and political boundaries, archaeological evidence of metallurgy in this area is evident in the Bronze and Iron Ages; in fact, Tell Hammeh, the site of early iron smelting discussed in Chapter Two, is in this same region.[122]

It is once again necessary, however, to note that a definitive link between Solomon and any 10th century metallurgical sites cannot be made. Despite this challenge regarding a historical Solomon, the activity in the Jordan Valley and the Arabah provides us with valuable context for understanding the period. The new demand for metals, especially copper and bronze, would have been driven by elites – both as consumers and gatekeepers. Local elites who could control access and production in the Jordan Valley and the Arabah stood to gain economically and in prestige. We should not be surprised to find that resource areas and production sites were closely connected to the main routes to and through the Jordan Valley. We can also observe that the DH preserves memory of a king's acquisition of a large amount of copper/bronze, as well as his involvement in local metallurgical activity and, importantly, that this metallurgical activity had ceased prior to the earliest periods associated with the composition of what became the Solomon Narrative. It appears most likely that the biblical account of Solomon's participation was influenced by general knowledge that elites controlled the earlier operations in the Jordan Valley and the Arabah. Later historians attributed that activity to the most famous elite consumer in their historical tradition.

Silver and Gold

According to the DH, Solomon deposited silver and gold vessels from the time of David in the completed temple (1 Kgs 7:51) and expanded his stores of silver through his maritime ventures, tribute, and horse trade (1 Kgs 10:22, 25, 29). The history famously states that he made silver as common as stones in Jerusalem (1 Kgs 10:27). Similarly, the DH reports lavish gold ornamentation in the temple and palace (1 Kgs 6; 7:48–50; 10:16–21), and notes that some of Solomon's exchange with Hiram involved gold (1 Kgs 9:10–14, 27–28; 10:11–12). Much of these reports are clearly hyperbolic, but the importance of nonlocal, precious metals in the lives of monarchs is well-attested throughout the Iron Age. For the early Iron Age specifically, the extreme extent to which an Egyptian elite could have significant quantities of silver and gold is demonstrated in the burials of Third Intermediate Period pharaohs and high officials, and the 'Tale of Wenamun' describes the use of the metals in trade.[123] Egyptian contexts cannot be compared to other areas without qualification, but it is illustrative to see what kind of wealth in these metals was available in the eastern Mediterranean for those with the most access.

Based on archaeological, historical, and literary sources, we have long known that silver was imported to the southern Levant and Egypt from Anatolia, the Aegean, and the western Mediterranean, but recent research is pinpointing key changes in the supply and exchange systems that were involved. Most critical for the present discussion is that lead isotope analysis shows that, in response to a critical silver shortage related to the LBA collapse, debasement practices began around 1200 BCE.[124] By the early Iron Age, debased silver appears to have been an acceptable substitute until Phoenician exploitation of the western Mediterranean took off in the late 10th century and replenished the silver supply. Notable in this process is that Arabah copper was the main element used for debasing silver.

There are many exciting connections between these archaeological findings and the overall picture provided by the Solomon Narrative. Among the most important are the social and economic contexts: silver was in high demand but low supply earlier in the Iron Age (ca. 12th and 11th centuries), to which Phoenician trade, concentrated in and around Tyre, responded with new supplies of silver by the end of the 10th century. To be absolutely clear, there is no relationship to a historical Solomon or Hiram in this archaeological evidence. The traders, artisans, and consumers remain anonymous, and excavations in Jerusalem have not produced quantities of silver to test. It is exceptional, however, that the narrative corresponds to the findings. Biblical authors situated relevant activities in the Solomonic era: both the collection/hoarding of silver in a temple – which would have served as a sort of state treasury, as temples commonly did – and the dramatic increase of silver, which we might correlate either to debasement that extended silver hoards or to new sources of the metal supplied by Phoenician trade via Tyre. Although these narrative accounts may not instill confidence in precise reconstructions of the monarchs' lives, we should be open to the notion that cultural memory of early Iron Age economic changes informed this particular part of the Solomon story.

The same kind of evidence for contemporary trade in gold has not been found, but there is no doubt that gold items existed and were exchanged, especially among 10th century elites. The nearest sources for gold were in southern Egypt, Nubia, the Arabian Peninsula, Anatolia, and the Zagros mountains.[125] As one of the most desired metals, it is not surprising that gold has only been recovered in extraordinary circumstances.[126] We should also keep in mind that the regular practice of holding/exchanging heirloom pieces, and of recycling older items into new forms, would have complemented any new supply through trade and potentially sustained demand for gold in times of scarcity due to decreased network interactions. Contemporary epigraphic sources about exchanging gold do not exist in the southern Levant, but Egyptian sources testify to royal stores of the metal, for example in the quarry inscription describing Shoshenq I's preparations for his Karnak monument, and in Osorkon I's record of gifts of gold and various luxury goods (e.g., silver, copper, lapis lazuli, vessels) to temples throughout Egypt.[127]

As I noted above, however, epigraphic evidence of imported gold within the southern Levant, especially from Ophir, does not appear until the 8th century. These 10th century contexts and examples demonstrate that the use of gold in the description of Solomon's royal building projects should be considered fitting to how a king should act. In other words, if a historical Solomon did such things, he was following the model for a monarch, but this model existed across centuries. It is true of kings from the LBA through the Iron Age. The DH's Solomon may reflect cultural memory of a 10th century king's conspicuous display of social and economic power, but that imagery is indistinguishable from what 8th to 6th century contexts would dictate. Thus, the great tribute that came to Solomon, described throughout 1 Kings 10, cannot be relied on for a history of the early Iron Age.

Overall, there is substantial material evidence for the production and exchange of copper, iron, silver, and gold in the 11th through 9th centuries in the region. Although none of material summarized above confirms details about a historical Solomon, it does show us that, in respect to metallurgy, the depiction in the DH is not anachronistic for a Solomonic era. In fact, the chronological limits of the Arabah copper operations allow us to go a step further, to say that cultural memory retained in the Solomon Narrative may be a critical detail in understanding to what extent portions of the DH convey historical memory about early Iron Age exchange and the transition to local monarchies.

Preliminary Conclusions: Long-Distance Interactions

Interregional interactions are essential in the depiction of Solomon, but our reliance on 1 Kings 3–11 for historical inquiry is complicated by its compositional history – the literary-formation processes, so to speak. Older sources provided a foundation for the depiction of extensive long-distance exchange. Historical circumstances and literary material from the 8th through 6th centuries influenced the presentation of Solomon's career. The later layer in the narrative is rooted in the Dtr's day, at the end of the monarchy, when Solomon's history provided a foundation for hope of an expanded kingdom and renewed success from Jerusalem. The most influential time in the text's composition was during the 8th century, perhaps during the period when Jerusalem stood out among its neighboring capital cities in the wake of Assyrian conquests. Solomon's reputation was explained according to the idiom of successful kingship of the time. The 10th century icon provided a fitting measure for Hezekiah's accomplishments. Much of the boasting of the Solomon Narrative must be situated in these later contexts: international horse trade, gold from Ophir, Sheba's queen, 'model letters,' and the 'adversaries.'

In contrast, some of the narrative's activities may have better historical grounding. Egyptian elites were engaged in interactions with the Levant through consumption of Arabah copper, deposition of statues/stele, and at least one large-scale military campaign. Rulers in Tyre and Jerusalem/Israel may have negotiated an agreement involving goods, services, and land. In addition, a good case for contemporary trade in metals exists, based in the archaeological evidence, and may be evident in the accounts of Solomon's activities in the Jordan Valley and relations with Arabia.

In addition to whether or not any of these interactions took place, we confirm several important issues when scrutinizing the biblical text. First, for historical inquiry, the biblical text cannot stand on its own. This is an obvious statement, but the material in this chapter provides an opportunity to reflect on historical-critical method. It is impossible to require that every detail in the Solomon Narrative have corroboration with extrabiblical sources in order to be of use historically, and, in fact, that standard is not adhered to for other ancient accounts, but close attention to extrabiblical evidence of various periods is necessary for an evaluation of plausibility. Second, looking at the exchange partners and partner regions described in the narrative draws attention to 10th century elites that are attested through historical and material remains. These figures, even if they cannot be connected to the details of the Solomon Narrative, help us understand specialized elite culture of the period. Third, the message we can take from the later, more extravagant accounts of Solomon's history is that interregional interactions were essential to describing his reign because exchange was a defining characteristic of the period when local monarchies found their footing, and presumably a memorable characteristic of a Solomonic era, even if it was not as grand as the biblical text proclaims.

'Domestic' Economic Development

We turn now to exchange and interactions that took place within the territory that the Solomon Narrative asserts to be his kingdom. Based on the list of administrators in 1 Kings 4:8–19, the land stretched from the northern reaches of the Galilee to the Red Sea, and from across the Jordan Valley to the Mediterranean coast. The DH devotes significant attention to Solomon's policies for these areas. The history details changes that Solomon made in the economic organization of Israelite territory, and in his use of the region's resources to carry out large-scale building projects. Even though these activities are understood to be domestic, they were an integral part of regional and interregional interactions. Based on the DH's presentation of events, Solomon's reorganization of his territory's resources reveals an effort to dominate important trade areas, and the construction activities provided necessary infrastructure for his administrative system and control of key cities, as well as physical reminders of dominance to inhabitants and travelers through the region.

Solomon's Administrative Districts

The administrative data in 1 Kings 4:8–19 appear to reveal historical details of Solomon's economic policies. The text consists of a list of administrators who were stationed throughout Israel and sent provisions to the royal court. The form and condition of the list suggest that the Dtr imported this information from older source material. *If* the source dates to Solomon's reign, then we would have critical information regarding how Solomon organized his kingdom, consolidated resources, and controlled territories, possibly in the interest of becoming competitive in interregional exchange. The text, however, is difficult and cannot be dated with certainty, so understanding the list and assessing its historical value are challenging. Despite the difficulties, the source material appears to be closely linked to Solomon's administration and reveals strategic use of the land and royal officials for economic and trade gains.

For much of 20th century scholarship, this list was touted as the most historically reliable portion in the Solomon Narrative. Arguments by Alt, Albright, and Wright laid the foundation for confidence that we had a view into accurate records from Solomon's day.[128] Typically, studies of Solomon's administration followed in this vein, until scholars moved to a more critical view of the material. Today, scholars hold more reservations about whether the information conveys accurate details of the 10th century but, more often than not, continue to label the list as 'early' or 'old.'[129] The text has retained its status as one of the oldest sources in the Solomon Narrative, but scholars are more cautious in their application of the material to historical reconstruction. In the analysis here, we will look at the nature of the text and, with cautious acceptance of an 'early' date, examine what it conveys of exchange in the early Iron Age.

The older source material is easily separated from the surrounding narrative due to editorial seams in the text. A summary introduces the list: 'Solomon had twelve officials (נִצָּבִים) stationed over all of Israel, and they supported the king and his household, each providing for one month of the year. And these are their names…' (1 Kgs 4:7–8a). The character of the verses is similar to statements elsewhere in the DH describing the extent of the kingdom or the length of a king's reign. The phrase 'over all of Israel' (עַל־כָּל־יִשְׂרָאֵל), for example, appears a number of times in 2 Samuel and 1 Kings, in summary statements that appear to be the Dtr's.[130] At the end of the list of officials is a general conclusion, 'Judah and Israel were as numerous as the sand by the sea; they ate and drank and were happy' (1 Kgs 4:20), which completes the discussion of domestic matters and returns the reader to the greater narrative of 1 Kings 3–11. The introduction and conclusion that bookend the list stand in contrast to the literary character of the catalog of officials, which allows us to isolate the source material.

The text of 1 Kings 4:8–19 is made up of individuals' names followed by their geographic locations but is not in ideal condition. There is very little in the way of narrative explanation, contextualization, or transition from one item to the next. The source has been damaged or the text corrupted. For example, some individuals are listed with a personal name and a patronym while others are not; compare יהושפט בן־פרוח in verse 17 to בן־דקר in verse 9. The source may have been inconsistent in identifying the officials, or, if originally consistently formulaic, it was damaged or altered long ago.[131] There is also evidence of additions to the source. In some cases, the geographic notes are more extensive than others. Compare verses 13 and 14:

13 בן־גבר ברמת גלעד
לו חות יאיר בן־מנשה אשר בגלעד
לו חבל ארגב אשר בבשן ששים ערים
גדלות חומה ובריח נחשת
14 אחינדב בן־עדא מחנימה

13 Ben-Geber in Ramoth Gilead:
    to him were the villages of Jair ben-Manasseh, which are in Gilead,
    to him was region of Argob, which is in Bashan, sixty great cities,
    walled and barred with copper/bronze.
14 Ahinadab ben-Iddo in Mahanaim.

In verse 13, substantial explanation follows the initial listing of the individual's name and location, but verse 14 is concise. It is more likely that the shorter entry represents the older form and verse 13 was subjected to elaborations.[132] There are additional complications when we try to make sense of the overall content. For example, the repetition or confusion between verses 13 and 19 – where the individual's name contains 'Geber' and the region described is Gilead – causes concern and raises more questions: has the repetition resulted from problems in transmission or textual corruption?[133] Was there a father *and* son (Ben-Geber in verse 13 and Geber ben-Uri in verse 19) governing areas in the Transjordan, or was the office passed from father *to* son? There is also confusion as to the presence or absence of Judah in the list or in the administrative system.[134] Overall, however, the material and arguments are relatively strong in support of the conclusion that 1 Kings 4:8–19 preserves a significant amount of historical data, even if it has changed or was manipulated over time.

There is little doubt that the historian used a source when composing this section of 1 Kings 4. In fact, the many problems in the text bolster arguments that the material comes from an older source. We might expect a source closer to the historian's day to be more cohesive, less corrupt or confused, and we know that the Dtr was capable of much better narrative composition than we have in these verses.[135] The debates now lie in how much older the source was, how it was preserved or transmitted prior to the historian's time, and whether the information can be reliable for history writing today, all of which impact whether or not this material should be considered when assessing 10th century economic or commercial interactions.

Proposals for the source's antiquity range from a point during Solomon's reign, mid-10th century, to just about any point prior to the Dtr in the late 7th century.[136] Before becoming part of the DH, the source could have been preserved in a pre-Dtr history that chronicled Solomon or among court/administrative records. Despite the chronological range of possibilities, most scholars continue to look to Solomon's reign for the *origin* of the information, even if the source preserved in 1 Kings 4 is a later product.[137] For example, Na'aman has 'no doubt' about a 10th century origin for the information in the list, but he also argues that administrative records like this list were part of a corpus used in later periods for scribal training, and that this list was influenced by later Judahite and Assyrian contexts.[138] Ash argues that the material stems from the 10th century but could have been a written source only after writing became standard in the 8th century; prior to that, the information must have been transmitted orally.[139] Halpern argues for a 10th century or, at the latest, early 9th century provenance for most of the material in the list, which, he claims, was incorporated into a history composed during Hezekiah's reign.[140] Just as in these examples, the general trend in scholarship situates the origins of the list's core content in the late 10th century, or soon after, with the acknowledgment that some manipulation occurred over time.

The problems notwithstanding, the administrative list seems to have roots (oral or written) in the 10th century and is among the oldest sources related to Solomon's era that we can discern in the DH. This conclusion is based on the condition of the source, some continuity between individuals in the narrative of David's reign and officials in the list, and on the Dtr's assertion that the list represents an administrative policy under Solomon.[141] Additionally, the list does not exclusively describe any other period in the region's history.[142] Even though the list was not perfectly preserved, and was enhanced in certain verses, the Dtr (or other editors or revisers) was not overly liberal in smoothing out these issues. If he had been, there should be far fewer problems with the list. Although the date cannot be confidently narrowed to a particular decade, there is not strong enough evidence to remove the material entirely from a Solomonic era. No alternative interpretation has been argued well enough to settle uncertainty. As Van Bekkum has recently demonstrated, the combined weight of current archaeological evidence works against arguments for a later origin and may in fact situate this text most securely in an earlier Iron II context.[143] For these reasons, the list of administrators and districts list will contribute to the present discussion of interregional exchange in the late 10th century.

The geographic organization of Solomon's administrative system aimed to maximize the economic contribution from the districts (Figure 3.2).[144] Typically, the notes in 1 Kings 4:7 and 5:7, which are separate from the older source in 1 Kings 4:8–19, led interpreters to the understanding that the district officials, each assigned one month of the year, provided food (וְכִלְכְּלוּ) collected from each region. The list itself, however, does not specify that food provisions per se were the concern of the officials, and there is good reason to believe that the districts contributed in broader terms.[145] Based on the land's potential, certain districts were better equipped than others to provide agricultural produce to the crown. For example, the first district, Har Ephraim, was the agricultural heartland of the region, which easily could have supplied foodstuffs. Similarly, Bashan and Gilead were prime grazing lands, as well as agricultural resources. Other districts, however, may have been better off supplying different types of provisions. Several areas appear to be arranged around alternate assets. For example, the third district (central coast), fourth (Naphath-Dor), and fifth (including the Jezreel and Jordan Valleys) appear best suited to exploit transit routes and port facilities.

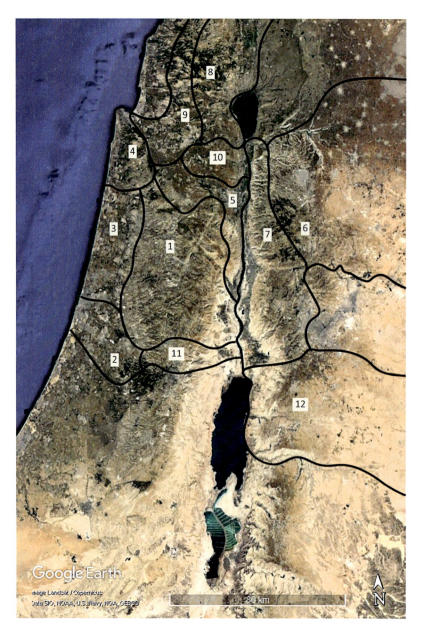

Figure 3.2: Map of administrative districts. Borders based on Rainey and Notley, *The Sacred Bridge* (Jerusalem: Carta, 2006), 175. Map: Google Earth, © 2020.

The fifth district is an illustrative example of how such areas could be linked to trade resources. The district stretched from Megiddo to Beth-Shean, and then some distance south along the Jordan Valley. The description of this area requires considerably more detail than the others due to its unique shape. Surprisingly, it excludes the agricultural lands to the south and north. These were assigned to other districts (to the first and tenth, respectively). The delimitation follows two major valley systems, the Jordan and Jezreel.

The valleys are the natural resource of the district and determine its extent in the same way that other resources (e.g., pasture or agricultural lands) dictate the orientation of neighboring districts. The key attribute of the fifth district is the transportation corridor formed by the valleys that connected distinct natural and cultural areas. These valley systems served the region in this way long before and after Solomon's day.[146] Unifying them into one administrative unit would have been a strategic approach to managing (and exploiting) already existing activities. Thus, the fifth district served as a channel that facilitated local-resource consolidation and longer-distance exchange, especially traffic moving along international routes.

It is likely that the main responsibility of administrators of the fifth, fourth, and third districts would have been oversight of port and highway traffic. It is useful to ask: if these responsibilities were not the task of the officials, why would the districts take this particular form? Or, to look at it from another angle, if *food* provisions were the goal of the reorganization of land, Solomon's districts were not strategically assigned. From this perspective, the orientation of the districts reveals the philosophy behind them: they were organized in the interest of exploiting the local territories, whether the resources were domestic products or the landscape's potential in long-distance transportation and exchange. There is no doubt that the economic advantage from these different types of resources would provide for the crown, though not in the ways that the districts are traditionally understood.

Examination of the district officials may illuminate further how each contributed to a centralized economic strategy. The officials' title, נצב/נציב, suggests someone 'stationed' in a place or over a thing. It is derived from the same root as the terms used to describe Philistine installations during the time of Saul, but in this source, the position is generally understood to be something like a tax official (appropriate whether collecting produce or other goods/income) who would gather resources from his district and send them to Jerusalem. While this job description appears sound, the nature of the districts indicates that these men were not simply collecting taxes. They must have acted as monitors of each territory, overseeing the resources that were most valuable to Solomon's operation.

The corporate nature implied by the list – that is, Israelite officers managing fellow countrymen – belies the complications that would have existed 'on the ground' in the 10th century. A broad overview of the DH leads us to believe that there was a distinct entity called 'Israel' that was active for centuries by the time of Solomon. Closer inspection, however, demonstrates that Israel's transition to a centralized state was recent by Solomon's reign, if fully accomplished even then. Based on historical, biblical, and archaeological evidence, there were many tensions throughout the Late Bronze Age, Iron I, and Iron IIA periods: between Israelites and others (e.g., Philistines, Canaanites, etc.); between north and south or highland and coastal; between local or tribal and centralized; and between urban and rural.[147] If Solomon indeed united these lands into one system, we have to keep in mind the context that for at least a century prior, tribal or local autonomy allowed for the management of resources and exchange. If historical, Solomon's districting attempted to change this practice and imposed unwelcome policies on the traditional holders of authority or local elites. It is worth considering whether some of the figures listed as officials were more likely peers to Solomon, who no doubt would have described their relationship to a ruler in Jerusalem differently. Whatever the precise circumstances and relationships, Solomon's district officers would have been saddled with the challenge of negotiating one or more of these tensions.[148]

The examples of the fourth (Naphath-Dor) and eighth (Naphtali) districts provide an opportunity to explore factors at play in the districts and among their officials. These two stand out, in part, because of the notices in the text that the officials were each married to a daughter of Solomon: Ben-Abinadab, overseeing the region of Dor, married Taphath (1 Kgs 4:11), and Ahimaaz of Naphtali married Basemath (1 Kgs 4:15). The inclusion of such information – that is, regarding daughters' lives – is unusual in both the list and the Solomon Narrative. One might suggest that the marriage notices were expansions, as is the case for some of the other notes in the list (e.g., 1 Kgs 4:13 quoted above), but it is difficult to detect a reason for the later addition of their names. We do not otherwise hear of any of Solomon's children (male or female) in 1 Kings 3–11, and these daughters do not reappear in the DH.[149] The inclusion of their names does not resemble the more obvious expansions in verses 13 or 19, which use stock characterizations known from other texts. Further, the references to Solomon's daughters do not echo any other descriptions of women in the narrative, so they do not fit with the narrative's use of female figures like the prostitute-mothers (1 Kings 3) or Solomon's 'many foreign wives' (1 Kgs 11). In other words, the daughters' appearance does not contribute to the aggrandizement or condemnation of Solomon. We are left with the reason that their inclusion is due to their importance to the core purpose of the text (i.e., regarding administrative and economic matters), and it is likely that their place in the list is relatively early.

The marriages linking Solomon's daughters to the district officials are generally, and with good reason, assumed to be political or diplomatic in nature. These districts had the potential to connect Israelite territory to more distant (or non-allied) regions, especially for economic benefit, and provided access from the hill country to Mediterranean, Phoenician, Aramean, and Mesopotamian interaction networks. At the same time, the fourth and eighth districts lay far from Jerusalem and had the potential to be more closely allied to northern neighbors than to Solomon's headquarters. Both districts may have had more in common culturally with Phoenicia and Aram than Jerusalem, a problem particularly evident in the case of Dor, which was more closely linked culturally and politically to the Sea Peoples and their descendants than those typically thought of as Israelite.[150] Additionally, studies of border and port territories with economic resources suggest that these locales tend to act independently or become targets or bargaining chips for larger powers.[151] These very conditions are described for both Dor and Naphtali in subsequent periods (e.g., 1 Kgs 15, 20). Recall similar issues described in 1 Kings 9 for the district in between Naphtali and Naphath-Dor, the ninth district which contained the land Solomon gave to Hiram, the Cabul. We might consider these districts more as peer polities within the southern Levant than as parts of a cohesive Israelite whole, especially from the perspective of a Jerusalem base. In this respect, the examples from Third Intermediate Period Egypt discussed above also come to mind, whereby marriages aided in Shoshenq I and other elites' efforts to consolidate power that was not (or only tenuously) centralized. A Jerusalemite ruler would have had strong incentives to secure distant territories through diplomatic marriage. Establishing daughters in each local power base might have aligned the regions with Jerusalem and assuaged tendencies toward loyalty to nearer powers (e.g., Damascus or Tyre), thus securing economic gains from these trade-friendly regions for Solomon's holdings.

Whether it was to centralize Israel's domestic products or to capitalize on goods that were transported through Israel, Solomon's districts reveal an economy-oriented approach to administering a territory. Underlying this policy may have been concerns for negotiating among ancestral claims to land, competition for loyalty, and smaller-scale diplomatic arrangements within the southern Levant. Scholars' attempts to make any one explanation (especially that each area supplied equal agricultural provisions) account for all the districts have not resulted in fully satisfying answers for the precise division and organization in the text. Admittedly, only a selection is examined here; however, when the economic advantages of individual districts are the focus, without requiring each to make the same contribution to the center, we see how the divisions of land can be explained according to regional variation and the discrete attributes that any one territory had to offer.

Solomon's *Mas* and Building Projects

In addition to his administrative reorganization, Solomon is reported to have ordered large-scale fortification and building projects during his reign. These projects are relevant to local and interregional exchange in a number of ways. The constructions, as described in the DH, required the import of resources and artisans from outside of Israel, most notably from Phoenicia. The resulting fortifications would have improved Israel's ability to control trade along highways or routes. In addition, Solomon's transformation of Jerusalem would have elevated the city's status to that of an economic and diplomatic center, thus increasing Jerusalem's ability to compete in the growing trade of the time. This last examination will evaluate the policies that supported Solomon's construction efforts and the possible impact they had on Israel's role in long-distance exchange.

Solomon's building campaign is described throughout 1 Kings 5–10. The majority of the material is devoted to the temple and palace complexes.[152] The DH also records projects outside of Jerusalem, and the policies necessary for the completion of the work.[153] The foundation for all of the projects is the conscripted labor policy, the *mas* (מס), which is referenced several times in the Solomon Narrative (1 Kgs 4:6; 5:27–32; 9:15–25).[154] The descriptions of the *mas* differ, revealing both source material and the Dtr's editorial work and commentary.

The first note on the *mas*, 1 Kings 4:6, appears in the list of Solomon's chief officers and states that Adoniram oversaw the *mas*. This reference does not describe what the *mas* was or why or how it was used, but it may be suggestive of the policy's antiquity.[155] The list of high officials (1 Kgs 4:2–6), like the list of administrators discussed above, is thought to be based on relatively old records, possibly from sources close to Solomon's administration. Solomon's *mas* official, Adoniram (alternatively Adoram), is noted to have also governed over the *mas* under David (2 Sam 20:24) and Rehoboam (1 Kgs 12:18). These references do not appear to be editorial insertions to link the episodes, suggesting that they too stem from older sources.

The additional discussions are situated in narrative sections in 1 Kings 5 and 9. Toward the end of 1 Kings 5, the *mas* pericope follows the dialogue between Hiram and Solomon that dramatized their cooperative alliance and treaty agreement. After the dialogue, the narrative turns to the details of the *mas*. According to this account, Solomon drew from all of Israel to put together his labor force (מס מכל־ישראל), which Adoniram oversaw. The laborers numbered 30,000 and would work in Lebanon in shifts (1 Kgs 5:27–28). There were additional porters and stonemasons, as well as specialized craftsmen from Israel, Lebanon, and Byblos (1 Kgs 5:29–32). After the detailed discussion of the palace and temple (1 Kgs

6–7), and another exchange between Hiram and Solomon (1 Kgs 9:10–14), the DH notes explicitly that the *mas* contributed to the main Jerusalem constructions, as well as the Millo, Jerusalem's wall, Hazor, Megiddo, Gezer, Lower Beth-Horon, Baalath, Tamar, and other royal properties (1 Kgs 9:15–19). The DH then moves to yet another account of the *mas*, which states that it was composed of descendants of the pre-Israelite nations, *not* Israelites. Instead, the Israelites filled other positions, those not linked to servitude (1 Kgs 9:20–23).

The critical distinctions among these accounts lie in the make-up of the *mas* and slight but significant differences in terminology. In the first part of the narrative, Solomon's forced labor is referred to simply as מס and המס (1 Kgs 4:6 and three occurrences in 1 Kgs 5:27–28). In 1 Kings 9, it is first introduced as דבר־המס (9:15) and later discussed as מס־עבד (9:21). While any one author may use a variety of terms, the differences suggest that we are looking at multiple accounts. An examination of the nature of the *mas* results in the same conclusion. Earlier in the history, the Israelites are the labor force (1 Kgs 5:27). Later, the DH states emphatically that it is not the Israelites but remaining pre-Israelites who made up the *mas* (9:20). The Israelites, according to this version, and in contrast to the previous, were officers and overseers (1 Kgs 9:20–23). These discrepancies point not only to more than one source, but also to distinct disagreements about the workforce.

The difference of opinion helps to identify certain influences in these accounts. First Kings 9:20–21 states that the laborers, who were descendants of the unconquered nations, had remained in conscripted labor 'until this day': (למס־עבד עד היום הזה). These verses expose the Dtr's involvement in several ways. The list of nations in 1 Kings 9:20 is similar to other iterations in the DH.[156] The phrase 'until this day' in 1 Kings 9:21 is a hallmark of Dtr commentary, and the discussion of forced labor is reminiscent of other Deuteronomistic passages.[157] The closest parallel in terminology and content is Joshua 16:10: 'But they did not drive out the Canaanites who dwelt in Gezer, so the Canaanites dwell in the midst of Ephraim to this day, but they are forced labor' (עד היום הזה ויהי למס־עבד). Very similar language occurs in Deuteronomy 20:11 in describing how to treat the inhabitants of a city that surrenders peaceably during war: '…then all who are found in it shall be your forced labor and shall serve you' (יהיו לך למס ועבדוך). Based on these parallels and characteristic phrasing, we can conclude that the depiction in 1 Kings 9:20–21 was composed or thoroughly edited by the Dtr.

Immediately following the Dtr's description of the *mas*, which removed the Israelites from the labor force and promoted them to the role of overseers, the narrative returns to the Jerusalem constructions. We are told that Solomon built the altar and worshiped at it three times a year; the narrative then concludes with the note that Solomon finished the construction of the temple (1 Kgs 9:25). It is common to view this material as an apologetic account, seeking to defend Solomon against less flattering views (e.g., the *mas* in 1 Kgs 5 or pagan worship in 1 Kgs 11). This version is indeed a defense, but it may be less concerned with Solomon and more with Jerusalem's character. The Dtr's shaping of this version serves his theological positions concerning Jerusalem as YHWH's residence, so that Solomon's *mas* policy was aligned with Deuteronomic instruction and the Dtr's version of history.[158]

The parallels noted above (e.g., Deut 20:10–11; Josh 16:10), along with Deuteronomy 16:16 and Joshua 9:27, shed light on the issue. Using this evidence base, J. Geoghegan has identified a connection between the Dtr and depictions of a מס־עבד.[159] Geoghegan argues that the Dtr, informed by Deuteronomy 20:10–11, accounts for non-Israelite service at the temple during his own day through precedents like Joshua 9:27, where Gibeonites provided services for YHWH worship 'until this day, at the place that he will choose.' The relationship between Deuteronomy and the examples that the Dtr creates justifies the involvement of non-Israelites in what appear otherwise to be Israel-exclusive locations and activities. We see yet another allusion to Deuteronomic law in 1 Kings 9:25, with Solomon's worship at YHWH's altar, which conforms to the instruction for all males to appear 'before YHWH at the place that he will choose' for the three major festivals (Deut 16:16). This version of the *mas* legitimizes the origins of the Jerusalem cult center according to Deuteronomistic theology and practices observed 'until this day.' The Dtr interjects the final word concerning Solomon's policy and, in doing so, obscures the historical record by prioritizing his ideological revision.

In contrast, in 1 Kings 5:27, there is no hint of apology for the use of Israelite labor. It is nearly a reverse of 1 Kings 9:20–23; the Israelites are the *mas*, and the higher-level artisans come from both Israel and Phoenicia. This is a dramatically different account and can be interpreted in two ways. It either assumes the inevitability of conscripted labor for subjects of a kingdom or attempts to expose Solomon's treatment of the ancient Israelites. The former appears more likely. Regarding the latter, there is not an overtly negative presentation of the policy to suggest that the account was an objection to Solomon's activities.[160] In fact, conscripted labor was not an unusual form of tax.[161] Though it may have been undesirable – as taxes often are – it does not seem to be out of the ordinary or even exorbitant for an Iron Age monarch, and the depiction in 1 Kings 5:27 reflects this perspective.

One clue to the historical value of 1 Kings 5:27–32 is that the Dtr-preferred account in 1 Kings 9:20–23 is undoubtedly speaking against some historical memory of an Israelite *mas*. The version in 1 Kings 5:27–32 may not have been the only source of such information, but because the Dtr edited the Solomon Narrative, we can be confident that he was familiar with the text and thus the claims it makes. First Kings 5:27–32 must antedate the Dtr. By just how much is very difficult to determine. The account follows the Hiram and Solomon dialogue of 1 Kings 5:15–25. And while the *mas* account is not cut from the same cloth as the correspondence, it may come from a pre-Dtr history.[162] The account is preferable to 1 Kings 9:20–23 as a historical source, as it does not obviously aggrandize or disparage Solomon or conform to Deuteronomic ideals. Without obvious biases, it is better for our historical reconstruction: Solomon used Israelite labor for his projects, and he was well known for this behavior in periods of Israelite history writing.

The last reference to consider is 1 Kings 9:15–19. This one is silent on the makeup of the workforce, but fills in where the others leave off by providing details on which constructions were created through the *mas*. It has some similarities to 1 Kings 4:8–19; it is brief and annalistic, and exhibits evidence of supplementation to an older, original source. Expansions are apparent in 1 Kings 9:16, where Gezer receives unusual attention compared to the other sites, or in 1 Kings 9:19, where the narrator broadens the scope of the projects to include grander claims (e.g., '…and whatever Solomon desired to build, in Jerusalem, in Lebanon, or in all of his dominion'). The older core of this material appears to be the list of projects that possibly included Jerusalem, Hazor, Megiddo, Gezer, Lower Beth-Horon (and Upper Beth-Horon[163]), Baalath, and Tamar.[164] There is Deuteronomistic material in the surrounding narrative (especially evident in 1 Kgs 9:1–9 and in 1 Kgs 9:20–25), but the verses 1 Kings 9:15, 17–18 do not exhibit language characteristic of the Dtr.[165] These verses can be treated in the same way as the administrative districts list. They antedate the Dtr and were incorporated into the history by him or were retained as part of an earlier history of Solomon. The reliability of the list is difficult to assess based on the biblical text alone, but it can function as a starting place when considering the impact of the construction projects.

Figure 3.3: Solomon's fortifications, as described in 1 Kings 9:15–18. Map: Google Earth, © 2020.

As a result of these evaluations, we can state some conclusions before applying the material to questions of 10th century trade. Regarding the *mas*, the DH contains four separate accounts in the Solomon Narrative. Of these four, all agree that there was some kind of *mas* policy. Those with potential to be the oldest are 1 Kings 4:6 and 9:15, 17–18. The account in 1 Kings 9:20–23 is the most recent, and was thoroughly shaped, if not composed wholly, by the Dtr. The account in 1 Kings 5:27–28, though not likely to be a 10th century report, presents the more reliable account of the policy – that is, that Solomon used conscription of Israelites for his building campaigns, which might be reconstructed based on 1 Kings 9:15, 17–18.

We may now entertain the topic of the constructions themselves. The fortifications were situated on known roads and strategic crossroads (Figure 3.3). They would have allowed for defense as well as control over the movement of goods, within an Israelite (or Jerusalem-based) state and across its borders.[166] All sites were arguably important for a growing kingdom, especially in relation to interregional affairs. Hazor would have negotiated the north and east, and neighbors such as Aram. Megiddo guarded a critical point in the Via Maris and entry to the Jezreel Valley from the west. Gezer, Baalath, and Lower (and Upper?) Beth-Horon would have guarded passage between the west and Jerusalem, while Tamar would have secured movement in relation to the Arabah. If there had been construction activity to this extent in the 10th century, it would have made a clear statement in Israel and the region that Solomon was sovereign over these important locations and, as Halpern has noted, have 'precluded the local Israelites from taking advantage of these strategic positions for commerce.'[167] Construction projects like the ones described in 1 Kings 9:15, 17–18 would have been necessary steps in asserting Solomon and Jerusalem's authority to Israelites, to regional inhabitants, to neighboring kings and states, and in entering into long-distance exchange beyond the southern Levant's boundaries. The greatest problem in assessing the historical value of these fortifications is, of course, the archaeological material. However, even without connecting the list to any particular material remains, we can conclude that there was a strong tradition linking a *mas* policy to strategic fortifications, and *if* a correlation to any of the locations cited by the text can be demonstrated with extrabiblical evidence, it is fairly certain that the site or sites were influential in interregional affairs.

Preliminary Conclusions: 'Domestic' Affairs

Even from those who are skeptical that there was an extensive written record from Solomon's day that made its way to the 7th or 6th centuries, there is acknowledgment that there may be a historical basis in references like the districts list (1 Kgs 4:9–18), the constructions list (1 Kgs 9:15, 17–18), or accounts of Solomon's *mas* policy (e.g., 1 Kgs 5:27–28). We have sufficient evidence through the variety in the DH's sources to support the claim that Solomon attempted to employ domestic policies that would have improved infrastructure and administrative strength to the advantage of the centralized authority. Solomon likely used a workforce (*mas*, overseers, and administrators) made up of Israelites and non-Israelites (though *not* in the sense of 1 Kgs 9:20–21) to build a capital city and tie together relatively independent lands. His division and organization of his territory focused on consolidating the strengths of each region, creating one polity able to compete with other emerging states and exchange systems.

Chapter Conclusions

Portions of Solomon's story are larger than life. It is apparent that the ancient authors who wrote about him attempted to convey his successes according to the standards of their own times. For example, an 8th century historian created Solomon the horse trader, the Dtr crafted the worldly Solomon who was distracted from YHWH, and an even later writer may have enhanced the international reach of Solomon's trade connections. Nevertheless, it is also apparent that information from even earlier times has been retained in the source material. The later contributions complicate, but do not negate, the value of this earlier information.

This examination of 1 Kings 3–11 indicates that some of the history can be included in a reconstruction of interregional interactions for the second half of the 10th century, even if precise details must be excluded, or the evidence informs the region's history more so than Solomon's. The most promising information from this history includes the notions that there were diplomatic and contentious relations with both Egypt and Tyre/Phoenicia; organization that monitored exchange activities within and through Solomon's territory; another system that required labor for construction projects; and geographic information related to the districts and fortifications.

The most suggestive evidence in favor of Solomon's involvement in interregional interactions comes from descriptions of Solomon's management of what is reported to be his territory. The organization of his districts implies a concern for ports and main transportation corridors, particularly those related to the Mediterranean coast, Jezreel Valley, and Jordan Valley. The locations of his fortifications suggest there was a strategy in place to monitor traffic on key roads and at entry points to the region. In addition, strengthening his connection to the northern districts through marriage hints at the possibility that relations with some officials may have resembled peer-polity interactions more than the biblical history lets on.

Regarding long-distance activity, exchange networks, especially those related to metallurgy, did exist during the time of Solomon, but a direct link to the monarch or Jerusalem is not currently possible. Of the events described in the history, relations with Phoenicia and Egypt are the most likely to have been rooted in historical events. Underneath the narrative of diplomatic correspondence between Solomon and Hiram lies an event that determined control of territory in the north in exchange for Phoenician assistance in Solomon's building projects. Solomon's relationship to Egypt through a diplomatic marriage cannot be substantiated. In contrast, exchange relations between the southern Levant and Tanis were in place, and Egyptian influence on the architectural character of Jerusalem's royal complex is hinted at in the narrative.[168] At the same time, political security in either state was fleeting, and relations with Egypt would have varied, which the campaign of Shishaq in 1 Kings 14:25–26 illustrates well. In sum, even though substantial portions of the Solomon Narrative cannot be related to 10th century events with confidence, some key accounts are more likely to have their origins close to his reign. From these sources, we are able to propose a number of exchange-related interests and policies, which will figure into the comprehensive discussion at the end of this study.

Notes

1. The other historical account comes from the Chronicler, which was often informed by the DH or by a common source. In the case of Solomon, the Chronicler preferred accounts that favored the monarch, which results in a less critical portrayal than the Deuteronomistic presentation. Other depictions of Solomon come from legendary characterizations that do not contribute to a historical discussion (e.g., Ecclesiastes or the Song of Songs). For this chapter, the Deuteronomistic History will be the main concern. As a historical work, it and its sources were closer in proximity to the time of Solomon; most importantly, it was early enough not to have been heavily influenced by the Persian Era (with the exception of a small number of additions to the text). In general, Chronicles and other depictions of Solomon reflect values and assumptions of postexilic Yehud/Judea, which differ significantly from the time of the monarchy. For a more detailed focus on the relationship between the DH and Chronicles, as well as the Chronicler's treatment of Solomon, see Baruch Halpern, "Sacred History and Ideology: Chronicles' Thematic Structure – Indications of an Earlier Source," in *The Creation of Sacred Literature: Composition and Redaction of the Biblical Text*, ed. Richard Elliott Friedman (University of California Publications Near Eastern Studies 22; Berkeley; Los Angeles: University of California Press, 1981), 35–54; Isaac Kalimi, *The Reshaping of Ancient Israelite History in Chronicles* (University Park: Penn State University Press, 2021); idem, *Writing and Rewriting the Story of Solomon in Ancient Israel* (Cambridge: Cambridge University Press, 2018).
2. Yigal Yadin's conclusions were based on his own excavations at Hazor, where he uncovered a large city gate 'identical in plan and measurements with' Megiddo's. Guided by the passage in 1 Kings 9:15, he reviewed R. A. S. Macalister's excavations of Gezer and found yet another, strikingly similar gate complex; see Yigal Yadin, "Solomon's City Wall and Gate at Gezer," *IEJ* 8 (1958): 80–86; see also idem, "New Light on Solomon's Megiddo," *BA* 23, no. 2 (1960): 62–68.
3. Revisions to Miller and Hayes's widely used history, *A History of Ancient Israel and Judah*, reveal the effects of these debates. Comparison of the chapters on Solomon shows significant movement from the authors' 1986 position, where they cite the fortifications as proof that history and archaeology agree in the period of Solomon (*A History of Ancient Israel and Judah*, 1st ed. [Philadelphia: Westminster Press, 1986], 189–190). In the 2006 edition, they are much more tentative, emphasizing scholars' uncertainty while attempting to provide a historical synthesis from biblical and archaeological material (*A History of Ancient Israel and Judah*, 2nd ed., 197–204). See also Gary N. Knoppers, "The Vanishing Solomon: The Disappearance of the United Monarchy from Recent Histories of Ancient Israel," *JBL* 116, no. 1 (1997): 19–44.
4. See Chapter One.
5. Examples include Pablo A. Torijano, *Solomon the Esoteric King: From King to Magus* (Supplements to the Journal for the Study of Judaism 73; Leiden; Boston: Brill, 2002); Walter Brueggemann, *Solomon: Israel's Ironic Icon of Human Achievement* (Studies on Personalities of the Old Testament; Columbia: University of South Carolina, 2005); Israel Finkelstein and Neil Asher Silberman, *David and Solomon: In Search of the Bible's Sacred Kings and the Roots of Western Tradition* (New York: Free Press, 2006); Steven Weitzman, *Solomon: The Lure of Wisdom* (Jewish Lives; New Haven: Yale University Press, 2011); John W. Herbst, *Development of an Icon: Solomon before and after King David* (Wipf and Stock Publishers, 2016); Kalimi, *Writing and Rewriting the Story of Solomon in Ancient Israel*.
6. For example, Russell, *Space, Land, Territory*; Wilson, *Kingship and Memory in Ancient Judah*; Pioske, *Memory in a Time of Prose*; Sarah Shectman, "Back to the Past: An Overview of Feminist Historical Criticism," in *Feminist Interpretation of the Bible in Retrospect*, ed. Susanne Scholz, vol. 3 (Sheffield: Sheffield Phoenix Press, 2016), 55–73; Shawna Dolansky and Sarah Shectman, eds., "What Is Gendered Historiography and How Do You Do It?," *The Journal of Hebrew Scriptures* 19 (2019): 3–18.
7. There are varied opinions on identifying the beginning and end of a Solomon Narrative. See, for example, the exchange between Amos Frisch and Kim Ian Parker in *Journal for the Study of the Old Testament* 51 (1991) for debates regarding the narrative's structure and extent: Amos Frisch, "Structure and Its Significance: The Narrative of Solomon's Reign (1 Kings 1-12.24)," *JSOT* 16, no. 51 (1991): 3–14; idem, "The Narrative of Solomon's Reign: A Rejoinder," *JSOT* 16, no. 51 (1991): 22–24; Kim Ian Parker, "The Limits to Solomon's Reign: A Response to Amos Frisch," *JSOT* 16, no. 51 (1991): 15–21. First Kings 3–11 constitutes the narrowest proposal, but others detect the narrative's beginning at 1 Kings 1 or 2 and end at or within 1 Kings 12. For additional discussions of the narrative's structure, see Marc Brettler, "The Structure of 1 Kings 1–11," *JSOT* 16, no. 49 (1991): 87–97; Jerome T. Walsh, "Symmetry and the Sin of Solomon," *Shofar* 12 (1993): 11–27; David S. Williams, "Once Again: The Structure of the Narrative of Solomon's Reign," *JSOT* 86 (1999): 49–66; John W. Olley, "Pharaoh's Daughter, Solomon's Palace, and the Temple: Another Look at the

Structure of 1 Kings 1–11," *JSOT* 27, no. 3 (2003): 355–69. Regardless of one's position on the theory of the Succession Narrative, there is a thematic shift between 1 Kings 1–2 and 3–11, where the latter recounts Solomon's deeds once he secured kingship. Prior to 1 Kings 3, the focus is on succession, not economic or interregional relations. Similarly, whether or not any sources or literary structure extend beyond the report of Solomon's death, the summary of his life activities is complete with 1 Kings 11. For the purposes here, 1 Kings 3–11 functions as the primary source.

8   It is important to note that the DH contains many arguments that are anachronistic for the 10th century, or aspirational. These impact the telling of Solomon's history. Among these claims are that there was an exclusive monotheism and that Jerusalem was recognized as the religious and political center for all Israelites. The history is also heavily influenced by Deuteronomic laws and ideology, especially regarding kingship and intermarriage. See Halpern, *Constitution of the Monarchy in Israel*, 243–249; Brettler, "The Structure of 1 Kings 1–11"; Gary N. Knoppers, *Two Nations Under God: The Deuteronomistic History of Solomon and the Dual Monarchies*, 2 vols. (HSM 52–53; Atlanta: Scholars Press, 1993), 1.145–146; Marvin A. Sweeney, "The Critique of Solomon in the Josianic Edition of the Deuteronomistic History," *JBL* 114, no. 4 (1995): 607–22.

9   For discussion of potential sources, see Halpern, "Sacred History and Ideology"; Nadav Naʾaman, "Sources and Composition in the History of Solomon," in *The Age of Solomon: Scholarship at the Turn of the Millennium*, ed. Lowell K. Handy (SHCANE 11; Leiden; New York: Brill, 1997), 57–80.

10 Along with the scholarship cited above, the following studies focus on the sources that underlie the Deuteronomistic treatment of Solomon: Steven L. McKenzie, *The Trouble with Kings: The Composition of the Book of Kings in the Deuteronomistic History* (VTSup 42; Leiden; New York: Brill, 1991); various studies in Handy, ed., *The Age of Solomon*; Halpern, *David's Secret Demons*.

11 Such as the 'Book of Solomon's Acts' that is mentioned at the end of the unit (1 Kgs 11:41). Much of one's position on these matters is based on various directions in scholarship on the DH. Another key factor is that there are important differences between the MT and the LXX in the development of Kings, indicating considerable fluidity in the texts even when other biblical material had become fixed. See D. W. Gooding, "Pedantic Timetabling in 3rd Book of Reigns," *VT* 15, no. 2 (1965): 153–66; idem, "The Septuagint's Version of Solomon's Misconduct," *VT* 15, no. 3 (1965): 325–35; McKenzie, *The Trouble with Kings*; Knoppers, *Two Nations Under God*; P. S. F. van Keulen, *Two Versions Of The Solomon Narrative: An Inquiry Into The Relationship Between MT 1 Kgs. 2–11 And LXX 3 Reg. 2–11* (Leiden: Brill, 2005); Andrzej S. Turkanik, *Of Kings and Reigns: A Study of Translation Technique in the Gamma/Gamma Section of 3 Reigns (1 Kings)* (Tübingen: Mohr Siebeck, 2008).

12 The history walks an ideological tightrope here: because of the Deuteronomistic covenant theology, Israel as a people and state must surpass all other nations, but being led by a king was a challenge to divine authority (see 1 Sam 8 and Deut 17).

13 The exceptions include portions of this introduction to Solomon's story (1 Kgs 3:4–28), prayer or communication between Solomon and YHWH (e.g., 1 Kgs 8:1–9:9), and portions of the end of Solomon's reign (e.g., 1 Kgs 11:9–13), all of which contain large compositions from the Dtr. There is a broad structure apparent in the narrative that accounts for these concentrations, although scholars debate many of the details, including how much of this order was the work of the Dtr. The focus on the temple and close connections to Deuteronomistic ideology (in light of Deut 17:14–20) that appear in the text's arrangement suggest a Deuteronomic-minded redactor. The temple construction is at the center, with corresponding content before and after. Wealth and wisdom (or trade and economic matters) are detailed on either side of the temple material, possibly with criticism or irony in the second half of the narrative in response to the international character of Solomon's leadership approach and capital city (see Chapter Four). Solomon's rise and fall bookend the work.

14 It is not uncommon to see the 'Book of Solomon's Acts' (1 Kgs 11:41) used to refer to the entirety of non-Deuteronomistic material in 1 Kings 3–11. While it is possible that the historian revealed the name of an extensive source, it is unlikely, based on the analysis in this chapter, that it was his *only* source. Further, we have no way of knowing the precise contents of this work or its importance relative to other sources. A more responsible position is that the historian reproduced material from a variety of sources, which may have included content from 'Solomon's Acts.'

15 Notably, Shishaq (to be identified with Shoshenq I, see next note) is the first pharaoh in the DH referred to by name. He is connected to Solomon's reign indirectly through his support of Jeroboam, and in the DH, he returns to the narrative in 1 Kings 14:25–26, which records Shishaq's looting of Jerusalem's royal and sacred areas in the fifth year of Solomon's successor, Rehoboam's reign.

16 There is a fair amount of agreement that the biblical Shishaq is Shoshenq I of the 22nd Dynasty, but scrutiny of this association continues. For those who are not convinced, the absence of Jerusalem in Shoshenq's Karnak inscription is a significant problem as is the chronological distance between the Dtr and the 10th century; see Peter James and Peter van der Veen, eds., *Solomon and Shishak: Current Perspectives from Archaeology, Epigraphy, History and Chronology: Proceedings of the Third BICANE Colloquium Held at Sidney Sussex College, Cambridge 26-27 March, 2011* (BAR International Series, 2732; Oxford: Archaeopress, 2015). In my view, discrepancies between Shoshenq's formal inscription and biblical, cultural memory of the period are not problematic. Full agreement among ancient sources, even when contemporary, is exceptional. This point aside, consideration of the critique is important, but the present discussion follows the convention that the biblical Shishaq should be understood to be Shoshenq I.

17 There are some textual difficulties here, involving variations of the place names discussed below, quantities (600 measures of silver for a chariot in the MT versus 100 in the Greek and 150 versus 50 regarding horses) and the manner of transport (בידם 'into their hand' versus the Greek's κατα θαλασσαν 'by sea,' [*בים]), all of which can be attributed to scribal errors. The MT's בידם is to be preferred and is in agreement with the parallel in 2 Chronicles 1:16.

18 Que is the Assyrianized version of Hiyawa. The identification has long been known, but new inscriptions have enlivened discussion about early Iron Age states in the region and the transition from the Late Bronze Age (Trevor Bryce, "The Land of Hiyawa [Que] Revisited," *Anatolian Studies* 66 [2016]: 67–79).

19 Hayim Tadmor, "Que and Muṣri," *IEJ* 11, no. 3 (1961): 143–50. For summary of the arguments and refutations, see Paul S. Ash, *David, Solomon and Egypt: A Reassessment* (JSOTSup 297; Sheffield: Sheffield Academic Press, 1999), 119–20, footnote 64.

20 Naʾaman, "Sources and Composition in the History of Solomon."

21 Lisa A. Heidorn, "The Horses of Kush," *Journal of Near Eastern Studies* 56, no. 2 (1997): 105–14; Stephanie Dalley, "Foreign Chariotry and Cavalry in the Armies of Tiglath-Pileser III and Sargon II," *Iraq* 47 (1985): 31–48.

22 For cavalry, they preferred *mesaya* horses – that is, horses from Mesu in present-day Iran (Dalley, "Foreign Chariotry and Cavalry in the Armies of Tiglath-Pileser III and Sargon II"). Note that Dalley is uncritical of the 1 Kings 10:28–29 account and includes it in support of part of her discussion regarding Sargon II (ibid., 43.). The reverse is in fact a better argument; the Sargon material contributes to a better understanding of the Solomon Narrative.

23 Ibid., 45–46.

24 Ibid.

25 Miriam Lichtheim (ed.), *Ancient Egyptian Literature: Volume III: The Late Period* (Berkeley: University of California Press, 2006), 66–83.

26 Heidorn, "The Horses of Kush."

27 Sarah A. Schrader et al., "Symbolic Equids and Kushite State Formation: A Horse Burial at Tombos," *Antiquity* 92, no. 362 (2018): 383–97.

28 The tomb itself had been prepared and used in the New Kingdom, later looted, but then reused in the early Third Intermediate Period (ibid.).

29 Although circumstantial evidence is mounting with discoveries related to an early Iron Age spice trade. If cinnamon and other trade goods journeyed to the eastern Mediterranean via the Indian Ocean, the exchange networks were in place to connect Nubian and south Arabian elites to the southern Levant, although likely very indirectly. See later in this chapter and discussion in Chapter Six.

30 In accordance with Naʾaman, "Sources and Composition in the History of Solomon," 70–72.

31 This confusion similarly plagues the related material in 2 Samuel 8 concerning David's relations with these neighbors. The redundancy in the confusion between the Hadad and Rezon episodes would suggest some Aramean element in the Dtr's source(s). In fact, André Lemaire argues that Hadad was Aramean and that in this source we have evidence of Aram's first king ("Edom and the Edomites," in *The Books of Kings: Sources, Composition, Historiography and Reception*, ed. André Lemaire, Baruch Halpern, and Matthew Joel Adams [VTSup 129; Leiden: Brill, 2010], 225–240, esp. 225–230; idem, "Les Premiers Rois Araméens Dans La Tradition Biblique," in *The World of the Aramaeans I: Biblical Studies in Honour of Paul Eugène Dion*, ed. P. M. Michèle Daviau et al. [JSOTSup 324; Sheffield: Sheffield Academic Press, 2001], 113–43.).

32 For an extended exploration of the differences, see van Keulen, *Two Versions of The Solomon Narrative*; Turkanik, *Of Kings and Reigns*.

33 Diana V. Edelman, "Solomon's Adversaries Hadad, Rezon and Jeroboam: A Trio of 'Bad Guy' Characters Illustrating the Theology of Immediate Retribution," in *The Pitcher Is Broken: Memorial Essays for Gösta W.*

Ahlström, ed. Steven W. Holloway and Lowell K. Handy (JSOT Supplement Series 190; Sheffield: Sheffield Academic Press, 1995), 166–91.

34 Ibid.
35 For a recent, in-depth analysis of this figure's name/title, see Christoffer Theis, "Θεκεμείνας Und תַּחְפְּנֵיס in 1 Könige 11,19," *Journal of Septuagint and Cognate Studies* 49 (2016): 50–60, and discussion below.
36 By that time, there is sufficient evidence of regional interactions such as those described in 1 Kings 11. The Tel Dan stele and the Mesha stele, for example, make clear that there were regional kings and upstarts antagonizing each other, but the biblical material remains the only description for the 10th century. See Mark W. Chavalas, "Inland Syria and the East-of-Jordan Region in the First Millennium BCE before the Assyrian Intrusions," in *The Age of Solomon: Scholarship at the Turn of the Millennium*, ed. Lowell K. Handy (SHCANE 11; Leiden; New York: Brill, 1997), 168–71; J. C. L. Gibson, *Textbook of Syrian Semitic Inscriptions II: Aramaic Inscriptions Including Inscriptions in the Dialect of Zenjirli* (Oxford: Clarendon Press, 1975); idem, *Textbook of Syrian Semitic Inscriptions III: Phoenician Inscriptions Including Inscriptions in the Mixed Dialect of Arslan Tash* (Oxford: Clarendon Press, 1982).
37 Nadav Naʾaman, "Israel, Edom and Egypt in the 10th Century B.C.E.," *TA* 19 (1992): 71–93.
38 His more recent arguments focus on the newer archaeological evidence of the 10th century from the Arabah and Faynan, as well as 8th century tensions between Aram, Israel, and Edom and commerce east of the Jordan and Arabah Valleys. See Nadav Naʾaman, "Judah and Edom in the Book of Kings and in Historical Reality," in *New Perspectives on Old Testament Prophecy and History. Essays in Honour of Hans M. Barstad*, ed. Rannfrid I. Thelle, Terje Stordalen, and Mervyn E. J. Richardson (Vetus Testamentum Supplements 168; Leiden; Boston: Brill, 2015), 197–211; idem, "Hiram of Tyre in the Book of Kings and in the Tyrian Records," *JNES* 78, no. 1 (2019): 75–85.
39 And, as we have already observed indirectly in the case of David's 'rescue' of Qeʿilah in Chapter Two; the Amarna correspondence details very similar regional conflicts in the 14th century as the books of Samuel portray in the 10th century. For a discussion of Jerusalem's depiction in the Amarna letters, see Chapter Four.
40 Naʾaman, "Sources and Composition in the History of Solomon"; idem, "Judah and Edom in the Book of Kings and in Historical Reality"; idem, "Hiram of Tyre in the Book of Kings and in the Tyrian Records."
41 And later; Bernd U. Schipper argues that period of the 25th and 26th Dynasties provided the greatest opportunity for direct cultural contact and influence between Egypt and Jerusalem ("Egypt and Israel: The Ways of Cultural Contacts in the Late Bronze Age and Iron Age [20th–26th Dynasty]," *Journal of Ancient Egyptian Interconnections* 4, no. 3 [2012]: 30–47).
42 Alan R. Schulman, "Diplomatic Marriage in the Egyptian New Kingdom," *JNES* 38, no. 3 (1979): 177–93; Trevor Bryce, *Letters of the Great Kings of the Ancient Near East: The Royal Correspondence of the Late Bronze Age* (London: Routledge, 2004); Tracy Maria Lemos, *Marriage Gifts and Social Change in Ancient Palestine: 1200 BCE to 200 CE* (Cambridge: Cambridge University Press, 2010); Amanda H. Podany, *Brotherhood of Kings: How International Relations Shaped the Ancient Near East* (Oxford; New York: Oxford University Press, 2010).
43 The LXX provides a longer, explicitly royal Ammonite pedigree for Naamah. Regarding David's marriages, see Jon D. Levenson and Baruch Halpern, "The Political Import of David's Marriages," *JBL* 99, no. 4 (1980): 507–18.
44 In addition to textual issues with 1 Kings 11:19, scholars debate whether תחפניס should be understood to be a distinct personal name or an Egyptian title later understood by the biblical author(s) and/or LXX translators as a name. Complicating things further is the LXX's account of Jeroboam's marriage; this account seems to have been influenced by the Hadad tradition, which was used to flesh out some details of Jeroboam's history (1 Kgs 11:26–14:20). See R. P. Gordon, "The Second Septuagint Account of Jeroboam: History or Midrash?," *VT* 25, no. 2 (1975): 368–93; Marvin A. Sweeney, "A Reassessment of the Masoretic and Septuagint Versions of the Jeroboam Narratives in 1 Kings/3 Kingdoms 11–14," *Journal for the Study of Judaism in the Persian, Hellenistic, and Roman Period* 38, no. 2 (2007): 165–95; and recently, Theis, "Θεκεμείνας Und תַּחְפְּנֵיס in 1 Könige 11,19."
45 This sort of idea would influence even later understanding, especially concerning traditions of Sheba's queen stemming from 1 Kings 10:1–10. According to Ethiopian tradition, the Queen's visit included marriage, and the two produced a son, Menelik I, founder of the Ethiopian dynastic line claimed by Yekuno Amlak in the 13th century CE. Ironically, in the DH, Sheba's queen is the only foreign royal woman not linked to the king through marriage.
46 Although Solomon's construction of shrines to his wives' foreign gods is described in 1 Kings 11:7–8, it is different in literary character than the other verses and refers to a separate part of the Jerusalem landscape.

47 Shaye Cohen's study of the Pharaoh's daughter supports the argument that there was an older source for the marriage alliance report ("Solomon and the Daughter of the Pharaoh: Intermarriage, Conversion, and the Impurity of Women," *JANES* 16–17 [1984]: 23–37). For a contrasting view, see Knoppers, *Two Nations Under God*, 1.145–146. For a complete dismissal, see Miller and Hayes, *A History of Ancient Israel and Judah*, 2nd. ed., 208.

48 Knoppers, *Two Nations*, 1:141; idem, "Sex, Religion, and Politics: The Deuteronomist on Intermarriage," *Hebrew Annual Review* 14 (1994): 121–41.

49 This is in contrast to the prostitute-mothers of 1 Kings 3 or the collective character of his other foreign wives in 1 Kings 11, from which the historian makes statements about Solomon's quality. Adele Reinhartz treats the figure of the Pharaoh's daughter as the same type of character as other women in the narrative, but she also notes that there is something different about her ("Anonymous Women and the Collapse of the Monarchy: A Study in Narrative Technique," in *The Feminist Companion to Samuel and Kings*, ed. Athalya Brenner [Feminist Companion to the Bible 5; Sheffield: Sheffield Academic, 1994], esp. 46–48).

50 Schipper has suggested that an Egyptian-style building in Jerusalem may have been the inspiration for the idea that Solomon married an Egyptian princess ("Salomo und die Pharaonentochter – zum historischen Kern von 1 Kön 7,8," *BN* 102 [2000] 84–94). Separately, I have presented a very similar argument: that Egyptian influence during the New Kingdom contributed to an Egyptian character to the city's architecture whose origin was not remembered by the time the sources were composed (Sarah Malena, "A Woman's Place[s]: Pharaoh's Daughter, Jerusalem's Landscape, and Layers of Meaning," paper presented at the Society of Biblical Literature annual meeting, San Diego, 2019). For additional discussion, see Chapter Four. Other scholars have focused on the association between the Pharaoh's daughter and Solomon's constructions, but with different research questions. Olley argues for a connection between the Pharaoh's daughter and the discussions of architecture, but his focus is on literary structure not historical relationships ("Pharaoh's Daughter, Solomon's Palace, and the Temple"). Cohen also notes the connection between the Egyptian wife and locations in Jerusalem, but his focus is on the notions of intermarriage and reception history ("Solomon and the Daughter of the Pharaoh").

51 Halpern elaborates on Solomon's emulation of a more prestigious Egypt (*David's Secret Demons*, 397–398). Michael D. Oblath argues that Solomon's possible emulation of Egypt may have influenced Israelites' perception of him as a pharaoh-like oppressor or the possibility that Solomon's labor policies gave rise to the oppressive Pharaoh story ("Of Pharaohs and Kings – Whence the Exodus?," *JSOT* 87 [2000]: 23–42). The fact that the Exodus features another important Pharaoh's daughter is provocative.

52 Anson F. Rainey, *The El-Amarna Correspondence: A New Edition of the Cuneiform Letters from the Site of El-Amarna Based on Collations of All Extant Tablets*, ed. William M. Schniedewind (Leiden; Boston: Brill, 2014), 73.

53 EA 1–5.

54 For general summaries of the period from differing positions on the issue of intermarriage and biblical reliability, see Kenneth Kitchen, *The Third Intermediate Period in Egypt*, 2nd ed. with supplement (Warminster: Aris & Phillips, 1995), 3–81; John Taylor, "The Third Intermediate Period (1069–664 BCE)," in *The Oxford History of Ancient Egypt*, ed. Ian Shaw (Oxford: Oxford University Press, 2002), 324–63. Marc Van De Mieroop, *A History of Ancient Egypt*, 2nd ed. (Hoboken: Wiley Blackwell, 2021), 249–71.

55 In the transition between the 20th and 21st Dynasties, there was fluidity in titles, perhaps depending on one's audience (e.g., the power struggle between Herihor and Piankh). See Ben Haring, "Stela Leiden V 65 and Herihor's 'Damnatio Memoriae,'" *Studien Zur Altägyptischen Kultur* 41 (2012): 139–52; Gerard P. F. Broekman, "The Leading Theban Priests of Amun and Their Families under Libyan Rule," *The Journal of Egyptian Archaeology* 96 (2010): 125–48.

56 The term 'Libyan' here is a generalization for a number of tribes from the western Delta. Egyptian records (epigraphic and pictorial) record names and differences in some cases, but also stereotype in others. By the end of the 20th Dynasty, Libyan elites become conspicuous in written records due to incorporation into the military (Linda Hulin, "The Libyans," in *The Oxford Handbook of Egyptology*, ed. Ian Shaw and Elizabeth Bloxam [Oxford: Oxford University Press, 2020]).

57 The Libyan cultural and ethnic identity was not confined to traditional titles. M. Anthony Leahy's research demonstrates the cultural difference through burial practices, names, political organization, and writing/language ("The Libyan Period in Egypt: An Essay in Interpretation," *Libyan Studies* 16 [1985]: 51–65); see also Broekman, "Leading Theban Priests"; Haring, "Stela Leiden V 65 and Herihor's 'Damnatio Memoriae'"; Troy L. Sagrillo, "The Geographic Origins of the 'Bubastite' Dynasty and Possible Locations for the Royal Residence and Burial Place of Shoshenq I," in *The Libyan Period in Egypt: Historical and Cultural Studies into the 21st-24th Dynasties: Proceedings of a Conference at Leiden University, 25-27 October 2007*, ed. Gerard P. F. Broekman, Robert Johannes Demarée, and Olaf E. Kaper (Leiden: Peeters, 2009), 341–60.

58 Kenneth Kitchen draws attention to this practice in his influential history of the Third Intermediate Period (*The Third Intermediate Period in Egypt*, §§241–249). The work is detailed and comprehensive but also asserts the reliability of the biblical material pertaining to the 10th century, which lessens its effectiveness. See sources below for those who continue to work on the issue of strategic marriages in the 21st and 22nd Dynasties.

59 Broekman, "Leading Theban Priests," 129–33; Karl Jansen-Winkeln, "Beiträge Zur Geschichte Der 21. Dynastie," *The Journal of Egyptian Archaeology* 102 (2016): 73–96. Shoshenq's son continued this practice by marrying Maatkara, who was the daughter of Psusennes I, last king of the 21st Dynasty who was also High Priest of Amun (John Taylor, "The Third Intermediate Period [1069–664 BCE]," 335).

60 Chronologically, we could also consider Psusennes II, who reigned between Siamun and Shoshenq and was the high priest of Amun in Thebes before also taking over leadership in the north. He is not normally considered among the likely candidates because he did not leave any record of interaction in the southern Levant.

61 Some scholars rely on this depiction as extra-biblical evidence that Siamun indeed campaigned *at* Gezer and must be the pharaoh of 1 Kings 9:16; however, there is no written identification of the enemy or location on the relief. The argument begins with Pierre Montet's discovery and publication of the relief, and gained in popularity after Jacob Goldwasser's article, "The Campaign of Siamun in Palestine," *BJPES* 14 (1948): 82–84. See also Alberto R. Green, "Solomon and Siamun: A Synchronism between Early Dynastic Israel and the Twenty-First Dynasty of Egypt," *JBL* 97 (1978): 353–67. For arguments against these interpretations, see Ash, *David, Solomon and Egypt*, 37–46.

62 Shmuel Yeivin, "Did the Kingdoms of Israel Have a Maritime Policy?," *JQR* 50 (1960): esp. 198–207.

63 Cross, *Canaanite Myth and Hebrew Epic*, 263; see also Halpern, *David's Secret Demons*, 331.

64 If we use scholarly interest and debate as a measure of the potential for one of these kings to be engaged with 10th century Levantine rulers, Shoshenq is the clear frontrunner. His monuments and inscriptions, as well as the likely identification as biblical Shishaq, have been the focus of international conferences and numerous publications over the last two decades (see notes below). The case for Siamun has essentially faded into the 20th century (CE) background.

65 If he is indeed the same pharaoh as biblical Shishaq, which is the operating assumption here, these attestations provide critical historical and archaeological links in the region and allow scholars to connect relative and absolute chronologies across archaeological, epigraphic, and biblical evidence. See Troy L. Sagrillo, "Shoshenq I and Biblical Šîšaq: A Philological Defense of Their Traditional Equation," in *Solomon and Shishak: Current Perspectives from Archaeology, Epigraphy, History and Chronology; Proceedings of the Third BICANE Colloquium Held at Sidney Sussex College, Cambridge 26–27 March, 2011* (BAR International Series 2732; Oxford: Archaeopress, 2015). For a recent argument to the contrary, see Ronald Wallenfels, "Shishak and Shoshenq: A Disambiguation," *JAOS* 139, no. 2 (2019): 487–500.

66 Shoshenq's familial claims to power reach into the 21st Dynasty through his father, the prior Chief, and his uncle Osorkon, who ruled as king before Siamun in Tanis (Taylor, "The Third Intermediate Period"; Kitchen, *The Third Intermediate Period in Egypt*).

67 This event is famously documented on the Bubastite Portal at Karnak. It is typically also understood to be the campaign described in 1 Kings 14:25. With the reevaluation of the historicity of the biblical material of the early kings and 10th century chronologies, the event's status as the first synchronism between biblical and extrabiblical evidence is under more scrutiny.

68 See also Chapters Six and Seven. This explanation was suggested by Aharoni (*The Land of the Bible*, 290) and taken up by Rainey in *The Sacred Bridge* (185–189) before becoming more frequently discussed more recently. It is most convincingly supported in the case of the southern sites (i.e., the Negev and Beersheba Valley) due to their involvement in the copper exchange network; see Thomas E. Levy, Mohammad Najjar, and Erez Ben-Yosef, "Conclusion," in *New Insights into the Iron Age Archaeology of Edom, Southern Jordan: Surveys, Excavations and Research from the University of California, San Diego & Department of Antiquities of Jordan, Edom Lowlands Regional Archaeology Project (ELRAP)*, ed. Thomas E. Levy et al., 2 vols. (Monumenta Archaeologica 35; Los Angeles: The Cotsen Institute of Archaeology Press, 2014), 985. In many cases, however, the trade motivation is often put forward but not fully argued or simply assumed; see for example, Gösta Werner Ahlström, "Pharaoh Shoshenq's Campaign to Palestine," in *History and Traditions of Early Israel: Studies Presented to Eduard Nielsen, May 8th 1993*, ed. André Lemaire, Benekikt Otzen, and Eduard Nielsen (VTSup 50; Leiden: Brill, 1993), 1–16; Frank Clancy, "Shishak/Shoshenq's Travels," *JSOT* 86 (1999): 3–23; Finkelstein, "The Campaign of Shoshenq I to Palestine: A Guide to the 10th Century BCE Polity," *ZDPV* 118 (2022): 109–35; idem, "The Impact of the Sheshonq I Campaign on the Territorial History of

the Levant: An Update" Accessed on academia.edu, February 25, 2023 (forthcoming); Halpern, *David's Secret Demons*, esp. 465 and note 76 relating to Solomon's districts; Herzog and Singer-Avitz, "Redefining the Centre," 232–233; Amihai Mazar, "Archaeology and the Biblical Narrative: The Case of the United Monarchy," in *One God – One Cult – One Nation. Archaeological and Biblical Perspectives*, ed. Reinhard G. Kratz and Hermann Spieckermann (BZAW 405; Berlin; New York: De Gryter, 2010), 30–31; Schipper, "Egypt and Israel." Even if other areas of the campaign have not yet been connected to trade interests, the circumstantial evidence is compelling. Shoshenq's conquered sites correspond to many of the critical areas surveyed in this study: those associated with interactions with Philistines (see Chapter Two), Solomon's affairs, and sites associated with the extrabiblical evidence surveyed in Chapters Five and Six.

69 See discussions in Chapters One and Five.
70 Another suggestion offered in Schipper's exploration of the Pharaoh's daughter problem ("Salomo und die Pharaonentochter").
71 Shirly Ben-Dor Evian et al., "Pharaohs Copper: The Provenance of Copper in Bronze Artifacts from Post-Imperial Egypt at the End of the Second Millennium BCE," *JASREP* 38 (2021); Veit Vaelske, "Early Iron Age Copper Trail between Wadi Arabah and Egypt during the 21st Dynasty: First Results from Tanis, ca. 1000 BC (with Michael Bode, DBM)," *Zeitschrift Für Orient-Archäologie* (n.d.), 190–91.
72 Ibid.
73 See Chapter Five.
74 Gunnar Lehmann, "The Emergence of Early Phoenicia," *Jerusalem Journal of Archaeology* 1 (2021): 280.
75 See Chapter Six.
76 María Eugenia Aubet, "Phoenicia during the Iron Age II Period," in *The Oxford Handbook of the Archaeology of the Levant: C. 8000-332 BCE*, ed. Margreet L. Steiner and Ann E. Killebrew (Oxford: Oxford University Press, 2014), 706–16.
77 Josephus cites Menander of Ephesus as his source, who, according to Josephus, had translated Tyre's royal archives from Phoenician into Greek (*Antiquities of the Jews* 8.5.3; *Against Apion* 1.18).
78 The language of Hiram's correspondence with David and Solomon has been argued to reflect known treaties and diplomatic etiquette. In the middle of the last century, there was much more confidence in the usefulness of ancient Near Eastern parallels for supporting the historical reliability of such a treaty; see, for example, F. C. Fensham, "The Treaty between Solomon and Hiram and the Alalakh Tablets," *JBL* 79 (1960): 59–60; idem, "The Treaty between the Israelites and the Tyrians," in *International Congress for the Study of the Old Testament, Rome*, ed. John Adney Emerton (VTSup 17; Leiden: Brill, 1969), 71–87; William L. Moran, "The Ancient Near Eastern Background of the Love of God in Deuteronomy," *CBQ* 25 (1963): 77–87; J. Priest, "The Covenant of Brothers," *JBL* 84 (1965): 400–406. If all of the royal correspondence is viewed together (2 Sam 5:11; 1 Kgs 5:15–25; 1 Kgs 9:10–14), there appears to be conformity to the ancient parallels (e.g., the terminology 'brother,' 'know,' 'love,' 'peace,' and exchange of gifts); however, the historical conclusions characteristic of the earlier studies have not held up as well as the form-critical aspects. More recently theoretical discussions, especially informed by the social sciences, have dominated research in this area; see, for example, Saul M. Olyan, "Honor, Shame, and Covenant Relations in Ancient Israel and Its Environment," *JBL* 115 (1996): 201–18; Victor H. Matthews, "The Unwanted Gift: Implications of Obligatory Gift Giving in Ancient Israel," *Semeia* 87 (1999): 91–104; Simkins, "Patronage and the Political Economy of Monarchic Israel"; Gary Stansell, "The Gift in Ancient Israel," *Semeia* 87 (1999): 65–90; R. Westbrook, "Patronage in the Ancient Near East," *JESHO* 48 (2005): 210–33.
79 Na'aman, "Sources and Composition in the History of Solomon," 65–67. He explains, 'The epistolary language, the diplomatic and legal terminology and the commercial details, were all borrowed from the reality of his time and outwardly look authentic. Yet the letter is non-historical, and save for a few details (e.g., the contemporaneity of Hiram and Solomon and their possible commercial relations), mainly illustrates the outlines of negotiation and the conclusion of commercial agreements in the author's time' (ibid., 67). The 8th century is probable for a number of reasons (including our knowledge of a firmly established court system in Jerusalem and evidence of scribal activity in general), but above all the relationship between Solomon's history and Hezekiah's point to Hezekiah's reign as a likely period for the composition of a (favorable) Solomonic account; see Halpern, "Sacred History and Ideology"; Richard Elliott Friedman, "Solomon and the Great Histories," in *Jerusalem in Bible and Archaeology: The First Temple Period*, ed. Andrew G. Vaughn and Ann E. Killebrew (Atlanta: Society of Biblical Literature, 2003), 171–80.
80 The characterization of this land, as either Israelite or Phoenician, is difficult. Archaeologists once considered there to be clear lines in material culture between the two lands that corresponded to biblical boundaries. Sites in this region were often confounding, as they exhibited what were considered to be

both Israelite and Phoenician elements. More recent interpretation understands that identity is more complex than political boundaries and styles of pottery.

81 Halpern suggests that this part of the history is 'masking' a loss of this territory and/or the 'alienation of Israelites from the national state.' In his interpretation, Hiram's payment was part of the kings' maritime arrangement (*David's Secret Demons*, 408–410).

82 Based on extrabiblical evidence, this region was also important for exchange relations between the Levant and Cyprus, which were growing in the 10th century. For additional discussion, see below and Chapter Six.

83 For summaries of recent archaeological evidence of Assyrian impact on the southern Levant, see Avraham Faust, "Settlement, Economy, and Demography under Assyrian Rule in the West: The Territories of the Former Kingdom of Israel as a Test Case," *JAOS* 135, no. 4 (2015): 765–89, esp. pp. 767–68 for the Galilee.

84 The variation between the reports (that is, whether the exchange was in goods or land) is not necessarily incompatible. Agricultural produce may have been viewed as synonymous with the land, especially if the produce taken was considered excessive. Excavator Zvi Gal has identified the archaeological site Horvat Rosh Zayit with the Cabul and sees a correlation between the site and this history. The site was occupied from the 10th to the 8th century and yielded diverse archaeological remains (Gal describes a mixture of Phoenician and Israelite culture) as well as facilities for large-scale agricultural storage; see Zvi Gal and Yardenna Alexandre, *Horbat Rosh Zayit, an Iron Age Storage Fort and Village* (Jerusalem: Israel Antiquities Authority, 2000).

85 Note that this 'common historical situation' may or may not have involved a historical Solomon, but that exchange relations between Israelite and Tyrian lands/interests prior to the 9th century were remembered as part of a Solomonic era.

86 *HALOT*, 1731. In general, the luxury goods in the verse have troubled translators and interpreters from ancient times to present; for a full variety of translations and possibilities, see entries in *HALOT*. Halpern makes a strong case that some of the more exotic (and typically considered far-fetched) trade in the accounts can be supported through extrabiblical parallels involving other areas of the ancient Near East, and therefore 'a trading state' in the 10th century, based in Jerusalem, is likely in his view (*David's Secret Demons*, 209–210).

87 Edward Lipiński, *Itineraria Phoenicia* (Ola 127; Studia Phoenicia 18; Leuven; Dudley: Uitgeverij Peeters en Departement Oosterse Studies, 2004), 225–226. He argues that the meanings of the words were only vaguely understood (as related to cutting) by the time they were translated into Greek and were completely misunderstood by the author of Targum Jonathan.

88 The parallel account in 2 Chronicles 9:10–11 has an alternate form of the word, אלגומים (also in 2 Chr 2:7). The difference between the two is a deceivingly simple metathesis between מ and ג. The Chronicles version may be related to or influenced by the Arabic *al + gamīm*, 'lush plant,' but there is no widespread acceptance of etymologies for either of the words to determine which is original. Ancient sources also appear to be uncertain of the material (see *HALOT*). There is slight disagreement between Kings and Chronicles on the use of the wood. The discrepancies appear in just two words that happen to be adjacent to one another. The Chronicler relied on the same source or the Kings report, but it is unclear why the name of the wood and its use are different between the two accounts. The words were either unknown by the time of the Chronicler and suitable replacements supplied, or the words were corrupted in the Kings version after Chronicles was composed. The former seems more probable, as the Chronicler adapted other parts of the verse (and his work) to be appropriate for his situation. The Chronicler would also be more likely to emend an unknown material to the form *al + gamīm* noted above. If the Kings version is original, then there is additional reason to view the other information in 1 Kings 10:11–12 as derived from older sources.

89 1 Kings 10:22 does not state where the ships imported goods from, but it would not be odd for Ophir to be the assumed location. If the verse was appended to the account later on, there would be no need to restate 'Ophir.'

90 The ostracon was found on the surface of the site and has been dated based on the epigraphy (8th to 6th centuries) and the site's archaeological record (destroyed by the Assyrians in the 8th century); see Benjamin Maisler [Mazar], "Two Hebrew Ostraca from Tell Qasile," *JNES* 10 (1951): 265–87; A. Mazar, *Excavations at Tell Qasile*.

91 Lipiński provides an extensive exploration of possible locations for Ophir, as well as a reconstruction of the composition and redaction process that led to the association between Solomon, the 8th century's Hiram (II), and Ophir trade (*Itineraria Phoenicia*, 189–224, esp. 217–218).

92 Maritime travel between the Levant and India via the Red Sea is better known from the Hellenistic and Roman eras. The recent discovery of cinnamon in early Iron Age flasks has renewed questions about the nature and extent of trade between the eastern Mediterranean and the Indian subcontinent; see Chapter Six.
93 John Day, "Where Was Tarshish?," in *Let Us Go Up to Zion: Essays in Honour of H. G. M. Williamson on the Occasion of His Sixty-Fifth Birthday*, ed. Iain Provan and Mark Boda (Leiden: Brill, 2012), 359–70; Christine M. Thompson and Sheldon Skaggs, "King Solomon's Silver? Southern Phoenician Hacksilber Hoards and the Location of Tarshish," *Internet Archaeology* 35 (2013).
94 For a detailed discussion of these connections, see Na'aman, "Judah and Edom in the Book of Kings and in Historical Reality"; idem, "Hiram of Tyre in the Book of Kings and in the Tyrian Records."
95 That is, later than the 10th century. We do not yet know the identity of the lowland polities of the 10th century. Biblical Edom, meaning the plateau kingdom, was well situated to take control of the area, but appears to have been a vassal rather than an independent actor in the repeated shifts of power over Elath/Ezion-geber. In both 1 Kings 22:48–50 and 2 Kings 14, Israel was more powerful than Edom and Judah, and control of Elath was Judah's attempt to gain power or independence. See Nadav Na'aman, "Azariah of Judah and Jeroboam II of Israel," *VT* 43 (1993): 227–34; Miller and Hayes, *A History of Ancient Israel and Judah*, 2nd ed., 304, 319.
96 As discussed above, the similarity between ר and ד has caused problems in the history. There has been confusion between ארם and אד(ו)ם in various mss. and versions throughout this verse. The reading assumed here is that Rezin, king of Aram, reclaimed Elath for Aram, and Edomites (possibly also Arameans) settled there.
97 Examples of the Dtr's work include 2 Kings 16:6, which begins with בעת ההיא, 'at that time,' and ends with עד היום הזה, 'until this day.' The entire episode (beginning 2 Kgs 16:1) is set with highly characteristic phrasing. Also, 1 Kings 22:50 fits a pattern attributed to the Dtr, אז + imperfect; see James A. Montgomery, "Archival Data in the Book of Kings," *JBL* 53, no. 1 (1934): 46–52, esp. 49. Interest in Elath and Ezion-geber is related, in part, to the Dtr's concern for Judah-Edomite relations, which the DH ultimately traces back to the wilderness period; see Jeffrey C. Geoghegan, "'Until This Day' and the Preexilic Redaction of the Deuteronomistic History," *JBL* 122, no. 2 (2003): 201–227, esp. 222–223.
98 Archaeology has confirmed that the area was important in the later Iron Age, but there is not currently strong evidence for the 10th century. The site identified as Ezion-geber, Tell el-Kheleifeh, was initially considered Solomonic by Glueck, but further examination has focused on the fact that the most concrete evidence (e.g., ceramics) dates to the 8th to 6th centuries BCE. The evidence that continues to provoke questions about occupation in the Iron I–IIA is the recovery of Qurayyah Painted Ware, which first appears in the Late Bronze Age but is also found into the 10th century in the Arabah and Faynan. For further discussion of this pottery, see Chapter Six. For renewed discussion of the QPW and the site, see Marta Luciani, "Pottery from the 'Midianite Heartland?' On Tell Kheleifeh and Qurayyah Painted Ware. New Evidence from the Harvard Semitic Museum," in *To the Madbar and Back Again: Studies in the Languages, Archaeology, and Cultures of Arabia Dedicated to Michael C.A. Macdonald*, ed. Laïla Nehmé and Ahmad Al-Jallad (Leiden: Brill, 2017), 392–438. For previous assessments, see Gary D. Pratico, "Nelson Glueck's 1938–1940 Excavations at Tell El-Kheleifeh: A Reappraisal," *BASOR* 259 (1985): 1–32; idem, *Nelson Glueck's 1938–1940 Excavations at Tell El-Kheleifeh – A Reappraisal* (Atlanta: Scholars Press, 1993); Virginia Egan, Patricia M. Bikai, and Kurt Zamora, "Archaeology in Jordan," *American Journal of Archaeology* 104, no. 3 (2000): 577–578; Neil G. Smith and Thomas E. Levy, "Iron Age Ceramics from Edom: A New Typology," in *New Insights into the Iron Age Archaeology of Edom, Southern Jordan: Surveys, Excavations and Research from the University of California, San Diego & Department of Antiquities of Jordan, Edom Lowlands Regional Archaeology Project (ELRAP)*, ed. Thomas E. Levy et al., 2 vols. (Monumenta Archaeologica 35; Los Angeles: The Cotsen Institute of Archaeology Press), 412.
99 Dvory Namdar et al., "Cinnamaldehyde in Early Iron Age Phoenician Flasks Raises the Possibility of Levantine Trade with South East Asia," *Mediterranean Archaeology and Archaeometry* 12, no. 3 (2013): 1–19; Ayelet Gilboa and Dvory Namdar, "On the Beginnings of South Asian Spice Trade with the Mediterranean Region: A Review," *Radiocarbon* 57, no. 2 (2015): 265–83.
100 Gilboa and Namdar, "On the Beginnings of South Asian Spice Trade." The researchers stress that a precise route cannot be determined and that there may have been various fluctuating and/or competing routes, perhaps some via Mesopotamia.
101 Ibid., 276.

102 In addition to creating a Solomonic precedent for control of Ezion-geber, it is possible that inspiration for the southern orientation of these accounts was influenced by cultural memory of the 10th century copper exchange network that was active in the south; see Chapters Six and Seven.

103 Kenneth Kitchen, "Sheba and Arabia," in *The Age of Solomon: Scholarship at the Turn of the Millennium*, ed. Lowell K. Handy (SHCANE 11; Leiden; New York: Brill, 1997), 126–53; Sarah Malena, "Spice Roots in the Song of Songs," in *Milk and Honey: Essays on Ancient Israel and the Bible in Appreciation of the Judaic Studies Program at the University of California, San Diego*, ed. Sarah Malena and David Miano (Winona Lake: Eisenbrauns, 2007), 176–180.

104 The queen's speech (1 Kgs 10:6–9) echoes Hiram's and Solomon's words in 1 Kings 5, but it is not entirely clear if the texts are of the same authorship. R. B. Y. Scott sees the queen's words as inspired by Hiram's, as opposed to being related in authorship, and argues that the text contains post-exilic elements, especially in vocabulary and idiom ("Solomon and the Beginnings of Wisdom in Israel," in *Wisdom in Israel and in the Ancient Near East Presented to Professor Harold Henry Rowley*, ed. Martin Noth and D. Winston Thomas [VTSup 3; Leiden: Brill, 1960], 262–79).

105 The last of the list, the פחות הארץ or 'governors of the land,' is the most informative element. The noun פחה, 'governor' (translated in the LXX as των σατραπων, 'satraps') is a loan word from Akkadian and indicates a later period of composition. Notably, the term was used for governors who served the Persian Empire, but it is also related to officials under the Neo-Assyrian and Neo-Babylonian periods. It is most frequent in later biblical texts. See *HALOT*, 923.

106 See Chapter Six.

107 Marta Luciani and Abdullah S. Alsaud, "Qurayyah 2015: Report on the First Season of the Joint Saudi Arabian-Austrian Archaeological Project," *ATLAL, Journal of Saudi Arabian Archaeology* 28 (2020): 47–78; Marta Luciani, "Qurayyah," in *Roads of Arabia: Archaeological Treasures from Saudi Arabia*, ed. Alessandra Capodiferro and Sara Colantonio (Milan: Electa, 2019), 140–55; Peter J. Parr, "Contacts between North West Arabia and Jordan in the Late Bronze and Iron Ages," in *Studies in the History and Archaeology of Jordan*, ed. A. Hadidi (Amman: Hashemite Kingdom of Jordan, Department of Antiquities, 1982), 127–33.

108 See Chapters Four and Six.

109 Eilat Mazar, *Discovering the Solomonic Wall in Jerusalem: A Remarkable Archaeological Adventure* (Jerusalem: Shoham Academic Research and Publication, 2011); Smith and Levy, "Iron Age Ceramics from Edom," 327; Neil G. Smith, Yuval Goren, and Thomas E. Levy, "The Petrography of Iron Age Edom: From the Lowlands to the Highlands," in *New Insights into the Iron Age Archaeology of Edom, Southern Jordan: Surveys, Excavations and Research from the University of California, San Diego & Department of Antiquities of Jordan, Edom Lowlands Regional Archaeology Project (ELRAP)*, ed. Thomas E. Levy et al., 2 vols. (Monumenta Archaeologica 35; Los Angeles: The Cotsen Institute of Archaeology Press, 2014), 476, 479, 488.

110 Eleanor Bennett, "The 'Queens of the Arabs' during the Neo-Assyrian Period" (Doctoral Dissertation, University of Helsinki, Helsinki, 2021).

111 Nadav Na'aman, "The Contribution of the Suḫu Inscriptions to the Historical Research of the Kingdoms of Israel and Judah," *JNES* 66 (2007): 107–22.

112 George Hatke, "For ʾIlmuquh and for Sabaʾ: The Res Gestae of Karibʾīl Watar Bin Dhamarʿ Alī from Ṣirwāḥ in Context," *Wiener Zeitschrift Für Die Kunde Des Morgenlandes* 105 (2015): 87–133; Na'aman, "The Contribution of the Suḫu Inscriptions," 107–22.

113 Hatke, "For ʾIlmuquh and for Sabaʾ," 94–95.

114 RINAP 3/1 Sennacherib 168.

115 Also notable here is the detail the DH provides about the main artisan: Solomon summoned from Tyre a man named Hiram, whose mother was a Naphtalite widow and whose father had been a Tyrian smith (איש־צרי חרש נחשת) (1 Kgs 7:13–14).

116 Erez Ben-Yosef et al., "Ancient Technology and Punctuated Change: Detecting the Emergence of the Edomite Kingdom in the Southern Levant," *PLOS ONE* 14, no. 9 (2019): e0221967; Erez Ben-Yosef et al., "A New Chronological Framework for Iron Age Copper Production at Timna (Israel)," *BASOR* 367 (2012): 31–71; Thomas E. Levy et al., eds., *New Insights into the Iron Age Archaeology of Edom, Southern Jordan*.

117 Erez Ben-Yosef et al., "Ancient Technology and Punctuated Change." Identifying this polity as 'Edomite' has caused considerable debate; see most recently, Erez Ben-Yosef, "And Yet, a Nomadic Error: A Reply to Israel Finkelstein," *Antiguo Oriente* 18 (2020): 33–60.

118 Vaelske, "Early Iron Age Copper Trail between Wadi Arabah and Egypt during the 21st Dynasty."

119 Moritz Kiderlen et al., "Tripod Cauldrons Produced at Olympia Give Evidence for Trade with Copper from Faynan (Jordan) to South West Greece, c. 950–750 BCE," *Journal of Archaeological Science: Reports* 8 (2016): 303–13.

120 Tzilla Eshel et al., "Debasement of Silver throughout the Late Bronze-Iron Age Transition in the Southern Levant: Analytical and Cultural Implications," *Journal of Archaeological Science* 125 (2021): 1–24.
121 Regarding the method of casting, the text reads literally 'in the thick of the earth' (במעבה האדמה).
122 The metallurgical activity in this area is known from investigations of the larger mounds like Tell Deir 'Alla. Smaller sites like Tell Hammeh, which is roughly 2.5 km east of Tell Deir 'Alla, may have also been critical in production, but they are only recently the subject of investigation.
123 Claus Jurman, "'Silver of the Treasury of Herishef' – Considering the Origin and Economic Significance of Silver in Egypt during the Third Intermediate Period," in *The Mediterranean Mirror: Cultural Contacts in the Mediterranean Sea between 1200 and 750 B.C.*, ed. Andrea Babbi et al. (RGZM – Tagungen 20; Mainz: Verlag der Römisch-Germanischen Zentralmuseums, 2015), 51–68.
124 Eshel et al., "Debasement of Silver"; Tzilla Eshel et al., "Lead Isotopes in Silver Reveal Earliest Phoenician Quest for Metals in the West Mediterranean," in *Proceedings of the National Academy of Sciences* (February 2019). Note that Eshel et al. distinguish their arguments from Thompson and Skaggs, who used different methods but also argue for renewed and Phoenician-initiated silver trade in the early Iron Age (Thompson and Skaggs, "King Solomon's Silver?"). For historical and archaeological arguments focused on Phoenician-Aegean interactions, see Susan Sherratt, "Phoenicians in the Aegean and Aegean Silver, 11th–9th Centuries BC," in *Les Phéniciens, Les Puniques et Les Autres: Échanges et Identités En Méditerranée Ancienne*, ed. Luisa Bonadies, Iva Chirpanlieva, and Élodie Guillon (Orient & Méditerranée 31; Paris: Éditions de Boccard, 2019).
125 Lloyd Weeks, "Metallurgy," in *A Companion to the Archaeology of the Ancient Near East*, ed. Daniel T. Potts (Malden: Wiley-Blackwell, 2012), 295–316; Stager and King, *Life in Biblical Israel*, 170–171.
126 These discoveries usually come from lost caches and undisturbed graves, such as the Middle Bronze Age hoard from Tell el-'Ajjul and the extravagant 8th century gold luxuries from Ashurnasirpal II's Nimrud palace (Ora Negbi, *The Hoards of Goldwork from Tell El-'Ajjul* [Studies in Mediterranean Archaeology 25; Göteborg: Studies in Mediterranean Archaeology, 1970]; J. E. Curtis et al., eds., *New Light on Nimrud: Proceedings of the Nimrud Conference 11th–13th March 2002* [London: British Institute for the Study of Iraq, 2008]).
127 James H. Breasted, *Ancient Records of Egypt: Historical Documents from the Earliest Times to the Persian Conquest, Vol. IV: The Twentieth to the Twenty-Sixth Dynasties* (Chicago: University of Chicago Press, 1906), 344–347, 362–366. Notably, Osorkon is described in terms familiar from depictions in the Deuteronomistic History: '…their bodies repose in all their favorite places; [there is none hostile toward them --], since the time of former kings; there is none like thee in this land. Every god abides upon his throne, and enters his abode with glad heart, [since] thou art installed to be [king] ---------- thee, building their houses, and multiplying their vessels of gold, silver, and every genuine costly stone, for which his majesty [gave] instructions, in his capacity as Thoth' (ibid., 4.362–363, §730). Alan R. Millard collects examples of similar reports of lavish uses of gold among rulers of the ancient world. While his comparisons show that the Bible's reports are similar, they do not situate the depiction in the 10th century ("Does the Bible Exaggerate King Solomon's Golden Wealth," *BAR* 15, no. 3 [1989]: 20–29, 31, 34).
128 Albrecht Alt, "Israels Gaue Unter Salomo," in *Kleine Schriften Zur Geschichte Des Volkes Israel, Volume 2*, ed. Martin Noth (Munich: Beck, 1953), 2.76–89; idem, "The Formation of the Israelite State in Palestine," in *Essays on Old Testament History and Religion*, trans. R. A. Wilson (Garden City: Doubleday, 1967); William Foxwell Albright, "The Administrative Divisions of Israel and Judah," *JPOS* 5 (1925): 15–54, esp. 25–26; G. E. Wright, "The Provinces of Solomon," *ErIsr* 8 (1967), 58*–68*. These studies were followed by Frank Moore Cross and G. E. Wright, "The Boundary and Province Lists of the Kingdom of Judah," *JBL* 75 (1956): 202–26; Tryggve N. D. Mettinger, *Solomonic State Officials: A Study of the Civil Government Officials of the Israelite Monarchy* (Coniectanea Biblica Old Testament Series 5; Lund: Gleerup, 1971); Baruch Halpern, "Sectionalism and the Schism," *JBL* 93 (1974): 519–532, esp. 528–531; Eric William Heaton, *Solomon's New Men: The Emergence of Ancient Israel as a National State* (New York: Pica Press, 1975); Yohanan Aharoni, "The Solomonic Districts," *TA* 3 (1976): 5–15; Gösta Werner Ahlström, "Administration and Building Activities in the Davidic-Solomonic Kingdom," in *Royal Administration and National Religion in Ancient Palestine* (SHANE 1; Leiden: Brill, 1982), 27–43.
129 More recent work includes Nadav Na'aman, *Borders and Districts in Biblical Historiography: Seven Studies in Biblical Geographic Lists* (Jerusalem Biblical Studies 4; Jerusalem: Simor, 1986), 167–201; idem, "Sources and Composition in the History of Solomon," 57–80; idem, "Solomon's District List (1 Kings 4, 7–19) and the Assyrian Province System in Palestine," *UF* 33 (2001): 419–36; Halpern, *David's Secret Demons*, 412–419; Stager, "The Patrimonial Kingdom of Solomon"; Rainey and Notley, *The Sacred Bridge*, 174–179.

More recent examination of the נְצִיב/נִצָּב specifically comes from Nili Sacher Fox, *In the Service of the King: Officialdom in Ancient Israel and Judah* (Monographs of the Hebrew Union College 23; Cincinnati: Hebrew Union College Press, 2000), 141-149. Paul S. Ash has been the most ardent critic of the list ("Solomon's? District? List," *JSOT* 67 [1995]: 67-86).

130 E.g., 2 Samuel 5:5; 8:15; 1 Kings 4:1, 7; 11:42; 12:20; 15:33. There is inconsistency in the use of the phrase to refer either to the northern tribes, to the exclusion of Judah, or to the entirety of the Israelite tribes as a state, which includes Judah. Paul S. Ash's characterization of 'all Israel,' presumably כל־ישראל, may be slightly misleading; see Ash, 'Solomon's? District? List," 77. There appears to be significance to the longer phrase; consider 2 Samuel 5:5, where the narrator states that from Jerusalem David ruled for 33 years 'over all of Israel and Judah' (על־כל־ישראל ויהודה). The phrase also appears within dialogue in 1 Samuel 11:2, which is likely the Dtr's composition.

131 There are several arguments for the inconsistency in the list of names. It has been proposed that the historian's source was a damaged document that followed the formula personal name + בן + patronym; see Albright, "The Administrative Divisions of Israel and Judah"; Wright, "The Provinces of Solomon"; Halpern, *David's Secret Demons*, 418. Joseph Naveh argues that there is not good reason to demand consistency among the names, and that the men were recorded according to their known names ("Nameless People," *IEJ* 40 [1990]: 108-23). See, more recently, Pamela Tamarkin Reis, "Unspeakable Names: Solomon's Tax Collectors," *ZAW* 120 (2008): 261-66. Reis argues that the source was intentionally altered to condemn the individuals.

132 Verse 13 is a particularly good example. The description of the villages of Jair and the depiction of Bashan are very similar to Deuteronomy 3:1-17 but also incorporate information from other parts of the DH; see Ash, "Solomon's? District? List," 75-78. Likewise, verse 19 invokes familiar or stock phrases and descriptions (e.g., kings Sihon and Og). Both verses contain later additions to an older record.

133 In addition to problems discussed in the previous note, some Greek versions lack 'Geber' in verse 19 and read 'Gad' for 'Gilead'; Greek versions in general read υιος Αδαι for בן־ארי (due to common confusion between ר and ד discussed above). Similarly, there are problems with verse 13, where Greek versions lack the segment describing Jair's villages. Ash argues well for the authority of the MT over the Greek versions for this list (ibid., 76, note 41).

134 The Greek adds Judah to the end of verse 19. There are textual and exegetical arguments to support the shorter MT reading (e.g., the final clause may have been a gloss or editorial addition). Na'aman argues for the presence of Judah in the list, claiming that a scribe added the second Gilead district to conceal Solomon's taxation of Judah (*Borders and Districts*, 176). The Greek addition, however, is more likely an attempt to present a more unified Israel or administrative program and should be viewed as an expansion.

135 Ash expresses this type of sentiment even in an argument against reliance on the list for historical reconstruction ("Solomon's? District? List," 79-80). That we have received a text without too much editing by the historian seems to be the case. The many textual problems among witnesses are attempts to improve upon a difficult text.

136 The latest possible date is straightforward: the composition of the DH. This date is unlikely and not popular even among scholars who argue against relying on the list for historical investigations. Most of the material in 1 Kings 4:8-19 does not contain language characteristic of the Dtr, and, as I commented above, the verses are framed by introduction and summary that are distinct from the list. The list must be significantly older than the Dtr.

137 An exception is the proposal by Finkelstein and Silberman that the list reflects the time and administrative policies of Jeroboam II (*David and Solomon*, 161-62.).

138 Na'aman, *Borders and Districts*, 176; idem, "Sources and Composition in the History of Solomon," 77. In the latter, he identifies this corpus with the 'Book of Solomon's Acts' from 1 Kings 11:41.

139 Ash, "Solomon's? District? List," 84-85. Ash's reconstruction is based in his argument about the relationship between scribal administrative work and complex statehood that I discuss further in Chapter Five. In contrast to Albright and others' arguments that the source was a 10th century written document, Ash concludes that, based on the scant written remains available from the 10th century, we must understand this source (*if* it contains material from Solomon's day) to have been transmitted orally at least in earlier stages (ibid., 71-72). He makes important observations about scholars' assumptions and the list's problems, but his arguments for oral transmission are not as convincing. For additional comments on Ash, see Halpern, *David's Secret Demons*, 220, note 23; Na'aman, "Sources and Composition in the History of Solomon," 60, note 6.

140 Halpern, "Sectionalism and the Schism," 529-530; idem, *David's Secret Demons*, 412-417.

141 For the continuity between David's and Solomon's administrations, see Halpern, "Sectionalism and the Schism," 529–530; idem, *David's Secret Demons*, 412–417. That the list was connected to Solomon is not typically questioned, but Ash notes that nowhere in the older source (i.e., setting aside editorial framing/commentary) does the list claim to be from Solomon's reign ("Solomon's? District? List").

142 Naʾaman argues that the text may have grown from an older list of names and was supplemented by a late 8th century author, but that the list most closely reflects a combination of Judahite districts and formerly Israelite (i.e., northern) districts that the Assyrian empire inherited ("Solomon's District List"). This argument does not address what would make the list exclusively 8th century. Why should Assyrian-era organization that recognized Dor or Megiddo, for example, as logical administrative units trump any other era's tendency to do the same? While Naʾaman acknowledges that the Assyrians largely continued some of the organizational structures of Israel and Judah, he does not convincingly argue that the list in 1 Kings 4:7–19 *must* be situated in the period of Assyrian administration.

143 Koert van Bekkum, "'The Situation Is More Complicated': Archaeology and Text in the Historical Reconstruction of the Iron Age IIA Southern Levant," in *Exploring the Narrative: Jerusalem and Jordan in the Bronze and Iron Ages: Papers in Honour of Margreet Steiner*, ed. Noor Mulder-Hymans, Jeannette Boertien, and Eveline van der Steen (Library of Hebrew Bible/Old Testament Studies 583; London; New York: Bloomsbury T&T Clark, 2014).

144 Economic motivation and coordination of regional elites are among the explanations proposed by Hermann Michael Niemann, but he sees the geographic arrangement as lacking a clear strategy ("The Socio-Political Shadow Cast by the Biblical Solomon," in *The Age of Solomon: Scholarship at the Turn of the Millennium*, ed. Lowell K. Handy [Studies in the History and Culture of the Ancient Near East 11; Leiden; New York: Brill, 1997], 279–88.).

145 There is debate about whether each district could have supplied for the crown in the way described in 1 Kings 4:7 and 5:7, and if וְכִלְכְּלוּ should be taken to mean (food) provisions from all districts in like kind. G. E. Wright sees the districts as comparable in their resources, though others disagree; see, for example, Naʾaman, *Borders and Districts*, 170. Yohanan Aharoni argues against the claim that there was an effort to create districts of equal area and 'economic potential,' but he also argues this point in order to maintain that Solomon's districts were arranged 'to preserve the tribal unit' (*Land of the Bible*, 315–16). In the interpretation argued here, allegiance to the tribal boundaries is not necessary. There are extra-biblical examples demonstrating that similar administrative districts were in place in the ancient Near East. Naʾaman uses 9th century Assyrian texts, which show that during its expansion, Assyria converted annexed kingdoms into administrative units. There would not have been consistency in size, resources, or contribution of each district through this kind of process (*Borders and Districts*, 170–71). Naʾaman also notes that these practices could have contributed in ways other than taxes; the districts could have provided other needs like military or temple service (which is the position Aharoni favors; Aharoni, *Land of the Bible*, 316; Naʾaman, *Borders and Districts*, 172). Another alternative is that the list describes not administrative districts but royal estates. In this view, the officials would have served as custodians of these properties; see Miller and Hayes, *A History of Ancient Israel and Judah*, 2nd ed., 212–13. Regardless of the goods, income, or service provided, or whether provisions came once a year or services were provided throughout a year, the list attests to a system of oversight throughout the land that appears to have supported the crown's interests. Actually, the many proposals are not all exclusive. The officials' responsibilities could have involved a combination of the options presented here: collecting local resources from the district, negotiating between state and local authority, maintaining royal properties, and monitoring passage and exchange through the lands.

146 These systems are examined in more detail in Chapters Six and Seven. Worthy of note here, however, are the many excavations that have fleshed out our understanding of the substantial economic value of the region (e.g., the impact of Tel Reḥov), and the use of the valleys for consolidation of agricultural resources in the early Iron Age (Omer Sergi et al., "Ḥorvat Ṭevet in the Jezreel Valley: A Royal Israelite Estate," in *New Studies in the Archaeology of Northern Israel*, ed. Karen Covello-Paran, Adi Erlich, and Ron Beeri [Jerusalem: Israel Antiquities Authority, 2021], 31*–48*). It is also important to emphasize that these excavations are contributing to a richer picture of local centers of authority, in contrast to the biblical depiction of a singular, centralized state.

147 Some of these tensions have always been apparent through the biblical texts. Other evidence and scholarship, especially from archaeology and through anthropological interpretation, are making clearer how tensions may have persisted and/or shifted despite ethnographic labels, issues that we will return to later in this volume. The more sophisticated our approach to the cultural, ethnic, and political variations in the region, the better we can approximate the complexity of the district official's job.

148 Halpern, *The Constitution of the Monarchy in Israel*, 245–249.
149 We learn of descendants only when the matter of succession is raised in 1 Kings 12. As for Solomon's daughters, the name Taphath ('abundant'?) is otherwise unattested in the Bible; the name Basemath ('spice/perfume') occurs elsewhere only in the case of Esau's wife (Gen 26:34; 36:1–17). These figures receive little attention from scholars other than brief discussion that their marriages must have been political in nature and useful in securing relationships between Jerusalem and the more distant districts; see, for example, Diana V. Edelman, "Taphath," in *Women in Scripture: A Dictionary of Named and Unnamed Women in the Hebrew Bible, the Apocryphal/Deuterocanonical Books, and the New Testament*, ed. Carol Meyers (Grand Rapids: Eerdmans, 2001), 165; Carol Meyers, "Basemath 2," in *Women in Scripture: A Dictionary of Named and Unnamed Women in the Hebrew Bible, the Apocryphal/Deuterocanonical Books, and the New Testament*, ed. Carol Meyers (Grand Rapids: Eerdmans, 2001), 57.
150 Such is the impression given in the account of Wenamun, which leads us to believe that Dor was an independent principate in the 11th to 10th centuries. See Chapters Five and Six for further discussion of the historical and archaeological evidence.
151 Explorations in the mid-20th century under the influence of Karl Polanyi resulted in supporting evidence across cultures and disciplines. Examples include Revere, "'No Man's Coast'"; Rosemary Arnold, "A Port of Trade: Whydah on the Guinea Coast," in *Trade and Market in the Early Empires: Economies in History and Theory*, ed. Karl Polanyi, Conrad M. Arensberg, and Harry W. Pearson (Glencoe: Free Press, 1957), 154–76; Francisco Benet, "Separation of Trade and Market: Great Market of Whydah," in *Trade and Market in the Early Empires: Economies in History and Theory*, ed. Karl Polanyi, Conrad M. Arensberg, and Harry W. Pearson (Glencoe: Free Press, 1957), 177–87; as well as Karl Polanyi, "Ports of Trade in Early Societies," in *Primitive, Archaic, and Modern Economies: Essays of Karl Polanyi*, ed. G. Dalton (Boston: Beacon Press, 1971), 238–60. While Polanyi's theories continue to promote debate, some of the foundations from the earlier studies remain influential; for example, see Joanna Luke, *Ports of Trade, Al Mina and Geometric Greek Pottery in the Levant* (BAR International Series 1100; Oxford: Publishers of the British Archaeological Reports, 2003).
152 1 Kings 5:16–6:38; 7:1–51; 9:10–25; 10:12, 16–20.
153 1 Kings 5:16–32; 7:13–14; 7:45–46; 9:10–28.
154 The DH discusses the *mas* before and after the temple and palace descriptions in 1 Kings 6–7. The narrative's structure in this respect is intentionally symmetrical. The *mas* and the exchanges with Hiram were both necessary for Solomon to undertake his building campaign, and both of them were incorporated into the symmetrical structure. They are introduced in 1 Kings 4–5 and revisited in 1 Kings 9. The repetition should be interpreted as a stylistic choice in the construction of the narrative, as a result of having a variety of views of the same or related events rather than repeated actions or a chronologically accurate depiction of the events.
155 *Mas* policies (Akkadian *massu*) are known from other cultures in the ancient Near East, from the Old Babylonian and Amarna Periods through the Iron Age; see Anson F. Rainey, "Compulsory Labour Gangs in Ancient Israel," *IEJ* 20 (1970): 191–202.
156 The 'remaining peoples' in this verse consist of Amorites, Hittites, Perizzites, Hivites, and Jebusites. The LXX includes Canaanites and Girgashites. In other words, it is the (seven) mighty nations often invoked in Deuteronomistic tradition (see Deut 7:1). The list is not exclusive to the Dtr but is frequent in texts associated with him: Deuteronomy 7:1; 20:17; Joshua 3:10; 12:8; 24:11; and Judges 3:5. Very similar lists also occur in Exodus 3:8, 17; and 23:23. The same list occurs in 2 Chronicles 8:7 in the parallel to 1 Kings 9:20.
157 Geoghegan, "Until This Day," 214–215.
158 The reformed *mas* and comment regarding Solomon's worship does establish a Solomon who acts in accord with Deuteronomic instruction for part of his reign, only to act against it toward the end, thus setting up a literary rise and fall of Solomon as well as supportive evidence for the Deuteronomistic explanation for the division of the monarchy. There is no doubt that these elements are deliberate, but they would lose their explanatory power without the theological foundations that rely on the sanctity of Jerusalem's holiest residence, the temple.
159 Ibid., 214–215.
160 There is significant debate on this matter, and many argue that there is a subtle but strong criticism of Solomon in these verses. See Sweeney, "The Critique of Solomon in the Josianic Edition of the Deuteronomistic History"; David A. Glatt-Gilad, "The Deuteronomistic Critique of Solomon: A Response to Marvin A. Sweeney," *JBL* 116 (1997): 700–703. The view presented here agrees with Glatt-Gilad and is contra Sweeney. Solomon's policies were very likely viewed negatively at some points in history, but the earlier material in 1 Kings 5 does not reveal such criticism. For arguments in favor of critical depictions

at various times, see Jerome T. Walsh, "The Characterization of Solomon in First Kings 1–5," *CBQ* 57 (1995): 471–93; J. Daniel Hays, "Has the Narrator Come to Praise Solomon or to Bury Him? Narrative Subtlety in 1 Kings 1–11," *JSOT* 28, no. 2 (2003): 149–74. Oblath suggests a different type of veiled criticism by arguing that the Exodus story was based on Jeroboam's heroic secession from Solomon and Rehoboam ("Of Pharaohs and Kings"). He argues that the Moses character was based on Jeroboam and the Exodus Pharaoh based on Solomon, with a key parallel being the *mas* and its use to build store cities (ערי [ה]מסכנות; Exod 1:11; 1 Kgs 9:19). If Oblath's theory is correct, the Exodus story is yet another (though possibly not fully independent) source regarding Solomon's *mas*. While intriguing, it is not strong enough to be relied on for a history of Solomon or the 10th century.

161 R. A. Oded, "Taxation in Biblical Israel," *Journal of Religious Ethics* 12, no. 2 (1984): 162–182; esp. 165–167.
162 There is evidence of some editorial activity that relates the *mas* account to 1 Kings 4:1–6 (compare to 1 Kgs 5:28, 30), but it is not obviously Deuteronomistic in character. While there is evidence of Deuteronomistic editing in portions of the correspondence, there is no such evidence in 1 Kings 5:27 where the composition of the *mas* is stated.
163 Included in the parallel list in 2 Chronicles 8:5; see Rainey and Notley, *The Sacred Bridge*, 166.
164 The debates pertaining to this list and its relationship to archaeological sites and strata are dynamic, in no small part because of the chronological debates discussed in Chapter One. There is good reason to be careful with any of the cities in the list. The importance of Jerusalem, for example, would attract later manipulation. It is safest to say that there were likely some Jerusalem constructions at the core of the tradition of Solomon's building campaign (see Chapter Four). The list should also be considered a composite, even in its earliest form as a historical document; see Volkmar Fritz, *1 and 2 Kings* (Continental Commentaries; Minneapolis: Fortress Press), 108–109; Rainey and Notley, *The Sacred Bridge*, 165–168; Schniedewind, "Excavating the Text of 1 Kings 9." See below for the geographic significance of the locations.
165 The Dtr or another historian/redactor would have been responsible for the introductory וזה דבר־המס. There are similar constructions in Deuteronomy 15:2, regarding the Sabbath year and release of debts, and in Deuteronomy 19:4, regarding cities of refuge. The parallels are not necessarily suggestive of Dtr composition; rather, the form indicates that the material was incorporated from a separate (older) source into the history.
166 The correlation (or dismissal of) the list of fortifications to archaeological remains has been a heated topic for decades. The discussion here does not seek to determine if known remains of fortifications can in fact be *the* Solomonic fortifications. Instead, the focus here is on the significance in the reported locations in relation to exchange relations. Most of these places are known. The less certain are the sites of Baalath and Tamar. Baalath has not yet been identified; Fritz proposes either Qatre or el-Muğar, 'probably a fortified outpost against the Philistine cities of the southern coastal plain' (*1 and 2 Kings*, 111). The site of Tamar may be identified with En Haseva, which has a large Iron Age fortification and yielded evidence of Qurayyah Painted Ware (see Chapter Six; Rudolf Cohen and Yigal Yisrael, "The Excavations of ʿEin Hazeva, Israelite and Roman Tamar," *Qadmoniot* 112 [1996]: 78–92).
167 Halpern, *David's Secret Demons*, 406.
168 See Chapter Four for further discussion.

4 The Special Case of Jerusalem – A Discussion

Despite the prominence of the city in the biblical narratives, I have intentionally set aside the topic of Jerusalem in the previous discussions. While the development of the royal city is critical to the biblical depiction of interactions, historical and archaeological investigation of early Iron Age Jerusalem has been fraught with difficulty.[1] Limitations to research have existed since archaeologists began investigating the city in the 19th century. Today, the city is densely inhabited, and the most ancient areas of the city center are among the most contested. Current research suggests that the core of early Iron Age Jerusalem was situated along the ridge between the Tyropoeon and Kidron Valleys, where residents had access to a reliable spring, the Gihon.[2] The location was in continuous use throughout the Iron Age, limiting what archaeologists can know, since buildings and walls were frequently reused until the Neo-Babylonian destruction in 586 BCE. Later building activity in the Roman era further impacted any Iron Age remains, by clearing construction areas to bedrock. In addition to challenges to physical examination, the 'minimalist' critique that cast doubt on the existence or extent of Davidic or Solomonic kingdoms focused on the limited amount of early Iron Age remains recovered from the city. Reconstructions of the ancient city from this perspective propose that the absence of evidence is evidence of an invented history, concluding that a capital in Jerusalem did not exist until the 8th or 7th centuries BCE (at the earliest); it was merely a town with local significance.[3] Recent excavations and new arguments force additional reevaluation of the nature of early Iron Age Jerusalem. (Also see note 1.) Because of this complicated history of investigation, it is best to address the 'problem with Jerusalem' in one discussion, here, following the examination of the biblical material (Chapters Two and Three) and before venturing into the extrabiblical evidence (Chapters Five and Six).[4] This chapter will briefly introduce the current evidence regarding Jerusalem and situate the most relevant evidence into the context of an analysis of interactions.

Jerusalem and Interactions

Jerusalem is at the crux of the biblical claims for a sophisticated polity that engaged in interregional interactions and exchange. According to the biblical narratives, a Jebusite town or stronghold preexisted an Israelite monarchy. Although the location did not play an obvious role in the narrative describing Saul's activities, David's forceful acquisition of the site begs the question of its regional importance, at least in the narrative's worldview

(2 Sam 5:6–9). Solomon's history credits him with the construction of the city's administrative infrastructure, a royal complex, and of course the first temple to YHWH. The biblical history also claims that Egypt's king Shishaq (Shoshenq I of the 22nd Dynasty) marched to Jerusalem and pillaged the palace and temple early in Rehoboam's reign (1 Kgs 14:25–26). Although the historical reliability of this claim is not corroborated by Shoshenq's victory monument in Egypt, the biblical account of Jerusalem as a target for the Egyptian king is, in itself, a claim by the biblical sources for Jerusalem's importance as a contender in interregional affairs.[5]

Looking outside of these biblical claims, there is little doubt that Jerusalem long held regional importance. The hilltop site with an adjacent source of water from the Gihon spring would have attracted regular use from pastoralists, agriculturalists, and travelers. The rich history of burials dating at least as far back as the Intermediate Bronze Age also suggests a lengthy tradition of a sacred nature at the location.[6] In the Middle Bronze Age, activity in the area intensified, and occupants constructed large-scale water and defense systems related to the spring.[7] These structures were so substantial that they influenced later settlement and were reused and adapted well into the Iron Age. Jerusalem's position, situated where important east-west passages cross the main north-south route through the hill country, further point to the strategic role the site played. D. Dorsey explains that Jerusalem sat at 'the northern end of the bottleneck' on the Ridge Road, 'at the point where this highway reached the end of the confining ridge from Bethlehem and arrived at the southern end of the broad, fertile plateau of Benjamin, from which important roads fanned out in various directions to the east, north, and west.'[8] The site's strategic location and resources are sufficient to demonstrate why people were attracted to the location, but the more debated issue is how much that place mattered in its immediate environs, as well as in the greater dynamics of southern Levantine and ancient Near Eastern affairs.

Both before and after the period of focus in this chapter, we have strong, even if not abundant, historical and epigraphic evidence of Jerusalem's participation in long-distance interactions across many centuries. To set the scene briefly, the earliest mention of Jerusalem comes from Egyptian execration texts of the Middle Kingdom (12th and 13th Dynasties).[9] As we examine below, the Amarna letters provide an important source for the Late Bronze Age. We also have clear evidence from the succession of empires in the 1st millennium BCE that control of Jerusalem was highly strategic. The early Iron Age poses a challenge, however, in that there is a significant lack of written evidence regarding Jerusalem. Given the profound decline in scribal activity in the Mediterranean and ancient Near East following the LBA collapse (see Chapter Five), we should not be surprised by the absence, yet expectations informed by the long-term trends just noted, and by the biblical accounts, intensify scholarly scrutiny of Jerusalem's importance in this critical period.

Late Bronze Age

In the Late Bronze Age, Egypt succeeded in dominating much of the southern Levant. Following military campaigns, Egypt initially ruled through vassal kings and touring administrators during the 18th Dynasty. In the Ramesside dynasties, Egypt more fully embraced an imperial model. Much of these efforts are well-documented in historical and material evidence throughout the southern Levant, but physical and epigraphic remains in Jerusalem are especially modest. The classic illustration for understanding the difficulty inherent in reconstructing Late Bronze Age Jerusalem comes from Egypt's Amarna letters, which date to the mid-14th century and the reigns of Amenhotep III and his son Akhenaten. By this time, Egypt had firmly established its dominance of the southern Levant and had considerable control over the political makeup and economic activities of the region – that is, from the Egyptian point of view. Correspondence from the local leaders, however, suggests there was significant strife. Among the Amarna letters are six from Jerusalem's ruler, ʿAbdi-Ḫeba (EA 285–290).[10] His communications focus on two issues: 1) defense of his loyalty to Egypt against accusations by contemporary Levantine rulers; and 2) requests for support in securing lands related to Jerusalem's political and economic position in the region.[11] What becomes clear from these letters is that there was competition between the rulers of locations like Jerusalem, and that these rulers portrayed themselves as men of means who controlled troops and had access to luxury goods and expendable staff. In short, they fit the bill for ancient Near Eastern rulers. This portrayal contributes to the expectation that we should find the trappings of a Late Bronze Age 'kingdom' of Jerusalem, but archaeological investigations have produced quite the opposite.

Despite being the focus of constant archaeological inquiry since the 19th century, no compelling evidence of a LBA urban polity has been found – that is, assuming such an entity would have had monumental structures such as fortifications, palaces, temples, etc. In fact, over the course of more than 100 years, various excavations of the presumed city center, the area south of the Old City walls, have yielded very little evidence of LBA settlement.[12] Even if we assume that Jerusalem's leadership made use of the substantial Middle Bronze Age features as part of the LBA landscape, the scanty remains strike us as being at odds with the presentation from the Amarna letters.[13] A common explanation for this disconnect is that intensive habitations, renovations, and destructions that the city has seen eradicated the LBA remains. A. De Groot argues that builders routinely cleared previous constructions to bedrock because the steep eastern slope of the City of David made rebuilding atop ruins too risky. Thus, the LBA remains are simply gone and unrecoverable.[14] Situating Jerusalem in the broader context of the period is also helpful for interpretation. K. Prag, who has published K. Kenyon's excavation results, situates the sharp dip in archaeological contexts that yielded LBA pottery, compared to Middle Bronze and Iron Age contexts, in a demographic decline evident in the Late Bronze Age southern Levant generally.[15]

The discrepancy in remains versus expectations based on textual evidence has led to a reevaluation of the period. Rather than presume that Amarna-era Jerusalem must have been a substantial city with a royal center, a 'kingdom' in conventional understanding, scholars suggest that we understand it as only a small, minimally staffed Egyptian garrison, or as the domain of a locally prominent ruling family that drew on the resources from its surrounding territory.[16] It has even been suggested, although without lasting impact, that the Urusalim of the Amarna letters should not be identified with the Jerusalem of the Judean hills but some other Levantine site.[17] This claim can no longer be entertained now that analysis has confirmed that the majority of ʿAbdi-Ḫeba's tablets were made from Jerusalem clay, but it accentuates the problem: scholarly expectations, based on interpretation of the Amarna-era rulers' presentations, do not correspond to what we are seeing in the archaeological remains of the 14th century.[18]

Our understanding of Jerusalem's affairs after ʿAbdi-Ḫeba's tenure and the Amarna period is even more limited. We are lacking written records from Jerusalem, and no

Egyptian records refer directly to the city, its leadership, or its occupants. There are, however, a number of artifacts that suggest some kind of relationship to Egypt (or Egyptian culture) in the period of the 19th and 20th Dynasties, but many details about them are uncertain. Some of the artifacts are known only from the records of early excavations, some are held in museums, some in storage areas, and others remain a part of the Jerusalem landscape.[19] Combined, the studies have identified two alabaster vessels, an alabaster lid, a stele fragment, two offering tables(?), palm-style capitals, as well as figurine and statue/tte fragments.[20] Other Egyptian or Egyptianizing finds, such as 'balustrade' fragments, have been recorded from tombs in the Jerusalem area.[21] These remains appear to date to the Ramesside dynasties, but the objects themselves do not convey how or why Egyptian and Egyptian-style goods came to be in Jerusalem during this period. D. Bahat and G. Barkay each propose that there was an Egyptian temple on the northern edge of the settlement on the road to Shechem.[22] P. van der Veen reconstructs a more elaborate Egyptian influence, invoking C. Higginbotham's arguments that Egyptian kings of the 19th Dynasty continued to use vassal rulers, much like their 18th Dynasty predecessors, and that these local rulers emulated their Egyptian suzerains.[23]

Higginbotham's arguments are based on more extensive evidence than Jerusalem can provide; instead, her work is based on a survey of Egyptian and Egyptianizing material culture across the southern Levant and is notably not inclusive of this Jerusalem evidence. Nevertheless, the Jerusalem finds do attest to Egyptian-inspired architecture and cultural influences in Jerusalem toward the end of the Late Bronze Age, and currently, Higginbotham's explanation of elite emulation appears to be the best fit for the evidence. In her analysis, she finds little support for the proposal that Ramesside pharaohs adopted a 'direct rule' approach, meaning that it was rare for Egyptians to live in southern Levant cities and settlements (with some notable exceptions, such as at Beth-Shean). In other words, the presence of Egyptian-looking goods does not mean that Egyptians were responsible for their transport, acquisition, use, and deposition. Instead, the Egyptian state ruled through its vassals, along with the support of circuit officials and mobile garrisons. The vassal rulers signaled their relationship to Egyptian power through cultural emulation.

Although we don't know from epigraphic sources who lived in and governed Jerusalem outside of the narrow depiction in the Amarna correspondence, burial contexts support the case for a stable, centuries-long tradition of a sedentary population (even if it was not an intensively urban one).[24] Notably, the finds from the tombs include a high percentage of imported goods (mainly from Cyprus) and Egyptian-influenced elements indicating that 'there was certainly one level of society which was prosperous and could afford to bury imported goods with the dead.'[25] We have a good idea from written records about one such person, who must have been counted among the prosperous in the 14th century, ʿAbdi-Ḫeba. In addition to his privileged position in respect to the Egyptian state, we know that he employed a highly accomplished scribe and was able to afford gifts and tribute for his suzerain.[26] The elite nature of the burial evidence, however, challenges us not to limit our understanding of LBA Jerusalem elite to ʿAbdi-Ḫeba's career. The imported goods and assorted Egyptian-influenced material culture that have survived to present day attest to a succession of prominent elite and special relations with Egypt well into the Ramesside era. Taken with the Amarna-era evidence, we have a case for both a lengthy history of interactions and a long-standing elite cultural tradition for those who held sway in the region.

11th–10th Century Jerusalem in Biblical Narratives

Before addressing the evidence of the early Iron Age, it is important to note that expectations (both ancient and modern) of what Jerusalem was like in the 11th and 10th centuries (namely the understanding of it as an already important capital city) has played a significant role in the debates regarding the nature of Jerusalem and its role in the region. Indeed, this issue is already evident in the scholarly debates, discussed above, regarding the LBA. It is perhaps even more important to emphasize that contexts matter in our interpretations. D. Pioske's research points to the impact of comparative contexts. Examined in light of contemporary state centers such as Tanis or Assur, Jerusalem was an exceptionally small settlement.[27] Compared to other early 10th century southern Levantine sites, however, Jerusalem was in line with its contemporaries, sites of prominence in their respective spheres of influence, such as Khirbet Qeiyafa, Beth-Shemesh, Tel Reḥov, and Tell el-Farʿah (N).[28] Additionally, the challenges scholars face when researching early Iron Age Jerusalem is strikingly similar to the difficulties related to the study of other Levantine cities that became regional capitals, and whose significance stretches into modern times – sites such as Tyre or Damascus.[29]

Compounding an already complicated tension between biblical sources, archaeological sources, and scholarly expectations/debates is the fact that the DH is not internally consistent about the nature of Jerusalem prior to David's acquisition of the city and Solomon's building campaign. The general impression from both archaeology and the biblical depiction of the region around Jerusalem is that we should understand the location as part of an agrarian community, much like its contemporary hill-country towns.[30] Biblical discussion of the Jebusite settlement itself, however, is succinct, with the 'the stronghold of Zion' (מצדת ציון) in 2 Samuel 5:7 as the only descriptive clue offered by the narrator.[31] Also noticeably absent is any information on Jebusite leadership at the time of David's attack.[32] In fact, for all of the importance that Jerusalem will come to have in the biblical discussion after 2 Samuel 5, it is conspicuously absent earlier in the DH, with the exception of geographic notes aimed at the narrative's audience and Joshua's legendary battle with the five 'kings of the Amorites,' one of whom is identified as Adoni-zedek, 'king of Jerusalem' (מלך ירושלם; Josh 10:1–27).[33] Though potentially notable for the notion of a history and/or memory of kingship in the region, the story says nothing about the nature of Jerusalem itself. Overall, the DH appears to guard aspects of the history in respect to Jerusalem's character, its position in the region, its elite institutions, and the transition to David's control.

Analysis of the actions recounted in David's history, however, reveals that there were a number of strategic advantages to the acquisition of Jerusalem and relocation from Hebron.[34] Conventionally, David's selection of Jerusalem has been explained as a clever move to create a neutral capital for the Israelite tribes.[35] It is more likely, however, that David's selection of the hilltop stronghold served his interests in expanding his reputation, territory, and economic gains. To begin with, Jerusalem's past as a regional center of power would not likely have been lost on the 11th and 10th century inhabitants in the region. Pioske argues convincingly that assuming control of Jerusalem would have aligned David with a history of kingship and authority associated with that place.[36]

Moving from Hebron to Jerusalem ensured that David could monitor the activities of his main rivals. Although we have no information about Jerusalem's prior leadership, the biblical text provides details about David's treatment of Saul's house. Saulide descendants and loyalists were established only about five miles to the north of Jerusalem. This proximity was critical. The territory was not easily subdued, according to the biblical history. Even after David and his supporters defeated Ishbaal and his men for control of Saulide Gibeon (2 Sam 2–4), David maintained a close watch on Saul's descendants (2 Sam 9) and was subjected to challenges by Saulide loyalists (2 Sam 16).[37] Headquarters in Jerusalem would have provided David with tight controls over his newly acquired territory and the routes through Benjamin that Saul and Jonathan reportedly secured.

When we look at the region's interactions more broadly, taking into consideration the events involving Philistia, Saul, and David, as well as potential connections across longer distances (e.g., involving Transjordan), we have even stronger indications that Jerusalem sat in a prime location for exchange. The biblical text in Samuel, however, is silent on the site's role as an interaction partner with any of its neighbors. There are various ways to interpret the silence, including the accidents of the historical process, but the interaction patterns suggest that either Jerusalem remained isolated from the region's interactions, which is highly unlikely, or that it was an important part of the region's exchange networks.

For David's interests, the Jebusite stronghold was better located than Hebron to monitor exchange through the central hill country and the south, which included long-distance traffic passing through the region.[38] Building on my discussion in Chapter Two, the Philistines would also have had reasons to involve themselves in the fate of Jerusalem. The outposts at the Michmash Pass and Bethlehem may indicate that the Philistines had been attempting to bypass Jerusalem in their exchange activities. Perhaps the Jebusite stronghold dominated its environs enough to make Philistine installations outside of its reach worthwhile, even if it meant costly battles with Saul and David to either side. An alliance between David and Achish that included cooperation along the region's highways could easily have led to a joint effort to take Jerusalem. It is not difficult to reconstruct a plausible historical scenario for the alliance, or to correlate it to the biblical version of how events played out. As I discuss in Chapter Two, Saul and the Jebusites were antagonistic to Philistine traffic moving between the Jordan Valley and the Mediterranean coast. An effort to control the hill country and its critical Ridge Road had to contend with both parties. David would create problems for Saul in the south; the Philistines in their own alliance would draw Saul into battle in the west and eventually north. The overextended Saul would easily be beaten. In exchange for this coordinated effort, David could have agreed to leave the Jezreel Valley to the Philistines (or whoever Saul's opponent was). The Philistines may have assisted David's defeat of Saul's successor Ishbaal and Jerusalem in exchange for a cooperative partner in the hill country.[39] In light of these complex interactions, the importance of Jerusalem was in its relation to a tradition of power, its relation to contemporary regional powers (i.e., Gath, Gibeah, and Hebron), and the exchange networks that moved through or near the hill country (i.e., the Ridge Road and its crossroads).

As we move to David's successor, we see a very different image of Jerusalem. The DH claims that Solomon not only put Jerusalem at the center of his economic programs, but also increased fortifications and royal complexes, transforming the town into a world center for economic and cultural activity. The Solomon Narrative details efforts to connect Jerusalem to longer-distance interactions both within the southern Levant and beyond it. The key to doing so would have been in making sure that Jerusalem was not isolated from other regions. As I argue in Chapter Three, integrating Jerusalem into exchange networks could have been achieved through diplomatic efforts, which the DH reports regarding Egypt, Phoenicia, and the northernmost administrative districts that were most at risk of allying with neighboring states. The DH account that Solomon constructed shrines in the vicinity of Jerusalem dedicated to foreign deities (1 Kgs 11:7–8) should be considered in relation to interaction strategies. Although it cannot be verified, if the account was derived from knowledge of shrines in the vicinity of Jerusalem, such worship places may have provided travelers, traders, and envoys the opportunity to perform rituals for protection during their journeys.[40] Solomon's administrative districts may have imposed structure on regional exchange networks and laid claim to routes and goods to which each district had access. With a decree that provisions be sent to Jerusalem, Solomon's city would have been formally connected to these exchange activities. Finally, fortification projects in Jerusalem and other key locations in Solomon's territory would have provided a physical infrastructure for a Jerusalem network, as well as propaganda to enforce the idea that Solomon's kingdom was well connected in 'global' affairs.

The biblical depiction of the city itself, especially its royal and religious precincts, gives the impression that Jerusalem was influenced by consequences of participation in interregional interactions. The Egyptian and Syro-Phoenician styles that have been most intensely examined in relation to Solomon's temple may expose the artistic influences of Jerusalem's location and interactions (directly or indirectly) in the broader region.[41] Descriptions of key characteristics of the royal quarters, in particular, appear to align closely with references to Solomon's Egyptian wife, implying the princess may have provided a route through which Egyptian influence came to be evident in the city's landscape.[42] This literary arrangement gives the distinct impression of cultural and artistic influence and may also imply political involvement (in the same vein as the reference to the Pharaoh's conquest and transfer of Gezer in 1 Kgs 9:16). Given that a historical marriage cannot be established, it is possible that the report was an interpretive tradition to account for a building or architectural style with undeniably Egyptian character.[43] Bearing in mind the extensive cultural influence that resulted from the New Kingdom's control of the Levant, reviewed above, it is possible that later residents of Jerusalem explained the city's Egyptian features through a proposed (i.e., invented) diplomatic marriage.

Other features in the biblical narrative that have received scholarly attention for proposed cultural parallels include palace and temple accoutrements, such as Solomon's ivory and gold throne (1 Kgs 10:18–20) and other furnishings, vessels, and shields. The descriptions of these items resemble 'international' artistic styles once preferred by elites across the eastern Mediterranean and ancient Near East, known to us through artifacts, reliefs, and non-biblical written sources from throughout the Iron Age.[44] Similarly, Solomon's intellectual pursuits (1 Kgs 5:10–13; 10:23–25) fit with depictions of ancient Near Eastern kings who used learning to convey mastery of the world.[45] While researchers have made suggestive cases for the appropriateness of such features for 10th century rulers, it is critically important to emphasize that elite styles persisted over many centuries.

The exercise of seeking cross-cultural comparisons reveals a broader, 'international' context that informed expectations for the appearance and activities of royalty and their environments. Relevant examples can be found from LBA as well as 9th century and later Iron Age evidence.[46] The resulting conclusions must be that, while we can argue that the character of Solomonic Jerusalem that is put forward by the DH is not entirely inappropriate for Solomon's day, it is not exclusive to the 10th century BCE. The most logical explanation for the overall biblical depiction is that the later writers of the 8th through 6th centuries BCE enhanced the king's and the city's depiction. At the same time, it appears likely that the motivation for later authors to augment the international character of

Solomon, as well as Solomonic Jerusalem and his kingdom, may have derived from traditions and memories of an earlier ruler (or various rulers) who connected a growing polity to rapidly increasing long-distance exchange networks that, based on the material surveyed in the next two chapters, included communities from east and west of the Jordan River, Egypt, Philistia, Syria, Phoenicia, and into the Mediterranean.

Archaeological Remains and Debates

Despite what *appears* to be a significant history of interactions based in Jerusalem, as we noted above, archaeological remains have generally been considered supportive of only a modest agrarian settlement during the early Iron Age, which some scholars have considered too small to be reconciled with the biblical history.[47] The failure to reveal the expected evidence of an urban, administrative center that could be identified with Jebusite, Davidic, or Solomonic Jerusalem, after more than a century of excavations, has played an important role in discussions of ancient Israel's history for some time.[48] Prior to more recent discoveries in the Ophel and City of David excavations, the Iron I–IIA evidence from ancient Jerusalem consisted of the 'Stepped Stone Structure' (SSS) and supporting 'terraces' below it, some wall fragments, small amounts of pottery, a proto-Aeolic capital, a bronze fist fragment from a figurine, and a cult stand fragment.[49] In response, most scholars tended toward one of two interpretive options. Either early Iron Age Jerusalem was not the urban center or administrative capital that the Bible describes, but instead merely a 'cow town'; or it had been a significant city, but its remains are not accessible to us because they were destroyed centuries ago through conquest and rebuilding, or lie below sacred and contested locations that cannot be investigated.[50]

E. Mazar committed to yet another position, which is that excavation possibilities have not yet been exhausted, and, in 1997, she asserted that her future excavations would not only discover more Iron I and IIA remains but spectacularly 'King David's Palace.'[51] Mazar's project did indeed contribute new early Iron Age evidence to the discussion. Although her historical reconstructions of 'David's Palace' and 'Solomonic' fortifications have not persuaded many, her excavations dramatically changed the picture of early Iron Age Jerusalem. Most notable is the 'Large Stone Structure' and additional excavation of Iron IIA towers/fortifications in the Ophel. Her excavations yielded additional pottery from the Late Bronze Age through Iron IIA periods, including assemblages recovered from surfaces, 'collared-rim' storage jars, evidence of metalworking, the top portion of a Sekhmet figurine, a Cypriot Black-on-Red (BoR) imported jug, and ivory handle inlays; and, from the Ophel excavations, an Iron IIA black juglet and an inscribed potsherd.[52]

Despite this impressive summary of finds, there remains significant debate about what it all means. E. Mazar repeatedly maintained her historical attributions, first and foremost. She selected her excavation area with the explicit intention of finding David's palace, based in no small part on her reading of the biblical text.[53] With her theory seemingly validated by such impressive remains, her reliance on the biblical narrative appeared, for her, justified. Such confidence allowed her to conclude further that the Large Stone Structure was constructed by Phoenicians for David, as described in 2 Samuel 5:11, even without physical evidence to corroborate the theory. Needless to say, this line of reasoning has not satisfied many archaeologists or historians. While Mazar's initial claims of a 'palace' were met with much skepticism, subsequent excavation and publication of the project have convinced more scholars of other important notions, namely that the large structure was, in fact, built in the early Iron Age and functioned in an administrative or royal capacity.[54]

Critical to interpretation are the relationships among the monumental constructions. Mazar emphasized a relationship between the Large Stone Structure and the Stepped Stone Structure, which she argues were integrated during their construction, so that the latter supports the former.[55] This finding is gaining ground and provides a purpose for the Stepped Stone Structure. The more controversial part of Mazar's claims, however, are the chronological relationships. Before Mazar's excavation of the Large Stone Structure, M. Steiner (based on K. Kenyon's excavations) and J. Cahill (based on Y. Shiloh's excavations) each dated the pottery associated with the SSS to the Iron I.[56] Mazar's excavations have provided evidence that no pottery later than Iron I lies beneath the foundations and floors of the Large Stone Structure. From these findings, several scholars have suggested that the two structures likely predate an Israelite (or Davidic) phase of the settlement.[57] To maintain the Davidic attribution, however, Mazar argues that the Large Stone Structure was built in the transition period between the late Iron I and the early Iron IIA, thus situating the construction in the mid-10th century.[58] Despite her convictions, the monumental constructions are better understood as Iron I fortifications, which probably had a royal/administrative function that continued in use through the Iron IIA.[59]

Mazar also excavated in the Ophel, just south of the Temple Mount. Like the City of David, this area has been investigated a number of times since the 19th century (by C. Warren, K. Kenyon, B. Mazar, and E. Mazar with B. Mazar). In 1989, E. Mazar published her earlier findings (from excavations in the 1980s) along with the findings of B. Mazar's excavations in the 1960s and 1970s, arguing that the complex was a royal gateway constructed in the 9th century.[60] Since her earlier publications, she later revised her chronological determinations for the structures to the late 10th century and dated additional structures more recently uncovered to the early Iron IIA.[61] Her shift in dating corresponds to a revised historical interpretation that this area was part of Solomon's fortification project described in 1 Kings 9:15.

Similar to the issues with Mazar's arguments regarding David's palace, attributing these structures to Solomon cannot be done with certainty, in part because we lack epigraphic evidence, but more importantly because the chronological ranges related to the associated finds are not narrow enough to exclude, in this case, the 9th century. The most suggestive evidence for an earlier date, however, is the ceramic assemblage from the 'Large Tower' and nearby fills that has strong parallels to Khirbet Qeiyafa.[62] This fortified site, located ca. 30 km southwest of Jerusalem, was founded in the 11th century and destroyed near the beginning of the 10th century.[63] Thus, Mazar's Ophel excavations have produced ceramic evidence that may be situated in the late Iron I, along with pottery that has a range of use from the 10th through the 9th centuries. Her Ophel excavations cannot be limited to the 10th century, but there may be evidence of activity early in that century.

The overly ambitious historical claims notwithstanding, Mazar's excavations in the Ophel have succeeded in bringing to light additional evidence of potential administrative operations in the late Iron I and early Iron IIA periods and some indications of Jerusalem's place in interregional interactions. Finds include numerous storage jars, collared-rim pithoi, two Sekhmet figurine fragments, an Akkadian cuneiform tablet fragment (Amarna period?), an inscribed potsherd, bullae, stamped jar handles, figurine fragments, and an ivory inlay of a goat.[64] Of these, only a few – the collared-rim pithoi, the inscribed pithos fragment, a scarab (and possibly the black juglet) – can be linked to the Iron I–early Iron

IIA periods.[65] From these few finds, we could tentatively conclude that there was some type of storage operation in the area, interregional interaction related to Egypt resulting in the acquisition of a scarab, and a level of status or wealth that allowed for a scribe and possibly luxuries such as perfumed oil that may have been stored in the black juglet.

Iron I–IIA Interactions Involving Jerusalem

Although historical, biblical, and archaeological evidence do not correspond closely enough for an uncomplicated case, there are strong indications that Jerusalem was active in interregional relations and served as a regional center in the Iron I and early Iron IIA periods. Given the evidence of interactions and elite culture from the Amarna Period on, it is likely that a history of interregional relations assisted in keeping Jerusalem connected even when long-distance exchange lessened during the period between the decline of the Ramessides and the rise of Shoshenq I. Connections to other regions are more difficult to support based on Jerusalem-related evidence alone, but the BoR juglet and ivory inlays, both discovered in the early Iron IIA expansion to the Large Stone Structure, suggest that Jerusalem was integrated in exchange networks that carried luxury goods inland from the Phoenician coast. In addition, collared-rim storage jars and an incised pithos rim from the Ophel speak to the collection of goods and wealth, and the employment of scribes, in this early period.[66] Lastly, even without a definitive label or more precise knowledge of its origins, the monumental architecture indicates that an elite leadership had the resources to command the construction of these buildings. The impressive scale undoubtedly had a defensive function, but one cannot help but also imagine the psychological effect they would have had.[67] We must wonder, was this great effort extended to impress the local hill-country inhabitants, or was there a different audience in mind? I imagine that these massive structures were intended to have an impact both on locals and on visitors from farther afield.

Moving from the archaeological picture back to the historical and biblical accounts makes some of the biblical claims about the 10th century monarchs less surprising. The idea that a relatively local contender such as the biblical David would have had an interest in taking Jerusalem seems to be more logical if the site was already well equipped for his new headquarters and well integrated into interaction networks in the southern Levant. Solomon's 'upgrade' in his administrative systems and fortifications (whether or not they are to be identified with E. Mazar's Ophel structures) is also easier to imagine with the understanding that a large-scale infrastructure and long-distance exchange networks involving Jerusalem were already in place. In addition, the Egyptian character attributed to Solomon's projects in the DH is quite in line with the smattering of Egyptian cultural remains that have been identified from the limited evidence of the LBA through Iron IIA periods. While the biblical and material records do not closely correspond, it is much more difficult to maintain that Jerusalem was an isolated, regionally insignificant settlement in the early Iron Age than it was a decade or two ago. Instead, the site appears to have been a regional competitor, along with locations such as Tell eṣ-Ṣafi/Gath, Beth Shemesh, Khirbet Qeiyafa, and Gezer, and the more distant contemporaries Khirbat en-Nahas, Tel Reḥov, Megiddo, and Tyre.

Notes

1. For recent summaries of the history of excavation and work most relevant to the Iron I–IIA (although with differing views of those periods), see Hillel Geva, "Archaeological Research in Jerusalem from 1998 to 2018: Findings and Evaluations," in *Ancient Jerusalem Revealed: Archaeological Discoveries, 1998-2018*, ed. Hillel Geva (Jerusalem: Israel Exploration Society, 2019), 1–31; Kay Prag, *Re-Excavating Jerusalem: Archival Archaeology* (Oxford: Oxford University Press, 2018); Alon De Groot, "Discussion and Conclusions," in *Excavations at the City of David 1978-1985 Directed by Yigal Shiloh, Volume VIIA: Area E: Stratigraphy and Architecture: Text*, ed. Alon De Groot and Hannah Bernick-Greenberg (Qedem 53; Jerusalem: Institute of Archaeology, Hebrew University of Jerusalem, 2012), 141–86; Henk J. Franken, "A History of Excavation in Jerusalem," in *Jerusalem before Islam*, ed. Zeidan Abdel-Kafi Kafafi and Robert Schick (BAR International Series 1699; Oxford: Archaeopress, 2007), 45–53; Larry G. Herr, "Jerusalem in the Iron Age," in *Jerusalem before Islam*, ed. Zeidan Abdel-Kafi Kafafi and Robert Schick (BAR International Series 1699; Oxford: Archaeopress, 2007), 74–85. For E. Mazar's published results, see below. Following the completion of this manuscript, new radiocarbon evidence for Jerusalem's Iron Age was published, which includes samples dating to the early Iron Age (Johanna Regev et al., "Radiocarbon Chronology of Iron Age Jerusalem Reveals Calibration Offsets and Architectural Developments," *PNAS* 121, no. 19 [May 7, 2024]: e2321024121, https://doi.org/10.1073/pnas.2321024121).
2. This is the majority view of early Iron Age Jerusalem's location. For an alternative, see Israel Finkelstein, Ido Koch, and Oded Lipschits, "The Mound on the Mount: A Possible Solution to the 'Problem with Jerusalem,'" *Journal of Hebrew Scriptures* 11 (2011).
3. E.g., Jamieson-Drake, *Scribes and Schools*; Thomas L. Thompson, *Early History of the Israelite People: From the Written and Archaeological Sources* (Leiden; New York: Brill, 1992). Jamieson-Drake's book became the foundation for many subsequent arguments in the same vein.
4. Finkelstein, Koch, and Lipschits, "The Mound on the Mount."
5. There continues to be debate over the reading of Shoshenq's toponyms, as well as the expectation for corroboration from Egyptian sources for this event in Jerusalem's history. See Chapters Three and Six for further discussion.
6. Kay Prag, "Jerusalem in the Third and Second Millennia BC: The Archaeological Evidence," in *Jerusalem before Islam*, ed. Zeidan Abdel-Kafi Kafafi and Robert Schick (BAR International Series 1699; Oxford: Archaeopress, 2007), 54–68.
7. Ronny Reich and Eli Shukron, *Excavations in the City of David, Jerusalem (1995-2010)* (University Park: Penn State University Press, 2021); idem, "The Middle Bronze Age II Water System in Jerusalem," in *Jérusalem Antique et Médiévale. Mélanges En l'honneur d'Ernest-Marie Laperrousaz*, ed. C Arnould-Béhar and André Lemaire (Paris: Peeters, 2011), 17–29; idem, "A New Segment of the Middle Bronze Fortification in the City of David," *TA* 37 (2010): 141–53; Prag, *Re-Excavating Jerusalem*; Johanna Regev et al., "Middle Bronze Age Jerusalem: Recalculating Its Character and Chronology," *Radiocarbon* 63, no. 3 (2021): 853–83.
8. Dorsey, *Roads and Highways*, 124.
9. Katharina Streit, "A Maximalist Interpretation of the Execration Texts – Archaeological and Historical Implications of a High Chronology," *Journal of Ancient Egyptian Interconnections* 13 (2017): 59–69. Interactions are also attested through the discovery of a scarab impression (Shirly Ben-Dor Evian et al., "An Egyptian Private-Name Scarab Impression on a Clay Sealing from the City of David," *Journal of Ancient Egyptian Interconnections* 24 [2019]: 1–15).
10. An additional letter EA 291 is included in this collection, but it is too fragmentary to contribute additional historical details (Anson F. Rainey, *The El-Amarna Correspondence: A New Edition of the Cuneiform Letters from the Site of El-Amarna Based on Collations of All Extant Tablets*, ed. William M. Schniedewind [Leiden; Boston: Brill, 2014], 1597).
11. Rainey, *The El-Amarna Correspondence*.
12. The most extensive and systematic excavations occurred under the direction of Kenyon, Shiloh, B. Mazar, and E. Mazar.
13. Here too there is a conspicuous absence of LBA and early Iron Age ceramic evidence, although there is evidence that later Iron Age residents made use of the Middle Bronze Age water system (Reich and Shukron, "The Middle Bronze Age II Water System in Jerusalem").
14. De Groot, "Discussion and Conclusions," 141.
15. Prag, *Re-Excavating Jerusalem*, 21–25, see especially Table 3.1.

16 For example, Margreet L. Steiner, "Jerusalem in the Late Bronze and Iron Ages. Archaeological Versus Literary Sources?," in *Jerusalem before Islam*, ed. Zeidan Abdel-Kafi Kafafi and Robert Schick (BAR International Series 1699; Oxford: Archaeopress, 2007), 69–74; Israel Finkelstein, "The Rise of Jerusalem and Judah: The Missing Link," *Levant* 33 (2001): 105–15.

17 Although Steiner later abandoned this claim, see H. J. Franken and Margreet L. Steiner, "Urusalim and Jebus," *ZAW* 104 (1992), 110–11]; Margreet L. Steiner, "Re-Dating the Terraces of Jerusalem," *IEJ* 44, no. 1 (1994): 13–20.

18 Yuval Goren et al., *Inscribed in Clay: Provenance Study of the Amarna Tablets and Other Ancient Near Eastern Texts* (Tel Aviv: Emery and Claire Yass Publ. in Archaeology of the Institute of Archaeology, 2004). The more recent find of a cuneiform tablet from the Ophel was also made in Jerusalem (Eilat Mazar et al., "A Cuneiform Tablet from the Ophel in Jerusalem," *IEJ* 60, no. 1 [2010]: 4–21).

19 Gabriel Barkay, "A Late Bronze Age Egyptian Temple in Jerusalem?," *IEJ* 46, no. 1 (1996): 23–43; idem, "What's an Egyptian Temple Doing in Jerusalem?," *BAR* 26, no. 3 (2000): 48–57, 67); Peter van der Veen, "When Pharaohs Ruled Jerusalem," *BAR* 39, no. 2 (2013): 42–48, 67. See also Simone Burger Robin, "Analysis, Interpretation and Dating of a Problematic Egyptian Statuary Fragment Discovered in Jerusalem," in *Solomon and Shishak: Current Perspectives from Archaeology, Epigraphy, History and Chronology: Proceedings of the Third BICANE Colloquium Held at Sidney Sussex College, Cambridge 26-27 March, 2011*, ed. Peter James and Peter van der Veen (BAR International Series, 2732; Oxford: Archaeopress, 2015), 258–63.

20 Barkay, "A Late Bronze Age Egyptian Temple in Jerusalem?"; van der Veen, "When Pharaohs Ruled Jerusalem". Barkay notes a report of a large scarab that is held at the Catholic school at St. Paul's hospice; he argues it should be considered contemporary to the finds in his article ("A Late Bronze Age Egyptian Temple in Jerusalem?," 43, note 43). Kitchen questions the 'Egyptian' characterization and date of one of the 'offering tables' ("Jerusalem in Ancient Egyptian Documentation," in *Jerusalem before Islam*, ed. Zeidan Abdel-Kafi Kafafi and Robert Schick [BAR International Series 1699; Oxford: Archaeopress, 2007], 33).

21 Prag notes that these are characteristic of Egyptian influence in the 12th century (*Re-Excavating Jerusalem*, 24–25).

22 Dan Bahat, *The Carta Jerusalem Atlas*, 3rd updated and expanded ed. (Jerusalem: Carta, 2011); Barkay, "A Late Bronze Age Egyptian Temple in Jerusalem?"

23 van der Veen, "When Pharaohs Ruled Jerusalem"; Peter van der Veen and David Ellis, "'He Placed His Name in Jerusalem': Ramesside Finds from Judah's Capital," in *Solomon and Shishak: Current Perspectives from Archaeology, Epigraphy, History and Chronology*, 264–73; Carolyn R. Higginbotham, *Egyptianization and Elite Emulation in Ramesside Palestine: Governance and Accommodation on the Imperial Periphery* (Culture and History of the Ancient Near East 2; Leiden; Boston: Brill, 2000).

24 Prag, *Re-Excavating Jerusalem*, 22–25; idem, "Jerusalem in the Third and Second Millennia BC," 61.

25 Prag, "Jerusalem in the Third and Second Millennia BC," 62.

26 William L. Moran, "The Syrian Scribe of the Jerusalem Amarna Letters," in *Amarna Studies: Collected Writings* (Harvard Semitic Studies 54; Leiden: Brill, 2003), 249–74.

27 Jerusalem at ca. 4 hectares was a fraction of the size of Tanis at ca. 177 hectares and Assur at ca. 120 (Pioske, *David's Jerusalem*, 182–97).

28 Ibid., 183.

29 Ibid., 186–89.

30 Ibid., 194–209.

31 Ibid., 229–31.

32 The critical passage that sets up the confrontation, 2 Samuel 5:6, is unspecific in a variety of ways that are vexing for literary or historical interests.

33 Although told in legendary terms, the conflict touches on the expected major centers for power and interaction in the central/southern hill country (later Benjamin and Judah) and Shephelah. Regardless of the historicity of the story, the contending parties represent important connections between the hill country and coastal plain, and parallel much of the geography of conflict and interaction known from various periods including what is in Samuel and in the Amarna correspondence (Rainey and Notley, *The Sacred Bridge*, 126).

34 As I discussed in Chapter Two, the account in 2 Samuel 5 is problematic, but I do not take issue with the notion that David's influence eventually extended to Jerusalem. Even though this part of the text is difficult and not historically informative in its details, it is the only account of a transition, and based on greater historical circumstances, we must assume that some leadership transition took place.

35 But this interpretation is anachronistic and idealized based on the Deuteronomistic assertion of 'all of Israel' and traditional scholarly views of a unified kingdom. Jerusalem's location was not the most central, and Jerusalem was not the only non-Israelite city in the region. Judging from the period before and after David, much more needed to be done to unite the region than the selection of a 'neutral' capital location. According to the DH, the tribes were rarely united in the Judges period, and there is no persuasive evidence of unity in Saul's history. The attempts to unify through administrative means (i.e., Solomon's officials and extraction of resources and Rehoboam's threat to intensify Solomon's policies) highlight the difficulty of achieving a cohesive state. David's motivations likely had little to do with pleasing his new constituents.

36 Pioske, *David's Jerusalem*, 216–54.

37 For detailed analysis of the political calculations involved, see Halpern, *David's Secret Demons*, 306–316, 341–344.

38 We must assume that David's time in Hebron and the south had secured important interactions through the Beersheba Valley, and that he would have established some way of maintaining control even from a residence further north; see Edelman, "Tel Masos, Geshur, and David," 253–58.

39 Halpern, *David's Secret Demons*, 303–6.

40 The note may also or alternatively reflect an attempt by the later biblical authors to delegitimize Jerusalem-area temples (or memories of them) that were not in line with the DH's theological preference for centralization at the official temple associated with the royal complex. The recently excavated temple complex at Tel Motza comes to mind as an intriguing example.

41 See John Monson, "The New 'Ain Dara Temple: Closest Solomonic Parallel," *BAR* 26, no. 3 (2000): 20–30, 32–35, 67. Relying too heavily on a comparison of details between the Solomon Narrative and Near Eastern parallels has its problems. Indeed, the Dtr reveals a *late* Iron Age perspective and eye-witness report of the royal and temple complexes when reporting that some of Jerusalem's features were known 'to this day.' We would have to suppose that the historian either had an earlier description of the structures in order to give an accurate 10th century depiction or intimately knew the history of the city center's various renovations over centuries, if we were to claim that he was not relying on knowledge of his day in describing Solomon's constructions.

42 Each mention of the Pharaoh's daughter is tightly connected to descriptions of Jerusalem's built environment: 1 Kings 3:1–2; 7:8–12; 9:10–25; and although potentially a later addition, 1 Kings 11:1–8 appears to follow suit by associating the foreign women with Solomon's constructions.

43 This proposal was put forward previously by Bernd U. Schipper ("Salomo und die Pharaonentochter"; see also Bernd U. Schipper, "Nocheinmal zur Pharaonentochter – ein Gespräch mit Karl Jansen-Winkeln," *BN* 111 [2002] 90–98; Karl Jansen-Winkeln, "Anmerkungen zu 'Pharaos Tochter,'" *BN* 103 [2000]: 23–29). I became aware of Schipper's proposal to this effect after coming to similar conclusions in my research for Chapter Three. I will be exploring the inspiration (from material culture, historical, and literary sources) and reaction to the traditions of the Pharaoh's daughter in future research.

44 Feldman, *Communities of Style*. The recent discovery of furniture inlays in Jerusalem excavations provide yet another example of elite material culture and how such physical objects may have influenced the ancient historians' portrayals; for one report of their discovery, see Ruth Schuster, "In First, Ivory Panels Mentioned in Bible Found in Jerusalem – Archaeology," *Ha'aretz*, September 8, 2022.

45 See Halpern, *David's Secret Demons*, 113–124.

46 Despite the scholarly tendency to emphasize that there must be a gulf between the LBA and later influences here, it appears increasingly likely that there was a continuous practice among Iron Age elites of emulation of predecessors, including those of the Bronze Ages. This may have taken place through generational transmission or through inspiration from LBA objects and architecture that were evident to later residents. For a discussion of the indirect contact between Egypt and the Levant via the 'leftovers' of the New Kingdom's involvement in the region, see Schipper, "Egypt and Israel."

47 For example, E. A. Knauf, "Jerusalem in the Late Bronze and Early Iron Ages: A Proposal," *TA* 27 (2000): 75–90; Finkelstein, Koch, and Lipschits, "The Mound on the Mount."

48 Many critiques have taken inspiration from the foundation laid by Jamieson-Drake (*Scribes and Schools*), especially concerning the point at which Jerusalem could be considered the capital of a state. The debate hinges of the nature of Jerusalem before the 8th century, and it carries on (see, for example, Yuval Gadot and Joe Uziel, "The Monumentality of Iron Age Jerusalem Prior to the 8th Century BCE," *TA* 44, no. 2 [2017]: 123–40, or, in contrast, Prag, *Re-Excavating Jerusalem*, 37–38).

49 Prag, *Re-Excavating Jerusalem*, 25-38; Jane M. Cahill, "Jerusalem at the Time of the United Monarchy: The Archaeological Evidence," in *Jerusalem in Bible and Archaeology: The First Temple Period*, ed. Andrew G. Vaughn and Ann E. Killebrew (SBL Symposium Series 18; Atlanta: Society of Biblical Literature, 2003), 13-80.
50 Nadav Na'aman, "Cow Town or Royal Capital? Evidence for Iron Age Jerusalem," *BAR* 23, no. 4 (1997): 43-47, 67; Knauf, "Jerusalem in the Late Bronze and Early Iron Ages"; Herzog and Singer-Avitz, "Redefining the Centre"; Finkelstein, Koch, and Lipschits, "The Mound on the Mount."
51 Eilat Mazar, "Excavate King David's Palace!," *BAR* 23, no. 1 (1997): 50-57, 70.
52 Eilat Mazar, *Preliminary Report on the City of David Excavations 2005 at the Visitors Center Area* (Jerusalem; New York: Shalem Press, 2007), 61; idem, *The Palace of King David: Excavations at the Summit of the City of David, Preliminary Report of Seasons 2005-2007* (Jerusalem; New York: Shoham Academic Research and Publication, 2009), 38-41, 59-65; idem, *Discovering the Solomonic Wall in Jerusalem*; Eilat Mazar, David Ben-Shlomo, and Shmuel Aḥituv, "An Inscribed Pithos from the Ophel, Jerusalem," *IEJ* 63 (2013): 39-49.
53 Mazar, "Excavate King David's Palace!"; idem, "Did I Find King David's Palace?," *BAR* 32, no. 1 (2006): 16-27, 70.
54 For early criticism, prior to the official publications of the excavations, see Israel Finkelstein et al., "Has King David's Palace in Jerusalem Been Found?," *TA* 34, no. 2 (2007): 142-64; and a measured review from Margreet Steiner, "The 'Palace of David' Reconsidered in the Light of Earlier Excavations," *Bible and Interpretation*, September 2009. For reactions since the official publications, see below.
55 Mazar, *The Palace of King David: Excavations at the Summit of the City of David, Preliminary Report of Seasons 2005-2007* (Jerusalem; New York: Shoham Academic Research and Publication, 2009), 56-57.
56 Steiner, "Jerusalem in the Late Bronze and Iron Ages. Archaeological Versus Literary Sources?" Prag, in her recent reevaluation of Kenyon's work, suggests revising Kenyon's identifications of Iron I to IIA (*Re-Excavating Jerusalem*, 34-37).
57 Mazar, "Archaeology and the Biblical Narrative"; Avraham Faust, "Did Eilat Mazar Find David's Palace?," *BAR* 38, no. 5 (2012): 47-52, 70; Daniel D. Pioske, "David's Jerusalem: A Sense of Place," *NEA* 76, no. 1 (2013), 5; idem, "Placing the Past: On Writing a History of 'David's Jerusalem,'" *The Bible and Interpretation*, October 2014.
58 She lays out her position quite plainly (emphasis in original): 'The Large Stone Structure was built in a *transitional phase* between the Iron Age I, which ended at the beginning of the 10th century BCE, and the Iron Age IIA. Since I hold that *it was built by the Phoenicians during King David's reign* in Jerusalem..., I have decided to present its remains in the chapter on the Iron Age IIA, despite the fact that the pottery associated with its construction and its initial phases of use is mainly characteristic of the Iron Age I'; Mazar, *The Palace of King David*, 18. Even while adhering to her theory that this is David's palace, E. Mazar also explains that there must have been a Canaanite fortress that was used by the Jebusites in the Iron I, since 2 Samuel 5:7 states that 'David took the stronghold of Zion, which is the City of David.' Mazar assumes the presence of an Iron I fortress, acknowledges that the Stepped Stone Structure has also been determined to have been constructed in the Iron I, and admits that the Large Stone Structure was founded in the Iron I (she argues late in the Iron I). As others have observed, rather than having discovered David's 'palace,' her reading of the biblical text should indicate that she has uncovered the Jebusite fortification later conquered by David. These complications aside, the greater problem in her historical approach is an uncritical use of the biblical history, particularly in the case of 2 Samuel 5 (see Chapter Two) and apparent ignorance of or no need for critical biblical scholarship; see also Todd Bolen, "Identifying King David's Palace: Mazar's Flawed Reading of the Biblical Text," *The Bible and Interpretation*, September 2010.
59 Additional rooms were added on to the structure that can be confidently dated to the Iron IIA (Mazar, *The Palace of King David*, 47-56).
60 Eilat Mazar and Benjamin Mazar, *Excavations in the South of the Temple Mount* (Qedem 29; Jerusalem: Institute of Archaeology, the Hebrew University of Jerusalem, 1989).
61 She focuses on the presence of a black juglet, which is known from the 10th *and* 9th centuries, and argues that she had earlier selected the latest possible date for this artifact but now prefers the earlier date based on its broader chronological range of use; Mazar, *Discovering the Solomonic Wall in Jerusalem*, 70-71. See also Mazar, Ben-Shlomo, and Aḥituv, "An Inscribed Pithos from the Ophel, Jerusalem."
62 Mazar, *Discovering the Solomonic Wall in Jerusalem*, 148.
63 Yosef Garfinkel and Saar Ganor, eds., *Khirbet Qeiyafa Volume 1, Excavation Report 2007-2008* (Jerusalem: Israel Exploration Society; Institute of Archaeology, Hebrew University of Jerusalem, 2009); Yosef Garfinkel, Saar Ganor, and Michael G. Hasel, "The Iron Age City of Khirbet Qeiyafa after Four Seasons of

Excavations," in *The Ancient Near East in the 12th–10th Centuries BCE: Culture and History. Proceedings of the International Conference Held at the University of Haifa, 2–5 May, 2010*, ed. Gershon Galil et al. (Alter Orient und Altes Testament 392; Münster: Ugarit-Verlag, 2012), 149–74.

64 Mazar, *Discovering the Solomonic Wall in Jerusalem*.

65 Parallels and additional interregional connections for some of these finds are explored in Chapters Five and Six.

66 For more on this inscription see Chapter Five. The presence of collared-rim pithoi in both the City of David and Ophel excavations may supply additional information regarding early Jerusalem's ethnic orientation or commercial activities, depending on one's understanding of the vessels. See the review of theories in Faust, *Israel's Ethnogenesis*, 191–205. Faust ultimately settles on an updated version of the theory that the vessels are indicative of Israelite ethnic identity.

67 Mazar, *The Palace of King David*, 65.

5 Epigraphic Evidence Relating to Exchange[1]

The first step in any historical investigation would normally be a survey of contemporary written evidence of the period in question, in our case the late 11th and 10th centuries BCE, but these years have long been characterized as a historically 'dark' age. Investigations into the southern Levant have produced inscribed objects from the period, but of a limited number and none of a monumental or narrative character. At first glance, the short inscriptions appear to have little to contribute to a discussion of trade and exchange. They do not note quantities of goods or inventories of taxes or tribute. The vast majority of them consist of only a personal name. Nevertheless, this limited corpus makes clear that the use of scribal services, though rare, was in demand in certain circles. My research suggests that it was regional elites who created the demand for the inscribed objects, and thus supported the work of scribes. Those who possessed inscriptions sought membership in an elite network linked to the greater eastern Mediterranean world. Contemporary evidence from the better-attested regions of Byblos and Egypt shows parallel developments. While these polities were obviously of a different complexity compared to Levantine elites, they provide important comparisons for the role of inscriptions in the processes of political reorganization, eventual stabilization, and interregional activity.

The Nature of the Evidence and Scholarly Debates

Although a recent wave of discoveries has more than doubled the corpus of early Iron Age inscriptions, a sober look at the evidence reminds us that, compared to the Late Bronze Age or later phases of the Iron Age, there is very little to work with regarding the late 11th and 10th centuries.[2] Epigraphic evidence, which is the focus of this discussion, consists of short inscriptions and ostraca, plus a quantity of inscribed arrowheads. Due to the growth of the corpus, the majority of the evidence, aside from the arrowheads, which are mostly unprovenanced, now comes from stratigraphically sound discoveries.[3]

Considering that we are still dealing with a small number of inscriptions, it is worth exploring what other evidence contributes to our knowledge of early Iron Age writing. Additional indications might include various equipment used by scribes, such as implements (for writing, impressing, incising; knives for cutting papyrus), papyrus or parchment, and cordage for tying scrolls, etc. (cf. Jeremiah 36); however, few such items are typically recovered. Seals and stamped clay bullae used to secure ancient writings offer yet additional evidence of scribal practices, and, fortunately, recovery of these items has been more plentiful, as they are constructed of more durable materials.[4] Bullae discoveries are particularly valuable as a testament to the long-lost papyri and parchment they once sealed. Not surprisingly, concentrations of bullae are understood to signal scribal and/or administrative activities and are more commonly discovered in later Iron Age contexts (ca. 8th–6th centuries). Like inscriptions, this type of evidence is less common in the early Iron Age, but a collection of six bullae from Tell Summeily provides further confirmation that scribal activity not only existed in this era but also might be recovered at various types of sites.[5] With the new wealth of material – relatively speaking – there is renewed discussion of the significance of inscriptions and scribal activity prior to the 9th century, when lengthier and monumental inscriptions typically associated with kings (e.g., Tel Dan and Mesha inscriptions) are attested.

Scholarly trends have had considerable influence on how we view the relationships between scribal activity and social complexity. The most critical is related to the tension between the extrabiblical and biblical evidence regarding centralized states. One school of thought, rooted in the work of D. Jamieson-Drake, maintains that centralized kingdoms could not operate without supporting scribal activity (of both administrative and monumental character).[6] These arguments rest in certain assumptions about the constellation of entities that support a state – things like a standing military, public and private spheres apparent through city planning and architecture, and government bodies that might include, for example, scribes. Another aspect of this issue is the influential biblical claim that premonarchic Israel was relatively egalitarian and slow to diversify in power.[7] Historians who are particularly loyal to (or swayed by) the biblical history attribute the advent of administrative offices (other than the priesthood) to Solomon's reign, with its dramatic transition to centralized administration (1 Kgs 4). It would be more realistic, however, to expect a less dramatic, less punctuated transition.

To make this point, we can focus on writing or scribal activity, often considered to be among the hallmarks of statehood – and for good reason. Writing is extremely useful in the operations of a state. Its applications range from basic record keeping necessary for taxes to more elaborate applications like court histories, monumental inscriptions, or propaganda, but these uses come at an advanced stage of a state. We should not necessarily expect them in the formative stages (e.g., in the 11th and 10th centuries). R. Byrne proposes a more nuanced relationship, with attention to different stages of both the state's and writing's development, concluding: 'The state facilitates the alphabet's segue from a curiosity to the sine qua non.'[8] The development of both institutions, alphabetic writing and the state influenced each other. Based on his evaluation of southern Levantine, Ugaritic, and Byblian evidence, Byrne argues that we should not expect standardization in scribal institutions before an established state, and not even at the early stages of a state system. This perspective eases pressures to fit the limited epigraphic material into any particular depiction of political organization.

Inscriptions from the Southern Levant

The number of inscriptions that date to the late 11th and 10th centuries now number at least 17 (again excepting the arrowheads; Table 5.1).[9] They are all written in linear alphabetic script, and most appear to be in Northwest Semitic languages (most likely Hebrew, Phoenician, or Aramaic), with a notable, possible exception from Tell eṣ-Ṣafi (Gath).[10] By far the most common type of inscription is the name formula, used to mark the possession or dedication of an object, but there are also examples of educational or scribal exercises (e.g., Gezer calendar and Tel Zayit abecedary), and others whose readings cannot yet be classified (e.g., Khirbet Qeiyafa ostracon). The inscriptions come from ten sites: Kefar Veradim, Tel ʿAmal, Tel Reḥov, the Ophel/Jerusalem, Gezer, Tel Batash, Beth-Shemesh, Khirbet Qeiyafa, Tell eṣ-Ṣafi (Gath), and Tel Zayit.[11] Of these, seven have produced one inscription from the period in question here. Tel Reḥov, Tell eṣ-Ṣafi, and Khirbet Qeiyafa are exceptional in yielding multiple inscriptions from controlled excavations that date to the Iron IIA more broadly. Tel Reḥov boasts ten dating to the Iron IIA (10th–9th centuries); three to five of these fall within the Iron I–IIA transition period.[12] Tell eṣ-Ṣafi (Gath) has yielded seven from the Iron IIA generally, two of which fall within the Iron I–IIA transition.[13] Excavations at Khirbet Qeiyafa have uncovered three from the Iron I–IIA transition.[14] Tel Reḥov, Beth-Shemesh, and Tell eṣ-Ṣafi (Gath) have yielded multiple inscriptions from the even larger span of the Iron I and IIA periods combined, which helps to illustrate the fairly continuous use of linear alphabetic scripts in the southern Levant in the early Iron Age.[15]

Table 5.1: Southern Levantine inscriptions from the Iron I–IIA transition.

Site	Object Description	Reading	Personal Name
Kefar Veradim[16]	engraved bronze bowl	ks psḥ bn šmʿ	psḥ bn šmʿ
Tel ʿAmal[17]	hippo storage jar	lnmš	nmš
Tel Reḥov[18]	No. 1: storage jar, inscribed near base (str. VI, Area C)	ʿy	?
	No. 2: narrow storage jar, inscribed twice with the same inscription (str. VIB, Area C)	mtʾ	mtʾ
	No. 3: inner side of a storage jar (str. VI, Area C)	l	?
	No. 4: storage jar (str. VI, Area B)	lnḥm? or lnbʾ?	nḥm?
	No. 5: hippo storage jar (str. V, Area C, apiary)	lnmš	nmš
Ophel/Jerusalem[19]	neckless pithos	ḥ]mr lḥnn[	ḥnn
Gezer[20]	calendar/writing exercise on limestone	Describes agricultural activity of different months.	ʾbyh
Tel Batash[21]	ceramic bowl body sherd	n|ḥnn	[b]n|ḥnn
Beth-Shemesh[22]	game board fragment	ḥnn	ḥnn
Tell eṣ-Ṣafi (Gath)[23]	ceramic bowl rim sherd	ʾlwt|wlt[	ʾlwt|wlt[Philistine? names Alyattes and Oletas[24]
Khirbet Qeiyafa[25]	ostracon	Not yet definitive.	possible (Phoenician) names include bdmlk, ʿbdʾ, špṭ, grbʿl, nqmy, ʾltʾš[26]
	storage jar	ʾšbʿl |ʿbn`|bdʿ	ʾšbʿl |ʿbn`|bdʿ
	additional inscription	Not yet published.	?
Tel Zayit[27]	abecedary on stone	above abecedary: ʿzr line 1: ʾ b g d w h ḥ z ṭ y l k m n ˹s˺ ˹p˺ ˹ˊ˺ ˹ṣ˺ line 2: ˹q˺ ˹r˺ š ˹t˺	ʿzr
Various locations[28]	bronze arrowheads	various	various

Figure 5.1: Find locations of late 11th–10th century BCE inscriptions. Map: Google Earth, © 2020.

Since our interest here is exchange and interactions, it is necessary to be oriented to the geographic distribution of the finds. The inscriptions are mostly concentrated in two areas, easily divided into a northern and a southern group (Figure 5.1). In the south, there is a cluster of sites in the Shephelah, primarily in the contact zones between Philistia and the hill country. Some sites can be characterized fairly easily. Tell eṣ-Ṣafi (Gath) was a Philistine center; Khirbet Qeiyafa appears to have been part of an emerging hill-country culture. Some others, however, seem to be border communities with diverse populations and cultural contacts, such as Beth-Shemesh.[29] The southern group also includes Jerusalem. Although it was outside of the border region, it was closely connected by major roads and can be considered part of a larger interaction unit. The frequency of epigraphic finds in an area that, according to both archaeological and historical research, was an intense contact zone among emerging Iron Age polities, suggests that the intensification in interactions corresponded to an increase in scribal activities.

The other concentration of inscriptions is in the north. As in the southern group, the sites where inscriptions have been found correspond to areas that saw more exchange and cultural interaction, but rather than being clustered together, these sites are related to 'international' routes. For example, Tel Reḥov and neighboring Tel ʿAmal essentially guarded the intersection of the eastern extension of the Jezreel Valley highway (i.e., the Harod Valley) and the Jordan Valley corridor. These crossroads witnessed north-south traffic along the Jordan Valley, which would have included activity from iron and copper metallurgical trade, travelers using the Jezreel to pass through the hill country between the Mediterranean and the eastern routes, or those seeking access to the Great Trunk Road linking Egypt and Syria/Mesopotamia. All of these routes were well traveled during the Iron I–IIA transition period.[30]

At the northern extent of the region examined here, and in close proximity to the Mediterranean port regions of Acco and Achziv, excavators found a rich burial deposit at Kefar Veradim (Cave 3).[31] Among the goods was an exceptional example of an engraved bronze bowl. Its inscription reads *ks pšḥ bn šmʿ*, 'cup of Psḥ son of Šmʿ.' It is clear from the quality (the object as well as the inscription), and from the associated finds, that the family who used the burial cave was not only wealthy, but also well integrated into the Mediterranean exchange systems of the time. In fact, the bowl has striking parallels in burial deposits in Crete and Egypt. The parallel from Crete was found in Tekke Tomb J near Knossos. It is also on a bronze bowl (but of a different shape) and similarly reads *ks.šmʿ [ ] bn lʾ [ ] [ ]*, 'the cup of Šemaʿ, son of L[ ].'[32] Both the Cretan and Kefar Veradim burials contained a wealth of grave goods, many of which were imported and luxury items, including BoR vessels and, not insignificantly, the use of the Phoenician script.[33] The Egyptian parallel is from the Tanite burial of Wendjebauendjed, the Egyptian official buried with Faynan copper and other luxuries, discussed in Chapter Three. Among Wendjebauendjed's numerous burial goods were many exquisite vessels made of combinations of gold, silver, electrum, and glass paste. Several are inscribed with Wendjebauendjed's name and titles, including the stylistic parallel to Kefar Veradim's bowl.[34]

There can be little doubt that, in each of these cases, we are looking at the burials of elite figures/families well connected to long-distance exchange, and that each had the means to make use of a scribe. The richness of the Tanite burial is not surprising in its royal context, but for the Levantine and Cretan burials, we have clear statements of exceptional family wealth. In each, a family devoted resources through the dedication of rare goods, possibly valued heirlooms, to a use that eliminated this wealth from the activities of the living.[35]

Although our other examples may not come from contexts as luxurious and 'international' as the Kefar Veradim bowl, the contexts of the epigraphic finds indicate that they should be considered in the class of trade and prestige goods.[36] Many of the possession inscriptions have been found on large storage jars, indicating that scribes were employed to mark collected or commercial goods. Most sites (eight of ten) where inscriptions have been found have also produced evidence of imported pottery, usually from the Mediterranean.[37] Some sites provide more comprehensive evidence of the potential for wealth at this time. Remains of a smithy's workshop, another specialized and high-value industry, have been uncovered at Beth-Shemesh.[38] The inscription from this site is on the side of a game board. In the Iron 1 and early IIA period remains at Tell eṣ-Ṣafi (Gath), there is evidence of large-scale fortifications; interregional exchange; a cult center (temple?) with concentrations of potentially sacred and dedicated objects; metallurgical activity; and elite practices such as feasting.[39] Excavations at Tel Reḥov have also brought to light evidence of an elaborate elite culture. In addition to inscriptions and Mediterranean imports (including from the Aegean), there is evidence of feasting and a large apiary.[40] Overall, the evidence is adding up that the use of scribes in the late 11th and 10th centuries coincided with uncommon wealth and status, and that writing was used to demonstrate ownership or patronage of some kind.

These connections are underscored by the fact that nearly every inscription from this period documents personal names. In the majority of cases, the purpose of the inscription was to signify ownership – for example, the owner/producer of goods in storage jars, or the identity of a lord or patron, as on the arrowheads. Even in the texts that would not fall into the category of a possession inscription, however, we find the inclusion of names. The Tel Zayit abecedary and the Gezer calendar each appear to have a name inscribed near the primary text, and the Khirbet Qeiyafa ostracon, according to some readings, may be a list of names, rather than a narrative composition.[41] According to the current body of evidence, a significant aspect of the scribe's work was documenting personal names. Assuming that the knowledge of a specialist was required, we have a growing list of individuals or families who employed scribes (on at least one occasion) or even the names of some of the scribes themselves (Table 5.1). There was a varied application of this practice. Names accompany commercial goods (e.g., storage jars), personal items (e.g., the Beth-Shemesh game board), grave goods (e.g., the Kefar Veradim bronze bowl), symbols of power (e.g., bronze arrowheads), and possibly intellectual or academic material as well (e.g., scribal exercises).

In at least two cases, we have the repetition of a name in more than one location. We must note upfront that it is possible that these instances represent multiple, unrelated individuals who happened to share a common name.[42] At the same time, it is worth exploring possible connections among the occurrences. The most recently published inscription from Tell eṣ-Ṣafi/Gath appears to bear the name *bdʿ*, the same name as the patronym on Khirbet Qeiyafa's ʾIšbaʿal inscription.[43] The name *ḥnn* was written on the side of a bowl from Tel Batash (Timnah), and on the game board discovered at Beth-Shemesh (as well as on an Iron I ostracon also from Beth-Shemesh).[44] The name has also been proposed in readings of Jerusalem's Ophel inscription.[45] In addition, the place name Elon-Beth-Ḥanan follows Beth-Shemesh in the description of the Solomon's second district in 1 Kings 4:9.[46] The find locations were connected by a road that led from Jerusalem to the Mediterranean via the Soreq Valley, and Tel Batash and Beth-Shemesh are only about 7.5 km apart on that route.[47] While the name ḥnn and variations of it were common (e.g., Jehu son of Ḥanani in 1 Kgs 16; the 'false' prophet Ḥananiah in Jeremiah 28), the geographic and chronological proximity of the ḥnn finds is intriguing.[48] We cannot help but wonder: was there a prominent ḥnn family in the Soreq Valley in the early Iron Age?[49] We cannot say conclusively that these references all belonged to one ḥnn family, but if they were related, we would have an excellent case for exploring the regional leadership of an elite lineage.

A parallel situation exists in the northern Jordan Valley. The personal name nmš is attested on the Tel ʿAmal sherd and on two inscriptions at Tel Reḥov, one of which was found in the apiary, as well as in later periods on an inscription, several seals, and in the Hebrew Bible (notably, for example, Jehu's family; 2 Kgs 9).[50] Multiple nmš inscriptions in close proximity (also about 7.5 km apart) compel us to consider whether they could be related. Like ḥnn, nmš was not an uncommon name, but the inscribed vessels (all storage jars) are similar and were part of comparable ceramic assemblages. In addition, there is some epigraphic affinity between the sites.[51] S. Aḥituv and A. Mazar venture that, indeed, these are all related, and that the 'Nimshi clan' was a prominent, elite family in the region, with Tel Reḥov as their hometown 'just before and during the reign of Jehu.'[52] As with the Soreq Valley examples, we will need additional evidence to be sure, but the connections provide an opportunity to explore ideas about prominent individuals or families, and their leadership in local networks.

The Assertion of Elite Status through Writing

While it is a fairly common notion that literacy would have been limited in the ancient world, there have been some persistent assumptions in conflict with this understanding regarding literacy in the southern Levant. S. Sanders and C. Rollston draw our attention to the predominance of the scholarly view that becoming fluent in the Semitic alphabetic scripts would have been a swift and simple process.[53] This kind of thinking might lead to the idea that anyone could easily have become literate in ancient Israel, and that writing was not a limited or privileged activity. Such a notion conforms well with another assumption about early Israel, that it was relatively egalitarian (and therefore the antithesis of urbanized and elite Canaanite society). In this idyllic depiction, we might imagine a classless society where cultural wisdom, including literacy, passed to all members of small, peaceful hamlets. More recent investigations, however, demonstrate that many settlements were culturally complex, and the material evidence shows diversity in wealth and status. We can no longer hold to the earlier views, that Iron II Israel developed from an egalitarian and homogenous Iron I existence.

R. Byrne argues convincingly for the use of alphabetic writing as a status statement in this transitional period:

> The survivability of the alphabetic *haute couture* in the centuries after the ebb of Canaanite cuneiform ironically hinged on its own irrelevance, i.e., in its relevance to those who could afford the *luxury*. Perhaps this illuminates a peculiar pericope about the primordial monarchy. In each of David's entourage lists (2 Sam 8:16–18; 20:23–26), the king boasts a single scribe (Seraiah and Sheva, respectively). Some have taken this to represent a larger bureaucracy (or worse still, an Egyptian derivative), but the text makes more sense at face value. David retains a scribe when scribes are curiosities. The narrative is less interested in the

hint of a chancery (certainly an anachronism) than the accentuation of a status retainer fashionable for the time. These scribes were less administrators than hagiographers.[54]

In this depiction, one's employment of a scribe conveyed one's ability to 'afford the luxury,' which would, in turn, convey distinction and power. When we see conspicuous consumption, even in a way that appears subtle compared to monumental creations like structures or statuary, we should expect that it arose in response to others' similar behavior, or to an accepted model for elite behavior. The elite retainer would have been emulating well-known models of power and competing with more localized individuals or groups. For this point, it is important to keep in mind the appropriate cultural context. In the southern Levant at this time, the employment of a scribe may have been quite distinguishing. Rather than view the few inscriptions that we know of as anomalous or insignificant, being 'only a name,' we can posit that they indicate rising elites who were competing for recognition as the region was transitioning through economic and cultural disruption from the end of the Late Bronze Age, the withdrawal of Egypt, and the arrival of new population groups.[55]

The excavations at Tel Reḥov provide an interesting test case for both the relationships among writing, elites, and exchange, and the role of scholarly expectations. A. Mazar, principal investigator of the excavations, has previously interpreted the wealth of inscriptions from the site as a general increase in literacy in society, and as evidence against the proposal that the amount of inscriptions from a society correlates to the presence of state-level organization. In various publications, Mazar stresses that the early inscriptions in general, and the Tel Reḥov finds particularly, are evidence of 'everyday use of writing,' 'writing on everyday objects,' and 'the spread of literacy in daily activities' and 'for routine purposes.'[56] In these examples, he is building a case for the possibility of a complex state prior to evidence of major institutions of writing, such as royal administrations and monumental inscriptions. In his effort to demonstrate that there is enough evidence of writing to support the advent of monarchy, he rules out another important interpretation.

Mazar acknowledges, but downplays, the possibility that writing should be viewed as an elite activity at Tel Reḥov. His initial comment to this effect is tucked away in the final footnote of his 2003 report on the first three inscriptions discovered at the site. It was prompted by comments from D. Edelman that the 9th century inscriptions came from what might be a public building and should be attributed to an elite, not common, use of writing.[57] Mazar responds:

> ...the general argument against literacy before the 8th century is that it either did not exist at all or was limited to the royal court. Even if the *Tēl Reḥōv* inscriptions are related to elite activity, this was a local elite of priests, merchants, etc. Thus, the inscriptions should signify the spread of literacy to a broad spectrum of Israelite society.[58]

A critical assumption here is that the 'local elite' were part of 'a broad spectrum' who presumably received their knowledge through a relationship to a centralized (i.e., Davidic) state. Literacy, in Mazar's implied argument, emanated from a central Israelite power.

In addition, his response to the nature of the archaeological context glossed over critical information about the site. The assemblages corresponding to the inscriptions speak to *uncommon* wealth and connections, even at the time of the 2003 publication. In addition to evidence of scribal activity and significant wealth, Aegean ceramic imports were discovered at Tel Reḥov in the same periods as the inscriptions (i.e., in 10th and 9th century contexts). It is notable that, at present, eight of the ten inscriptions found during the excavations, and three of eight imported Greek sherds, were found in Area C.[59] In addition, most of the inscriptions were found on storage vessels, including hippo jars, which may have been part of an organized, commercial operation in the region.[60] In Mazar's 2003 interpretation, he ruled out the possibility that local elite groups were important, independent players in regional and longer-distance interactions. Since that report, excavations have uncovered a unique apiary complex (Area C), an elite 'patrician' house (Building F in Area C), an ivory statuette (Area C, near Building F), and zooarchaeological evidence of feasting at the site.[61] This additional evidence of economic stratification and interregional exchange changes the characterization of the site during the Iron IIA period. The importance of a well-established elite group (probably not exclusively 'Israelite') is now acknowledged.[62] Even so, Mazar continues to stress that inscriptions were found in mundane contexts throughout the site, ruling out exclusively elite activities.[63]

S. Sanders has argued for a more nuanced understanding of the scribal enterprise at this time, emphasizing that writing need not be confined to the category of a state bureaucracy:

> The simplest explanation for the persistence of the linear alphabet between the Late Bronze Age collapse and the Iron IIB renaissance of writing is that writing was a small-scale luxury craft (Byrne 2007). The goal of these scribes' work was to signify local powers such as the king of Amurru (witness the arrowheads bearing his name) but through inscriptions on portable luxury items such as engraved weapons, not monuments. The linear alphabet's durability was tied to a small-scale, adaptable craft tradition serving elites but free of allegiance to any specific dialect or regime.[64]

This alternate sphere of activity and influence creates a space in which the late Iron I–early Iron IIA inscriptions can be situated. There is no need to force the characterization of a state system or reconstruct a court-sponsored scribal education that made these texts possible. Elite patronage seems a more likely explanation. The inscriptions and their corresponding evidence (i.e., ceramic assemblages, geographic locations, long-term history of the sites) suggest that elite families become visible in these 11th and 10th century remains. Even the diversity of contexts in which the Tel Reḥov inscriptions have been found fits this interpretation. The scribal activity may have been sponsored by the elite leadership, whose reach went beyond specialized residences or structures. It seems plausible that those who emerged in status at this time came from entities (whether families or locales) that weathered economic and cultural transitions better than most. Still others may have filled niches that translated into local status – for example, a person in a position of leadership over a border zone (e.g., Beth-Shemesh, Tel Zayit) or a major traffic area (e.g., Tel Reḥov), or a member of an immigrant community who retained connections to another region (e.g., Tell eṣ-Ṣafi).[65]

Cross-Cultural Material: Byblos and Egypt

We can turn to neighbors of the southern Levant, Byblos and Egypt, for a comparison of how writing and scribes were employed in the early Iron Age. Admittedly, comparing Egypt and Byblos on the one hand, and the southern Levantine sites on the other, is not a simple issue. The nature of the Byblian and Egyptian evidence is distinct from that of the southern Levant; we have monumental royal inscriptions, many elites documented through inscriptions on smaller objects as discussed above, and a contemporary Egyptian narrative source, the Report of Wenamun. In addition, these cultures have dramatically different histories from the smaller, and typically younger, southern Levantine sites, but all locations sought new directions in the wake of the Late Bronze Age collapse. Not surprisingly, Byblian and Egyptian inscriptions of this time stress the power and legitimacy of new leadership. Elites used scribes and inscriptions to promote their authority, legitimacy, and distinction from others. While we cannot transfer all of this information, unaltered, to the southern Levant, we can see similar trends in the evidence, albeit on a different scale.

Four royal inscriptions from Byblos illustrate how new rulers used scribes as a part of their campaigns for legitimacy during the Iron I–IIA period.[66] These are the Aḥiram sarcophagus, commissioned by his son 'Ittobaʿal (late 11th/10th century); the Abibaʿal inscription (second half of the 10th century); and inscriptions by Yeḥimilk and his son Elibaʿal (10th to early 9th century).[67] In general, these documents paint a picture of emerging status, but not necessarily of overwhelming power. The inscriptions document the rulers' good deeds and successes in carrying out quintessentially royal duties, especially the creation of, and care for, monuments, which we should understand as a method for establishing authority. With the exception of the sarcophagus, the texts describe dedication to Byblos' patron goddess, Baʿalat Gebal, the Mistress of Byblos – again, cultivating legitimacy.[68] At the same time, the inscriptions hint at political instability. Aḥiram's sarcophagus contains warnings to future rulers against disturbing the burial (ironic, since the tomb and sarcophagus were reused for Aḥiram).[69] Yeḥimilk's inscription lacks a statement of a hereditary claim to the throne, instead asserting that he is 'the legitimate and rightful king' of Byblos, a description fitting of a usurper.[70] Abibaʿal and Elibaʿal placed their inscriptions on statues of pharaohs (Shoshenq I and Osorkon I, respectively). While the monuments of early 22nd Dynasty kings in Byblos stand as a testimony to renewed relations between the two states, and Byblian participation in that exchange appears to have been meaningful for supporting a king's authority, we should be thoughtful about why these kings chose Egyptian statuary for their declarations.[71] Were they not in command of enough resources to have their own monuments crafted? Did the Egyptian monuments offer additional prestige (an indirect/involuntary endorsement?) for the local kings? Or were the Byblian kings building on the prestige of, or asserting themselves *over*, their Egyptian contemporaries? Whatever the motivation, their scribes served a powerful role as the agents of appropriation and monument creation, particularly when the rulers may have felt limitations in their authority.[72]

The Egyptian evidence is more plentiful, although still scant compared to other periods in Egyptian history. Even so, rulers and officials left significant evidence of their activities in inscriptions.[73] The 10th century rulers Siamun, Shoshenq I, and Osorkon I recorded their accomplishments, including relations with the Levant.[74] Their documents illustrate a more fully realized exhibition of power through inscribed monuments. In emulation of classic New Kingdom displays of power, Siamun and Shoshenq I depicted campaigns against foreigners in monumental inscriptions, the first since the end of the Ramessides.[75] The use of this convention, which relied on professional artists and scribes, makes the claim that they were worthy and powerful kings, rightfully situated alongside their great predecessors. In the same vein, Shoshenq and Osorkon recorded tribute, temple gifts, and offerings, drawing attention to their abilities to amass a significant amount of wealth and dominate other regions.[76] Perhaps the most impressive for this period is the epigraphic evidence of these kings outside of Egypt. As we have noted, Shoshenq and Osorkon gave statues to the Mistress of Byblos, long associated with the Egyptian goddess Hathor.[77] In addition, a stele fragment found in Megiddo bears Shoshenq's name, presumably installed as a reminder of his Levantine campaign,[78] and a scarab bearing the name of Shoshenq was found in the Faynan region in Jordan, possibly as a result of the campaign or of Egyptian involvement in the region's copper trade.[79]

Finally, the Report of Wenamun, probably best characterized as a work of historical fiction, follows an Egyptian official on a journey along the Levantine coast to acquire cedar for the Barque of Amun in Karnak.[80] The story, set in the early 11th century and composed in the 11th or 10th century, provides a glimpse at changes in elite status and exchange relations across the eastern Mediterranean at the turn of the millennium.[81] In the tale, former vassals no longer treat Egypt with the deference that was customary in previous years. Instead, centers like Dor and Byblos assert new-found authority. The tale is also a rich resource for attitudes about the authority of the written word in establishing one's bona fides, and in negotiating international relations. At the beginning of the text, Wenamun shows his papers in northern Egypt in order to outfit himself for his journey, but his lack of papers in Byblos (because he left them in Egypt) causes great hardship when trying to do business with the Byblian prince, Zakar-Baal. Wary of the undocumented Wenamun, the prince consults royal annals that preserve a history of relations between Byblos and Egypt. Eventually, the men arrive at a solution, and Zakar-Baal calls on his scribe to provide new papers for Wenamun's return. Within the narrative, and from the perspective of the author, we see that scribes and written documentation provided evidence of identification and authority in what is characterized as a very chaotic and confusing time in international relations. Notice that the author draws a stark contrast between Wenamun, lacking official papers or a means to produce new ones (i.e., a scribe), and Zakar-Baal, who both retains a scribe and has access to the authority of written precedents.

An examination of these contemporary records situates Egypt as the most established in the use of scribes, which included the creation of new monumental works, but we also know, from both historical and archaeological sources, that Egypt was not the world power it was previously, and that stable, familial dynasties were not the norm. New rulers had to vie for their position and legitimacy through visible and powerful means: construction, conquest, and conspicuous inscriptions. The Report of Wenamun suggests that authority and legitimacy accompanied the possession of written documents, and that one who could produce such items held significant power. In both Egypt and Byblos, new rulers and dynasties declared their status through inscriptions. Egypt provides the best evidence of elites both creating monuments and documenting power on them. In contrast, Byblian leaders added their statements to preexisting objects, but these illustrate this same sentiment. They employed scribes in order to establish their status, even if they could not secure the wealth and authority required to commission original monumental works. If other luxuries were lacking, one could 'make a statement' through an inscription. This practice puts a spin on the association between monumental inscriptions and complex states – Byblian elites 'created' monumental inscriptions through graffiti and associated themselves with recognized elites, thereby elevating themselves in their sphere of influence.

Conclusions

We return now to the southern Levantine inscriptions. The examples from Byblos or Egypt cannot be compared without qualification. Instead of expecting the same scale from the southern Levant, we should look for indications of relative forms of distinction.

New pharaohs modeled themselves and their inscriptions on the greats of Egyptian history. Elite officials asserted their status through documents, evidence of their names and titles, as well as the possession or trade of foreign, luxury goods. Byblian and southern Levantine elites were engaged in similar emulation processes, but in ways relative to their respective locations and wealth.[82] Individuals were documenting their status on materials that may have already testified to their elevated social positions. In the southern Levant, name formulae appear on prestige items: a fine bronze bowl, bronze arrowheads, a game board, or a dedication vessel. In other cases, names were placed on storage vessels, likely documenting the status of the producer or regional ruler. In the context of limited literacy, it is not so much the content of the written word that mattered, but its presence, its conspicuousness.

In all regions, the apparent increase in epigraphic finds corresponds to the rise of new elite groups and intensifying cultural interactions. The new leaders promoted their status through inscribed objects and other luxury goods in order to gain prominence within their emerging territories, and in their competition for regional power. This image of various, competing elites contradicts the biblical image of a lack of diversity in wealth in pre-Solomonic eras. The Bible recounts that outstanding individuals like the Judges, Saul, or David were plucked from a common mass, with dynastic succession endorsed only after David proved his piety. The history conspicuously denies hereditary status or dynastic succession for anything but the priesthood or Davidic line. Despite these efforts, the illusion is not completely successful. Elite status is apparent in minor characters like the wealthy Nabal (1 Sam 25) or wealthy and influential Barzillai (2 Sam 19).[83] If we overlook the biblical argument regarding wealth, the emergence of regional leadership is apparent in the inscribed materials and other testaments to elevated status.

The scribes who were employed by these elites played a significant role in drawing a line between an emerging class of power players and everyone else, the common people of the land. While there remains the view that a range of social classes participated in writing and literacy, when we re-situate the inscribed artifacts in the contexts where they have been found, and in the relative contexts of how inscriptions were being used in the late 11th and 10th centuries, I find the depictions of Byrne and Sanders to be the more likely characterizations of who the scribes were and how they operated. They made themselves first useful and later necessary to those who were involved in rapidly intensifying cultural, commercial, and political interactions. By doing so, they furthered their own distinction and aligned with the future ruling classes.

The evidence surveyed in this chapter also confirms that the presence of writing in the material record is a strong indicator that other types of activities (i.e., interaction beyond one's immediate environs and with other elites) were also taking place. The inscriptions that have been found show a strong correlation to interactions: where interregional traffic was frequent (especially in the northern examples), and where regional competition may have been particularly intense (southern group). In a few cases, we have suggestive evidence that certain families may have dominated some of these key areas. Ultimately, this focus on epigraphic evidence demonstrates that there is much more to these 'simple' texts. They do not need to document interactions explicitly, in the form of an inventory of commodities or an agreement of trade between elites. Perhaps more importantly, we see a strong case for the *association* of certain types of evidence, social status, and behaviors that point us toward emerging elites and their relationships in the southern Levant and eastern Mediterranean.

Notes

1. The chapter was previously published as 'Influential Inscriptions: Resituating Scribal Activity during the Iron I-IIA Transition,' in *Scribes and Scribalism*, ed. Mark Leuchter (The Hebrew Bible in Social Perspective; London; New York: Bloomsbury Publishing, 2020), 13–27. It is reproduced here (with some revisions) with kind permission from Bloomsbury.
2. Recently, Israel Finkelstein and Benjamin Sass published an updated summary of the evidence with new analysis regarding discrete changes in alphabetic writing based on regional variation and chronological factors (e.g., proximity to LBA administrative centers). Their chronological and geographic parameters (notably including northern Levantine inscriptions as well) are slightly different from what is examined here, and their count lists 49 inscriptions ("The Exceptional Concentration of Inscriptions at Iron IIA Gath and Rehob").
3. There are more than 60 now known. They have been found and purchased throughout the Levantine region, in Lebanon, Israel/Palestine, and Jordan. Only one from Ruweiseh, Lebanon was found in a secure (albeit disturbed) archaeological context. Many may be forgeries, but there is a consensus that *some* are authentic and thus the practice of inscribing arrowheads can be situated in the late 11th–10th centuries. See most recently André Lemaire, "Levantine Literacy ca. 1000–750 BCE," in *Contextualizing Israel's Sacred Writing: Ancient Literacy, Orality, and Literary Production*, ed. Brian B. Schmidt (Atlanta: SBL Press, 2015), 13-14; idem, "From the Origin of the Alphabet to the Tenth Century B.C.E.: New Documents and New Directions," in *New Inscriptions and Seals Relating to the Biblical World*, ed. Meir Lubetski and Edith Lubetski (Atlanta: Society of Biblical Literature, 2012), 1–20. For a discussion of their social significance, see Seth L. Sanders, *The Invention of Hebrew* (Urbana: University of Illinois Press, 2009), 55, 106–8.
4. For a recent summary of this evidence, see Matthieu Richelle, "Elusive Scrolls: Could Any Hebrew Literature Have Been Written Prior to the Eight Century BCE?," *VT* 66 (2016): 1–39, esp. 4–6. See also Sanders, *The Invention of Hebrew*, 108, 212 note 6; Othmar Keel and Amihai Mazar, "Iron Age Seals and Seal Impressions from Tel Reḥov," *Eretz-Israel* 29 (2009): 57*–69*.
5. James W. Hardin, Christopher A. Rollston, and Jeffrey A. Blakely, "Iron Age Bullae from Officialdom's Periphery: Khirbet Summeily in Broader Context," *NEA* 77, no. 4 (2014): 299–301; Kara Larson, Elizabeth Arnold, and James W. Hardin. "Resource Allocation and Rising Complexity during the Iron Age IIA: An Isotopic Case Study from Khirbet Summeily, Israel." *Quaternary International* (2022).
6. Jamieson-Drake, *Scribes and Schools in Monarchic Judah*. Jamieson-Drake has been a favorite among the so-called minimalist scholars. His approach has strengths in proposing ways to measure cultural activities and in his warnings about the nature of the evidence. It does not, however, provide a framework for making meaning of *all* of the results, especially more subtle changes and in discussions of the 11th to 8th centuries. In addition, Jamieson-Drake assumes that literacy should have been widespread or 'democratic' in order to recognize social change, which obscures important trends in his evidence. I maintain a very different premise, that scribal activity would have been a tool of the elite in the process of social change and not easily acquired or readily available to a broader population (see further discussion and references below). With this model, we should expect small numbers of inscriptions and other 'luxury items' for some time, which produces a better correlation between the data and interpretation. As Jamieson-Drake admits, 'If a datum must be interpreted in an unnatural way in order to fit into our model, we must consider modifying or overhauling the model' (ibid., 149). In this case, it is the model regarding literacy that needs to be changed.
7. This idea is implicit in many archaeological and historical interpretations, but Faust calls attention to it directly, what he deems an 'egalitarian ethos' in his book *Israel's Ethnogenesis*. Kletter critiques in detail assumptions underlying Faust's egalitarian argument ("Water from a Rock: Archaeology, Ideology, and the Bible," *SJOT* 30, no. 2 [2016]: 161–84).
8. Ryan Byrne, "The Refuge of Scribalism in Iron I Palestine," *BASOR* 345 (2007): 23. Note that the state precedes a large-scale scribal institution here, rather than the reverse. This reconstruction better fits our archaeological evidence.
9. There continues to be significant debate about the chronology of the late Iron I and Iron IIA, and the archaeological and historical periodization may not correspond well to paleographic developments. Finkelstein and Sass, using the low chronology and corresponding paleographic considerations differ in their classification of Late Iron I and early Iron IIA inscriptions ("The West Semitic Alphabetic Inscriptions, Late Bronze II to Iron IIA: Archeological Context, Distribution and Chronology," *Hebrew Bible and Ancient Israel* 2 [2013]: 149–220). Other recent discussions of the corpus may be found in Richelle,

"Elusive Scrolls"; Gordon J. Hamilton, "Two Methodological Issues Concerning the Expanded Collection of Early Alphabetic Texts," in *Epigraphy, Philology, and the Hebrew Bible: Methodological Perspectives on Philological and Comparative Study of the Hebrew Bible in Honor of Jo Ann Hackett* (Ancient Near Eastern Monographs 12; Atlanta: SBL Press, 2015), 127–56; Shmuel Aḥituv and Amihai Mazar, "The Inscriptions from Tel Reḥov and Their Contribution to Study of Script and Writing During the Iron Age IIA," in *"See, I Will Bring a Scroll Recounting What Befell Me" (Ps 40:8): Epigraphy and Daily Life - From the Bible to the Talmud Dedicated to the Memory of Professor Hanan Eshel*, ed. Esther Eshel and Yigal Levin (Journal of Ancient Judaism Supplements 12; Göttingen; Bristol: Vandenhoeck and Ruprecht, 2014), 39–68; Chris A. Rollston, *Writing and Literacy in the World of Ancient Israel: Epigraphic Evidence from the Iron Age* (Atlanta: Society of Biblical Literature, 2010).

10 For discussions of distinctions in script and language, see Finkelstein and Sass, "The Exceptional Concentration"; Christopher A. Rollston, "The Phoenician Script of the Tel Zayit Abecedary and Putative Evidence for Israelite Literacy," in *Literate Culture and Tenth-Century Canaan: The Tel Zayit Abecedary in Context*, ed. Ron E. Tappy and P. Kyle McCarter (Winona Lake: Eisenbrauns, 2008), 61–96; Seth L. Sanders, "Writing and Early Iron Age Israel: Before National Scripts, Beyond Nations and States," in *Literate Culture and Tenth-Century Canaan: The Tel Zayit Abecedary in Context*, ed. Ron E. Tappy and P. Kyle McCarter (Winona Lake: Eisenbrauns, 2008), 97–112; Sanders, *The Invention of Hebrew*.

11 Two additional inscriptions are worth noting: 1) A recent find from Megiddo may need to be added to the Iron I–IIA transition group. Sass and Finkelstein published a linear alphabetic inscription from Megiddo, stratum VB/VAIVB, which they date to the 9th century. It is a two-letter inscription on a jug, written in ink prior to firing. They propose that it was a dedicatory inscription, reading *hb* with a possible reconstruction of the personal name [n']hb ("The Swan-Song of Proto-Canaanite in the Ninth Century BCE in Light of an Alphabetic Inscription from Megiddo," 2). Excavators of Khirbet al-Ra'i have recently published an Iron I inscription, that appears to read *yrb'l*, Jerubba'al. Three inscribed sherds, all from the same vessel, were found in a silo that contained household waste. Both the archaeological contexts and the palaeographic analysis point to the late 12th to early 11th century as a date (Christopher Rollston et al., "The Jerubba'al Inscription from Khirbat Al-Ra'i: A Proto-Canaanite (Early Alphabetic) Inscription," *Jerusalem Journal of Archaeology* 2 [2021]: 1–15).

12 Aḥituv and Mazar, "The Inscriptions from Tel Reḥov." An additional sherd, typically dated to the Iron I, was found out of context in 1939. Finkelstein and Sass date it to early Iron IIA (partly out of a determination that any linear alphabetic inscription found outside of Philistia must be later than the Iron I; "West Semitic Alphabetic Inscriptions," 160–61, 177, 186, 209).

13 The most recently published example from Tell eṣ-Ṣafi (Gath) is dated to the late Iron I to early Iron IIA based on the inscription and pottery characteristics, but it was found in a later context (Esther Eshel et al., "Two Iron Age Alphabetic Inscriptions from Tell Eṣ-Ṣâfi/Gath, Israel," *BASOR* 388 [2022]: 31–49).

14 Yosef Garfinkel et al., "The 'Išba'al Inscription from Khirbet Qeiyafa," *BASOR* 373 (2015): 217–33; Haggai Misgav, Yosef Garfinkel, and Saar Ganor, "The Ostracon," in *Khirbet Qeiyafa Vol. 1, Excavation Report 2007-2008*, ed. Yosef Garfinkel and Saar Ganor (Jerusalem: Israel Exploration Society; Institute of Archaeology, Hebrew University of Jerusalem, 2009), 243–57; Ada Yardeni, "Further Observations on the Ostracon," in *Khirbet Qeiyafa Vol. 1, Excavation Report 2007-2008*, ed. Yosef Garfinkel and Saar Ganor (Jerusalem: Israel Exploration Society; Institute of Archaeology, Hebrew University of Jerusalem, 2009), 259–60.

15 These examples are compiled in Finkelstein and Sass, "The Exceptional Concentration"; idem, "West Semitic Alphabetic Inscriptions." The researchers also note the only LBA linear alphabetic texts from reliable contexts come from sites within the geographic zone of their Shephelah-Philistia group (or the southern cluster in this chapter; "The Exceptional Concentration," 127). Nadav Na'aman explores the potential processes of an LBA–Iron I transmission in the Levant in "Egyptian Centres and the Distribution of the Alphabet in the Levant, *TA* 47, no. 1 (2020), 29–54.

16 Yardenna Alexandre, "A Canaanite-Early Phoenician Inscribed Bronze Bowl in an Iron Age IIA–B Burial Cave at Kefar Veradim, Northern Israel," *Maarav* 13, no. 1 (2006): 7–41, 129–32.

17 F. W. Dobbs-Allsopp et al., *Hebrew Inscriptions: Texts from the Biblical Period of the Monarchy with Concordance* (New Haven: Yale University Press, 2005), 3.

18 Aḥituv and Mazar, "The Inscriptions from Tel Reḥov."

19 Mazar et al., "An Inscribed Pithos from the Ophel, Jerusalem," 39–49.

20 W. F. Albright, "The Gezer Calendar," *BASOR* 92 (1943): 16–26; Dobbs-Allsopp et al., *Hebrew Inscriptions*, 155–65.

21 George L. Kelm and Amihai Mazar, "Tel Batash (Timnah) Excavations: Third Preliminary Report, 1984–1989," BASORSup 27 (1991): 47–67; Dobbs-Allsopp et al., *Hebrew Inscriptions*, 113–14.

22. Shlomo Bunimovitz and Zvi Lederman, "Beth-Shemesh: Culture Conflict on Judah's Frontier," *BAR* 23, no. 1 (1997): 42–49, 75–77.
23. A. Maeir et al., "A Late Iron Age I/Early Iron Age II Old Canaanite Inscription," 39–71.
24. Gordon J. Hamilton has a slightly different reading of the first name: ʾlgwt; interpreting it as West Semitic name ("From the Seal of a Seer to an Inscribed Game Board: A Catalogue of Eleven Early Alphabetic Inscriptions Recently Discovered in Egypt and Palestine," *The Bible and Interpretation* [February 2010]: 12).
25. Garfinkel et al., "The ʾIšbaʿal Inscription"; Misgav, Garfinkel, and Ganor, "The Ostracon"; Yardeni, "Further Observations on the Ostracon"; Aaron Demsky, "An Iron Age IIA Alphabetic Writing Exercise from Khirbet Qeiyafa." *IEJ* 62, no. 2 (2012): 186–99.
26. Edward M. Cook, "Olive Pits and Alef-Bets: Notes on the Qeiyafa Ostracon," *Ralph the Sacred River*, March 14, 2010.
27. Ron E. Tappy et al., "An Abecedary of the Mid-Tenth Century B.C.E. from the Judaean Shephelah," *BASOR* 344 (2006): 5–46; Rollston, "The Phoenician Script of the Tel Zayit Abecedary."
28. For examples, see Josette Elayi, "Four New Inscribed Phoenician Arrowheads," *Studi Epigrafici e Linguistici* 22 (2005): 35–45; Finkelstein and Sass, "West Semitic Alphabetic Inscriptions," 163, 210–12; Lemaire, "From the Origin of the Alphabet," 1–20; idem, "Levantine Literacy ca. 1000–750 BCE," 13–14.
29. Bunimovitz and Lederman, "Beth-Shemesh," 42–49, 75–77. Although a bit further south, the bullae finds at Tell Summeily noted above should be considered a part of this same cluster of scribal activity.
30. Dorsey, *Roads and Highways*, 93–116.
31. The corresponding ceramic assemblage fits in the 10th to 8th century range broadly. Yardenna Alexandre assigns the burial to the 10th century based, in part, on the style of the bronze bowl (with the late 11th century parallel in Tanis) and the Cyriot Black-on-Red pottery (BoR), especially the kraters and jugs ("A Canaanite-Early Phoenician Inscribed Bronze Bowl," 13–20). Benjamin Sass has proposed a later date based on Assyrian parallels, among other factors, but his position has not convinced many; see review of his claim in Rollston, *Writing and Literacy*, 27–29; and Aḥituv and Mazar, "The Inscriptions from Tel Reḥov," 54–55.
32. Judith Muñoz Sogas, "Was Knossos a Home for Phoenician Traders?," in *Greek Art in Motion: Studies in Honour of Sir John Boardman on the Occasion of His 90th Birthday*, ed. Rui Morais et al. (Oxford: Archaeopress, 2019), 408–416.
33. Noted by Seth Sanders (personal communication).
34. Pierre Montet, *Les Constructions et le Tombeau de Psousennès á Tanis*, vol. 2 of *La Nécropole Royale de Tanis* (Paris: s.n., 1951), 82–83, plate 54. This parallel, a fluted drinking vessel, is exceptional in its similarity in shape to the Kefar Veradim bowl. Marian Feldman examines the 'international' popularity and significance of these types of drinking vessels, although mostly concerning later Iron Age contexts (*Communities of Style*, 111–38).
35. In both cases, there has been debate about dating both the inscriptions and the archaeological contexts. The paleographic analysis results in an earlier date than the ceramic assemblages. The inscriptions appear to date to the 11th–10th centuries. Wendjebauendjed's burial dates to the 11th century. See Sogas, "Was Knossos a Home for Phoenician Traders?," 412, with references; Rollston, *Writing and Literacy*; Alexandre, "A Canaanite-Early Phoenician Inscribed Bronze Bowl."
36. Jamieson-Drake argues well why inscriptions should be viewed as prestige goods (*Scribes and Schools*, 107–35).
37. These include Kefar Veradim, Tel ʿAmal, Tel Reḥov, Gezer, Beth Shemesh, Tell eṣ-Ṣafi (Gath), Khirbet Qeiyafa, and the Ophel/Jerusalem.
38. Trade in copper and iron was important in the Iron I–IIA and involved both of the areas where epigraphic discoveries have been most intense; see Chapters Two, Three, and Six.
39. Aren M. Maeir, "Chapter 1: Introduction and Overview" in *Tell es-Safi/Gath II: Excavation and Studies*, ed. A. M. Maeir and J. Uziel (Ägypten und Altes Testament 105; Münster: Zaphon, 2020), 3–52, esp. 19–27.
40. See references below.
41. Cook, "Olive Pits and Alef-Bets"; Matthieu Richelle, "Quelques Nouvelles Lectures Sur L'ostracon de Khirbet Qeiyafa," *Semitica* 57 (2015): 147–62. Although see also, most recently, a new proposal for the text as a narrative composition related to legal proceedings (Brian Donnelly-Lewis, "The Khirbet Qeiyafa Ostracon: A New Collation Based on the Multispectral Images, with Translation and Commentary," *BASOR* 388 [2022]: 181–210).
42. Regarding ḥnn, see Hamilton, "Two Methodological Issues," 151, note 41.
43. Eshel et al., "Two Iron Age Alphabetic Inscriptions."

44 Bunimovitz and Lederman, "Beth-Shemesh," 42–49, 75–77.
45 Aaron Demsky, "The Jerusalem Ceramic Inscription," Sidebar in "Artifact Found Near Temple Mount Bearing Canaanite Inscription from the Time before King David," *Foundation Stone*, July 7, 2013; Hamilton, "Two Methodological Issues."
46 Frank Moore Cross, "The Origin and Early Evolution of the Alphabet," *Eretz-Israel* 8 (1967): 8*–24*; Bunimovitz and Lederman, "Beth-Shemesh."
47 Dorsey, *Roads and Highways*, 186–89.
48 For commonness of ḥnn, see Hamilton, "Two Methodological Issues," 151, note 41.
49 This possibility was first entertained by Amihai Mazar, who excavated Tel Batash ("The Northern Shephelah in the Iron Age: Some Issues in Biblical History and Archaeology," in *Scripture and Other Artifacts: Essays on the Bible and Archaeology in Honor of Philip J. King*, ed. Michael David Coogan, J. Cheryl Exum, and Lawrence E. Stager [Louisville: Westminster John Knox Press, 1994], 255). See also Koert Van Bekkum, "'The Situation Is More Complicated': Archaeology and Text in the Historical Reconstruction of the Iron Age IIA Southern Levant," in *Exploring the Narrative: Jerusalem and Jordan in the Bronze and Iron Ages: Papers in Honour of Margreet Steiner*, ed. Noor Mulder-Hymans, Jeannette Boertien, and Eveline van der Steen (Library of Hebrew Bible/Old Testament Studies 583; London; New York: Bloomsbury T&T Clark, 2014), 233, note 31; Shlomo Bunimovitz and Zvi Lederman, "The Early Israelite Monarchy in the Sorek Valley: Tel Beth-Shemesh and Tel Batash (Timnah) in the 10th and 9th Centuries BCE," in *"I Will Speak the Riddles of Ancient Times": Archaeological and Historical Studies in Honor of Amihai Mazar on the Occasion of His Sixtieth Birthday*, ed. Aren M. Maeir, Pierre De Miroschedji, and Amihai Mazar (Winona Lake: Eisenbrauns, 2006), 422, note 10.
50 Dobbs-Allsopp et al., *Hebrew Inscriptions*, 3.
51 Amihai Mazar, "Three 10th–9th Century B.C.E. Inscriptions From Tēl Reḥōv," in *Saxa Loquentur: Studien zur Archäologie Palästinas/Israels. Festschrift für Volkmar Fritz* ed. Cornelis G. Den Hartog, Ulrich Hübner and Stefan Münger (AOAT 302; Münster: Ugarit Verlag, 2003), 171–84; Aḥituv and Mazar, "The Inscriptions from Tel Reḥov," 43–44, 64.
52 Aḥituv and Mazar, "The Inscriptions from Tel Reḥov," 64.
53 Propagated by Albright, Cross, and others; see Seth L. Sanders, "What Was the Alphabet For? The Rise of Written Vernaculars and the Making of Israelite National Literature," *Maarav* 11, no. 1 (2004): 34–42; Rollston, "The Phoenician Script of the Tel Zayit Abecedary," 67–70. More recently, Alan Millard has also asserted that, since the Khirbet Qeiyafa inscription does not appear to be by a skilled hand, writing must have been widespread ("The Ostracon from the Days of David Found at Khirbet Qeiyafa," *TynBul* 62, no. 1 [2011]). Similarly, Gordon Hamilton suggests that the newer discoveries (from Middle Bronze through Iron Age) indicate 'the use of alphabetic scripts along a spectrum from formal to informal levels of writing' and 'among people of various social classes' ("From the Seal of a Seer").
54 Byrne, "The Refuge of Scribalism," 23; emphasis in the original.
55 Paul S. Ash is dismissive of the value of the 10th century inscriptions for conveying information about social status or change in this period. For example, he refers to the Tel Batash inscription as 'a potter's name' and the Tel 'Amal inscription as 'only a personal name' and 'graffito' ("Solomon's? District? List," 72, note 22).
56 Mazar, "Three 10th–9th Century B.C.E. Inscriptions"; Amihai Mazar, "Reḥob," in *The Oxford Encyclopedia of Bible and Archaeology*, ed. Daniel M. Master et al. (New York: Oxford University Press, 2013), 226; Aḥituv and Mazar, "The Inscriptions from Tel Reḥov," 63.
57 Their debate implicitly references Jamieson-Drake's arguments about scribal schools appearing no earlier than the 8th century. The two sides have in common the assumption that literacy was accessible and had to be widespread, which is also derived from Jamieson-Drake's arguments although he is somewhat inconsistent on the matter (*Scribes and Schools*, 148–53).
58 Mazar, "Three 10th–9th Century B.C.E. Inscriptions," note 16. It is notable that although he refers to a 'scribe' when discussing the character of the inscriptions, Mazar does not acknowledge or consider those who would have such knowledge necessarily to be in or employed by an elite group.
59 John Nicolas Coldstream and Amihai Mazar, "Greek Pottery from Tel Rehov and Iron Age Chronology," *IEJ* 53 (2003): 29–48; Aḥituv and Mazar, "The Inscriptions from Tel Reḥov."
60 Yardenna Alexandre, "The 'Hippo' Jar and Other Storage Jars at Hurvat Rosh Zayit," *TA* 22, no. 1 (1995): 77–88; Leore Grosman et al., "Archaeology in Three Dimensions: Computer-Based Methods in Archaeological Research," *Journal of Eastern Mediterranean Archaeology & Heritage Studies* 2, no. 1 (2014): 62.

61 Amihai Mazar, "An Ivory Statuette Depicting an Enthroned Figure from Tel Reḥov," in *Bilder Als Quellen, Images as Sources: Studies on Ancient Near Eastern Artefacts and the Bible Inspired by the Work of Othmar Keel*, ed. Susanne Bickel et al. (Orbis Biblicus et Orientalis; Fribourg; Göttingen: Academic Press; Vandenhoeck & Ruprecht, 2007), 101–10; Amihai Mazar and Nava Panitz-Cohen, "It Is the Land of Honey: Beekeeping at Tel Reḥov," *NEA* 70, no. 4 (2007): 202–19; Nimrud Marom et al., "Backbone of Society: Evidence for Social and Economic Status of the Iron Age Population of Tel Rehov, Beth-Shean Valley, Israel," *BASOR* 354 (2009): 1–21; Mazar, "Reḥob"; Aḥituv and Mazar, "The Inscriptions from Tel Reḥov."

62 Mazar, "Reḥob."

63 Aḥituv and Mazar, "The Inscriptions from Tel Reḥov," 63.

64 Seth L. Sanders, "From People to Public in the Iron Age Levant," in *Organization, Representation, and Symbols of Power in the Ancient Near East: Proceedings of the 54th Rencontre Assyriologique Internationale at Würzburg 20–25 July 2008*, ed. Gernot Wilhelm (Winona Lake: Eisenbrauns, 2012), 106.

65 Despite the anachronistic language, the Iron I period was a time of widespread displacement and migration. We should expect that not all connections were lost even across long distances.

66 This discussion follows the conventional scheme for the early Phoenician rulers and their approximate dates. Benjamin Sass has argued for a dramatic down-dating of the inscriptions that seems unnecessary (*The Alphabet at the Turn of the Millennium: The West Semitic Alphabet ca. 1150–850 BCE: The Antiquity of the Arabian, Greek and Phrygian Alphabets* [Tel Aviv: Emery and Claire Yass Publications in Archaeology, 2005]; Finkelstein and Sass, "West Semitic Alphabetic Inscriptions," 181–83). For a detailed critique of Sass, see Christopher A. Rollston, "The Dating of the Early Royal Byblian Phoenician Inscriptions: A Response to Benjamin Sass," *Maarav* 15, no. 1 (2008): 57–93. Sass has revisited the arguments in a number of more recent publications, for example, "The Emergence of Monumental West Semitic Alphabetic Writing, with an Emphasis on Byblos," *Semitica* 59 (2017): 109–41.

67 For a general review of the inscriptions, see Gibson, *TSSI III*, 12–24. See also William Foxwell Albright, "The Phoenician Inscriptions of the Tenth Century B. C. from Byblus," *JAOS* 67, no. 3 (1947): 153–60; Yitzhak Avishur, *Phoenician Inscriptions and the Bible: Select Inscriptions and Studies in Stylistic and Literary Devices Common to the Phoenician Inscriptions and the Bible* (Tel Aviv: Archaeological Center Publication, 2000), 103–4; Marilyn J. Lundberg, "Editor's Notes: The Aḥiram Inscription," *Maarav* 11, no. 1 (2004): 81–93.

68 Most translations of Yeḥimilk's inscription emend *b'l gbl* to *b'lt gbl* because of the frequency of the latter and infrequency of the former. For an argument against the emendation, see Aaron Schade, "The Syntax and Literary Structure of the Phoenician Inscription of Yeḥimilk," *Maarav* 13, no. 1 (2006): 119–22.

69 Matthew James Suriano, "The Formulaic Epilogue for a King in the Book of Kings in Light of Royal Funerary Rites in Ancient Israel and the Levant" (Doctoral Dissertation, University of California, Los Angeles, 2008), 152.

70 Eliba'al's text (and his son Shipitba'al's) establishes his legitimacy through Yeḥimilk.

71 John Gibson suggests that these inscriptions on Egyptian monuments served to elevate the reputation and status of the Byblian king to the level of a pharaoh (*TSSI III*, 22). The Report of Wenamun, however, presents a power reversal, where Egyptian authority was not well respected by Levantine rulers (see below). Does the Byblian kings' defacing/appropriating of these statues corroborate the Egyptian tale? Rather than interpret the act as a resourceful way for a king to 'create' a monumental inscription, we could also view it as a type of dominance, Byblos over Egypt, where the king appropriates the status object and presents it to the goddess under his name.

72 For analysis of similar appropriation and emulation of sculpture, see Virginia R. Herrmann, "Appropriation and Emulation in the Earliest Sculptures from Zincirli (Iron Age Sam'al)," *American Journal of Archaeology* 121, no. 2 (2017): 237–74.

73 An Egyptian official, 'Pa-di-iset, the justified, son of Apy,' 'the only renowned one, the impartial envoy of Philistine Canaan,' had himself immortalized by removing the inscription from a Middle Kingdom official's statue and replacing it with his own. Pa-di-iset may have served a 22nd Dynasty king. The inscription is often dated to the 10th century, but there is not enough evidence to pin down a more precise date. The inscription's character fits the model of reuse and assertion that we have seen, though this combination is not exclusive to the period by any means. See Georg Steindorff, "The Statuette of an Egyptian Commissioner in Syria," *JEA* 25, no. 1 (1939): 30–33, plate VII; Walter's Art Gallery "Statue of a Vizier, Usurped by Pa-di-iset."; Singer, "Egyptians, Canaanites, and Philistines," 330.

74 Egyptian chronology of this period is also debated. See Kenneth Kitchen, "Establishing Chronology in Pharaonic Egypt and the Ancient Near East: Interlocking Textual Sources Relating to C. 1600–664 BC," in *Radiocarbon and the Chronologies of Ancient Egypt*, ed. Andrew J. Shortland and Christopher Bronk

Ramsey (Oxford: Oxbow Books, 2013), 1–18; Andrew Shortland, "Shishak, King of Egypt: The Challenges of Egyptian Calendrical Chronology in the Iron Age," in *The Bible and Radiocarbon Dating: Archaeology, Text and Science*, ed. Thomas E. Levy and T. Higham (London; Oakville: Equinox Publishing, 2005), 43–54; Taylor, "The Third Intermediate Period."

75 Kenneth Kitchen, "Egyptian Interventions in the Levant in the Iron Age II," in *Symbiosis, Symbolism, and the Power of the Past: Canaan, Ancient Israel, and Their Neighbors from the Late Bronze Age through Roman Palaestina. Proceedings of the Centennial Symposium, W.F. Albright Institute of Archaeological Research and American Schools of Oriental Research, Jerusalem, May 29/31, 2000*, ed. William G. Dever and Seymour Gitin (Winona Lake: Eisenbrauns, 2003), 118–19, 121–25. For Siamun's relief, see Pierre Montet, *La Nécropole Royale de Tanis, Volume 1: Les Constructions et le Tombeau d'Osorkon II à Tanis* (Paris, 1947), plate 9A. For Shoshenq's Karnak inscription, see Rainey and Notley, *The Sacred Bridge*, 185–89.

76 Breasted, *Ancient Records of Egypt*, secs. 723, 729–737.

77 Susan Tower Hollis, "Hathor and Isis in Byblos in the Second and First Millenniua BCE," *Journal of Ancient Egyptian Interconnections* 1, no. 2 (2009): 1–8.

78 Robert S. Lamon and Geoffrey M. Shipton, *Megiddo I: Seasons of 1925-1934, Strata I–V* (Oriental Institute Communications 42; Chicago: University of Chicago Press, 1939), 60–61, fig. 70. The choice of Megiddo for such a display of power must have been related to the international traffic that passed through the site. The logistics of this are intriguing: were Egyptian scribes part of the campaign and left to commemorate it? Was the stele later shipped from Egypt? And what was the impact of this monumental inscription on the scribes of the southern Levant's elites?

79 Stefan Münger and Thomas E. Levy, "The Iron Age Egyptian Amulet Assemblage," in *New Insights into the Iron Age Archaeology of Edom, Southern Jordan: Surveys, Excavations and Research from the University of California, San Diego & Department of Antiquities of Jordan, Edom Lowlands Regional Archaeology Project (ELRAP)*, ed. Thomas E. Levy et al. (Monumenta Archaeologica 35; Los Angeles: The Cotsen Institute of Archaeology Press, 2014), 748–49, 758.

80 The account probably relied on real-life experiences of travel in the region; see Miriam Lichtheim, *Ancient Egyptian Literature: A Book of Readings, Volume II: The New Kingdom* (Berkeley: University of California Press, 1973), 224, 229–30.

81 The tale is typically understood to date to the 11th century. Edward F. Wente Jr. and Benjamin Sass have, separately, proposed arguments for the 10th century: Wente proposing authorship during the 21st Dynasty ("The Report of Wenamun" in *The Literature of Ancient Egypt: An Anthology of Stories, Instructions, Stelae, Autobiographies, and Poetry*, ed. William Kelly Simpson [New Haven; London: Yale University Press, 2003], 116); Sass argues for Shoshenq I's reign ("Wenamun and His Levant – 1075 B.C. or 925 B.C.?," *Egypt and the Levant* 12 [2002]: 247–55) Sass's arguments are not as convincing, but the historical situations of either the 11th or 10th centuries are plausible settings for the story's creation.

82 Other studies have shown that emulation was an important factor in the growth of Iron Age leadership in the region. See Higginbotham, *Egyptianization and Elite Emulation in Ramesside Palestine*; Alexander H. Joffe, "The Rise of Secondary States in the Iron Age Levant."

83 Sarah Malena, "History without Texts: Interdisciplinary Interpretive Methods for Understanding the Early Iron Age," in *"And in Length of Days Understanding" (Job 12:12): Essays on Archaeology in the Eastern Mediterranean and Beyond in Honor of Thomas E. Levy*, ed. Erez Ben-Yosef and Ian W. N. Jones (Interdisciplinary Contributions to Archaeology; Cham: Springer, 2023), 535–54.

6 Nonlocal Ceramics in the Iron I–IIA Transition

Our examination now turns to another form of conspicuous material culture, nonlocal ceramics, and examines how such items contribute to the evidence of interregional interaction in the late Iron I to early Iron IIA. Ceramics produced in northwest Arabia, Cyprus, and the Aegean have been unearthed in excavations throughout the southern Levant, from northern Israel/southern Phoenicia to the southern desert zones, and both west and east of the Jordan and Arabah Valleys.[1] These different wares were not integrated into one trade operation. The pottery from northwest Arabia was associated with the copper exchange network in the south and was most prevalent later in the LBA and into the early Iron Age. Interactions in the eastern Mediterranean were reestablished by the end of the 11th century BCE, evidenced by a limited amount of pottery from Cyprus and the Aegean. Mediterranean imports are rare in excavated contexts dating to the earlier years of the Iron I–IIA transition, suggesting a more exclusive exchange community at that time. By the end of the 10th century, however, Cypriot trade had expanded to reach most areas of the southern Levant. These ceramic groups demonstrate that, even as the major LBA exchange networks dissolved, some exchange relations persisted and new connections were established, filling the gap in long-distance interactions that were experienced elsewhere.

Spatial distributions of the imported wares make clear that there was a variety of consumers. Combined, the imports stretch from Tyre to the Gulf of Aqaba/Eilat, and from all along the Mediterranean coast to the Jordan Valley, including in the Negev and Jordanian deserts. Involvement in the exchange networks, however, was limited to zones near entry points to the region and strategically positioned sites (i.e., those near key transportation routes, at well-defensible locations such as major tells, or those that governed over crossroads and important resource areas). Based on these geographic observations, participation in the early stages was dominated by those who were closest to primary routes and in control of key resources. In some cases, however, exchange penetrated beyond the expected exchange zones, suggesting that the transport of these vessels to more distant locations was the result of a deliberate demand for the wares and their associated goods. Analysis of these contexts and circumstances demonstrates that this special exchange was most active among elites.

Archaeological Evidence of Exchange

Ceramics are not the only archaeological indicator of exchange activities, and recent discoveries have demonstrated two important points: 1) that researchers now have a number of indicators for understanding early Iron Age trade; and 2) that older characterizations of the Iron I and early Iron II as a period of insularity and isolation are no longer accurate. This shift in our knowledge is very recent and has important implications for our understanding not only of trade and exchange in the Iron I and early Iron IIA, but also of cultural identity, social organization, and state formation. There is not room here for a full survey of all the new evidence, but before examining the ceramic groups, I note briefly examples from some of the most consequential developments. The findings from research into these other exchange goods is complementary to the conclusions reached in this chapter.

Spice Trade

In the mid-8th century, Tiglath-Pilesar III boasted of capturing Levantine coastal cities and claiming them as Assyrian emporia.[2] As any critical reader of his inscriptions would surmise, the cities were well-known trade centers before the Assyrian king assumed the throne, but what was not proven until recently is just how 'international' they were. Recent residue analysis from small flasks demonstrates that cinnamon was being imported to the Levantine coast in the Iron I–IIA transition (ca. 11th and 10th centuries). The type of vessel that was tested has been found in many types of contexts, and should not be considered a rarity, but they 'are especially common in ritual and elite contexts.'[3] Ten vessels (five from Dor, four from Tel Qasile, one from Kinneret), which made up nearly 40% of the study, tested positive for cinnamaldehyde, a major component of cinnamon, which at the time was grown only in south and southeast Asia.[4] The networks responsible for bringing cinnamon to the eastern Mediterranean most likely involved sea trade in the Indian Ocean, and would have also connected goods and peoples in east Africa and Arabia, but the trade was not centrally organized or dominated by one or even a few major states.[5] As Gilboa and Namdar argue, '...at least in the early Iron Age this trade and the cultural contacts it generated involved entrepreneurs in small-scale societies, and undoubtedly some down-the-line mechanism.'[6] The proposed scope of the networked communities would have linked resource zones of not only cinnamon and other plants in the 'spice' category, but also incense, gold, shells, and rare stones, as well as foodstuffs such as nonlocal fish and grains.

Dyed Textiles

The famed purple dye that was a signal of elite status for centuries has also recently been discovered in early Iron Age archaeological contexts. Textiles found in excavations at Timna Site 34 have been identified conclusively as having been dyed with the 'royal purple' and are, for the southern Levant's Iron Age, the oldest direct, physical evidence of textiles dyed with the murex-derived substance.[7] Interregional exchange is the only explanation for the presence of the dyed textiles in the Arabah, since the source of the dye was the central Levantine coast – in other words, Phoenicia. The requirements for producing the dye and the process of dying textiles with it were intensive and needed to be located close to the source of the murex sea snails. The importance of this discovery is not limited to the fact that we have yet another type of long-distance exchange item now in evidence; it is also suggestive of who was involved in this exchange. Due to the rarity and difficulty in producing the dye, textiles colored with it were reserved for the most elite figures in the ancient Mediterranean, throughout the 2nd millennium BCE and into the 1st millennium CE. The presence of dyed fibers is overwhelming evidence in favor of the presence of elites, both in locations where it is found, and in systems related to its exchange. In this case, we have strong evidence of elite involvement in the exchange affiliated with Timna.[8]

Metals

As I introduced in Chapters Two and Three, the southern Levant witnessed a very active trade in metals during the Iron I–IIA period. Both copper and iron were sourced and produced in the region, and the former is proving to have been among the most important regional resources of the period.[9] The interregional impact of this industry is coming to light with the recent discoveries that Arabah copper was used to produce objects found as far away as northern Egypt and Greece.[10] Silver was also in high demand but could not be sourced locally – rather, it was a product from Anatolia, the Aegean, and western Mediterranean.[11] During shortages in the metal due to the end of the LBA crisis, those who specialized in the silver trade debased it with Arabah copper to stretch what was still available.[12]

Based on early Iron Age evidence in neighboring regions, we should also understand that gold remained a prized commodity, but our direct evidence of its trade in the southern Levant is, at present, limited to depictions of exchange in the Report of Wenamun. In this text, silver and gold are the currency of diplomacy and commercial exchange, as well as targets for theft.[13] Indirect evidence in this period includes small finds in burial contexts and descriptions of dedicatory gifts by rulers.[14] The resource zones for gold (primarily modern day Sudan) and the exchange systems that may have brought it to the southern Levant were by no means out of reach considering the new evidence of other long-distance trade in spices that came to the southern Levant via Arabian networks and exchange in copper between the Egyptian Delta and the Arabah.

Ceramics as Evidence of Exchange

Although these newer discoveries provide insights into the commodities that were circulating, the recovery of metals, textiles, and spices is challenged by the rarity of these goods in ancient times, along with issues of consumption, reuse, and preservation. In contrast, pottery is ubiquitous in the archaeological record. It is easy to produce and preserves relatively well. As a result, archaeologists have access to a large body of evidence and examples. Pottery can also reflect cultural interaction in various ways. Vessel shape and decoration can easily be adapted and might indicate influence from other cultures. Conversely, the persistence of distinct styles despite frequent interactions with other groups might indicate the maintenance of deliberate cultural boundaries.[15] Analysis of a vessel's fabric provides information about clay sources and thus the pot's place of manufacture.[16] In addition, distribution studies show how widespread the use of a ceramic type was.[17] Once provenance and distribution are determined, we can explore questions about the significance of exchange.[18] This chapter relies on such archaeological principles and on previous research that has laid the groundwork in provenance studies, catalogs and inventories, and geospatial information.

Issues Particular to the Southern Levant

Before addressing the specific pottery groups, there are some critical issues that are shaping current archaeological discussions that need to be addressed, especially concerning interactions of various populations, relationships between sites, and historical events.

Ethnicity, Pots, and Peoples

Debates about the relationship between pottery and population groups are ongoing and necessary. On the one hand, there is good reason to ask if a type of pottery can be an indication of a certain people; populations may have a distinct cultural assemblage. On the other hand, diversity within a society is now well recognized, and anthropology has provided more approaches to exploring identity formation and cultural interaction. Revolutions in these approaches gained ground in the 1960s; F. Barth's *Ethnic Groups and Boundaries* remains an influential example.[19] In the 1970s and 1980s, I. Hodder led a new approach that challenged the way scholars examined people's relationships to things.[20] Despite these trends in social scientific circles, it was still necessary in 1997 for J. Waldbaum to remind her audience that Greek pottery found in the Levant did not necessarily mean there were Greek peoples in the Levant,[21] and discussions of ethnicity in the Iron Age and the Bible have only applied sociological and anthropological approaches relatively recently to archaeological and historical discussions.[22] Some of the evidence surveyed in this chapter has been interpreted in previous scholarship as evidence of migrations, and the early Iron Age was indeed an age of migration for many population groups. Nevertheless, my point of departure is that pottery of foreign origins may have reached the Levant through other exchange mechanisms. We will see that these were primarily trade and elite exchange networks.

Chronological Debate

One of the greatest challenges to archaeological discussions today remains chronology. The ongoing refinement touches any discussion of Iron Age archaeology, but it is particularly germane to a discussion of imported goods. That is because early biblical archaeology and biblical stories of trade not only laid the foundation for the chronology of ancient Israel and Palestine, but also provided anchors for the early Iron Age chronologies of Phoenicia, Cyprus, and the Aegean.[23] The biblical tales of Solomon's trade with Arabia, Mesopotamia, Egypt, and his acquisition of metals for construction projects informed the analysis of scholars like N. Glueck, who conducted the first archaeological surveys of the southern desert regions in the 1930s–1960s. Throughout the first half of the century, W. F. Albright, G. E. Wright, Y. Yadin, and others, excavating the region's most spectacular tells, established their chronologies, trusting in biblical history (including David's conquests and Solomon's great building efforts, which they associated with the remains they found). A handful of imported sherds from these digs were coordinated with the imports' lands of origins, thus setting anchor points for all the regions, based on methods that no longer meet standards of excavation or scholarship.

Several key problems have resulted from this research history. The chronologies of the ceramic sequences of the Aegean, Cyprus, and Phoenicia developed independently *after* their initial correlation to the earlier southern Levantine excavations. Until recently, adjustments to chronologies did not address the underlying link between the regions, and one region's chronology would continue to reinforce or rely on chronological anchors that were no longer maintained in other regions (e.g., Cypriot chronology's reliance on a Megiddo context that is no longer an anchor for southern Levantine chronology).[24] Regional specialists for the Aegean, Cyprus, Phoenicia, and the southern Levant are all reexamining these foundations, and as each region is experiencing revision, it is difficult to keep parallels current. Until new anchors are determined, a comprehensive, absolute chronology for the Mediterranean remains a moving target. Despite these problems, the three pottery groups that are examined below span the time period in question, and recently recovered examples of these wares are allowing for more confidence in our understanding of each group. Thus, even with continued debate, the material in this chapter provides evidence for long-distance exchange during the region's transition period from the late Iron I to the early Iron IIA.

Imported Wares by Region of Origin

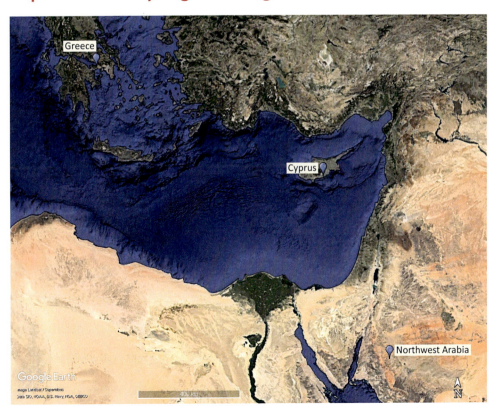

Figure 6.1: Lands of origin of ceramic imports. Map: Google Earth, © 2020.

Northwest Arabia

Qurayyah Painted Ware (QPW), frequently referred to as 'Midianite' ware, is best known from surveys and excavations in the Arabah Valley. The vast majority of QPW finds in the southern Levant have come from Timna, a complex of archaeological sites in the southwest Arabah Valley, whose primary function was smelting and processing locally mined copper. The pottery is also well known from the region's other copper processing center, the Faynan in southern Jordan, and along the copper trade routes, as far as eastern Egypt. There is an undeniable correlation between the ancient copper industry and QPW, but the pottery has also been recovered from non-metallurgical contexts, as far north as Amman and Gezer, which raises questions about QPW's role in trade activities. Often, the ware was associated with other imported and luxury goods, suggesting that it was valued as a prestige item.

Because of its distinctive painted designs and characterization as a fine ware, excavators have been recording their discoveries of QPW in one way or another for more than a century, but it was only in the latter half of the 20th century that scholars worked toward a formal classification of the ware. Prior to a consensus, this pottery group was recorded under a variety of names, or through idiosyncratic descriptions, so that there was little consistency among researchers and publications.[25] P. Parr's research in northwest Arabia and B. Rothenberg's research in the Timna region laid the foundation for all subsequent investigations.[26] In 1983, Rothenberg and Glass published results of petrographic testing that confirmed an origin for the pottery in the Hejaz region of northwest Arabia.[27] Parr's surveys in that area had already provided evidence for a probable site of production, Qurayyah, for which the pottery is now named.[28] M. Luciani's recent excavations demonstrate that QPW grew out of large-scale, local pottery production at the site that began in the first half of the 2nd millennium BCE.[29] Instrumental Neutron Activation Analysis (INAA) performed on Levantine samples of QPW further confirms a relationship to the northern Hejaz. There is enough variation in fabric that there may have been multiple production centers, but samples of finer fabrics appear to have come from one production location.[30] A few exceptions to an Arabian origin have been reported, namely sherds from the Arabah sites in the Faynan and possibly Timna, and these examples indicate that there may have been local production in this region.[31]

As is the case with most archaeological evidence from the southern Levant, the chronological range of QPW's production and use is debated. Prior to Rothenberg's Timna excavations, contexts associated with this pottery were dated to the 10th century, based on assumptions that the sites were connected to Solomon's metallurgical efforts (such as that described in 1 Kgs 7:46); Rothenberg's excavations, however, produced evidence of QPW along with Egyptian activity of the 13th and 12th centuries BCE.[32] Additional excavation at Timna, along with excavations in the Faynan, Tayma, Qurayyah, and the reevaluation of some key find sites (e.g., Tell el-Kheleifeh), have provided critical new data for assessing periods when QPW was produced and in use.[33] A. Intilia's comprehensive analysis indicates that the main period of use in the Levant occurred during the 13th through 11th centuries.[34] Excavation of sites in northwest Arabia confirm that QPW had been in production and use there since the mid-2nd millennium.[35] The end of QPW's use has been a more challenging question. Recent excavations at Timna and the Faynan have shifted focus again toward the Iron IIA. Some QPW sherds were found associated with 10th century metallurgical activity at Timna Site 30.[36] More than 30 sherds of QPW have been recovered from Khirbat en-Nahas (KEN) in the Faynan.[37] The main metallurgical phases at KEN began in the 11th century and ended by the end of the 9th, and the contexts associated with the QPW date primarily to the 10th century.[38] The Arabah evidence may demonstrate that QPW went out of use slightly later than in northwest Arabia. Alternatively, a number of scholars argue that the sherds recovered from the early Iron IIA contexts in the Arabah should be considered residual finds of earlier phases of activity (i.e., not later than the 11th century).[39] As research in both areas remains active, the presence of QPW in the Iron IIA will continue to be debated, but it appears quite certain that it was in use in the Arabah in the 11th century, at the start of the transition between the Iron I and IIA.

Northwest Arabia and Interaction

Prior to recent excavations at Qurayyah, scholars thought QPW developed its distinctive style as a result of interregional interaction toward the end of the LBA. What looked like a hybridization of Aegean, Egyptian, and Levantine characteristics from the LBA, is now understood to have developed from local ceramic traditions of the 17th and 16th centuries BCE. The earliest phase of QPW, termed 'Standard Qurayyah Painted Ware' by Luciani, 'is contemporaneous with similar assemblages found in the eastern Mediterranean, such as the Cypriot and Levantine Bichrome Ware, Chocolate-on-White Ware and Cypriot White Slip I.'[40] Luciani emphasizes that QPW was not an imitation of these wares.[41] This emphasis is important for underscoring the extent of the ceramic tradition at Qurayyah, but it is also notable that like their contemporaries, the originators and producers of QPW were engaged in the broader LBA cultural milieu and made a distinct contribution to cultural exchange.[42]

Qurayyah sits at an advantageous location in relation to water resources and along one of the only routes that provided passage through the mountainous terrain to the interregional roads along the Gulf of Aqaba.[43] Systematic excavations have made clear that the site supported sizeable communities from the Neolithic to Nabatean periods. Occupants as early as the 3rd millennium BCE maximized the setting with a dam and other features to create a 'human-made oasis.'[44] Qurayyah's resources, as well as its public and domestic areas, were surrounded by a mudbrick enclosure, which Luciani describes as 'a bounded landscape.'[45] At various points in the site's history, residents cultivated olive groves and smelted copper.[46] The residents of the Middle and Late Bronze Ages produced distinctive wares, including QPW, on an industrial scale.

The precise reasons that QPW came to be distributed outside of its region of origin are not fully understood, but vessel forms and contexts from which QPW has been recovered offer some clues. Most examples come from open vessels, indicating that the pottery was not simply a container holding a commodity. It may have moved with certain populations as a preferred tableware, or QPW may itself have been traded as a commodity.[47] While the strongest associated activity is with the copper industry (see below), burial contexts illustrate the potential for QPW to have been valued as a luxury ware. A QPW bowl and additional sherds were discovered in the 'Airport structure' in Amman. The unique building, which may have been a mortuary installation, contained imports from throughout the ancient Near East (from the Aegean, Cyprus, Mesopotamia, and Egypt).[48] QPW has also been found in burial contexts, the most striking of which is a burial cave at Tel Jedur (biblical Gedor), where a small QPW bowl was discovered among a rich LBA assemblage. The burial contained Aegean and Cypriot pottery, weapons, jewelry, Nile shells, glass vessel fragments, and two alabaster vessels.[49] There is no doubt that these burial goods belonged to a family of unusual wealth. The presence of QPW in these rich assemblages suggests that it too held significance as a valued, imported good.

The complicating factors in these burial contexts are that they were used over a long period of time for multiple burials, and that heirloom items may have been included in them.[50] As a result, determining the precise date of an item's deposition or the relationships among deposited goods is challenging. If QPW was contemporary to the LBA materials, then we have an indication that it was used as a luxury ware before the end of the LBA. If QPW was a later addition to a burial deposit (i.e., after the disruption of the LBA maritime trade networks), it could have served as a substitute for decorated wares that were no longer available. The burial at Tell el-Farʿah (S), Tomb 542 (one of Petrie's 'Tombs of the Philistine Lords') dated to the 12th–11th centuries, may illustrate this possibility. It contained a QPW vessel, along with other imported pottery (Phoenician, Egyptian, and 'Egyptianizing' wares), metal vessels, and weapons.[51] Although precise dating is uncertain, especially in respect to the availability of elite goods known from earlier in the LBA, this assemblage may demonstrate a continuation of LBA elite burial practices during the transition between the LBA and Iron I.

QPW and Copper Exchange Networks

The clearest context associated with QPW remains the copper trade, but the precise relationships among this pottery group and the copper industry, metallurgists, and trade routes are still unclear. Timna's excavations have produced the greatest amount of QPW, followed by the Faynan region. In smaller quantities, QPW is distributed along the highways that linked the copper sources and production sites with areas to the north and west. While QPW was oftentimes found alongside evidence of metalworking, the ware was not intimately linked to the technology of metallurgy. Rothenberg proposed that the pottery, which he labeled 'Midianite,' was brought to Timna by metalsmiths from northwest Arabia (biblical Midian), who served Egyptian interests.[52] Although we cannot maintain the precise historical reconstruction Rothenberg proposed, the evidence seems best explained as a close connection between the occupants of the Timna sites and cultural practices shared between the southern Arabah and the northern Hejaz.[53] We are still without direct confirmation of who the peoples of either of these regions understood themselves to be, at least in respect to historically attested cultures. The principal investigators from the Central Timna Valley (CTV) and Edomite Lowlands Regional Archaeology Project (ELRAP) argue that those who ran and worked the Arabah copper sites were part of a local, pastoral-nomadic society that gave rise to the Edomite Iron Age polity.[54] Luciani suggests another perspective, whereby we understand Timna and other southern Arabah sites 'as part of the material world of north Arabian oases.'[55]

Excavations at the Faynan's largest copper production site, Khirbat en-Nahas (KEN), turned up 49 QPW sherds but none of the evidence that Rothenberg relied on for a theory of resident Midianite smiths.[56] The KEN excavations have, rather, demonstrated that the site was a locally-run enterprise that was part of a rich Iron I–IIA network, which also included the Timna region and its copper production.[57] Evidence of interregional interaction from KEN, such as unusual jewelry, Egyptian amulets, Cypriot Black-on-Red (BoR) pottery, and other ceramic imports from the Negev and Jerusalem, became part of the site's assemblage as a result of the copper trade.[58] The associated contexts at KEN have been securely radiocarbon dated to the late Iron I to early Iron IIA, and the evidence does not indicate that the vessels had been preserved as heirlooms.[59] Interestingly, QPW, along with pottery imported from or via the western Negev, was found in metallurgical areas within KEN, but the overall quantity compared to the full ceramic assemblage from the site shows that these imports were small in number (e.g., QPW makes up 4% of the overall assemblage).[60] Smith and colleagues conclude that, 'even among the wheel-made red-slipped bowls from the western Negev and the painted Qurayyah wares, they should be considered rare, infrequent imports rather than a contingent of foreigners living at the site.'[61] Thus, the QPW found at KEN better fits into the context of an active exchange network associated with the culture of the copper trade than into Rothenberg's foreign smiths theory.

The full distribution of QPW highlights the close relationship with the copper trade, but, to reiterate, it is not limited to metallurgical production. QPW has been found along the routes leading from northern Arabia to the southern Levant, as well as the routes that distributed Timna and Faynan copper products to the west, along the Dharb el-Ghazza (including Tell el-Qudeirat/Kadesh Barnea[62]), throughout the Arabah Valley and Beersheba Valley. These associations indicate that QPW moved through the same channels as copper products, possibly as a traded commodity in its own right.[63]

The remains at Tel Masos, the most prominent site along the Beesheba Valley during this period, provide a view from another side of the exchange network. During the 12th to 10th centuries, Tel Masos was a thriving center of interregional exchange.[64] Its prosperity was due in part to its position, guarding passage through the Beersheba Valley as well as the routes into the Judahite hill country to the north and a road to Tell el-Qudeirat (Kadesh Barnea) to the south. The architecture of Tel Masos exhibits Canaanite and Egyptianizing styles (a local adaptation of the Egyptian 'Center Hall House,' i.e., 'Governor's Residency'[65]), and its inhabitants accumulated many imported goods and a diverse material culture: QPW from the Hejaz; copper from the Arabah/Faynan; Philistine bichrome pottery; Phoenician bichrome; a 'Negebite' vessel; Egyptian wares and small objects (e.g., scarabs); a Canaanite-style carved ivory lion's head; and possibly also Cypriot BoR.[66] The wealth of imports mimics prestige culture known from the LBA, suggesting select residents emulated the LBA models of elite behavior and did so with the styles and imports that were available at the time.[67] Similar behaviors may account for the rich burial at Tell el-Farʿah (S) described above, and the diversity of imported goods at Khirbat en-Nahas. We should understand these communities and the similarities among them as the result of participation in the copper exchange system, particularly by residents in leadership positions.[68]

In both the copper production areas and along the routes, local, Iron Age leadership directed successful operations. The retraction of Egyptian control in the 12th century allowed for local leaders to take over the network.[69] Tel Masos and Khirbat en-Nahas provide an archaeological picture of elite leadership within this exchange network. Similarly, residents of Tell el-Farʿah (S) and Tell el-Qudeirat (Kadesh Barnea), sites that occupied strategic positions along the routes, must have taken advantage of their location, and the lapse in Egyptian oversight, to secure operations along the exchange network.

Distribution Overview

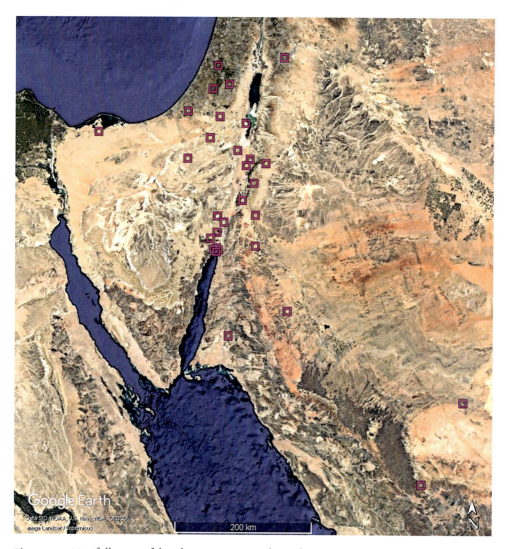

Figure 6.2: QPW full range of distribution. Map: Google Earth, © 2020.

QPW has been recovered from dozens of sites from northwestern Arabia, the Arabah, the Negev, northern Sinai, southern Jordan, the Shephelah, and the hill country near Hebron (Table 6.1).[70] Its distribution follows a pattern that we will see again with Aegean and Cypriot imports below. The sites correspond to major routes and prominent locations, and the distribution indicates that the Arabah and Beersheba Valleys were most significant outside of the Hejaz. These valleys also coincide with the copper exchange network that linked Arabah copper resources with the rest of the southern Levant and Egypt. Whoever transported the pottery and other goods likely traveled by foot, with donkeys or camels to assist with loads.[71] A day's journey could cover about 18–20 miles, or about 30 km (see Table 6.2).[72]

Table 6.1: Find locations of Qurayyah Painted Ware.

Arabia	Arabah & Southern Exchange Routes	Northern Sites	Northern Sinai
al ʿUla	Barqa al-Hatiya	Negev Highlands	Bir el-ʿAbd
Mughair Shuayb	En Hazeva	Rujm Hamra Ifdan	
Qurayyah	Ghrareh	Tawilan	
Tayma	Har Shani	T. el-Farʿah (S)	
	Jezirat Faraʿun	T. el-Kheleifeh	
	Kh. Duwar	T. Masos	
	Kh. en-Nahas	T. el-Qudeirat	
	Kh. esh-Shedeiyid	Timna	
	Mezad Gozal	Um Guweah	
	Nahal Amram	Uvda Valley	
	Nahal Shlomo	Yotvata	

Table 6.2: Distances from Qurayya.

Find location	Approximate travel distance from Qurayyah (km)	Approximate journey time from Qurayyah (days)
Timna	150	5–6
Faynan	250	8–9
Kadesh-Barnea	265	8–9
Bir el-ʿAbd	450–550	15–19
Gezer	425–450	14–16

The Arabah Valley was by far the most critical zone for QPW distribution (Figure 6.3). Stretching from the southern tip of the Dead Sea to the Gulf of Aqaba, the Arabah dominates the landscape of the south. Modern borders follow the low valley, separating today's nation-states, but its natural, funnel-like quality impacted ancient communities differently. The wadi systems from the highlands to the west and east drain into in this section of the Great Rift Valley. These drainages dictated travel and settlement patterns. As a result, the Arabah was a major corridor connecting the more populous areas of the southern Levant to the Red Sea and to routes leading to Arabia. Given QPW's origins in the Hejaz, the Arabah would inevitably be the main passage to sites in the Levant, which means the ware's presence at Arabah sites is to be expected. Considering the importance of copper production at Timna and the Faynan, and the trade resulting from it, it is logical that there are large quantities of QPW in these areas.

All routes connecting the Levant to Arabia merged in the Gulf of Eilat/Aqaba region. The Hebrew Bible indicates the area's importance, with reports of kings' efforts to control maritime activities through the port/fortress of Ezion-geber (1 Kgs 9:26, but see analysis in Chapter Three; 1 Kgs 22:49), which some scholars identify with Tell el-Kheleifeh.[73] With QPW reported from several sites in the area, this was the entry to the southern Levant for QPW's carriers/users.[74]

QPW has been found in the northeastern Arabah (the Faynan region), on the southern Jordanian plateau (Um Guweah, Khirbet esh-Shedeiyid, Ghrareh, Tawilan, Khirbet Duwar), and as far north as Amman. Two main roads ran north from the gulf. One followed the eastern edge of the Arabah Valley, and the other, the King's Highway, followed the plateau.[75] Sites on the plateau could have been reached by routes leading east from the Arabah road, but the ascent to the highland sites involved a steep climb.[76] Travel to sites such as Tawilan would necessarily have occurred via easier ascents further south, or at a limited number of more accessible passages.[77] The lowland Faynan sites (e.g., Barqa al-Hatiya, Khirbat en-Nahas) would have been reached directly from the Arabah. Further north, Amman sat at a convergence of highland roads and passage west to the Jordan Valley, where fords allowed travelers to cross the river.

Figure 6.3: QPW in southern Levantine sites. Map: Google Earth, © 2020.

Distribution west of the Jordan suggests that QPW was transported through sites that supported long-distance exchange. From the gulf, travel to the northwest followed two main routes that ultimately joined again in southern Philistia: 1) the Darb el-Ghazza; or 2) along the Arabah and Beersheba Valleys. The most direct route, the Darb el-Ghazza, led through the Sinai desert, along the southwestern fringe of the Negev Highlands. Travelers on this road passed Kadesh Barnea (Tell el-Qudeirat) en route to Gaza, where the road met the international coast highway, the Via Maris.

The Arabah-Beersheba route also began in the vicinity of Eilat/Aqaba but headed north along the western edge of the Arabah. This first leg of the journey served the Timna region. Traffic that continued north passed by several sites that were fortified for at least some of their existence, and which have produced QPW (e.g., Tell el-Kheleifeh, Yotvata, En Haseva, Mesad Gozal). As traffic reached the southern tip of the Dead Sea, it joined with the eastern extent of the Beersheba Valley. The road through the Beersheba Valley was the most important transportation corridor in the south.[78] It connected the west (Egypt and the Mediterranean coast), the international coastal highway (Via Maris), northern sites in the Shephelah, and highland regions with the Arabah, Transjordan, or Arabia. Tel Masos guarded the crossroads between the east-west valley route and the north-south Ridge Road throughout the Iron Age.[79]

From the core of the Beersheba route, passage further west could continue along a few roads. One followed the Nahal Besor, which directed traffic to Tell el-Farʿah (S). QPW from Tell el-Farʿah (S) was discovered in the Egyptian 'Governor's Residence' or 'Center Hall House,' an administrative building characteristic of Egyptian hegemony in the region, and in the elite burial discussed above.[80] These contexts were undoubtedly associated with the importance of the site in relation to the major roads. From the Mediterranean coast, a segment of the 'Ways of Horus' led directly to the Egyptian Nile Delta and was equipped with fortified stations along the way. This infrastructure was established to facilitate Egyptian control over Canaan. Based on the route described so far, it should come as no surprise that QPW sherds were found at one of these administrative forts, Bir el-ʿAbd. With the new knowledge of the distribution of Faynan and Arabah copper to northern Egypt, we can be quite confident that various luxury goods from the east passed through this route to reach elite consumers of the 21st and 22nd dynasties.[81]

Sites in the Shephelah and the neighboring highlands would have been reached via roads north from the Beersheba Valley. Three sites produced QPW: Lachish, Gezer, and Tel Jedur. Tel Jedur sat just off the Ridge Road between Hebron and Bethlehem, on the east-west route leading to Adullam, the Elah Valley, and ultimately the coastal plain.[82] Situated at busy crossroads, both Lachish and Gezer were strategically positioned to monitor the eastern extent of routes that followed the coastal plain and the Shephelah, the transition zone between the coastland and highland regions, valued for its agricultural potential, which often functioned as a border zone between ethnic and political groups.

Examining the distribution of QPW reveals several important things. The pottery coincided with major roads (e.g., the Arabah Valley, the King's Highway, the Darb el-Ghazza, and the Beersheba Valley) and routes related to the copper trade. The use of these roads indicates that QPW was one element in an active exchange system in the south. The presence of QPW along these routes and in distinct regions also provides evidence that QPW acquisition occurred across different cultural groups. Finally, QPW found at more distant locations tended to be associated with elite and/or administrative contexts.

Summary

Although the overall chronology of QPW is still debated, it is apparent that during the later days of the LBA, the pottery was prevalent in Timna and was important as a prestige ware as distance from the copper region increased. At the close of the LBA and into the Iron I, QPW appeared, along with other imported goods, at sites in the south that were associated with the copper trade network that reached from the Arabah to the Mediterranean coast and beyond. As a painted fine ware, QPW may have functioned in banqueting practices and may have served as a counterpart or substitute for popular Mediterranean wares that were not available due to distance or as LBA networks waned. The wealth and concentration of imported goods at sites such as Tel Masos and Khirbat en-Nahas hint at the possibility that, during the transition to the Iron Age, those who were in positions of power in the region participated in a shared culture related to the exchange activities of the copper network. The participants in the copper trade and related exchange formed an elite cultural sphere that reached from northwest Arabia to at least as far as Amman, Gezer, the Mediterranean coast, and Egypt.

Cyprus

Cypriot imports provide evidence of early Iron Age exchange between the island and the southern Levant. White Painted (WP) and Bichrome wares appear first in the transition between the Iron I and II periods, followed by (and overlapping with) 'Cypro-Phoenician' Black-on-Red (BoR) pottery, which became the most popular Cypriot commodity in the Iron IIA.[83] All three types begin to decrease during the 9th century. Two studies underscore the relevance of these imports for examining exchange relations: N. Schreiber's study of BoR and A. Gilboa's concentration on Cypriot barrel juglets, which appear in WP, Bichrome, and BoR wares (although not in equal frequency).[84] Both scholars demonstrate that Cypriot wares were among the earliest Iron Age imports from the Mediterranean to appear in the southern Levant, and their findings suggest that small containers (e.g., jugs, juglets, and bowls) were part of a specialized trade between Cyprus and particular consumer groups. The predominance of closed containers (i.e., jugs and juglets) suggests that the vessels carried perfumed oils. The fine quality of the Cypriot wares, combined with the recovery of open vessels (i.e., small bowls, although in smaller quantities but among the earliest of the imports), indicates that pottery itself was likely acquired as value items as well.[85] Within the southern Levant, Cypriot vessels have been found in Phoenicia, the coastlands, the Shephelah, the northern and southern hill country, the Jordan Valley, and as far south as the Negev and the Arabah.

The origin of Cypriot White Painted and Bichrome wares is not disputed, but there has been significant debate about the source and absolute chronology of BoR pottery. The 'Cypro-Phoenician' designation reveals the confusion that has persisted. Based on forms and decoration, BoR appears to be closely related to the preceding Cypriot White Painted and Bichrome wares but also shows similarities to Phoenician Red-Slip. Due to problems aligning chronologies throughout the eastern Mediterranean, some examples of BoR in the southern Levant appeared to be earlier than BoR in the north and on Cyprus.[86] Combined with the pottery's prevalence in Phoenicia, scholars argued that it must have been produced in Phoenicia and traded to Cyprus. Ultimately, Atomic Absorption Spectrometry (AAS) helped to determine that the pottery was indeed manufactured in Cyprus. N. Brodie and L. Steel's results indicate Amathus or Kourion in the southern part of the island were the sources of samples from Tell el-Ajjul and Tell el-Farʿah (S) (Figure 6.4).[87] Subsequent studies also confirmed a Cypriot origin for BoR, with more than one production center.[88] The confusion that has surrounded BoR's origins draws attention to its interregional character. The BoR style appears to have developed in response to exchange activities already in place between Cyprus and the Levant. Despite debate regarding its earliest phases, and in coordinating chronologies between Cyprus and the Levant, it is firmly situated in the Iron IIA/late 10th and 9th centuries and demonstrates that exchange was well established.[89]

NONLOCAL CERAMICS IN THE IRON I–IIA TRANSITION   167

Figure 6.4: BoR samples of southern Levant and Cypriot origins. Map: Google Earth, © 2020.

Gilboa's analysis of barrel juglets provides a context for the developments of Cypriot exchange. She explains that barrel juglets 'exemplify a commercial phenomenon starting towards the end of the CG [Cypro-Geometric] IB/II horizon, *prior* to the extensive production and export of BoR containers. The fact that from the moment these vessels were produced, they were also used for overseas shipment, indicates that the shape was *inter alia* meant to serve this endeavor.'[90] The barrel juglets have a barrel-shaped body with a narrow, flared neck. They are also very small. For example, a recently unearthed, complete miniature juglet from Khirbet Qeiyafa measures 8.8 cm tall, 6 cm long, and 5.2 cm wide.[91] The size and distinctive shape suggest that expensive, perfumed oils were the traded commodities; the different wares (WP and Bichrome versus BoR) may have contained different varieties of oils.[92]

Distribution Overview

Table 6.3: Sites with Cypriot imports.

White Painted	Bichrome	BoR (Phase 1 & Iron IIA*)	
Achziv	Achziv	Achziv	T. el-Ajjul
Ashdod	Dor	Beersheba	T. el-Far'ah (N)
Beth-Shean	Kh. Qeiyafa	Beth-Shean	T. el-Far'ah (S)
Beth-Shemesh	Lachish	Beth-Shemesh	T. el-Ful
Dor	Megiddo	Beth-Zur	T. el-Hammeh
Kh. Qeiyafa	Tyre	Carmel	T. el-Qudeirat
Megiddo		Dor	T. en-Nasbeh
Shiqmona		En Gev	T. Halif
T. Abu Hawam		Gezer	T. Jemmeh
T. Beit Mirsim		Hazor	T. Jezreel
T. el-Far'ah (S)		Hurvat Rosh Zayit	T. Keisan
T. el-Ful		Jerusalem*	T. Masos
T. es-Safi		Kh. en-Nahas*	T. Mevorakh
T. Gerisa		Lachish	T. Michal
T. Qasile		Megiddo	T. Qasile
T. Zeror		Pella	T. Qiri
Tyre		Shiqmona	T. Rehov
		T. Abu Hawam	T. Taanach
		T. Abu al-Kharaz*	T. Yoqneam
		T. 'Amal	T. Zeror
		T. Azor	Tyre
		T. Beit Mirsim	*Locations added to
		T. Dan	Schreiber's list (2003)

The early Iron Age import of Cypriot goods began with White Painted and Bichrome wares (including barrel juglets) during the end of the Iron I and the Iron I–II transition (from the 11th to mid-10th centuries), and BoR vessels started to arrive during the early Iron IIA (late 10th to early 9th centuries).[93] The distribution of these goods appears to have been tailored to specific places (Table 6.3; Figure 6.5). The earlier phase of barrel juglet imports (WP and Bichrome) are almost exclusively distributed in the southern Levant, especially in southern Phoenicia/northern Israel, with a few examples known from Syria, a few from Egypt, and one notable example found in a grave at Lefkandi.[94] The distribution of the earlier WP and Bichrome wares, more generally, shows that ports and coastal centers (from

Sarepta to Ashdod, but especially Dor and Tyre) were the first to receive the items. From these entry points, the wares traveled along main roads and wadi systems to a handful of inland sites: Megiddo, Beth-Shean, Tell el-Ful, Khirbet Qeiyafa, Tell eṣ-Ṣafi, Lachish, Tell el-Farʿah (S).[95] These sites were among the largest and most strategic in this period.

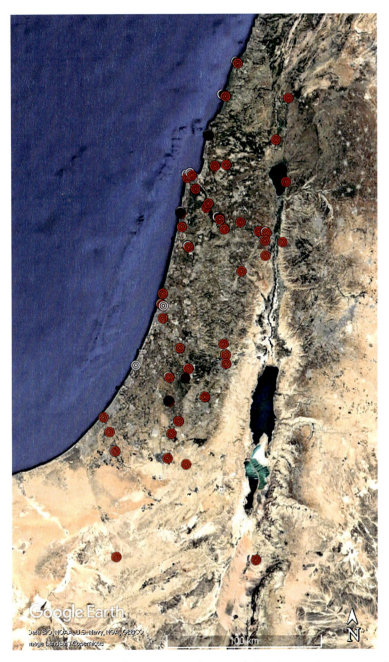

Figure 6.5: Full distribution map of Cypriot wares (map symbols: white circle = WP ware; dark red circle = Bichrome; bright red = BoR). Map: Google Earth, © 2020.

Not surprisingly, BoR distribution follows roughly the same pattern. The highest density of sites and quantity of finds are in the Carmel/Akko region, indicating that this area became the gateway to the inland sites.[96] In smaller quantities, Cypriot imports have also been recovered along the coast south of Akko. Coastal sites with BoR include, from north to south, Tyre, Achziv, Tell Abu Hawam, Shiqmona, Dor, Tel Mevorakh, Tel Michal, and Tell Qasile.

Exchange followed road systems away from the coast, spreading farther east and south to reach more sites throughout the region. Notable additions to the earlier list of inland sites include Dan, Hazor, Bethsaida,[97] and En Gev in the north; Gezer, Tell en-Nasbeh, Jerusalem, Beth-zur, Tel Halif, Beersheba, and Tel Masos[98] farther south; and Tell el-Qudeirat and Khirbat en-Nahas in the southern deserts.[99] The area with the most intensification was the Jezreel Valley, where BoR distribution closely follows the route from the port of Tell Abu Hawam through the Jezreel Valley and across the Jordan Valley. Evidence of BoR exchange has been found at the most prominent sites along this route: Tell Abu Hawam, Yoqneam, Tel Qiri, Megiddo, Taanach, Jezreel, Tel ʿAmal, Beth-Shean, Tel Reḥov, Tell el-Hammeh, Pella, Tell Abu al-Kharaz, and, slightly off this route but related to traffic along it, Tell el-Farʿah (N).[100] There is a notable near-absence of Cypriot wares in the central hill country (to be discussed below).

Transport and Routes

As I mentioned previously, evident in this survey of Cypriot wares is the concentration in the Carmel/Akko region. The distribution aligns well with the best sailing patterns between Cyprus and the southern Levant.[101] Scholars estimate that a merchant ship traveling from Cyprus could reach the Carmel region within a day.[102] The close relationship between maritime activities and Cypriot wares is further indicated by recovery of imports at coastal sites outside of Akko. In many cases, these sites were also located at the mouths of rivers, which may have served as harbors and facilitated transport of the wares inland. The distribution of imports suggests that exchange followed routes along rivers and riverbeds, filtering inland (Table 6.4).[103]

Table 6.4: Cypriot imports near rivers.

Location of Cypriot Imports	Location Type	Associated River
Tell Abu Hawam	coastal	Nahal Qishon
Yoqneam	inland	
Tel Qiri	inland	
Tel Qashish	inland	
Tel Mevorakh	coastal	Nahal Taaninim
Tel Zeror	inland	Nahal Hadera
Tel Qasile	coastal	Nahal Yarkon
Tel Ashdod	coastal	Nahal Lachish
Lachish	inland	
Tell el-Ajjul	coastal	Nahal Besor
Tell Jemmeh	inland	
Tell el-Farʿah (S)	inland	
Beersheba	inland	Nahal Beersheba

Finds along the coast and inland also correspond to travel along the main coastal highway, the Via Maris, that passed along the eastern side of Mount Carmel.[104] This tendency appears to be borne out in the BoR distribution, where there is a ring of sites around the mountain, from Dor to Tel Qiri, Yoqneam, Tell Abu Hawam, and Shiqmona. From Dor, there may have been another route running south of Mount Carmel to the Sharon Plain, which passed through the sites Tel Mevorakh and Tel Zeror before connecting to the Via Maris.[105]

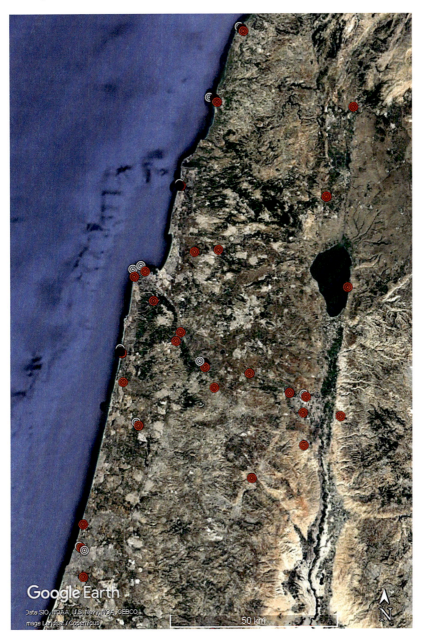

Figure 6.6: Cypriot imports, northern distribution. Map: Google Earth, © 2020 (Map symbols: white circle = WP ware; dark red circle = Bichrome; bright red = BoR).

The corridor from Carmel/Akko through the Jezreel Valley was by far the most important inland zone for the exchange of Cypriot imports (Figure 6.6). As we have seen in previous chapters, this valley was significant in a variety of interactions, including warfare, commercial ventures, and likely in connecting elite leadership groups.[106] The distribution of Cypriot wares illustrates the path of the main highway. Roughly one-third of sites in the southern Levant with BoR sat along this corridor. Most traffic passed from the coast to Megiddo,[107] then on to either the Beqaʿ Valley in the north (passing through Hazor and Dan along the way[108]) or through the Jezreel toward the Jordan Valley in the east (passing through the critical crossroads near Tel Reḥov and Beth-Shean and providing passage to Pella and routes in the east that might reach a site like En Gev). A relationship to the roads of the Jezreel and Jordan Valleys is also the most likely explanation for how BoR reached the site of Tell el-Farʿah (N).[109]

The cluster of sites of Tel Michal, Tell Qasile, and Tel Azor suggests another zone of exchange activity in the area of Joppa that relates to the distribution of Cypriot pottery in the southern half of the region (Figure 6.7). These coastal sites were well-positioned to function as port towns for maritime trade. Tel Michal sat on an alternative to the Via Maris that ran along the narrow pass between the Sharon and the Mediterranean. Tell Qasile was better positioned for organizing trade that was bound for the Shephelah and the hill country; its diverse archaeological remains support its characterization as a port city. Tel Azor, situated halfway between Joppa and the coast highway, sat at a convergence of routes.[110] Further south, the discovery of White Painted ware at Ashdod suggests another entry zone for the imports.

From these coastal sites, a number of routes led to the Shephelah and ascents into the hill country.[111] Ports in the region of Joppa connected to the most direct roads to Tell en-Nasbeh, Tell el-Ful, and Jerusalem, where Cypriot wares have been recovered. Similarly, the sites of Gezer, Tell eṣ-Ṣafi, Beth-shemesh, Khirbet Qeiyafa, and Lachish were well connected by roads to coastal areas, as well as to the hill country.[112] Imports at these sites were likely due to their positions at converging routes, and in the transition between different geographic, cultural, and political zones.

The southern exchange corridor along the Beersheba Valley also played an important role in the movement of Cypriot goods. Imports at Tell el-Ajjul, Tell Jemmeh, and Tell el-Farʿah (S) suggest that the Gaza region was yet another gateway for Mediterranean goods. From this southern entry point, imports may have moved to Beersheba and Tel Masos, where many routes led into the Shephelah and southern hill-country sites (including Lachish, Tell Beit Mirsim, Tel Halif, and Beth-Zur).[113] The recovery of BoR at Tell el-Qudeirat and Khirbat en-Nahas is undoubtedly due to movement of Cypriot goods through this southern corridor.

Understanding who was receiving these imports is more complicated than tracing their movement. Schreiber describes BoR's distribution pattern as a "filtering-through' trade from key points on the coast' into the Levant in 'small consignments.'"[114] This characterization creates an image of sporadic waves of imports that passed deeper inland with each shipment. Schreiber also finds that BoR was frequently associated with high-value items, especially in burial contexts (e.g., metal objects, jewelry, faience, other imports, figurines). She concludes, however, that the consumer base was not exclusively elite, since BoR finds became so frequent and were also associated with domestic contexts, which included cooking and storage vessels.[115]

Figure 6.7: Cypriot imports, southern distribution. Map: Google Earth, © 2020 (Map symbols: white circle = WP ware; dark red circle = Bichrome; bright red = BoR).

Gilboa's characterization differs somewhat. She emphasizes regional variations and suggests the shift in products and distribution was due to 'a significant change in clientele – the rising importance of (probably elite) customers in Israel, Philistia and Judah and concomitantly possibly also a reshuffle in trade networks.'[116] Similarly, Schreiber notes a 'disassociation' between BoR and Phoenician material culture.[117] Thus, there may have been a preference *away* from Cypriot imports in Phoenicia while it was more popular in other areas of the southern Levant. There is also a conspicuous absence of Cypriot wares in the hill country. The exceptions include Tell el-Farʿah (N), Tell en-Nasbeh, Tell el-Ful, Jerusalem, and farther south, at Beth-zur. If this pattern is not the result of variations in the intensity of modern excavation, a possible explanation is that the hill country was not well integrated into the exchange networks that were associated with BoR. It is also possible, perhaps even more likely, that the Cypriot goods were either not useful to the hill-country residents or were intentionally avoided.[118]

The importance of being well connected to the exchange networks is borne out in the distributions and site types. The imports' popularity spread to sites that had the best access to the earliest trade activities – for example, those along the major routes. Judging from the sites involved, there is an association with sites of significance, meaning prominent sites that guarded crossroads and strategic zones. Based on this tendency, it would appear that the Cypriot goods did in fact carry with them an air of prestige. Despite Schreiber's determination that BoR distribution was not limited to elites, there does appear to be some exclusivity in these patterns. The imported goods gravitated or were drawn to the more powerful sites.

The discoveries of BoR at Khirbat en-Nahas (KEN), the most distant location where BoR has been found, supports this perspective. Excavations have produced evidence of an elite, ruling or administrative class at KEN in the 10th and 9th centuries. Several elite residences and administrative structures have been unearthed in the excavations.[119] Their classification as elite is based on superior architectural plans and quality of construction; special installations in and around the structures (e.g., a dais and perimeter wall); and the presence of exceptional finds (e.g., imported pottery, scarabs, unusual vessels, a figurine fragment).[120] The team also discovered workers' residences and industrial areas that lacked the rarer luxury goods and special features, confirming that that there were separate social tiers present at the site.[121] The more exclusive BoR, along with black-burnished juglets imported from Jerusalem, were found within elite structures, but the southern-made QPW and western Negev ware were also found outside the elite buildings and in metallurgical contexts.[122] The various finds and the architecture associated with the elite contexts suggest that members of this group were in command of the exchange relations linking them to goods from the Judahite hill country, Phoenicia, and, by extension, Cyprus. While the possession of Cypriot imports may have been more commonplace, and thus less of a status symbol, near the Mediterranean port cities, these imports conveyed messages of exclusivity with increased distance from their origin.

Summary

The Cypriot imports were the largest component of the revival in Mediterranean trade in the early Iron Age. The renewal in this activity began toward the end of the Iron I with trade in precious oils (or a similar commodity) that were conveyed in small containers, first in WP and Bichrome wares and later also in BoR. As the distribution of these imports increased over time, the preference for different varieties (either of vessel or contents) correlates to distinct zones. While these distribution patterns might indicate different cultural identities, additional factors, such as the site's regional position (geographic and socio-political) and its proximity to the exchange networks, were significant in determining the extent of the trade and the social importance associated with the acquisition of Cypriot goods.

The Aegean

Early Iron Age Aegean imports (Sub-Mycenaean and Protogeometric sherds) have now been recovered from at least seven sites in the southern Levant (Figures 6.8 and 6.9).[123] The imports were discovered at Tyre, Tell Abu Hawam, Dor, Tel Hadar, Tel Reḥov, Megiddo, and Tell eṣ-Ṣafi (Gath), in contexts ranging from the late Iron I to IIA periods (late 11th to 9th centuries).[124] Scholars continue to refine the chronologies of the early Iron Age in the Aegean, Cyprus, and the Levant based on these imports.[125] Current research indicates that Early Protogeometric emerged in the second half of the 11th century, and Late Protogeometric wares extended through the 10th century. All but one or two of the Iron I–II Aegean imports came from Euboea (Table 6.5).[126] Unlike QPW and the Cypriot imports, there does not seem to be any other Aegean commodity closely associated with the Greek vessels, although some have been found in association with other imported and luxury goods.

Figure 6.8: Origins of Aegean wares and their distribution in the Levant. Map: Google Earth, © 2020.

Figure 6.9: Aegean imports in southern Levantine sites. Map: Google Earth, © 2020.

Table 6.5: Aegean imports.

Site and Strata	Aegean Imports (Origin)	Archaeological Phase	Excavators' Absolute Date
Tell eṣ-Ṣafi/ Gath A4–A5/A3	SM-EPG deep bowl (Argolid)	late Iron I to very early Iron IIA	10th century BCE
Tel Hadar IV	MPG-SPG lebes/krater (Euboean)	Iron I	early 10th century BCE
Tel Dor D2/8b	MGP-LPG open vessel, cup (Euboean)	Ir 1|2 to Ir2a	first half to mid-10th century BCE
Tyre XI–IX	SM-SPG a number of vessels including amphora, skyphoi, plate, tripod lebes (Euboean)	Ir 1|2 (acc. to Gilboa and Sharon)	(first half of 10th century BCE)
Tell Abu Hawam III	LPG-SPG skyphos, cup (Euboean)	Iron II	(uncertain)
Tel Reḥov VI–IV	LPG-SPG krater(s?), skyphoi, pyxis (Euboean)	Iron IIA	10th to mid-9th century BCE

From the Argolid

The fragment of a wavy-band deep bowl found at Tell eṣ-Ṣafi (Gath) appears to be the earliest Aegean import of the Iron Age.[127] Excavators suggest that the vessel and its contexts should be dated to the late Iron I or very early Iron IIA period, based on the fragment's type and decoration, the associated ceramic assemblage, and the site's stratigraphy.[128] Analysis of the sherd established that the vessel was produced in the Argolid region of Greece.[129] The discovery of this import was surprising both for its early date and because of Tell eṣ-Ṣafi's geographic position in relation to the other sites that have produced early Greek imports. All the other sites are in the north and closely related to the important international routes discussed above. If the Greek imports seem to be concentrated around access to exchange routes in the north, it may seem surprising to find the Argolid sherd on a route leading into the hill country. Tell eṣ-Ṣafi, however, was also in close proximity to the southern portion of the Via Maris and was one of the most important sites in the south during the Iron I–IIA transition, evidenced in archaeological and historical/biblical materials.[130] In addition, as discussed previously, the founders of Philistine communities in the Levant migrated from the Aegean. Perhaps some long-distance contacts were still in place, or the Greek import was sought out for its cultural affinity. With these factors in mind, Tell eṣ-Ṣafi is not a surprising place to find such a rare import at this time.

From Euboea

The remainder of the Greek imports originated from the island of Euboea. They have been discovered at Tyre,[131] Tell Abu Hawam,[132] Dor,[133] Tel Hadar,[134] Tel Reḥov,[135] and Megiddo.[136] By comparison, a small number of Euboean imports has also been reported at three sites in the northern Levantine coast: Al Mina, Ras al-Bassit, and Tell Sukas. Tel Reḥov has supplied by far the highest number of examples from a single site (eight items from the LPG/SPG or earlier), and these finds represent a long chronological range of activity, from the Iron IB to IIB. Each of these sites had in common an advantageous geographic position in relation to the most important interregional routes. Tyre, Tell Abu Hawam, and Dor were the busiest ports of this age. Tel Hadar, Tel Reḥov, and Megiddo each sat along inland routes that were critical for long-distance traffic. Tel Hadar and Tel Reḥov were situated at passages on the east and west sides of the Jordan Valley, connecting the southern Levant to Syria and beyond. Megiddo dominated its locale between the Carmel and the Jezreel valley for millennia. Both Megiddo and Tel Reḥov sat at crossroads formed by the most important interregional routes, such as the King's Highway, Jordan Valley routes, roads along the Jezreel, and the Via Maris. In addition to these notable positions, each site has produced evidence of unusual wealth during this period.

The source of this group of imports, the island of Euboea, is best known through excavations at Lefkandi, where an Iron Age settlement and nearby cemeteries have revealed a successful and prosperous community from the same period that Euboean imports begin to appear in the southern Levant. Excavations have established that the harbor settlement was active from the mid-12th to late 9th centuries. Among the burial goods in the cemeteries is evidence of Levantine imports and Levantine-inspired styles.[137] The exceptional amount of wealth and imported goods, best known from the elite 'Heroon' complex, proves that residents experienced Greece's 'Dark Age' crisis differently to other areas.[138]

Pottery from Lefkandi and the Euboean imports found in the Levant attest to a unique repertoire. Lefkandi's excavators attribute the settlement's artistic innovation and prosperity to a thorough engagement with long-distance trade.[139] It is fairly certain that Euboea's relations with the southern Levant, occurring as early as the late 11th century, were facilitated through exchange with Cyprus.[140] The earliest post-Mycenaean Greek imports to Cyprus are two PG Euboean vases found at Amathus, which was indicated as a possible source for BoR wares. In addition, the excavations at Lefkandi produced a Phoenician bichrome jug that is thought to have arrived via Cyprus.[141] The best explanation for these early imports is that southern Cyprus was essential in the transport of Greek wares to the east and Levantine goods to the west.

Discussion

Based on the Greek imports to the Levant and the excavations at Lefkandi, an extended, maritime exchange network was in place, at minimum between the Aegean and Cyprus and between Cyprus and the southern Levant, if not more directly between the Aegean and the Levant, during the Iron I to IIA transition. The small number of imports, however, speaks against any centrally organized trade operation or integration in an established network related to Aegean exchange (in contrast to the copper exchange production and the later Cypriot goods discussed above).[142] Instead, it is more likely that the demand for Greek vessels was driven by elites who were able to acquire these exotic or luxury wares.[143]

As in the previous import groups, the location of sites yielding the wares plays an important role. The port cities of Tyre, Dor, and Tell Abu Hawam were at the heart of the maritime trade, and thus had the best access to Mediterranean imports. Tell eṣ-Ṣafi Megiddo, Tel Reḥov, and Tel Hadar were each the premier location for their respective regions: Tell eṣ-Ṣafi for Philistia, Megiddo at the juncture of main roads and several regions

(Carmel coast, Sharon Plain, hill country, Galilee), Tel Reḥov for the northern Jordan Valley, and Tel Hadar for the eastern shore of the Sea of Galilee/Lake Kinneret.[144] Each of these sites was well integrated into long-distance exchange networks and exhibits other evidence of elite culture among a portion of the population.[145]

It is also evident that, generally, these sites fared better than many others in the years following the LBA collapse. The three port cities did not suffer major disruption that is known from centers like Ras Shamra (Ugarit).[146] As a result, they were able to participate in early Iron Age exchange that ultimately linked the Levantine coast to the Aegean. Tel Dor's excavators A. Gilboa and I. Sharon note that no evidence of a 'reurbanization' of Dor has been detected because the site did not experience the 'ruralization' of other regions.[147] The Tale of Wenamun, although somewhat a work of historical fiction, corroborates this with its description of Dor (and other ports).[148] In the story, the city was governed by an independent prince and maintained a role as an urban center and international port. The narrator, Wenamun, a representative of the Theban elite, must continue in his relations with Dor despite feeling mistreated. The stop at Dor was a necessary part of his journey along the coast to acquire wood from Byblos.[149] Although we cannot equate the history and the archaeology of Dor with Tell Abu Hawam and Tyre, it appears that their geographic positions, especially in relation to Cyprus and to routes inland, allowed them to remain active or to recover quickly when other cities faced more lasting hardship. As a consequence, they were best situated to become the commercial gateways between the Mediterranean and the southern Levant.

While we do not have comparable narrative sources for the inland sites (with the exception of the biblical history), it is apparent from the archaeological remains that they too were thriving at the time that the Greek imports arrived. All four sites were already established by the LBA and early Iron I. Most were relatively unaffected by the broader political and social turmoil of the 12th and 11th centuries, or, in the case of Tell eṣ-Ṣafi, were reestablished quickly.[150] Megiddo is an exception here, as the site experienced dramatic destructions, more than other sites, but there is also evidence of extraordinary wealth in the Iron I and IIA periods. During the late 11th and 10th centuries, most of these sites experienced growth or, as in the case of Tel Hadar, reached their height. Again excepting Megiddo, which experienced longevity not matched by the other locations, the sites' successes were limited to these earlier periods in the Iron Age, and they flourished precisely at the same time that Euboean pottery was imported to the Levant in small amounts – but presumably to key location or individuals. A. Mazar and N. Kourou recently noted the correspondence in Euboea's dominance of the Aegean (including in precious metals trade) and the success of some of these Levantine sites; the correspondence notably includes the decline of these apparent trade participants.[151] Euboean cultural and commercial dominance was supplanted by Attic involvement and the rise of the poleis at roughly the same time as notable transitions in the Levant. Tel Hadar suffered destruction during the Iron I–IIA transition. Tell eṣ-Ṣafi and Tel Reḥov were each destroyed in the mid to late 9th century.

With so few Aegean imports in the region, their distribution is best explained as the result of specialized exchange of luxury goods.[152] S. Martin situates the early imports in the context of an elite culture:

> In the early Iron Age, Mediterranean cultural exchange was fairly restricted to an elite realm where foreign vessels for drinking and other activities/rituals probably served as status markers in both Greece and the Near East. At minimum we can assume that these pots were perceived as exotic (even if their material lacked high intrinsic value). On the

other end of the interpretive spectrum, we might propose that they were used sometimes in more specific ways, even to evoke a heroic past. In the Ugaritic texts, the 'shades of the dead' (*rephaim*) were said to participate in the *marzeah*. In Greece, one can point to the so-called 'heroöns' of Lefkandi where foreign drinking vessels served as funerary goods.[153]

In fact, faunal analysis from Tel Reḥov indicates that a portion of its population did engage in feasting events.[154] The elite residents of the sites where the Greek imports have been found likely acquired the vessels through personal contacts with elites of other sites who were linked by key trade routes, ports, or specialized resources. In other words, contrary to Coldstream's earlier proposal of a diplomatic marriage alliance between Lefkandi and a Levantine king, it is not necessary or realistic that direct exchange relations existed between the elites at Lefkandi and elites in each of the sites where Euboean wares have been found. It is much more likely that elites in the Iron I–IIA span participated in a specialized culture to assert their status, a culture that included feasting and the conspicuous display of luxury goods. The acquisition of these goods was facilitated in some cases by participation in specialized trade of the day (e.g., in metals, honey). In other cases, diplomatic and regional security partnerships may have contributed to exchange. For some others, the prospect of enhancing prestige may have driven local rulers to join in the elite cultural practices. As we are now realizing, there was not a clean break between the LBA and Iron Ages, and, as Martin suggests, the wares may have supported claims of power. This select consumer group may have been emulating their LBA predecessors, among whom Mycenaean and Cypriot imports were status symbols. In the case of Tell eṣ-Ṣafi or Dor, the Greek wares may have been sought out in an effort to emphasize and perpetuate an Aegean heritage or Mediterranean-oriented identity.[155] Whatever the personal motives, the rarity of these items and the efforts that must have been involved in acquiring them suggest that the recipients were of exceptional status and may have been associates in an exclusive interaction network.

Reconstructing Iron I–IIA Exchange Networks

The distribution patterns of these imported wares expose regional exchange networks. From the north, maritime trade from Cyprus entered the southern Levant through the northern ports (e.g., Tyre, Achziv, Shiqmona, Tell Abu Hawam, Dor). These ports fell within a zone that allowed for efficient travel between Cyprus and the Levant. From this gateway, transportation followed river valleys and other routes inland. In the peak of BoR distribution in the late 10th–early 9th centuries, these networks grew to include sites, all along the coast, that were linked to river valleys, such as Tel Qasile on the Yarkon and Tell el-Ajjul on the Besor.[156]

Inland distributions correspond to the main roads and major crossroads. Aside from the coastal sites, the Jezreel corridor played the most significant role. The distribution of the Mediterranean imports traces the length of the route, from the port at Tell Abu Hawam to the Jordan Valley gateway sites of Beth-Shean, Tel Reḥov, Tell el-Hammeh, and Pella. We can discern still other strategic areas and routes. En Gev, Tel Hadar, Hazor, and Dan were each at significant crossroads and gateway zones in the north. Tell el-Farʿah (N), Tell en-Nasbeh, and Tell el-Ful seem to mark entrances to the central hill country via the main ridge highway. The Shephelah border zone contains a number of sites with Cypriot and other imports; each of these sites (Gezer, Beth-shemesh, Khirbet Qeiyafa, Tell eṣ-Ṣafi, and Lachish) guarded geological and traditional, cultural boundaries.

The southern exchange network is revealed through the overlap in Cypriot and northwest Arabian imports – although not all of these finds are contemporaneous.[157] Sites where both types of imports have been found include Gezer, Lachish, Tell el-Farʿah (S), Tell el-Qudeirat, and Khirbat en-Nahas. The copper network dominated exchange activity in the south, and based on the QPW distribution, we see the importance of the Arabah Valley as a southern gateway. The most important route in this network involved a series of roads connecting Gaza to the Arabah and Gulf of Eilat/Aqaba. The main route passed through the region of Beersheba/Tel Masos, from which other roads led north into the Shephelah and southern hill country, south to Tell el-Qudeirat, west to Gaza, and east to the Arabah. The Darb el-Ghazza was a significant alternate to the main route. It was a more direct route from the Gulf of Eilat/Aqaba (and northern Arabia) to Gaza and eventually Egypt, running along the edge of the Negev. Its most important site, Tell el-Qudeirat (Kadesh Barnea), sat at the center of that passage and was connected to the Beersheba Valley through an additional road to the north.

Comprehensive Discussion

What stands out the most in surveying these imported wares and their distributions is the cumulative evidence of active and far-reaching exchange networks during the 11th, 10th, and early 9th centuries. There can be no doubt that long-distance exchange was not only occurring but growing throughout the transition from the Iron I to the early Iron IIA. What was previously characterized as a period of regional isolation due to the breakdown of the LBA trade networks must now be viewed as a period of exciting and varied interactions among a number of communities.[158]

Those more likely to be involved in this new/renewed exchange were participants in towns that were located closer to major routes and in sites that guarded significant crossroads or resources. In addition to the importance of a site's location, how a site fared following the LBA collapse seems to have influenced its ability to be involved in long-distance exchange. Many of the sites with imported wares appear to have largely escaped regional turmoil and thrived in this period. For example, Tel Dor and Tel Reḥov in the north, Khirbat en-Nahas and Tel Masos in the south, and Tell eṣ-Ṣafi in the western Shephelah all flourished during the late Iron I–early IIA. The nature of the imported goods and their associated contexts compel us to recognize that the participants, especially in the earliest periods of the imports, and at the greatest distance from the wares' production, were local and regional elites. The fact that these characteristics and patterns are repeated throughout the region demonstrates that there was an elite class sharing both in this specialized exchange and in a distinct, elite cultural identity.

While not all sites with early imports experienced the successes of these examples, the majority appear to have achieved some stability or importance as a result of occupying strategic positions. This trend suggests that participation in long-distance trade was often dominated by and/or beneficial to persons of power.[159] However, judging from BoR's distribution, the exchange community broadened considerably in the 9th century, presumably from a general increase in stability in the region. The various sites also appear to have operated independently in their exchange activities. Indications of complex or centralized organization or standardized infrastructure behind the exchange networks are not presently apparent[160]; rather, the distributions reflect an opportunistic enterprise where goods 'filtered' along the major roads and were acquired most often by people of higher status. The Aegean imports provide the most suggestive evidence of an exclusive community of consumers who were linked by elite status rather than regional proximity.

If interregional interaction was a significant factor in social and political change in this period, the distribution patterns should indicate some potential areas for competition. Interactions were most intense in the northern ports, along the Jezreel Valley, in the Shephelah zone, and along the copper route in the south. These regions would have been the most lucrative to control, and thus potential targets for competition and military action.[161] More detailed discussion of these zones takes place in Chapter Seven, but it must be noted that some of the more spectacular conflicts that are known or remembered from this period happen to coincide with the areas of more intense interregional activity – for example, Saul's battle against the Philistines at Jezreel, wars between Israelites and Philistines in the Shephelah, and, of course, Shoshenq I's campaign into the Levant.

Notes

1. Egyptian pottery is another important group of nonlocal ceramics that are found in this period but is not included in this survey due to the nature of relations between Egypt and the Levant. The Egyptian influence and imperial administrative presence in the LBA and early Iron I periods complicates the characterization of Egyptian and Egyptianizing artifacts (i.e., were the artifacts in use by Egyptians in the Levant or by local populations who sought out foreign goods?). The three ceramic groups examined in this chapter arrived in the southern Levant as a result of long-distance trade and/or peer exchange relations. For discussion of Egyptian pottery in the region, see the work of Shirly Ben-Dor Evian ("Egypt and the Levant in the Iron Age I–IIA: The Ceramic Evidence," *TA* 38 [2011]: 94–119; idem, "Egypt and Israel: The Never-Ending Story," *NEA* 80, no. 1 [2017]: 30–39).
2. The ruler also boasts of the tribute gained from Levantine port cities, which included dyed textiles, gold, and silver (e.g., RINAP 1 Tiglath-pilesar III 49).
3. Gilboa and Namdar, "On the Beginnings of South Asian Spice Trade," 272.
4. Namdar et al., "Cinnamaldehyde in Early Iron Age Phoenician Flasks"; Gilboa and Namdar, "On the Beginnings of South Asian Spice Trade."
5. Gilboa and Namdar, "On the Beginnings of South Asian Spice Trade," 272–73, and references therein.
6. Ibid., 276.
7. Naama Sukenik et al., "Early Evidence of Royal Purple Dyed Textile from Timna Valley (Israel)," *PLOS ONE* 16, no. 1 (2021): e0245897.
8. Recent faunal analysis has provided even more support for such a proposal. In the later stages of Timna's occupation and copper production, there is evidence of the introduction of cattle and sheep, and eventually camels, compared to evidence of only goats and donkeys in earlier periods (Lidar Sapir-Hen and Erez Ben-Yosef, "The Emergence of a Nomadic Desert Polity: An Archaeozoological Perspective," *Archaeological and Anthropological Sciences* 14, no. 12 [2022]: 232). The shift indicates that there was increasing wealth among those who were able to support these additional herds, and in turn, those who could afford them exhibited their status through conspicuous husbandry, and presumably through the gifting or exchange of secondary products. There is parallel evidence of this shift in the Wadi Faynan copper region, testifying not only to the association between power and the copper production at the time but also to the close connection between these two copper production centers (ibid.).
9. For recent research of iron production in the southern Levant, see Chapter Two. In addition to the following, see references in Chapter Three and below ('Northwest Arabia' section) regarding Arabah copper production: Thomas E. Levy et al., eds., *New Insights into the Iron Age Archaeology of Edom, Southern Jordan*; Erez Ben-Yosef, "The Central Timna Valley Project."

10 Ben-Dor Evian, et al., "Pharaoh's Copper"; Kiderlen et al., "Tripod Cauldrons Produced at Olympia"; Veit Vaelske, Michael Bode, and Christian E. Loeben, "Early Iron Age Copper Trail between Wadi Arabah and Egypt during the 21st Dynasty: First Results from Tanis, ca. 1000 BC," *Zeitschrift Für Orient-Archäologie* 12 (2019), 184–203.
11 Eshel et al., "Debasement of Silver."
12 Eshel et al., "Debasement of Silver."
13 Gold and silver are also part of a larger payment that contains textiles, produce, fish, and other goods that are exchanged for timber (Miriam Lichtheim [translator], "The Report of Wenamun" in *Ancient Egyptian Literature: A Book of Readings, Vol. II: The New Kingdom*, ed. Miriam Lichtheim [Berkeley: University of California Press, 1973], 224–29).
14 See Chapter Three.
15 This kind of boundary maintenance has been proposed based on ceramic analysis of communities in the Cisjordan hill country versus the southern coastal area, and between the Faynan region in Jordan and its interaction partners in the Negev; see Faust, *Israel's Ethnogenesis*, 191–220; Smith and Levy, "Iron Age Ceramics from Edom."
16 There are a variety of techniques that might reveal the provenance of pottery. A vessel's form or decoration may be the first indicator, and evaluation of these aspects is performed in the field before any other analysis is attempted. This step provides information on the vessel's (and, theoretically, the context's) age and cultural identity (archaeological, not ethnic). If a sherd appears to be separate from the local or expected assemblage, additional testing may occur. Thin section petrographic analysis (TSPA) evaluates mineral elements and inclusions in the clay. When TSPA is not conclusive, ceramists turn to (I)NAA, (Instrumental) Neutron Activation Analysis, or AAS, Atomic Absorption Spectrometry, both of which can detect elements within the clay. When a mineralogical profile is determined for a pottery group, it is then matched to a region of origin based on a distinctive composition.
17 Analysis of the relationships between point of origin and distance from origin (such as fall-off analysis) have proven useful, but additional factors such as the type of imported good and the differences among consumer groups complicate this type of analysis; see Ian Hodder, ed., *The Spatial Organisation of Culture* (New Approaches in Archaeology; London: Duckworth, 1978).
18 The Edomite Lowlands Regional Archaeology Project (ELRAP) has shown that such analysis can indicate social interaction and exchange on various scales: between different segments of society within one site, between neighboring communities, through intraregional interaction, and through interregional exchange. See Smith and Levy, "Iron Age Ceramics from Edom"; Smith, Goren, and Levy, "The Petrography of Iron Age Edom."
19 Barth, *Ethnic Groups and Boundaries*.
20 Hodder, *The Spatial Organisation of Culture*; Ian Hodder and Clive Orton, *Spatial Analysis in Archaeology* (Cambridge: Camrbidge University Press, 1979); Ian Hodder, *Symbols in Action: Ethnoarchaeological Studies of Material Culture* (Cambridge; New York: Cambridge University Press, 1982).
21 Jane Waldbaum, "Greeks in the East or Greeks and the East? Problems in the Definition and Recognition of Presence," *BASOR*.305 (1997): 1–17. Waldbaum's argument was addressing the tendency to propose colonization to explain concentrations of Greek pottery in the east. Similar debates continue regarding the Philistines' relationship to their eastern neighbors and the Phoenicians' relationships to the west. Waldbaum's critiques of the different biases from scholars based on their western or eastern point of reference remain valid.
22 For example, Elizabeth Bloch-Smith, "Israelite Ethnicity in Iron I: Archaeology Preserves What Is Remembered and What Is Forgotten in Israel's History," *JBL* 122.3 (2003): 401–25; Killebrew, *Biblical Peoples and Ethnicity*; Faust, *Israel's Ethnogenesis*; Thomas E. Levy, "Ethnic Identity in Biblical Edom, Israel, and Midian: Some Insights from Mortuary Contexts in the Lowlands of Edom," in *Exploring the Longue Durée: Essays in Honor of Lawrence E. Stager*, ed. J. David Schloen (Winona Lake: Eisenbrauns, 2009), 251–61; and most recently the collection of articles edited by Lauren Monroe and Daniel Fleming dedicated to identity in *Hebrew Bible and Ancient Israel* 10, no. 2 (2021).
23 The history behind these relationships is succinctly recounted in Alexander Fantalkin, "Low Chronology and Greek Protogeometric and Geometric Pottery in the Southern Levant," *Levant* 33.1 (2001): 117–25.
24 Fantalkin, "Low Chronology and Greek Protogeometric and Geometric Pottery in the Southern Levant"; Kletter, "Chronology and United Monarchy"; Ilan Sharon et al., "Report on the First Stage of the Iron Age Dating Project in Israel: Supporting a Low Chronology," *Radiocarbon* 49, no. 1 (2007): 1–46.
25 This pottery group has been referred to by a variety of names: Midianite, Qurayya(h) Painted (or Painted Qurayyah), Tayma, Hejaz, sometimes identified as Edomite.

26 Peter J. Parr, G. Lankester Harding, and John E. Dayton, *Preliminary Survey in N.W. Arabia, 1968* (London: Institute of Archaeology, 1970); Beno Rothenberg, *Timna: Valley of the Biblical Copper Mines* (London: Thames and Hudson, 1972).

27 Beno Rothenberg and Jonathan Glass, "The Midianite Pottery," in *Midian, Moab, and Edom: The History and Archaeology of Late Bronze and Iron Age Jordan and North-West Arabia*, ed. John F. A. Sawyer and David J. A. Clines (JSOTSup 24; Sheffield: JSOT Press, 1983), 65–124. Jan Kalsbeek and Gloria London published a detailed discussion of the pottery prior to Rothenberg and Glass's analysis, but it was focused on finds at Yotvata rather than establishing a standardization for research of the pottery as a group ("A Late Second Millennium B. C. Potting Puzzle," *BASOR* 232 [1978]: 47).

28 Peter J. Parr, "Contacts between North West Arabia and Jordan in the Late Bronze and Iron Ages."

29 Marta Luciani, "Qurayyah," 141. For a detailed discussion of the relationship between QPW and the local and preceding Barbotine ware, see Marta Luciani and Abdullah S. Alsaud, "Qurayyah 2015," 53–54.

30 Arnulf Hausleiter, "Pottery Groups of the Late 2nd / Early 1st Millennia BC in Northwest Arabia and New Evidence from Tayma," in *Recent Trends in the Study of Late Bronze Age Ceramics in Syro-Mesopotamia and Neighbouring Regions: Proceedings of the International Workshop in Berlin, 2-5 November 2006*, ed. Marta Luciani and Arnulf Hausleiter (Orient-Archäologie 32; Leidorf: Rahden/Westf., 2014), see esp. 409–413; Andrea Intilia, "Qurayyah Painted Ware: A Reassessment of 40 Years of Research on Its Origins, Chronology and Distribution," in *The Archaeology of North Arabia. Oases and Landscapes: Proceedings of the International Congress Held at the University of Vienna, 5-8 December, 2013*, ed. Marta Luciani, 1st ed. (Vienna: Austrian Academy of Sciences Press, 2016), 175–255; J. Gunneweg et al., "'Edomite,' 'Negevite' and 'Midianite' Pottery from the Negev Desert and Jordan: Instrumental Neutron Activation Analysis Results," *Archaeometry* 33 (1991): 239-53.

31 Intilia notes that there are questions regarding the Timna evidence as reported in the earlier INAA results (i.e., Gunneweg et al., "'Edomite,' 'Negevite' and 'Midianite' Pottery"); it is not possible to determine with certainty if the sherds labeled 'Midianite' fit the QPW classification, but evidence from the Faynan is more suggestive (Intilia, "Qurayyah Painted Ware," 213–14).

32 For a historical review of investigations and debates, see John J. Bimson and Juan Manuel Tebes, "Timna Revisited: Egyptian Chronology and the Copper Mines of the Southern Arabah," *Antiguo Oriente* 7 (2009): 75–118; Erez Ben-Yosef et al., "A New Chronological Framework for Iron Age Copper Production at Timna (Israel)."

33 Ben-Yosef, "The Central Timna Valley Project:"; Intilia, "Qurayyah Painted Ware"; Levy et al., *New Insights into the Iron Age Archaeology of Edom, Southern Jordan*; Luciani and Alsaud, "Qurayyah 2015"; Luciani, "Pottery from the 'Midianite Heartland?'"; Lily Singer-Avitz, "The Earliest Settlement at Kadesh Barnea," *TA* 35.1 (2008): 73–81; idem, "The Qurayyah Painted Ware," in *The Renewed Archaeological Excavations at Lachish (1973-1994)*, ed. David Ussishkin (Tel Aviv: Emery and Claire Yass Publications in Archaeology, 2004), 1280–87; idem, "Epilogue: The Dating of Qurayyah Painted Ware in the Southern Levant," in *The Ancient Pottery of Israel and Its Neighbors from the Middle Bronze Age Through the Late Bronze Age (Volume 3)*, ed. S. Gitin (Jerusalem: Israel Exploration Society, 2019), 388–89.

34 Intilia, "Qurayyah Painted Ware," 194–211, and fig. 15.

35 Luciani and Alsaud, "Qurayyah 2015."

36 Ben-Yosef et al., "A New Chronological Framework for Iron Age Copper Production at Timna (Israel)," 50–52. The QPW sherds were found in secure contexts, closely associated with radiocarbon samples. Overall, the radiocarbon dating from the site shows that the earliest occupation began in the late 12th century, excluding the period of the 19th and 20th Egyptian Dynasties as an explanation for the metallurgical activity. Ben-Yosef et al. argue that the QPW should be dated to the 10th century; others argue it is residual from the earlier activity (see below).

37 These sherds have been identified through petrographic examination; see Smith, Goren, and Levy, "The Petrography of Iron Age Edom," 488.

38 Smith and Levy, "Iron Age Ceramics from Edom," 411–12.

39 Intilia, "Qurayyah Painted Ware," 195–211, 419–20. Evidence from Tayma also situates the end of QPW at that site by the end of the 11th century (Hausleiter, "Pottery Groups of the Late 2nd / Early 1st Millennia BC," 408).

40 Luciani, "Qurayyah," 141.

41 Luciani, "Qurayyah," 141. There is an important critique in Luciani's recent publications that we should not understand QPW to be imitative or derivative of other Near Eastern cultures. It is also important to note that Arabia was a contributor to the interregional relations of the ANE, and the region's role should

not be underestimated because of its geography or the absence of written records. For initial analysis of the ware, emphasizing both its distinctiveness and influence from Mediterranean and Levantine wares, see Peter J. Parr, "Pottery, People and Politics," in *Archaeology in the Levant: Essays for Kathleen Kenyon*, ed. Roger Moorey and Peter J. Parr (Warminster: Aris & Phillips, 1978); idem, "Contacts between North West Arabia and Jordan in the Late Bronze and Iron Ages"; idem, "Pottery of the Late Second Millennium B.C. from North West Arabia and Its Historical Implications," in *Araby the Blest: Studies in Arabian Archaeology*, ed. Daniel T. Potts (Copenhagen: Museum of Tusculanum Press, University of Copenhagen, 1988), 73–89. For more recent discussion, but prior to systematic excavation of Qurayyah, see Juan Manuel Tebes, "Pottery Makers and Premodern Exchange in the Fringes of Egypt: An Approximation to the Distribution of Iron Age Midianite Pottery," *Buried History* 43 (2007): 11–26; Hausleiter, "Pottery Groups of the Late 2nd / Early 1st Millennia BC."

42 Jesse M. Millek's research examines QPW along with other nonlocal goods during the transition from the LBA to the Iron Age. The results of that research are complementary to mine here, in the finding that the exchange taking place during the LBA–early Iron Age was varied and decentralized. Millek's argument is especially intriguing in its observations about changes that preceded the 'collapses' of that era, among them was disruption of the larger trade systems (*Exchange, Destruction, and a Transitioning Society: Interregional Exchange in the Southern Levant from the Late Bronze Age to the Iron I* [Tübingen: Tübingen University Press, 2019]).

43 Kalsbeek and London, "A Late Second Millennium B. C. Potting Puzzle," 53.

44 Luciani, "Qurayyah," 140.

45 Ibid.

46 Ibid.

47 Tebes argues that in areas where QPW appears in very small quantities, it may have been viewed as a luxury item and traded for that purpose ("Pottery Makers and Premodern Exchange," 19–22). Luciani suggests there may have been shared feasting practices and cultural identity between the Arabah and Hejaz ("Pottery from the 'Midianite Heartland?,'" 428).

48 Larry G. Herr, "The Amman Airport Structure and the Geopolitics of Ancient Transjordan," *BA* 46.4 (1983): 223–29. See also discussion in Intilia, "Qurayyah Painted Ware"; Luciani, "Pottery from the 'Midianite Heartland?'"

49 Sarah Ben-Arieh dates the cave's use to the 14th and 13th centuries ("Gedor, Tel," *NEAEHL*, 468). Singer-Avitz has extended the chronology to include the 12th century, which she considers a more likely range if QPW is present ("The Qurayyah Painted Ware," 1284).

50 For example, the Egyptian artifacts in the Amman structure included materials from as early as the Predynastic period and Middle Kingdom. The local pottery was dated to the 13th century (Herr, "The Amman Airport Structure and the Geopolitics of Ancient Transjordan").

51 Elizabeth Bloch-Smith, *Judahite Burial Practices and Beliefs about the Dead* (JSOTSup 123; Sheffield: JSOT Press for the American Schools of Oriental Research, 1992), 174–75. Other examples of QPW were found in the Egyptian administrative building (so-called 'Governor's Residence') at the site (Eli Yannai, "A Stratigraphic and Chronological Reappraisal of the 'Governor's Residence' at Tell El-Far'ah [South]," in *Studies in Archaeology and Related Disciplines*, ed. E. D. Oren and S. Aḥituv [Aharon Kempinski Memorial Volume, Beer Sheba XV; Beersheba: Ben-Gurion University of the Negev Press, 2002], 368–76).

52 Rothenberg, *Timna*. Rothenberg's theory was not based solely on the pottery. Persistence of occupation and metallurgy at Timna and the conversion of the Egyptian temple to a 'Semitic' (aniconic) shrine, along with evidence of QPW after the Egyptian activity at the site ended, does indicate that some group made use of the Timna sites. This group may have been from the desert regions of the Arabah, Negev, southern Jordan, or northwest Arabia. The difficulty in Rothenberg's argument is the characterization of the 'Midianite' people, of whom we have no contemporary evidence. The proposal that residents of these desert regions be associated with the Shasu known from Egyptian records has better historical grounding, but there remains considerable debate regarding the identity of folks in the region in this period, most recently regarding the proposal that the Arabah sites be associated with the people/polity of Edom (see below). For earlier arguments, see Levy, "Ethnic Identity in Biblical Edom, Israel, and Midian"; Marc Beherec, Mohammad Najjar, and Thomas E. Levy, "Wadi Fidan 40 and Mortuary Archaeology in the Edom Lowlands," in *New Insights into the Iron Age Archaeology of Edom, Southern Jordan: Surveys, Excavations and Research from the University of California, San Diego & Department of Antiquities of Jordan, Edom Lowlands Regional Archaeology Project (ELRAP)*, ed. Thomas E. Levy et al. (Monumenta Archaeologica 35; Los Angeles: The Cotsen Institute of Archaeology Press, 2014), 665–721; Ben-Yosef, "The Central Timna Valley Project," 59.

53 Luciani suggests that the southern Arabah sites '...shared tableware and feasting (?) practices that were current in Qurayyah and underscored their cultural identity with the northern Ḥijāz thereby underlining both otherness and belonging to other assemblages of the area (e.g., Bichrome Painted Ware, Cypriot or Chocolate-on-White).' ("Pottery from the 'Midianite Heartland?,'" 428). Juan Manuel Tebes has presented a modified and more complex version of Rothenberg's argument, claiming that the high concentration of QPW in the Arabah should be explained as the result of activities of nomadic groups, 'people straddling the interface between the northern Hejaz, Edom and the Negev' as well as Hejazi residents at Timna ("Pottery Makers and Premodern Exchange," 19).
54 Erez Ben-Yosef, "The Architectural Bias in Current Biblical Archaeology," *VT* 69.3 (2019): 361–87; idem, "And Yet, a Nomadic Error"; Erez Ben-Yosef, et al., "Ancient Technology and Punctuated Change." Israel Finkelstein is among the greatest critics of this argument; see "The Arabah Copper Polity and the Rise of Iron Age Edom: A Bias in Biblical Archaeology?" *Antiguo Oriente* 18 (2020): 11–32.
55 Luciani, "Pottery from the 'Midianite Heartland?,'" 429.
56 Smith and Levy, "Iron Age Ceramics from Edom," 411–12; Smith, Goren, and Levy, "The Petrography of Iron Age Edom," 488; Intilia, "Qurayyah Painted Ware," 217.
57 Erez Ben-Yosef et al., "Ancient Technology and Punctuated Change"; Levy, Najjar, and Ben-Yosef, "Conclusion." Contra various arguments by Israel Finkelstein: "Khirbet En-Nahas, Edom and Biblical History," *TA* 32 (2005): 119–25; Finkelstein and Silberman, *David and Solomon*; Alexander Fantalkin and Israel Finkelstein, "The Sheshonq I Campaign and the 8th-Century BCE Earthquake – More on the Archaeology and History of the South in the Iron I–IIA," *TA* 33 (2006): 18–42; Israel Finkelstein, Alexander Fantalkin, and Eliazer Piasetzky, "Three Snapshots of the Iron IIA: The Northern Valleys, the Southern Steppe, and Jerusalem," in *Israel in Transition: From Late Bronze II to Iron IIA (c. 1250–850 B.C.E.): Volume 1: The Archaeology*, ed. Lester L. Grabbe (Library of Hebrew Bible/Old Testament Studies 491; New York: T&T Clark, 2008), 37–39.
58 Thomas E. Levy et al., "Excavations at Khirbat En-Nahas, 2002–2009: An Iron Age Copper Production Center in the Lowlands of Edom," in *New Insights into the Iron Age Archaeology of Edom, Southern Jordan: Surveys, Excavations and Research from the University of California, San Diego & Department of Antiquities of Jordan, Edom Lowlands Regional Archaeology Project (ELRAP)*, ed. Thomas Evan Levy et al. (Monumenta Archaeologica 35; Los Angeles: The Cotsen Institute of Archaeology Press, 2014), 88–245.
59 Smith and Levy, "Iron Age Ceramics from Edom," 412. Smith and Levy propose that QPW continued to be manufactured in northern Arabia and traded to northern neighbors as late as KEN's major production phases, primarily during the 10th century. The more recent excavations at Qurayyah do not support that position, however (Luciani and Alsaud, "Qurayyah 2015").
60 Smith and Levy, "Iron Age Ceramics from Edom," 417; Smith, Goren, and Levy, "The Petrography of Iron Age Edom," 476.
61 Smith, Goren, and Levy, "The Petrography of Iron Age Edom," 488. For clarification about the ceramic assemblage that has traditionally been deemed 'Negebite,' especially in relation to the copper production and populations in the Arabah, see M. Martin et al., "Iron IIA Slag-Tempered Pottery in the Negev Highlands, Israel," *Journal of Archaeological Science* 40 (2014): 3777–92. The research demonstrates that the slag-tempered handmade vessels originated in the Arabah, and that the majority of wheel-made vessels were imported from north of the Negev Highlands.
62 The chronology of Kadesh Barnea continues to be debated. Singer-Avitz argued in 2008 that QPW did not extend beyond the 12th century. Based on this premise, QPW at Tell el-Qudeirat must have originated in the levels prior to the Iron IIA structure and/or the dating of the site must be incorrect. She dates the earliest levels according to her range for QPW and argues that the QPW from Tel Masos and Khirbat en-Nahas must also have originated in the earlier occupations at these sites ("The Earliest Settlement at Kadesh Barnea"). The updated publications from the Faynan force reconsideration of Singer-Avitz's commitment to the 12th century date for this pottery. The weight of this evidence was anticipated by Faust ("Review: Excavations at Kadesh Barnea [Tell El-Qudeirat] 1976–1982," *AJA* 113, no. 2 [2009]). Newer radiocarbon dating has also impacted this debate and provides a context in the 13th to 11th centuries; see Intilia, "Qurayyah Painted Ware," 200–201, and sources therein.
63 Tebes, "Pottery Makers and Premodern Exchange," 19–22.
64 Volkmar Fritz and Aharon Kempinski, *Ergebnisse Der Ausgrabungen Auf Der Hirbet El-Msas (Tel Masos) 1972–1975* (Abhandlungen Des Deutschen Palästinavereins Vol. I–III; Wiesbaden: Harrassowitz, 1983); Aharon Kempinski, "Masos, Tel," in *The New Encyclopedia of Archaeological Excavations in the Holy Land*, ed. Ephraim Stern (Jerusalem; New York: Israel Exploration Society & Carta; Simon & Schuster, 1993), 986–89; Israel

Finkelstein, *Living on the Fringe: The Archaeology and History of the Negev, Sinai, and Neighboring Regions in the Bronze and Iron Ages* (Monographs in Mediterranean Archaeology 6; Sheffield: Sheffield Academic Press, 1995), 103–26. See also Juan Manuel Tebes, "A New Analysis of the Iron Age I 'Chiefdom' of Tel Masos (Beersheba Valley)," *Aula Orientalis* 21 (2003): 63–78.

65 Higginbotham, *Egyptianization and Elite Emulation in Ramesside Palestine*, 273.
66 Kempinski, "Masos, Tel"; Finkelstein, *Living on the Fringe*, 103–26; Higginbotham, *Egyptianization and Elite Emulation in Ramesside Palestine*, 273; Tebes, "A New Analysis of the Iron Age I 'Chiefdom' of Tel Masos (Beersheba Valley)."
67 Herzog and Singer-Avitz note a close relationship between Stratum III finds and the LBA pottery tradition and provide a detailed evaluation of the evidence that indicates there was an elite group at the site ("Redefining the Centre," 222–27).
68 This scenario is more likely than what has been proposed by Fantalkin and Finkelstein that the entire corridor linking the coast, the Beersheba Valley, and the Faynan became a unified operation under the control of one site or power, namely Shoshenq ("The Sheshonq I Campaign and the 8th-Century BCE Earthquake"). For specific critiques against this position, see Amihai Mazar, "Archaeology and the Biblical Narrative"; Levy et al., *New Insights into the Iron Age Archaeology of Edom, Southern Jordan*.
69 Itamar Singer proposes that Philistines were the heirs to the Egyptian administrative system of the 19th and 20th Dynasties. This proposal is attractive as an explanation of the Philistine-related finds associated with the former Egyptian administrative buildings (so-called 'Governor's Residences'), especially in the south ("Egyptians, Canaanites, and Philistines in the Period of the Emergence of Israel"). There is not sufficient evidence, however, to support a claim that Philistines took over the copper exchange network, that Egypt was able to maintain its influence in this area (presumably during the late Iron I and early Iron II), or that Shoshenq was responsible for the surge in copper production and exchange activity along this network, as suggested by Fantalkin and Finkelstein ("The Sheshonq I Campaign and the 8th-Century BCE Earthquake," 27–28). It is much more plausible that the height of activity in the copper network in the 10th century drew the attention of Shoshenq and was a target of his campaign. See Chapter Seven; Levy, Najjar, and Ben-Yosef, "Conclusion."
70 For a recent, comprehensive catalog, including discussion of the difficulty in quantifying QPW, see Intilia, "Qurayyah Painted Ware," 186–89.
71 Ben-Yosef et al., "A New Chronological Framework for Iron Age Copper Production at Timna (Israel)," 65; Ben-Yosef, Najjar, and Levy, "Local Iron Age Trade Routes in Northern Edom," 513–14.
72 Dorsey, *Roads and Highways*, 12–15.
73 See Chapter Three.
74 Luciani, "Pottery from the 'Midianite Heartland?'"
75 Ben-Yosef, Najjar, and Levy, "Local Iron Age Trade Routes in Northern Edom," 544–47.
76 For example, elevation near Tawilan reaches 1500 m above sea level, and the modern highway 20 km to the west in the Arabah sits at about 150 m above sea level. See Ben-Yosef, Najjar, and Levy, "Local Iron Age Trade Routes in Northern Edom," 497–500.
77 Ben-Yosef, Najjar, and Levy, "Local Iron Age Trade Routes in Northern Edom," 521–35.
78 Dorsey, *Roads and Highways*, 200–201.
79 The Ridge Road followed the watershed of the highland mountain range that runs from the Negev mountains through Judah north into Samaria (Dorsey, *Roads and Highways*, 117).
80 See below. The Egyptian structure continued in use after the New Kingdom withdrew from the region.
81 See discussion in Chapter Three.
82 Dorsey, *Roads and Highways*, 182, 191–92.
83 Nicola Schreiber, *The Cypro-Phoenician Pottery of the Iron Age* (Culture and History of the Ancient Near East 13; Leiden; Boston: Brill, 2003); Ayelet Gilboa, "Cypriot Barrel Juglets at Khirbet Qeiyafa and Other Sites in the Levant: Cultural Aspects and Chronological Implications," *TA* 39, no. 2 (2012): 133–49; idem, "Iron Age I-II Cypriot Imports and Local Imitations," in *The Ancient Pottery of Israel and Its Neighbors: From the Iron Age through the Late Bronze Age*, ed. Seymour Gitin (Jerusalem: Israel Exploration Society, 2015), 483–507. Schreiber dates the pottery to the second half of the 10th century at the earliest and dates her 'Phase 1' to ca. 925–890/880 (*The Cypro-Phoenician Pottery*, 309–310). Herzog and Singer-Avitz emphasize how regular BoR vessels were as a part of the 'Jezreel cluster,' an assemblage characteristic of the first half of the late Iron IIA, which they date to the 9th century ("Sub-Dividing the Iron Age IIA in Northern Israel," 167–68). The difference between the two ranges is quite small but happens to coincide with one of the more contested transitions for historians and archaeologists (see Chapter One).

84 Schreiber, *The Cypro-Phoenician Pottery*; Gilboa, "Cypriot Barrel Juglets."
85 Recent studies of Cypriot White Painted and Bichrome wares further north at Tel Tayinat suggest the distinctive styles were in demand due to elite feasting practices (Steven Karacic and James F. Osborne, "Eastern Mediterranean Economic Exchange during the Iron Age: Portable X-Ray Fluorescence and Neutron Activation Analysis of Cypriot-Style Pottery in the Amuq Valley, Turkey," *PLOS ONE* 11, no. 11 [2016]: e0166399).
86 Assaf Kleiman et al., "The Date and Origin of Black-on-Red Ware"; Gilboa, "Iron Age I–II Cypriot Imports and Local Imitations"; M. Iacovou, "Phoenicia and Cyprus in the First Millennium B.C.: Two Distinct Cultures in Search of Their Distinct Archaeologies: Review Article," *BASOR* 336 (2004): 61–66; Schreiber, *The Cypro-Phoenician Pottery*, 230–32, 273–77; N. J. Brodie and L. Steel, "Cypriot Black-on-Red Ware: Towards a Characterization," *Archaeometry* 38.2 (1996): 263–78.
87 Ibid., 267–71. They also tested samples from Al Mina, which appear to have come from Kition or Kouklia. Note that these source areas are all on the southern side of the island. Brodie and Steel also note that samples from Salamis, the most likely candidate for a manufacture site based on historical and archaeological research and geographic position, were not sufficient to provide reliable results.
88 Kleiman et al., "The Date and Origin of Black-on-Red Ware," 534–40; Gilboa, "Iron Age I–II Cypriot Imports and Local Imitations."
89 Kleiman et al., "The Date and Origin of Black-on-Red Ware." Recent evidence from Megiddo's area Q provides a level of specificity for BoR and other Cypriot wares. WP was recovered from levels Q-6 (early Iron IIA) thorough Q-4 (late Iron IIA, and Bichrome sherds in level Q-4; and BoR appears first in level Q-5 (late Iron IIA). The bulk of BoR was found within levels Q-5 and Q-4, corresponding to the late 10th through the mid-9th centuries, which was confirmed through radiocarbon dating.
90 Gilboa, "Cypriot Barrel Juglets," 140; emphasis in the original. The CG IB–II phase corresponds roughly to the Iron I–IIA transition and the early Iron IIA period, and the 'Ir1|2 transitional horizon' for Phoenicia (Gilboa, "Cypriot Barrel Juglets," 136; see also Ayelet Gilboa and Ilan Sharon, "An Archaeological Contribution to the Early Iron Age Chronological Debate: Alternative Chronologies for Phoenicia and Their Effects on the Levant, Cyprus, and Greece," *BASOR* 322 [2003]: 1–75).
91 Gilboa, "Cypriot Barrel Juglets," 133.
92 Gilboa, "Cypriot Barrel Juglets," 143.
93 The discussion that follows (including the maps and tables) focuses on these earlier phases of Cypriot imports. Later imports, such as Schreiber's BoR Phase 2 and other 9th century and later examples, are not represented.
94 Gilboa, "Cypriot Barrel Juglets," 104–41; Gilboa, "Iron Age I–II Cypriot Imports and Local Imitations."
95 Schreiber, *The Cypro-Phoenician Pottery*, 28–46; Gilboa, "Cypriot Barrel Juglets," 136–38.
96 Schreiber provides the reconstruction of quantities as well as is possible, but there are many reasons why quantification of BoR is problematic. Excavation of sites with BoR has occurred over more than a century, and archaeological method has changed dramatically over that time. She explains that the most reliable information is the density of BoR compared across the region, as opposed to the density of BoR within one site. Overall quantities of ceramics were not consistently measured, and imported and decorated wares tend to be retained/recorded at a higher rate (all decorated sherds) than local ceramics (diagnostic sherds only). Bearing that in mind, a few sites appear to be exceptions to the general pattern. At most sites, BoR is a very small percentage of the overall ceramic finds. Exceptions include Megiddo (ca. 40 vessels?), Mt Carmel tombs (13 vessels, but these made up 40% of the pottery), Tell Abu Hawam (at least 40 vessels), Tell Keisan (more than 150 fragments), Tyre (29 sherds, but in a very small excavation area; see Schreiber, *The Cypro-Phoenician Pottery*, 26–28, 92–185; see also Faust, *Israel's Ethnogenesis*, 50, note 2.
97 BoR has been recovered from Bethsaida stratum VI (Iron IIA). Detailed analysis is not yet published (Rami Arav, "Bethsaida Excavations Project Report on the 2019 Excavation Season G-33/2019," *Bethsaida Excavations Project*, 1 February 2021).
98 Schreiber expresses some reservations about the date of BoR at Tel Masos (*The Cypro-Phoenician Pottery*, 9, 11).
99 Schreiber, *The Cypro-Phoenician Pottery*, 28–46, 85–169; Herzog and Singer-Avitz, "Redefining the Centre," 215–18; idem, "Sub-Dividing the Iron Age IIA in Northern Israel"; Gilboa, "Cypriot Barrel Juglets," 138–40; Smith and Levy, "Iron Age Ceramics from Edom," 327; Smith, Goren, and Levy, "The Petrography of Iron Age Edom," 479.
100 Schreiber, *The Cypro-Phoenician Pottery*, 85–169; Herzog and Singer-Avitz, "Sub-Dividing the Iron Age IIA in Northern Israel"; Peter M. Fischer, Teresa Bürge, and Eva Maria Wild, *Tell Abu Al-Kharaz in the Jordan Valley: Volume III: The Iron Age*. (Vienna: Austrian Academy of Sciences Press, 2013).

101 Schreiber, *The Cypro-Phoenician Pottery*, 76–78.
102 Based on the expertise of Avner Raban and Ezra Marcus (Schreiber, *The Cypro-Phoenician Pottery*, 77, note 48). As yet, there is no direct evidence of maritime exchange for this period (e.g., the likes of the LBA Uluburun shipwreck). There is no doubt, however, that the Cypriot imports (and Aegean wares discussed below) were part of maritime exchange networks.
103 Schreiber, *The Cypro-Phoenician Pottery*, 76–80.
104 Dorsey, *Roads and Highways*, 78–83.
105 Dorsey notes that the locations of Iron Age sites in the area suggest a route (I23), but if there was one it was not in use in later periods (*Roads and Highways*, 76–77).
106 Dorsey, *Roads and Highways*, 78–101.
107 Megiddo's large amount of BoR is most likely related to its position as a hub linking these international routes. The Q-5 BoR finds also correspond to Aegean imports, see below.
108 These sites were also situated at crossroads, each on west-east routes linking Damascus to the Mediterranean (to sites like Tyre and Achziv). See Aharoni, *The Land of the Bible*, 29–30, 48–49; Dorsey, *Roads and Highways*, 94–97.
109 Very few imports, Cypriot or otherwise, have been recovered from the highlands. See Faust, *Israel's Ethnogenesis*, 49–64.
110 Dorsey, *Roads and Highways*, 61–63.
111 Dorsey's J1 with alternate J2 (*Roads and Highways*, 181–84) and J8 (ibid., 61–64, 189).
112 Ibid., 183, 194.
113 Dorsey, *Roads and Highways*, 152. Schreiber expresses uncertainty about the context in which BoR was found at Tel Masos (*The Cypro-Phoenician Pottery*, 11).
114 Schreiber, *The Cypro-Phoenician Pottery*, 80.
115 Ibid., 56–73, 308.
116 Gilboa, "Cypriot Barrel Juglets," 139.
117 Schreiber, *The Cypro-Phoenician Pottery*, 48–51. Gilboa describes the cultural distance differently, but they appear to be describing the same phenomenon ("Cypriot Barrel Juglets," 139). They also define the limits of Phoenicia differently. Gilboa includes in 'southern Phoenicia' regions traditionally described as northern Israel: the coast of Galilee, the 'Akko plain, the Carmel coast and the western Jezreel Valley.
118 This is the argument Faust uses to explain the distribution patterns of Philistine pottery and collared-rim jars (*Israel's Ethnogenesis*, 191–220).
119 In Areas A, R, T, and W; see Levy et al., "Excavations at Khirbat En-Nahas, 2002–2009."
120 Levy et al., "Excavations at Khirbat En-Nahas, 2002–2009," 202–32.
121 Neighboring structures in Area W highlight the contrast (Levy et al., "Excavations at Khirbat En-Nahas, 2002–2009," 184–201).
122 Smith and Levy, "Iron Age Ceramics from Edom," 449.
123 The number of sites continues to grow; likely Aegean sherds have now been recovered from Tell Abel Beth-Maachah (Amihai Mazar and Nota Kourou, "Greece and the Levant in the 10th–9th Centuries BC: A View from Tel Rehov," *Opuscula* (2019): 369, footnote 3). The most important Aegean ceramics for this discussion come from the phases that preceded the Greek Geometric Age. These are the Sub-Mycenaean (SM) and the Protogeometric (PG) groups; the latter includes Early (EPG), Middle (MPG), Late (LPG), and Sub-Protogeometric (SPG) phases. Overall, Protogeometric is generally thought to have lasted from the 11th century to the 8th century. Archaeologists of the Aegean are having their own debates about these phases, their absolute dates, and regional distinctions (e.g., the distinctive Euboean group compared to Attic pottery).
124 The stratigraphy and chronology of Tyre is extremely complex and has been much discussed. The imported wares have been reviewed most recently by Gilboa and Sharon. They assign them to the same period as the Dor Ir1|2 horizon, roughly equivalent to the Iron I–IIA transition period (essentially early to mid-10th century) now incorporated into discussions of the MCC (Gilboa and Sharon, "An Archaeological Contribution," 68–70).
125 Alexander Fantalkin, Israel Finkelstein, and Eli Piasetzky, "Late Helladic to Middle Geometric Aegean and Contemporary Cypriot Chronologies: A Radiocarbon View from the Levant," *BASOR* 373 (2015): 25–48; Alexander Fantalkin et al., "Aegean Pottery in Iron IIA Megiddo: Typological, Archaeometric and Chronological Aspects," *Mediterranean Archaeology and Archaeometry* 20, no. 3 (2020): 135–47; Mazar and Kourou, "Greece and the Levant in the 10th–9th Centuries BC."

126 The exceptions are Tell-es Safi's painted sherd, which was produced in the Argolid, and one of the Megiddo vessels whose origin cannot be determined with certainty aside from likely having an Aegean origin; the excavators suggest Corinth or alternatively Cyprus. An additional sherd (Cat. No. 4) could not be confidently identified with known Aegean sources (Fantalkin et al., "Aegean Pottery in Iron IIA Megiddo").

127 Maeir, Fantalkin, and Zuckerman, "The Earliest Greek Import in the Iron Age Levant," 71-72. The closest parallel to the Gath sherd is a Tyre stratum XIV bowl or skyphos fragment (ibid., 73-74, note 94).

128 That is, late 11th to early 10th century in the MCC or mid to late 10th in the LC (Maeir, Fantalkin, and Zuckerman, "The Earliest Greek Import in the Iron Age Levant").

129 David Ben-Shlomo, Aren M. Maeir, and Hans Mommsen, "Neutron Activation and Petrographic Analysis of Selected Late Bronze and Iron Age Pottery from Tell Es-Safi/Gath, Israel," *JAS* 35 (2008): 956-64.

130 See Chapter Two and Aren M. Maeir, "The Tell Es-Safi/Gath Archaeological Project 1996-2010."

131 P. M. Bikai, *The Pottery of Tyre* (Warminster: Aris & Phillips, 1978); Gilboa and Sharon, "An Archaeological Contribution," 43-49.

132 Jacqueline Balensi, "Revising Tell Abu Hawam," *BASOR* 257 (1985): 65-74; M. D. Herrera Gonzalez and Jacqueline Balensi, "More about the Greek Geometric Pottery at Tell Abu Hawam," *Levant* 18 (1986): 169-71; Rosalinde Anne Kearsley, "The Redating of Tell Abu Hawam III and the Greek Pendant Semicircle Skyphos," *BASOR* 263 (1986): 85-86; Jane C. Waldbaum, "Early Greek Contacts with the Southern Levant, ca. 1000-600 B. C.: The Eastern Perspective," *BASOR* 293 (1994): 53-66; Gilboa and Sharon, "An Archaeological Contribution," 67-72.

133 Gilboa and Sharon, "An Archaeological Contribution"; Ayelet Gilboa and Ilan Sharon, "Between Carmel and the Sea," *NEA* 71, no. 3 (2008): 146-70.

134 Moshe Kochavi, "Hadar, Tel," in *The New Encyclopedia of Archaeological Excavations in the Holy Land*, ed. Ephraim Stern (Jerusalem: Israel Exploration Society & Carta, 1993), 551-52; idem, "The Eleventh Century BCE Tripartite Pillar Building at Tel Hadar," in *Mediterranean Peoples in Transition: Thirteenth to Early Tenth Centuries BCE* (Jerusalem: Israel Exploration Society, 1998), 468-78; Günter Kopcke, "1000 B.C.E.? 900 B.C.E.? A Greek Vase from Lake Galilee," in *Leaving No Stones Unturned: Essays on the Ancient Near East and Egypt in Honor of Donald P. Hansen*, ed. Erica Ehrenberg (Winona Lake: Eisenbrauns, 2002), 109-17.

135 Mazar and Kourou, "Greece and the Levant in the 10th-9th Centuries BC"; Coldstream and Mazar, "Greek Pottery from Tel Rehov and Iron Age Chronology."

136 Kleiman et al., "The Date and Origin of Black-on-Red Ware," 545-46.

137 Mervyn R. Popham, L. H. Sackett, and P. G. Themelis, eds., *Lefkandi I, the Iron Age* (British School at Athens Supplementary Volume 11; London: Thames and Hudson, 1979); Mervyn R. Popham, P. G. Calligas, and L. H Sackett, eds., *Lefkandi II: The Protogeometric Building at Toumba* (British School at Athens Supplementary Volume 22-23; London: British School of Archaeology at Athens, 1993); Mervyn R. Popham and Irene S. Lemos, "A Euboean Warrior Trader," *Oxford Journal of Archaeology* 14, no. 2 (1995): 151-57; Mervyn R. Popham, ed., *Lefkandi III: The Toumba Cemetery: The Excavations of 1981, 1984, 1986 and 1992-4* (British School at Athens Supplementary Volume 29; London: British School at Athens, 1996); Jane B. Carter, "Egyptian Bronze Jugs from Crete and Lefkandi," *Journal of Hellenic Studies* 118 (1998): 172-77; Georg Nightingale, "Lefkandi: An Important Node in the International Exchange Network of Jewellery and Personal Adornment," in *Between the Aegean and Baltic Seas: Prehistory across Borders: Proceedings of the International Conference Bronze and Early Iron Age Interconnections and Contemporary Developments between the Aegean and the Regions of the Balkan Peninsula, Central and Northern Europe, University of Zagreb, 11-14 April 2005*, ed. Ioanna Galanaki et al. (AEGAEUM [Annales d'archéologie Égéenne de l'Université de Liège et UT-PASP] 27; Liège, Belgique; Austin, TX: Université de Liège, Histoire de l'art et archéologie de la Grèce antique; University of Texas at Austin, Program in Aegean Scripts and Prehistory, 2007); Irene S. Lemos, "Lefkandi in Euboea: Amongst the Heroes of the Early Iron Age," *Minerva* (2008): 30-32; John H. Kroll, "Early Iron Age Balance Weights at Lefkandi, Euboea," *Oxford Journal of Archaeology* 27 (2008): 37-48.

138 The most famous residents are the elite couple from the 'Heroon' complex. Finds deposited with their remains included bronze and ceramic heirloom pieces from Mycenaean and Near Eastern cultures, gold jewelry, contemporary Cypriot imports, evidence of exchange with Macedonia, painted decoration of sailors and a ship on a vessel, thousands of faience and glass beads, and a sequence of merchants' weights that correspond to known commercial standards across the eastern Mediterranean (Popham and Lemos, "A Euboean Warrior Trader"; Nightingale, "Lefkandi").

139 Note, however, that John K. Papadopoulos warns against the imbalance that has occurred as a result of the sensational finds from Lefkandi and from the excavators' presentation of these discoveries. He notes

that the 'warrior/trader' characterization has led to an overemphasis on Euboean activity abroad to the detriment of investigations into interactions that reached Euboea ("Phantom Euboians," *JMA* 10.2 (1997): 191–219).

140 Cypriot maritime activity may have continued in the eastern Mediterranean (including with the southern Levantine coast) despite the upheaval following the LBA collapse. Based on Cypriot finds during the transition years, connections to Crete seem to have persisted throughout, which indicates that Cypriot relations to the Aegean more generally were possible at this early date (Nota Kourou, "The Aegean and the Levant in the Early Iron Age: Recent Developments," *BAAL* 6 [2008]: 361–74; idem, "Phoenicia, Cyprus and the Aegean in the Early Iron Age: J. N. Coldstream's Contribution and the Current State of Research," in *Cyprus and the Aegean in the Early Iron Age: The Legacy of Nicolas Coldstream*, ed. Maria Iacovou [Nicosia: Bank of Cyprus Cultural Foundation, 2012], 33–51).

141 Nancy H. Demand, *The Mediterranean Context of Early Greek History* (Oxford: Wiley-Blackwell, 2011), 226.

142 Although Sherratt argues for a strong Tyrian initiative in the exchange with Euboea ("Phoenicians in the Aegean and Aegean Silver, 11th–9th Centuries BC").

143 Mazar and Kourou have recently explored the possibility that Tel Reḥov functioned as a 'middleman' in the passage of Arabah copper to the Mediterranean ("Greece and the Levant in the 10th–9th Centuries BC"). While this is more in line with my arguments here than earlier proposals, such as Coldstream's suggestion of diplomatic marriage between Euboea and the Levant, the importance of elite interaction spheres greatly enhances our understanding of the evidence across the entire region, and of the long-distance exchange participants. For earlier explanations, see Popham and Lemos, "A Euboean Warrior Trader"; John Nicolas Coldstream, "The First Exchanges Between Euboeans and Phoenicians: Who Took the Initiative?," in *Mediterranean Peoples in Transition: Thirteenth to Early Tenth Centuries BCE*, ed. Seymour Gitin, Amihai Mazar, and Ephraim Stern (Jerusalem: Israel Exploration Society, 1998), 353–60; Kochavi, "The Eleventh Century BCE Tripartite Pillar Building at Tel Hadar"; Kopcke, "1000 B.C.E.? 900 B.C.E.?"

144 Tell eṣ-Ṣafi and Tel Reḥov have been introduced earlier (see Chapters Two and Five). Megiddo likely requires little introduction, but it is important to note that the Aegean sherds were found in level Q-5, which also yielded Cypriot imports, and near 'an elaborate public building, located at the highest point of the site' (Fantalkin et al., "Aegean Pottery in Iron IIA Megiddo," 143). As for Tel Hadar, it was a major regional center until its destruction in the late 11th-early 10th century. The site is situated at the point where the main route from Bashan joined passages to the southern Levantine international routes and to the Mediterranean coast. The site was fortified and included a 'citadel' area that appears to have served as an administrative and commercial center. The Greek sherd was found along with Phoenician vessels, suggesting the site was actively involved in long-distance exchange networks. The appearance of the Tel Hadar Greek import is unique and seems to have been made according to Levantine style of vessel shape with the Euboean quality and decoration. See Kochavi, "Hadar, Tel"; idem, "The Eleventh Century BCE Tripartite Pillar Building at Tel Hadar"; idem, "1000 B.C.E.? 900 B.C.E.?"

145 See previous note. For detailed examination of the routes around these sites, see Dorsey, *Roads and Highways*, 93–116, 181–201.

146 Tyre experienced some disruption (stratum XIV; Iron I) but continued to function (Bikai, *The Pottery of Tyre*, 73–74). Tel Reḥov also shows evidence of some disruptive event in the Iron I, but affected areas were rebuilt (Amihai Mazar, "Reḥov, Tel," in *The New Encyclopedia of Archaeological Excavations in the Holy Land*, ed. Ephraim Stern, Ayelet Lewinson-Gilboa, and Joseph Aviram [Jerusalem; New York: Israel Exploration Society & Carta; Simon and Schuster, 2008]).

147 Gilboa and Sharon, "Between Carmel and the Sea," 161–63. Tyre may have experienced a population shift from island to mainland at this time, but Bikai cautions that her investigation was too small to say for certain (*The Pottery of Tyre*, 73–74).

148 Lichtheim, *Ancient Egyptian Literature: Volume II*. See also Chapter Five.

149 Incidentally, the story ultimately leaves off with Wenamun being blown off course to Cyprus after leaving Byblos.

150 Destruction is evident in some of the LBA remains at Tell eṣ-Ṣafi, which is likely due to the arrival of a Philistine population (Maeir, "The Tell Es-Safi/Gath Archaeological Project 1996–2010," 16–20).

151 Mazar and Kourou, "Greece and the Levant in the 10th–9th Centuries BC," 384–87.

152 S. Rebecca Martin reviews critiques that Greek vessels were the primary traded item or that they were exchanged as gifts, but she concludes they may be 'indicative of a more personal level of exchange.' She explains, '...perhaps we can still locate Greek ceramics in the elite milieu by understanding that the very uppermost levels of the elite were exchanging gifts with greater intrinsic value, and a few of the lesser

elites (members of the *haute bourgeois*, if you will) may have imitated this practice by exchanging or seeking out for themselves fine ceramics' ("'Hellenization' and Southern Phoenicia: Reconsidering the Impact of Greece Before Alexander" [Ph. D. dissertation, University of California, Berkeley, 2007], 122–23, note 15).

153 Ibid., 155–56.
154 Marom et al., "Backbone of Society."
155 See Chapter Two.
156 Schreiber, *The Cypro-Phoenician Pottery*, 79.
157 Examples of QPW seem to decline as the Mediterranean imports increase. Perhaps the market for decorated wares was met by the Cypriot and later Aegean pottery, decreasing the demand for the Arabian style.
158 See also Susan Sherratt, "The Mediterranean Economy: 'Globalization' at the End of the Second Millennium B.C.E.," in *Symbiosis, Symbolism, and the Power of the Past: Canaan, Ancient Israel, and Their Neighbors from the Late Bronze Age through Roman Palaestina*, ed. William G. Dever and Seymour Gitin (Winona Lake: Eisenbrauns, 2003), 37–62.
159 Knowing the precise relationship here requires moving beyond the imports and distribution patterns – a comparative task too extensive for this book.
160 One potential exception has been put forward, which is the presence of 'Tripartite Pillared Buildings.' A number of these structures are found dispersed throughout the southern Levant. They have been interpreted as marketplaces or bazaars, which appears likely. What is less certain is whether their similarities are the result of a common form (not unlike gate or house structures now known to have been in use across ethnic boundaries), or a centralized effort to control trade. See Larry G. Herr, "Tripartite Pillared Buildings and the Market Place in Iron Age Palestine," *BASOR* 272 (1988): 47–67; Kochavi, "The Eleventh Century BCE Tripartite Pillar Building at Tel Hadar"; Jeffrey A. Blakely, "Reconciling Two Maps: Archaeological Evidence for the Kingdoms of David and Solomon," *BASOR* 327 (2002): 49–54. The structures are also noted in Rainey and Notley, *The Sacred Bridge*, 166.
161 This idea is discussed more generally in Sherratt, "The Mediterranean Economy," 51–54.

7 Synthesis and Conclusions

Any research into southern Levantine trade and exchange during the Iron I to II transition must confront obvious challenges. The biblical depiction of interaction in and around the 10th century BCE does not match up with the historical and archaeological evidence of the same period, and explicit extrabiblical evidence is meager. To be sure, the images of David's widespread conquests and Solomon's international trade empire have been heavily scrutinized and can no longer be considered historical in any uncomplicated way. Those who are skeptical of the biblical account's usefulness for historical questions point to the absence of contemporary historical evidence, and the discrepancy between how the Bible describes Israel's past and what the 10th century looks like according to archaeological evidence. With the exception of Shoshenq I's campaign to the Levant (ca. 925 BCE, referred to in 1 Kgs 14:25), it is not until the mid-9th century that inscriptions and biblical history begin to correspond (e.g., the Mesha stele and 2 Kgs 3, or Shalmaneser III's Black Obelisk and traditions of the house of Omri). It is rapidly becoming clearer that the interactions necessary for these connections did not develop suddenly; the southern Levant was not isolated during the 10th century, as many scholars proposed in the late 20th century. Based on the probability that diverse interregional interactions preceded the extrabiblical written evidence, I have looked for indications of exchange and interaction during the 100–150 years prior to the prominent 9th century monuments, primarily in the late 11th and 10th centuries. This research has found that interregional and intercultural interactions not only existed but were lively and influential on other important changes in the region, such as territorial organization and the development of new identities.

In the preceding chapters, I have explored biblical, epigraphic, and archaeological evidence, with several questions at the forefront of the inquiry. The first is the most basic: does this evidence attest to intercultural or interregional exchange? In all cases, the answer is, ultimately, yes – some directly, some indirectly – although that is not to say that the information from each type of evidence obviously relates to the others. Based on these indications of interactions, I have followed up with questions about who was participating, why they were interacting, and what the consequences were of venturing beyond a group's own boundaries. The participants and reasons for interacting are different based on the evidence at hand. According to biblical texts, Samuel's heroes fought the Philistines who were seeking passage east; Solomon used diplomatic connections and resource management to broaden his influence. Based on extrabiblical evidence, new leaders inscribed their names and stories on objects, implying they were members of an elite and interregional community. Possession of imported pottery made statements about wealth, stability, exotic connections, and group affiliations.

In this final chapter, I combine the results of the individual studies and more directly integrate the theoretical models introduced in Chapter One. The result is a synthesized view of the findings from the previous chapters, which shows that there is solid evidence of exchange and long-distance connections, including trade. The individual chapters shed light on distinct geographic regions, certain population groups, notions of identity, specific interaction niches, and different periods. When combined, that evidence provides greater coverage of the research area in both time and space, but it is admittedly both inconsistent and incomplete. It is done with this caveat: combining the evidence and preliminary conclusions is somewhat hazardous. A major source of inconsistency comes from reliance on the biblical texts, where bias and chronological distance from the events is especially apparent. The narratives prioritize certain interactions and geographic territories above others. An additional challenge comes from the fact that the different types of evidence do not clearly reference each other; there is a danger of both inflating and conflating the findings and significance. For example, there is no way to know, at present, how diverse evidence relates, despite provocative commonalities. Consider, for example, Samuel's Achish of Gath, Tell eṣ-Ṣafi's inscription, Tell eṣ-Ṣafi's Argolid import, and the ancient individuals who handled these artifacts. We can neither assume they were all related, nor that they were all independent. Addressing the evidence in sum, however, allows for another perspective and a comprehensive (though cautious) historical reconstruction. Before moving to the larger discussions, we will review the findings from the previous chapters.

Summaries of Interactions by Evidence Type

Interregional interaction, including long-distance trade, was taking place in the southern Levant during the late 11th and 10th centuries BCE. Our ability to state this fact so conclusively is largely a result of archaeological research of the last 15–20 years, but support for this initial conclusion stems from all the evidence types: epigraphic and contemporary historical materials; distribution of imported and rare goods; and portions of the biblical books of 1 and 2 Samuel and 1 Kings 3–11.

The biblical materials paint a picture of increasing interactions in the region from Samuel's day through Solomon's. Even if we have reservations about historical details of the main figures, the stories may represent the nature of the conflicts and interregional relations of earlier periods. Because we do not have corroborating evidence, the summaries below should be understood within the worldview of the biblical narrative. In the biblical depiction, the most intense relations were between Israelites and Philistines, first in the Shephelah and Benjamin, then in the Judahite hills and potentially as far north as the Jezreel Valley. Samuel, Saul, Jonathan, David, and other warrior-heroes represent various leaders who dominated smaller-scale territories. My analysis of these activities leads to the conclusion that most of the conflicts were related to Philistine and hill-country rivalries to dominate passage to the east, which, if successful, could have been used to exploit access to resources and inland highways, especially those related to metallurgical trade.

Saul and David's actions also portray competition that was not limited to the coast-versus-highlands divide. Having won control of the Michmash Pass, Saul engaged the Philistines (or a related? opponent) in the northern route to the east, the Jezreel Valley.

Alternately, David targeted areas in the south that would have impacted traffic between Philistia, Transjordan, and the Negev, and he used diplomatic ventures in addition to military might to secure his position. In the narrative, the competition among these leaders led to a consolidation of power. According to the DH, David's efforts were the most successful, gaining him control of multiple tribal territories.

Solomon's history describes diplomatic and administrative strategies that expanded regional and long-distance interactions in the mid to late 10th century. Although there are claims to many interregional interactions, much of which seem fanciful at first, there is reason to reconsider the text's claims about the era. Diplomatic marriages with Egyptian elite in the 10th century appear unlikely, but the practice of using strategic marriages to secure resources and power likely would have taken place among elites, perhaps across closer distances. Exchange agreements involving land (or territorial authority) and commodities with Phoenicia may reflect a historical practice of the era among southern elites and their northern counterparts. In terms of 'domestic' affairs, Solomon's policies regarding the Israelite territories included administrative efforts to control the region, through the reorganization and control of resources, a labor tax, and construction projects to demonstrate authority. Here too, it appears quite plausible that a 10th century Solomon (or a contemporary to such a figure) could have used diplomacy, in the form of his daughters' marriages, to strengthen loyalty from northern 'districts' (which may be better described as peer polities). The extraction of resources and wealth appears to be deeply connected to the idea of Solomon in the biblical narrative, and there is good reason to consider such an approach to the region as a plausible strategy for rulers of the time as well. The administrative districts reveal an organizational strategy based on commerce and wealth from natural resources, and the narrative's depictions of forced labor point to an important cultural memory. Whether or not these efforts were exclusively the work of a historical Solomon is less important than what we gain from the inquiry, which is a persuasive case in favor of such practices among 11th and 10th century elites to manage diverse territories and exploit interaction opportunities.

Based on the narrative evidence just reviewed, Jerusalem would seem to be an essential component of southern Levantine interactions in the 10th century; however, the role of Jerusalem in the biblical traditions has appeared at odds with the available archaeological remains of the city. Recent excavations have changed this picture to a certain extent, with the discovery of monumental architecture that was in use from the Iron I to IIA, and artifacts such as imported pottery, carved ivory objects, and epigraphic evidence. While the new discoveries do not provide explicit correspondence to biblical or historical figures, they do suggest that Jerusalem's elite participated in exchange networks throughout the southern Levant, and that they exhibited their significance through wealth and statements of power. The geographic context of the site and the evidence of its character in the Middle and Late Bronze Age periods further indicate that despite apparent discrepancies between textual and material remains, Jerusalem was integral in the region's interactions.

The epigraphic evidence appears, at first glance, to be both scant and silent regarding interaction; however, by situating scribal activity in a broader eastern Mediterranean context, we reach different conclusions. Evidence of scribal activity *is* evidence of elite interaction and competition. As contemporary Egyptian and Byblian material shows, interregional activities accompanied the employment of scribes. Although on a different scale, the short inscriptions in the southern Levant are testaments to competing small-scale elites who displayed their status through inscribed materials. The use of inscriptions went along with other elite activities, such as the collection of luxury goods (e.g., imported pottery or metals) and, in the case of Tel Reḥov, feasting and an exclusive beekeeping industry. Elites did not do this in isolation. The evidence appears in clusters, suggesting that the use of scribes was influenced by conspicuous display among neighboring sites. The repetition of names – ḥnn in the Shephelah and nmš in the northern Jordan Valley – may indicate that certain families dominated some of these territories.

The long-distance exchange of ceramics results in the most conspicuous and objective evidence of interregional exchange. Provenance testing has established that vessels produced in the Aegean, Cyprus, and northwest Arabia were transported into the southern Levant during the Iron I–IIA transition. These items were traded because they were desirable as prestige painted wares, as containers for other commodities such as perfumed oil, and probably also as important accoutrements to elite behaviors such as banqueting and burial deposits. The distributions show that the imported goods were more likely to be acquired at port cities, sites that were on significant roads, and other strategic locations. In addition, sites where imported wares have been found tended to have fared better in the Late Bronze to Iron Age transition, indicating that sociopolitical stability corresponded to participation in certain exchange networks. Like inscriptions, the distribution of imported wares appears in clusters, which may be evidence of an elite culture or competition among neighboring communities. The Aegean imports, in particular, reveal a highly exclusive network related to select sites.

Summaries of Interactions by Region

Because geography plays an important role in evaluating the different types of evidence, it is also useful to review the material of the preceding chapters according to distinct regions. Not all interactions would have been concurrent, but (with some exceptions for early examples of QPW) events and interactions should fall within 100–150 years of each other, which we might alternatively think of as a handful of generations. In reviewing the summaries below, it is important to keep in mind that the interactions, as described here, are based primarily on the evidence reviewed in the previous chapters and are not substantially supplemented by other studies of the regions. Also, because each of the previous chapters focused on a very specific source of interaction evidence, these summaries are biased based on the nature of that evidence and the activities that correspond to it.

Northern Coast

The northern coast (including Dor and nearby sites) is not emphasized in most of the biblical material from Chapters Two and Three; however, Solomon's district policies and his interactions with Hiram of Tyre deal directly with this region. Solomon reportedly traded part of the northern Israelite territory, the Cabul, to Hiram. Solomon's fourth and ninth administrative districts encompass the lands that acted as a gateway for early maritime exchange. These zones may have been designed to focus on that region's trade resources. Another revealing strategy in relation to the region is the marriage between Solomon's daughter Taphath and Ben-Abinadab – a wise move if the depiction of a highly independent prince and city of Dor in the Report of Wenamun conveys a historically accurate character for the city in this transition period. The entire area was impacted by renewed exchange with Cyprus, and three of the most important ports in this region have produced evidence of Euboean wares. Indications of exceptional wealth come from the burial at Kefar Veradim, which included an inscribed bronze bowl, Cypriot imports, and other prestige goods. The inscribed bowl alone testifies to extraordinary status and interregional connections.

Galilee and North

This area, the region around and north of the Sea of Galilee, was home to various peer leaders and states in the Iron Age (most consequentially, Aram), but it is present in only some of the previous discussions. Not surprisingly, the region is absent from the reports of relations with Philistines in Samuel (although other reports in David's history suggest interactions in this area; e.g., 2 Sam 8); however, Solomon's history devotes much attention to it. His eighth and tenth districts cover the territory north of the Jezreel Valley, to beyond Dan. Solomon reportedly secured these regions through his daughter Basemath's marriage to Ahimaaz and his fortifications in Hazor. The brief appearance of Damascus's ruler Rezon at the end of the Solomon Narrative may be suggestive of some memory of an early Iron Age contemporary elite or polity (although the conflicts involving Aram, Edom, Israel, and Judah in later generations muddy the historical waters here). The most conclusive evidence from the north comes in the form of material evidence of Mediterranean exchange, with Cypriot wares found at Hazor, Dan, and En Gev, and a Euboean vessel found at Tel Hadar.

Jezreel and Jordan Valleys

The Jezreel and Jordan Valleys had a distinct environmental, cultural, and political character. The Jezreel cuts through the hill country and provides passage from the Mediterranean coast to the Jordan Valley, which runs along the rift valley between the Dead Sea and the Sea of Galilee. In terms of interaction, the two valleys were among the most active transportation corridors of the southern Levant and were intimately connected due to long-distance travel and commerce.

We begin the review of evidence with the Jezreel Valley. In the biblical material, this area is featured in Saul's final war with the Philistines. The main conflict was at the heart of the Jezreel Valley, but Saul's remains were reportedly displayed on the wall of Beth-Shean, the massive guardian site at the international crossroad with the Jordan Valley. In Solomon's administration, the fifth district encompasses the related Jezreel and north Jordan Valley systems, undoubtedly due to their roles in interregional traffic. The text claims that Solomon fortified Megiddo, which guarded the juncture between the Via Maris and the Jezreel. Extrabiblical material parallels the biblical emphasis on these valleys. Local inscriptions have been found at Tel Reḥov and Tel ʿAmal, including the repeated name *nmš*. A stele fragment from Shoshenq was recovered from Megiddo, and his Karnak inscription names several sites in the region, tracing a path through both valley systems. Cypriot imports have been found throughout the Jezreel Valley, from the port cities through to

Pella, and Tel Reḥov has produced Greek sherds from the Euboean Protogeometric period and later.

Interactions involving the Jordan Valley are evident in select portions of the surveyed material. Although the motivation is not discussed explicitly in Samuel's history of the Philistines, the effort to expand eastward and establish outposts in the hill country suggests the Philistines had an interest in some activities in the Jordan Valley.[1] Solomon's districts included land east of the Jordan, and his metallurgical operations were reportedly situated in the valley. Intriguingly, the iron smelting site of Tell Hammeh is located in the vicinity indicated by the text, and Shoshenq's campaign appears to have focused on this same key area.[2] Regarding imported ceramics, BoR has turned up in Pella and Abu al-Kharaz, both situated close to the Jordan and Jezreel junction. Early QPW has been found at Amman, perhaps reflecting the southern orientation of the networks connected to that city. The most suggestive evidence is the relationship between the Jordan Valley and the metallurgical trade. As I cautioned above, we do not know what or if there was a direct relationship among any of these figures and events, but the importance of the central Jordan Valley in biblical and Egyptian sources, and the increasing evidence of metallurgical industry and trade in the region, are adding up. It appears likely that the biblical texts preserve, albeit imperfectly, cultural memories of the trade throughout this valley and the elite competition for control of it.

Central Coast and Sharon Plain

The central coast and Sharon Plain are not frequently mentioned in the examined biblical material, but they were of importance judging from the role Aphek plays in both the Ark Narrative and Saul's interactions with Philistines. Solomon's third district covered this region and presumably would have benefited from maritime and coastal traffic. Shoshenq's campaign trail seems to have moved through the Sharon, following a march through the Jordan and Jezreel Valleys. Additionally, the central coast's ports and inland routes became more important during the BoR phase of Cypriot imports, judging from the finds at Tel Michal, Tel Qasile, Tel Gerisa, Tel Azor, Tel Mevorakh, and Tel Zeror. For this region, the extrabiblical evidence provides a richer picture and demonstrates active exchange relations. More investigation is warranted to explore the reason for the limited coverage in the biblical narratives.

Central (Ephraimite) Hills

Although the central hill country is the focus of many early Iron Age discussions, it is barely represented in the interaction evidence surveyed here. The important site of Shiloh is on the margin of the Ark Narrative's main action, and Solomon's first district is equated with the Ephraim hills. The only ceramic evidence of interaction is Cypriot BoR found at Tell el-Farʿah (N), biblical Tirzah. The sparse representation of this region in the bodies of evidence examined in this study is conspicuous. The contrast compared to the other areas indicates that additional investigation is needed.

Benjamin

The Benjaminite hill country is, understandably, the focus in Saul's history, but it also plays a role in the Ark Narrative, when the ark rests at Kiriath-jearim and the troops rally at Mizpah. Armed conflict between the Philistines and Jonathan was located in Geba/Gibeah and the Michmash Pass, but there was also commercial interaction regarding smithing services in the neighboring lowland. Although David does not engage with the Philistines in this territory, it is possible that an alliance with them aided in his dominance over this area after Saul's death. In Solomon's activities, this region corresponds to the eleventh district, and Solomon is credited with fortifying Lower Beth-Horon, the most important ascent between the Shephelah and Benjamin's core. This same road was used in Shoshenq's campaign to pass through to the Jordan Valley. Other evidence of long-distance exchange is minimal, with Cypriot imports at Tell el-Ful and Tell en-Nasbeh.

Southern Hills and Jerusalem

The southern hill country was the site of repeated conflicts between Saul, David, and the Philistines (in Qeʿilah, Rephaim Valley, Bethlehem, and Adullam). This region becomes the focus of the biblical history as home to both of David's capitals, Hebron and Jerusalem. Solomon's history focuses on efforts to center administrative operations in Jerusalem and to expand the royal complex and building fortifications. Outside of the biblical accounts, there is evidence that this area was important in interregional interactions. Epigraphic evidence has been found in the form of inscribed arrowheads and the recent discovery of the Ophel pithos. Cypriot imports are known from Jerusalem, Beth-zur, Tell Beit Mirsim, and Tel Halif, and QPW was found in the Late Bronze Age burial cave at Tel Jedur. Many of the locations related to evidence of exchange activity, both within the biblical narratives and through extrabiblical indicators, were situated on key roads connecting to the Ridge Road, the Shephelah, and the Beersheba Valley.

Shephelah

The Shephelah was one of the most active areas according to each evidence group. The region figures prominently in the Ark Narrative, with events at Eben-ezer and Beth-shemesh. In David's history, he and his men battled the Philistines in a number of locations between Benjamin and Gath. According to Solomon's history, Solomon fortified Baalath and Gezer (which he purportedly acquired with his Egyptian wife), and his second district covered much of this territory. The extrabiblical evidence is strong. Six inscriptions have been recovered from the area, two of which bear the name ḥnn, and ceramic imports have been found at Gezer, Lachish, Beth-shemesh, and Khirbet Qeiyafa. From outside of the region, we may surmise from Shoshenq's relief that his campaign moved through the Shephelah, but without a precise itinerary or better preservation of the full list of place names, we rely on proposed reconstructions that continue to be debated. Nevertheless, it is the sum and variety of the different types of evidence, including a concentration of prestige goods and specialized metallurgical materials, that indicate intense interactions in this region.

Philistia

Interactions within the Philistine heartland are recorded in the Ark Narrative and in David's history, with his relations to Achish of Gath. While the biblical narratives focus on the Philistines outside of the core territory, extrabiblical evidence shows that the southern coast was well integrated into exchange networks. Tell eṣ-Ṣafi's inscription provides the earliest evidence of a Philistine alphabetic text, and the Argolid import is the earliest Aegean evidence in the region. Cypriot imports and/or QPW have also been found from Ashdod, Tell eṣ-Ṣafi, Tell el-Ajjul, Tell Jemmeh, and Tell el-Farʿah (S). Shoshenq's campaign passed through at least the southern portion of Philistine territory en route to other targets. If the biblical narratives can be relied on for a basic notion that the Philistines pursued interests inland, we might reconstruct a calculated effort to connect a base in Philistia with trade along the coast, to the east in the Jordan Valley, and potentially also to the Arabah. Our best candidate for that targeted activity is the iron and copper trade of the Iron I–IIA periods.

Negev and Northern Sinai

Interactions in the Negev are evident primarily along the routes that would have facilitated trade in copper and goods from Arabian exchange networks (e.g., cinnamon). QPW has been found in the Beersheva Valley at Tel Masos, as well as at Tell el-Qudeirat/Kadesh Barnea and various other Negev sites. That routes in this region facilitated other trade activities is evident in the discovery of Cypriot imports from Tel Masos, Beersheba, and Tell el-Qudeirat, and in the wealth and elite culture of Tel Masos. Shoshenq's campaign targeted the Beersheba region and Negev highland sites and may have penetrated as far as the Faynan. If the report of Solomon's fortification of Tamar (located either in this region or the Arabah) reflects memory of infrastructure in the south, we should understand such activity as related to the southern exchange networks.

Arabah

This region's land use, infrastructure, and interactions were heavily shaped by the early Iron Age copper industry. The Arabah sites' successes in the copper trade are apparent in unusual prestige goods, imports, and relative opulence in specific areas (e.g., keeping costlier livestock, architectural forms at Khirbat en-Nahas). It is also evident in the distribution of the copper itself, in elite products such as Wendjebauendjeb's shabti figurines, tripod cauldrons in Olympia, and debased silver in various Levantine hoards. The intensity of QPW in the region also remains intriguing, although its precise significance and longevity continue to be investigated. At the least, we can be certain that the connection between the Arabah and northwest Arabia would have had a profound impact on the exchange relations that facilitated the import of exotic goods such as spices. The inclusion of QPW in burials outside of the core distribution of the ware suggests an elite value associated with the vessels and perhaps their connection to other imported and prestige goods.

Despite this extraordinary archaeological evidence, the region is fully on the margin in the surveys of epigraphic and biblical evidence (unless the Tamar fortification is identified with an Arabah site such as En Haseva). In the biblical narrative, we may detect cultural memory of metallurgical trade in the affairs with the Philistines or of Solomon's reported smelting operations. In the territorial contestations, especially with David in the south, there are patterns that suggest attention to key routes leading between the Hebron and Judahite hill country and the copper and spice corridors to the south. Similarly, Shoshenq's campaign appears to have targeted extensions of these same networks. Focusing attention on the Arabah demonstrates that our most influential written sources, primarily the biblical narratives, have critical blind spots related to elites and exchange. Archaeology, however, provides the evidence that the Arabah had a great impact in the Levant and more distant regions in the 11th and 10th centuries.

Observations

Three sub-regions stand out for their exceptional intensity in interactions. Among the most important was the northern network that reached from the Carmel/Akko area to the Jezreel and Jordan Valleys. This sub-region is critical in the biblical histories of interactions with the Philistines and Solomon's activities. The Carmel/Akko region, including the large port of Dor, appears to have been the gateway for the earliest Mediterranean trade in the Iron Age and maintained its importance even as exchange broadened to include other coastal areas. The Jezreel and Jordan Valley road systems provided the best passage through the southern Levant, and sites in these valley systems controlled access into adjacent areas. The amount of imports in general, and the concentration of inscriptions in particular, show that residents at these sites (e.g., Tel Reḥov) were able to participate in specialized and elite activities.

The southern copper exchange network that ran from Timna and the Faynan to Gaza functioned similarly. The road networks had international importance, linking Egypt and the Mediterranean coast to southern Jordan and northwest Arabia, and routes into Arabia and along the eastern Jordan Valley. Tel Masos, Timna, and Khirbat en-Nahas demonstrate the amount of wealth and power that were possible for sites that dominated a portion of this network. While the biblical texts do not relate directly to this area, there are hints that its importance was felt by the hill country. The accounts of David's efforts to control the southern hill country and Solomon's southern fortification at Tamar were likely related to traffic moving northward. The southern portion of Shoshenq's campaign was similarly targeted at this active trade network.

Lastly, as I note above, biblical, epigraphic, ceramic imports, and archaeological evidence more generally, all indicate that the Shephelah was the site of frequent and intense interactions. The region was desirable for human habitation and for agriculture, and it was naturally disposed to be a border zone. The Shephelah is also home to several important valley systems that provided passage between the lowland and highland, and, as a result, sites along these routes grew to be prominent. Thus, it should not be surprising that an area such as the Elah Valley would be featured in biblical narrative and provide archaeological evidence of success in this period.

Interpretive Frameworks

The foundation for further interpretation is that interactions and trade were indeed occurring in the southern Levant throughout the transition from the Iron I to IIA. The positive evidence of interactions during this period is especially intriguing in light of the events that preceded it, namely the dissolution of Late Bronze Age powers and exchange networks. At the height of the LBA exchange, the eastern Mediterranean and ancient Near Eastern cultures were thoroughly interconnected through industry and commerce (elite-driven and other), expansive imperial policies, and diplomacy.[3] Mycenean and Cypriot imports, Egyptian material culture, Syrian-inspired art and architecture, prestige goods, and scribal activity were prevalent in southern Levantine contexts until the demise of the major power centers and support for the rich interregional relations. These disruptions resulted in chaos, when judged from sources that document exceptional change at this time.[4] In light of the evidence surveyed in the previous chapters, however, the Iron I and early Iron IIA periods, once thought of as an age of retrenchment, can now be understood as a period of renewal or intensification of eastern Mediterranean exchange.

Consequently, the new evidence of interactions introduces some challenging questions. Long-distance exchange usually implies that there were entities of considerable power, which created the demand as well as organized and facilitated the physical transport of goods. Since the southern Levant was left in a power vacuum resulting from a weakened Egypt, we have questions about who was involved in the early Iron Age interactions. Evidence of states, classically defined, remains wanting in the 10th century, and thus we are compelled to find alternative explanations for who was creating the demand for goods, who was organizing the supply and movement of goods, and what social dynamics were in place to support such activities.

The interpretive models that I introduced in Chapter One provide important analytical frameworks that enable a reconstruction. The evidence shows that the interactions took place across regions and cultures, including exchange *within* the southern Levant and *between* the southern Levant and Cyprus, the Aegean, Egypt, and Arabia. From this broad foundation, we can identify some trends. Geographic location played an important role in determining how long-distance interaction affected any particular site or population group. Gateways to the southern Levant experienced the most direct contact from external sources. Outside of that category, cities and towns that were on major roads, at significant crossroads and passes, or near resources were quite logically more likely to be involved in regional and interregional interactions. An additional trend emerges that is ripe for future study: sites that were strategically positioned *and* fared better during the years following the LBA collapse tend also to have strong evidence of engagement in long-distance exchange. It is not yet clear which of these factors influenced the others, but, in light of the LBA destructions at some locations that were also strategically located and heavily integrated in exchange networks, the contrast of destruction/abandonment versus continuity and/or growth invites attention.

Having established these trends, we can turn to some of the consequences of exchange activities. With the aid of the interpretive models of interaction spheres and peer polity interaction, I maintain that long-distance interactions led to a class of elite leaders who participated in a peer-based network. Exchange activities brought unusual goods into the southern Levant, and the people who were able to acquire them and participate in interactions became part of an elite group. We are able to identify this group in written and material sources, through their association with prestige goods. Membership in the elite group ensured that the leaders would engage in interactions, including trade and diplomacy, but also emulous behaviors and warfare. Due to the competitive nature of their peer relations and the added incentive of increased control of resources and exchange activities, certain portions of the elite community grew in influence. In some cases, that influence corresponded to a consolidation of territories.

Southern Levantine Interaction Spheres

The interaction sphere model, first proposed by Caldwell and adapted by Schortman and Urban, seeks to explain why some specific shared material culture turns up among distinct population groups.[5] It is worth considering whether the acquisition and creation of prestige goods indicates interaction spheres among elites in the southern Levant. Prestige items, which include imported ceramics, inscriptions, metals (including weaponry) and metallurgy, are found across numerous locations that do not generally share the same cultural assemblage: coastal, highland, east and west of the Jordan, north and south, and so on. This model allows scholars to recognize that more than one cultural identity may be evident in the material culture, and that each apparent identity group is not necessarily a fully distinct population at a site. In other words, we do not have to suppose that a foreign visitor or administrator must have been in residence to explain unusual, seemingly out-of-place finds. Rather, each local culture had its own distinct assemblage, but we also find evidence of an exclusive elite group that is conspicuous in our material evidence because of concentrations of nonlocal and rare goods.

I propose that the evidence accumulated in this study is the result of elite interaction spheres, and that the participants were engaged in a specialized network of long-distance exchange during the transition from the Iron I to IIA periods. They were the elite, potentially rulers, of key sites throughout the southern Levant. They were autonomous and may have governed over small territories, and these individuals or ruling families would have gained their leadership positions through their ties to the immediate community, probably through tribal affiliation and local lineages, through wealth, and through deeds. With greater local prominence, they established an association with other elites and became involved in the exchange network. These activities supported another identity exclusive to their interregional connections. The material expression of this identity would have included the acquisition and display of prestige goods, which are available to us in the material record. As these leaders became more integrated in the elite exchange network, their elevated position and cultural distinction in relation to their own territory would have increased even more.

Evidence from narrative sources and excavations supports the reconstruction of autonomous, local leaders who controlled small territories, ruling from sites in critical locations. The northern port cities provide illustrative examples. Their position as the gateway to exchange with Cyprus must have been a source of power and stability. The Report of Wenamun describes the rulers of Dor, Tyre, and Byblos as wealthy and holding more authority than the Egyptian envoy. From inscriptions, we know that Byblian leaders asserted their legitimacy based on lineage and exceptionalism (displaying Egyptian statues inscribed with their names and family lines). If we accept aspects of the biblical history but read against the DH's bias, Dor and Tyre's elites partnered with southern peers through diplomacy and exchange agreements.

The history in Samuel provides additional illustrations. Saul's power base was at the heart of the Benjaminite hill country, along the main road. His leadership qualifications included being from a family of substance. The son of a גבור חיל, *gibbor ḥayil*, a 'hero/man of substance,' he was striking and charismatic and proved himself as a successful warrior (1 Sam 9:1–2). He gained the loyalty of some neighboring populations, which resulted in extended influence and status. We have a similar picture of David, also described as a גבור חיל, a 'man of battle,' and a 'fine speaker' (1 Sam 16:12, 18). His strategic alliances and victories resulted in a southern territory, based in a number of key sites. The distinguishing quality in the cases of Saul and David is their membership in a particular elite class that included the label גבור חיל, an entourage, and physical symbols of social status, such as, personal, metal weaponry (e.g., 1 Sam 13:22) that set them apart from others.

Archaeological excavations do not tend to provide the colorful details of the narrative sources, but the material evidence contributes to a similar picture. For example, Tel Reḥov, Tel Masos, and Tell eṣ-Ṣafi were each commanding sites at strategic locations. Tel Reḥov and Tel Masos guarded interregional roads, and Tell eṣ-Ṣafi oversaw the boundary between the coastal plain and the Shephelah. All three of these sites have yielded extraordinary finds. Tel Masos had a unique blend of Egyptian and Canaanite-inspired architecture, imported and local pottery, and other prestige artifacts. Tel Reḥov's excavations have produced evidence of elite culture in feasting, a unique beekeeping industry, a variety of imports, and inscriptions. Tell eṣ-Ṣafi also shows evidence of an elite assemblage, and, judging from the site's size, there was considerable prosperity. In the case of biblical Gath (identified with Tell eṣ-Ṣafi), we can consider the traditions in Samuel, which remember the site as the residence of one of the south's most powerful leaders (Achish) and of a legendary warrior (Goliath).

This brief exploration emphasizes that there were many sites in the region that operated concurrently as small, independent polities, with local leadership. These polities did not necessarily have the characteristics of a state or an urban center, but certain inhabitants of smaller sites and territories were accumulating wealth and unusual goods, and becoming an elite class. These are our candidates for membership in the interaction spheres. According to the model, as these individuals accumulated nonlocal goods, they fueled a demand for interaction and linked themselves to extended regional and interregional networks. Participants developed or adopted an identity based on their elite exchange community. The members of this community would foster a distinct value system, legitimizing their participation and solidifying their roles in the network. This system would have its own code and symbolic language that became exclusively controlled by the elite participants.

We can identify such a code in the use of scribes and the display of inscriptions. Here, I continue the suggestions introduced in Chapter Five. Literacy and scribal activity were uncommon in this period. Where we see evidence of writing, we must acknowledge that it would have been commissioned by someone with power and status. The Egyptian and Byblian evidence provides a fuller picture; the elite use of scribes and inscriptions was closely linked to their interregional interaction. The evidence is literally written on exchanged material, the dedication statues to the Byblian goddess. Turning to the southern Levantine examples, it is useful to ask: who was the intended audience for small-scale inscriptions? In recognizing an interaction sphere, we have satisfying answers. The audience was both: 1) other participants in the elite exchange community who engaged in similar activity; and 2) locals from whom the elites were distinguishing themselves.[6] The inscriptions were symbolic of their membership. Indeed, most sites that have produced inscriptions from this period have also produced imported goods, other luxury items, or additional evidence of exchange.

The nature of the inscribed objects and their contexts strengthens the case that their message was intended for other elites, or to convey symbolically to non-elites, a message of difference. The dedication and possession formulae provide the clearest evidence. Several of the inscribed items were themselves uncommon or otherwise symbolic of status. The personalized game board from Beth-Shemesh implies wealth and leisure. The inscriptions from Tel ʿAmal and Kefar Veradim were found in burial deposits, a powerful, even if more private, statement of wealth – and presumably only a portion of the wealth that must have been displayed to the living world. The Kefar Veradim burial is an exceptional case, as I discuss earlier, as it, along with its parallels in Crete and Egypt, indicates a more integrated role in the most elite long-distance exchange relations of the eastern Mediterranean.

Metal objects were part of the symbolic code as well. Objects like the inscribed arrowheads, the weaponry attributed to Saul and Jonathan, or Solomon's display shields (or whatever objects inspired this imagery) must have made a significant statement in the hill country, which was a considerable distance (geographically and culturally) from the metal sources and production areas. As Sanders has argued, the commissioner of the bronze arrowheads put the 'means of communication' directly on the 'means of coercion,' combining symbols of exclusive, elite circles with physical power.[7]

In sum, even in this small selection of the available material from the studies presented in the previous chapters, we have ample and varied evidence in support of my proposed elite class during the Iron I–IIA transition years. Members are visible to us through their symbolic code of prestige goods like imported pottery, inscribed artifacts, metal objects, and the influence of foreign styles (e.g., artistic motifs, Egyptian architecture). The elites were linked to each other through interaction networks and through their own leadership culture, which perpetuated and increased the long-distance exchange in the region. Now that this group and its contacts are established, we can turn to the impact their activities had beyond their elite sphere. Their interactions led to increased competition and, ultimately, to significant changes in the social and geopolitical makeup of the southern Levant.

Peer Polity Interaction

At this point, it is useful to reorient to Renfrew's peer polity interaction model for understanding the Iron I–IIA transition. The aim of the model is to provide analytical options for examining interactions among 'autonomous socio-political units,' or polities, and evaluate the impact of such interactions on change over time. The model envisions a collection of peer units, where no one polity fully dominates a region. The interactions among the units are both cooperative and competitive, including warfare, commerce, emulation, and the exchange of ideas. Renfrew describes some typical characteristics of the peer polities:

> These usually include closely similar political institutions, a common system of weights and measures, the same system of writing (if any), essentially the same structure of religious beliefs (albeit with local variations, such as a special patron deity), the same spoken

language, and indeed generally what the archaeologist would call the same 'culture,' in whatever sense he might choose to use that term. The individual unit – the states – are often fiercely independent and competitive.[8]

He goes on to explain that the competitive nature often leads to political domination by one unit over the others, and, in Renfrew's explanation, consolidation through dominance often leads to a nation state or empire (a point we will return to below).[9]

Renfrew lays out a series of observations based on the application of the model.[10] He notes that where change is evident in one of the peer groups, comparable change will be evident in the others, at roughly the same time. This might take the form of changes in complexity, but also in social institutions, public or monumental architecture, communication and symbolic systems, special assemblages that are related to status, and customs that reinforce recent changes. These changes will also be evident in more than one peer group in the same period, and he stresses that these developments will not be explainable through diffusion; instead, the changes occur among the peer groups at the same time. Finally, there will be intensification in production and hierarchy within the peer groups.[11]

It is difficult not to envision the Levant's Iron Age kingdoms when reviewing the peer polity model. The Iron II polities shared the same measures and script, similar religious systems, but with distinct patron deities, and closely related languages and culture, sometimes indistinguishable in the material remains. These kingdoms were interconnected but independent and competed for resources and dominance in the region. It is important to acknowledge that there are reasons to be cautious about the notion of linear progression in the model. The biblical depiction of organizational change from kin-based tribes to a united Israelite state or even an empire under David and Solomon has proved difficult to escape in modern interpretations, influencing the focus on the 'origins' of Iron Age kingdoms and identities among scholars. Indeed, the idea of emerging polities is built into the framework of the present study, but this is precisely why a peer-oriented model is helpful. Contrary to the assertions of our historical and literary sources, the evidence speaks against a path to a singular, dominant state within the southern Levant. Instead, we see repeated attempts at control of resources and consolidation of territories, but without lasting success. The usefulness in the model is in its ability to accommodate diversity and concurrent power, and I would like to prioritize this element over the notion of inevitable large-scale states and empires. A focus on peer interactions shines a spotlight on how numerous and varied, but interconnected, the 'units' were at the beginning of the 1st millennium BCE, between the periods of external imperial control under the empires of the Egyptian New Kingdom and the Neo-Assyrians.

To illustrate, briefly, how the model helps us examine interconnectedness and diversity, we can look at changes that happened at roughly the same time across the region. A striking illustration of this phenomenon is the use of scribes. The earliest Iron Age inscriptions come from areas that were politically and culturally distinct, but which started using alphabetic inscriptions in close chronological proximity. In addition, intensification of production and consumption is apparent in various areas at the same time throughout the southern Levant: Tel Reḥov's apiary; smelting operations in Tell Hammeh, Khirbat en-Nahas, and Timna, as well as smaller metallurgical workshops; and production and distribution of BoR and its accompanying commodities. In accordance with the peer polity framework, we see indications of shared innovations and cultural intensification at roughly the same time, but not at the direction of a central authority (contra Solomon's history).

The importance of competition is critical in the peer polity model. Competitive interaction ranges from outright warfare to more subtle behaviors, such as emulation. Competition in the form of conspicuous display and consumption is evident in our survey of the narrative, historical, and archaeological material.[12] In possessing luxury goods, owners asserted their elevated status to those in their immediate community, but they were also responding to others in their elite interaction group, engaging in one-upmanship through the possession of rare goods. In the biblical material, we see conspicuous display remembered in stories of the ornate ark, Saul and Jonathan's weaponry, and in the case of Goliath's sword, which became a prize that changed hands from the Philistines to Saul, to the Nob priests, and to David, as the rival elites vied with each other.

The possession of imported pottery would have served the same competitive purpose, and the caches in burial deposits provide us with some hint to the excess that was possible for those of exceptional means. Competition is explicit in the epigraphic material, which ranges from possession formulae, perhaps the most succinct competitive statement, to the more elaborate display inscriptions of Byblos and Egypt. The competitive statement in these monumental examples occurs on multiple levels. More than the words inscribed on the objects, Byblian rulers claimed the prestigious Egyptian monuments by inscribing (or more accurately violating?) them, to claim them as their own.[13] Egypt's victory inscriptions are the clearest examples of all, combining the superiority of military victory with more implicit messages of dominance in wealth and artistic skill. Shoshenq's stele found at Megiddo (likewise his larger Karnak relief) shows us that the messages of competition and superiority were aimed at a mixed audience – as a monumental inscription, it was on display to the local population, to his peers in the Levant and southern Egypt, and to those who passed through Megiddo on the international roads.

Military action is the most direct, physical expression of competition between peer polities. It also tends to be well documented, as the victors took advantage of opportunities to commemorate their success, and destruction levels are recognizable in the archaeological record. Renfrew's peer polity model helps put military conflict into a new context, where it is but one of several types of interaction. In viewing it this way, and combining the results of the individual studies in biblical, epigraphic, and ceramic evidence, a new relationship between military competition, peer/elite interaction, and trade is apparent. As I argue in Chapter Two, the conflicts with the Philistines recorded in Samuel stemmed from competition to control critical routes and locations. Securing these passages would, in turn, create access to and provide control of international routes leading to resources such as the metal processing centers east of the Jordan. The distribution of imported ceramics and inscriptions corresponds to some of these routes, bolstering the case for their importance in long-distance interaction across a broad timeframe. Solomon's history calls attention to a number of these locations. Similarly, Shoshenq's reconstructed campaign trail targeted many of the same areas: Philistia and the Beersheba basin, the Ayalon Valley and Beth-Horon ascent to the hill country, the Jordan Valley (notably a metallurgy corridor), and the Jezreel Valley.

The recurrence of these key locations in a variety of evidence types suggests that they were among the most critical interaction areas during the 11th and 10th centuries, and, as such, they were the targets of the most intense competition for control. We can add to these locations three more territories that Shoshenq's campaign inscription did not name directly: the northern ports and the Shephelah feature prominently in narrative sources (biblical and the Report of Wenamun) and have a higher density of prestige objects and, in the case of the Shephelah, inscriptions. Lastly, the Arabah's intense metallurgical activity was quite clearly an essential component of the region's exchange networks and must have been of interest to the competing elites.

The peer polity model indicates that social changes occur as a result of the variety of interactions among the peer groups. We have just looked closely at those of a competitive nature. Interactions also took the form of shared innovation or 'symbolic entrainment,' which, for example, we can see in the highly specialized, shared metallurgical technology between Tell Hammeh and Beth-shemesh, between Timna and the Faynan, and, as mentioned above, in scribes' use of alphabetic scripts. An increased exchange of goods is another important category of interactions, which is particularly evident in Cypriot imports, and is remembered in the biblical depiction of Solomon's era (e.g., increases in the availability of silver). How do these various interactions add up to social change? To answer this question, we must focus especially on the elite identities and interaction spheres that I propose above.

The classic understanding of social change in the Iron I–IIA transition consists of a shift from tribal organization led by chiefs and elders to territorial states led by princes and kings, as famously described in the DH. In terms of the biblical narrative and its main figures, this change follows on the heels of the Judges era. Saul and David emerge as leaders, each deriving authority from their tribal lineage and identity, as well as from their dominance of neighboring groups. The narrative also clearly argues that they were the first kings of a new era. Solomon's reign is presented as the next stage, a tribal territory transformed into an efficient administration and a king ruling a fully realized monarchic institution. Implied in that depiction was a high level of social stratification and resource extraction, implicated in Deuteronomy 17:14–17 and 1 Samuel 8:4–18. The coupling of the elite spheres and peer polity approaches helps us create distance from this tidy reconstruction and recognize that early Iron Age leaders may have drawn on complex notions of identity that, on the one hand, bound them to their kin-based communities and, on the other, associated them with contemporaries beyond their local environments. Outside of the biblical narratives, we also observe the case of Shoshenq I, who maintained an emphasis on traditional Libyan authority rooted in his title as Chief of the Meshwesh, while also emulating traditional pharaonic ways. Rather than a linear transition from tribal leader to king, as argued by the biblical traditions, we can reconstruct a flexibility that accommodated various elite identities. When we look beyond the models of individual leadership to consider relations throughout the region, this flexibility may have facilitated interactions across differences in social organization, whether polities were urban, pastoral, emerging or established. The interconnected elite structures may have withstood various economic and political vacillations.

Concluding Thoughts

Long-distance and intraregional interactions had a dramatic impact on the southern Levant in the transition years between the Iron I and Iron II periods. My search to identify trade and exchange in the region during the years after the disruption of LBA systems, but before Neo-Assyrian involvement, results in a considerable amount of evidence of exchange and interaction in the region. Both direct and indirect evidence demonstrates that despite the typical characterization of the collapse and its aftermath, the southern

Levant as a whole was not devoid of interregional contacts and assertive, elite leadership during the 11th to early 9th centuries. Rather, long-distance relations were concentrated in certain locales and among certain communities. Sites that were in key locations and did not suffer significant hardships during the 12th and 11th centuries led in the early Iron Age exchange networks. Small-scale polities engaged in ambitious industries, trade, and competition for control of routes and resources. The leaders of these efforts are visible in biblical narratives, historical sources, and archaeological collections of unusual goods. This body of evidence reveals an elite community, and its members engaged in interactions, including trade and diplomacy but also competitive behaviors and warfare. Due to the nature of their peer interactions and the added incentive of increased control of exchange activities, various members of the elite community grew in influence and contended for dominance in their respective resource and geographic niches. The elites who were most successful in expanding their reach gave rise to the earliest 'kings' and 'princes' of the Iron Age.

Notes

1 Although not examined in detail in Chapter Two, Saul and David's histories each record activities in the Jordan Valley and to the east, independent from the accounts of interactions with Philistines.
2 Based on place names in the fifth line of the inscription (Rainey and Notley, *The Sacred Bridge*, 186).
3 Sherratt, "The Mediterranean Economy," 37–62; Sarah C. Murray, *The Collapse of the Mycenaean Economy* (Cambridge: Cambridge University Press, 2017).
4 Most sensationally depicted in historical sources related to the 'Sea Peoples' and the destruction of major centers of the Mycenaean world, Hattusa, Ugarit, etc., as well as the ancient traditional accounts of turmoil such as the Trojan War legends and the biblical Exodus, and the semi-historical Report of Wenamun.
5 Caldwell, "Interaction Spheres in Prehistory"; Schortman and Urban, "Modeling Interregional Interaction in Prehistory."
6 Contrary to arguments for common literacy or egalitarianism discussed in Chapter Five.
7 Sanders, *The Invention of Hebrew*, 107.
8 Renfrew, "Introduction," 2.
9 Ibid. Renfrew makes a point to explain that such transitions are not necessarily inevitable and that his model's applicability is not limited according to social complexity, but the theoretical framework is heavily influenced by traditional notions of complexity and his research in the Aegean.
10 Ibid., 7–8.
11 Ibid.
12 E.g., Solomon's numerous displays of wealth, especially in front of his foreign visitors; the inscribed game board from Beth-Shemesh; Byblian royal inscriptions on Egyptian statuary; feasting at Tel Reḥov; the rare early Greek imports potentially on display in feasting events.
13 It is probably not too much of a stretch to consider the relationship between the violent and violating nature of the inscription process and the symbolic damage done to the Egyptian competitor.

Bibliography

Adams, Robert McCormick. "Anthropological Perspectives on Ancient Trade." *Current Anthropology* 15, no. 3 (1974): 239–58. https://doi.org/10.1086/201466

Aharoni, Yohanan. *The Land of the Bible: A Historical Geography*. Philadelphia: Westminster Press, 1967.

———. "The Solomonic Districts." *Tel Aviv* 3 (1976): 5–15. https://doi.org/10.1179/033443576788529826

Aḥituv, Shmuel, and Amihai Mazar. "The Inscriptions from Tel Reḥov and Their Contribution to Study of Script and Writing During the Iron Age IIA." In *"See, I Will Bring a Scroll Recounting What Befell Me" (Ps 40:8): Epigraphy and Daily Life – From the Bible to the Talmud Dedicated to the Memory of Professor Hanan Eshel*, edited by Esther Eshel and Yigal Levin, 39–68. Journal of Ancient Judaism Supplements 12. Göttingen; Bristol: Vandenhoeck and Ruprecht, 2014. https://doi.org/10.13109/9783666550621.39

Ahlström, Gösta Werner. "Administration and Building Activities in the Davidic-Solomonic Kingdom." In *Royal Administration and National Religion in Ancient Palestine*, 27–43. Studies in the History of the Ancient Near East 1. Leiden: Brill, 1982.

———. "Pharaoh Shoshenq's Campaign to Palestine." In *History and Traditions of Early Israel: Studies Presented to Eduard Nielsen, May 8th 1993*, edited by André Lemaire, Benekikt Otzen, and Eduard Nielsen, 1–16. Supplements to Vetus Testamentum 50. Leiden: Brill, 1993.

Albright, William Foxwell. *Archaeology and the Religion of Israel*. 5th ed. Ayer Lectures. Baltimore: Johns Hopkins Press, 1968.

———. "New Light on the Early History of Phoenician Colonization." *Bulletin of the American Schools of Oriental Research* 83 (1941): 14–22. https://doi.org/10.2307/3218739

———. "The Administrative Divisions of Israel and Judah." *Journal of the Palestine Oriental Society* 5 (1925): 15–54.

———. "The Gezer Calendar." *Bulletin of the American Schools of Oriental Research* 92 (1943): 16–26.

———. "The Phoenician Inscriptions of the Tenth Century B. C. from Byblus." *Journal of the American Oriental Society* 67, no. 3 (1947): 153–60. https://doi.org/10.2307/596081

Alexandre, Yardenna. "A Canaanite-Early Phoenician Inscribed Bronze Bowl in an Iron Age IIA–B Burial Cave at Kefar Veradim, Northern Israel." *Maarav* 13, no. 1 (2006): 7–41, 129–32. https://doi.org/10.1086/MAR200613102

———. "The 'Hippo' Jar and Other Storage Jars at Hurvat Rosh Zayit." *Tel Aviv* 22, no. 1 (1995): 77–88.

Algaze, Guillermo. *The Uruk World System: The Dynamics of Expansion of Early Mesopotamian Civilization*. Chicago: University of Chicago Press, 1993.

Alt, Albrecht. "Israels Gaue Unter Salomo." In *Kleine Schriften Zur Geschichte Des Volkes Israel, Volume 2*, edited by Martin Noth, 76–89. Munich: Beck, 1953.

———. "The Formation of the Israelite State in Palestine." In *Essays on Old Testament History and Religion*, translated by R. A. Wilson. Garden City: Doubleday, 1967.

Arav, Rami. "Bethsaida Excavations Project Report on the 2019 Excavation Season G-33/2019." *Bethsaida Excavations Project*, 1 February 2021. https://bethsaidaarchaeologyorg.files.wordpress.com/2021/02/bethsaida-2019-field-report.pdf

Arnold, Patrick M. *Gibeah: The Search for a Biblical City*. Journal for the Study of the Old Testament Supplement Series 79. Sheffield: Journal for the Study of the Old Testament, 1990.

Arnold, Rosemary. "A Port of Trade: Whydah on the Guinea Coast." In *Trade and Market in the Early Empires: Economies in History and Theory*, edited by Karl Polanyi, Conrad M. Arensberg, and Harry W. Pearson, 154–76. Glencoe: Free Press, 1957.

Ash, Paul S. *David, Solomon and Egypt: A Reassessment.* Journal for the Study of the Old Testament Supplement Series 297. Sheffield: Sheffield Academic Press, 1999.

———. "Solomon's? District? List." *Journal for the Study of the Old Testament* 67 (1995): 67–86. https://doi.org/10.1177/030908929502006704

Aubet, María Eugenia. "Phoenicia during the Iron Age II Period." In *The Oxford Handbook of the Archaeology of the Levant: C. 8000-332 BCE*, edited by Margreet L. Steiner and Ann E. Killebrew, 706–16. Oxford: Oxford University Press, 2013.

Avishur, Yitzhak. *Phoenician Inscriptions and the Bible: Select Inscriptions and Studies in Stylistic and Literary Devices Common to the Phoenician Inscriptions and the Bible.* Tel Aviv: Archaeological Center Publication, 2000.

Bahat, Dan. *The Carta Jerusalem Atlas.* 3rd updated and expanded ed. Jerusalem: Carta, 2011.

Balensi, Jacqueline. "Revising Tell Abu Hawam." *Bulletin of the American Schools of Oriental Research* 257 (1985): 65–74. https://doi.org/10.2307/1356819

Barako, Tristan J. "The Philistine Settlement as Mercantile Phenomenon?" *American Journal of Archaeology* 104, no. 3 (2000): 513–30. https://doi.org/10.2307/507227

Barkay, Gabriel. "A Late Bronze Age Egyptian Temple in Jerusalem?" *Israel Exploration Journal* 46, no. 1 (1996): 23–43.

———. "What's an Egyptian Temple Doing in Jerusalem?" *Biblical Archaeology Review* 26, no. 3 (2000): 48–57, 67.

Barth, Fredrik. *Ethnic Groups and Boundaries: The Social Organization of Culture Difference.* Boston: Little, Brown, 1969.

Bauer, Alexander A. "Cities of the Sea: Maritime Trade and the Origin of Philistine Settlement in the Early Iron Age Southern Levant." *Oxford Journal of Archaeology* 17, no. 2 (1998): 149–68. https://doi.org/10.1111/1468-0092.00056

Bauer, Alexander A., and Anna S. Agbe-Davies. "Rethinking Trade as a Social Activity: An Introduction." In *Social Archaeologies of Trade and Exchange: Exploring Relationships among People, Places, and Things*, edited by Alexander A. Bauer and Anna S. Agbe-Davies, 13–28. Walnut Creek: Left Coast Press, 2010.

———. "Trade and Interaction in Archaeology." In *Social Archaeologies of Trade and Exchange: Exploring Relationships among People, Places, and Things*, edited by Alexander A. Bauer and Anna S. Agbe-Davies, 29–48. Walnut Creek: Left Coast Press, 2010.

Beherec, Marc, Mohammad Najjar, and Thomas E. Levy. "Wadi Fidan 40 and Mortuary Archaeology in the Edom Lowlands." In *New Insights into the Iron Age Archaeology of Edom, Southern Jordan: Surveys, Excavations and Research from the University of California, San Diego & Department of Antiquities of Jordan, Edom Lowlands Regional Archaeology Project (ELRAP)*, edited by Thomas E. Levy, Mohammad Najjar, Erez Ben-Yosef, and Neil G. Smith, 665–721. Monumenta Archaeologica 35. Los Angeles: The Cotsen Institute of Archaeology Press, 2014.

Bekkum, Koert van. "'The Situation Is More Complicated': Archaeology and Text in the Historical Reconstruction of the Iron Age IIA Southern Levant." In *Exploring the Narrative: Jerusalem and Jordan in the Bronze and Iron Ages: Papers in Honour of Margreet Steiner*, edited by Noor Mulder-Hymans, Jeannette Boertien, and Eveline van der Steen. Library of Hebrew Bible/Old Testament Studies 583. London; New York: Bloomsbury T&T Clark, 2014.

Ben-Arieh, Sarah. "Gedor, Tel." In *The New Encyclopedia of Archaeological Excavations in the Holy Land*, edited by Ephraim Stern, 468. Jerusalem: Israel Exploration Society & Carta, 1993.

Ben-Dor Evian, Shirly. "Egypt and Israel: The Never-Ending Story." *Near Eastern Archaeology* 80, no. 1 (2017): 30–39. https://doi.org/10.5615/neareastarch.80.1.0030

———. "Egypt and the Levant in the Iron Age I–IIA: The Ceramic Evidence." *Tel Aviv* 38 (2011): 94–119. https://doi.org/10.1179/033443511x12931017059422

Ben-Dor Evian, Shirly, Anat Cohen-Weinberger, Baruch Brandl, Yehudit Harlavan, and Yuval Gadot. "An Egyptian Private-Name Scarab Impression on a Clay Sealing from the City of David." *Journal of Ancient Egyptian Interconnections* 24 (2019): 1–15.

Ben-Dor Evian, Shirly, Omri Yagel, Yehudit Harlavan, Hadas Seri, Jessica Lewinsky, and Erez Ben-Yosef. "Pharaohs Copper: The Provenance of Copper in Bronze Artifacts from Post-Imperial Egypt at the End of the Second Millennium BCE." *Journal of Archaeological Science: Reports* 38 (2021). https://doi.org/10.1016/j.jasrep.2021.103025

Ben-Shlomo, David. "Pottery and Terracottas in Philistia during the Early Iron Age: Aspects of Change and Continuity." In *Change, Continuity, and Connectivity: North-Eastern Mediterranean at the Turn of the Bronze Age and in the Early Iron Age*, edited by Łukasz Niesiołowski-Spanò and Marek Węcowski, 141–57. Weisbaden: Harrassowitz Verlag, 2018.

Ben-Shlomo, David, Aren M. Maeir, and Hans Mommsen. "Neutron Activation and Petrographic Analysis of Selected Late Bronze and Iron Age Pottery from Tell Es-Safi/Gath, Israel." *Journal of Archaeological Science* 35 (2008): 956–64. https://doi.org/10.1016/j.jas.2007.06.020

Ben-Yosef, Erez. "And Yet, a Nomadic Error: A Reply to Israel Finkelstein." *Antiguo Oriente* 18 (2020): 33–60.

———. "Rethinking the Social Complexity of Early Iron Age Nomads." *Jerusalem Journal of Archaeology* 1 (2021): 155–79.

———. "Technology and Social Process Oscillations in Iron Age Copper Production and Power in Southern Jordan." Ph.D. dissertation. University of California, San Diego, 2010.

———. "The Architectural Bias in Current Biblical Archaeology." *Vetus Testamentum*, 69, no. 3 (2019): 361–87. https://doi.org/10.1163/15685330-12341370

———. "The Central Timna Valley Project: Research Design and Preliminary Results." In *Mining for Ancient Copper: Essays in Memory of Beno Rothenberg*, edited by Erez Ben-Yosef. Tel Aviv University Sonia and Marco Nadler Institute of Archaeology Monograph Series 37. Tel Aviv: Tel Aviv University, Sonia and Marco Nadler Institute of Archaeology, 2018.

Ben-Yosef, Erez, Brady Liss, Omri A. Yagel, Ofir Tirosh, Mohammad Najjar, and Thomas E. Levy. "Ancient Technology and Punctuated Change: Detecting the Emergence of the Edomite Kingdom in the Southern Levant." *PLOS ONE* 14, no. 9 (2019): e0221967. https://doi.org/10.1371/journal.pone.0221967

Ben-Yosef, Erez, Mohammad Najjar, and Thomas E. Levy. "Local Iron Age Trade Routes in Northern Edom: From the Faynan Copper Ore District to the Highlands." In *New Insights into the Iron Age Archaeology of Edom, Southern Jordan: Surveys, Excavations and Research from the University of California, San Diego & Department of Antiquities of Jordan, Edom Lowlands Regional Archaeology Project (ELRAP)*, edited by Thomas E. Levy, Mohammad Najjar, Erez Ben-Yosef, and Neil G. Smith, 493–575. Monumenta Archaeologica 35. Los Angeles: The Cotsen Institute of Archaeology Press, 2014.

Ben-Yosef, Erez, and Omer Sergi. "The Destruction of Gath by Hazael and the Arabah Copper Industry: A Reassessment." In *Tell it in Gath: Studies in the History and Archaeology of Israel, Essays in Honor of Aren M. Maeir on the Occasion of his Sixtieth Birthday*, edited by I. Shai, J. R. Chadwick, L. Hitchcock, A. Dagan, C. McKinny, and J. Uziel, 461–480. Münster: Zaphon, 2018.

Ben-Yosef, Erez, Ron Shaar, Lisa Tauxe, and Hagai Ron. "A New Chronological Framework for Iron Age Copper Production at Timna (Israel)." *Bulletin of the American Schools of Oriental Research* 367 (2012): 31–71. https://doi.org/10.5615/bullamerschoorie.367.0031

Benet, Francisco. "Separation of Trade and Market: Great Market of Whydah." In *Trade and Market in the Early Empires: Economies in History and Theory*, edited by Karl Polanyi, Conrad M. Arensberg, and Harry W. Pearson, 177–87. Glencoe: Free Press, 1957.

Bennett, Eleanor. "The 'Queens of the Arabs' during the Neo-Assyrian Period." Doctoral Dissertation, University of Helsinki, Helsinki, 2021.

Bikai, P. M. *The Pottery of Tyre*. Warminster: Aris & Phillips, 1978.

Bimson, John J., and Juan Manuel Tebes. "Timna Revisited: Egyptian Chronology and the Copper Mines of the Southern Arabah." *Antiguo Oriente* 7 (2009): 75–118.

Blakelock, Eleanor, Marcos Martinón-Torres, Harald Alexander Veldhuijzen, and Tim Young. "Slag Inclusions in Iron Objects and the Quest for Provenance: An Experiment and a Case Study." *Journal of Archaeological Science* 36 (2009): 1745–57. https://doi.org/10.1016/j.jas.2009.03.032

Blakely, Jeffrey A. "Reconciling Two Maps: Archaeological Evidence for the Kingdoms of David and Solomon." *Bulletin of the American Schools of Oriental Research* 327 (2002): 49–54. https://doi.org/10.2307/1357857

———. "The Location of Medieval/Pre-Modern and Biblical Ziklag." *Palestine Exploration Quarterly* 139, no. 1 (2007): 21–26. https://doi.org/10.1179/003103207x162988

Blenkinsopp, Joseph. "Kiriath-Jearim and the Ark." *Journal of Biblical Literature* 88, no. 2 (1969): 143–56. https://doi.org/10.2307/3262874

Bloch-Smith, Elizabeth. "Israelite Ethnicity in Iron I: Archaeology Preserves What Is Remembered and What Is Forgotten in Israel's History." *Journal of Biblical Literature* 122, no. 3 (2003): 401–25. https://doi.org/10.2307/3268384

———. *Judahite Burial Practices and Beliefs about the Dead*. Journal for the Study of the Old Testament Supplement Series 123. Sheffield: JSOT Press for the American Schools of Oriental Research, 1992.

Bloch-Smith, Elizabeth, and Beth Alpert Nakhai. "A Landscape Comes to Life: The Iron Age I." *Near Eastern Archaeology* 62, no. 2 (1999): 62–92, 101–27. https://doi.org/10.2307/3210703

Bolen, Todd. "Identifying King David's Palace: Mazar's Flawed Reading of the Biblical Text." *The Bible and Interpretation*, September 2010. http://www.bibleinterp.com/opeds/ident357928.shtml

Braudel, Fernand. *The Mediterranean and the Mediterranean World in the Age of Philip II*. Translated by Sian Reynolds. 2 volumes. Berkeley: University of California Press, 1995.

Breasted, James H. *Ancient Records of Egypt: Historical Documents from the Earliest Times to the Persian Conquest, Vol. IV: The Twentieth to the Twenty-Sixth Dynasties*. Chicago: University of Chicago Press, 1906.

Brettler, Marc. "The Structure of 1 Kings 1–11." *Journal for the Study of the Old Testament* 16, no. 49 (1991): 87–97. https://doi.org/10.1177/030908929101604905

Bright, John. *A History of Israel*. 4th ed. Philadelphia: Westminster Press, 2000.

Brodie, N. J., and L. Steel. "Cypriot Black-on-Red Ware: Towards a Characterization." *Archaeometry* 38, no. 2 (1996): 263–78. https://doi.org/10.1111/j.1475-4754.1996.tb00775.x

Broekman, Gerard P. F. "The Leading Theban Priests of Amun and Their Families under Libyan Rule." *The Journal of Egyptian Archaeology* 96 (2010): 125–48. https://doi.org/10.1177/030751331009600107

Brueggemann, Walter. *Solomon: Israel's Ironic Icon of Human Achievement*. Studies on Personalities of the Old Testament. Columbia: University of South Carolina, 2005.

Bryce, Trevor. *Letters of the Great Kings of the Ancient Near East: The Royal Correspondence of the Late Bronze Age*. London: Routledge, 2004.

———. "The Land of Hiyawa (Que) Revisited." *Anatolian Studies* 66 (2016): 67–79. https://doi.org/10.1017/S0066154616000053

Bunimovitz, Shlomo, and Zvi Lederman. "Beth-Shemesh: Culture Conflict on Judah's Frontier." *Biblical Archaeology Review* 23, no. 1 (1997): 42–49, 75–77.

———. "The Early Israelite Monarchy in the Sorek Valley: Tel Beth-Shemesh and Tel Batash (Timnah) in the 10th and 9th Centuries BCE." In *"I Will Speak the Riddles of Ancient Times": Archaeological and Historical Studies in Honor of Amihai Mazar on the Occasion of His Sixtieth Birthday*, edited by Aren M. Maeir, Pierre De Miroschedji, and Amihai Mazar, 407–28. Winona Lake: Eisenbrauns, 2006.

Bunimovitz, Shlomo, Zvi Lederman, and Dale W. Manor. "The Archaeology of Border Communities: Renewed Excavations at Tel Beth-Shemesh, Part 1: The Iron Age." *Near Eastern Archaeology* 72, no. 3 (2009): 114–42. https://doi.org/10.1086/NEA20697231

Byrne, Ryan. "The Refuge of Scribalism in Iron I Palestine." *Bulletin of the American Schools of Oriental Research* 345 (2007): 1–31. https://doi.org/10.1086/BASOR25066987

Cahill, Jane M. "Jerusalem at the Time of the United Monarchy: The Archaeological Evidence." In *Jerusalem in Bible and Archaeology: The First Temple Period*, edited by Andrew G. Vaughn and Ann E. Killebrew, 13–80. Society of Biblical Literature Symposium Series 18. Atlanta: Society of Biblical Literature, 2003.

Caldwell, Joseph R. "Interaction Spheres in Prehistory." In *Hopewellian Studies*, edited by Joseph R Caldwell and Robert L. Hall, 134–43. Illinois State Museum Scientific Papers 12. Springfield: Illinois State Museum, 1964.

Campbell, Antony F. *The Ark Narrative (1 Sam 4-6, 2 Sam 6): A Form-Critical and Traditio-Historical Study*. Society of Biblical Literature Dissertation Series 16. Missoula: Scholars Press, 1975.

———. "Yahweh and the Ark: A Case Study in Narrative." *Journal of Biblical Literature* 98, no. 1 (1979): 31–43. https://doi.org/10.2307/3265910

Carter, Jane B. "Egyptian Bronze Jugs from Crete and Lefkandi." *Journal of Hellenic Studies* 118 (1998): 172–77. https://doi.org/10.2307/632238

Chavalas, Mark W. "Inland Syria and the East-of-Jordan Region in the First Millennium BCE before the Assyrian Intrusions." In *The Age of Solomon: Scholarship at the Turn of the Millennium*, edited by Lowell K. Handy, 168–71. Studies in the History and Culture of the Ancient Near East 11. Leiden; New York: Brill, 1997.

Clancy, Frank. "Shishak/Shoshenq's Travels." *Journal for the Study of the Old Testament* 86 (1999): 3–23. https://doi.org/10.1177/030908929902408601

Cohen, Rudolf, and Yigal Yisrael. "The Excavations of 'Ein Hazeva, Israelite and Roman Tamar." *Qadmoniot* 112 (1996): 78–92.

Cohen, Shaye. "Solomon and the Daughter of the Pharaoh: Intermarriage, Conversion, and the Impurity of Women." *Journal for Ancient Near Eastern Studies* 16–17 (1984): 23–37.

Coldstream, John Nicolas. "The First Exchanges Between Euboeans and Phoenicians: Who Took the Initiative?" In *Mediterranean Peoples in Transition: Thirteenth to Early Tenth Centuries BCE*, edited by Seymour Gitin, Amihai Mazar, and Ephraim Stern, 353–60. Jerusalem: Israel Exploration Society, 1998.

Coldstream, John Nicolas, and Amihai Mazar. "Greek Pottery from Tel Rehov and Iron Age Chronology." *Israel Exploration Journal* 53 (2003): 29–48.

Cook, Edward M. "Olive Pits and Alef-Bets: Notes on the Qeiyafa Ostracon." *Ralph the Sacred River*, March 14, 2010. http://ralphriver.blogspot.com/2010/03/olive-pits-and-alef-bets-notes-on.html

Cross, Frank Moore. *Canaanite Myth and Hebrew Epic: Essays in the History of the Religion of Israel*. Cambridge: Harvard University Press, 1973.

———. "The Origin and Early Evolution of the Alphabet." *Eretz-Israel* 8 (1967): 8*–24*.

Cross, Frank Moore, and G. Ernest Wright. "The Boundary and Province Lists of the Kingdom of Judah." *Journal of Biblical Literature* 75 (1956): 202–26. https://doi.org/10.2307/3261922

Curtis, John E., Henrietta McCall, Dominique Collon, and Lamia al-Gailani Werr, eds. *New Light on Nimrud: Proceedings of the Nimrud Conference 11th-13th March 2002*. London: British Institute for the Study of Iraq, 2008.

Dalley, Stephanie. "Foreign Chariotry and Cavalry in the Armies of Tiglath-Pileser III and Sargon II." *Iraq* 47 (1985): 31–48. https://doi.org/10.2307/4200230

Davies, Philip R. *In Search of "Ancient Israel."* Journal for the Study of the Old Testament Supplement Series 148. Sheffield: JSOT Press, 1992.

Day, John. "Where Was Tarshish?" In *Let Us Go Up to Zion: Essays in Honour of H. G. M. Williamson on the Occasion of His Sixty-Fifth Birthday*, edited by Iain Provan and Mark Boda, 359–70. Leiden: Brill, 2012.

Demand, Nancy H. *The Mediterranean Context of Early Greek History*. Oxford: Wiley-Blackwell, 2011.

Demsky, Aaron. "An Iron Age IIA Alphabetic Writing Exercise from Khirbet Qeiyafa." *IEJ* 62, no. 2 (2012): 186–99.

Demsky, Aaron. "The Jerusalem Ceramic Inscription." Sidebar in "Artifact Found Near Temple Mount Bearing Canaanite Inscription from the Time before King David." *Foundation Stone*, July 7, 2013.

De Groot, Alon. "Discussion and Conclusions." in *Excavations at the City of David 1978-1985 Directed by Yigal Shiloh, Volume VIIA: Area E: Stratigraphy and Architecture: Text*, edited by Alon De Groot and Hannah Bernick-Greenberg, 141–86. Qedem 53. Jerusalem: Institute of Archaeology, Hebrew University of Jerusalem, 2012.

De Pury, Albert, Thomas Römer, and Jean-Daniel Macchi, eds. *Israel Constructs Its History: Deuteronomistic Historiography in Recent Research*. Journal for the Study of the Old Testament Supplement Series 306. Sheffield: Sheffield Academic Press, 2000.

Dobbs-Allsopp, F. W., Jimmy Jack McBee Roberts, Choon-Leong Seow, and R. E. Whitaker. *Hebrew Inscriptions: Texts from the Biblical Period of the Monarchy with Concordance*. New Haven: Yale University Press, 2005.

Dolansky, Shawna, and Sarah Shectman, eds. "What Is Gendered Historiography and How Do You Do It?" *The Journal of Hebrew Scriptures* 19 (2019): 3–18. https://doi.org/10.5508/jhs29396

Donnelly-Lewis, Brian. "The Khirbet Qeiyafa Ostracon: A New Collation Based on the Multispectral Images, with Translation and Commentary." *Bulletin of the American Society of Overseas Research* 388 (2022): 181–210. https://doi.org/10.1086/720558

Dorsey, David A. *The Roads and Highways of Ancient Israel*. American Schools of Oriental Research Library of Biblical and Near Eastern Archaeology. Baltimore: Johns Hopkins University Press, 1991.

Edelman, Diana V. *King Saul in the Historiography of Judah*. Journal for the Study of the Old Testament Supplement Series 121. Sheffield: Sheffield Academic Press, 1991.

———. "Saul Ben Kish in History and Tradition." In *The Origins of Ancient Israelite States*, edited by Volkmar Fritz and Philip R. Davies, 142–59. Journal for the Study of the Old Testament Supplement Series 228. Sheffield: Sheffield Academic, 1996.

———. "Solomon's Adversaries Hadad, Rezon and Jeroboam: A Trio of 'Bad Guy' Characters Illustrating the Theology of Immediate Retribution." In *The Pitcher Is Broken: Memorial Essays for Gösta W. Ahlström*, edited by Steven W. Holloway and Lowell K. Handy, 166–91. Journal for the Study of the Old Testament Supplement Series 190. Sheffield: Sheffield Academic Press, 1995.

———. "Taphath." In *Women in Scripture: A Dictionary of Named and Unnamed Women in the Hebrew Bible, the Apocryphal/Deuterocanonical Books, and the New Testaement*, edited by Carol Meyers, 165. Grand Rapids: Eerdmans, 2001.

———. "Tel Masos, Geshur, and David." *Journal of Near Eastern Studies* 47, no. 4 (1988): 253–58. https://doi.org/10.1086/373319

Egan, Virginia, Patricia M. Bikai, and Kurt Zamora. "Archaeology in Jordan." *American Journal of Archaeology* 104, no. 3 (2000): 561–88. https://doi.org/10.2307/507229

Elat, Moshe. *Economic Relations in the Lands of the Bible (ca. 1000–539 B.C.E.)*. Jerusalem: Bialik Institute, 1977.

———. "The Monarchy and the Development of Trade in Ancient Israel." In *State and Temple Economy in the Ancient Near East: Proceedings of the International Conference*, edited by Edward Lipinski, 527–46. Leuven: Departement Oriëntalistiek, 1979.

———. "Trade in the Period of the Monarchy." In *The World History of the Jewish People, Volume IV, part II: The Age of Monarchies: Culture and Society*, edited by A. Malamat, 174–86. Jerusalem: Massada Press, 1979.

Elayi, Josette. "Four New Inscribed Phoenician Arrowheads." *Studi Epigrafici e Linguistici* 22 (2005): 35–45.

Eliyahu-Behar, Adi, Naama Yahalom-Mack, Sana Shilstein, Alexander Zukerman, Cynthia Shafer-Elliott, Aren M. Maeir, Elisabetta Boaretto, Israel Finkelstein, and Steve Weiner. "Iron and Bronze Production in Iron Age IIA Philistia: New Evidence from Tell Es-Safi/Gath, Israel." *Journal of Archaeological Science* 39 (2012): 255–67. https://doi.org/10.1016/j.jas.2011.09.002

Emberling, Geoff. "Ethnicity in Complex Societies: Archaeological Perspectives." *Journal of Archaeological Research* 5, no. 4 (1997): 295–344. https://doi.org/10.1007/BF02229256

Eshel, Esther, Tania Notarius, Amit Dagan, Maria Eniukhina, Vanessa Workman, and Aren M. Maeir. "Two Iron Age Alphabetic Inscriptions from Tell Eṣ-Ṣâfi/Gath, Israel." *Bulletin of the American Society of Overseas Research* 388 (2022): 31–49. https://doi.org/10.1086/721690

Eshel, Tzilla, Yigal Erel, Naama Yahalom-Mack, Ofir Tirosh, and Ayelet Gilboa. "Lead Isotopes in Silver Reveal Earliest Phoenician Quest for Metals in the West Mediterranean." In *Proceedings of the National Academy of Sciences* (February 2019).

Eshel, Tzilla, Ayelet Gilboa, Naama Yahalom-Mack, Ofir Tirosh, and Yigal Erel. "Debasement of Silver throughout the Late Bronze-Iron Age Transition in the Southern Levant: Analytical and Cultural Implications." *Journal of Archaeological Science* 125 (2021): 1–24. https://doi.org/10.1016/j.jas.2020.105268

Fantalkin, Alexander. "Low Chronology and Greek Protogeometric and Geometric Pottery in the Southern Levant." *Levant* 33, no. 1 (2001): 117–25. https://doi.org/10.1179/lev.2001.33.1.117

Fantalkin, Alexander, and Israel Finkelstein. "The Sheshonq I Campaign and the 8th-Century BCE Earthquake – More on the Archaeology and History of the South in the Iron I–IIA." *Tel Aviv* 33 (2006): 18–42. https://doi.org/10.1179/tav.2006.2006.1.18

Fantalkin, Alexander, Israel Finkelstein, and Eli Piasetzky. "Late Helladic to Middle Geometric Aegean and Contemporary Cypriot Chronologies: A Radiocarbon View from the Levant." *Bulletin of the American Schools of Oriental Research* 373 (2015): 25–48. https://doi.org/10.5615/bullamerschoorie.373.0025

Fantalkin, Alexander, Assaf Kleiman, Hans Mommsen, and Israel Finkelstein. "Aegean Pottery in Iron IIA Megiddo: Typological, Archaeometric and Chronological Aspects." *Mediterranean Archaeology and Archaeometry* 20, no. 3 (2020): 135–47.

Faust, Avraham. "Between the Highland Polity and Philistia: The United Monarchy and the Resettlement of the Shephelah in the Iron Age IIA, with a Special Focus on Tel 'Eton and Khirbet Qeiyafa." *Bulletin of the American Schools of Oriental Research* 383 (2020): 115–36.

———. "Did Eilat Mazar Find David's Palace?" *Biblical Archaeology Review* 38, no. 5 (2012): 47–52, 70.

———. *Israel's Ethnogenesis: Settlement, Interaction, Expansion and Resistance*. London: Equinox Publishing, 2008.

———. Review of L. Singer-Avitz, "Excavations at Kadesh Barnea (Tell El-Qudeirat) 1976–1982." *American Journal of Archaeology* 113, no. 2 (2009).

———. "Settlement, Economy, and Demography under Assyrian Rule in the West: The Territories of the Former Kingdom of Israel as a Test Case." *Journal of the American Oriental Society* 135, no. 4 (2015): 765–89.

———. "The 'United Monarchy' on the Ground: The Disruptive Character of the Iron Age I–II Transition and the Nature of Political Transformations." *Jerusalem Journal of Archaeology* 1 (2021): 15–67.

Faust, Avraham, and Justin Lev-Tov. "The Constitution of Philistine Identity: Ethnic Dynamics in Twelfth to Tenth Century Philistia." *Oxford Journal of Archaeology* 30, no. 1 (2011): 13–31. https://doi.org/10.1111/j.1468-0092.2010.00357.x

Faust, Avraham, and Ehud Weiss. "Judah, Philistia, and the Mediterranean World: Reconstructing the Economic System of the Seventh Century B.C.E." *Bulletin of the American Schools of Oriental Research* 338 (2005): 71–92. https://doi.org/10.1086/BASOR25066890

Feldman, Marian H. *Communities of Style: Portable Luxury Arts, Identity, and Collective Memory in the Iron Age Levant*. Chicago; London: University of Chicago Press, 2014.

Fensham, F. C. "The Treaty between Solomon and Hiram and the Alalakh Tablets." *Journal of Biblical Literature* 79 (1960): 59–60. https://doi.org/10.2307/3264501

———. "The Treaty between the Israelites and the Tyrians." In *International Congress for the Study of the Old Testament, Rome*, edited by John Adney Emerton, 71–87. Supplements to Vetus Testamentum 17. Leiden: Brill, 1969.

Finkelberg, Margalit. *Greeks and Pre-Greeks: Aegean Prehistory and Greek Heroic Tradition*. Cambridge: Cambridge University Press, 2005.

Finkelstein, Israel. "A Great United Monarchy? Archaeological and Historical Perspectives." In *One God – One Cult – One Nation: Archaeological and Biblical Perspectives*, edited by Reinhard G. Kratz and Hermann Spieckermann, 3–28. Beihefte zur Zeitschrift für die alttestamentliche Wissenschaft 405. Berlin; New York: Walter de Gruyter, 2010.

———. "A Low Chronology Update: Archaeology, History and Bible." In *The Bible and Radiocarbon Dating: Archaeology, Text and Science*, edited by Thomas E. Levy and Thomas Higham, 31–42. London; Oakville: Equinox Publishing, 2005.

———. "First Israel, Core Israel, United (Northern) Israel." *Near Eastern Archaeology* 82, no. 1 (2019): 8–15. https://doi.org/10.1086/703321

———. "Khirbet En-Nahas, Edom and Biblical History." *Tel Aviv* 32 (2005): 119–25. https://doi.org/10.1179/tav.2005.2005.1.119

———. *Living on the Fringe: The Archaeology and History of the Negev, Sinai and Neighbouring Regions in the Bronze and Iron Ages*. Monographs in Mediterranean Archaeology 6. Sheffield: Sheffield Academic Press, 1995.

———. "Northern Royal Traditions in the Bible and the Ideology of a 'United Monarchy' Ruled from Samaria." In *Stones, Tablets, and Scrolls: Periods of the Formation of the Bible*, edited by Peter Dubovský and Federico Giuntoli, 113–26. Tübingen: Mohr Siebeck, 2020.

———. "Saul and Highlands of Benjamin Update: The Role of Jerusalem." In *Saul, Benjamin and the Emergence of Monarchy in Israel: Biblical and Archaeological Perspectives*, edited by Joachim J. Krause, Omer Sergi, and Kristin Weingart, 33–56. Atlanta: Society of Biblical Literature, 2020.

———. "Tell El-Ful Revisited: The Assyrian and Hellenistic Periods (with a New Identification)." *Palestine Exploration Quarterly* 143, no. 2 (2011): 106–18.

———. "The Arabah Copper Polity and the Rise of Iron Age Edom: A Bias in Biblical Archaeology?" *Antiguo Oriente* 18 (2020): 11–32.

———. "The Archaeology of the United Monarchy: An Alternative View." *Levant* 28, no. 1 (1996): 177–87. https://doi.org/10.1179/lev.1996.28.1.177

———. "The Campaign of Shoshenq I to Palestine: A Guide to the 10th Century BCE Polity." *Zeitschrift des deutschen Palästina-Vereins* 118 (2002): 109–35.

———. *The Forgotten Kingdom: The Archaeology and History of Northern Israel*. Ancient Near Eastern Monographs 5. Atlanta: Society of Biblical Literature, 2013.

———. "The Impact of the Sheshonq I Campaign on the Territorial History of the Levant: An Update." Forthcoming. Accessed on academia.edu, February 25, 2023. https://www.academia.edu/69280467/I_Finkelstein_The_Impact_of_the_Sheshonq_I_Campaign_on_the_Territorial_History_of_the_Levant_An_Update_forthcoming

———. "The Last Labayu: King Saul and the Expansion of the First North Israelite Territorial Entity." In *Essays on Ancient Israel and Its Near Eastern Context: A Tribute to Nadav Na'aman*, edited by Yairah Amit, 171–87. Winona Lake: Eisenbrauns, 2006.

———. "The Philistines in the Bible: A Late-Monarchic Perspective." *Journal for the Study of the Old Testament* 27, no. 2 (2002): 131–67. https://doi.org/10.1177/030908920202700201

———. "The Rise of Jerusalem and Judah: The Missing Link." *Levant* 33 (2001): 105–15.

Finkelstein, Israel, Shlomo Bunimovitz, Zvi Lederman, Salo Hellwing, and Moshe Sadeh. "Excavations at Shiloh 1981–1984: Preliminary Report." *Tel Aviv* 1985, no. 2 (1985): 123–80. https://doi.org/10.1179/tav.1985.1985.2.123

Finkelstein, Israel, Alexander Fantalkin, and Eliazer Piasetzky. "Three Snapshots of the Iron IIA: The Northern Valleys, the Southern Steppe, and Jerusalem." In *Israel in Transition: From Late Bronze II to Iron IIA (c. 1250–850 B.C.E.): Volume 1: The Archaeology*, edited by Lester L. Grabbe, 32–44. Library of Hebrew Bible/Old Testament Studies 491. New York: T&T Clark, 2008.

Finkelstein, Israel, Ido Koch, and Oded Lipschits. "The Mound on the Mount: A Possible Solution to the 'Problem with Jerusalem.'" *Journal of Hebrew Scriptures* 11 (2011). https://doi.org/10.5508/jhs.2011.v11.a12

Finkelstein, Israel, and Eli Piasetzky. "The Iron Age Chronology Debate: Is the Gap Narrowing?" *Near Eastern Archaeology* 74, no. 1 (2011): 50–54. https://doi.org/10.5615/neareastarch.74.1.0050

Finkelstein, Israel, and Benjamin Sass. "The Exceptional Concentration of Inscriptions at Iron IIA Gath and Rehob and the Nature of the Alphabet in the Ninth Century BCE." In *Oral et écrit dans l'Antiquité orientale: les processus de rédaction et d'édition*, edited by T. Römer, H. Gonzalez, L. Marti and J. Rückl, 127–73. Leuven: Peeters, 2021.

———. "The West Semitic Alphabetic Inscriptions, Late Bronze II to Iron IIA: Archeological Context, Distribution and Chronology." *Hebrew Bible and Ancient Israel* 2 (2013): 149–220.

Finkelstein, Israel, and Neil Asher Silberman. *David and Solomon: In Search of the Bible's Sacred Kings and the Roots of Western Tradition.* New York: Free Press, 2006.

———. *The Bible Unearthed: Archaeology's New Vision of Ancient Israel and the Origin of Its Sacred Texts.* New York: Free Press, 2001.

Finkelstein, Israel, Lily Singer-Avitz, Ze'ev Herzog, and David Ussishkin. "Has King David's Palace in Jerusalem Been Found?" *Tel Aviv* 34, no. 2 (2007): 142-64. https://doi.org/10.1179/tav.2007.2007.2.142

Fischer, Peter M., Teresa Bürge, and Eva Maria Wild, *Tell Abu Al-Kharaz in the Jordan Valley: Volume III: The Iron Age.* Vienna: Austrian Academy of Sciences Press, 2013.

Flannery, Kent V. "The Olmec and the Valley of Oaxaca: A Model for Inter-Regional Interaction in Formative Times." In *Dumbarton Oaks Conference on the Olmec*, edited by E. Benson, 79-110. Washington, D.C.: Dumbarton Oaks, 1968.

Fox, Nili Sacher. *In the Service of the King: Officialdom in Ancient Israel and Judah.* Monographs of the Hebrew Union College 23. Cincinnati: Hebrew Union College Press, 2000.

Henk J. Franken, "A History of Excavation in Jerusalem," in *Jerusalem before Islam*, ed. Zeidan Abdel-Kafi Kafafi and Robert Schick, 45-53. BAR International Series 1699; Oxford: Archaeopress, 2007.

Franken, Henk J., and Margreet L. Steiner. "Urusalim and Jebus." *Zeitschrift für die alttestamentliche Wissenschaft* 104 (1992): 110-111.

Frese, Daniel A., and David Noel Freedman. "Samaria I as a Chronological Anchor of Finkelstein's Low Chronology: An Appraisal." *Eretz-Israel* 25. Ephraim Stern Volume, edited by Joseph Aviram, 36*-44*. Jerusalem: Israel Exploration Society, 2009.

Frese, Daniel A., and Thomas E. Levy. "Four Pillars of the Iron Age Low Chronology." In *Historical Biblical Archaeology and the Future: The New Pragmatism*, edited by Thomas E. Levy, 187-202. London; Oakville: Equinox Publishing, 2010.

Friedman, Richard Elliott. "Solomon and the Great Histories." In *Jerusalem in Bible and Archaeology: The First Temple Period*, edited by Andrew G. Vaughn and Ann E. Killebrew, 171-80. Atlanta: Society of Biblical Literature, 2003.

———. *The Exile and Biblical Narrative: The Formation of the Deuteronomistic and Priestly Works.* Harvard Semitic Monographs 22. Chico: Scholars Press, 1981.

———. *The Hidden Book in the Bible: The Discovery of the First Prose Masterpiece.* San Francisco: Harper Collins, 1998.

Frisch, Amos. "Structure and Its Significance: The Narrative of Solomon's Reign (1 Kings 1-12.24)." *Journal for the Study of the Old Testament* 16, no. 51 (1991): 3-14. https://doi.org/10.1177/030908929101605101

———. "The Narrative of Solomon's Reign: A Rejoinder." *Journal for the Study of the Old Testament* 16, no. 51 (1991): 22-24. https://doi.org/10.1177/030908929101605103

Fritz, Volkmar. *1 and 2 Kings.* Continental Commentaries. Minneapolis: Fortress Press, 2003.

Fritz, Volkmar, and Aharon Kempinski. *Ergebnisse Der Ausgrabungen Auf Der Hirbet El-Msas (Tel Masos) 1972-1975.* Abhandlungen des Deutschen Palästinavereins Volumes I-III. Wiesbaden: Harrassowitz, 1983.

Gadot, Yuval, and Joe Uziel. "The Monumentality of Iron Age Jerusalem Prior to the 8th Century BCE." *Tel Aviv* 44, no. 2 (2017): 123-40.

Gal, Zvi, and Yardenna Alexandre. *Horbat Rosh Zayit, an Iron Age Storage Fort and Village.* Jerusalem: Israel Antiquities Authority, 2000.

Garfinkel, Yosef and Saar Ganor, eds. *Khirbet Qeiyafa Volume 1, Excavation Report 2007-2008.* Jerusalem: Israel Exploration Society; Institute of Archaeology, Hebrew University of Jerusalem, 2009.

Garfinkel, Yosef, Saar Ganor, and Michael G. Hasel. *In the Footsteps of King David: Revelations from an Ancient Biblical City.* London: Thames & Hudson, 2018.

———. "The Iron Age City of Khirbet Qeiyafa after Four Seasons of Excavations." In *The Ancient Near East in the 12th-10th Centuries BCE: Culture and History. Proceedings of the International Conference Held at the University of Haifa, 2-5 May, 2010*, edited by Gershon Galil, Ayelet Gilboa, Aren M. Maeir, and Dan'el Kahn, 149-74. Alter Orient und Altes Testament 392. Münster: Ugarit-Verlag, 2012.

Garfinkel, Yosef, Mitka R. Golub, Haggai Misgav, and Saar Ganor. "The ʾIšbaʿal Inscription from Khirbet Qeiyafa." *Bulletin of the American Schools of Oriental Research* 373 (2015): 217–33.

Geoghegan, Jeffrey C. "'Until This Day' and the Preexilic Redaction of the Deuteronomistic History." *Journal of Biblical Literature* 122, no. 2 (2003): 201–27. https://doi.org/10.2307/3268443

Geva, Hillel. "Archaeological Research in Jerusalem from 1998 to 2018: Findings and Evaluations." In *Ancient Jerusalem Revealed: Archaeological Discoveries, 1998–2018*, edited by Hillel Geva, 1–31. Jerusalem: Israel Exploration Society, 2019.

Gibson, John C. L. *Textbook of Syrian Semitic Inscriptions II: Aramaic Inscriptions Including Inscriptions in the Dialect of Zenjirli*. Oxford: Clarendon Press, 1975.

———. *Textbook of Syrian Semitic Inscriptions III: Phoenician Inscriptions Including Inscriptions in the Mixed Dialect of Arslan Tash*. Oxford: Clarendon Press, 1982.

Gilboa, Ayelet. "Cypriot Barrel Juglets at Khirbet Qeiyafa and Other Sites in the Levant: Cultural Aspects and Chronological Implications." *Tel Aviv* 39, no. 2 (2012): 133–49. https://doi.org/10.1179/033443512X13424449373669

———. "Iron Age I–II Cypriot Imports and Local Imitations." In *The Ancient Pottery of Israel and Its Neighbors: From the Iron Age through the Late Bronze Age*, edited by Seymour Gitin, 483–507. Jerusalem: Israel Exploration Society, 2015.

Gilboa, Ayelet, and Dvory Namdar. "On the Beginnings of South Asian Spice Trade with the Mediterranean Region: A Review." *Radiocarbon* 57, no. 2 (2015): 265–83. https://doi.org/10.2458/azu_rc.57.18562

Gilboa, Ayelet, and Ilan Sharon. "An Archaeological Contribution to the Early Iron Age Chronological Debate: Alternative Chronologies for Phoenicia and Their Effects on the Levant, Cyprus, and Greece." *Bulletin of the American Schools of Oriental Research* 322 (2003): 1–75. https://doi.org/10.2307/1357808

———. "Between Carmel and the Sea." *Near Eastern Archaeology* 71, no. 3 (2008): 146–70. https://doi.org/10.1086/NEA20361363

Glatt-Gilad, David A. "The Deuteronomistic Critique of Solomon: A Response to Marvin A. Sweeney." *Journal of Biblical Literature* 116 (1997): 700–703. https://doi.org/10.2307/3266554

Gnuse, Robert. "Spilt Water – Tales of David (2 Sam 23,13–17) and Alexander (Arrian, Anabasis of Alexander 6.26.1–3)." *Scandinavian Journal of the Old Testament* 12, no. 2 (1998): 233–48. https://doi.org/10.1080/09018329808585138

Goldwasser, Jacob. "The Campaign of Siamun in Palestine." *Bulletin of the Jewish Palestine Exploration Society* 14 (1948): 82–84.

Gooding, David W. "Pedantic Timetabling in 3rd Book of Reigns." *Vetus Testamentum* 15, no. 2 (1965): 153–66. https://doi.org/10.1163/156853365X00440

———. "The Septuagint's Version of Solomon's Misconduct." *Vetus Testamentum* 15, no. 3 (1965): 325–35. https://doi.org/10.1163/156853365X00198

Gordon, Robert P. "David's Rise and Saul's Demise: Narrative Analogy in 1 Samuel 24–26." *Tyndale Bulletin* 31 (1980): 37–64. https://doi.org/10.53751/001c.30594

———. "The Second Septuagint Account of Jeroboam: History or Midrash?" *Vetus Testamentum* 25, no. 2 (1975): 368–93. https://doi.org/10.1163/156853375X00674

Goren, Yuval, Israel Finkelstein, Nadav Naʾaman, and Michal Artzy. *Inscribed in Clay: Provenance Study of the Amarna Tablets and Other Ancient Near Eastern Texts*. Tel Aviv: Emery and Claire Yass Publ. in Archaeology of the Institute of Archaeology, 2004.

Gottlieb, Yulia. "Judah of Iron vs. Israel of Copper: The Metalworking Development in the Land of Israel and Its Historical Implications." In *Mining for Ancient Copper: Essays in Memory of Beno Rothenberg*, edited by Erez Ben-Yosef, 435–54. Tel Aviv University Sonia and Marco Nadler Institute of Archaeology Monograph Series 37. Tel Aviv: Tel Aviv University, Sonia and Marco Nadler Institute of Archaeology, 2018.

Gottwald, Norman K. *The Tribes of Yahweh: A Sociology of the Religion of Liberated Israel, 1250–1050 B.C.E.* Maryknoll: Orbis Books, 1979.

Grabbe, Lester L. "From Merneptah to Sheshonq: If We Had Only the Bible..." In *Israel in Transition 2, From Late Bronze II to Iron IIA (c. 1250-850 BCE): The Texts*, edited by Lester L. Grabbe, 62-129. The Library of Hebrew Bible/Old Testament Studies 551. London: Continuum International Publishing Group, 2011.

Green, Alberto R. "Solomon and Siamun: A Synchronism between Early Dynastic Israel and the Twenty-First Dynasty of Egypt." *Journal of Biblical Literature* 97 (1978): 353-67. https://doi.org/10.2307/3266164

Grosman, Leore, Avshalom Karasik, Ortal Harush, and Uzy Smilanksy. "Archaeology in Three Dimensions: Computer-Based Methods in Archaeological Research." *Journal of Eastern Mediterranean Archaeology & Heritage Studies* 2, no. 1 (2014): 48-64.

Gunneweg, Jan, T. Beier, U. Diehl, D. Lambrecht, and H. Mommsen. "'Edomite,' 'Negevite' and 'Midianite' Pottery from the Negev Desert and Jordan: Instrumental Neutron Activation Analysis Results." *Archaeometry* 33 (1991): 239-53. https://doi.org/10.1111/j.1475-4754.1991.tb00701.x

Halpern, Baruch. *David's Secret Demons: Messiah, Murderer, Traitor, King*. Grand Rapids: Eerdmans, 2001.

———. "Sacred History and Ideology: Chronicles' Thematic Structure – Indications of an Earlier Source." In *The Creation of Sacred Literature: Composition and Redaction of the Biblical Text*, edited by Richard Elliott Friedman, 35-54. University of California Publications Near Eastern Studies 22. Berkeley; Los Angeles: University of California Press, 1981.

———. "Sectionalism and the Schism." *Journal of Biblical Literature* 93 (1974): 519-32. https://doi.org/10.2307/3263829

———. "Sybil, or the Two Nations? Archaism, Kinship, Alienation, and the Elite Redefinition of Traditional Culture in Judah in the 8th-7th Centuries B.C.E." In *The Study of the Ancient Near East in the Twenty-First Century: The William Foxwell Albright Centennial Conference*, edited by Jerrold S. Cooper and Glenn M. Schwartz, 291-338. Winona Lake: Eisenbrauns, 1996.

———. *The Constitution of the Monarchy in Israel*. Harvard Semitic Monographs 25. Chico, Calif.: Scholars Press, 1981.

———. *The First Historians: The Hebrew Bible and History*. San Francisco: Harper and Row, 1988.

Hamilton, Gordon J. "From the Seal of a Seer to an Inscribed Game Board: A Catalogue of Eleven Early Alphabetic Inscriptions Recently Discovered in Egypt and Palestine." *The Bible and Interpretation* (February 2010). https://bibleinterp.arizona.edu/articles/seal357910

———. "Two Methodological Issues Concerning the Expanded Collection of Early Alphabetic Texts." In *Epigraphy, Philology, and the Hebrew Bible: Methodological Perspectives on Philological and Comparative Study of the Hebrew Bible in Honor of Jo Ann Hackett*, edited by Jeremy M. Hutton and Aaron D. Rubin, 127-56. Ancient Near Eastern Monographs 12. Atlanta: SBL Press, 2015).

Handy, Lowell K., ed. *The Age of Solomon: Scholarship at the Turn of the Millennium*. Studies in the History and Culture of the Ancient Near East 11. Leiden; New York: Brill, 1997.

Hardin, James W., Christopher A. Rollston, and Jeffrey A. Blakely. "Iron Age Bullae from Officialdom's Periphery: Khirbet Summeily in Broader Context." *Near Eastern Archaeology* 77, no. 4 (2014): 299-301.

Haring, Ben. "Stela Leiden V 65 and Herihor's 'Damnatio Memoriae.'" *Studien Zur Altägyptischen Kultur* 41 (2012): 139-52.

Hatke, George. "For ʾIlmuquh and for Sabaʾ: The Res Gestae of Karib ʾīl Watar Bin Dhamarʿ Alī from Ṣirwāḥ in Context." *Wiener Zeitschrift Für Die Kunde Des Morgenlandes* 105 (2015): 87-133.

Hausleiter, Arnulf. "Pottery Groups of the Late 2nd / Early 1st Millennia BC in Northwest Arabia and New Evidence from Tayma." In *Recent Trends in the Study of Late Bronze Age Ceramics in Syro-Mesopotamia and Neighbouring Regions: Proceedings of the International Workshop in Berlin, 2-5 November 2006*, edited by Marta Luciani and Arnulf Hausleiter, 399-434. Orient-Archäologie 32. Leidorf: Rahden/Westf., 2014.

Hays, J. Daniel. "Has the Narrator Come to Praise Solomon or to Bury Him? Narrative Subtlety in 1 Kings 1-11." *Journal for the Study of the Old Testament* 28, no. 2 (2003): 149-74. https://doi.org/10.1177/030908920302800202

Heaton, Eric William. *Solomon's New Men: The Emergence of Ancient Israel as a National State*. New York: Pica Press, 1975.
Heidorn, Lisa A. "The Horses of Kush." *Journal of Near Eastern Studies* 56, no. 2 (1997): 105–14. https://doi.org/10.1086/468525
Herbst, John W. *Development of an Icon: Solomon before and after King David*. Wipf and Stock Publishers, 2016.
Herr, Larry G. "Jerusalem in the Iron Age." In *Jerusalem before Islam*, edited by Zeidan Abdel-Kafi Kafafi and Robert Schick, 74–85. BAR International Series 1699. Oxford: Archaeopress, 2007.
———. "The Amman Airport Structure and the Geopolitics of Ancient Transjordan." *Biblical Archaeologist* 46, no. 4 (1983): 223–29. https://doi.org/10.2307/3209781
———. "Tripartite Pillared Buildings and the Market Place in Iron Age Palestine." *Bulletin of the American Schools of Oriental Research* 272 (1988): 47–67. https://doi.org/10.2307/1356785
Herrera Gonzalez, M. D., and Jacqueline Balensi. "More about the Greek Geometric Pottery at Tell Abu Hawam." *Levant* 18 (1986): 169–71. https://doi.org/10.1179/007589186790586047
Herrmann, Virginia R. "Appropriation and Emulation in the Earliest Sculptures from Zincirli (Iron Age Sam'al)." *American Journal of Archaeology* 121, no. 2 (2017): 237–74. https://doi.org/10.3764/aja.121.2.0237
Herzog, Ze'ev, and Lily Singer-Avitz. "Redefining the Centre: The Emergence of State in Judah." *Tel Aviv* 31 (2004): 209–44. https://doi.org/10.1179/tav.2004.2004.2.209
———. "Sub-Dividing the Iron Age IIA in Northern Israel: A Suggested Solution to the Chronological Debate." *Tel Aviv* 33 (2006): 163–95. https://doi.org/10.1179/tav.2006.2006.2.163
Higginbotham, Carolyn R. *Egyptianization and Elite Emulation in Ramesside Palestine: Governance and Accommodation on the Imperial Periphery*. Culture and History of the Ancient Near East 2. Leiden; Boston: Brill, 2000.
Hodder, Ian. *Symbols in Action: Ethnoarchaeological Studies of Material Culture*. Cambridge; New York: Cambridge University Press, 1982.
———, ed. *The Spatial Organisation of Culture*. New Approaches in Archaeology. London: Duckworth, 1978.
Hodder, Ian, and Clive Orton. *Spatial Analysis in Archaeology*. Cambridge: Cambridge University Press, 1979.
Holladay, Jr., John S. "The Kingdoms of Israel and Judah: Political and Economic Centralization in the Iron IIA-B (ca. 1000–750 BCE)." In *The Archaeology of Society in the Holy Land*, edited by Thomas E. Levy, 368–98. 2nd ed. New Approaches in Anthropological Archaeology. London: Leicester University Press, 1998.
Hollis, Susan Tower. "Hathor and Isis in Byblos in the Second and First Millenniua BCE." *Journal of Ancient Egyptian Interconnections* 1, no. 2 (2009): 1–8.
Hulin, Linda. "The Libyans." In *The Oxford Handbook of Egyptology*, edited by Ian Shaw and Elizabeth Bloxam. Oxford: Oxford University Press, 2020.
Hull, Eleanor. "David and the Well of Bethlehem: An Irish Parallel." *Folklore* 44, no. 2 (1933): 214–18. https://doi.org/10.1080/0015587X.1933.9718493
Iacovou, M. "Phoenicia and Cyprus in the First Millennium B.C.: Two Distinct Cultures in Search of Their Distinct Archaeologies: Review Article." *Bulletin of the American Schools of Oriental Research* 336 (2004): 61–66. https://doi.org/10.2307/4150089
Intilia, Andrea. "Qurayyah Painted Ware: A Reassessment of 40 Years of Research on Its Origins, Chronology and Distribution." In *The Archaeology of North Arabia. Oases and Landscapes: Proceedings of the International Congress Held at the University of Vienna, 5-8 December, 2013*, edited by Marta Luciani, 175–255. 1st ed. Vienna: Austrian Academy of Sciences Press, 2016.
James, Peter, and Peter van der Veen, eds. *Solomon and Shishak: Current Perspectives from Archaeology, Epigraphy, History and Chronology: Proceedings of the Third BICANE Colloquium Held at Sidney Sussex College, Cambridge 26-27 March, 2011*. BAR International Series 2732. Oxford: Archaeopress, 2015.

Jamieson-Drake, David W. *Scribes and Schools in Monarchic Judah: A Socio-Archeological Approach*. The Social World of Biblical Antiquity Series, 9. Journal for the Study of the Old Testament Supplement Series, 109. Sheffield: Almond Press, 1991.

Jansen-Winkeln, Karl. "Anmerkungen zu 'Pharaos Tochter.'" *Biblische Notizen* 103 (2000): 23–29.

———. "Beiträge zur Geschichte der 21. Dynastie." *The Journal of Egyptian Archaeology* 102 (2016): 73–96. https://doi.org/10.1177/030751331610200107

Joffe, Alexander H. "Defining the State." In *Enemies and Friends of the State: Ancient Prophecy in Context*, edited by Christopher Rollston, 3–24. Winona Lake: Eisenbrauns, 2018.

———. "The Rise of Secondary States in the Iron Age Levant." *Journal of the Economic and Social History of the Orient* 45, no. 4 (2002): 425–67. https://doi.org/10.1163/156852002320939311

Jurman, Claus. "'Silver of the Treasury of Herishef' – Considering the Origin and Economic Significance of Silver in Egypt during the Third Intermediate Period." In *The Mediterranean Mirror: Cultural Contacts in the Mediterranean Sea between 1200 and 750 B.C.*, edited by Andrea Babbi, Friederike Bubenheimer-Erhart, Beatriz Marín-Aguilera, and Simone Mühl, 51–68. RGZM – Tagungen 20. Mainz: Verlag der Römisch-Germanischen Zentralmuseums, 2015.

Kalimi, Isaac. *The Reshaping of Ancient Israelite History in Chronicles*. University Park: Penn State University Press, 2021.

———. *Writing and Rewriting the Story of Solomon in Ancient Israel*. Cambridge: Cambridge University Press, 2018.

Kalsbeek, Jan, and Gloria London. "A Late Second Millennium B. C. Potting Puzzle." *Bulletin of the American Schools of Oriental Research* 232 (1978): 47–56. https://doi.org/10.2307/1356700

Karacic, Steven, and James F. Osborne. "Eastern Mediterranean Economic Exchange during the Iron Age: Portable X-Ray Fluorescence and Neutron Activation Analysis of Cypriot-Style Pottery in the Amuq Valley, Turkey." *PLOS ONE* 11, no. 11 (2016): e0166399. https://doi.org/10.1371/journal.pone.0166399

Katz, Hayah, and Avraham Faust. "The Chronology of the Iron Age IIA in Judah in Light of Tel 'Eton Tomb C3 and Other Assemblages." *Bulletin of the American Schools of Oriental Research* 371 (2014): 103–27. https://doi.org/10.5615/bullamerschoorie.371.0103

Kearsley, Rosalinde Anne. "The Redating of Tell Abu Hawam III and the Greek Pendant Semicircle Skyphos." *Bulletin of the American Schools of Oriental Research* 263 (1986): 85–86. https://doi.org/10.2307/1356914

Keel, Othmar, and Amihai Mazar. "Iron Age Seals and Seal Impressions from Tel Rehov." *Eretz-Israel* 29 (2009): 57*–69*.

Kelm, George L., and Amihai Mazar. "Tel Batash (Timnah) Excavations: Third Preliminary Report, 1984–1989." *Bulletin of the American Schools of Oriental Research Supplements* 27 (1991): 47–67.

Kempinski, Aharon. "Masos, Tel." In *The New Encyclopedia of Archaeological Excavations in the Holy Land*, edited by Ephraim Stern, 986–89. Jerusalem; New York: Israel Exploration Society & Carta; Simon & Schuster, 1993.

Keulen, P. S. F. van. *Two Versions of The Solomon Narrative: An Inquiry into The Relationship Between MT 1Kgs. 2-11 and LXX 3 Reg. 2-11*. Leiden: Brill, 2005.

Kiderlen, Moritz, Michael Bode, Andreas Hauptmann, and Yannis Bassiakos. "Tripod Cauldrons Produced at Olympia Give Evidence for Trade with Copper from Faynan (Jordan) to South West Greece, c. 950–750 BCE." *Journal of Archaeological Science: Reports* 8 (2016): 303–13. https://doi.org/10.1016/j.jasrep.2016.06.013

Killebrew, Ann E. *Biblical Peoples and Ethnicity: An Archaeological Study of Egyptians, Canaanites, Philistines, and Early Israel, 1300-1100 B.C.E.* Atlanta: Society of Biblical Literature, 2005.

Killebrew, Ann E., and Gunnar Lehmann, eds. *The Philistines and Other "Sea Peoples" in Text and Archaeology*. Archaeology and Biblical Studies 15. Atlanta: Society of Biblical Literature, 2013.

Kitchen, Kenneth. "Egyptian Interventions in the Levant in the Iron Age II." In *Symbiosis, Symbolism, and the Power of the Past: Canaan, Ancient Israel, and Their Neighbors from the Late Bronze Age through Roman Palaestina. Proceedings of the Centennial Symposium, W. F. Albright Institute of Archaeological*

Research and American Schools of Oriental Research, Jerusalem, May 29/31, 2000, edited by William G. Dever and Seymour Gitin, 113–32. Winona Lake: Eisenbrauns, 2003.

———. "Establishing Chronology in Pharaonic Egypt and the Ancient Near East: Interlocking Textual Sources Relating to C. 1600–664 BC." In *Radiocarbon and the Chronologies of Ancient Egypt*, edited by Andrew J. Shortland and Christopher Bronk Ramsey, 1–18. Oxford: Oxbow Books, 2013.

———. "Jerusalem in Ancient Egyptian Documentation." In *Jerusalem before Islam*, edited by Zeidan Abdel-Kafi Kafafi and Robert Schick, 28–37. BAR International Series 1699. Oxford: Archaeopress, 2007.

———. "Sheba and Arabia." In *The Age of Solomon: Scholarship at the Turn of the Millennium*, edited by Lowell K. Handy, 126–53. Studies in the History and Culture of the Ancient Near East 11. Leiden; New York: Brill, 1997.

———. *The Third Intermediate Period in Egypt*. 2nd ed. with supplement. Warminster: Aris & Phillips, 1995.

Kleiman, Assaf, Alexander Fantalkin, Hans Mommsen, and Israel Finkelstein. "The Date and Origin of Black-on-Red Ware: The View from Megiddo." *American Journal of Archaeology* 123.4 (2019): 531–55. https://doi.org/10.3764/aja.123.4.0531

Kletter, Raz. "Chronology and United Monarchy: A Methodological Review." *Zeitschrift des deutschen Palästina-Vereins* 120 (2004): 13–54.

———. "Water from a Rock: Archaeology, Ideology, and the Bible." *Scandinavian Journal of the Old Testament* 30, no. 2 (2016): 161–84. https://doi.org/10.1080/09018328.2016.1226043

Knauf, E. A. "Jerusalem in the Late Bronze and Early Iron Ages: A Proposal." *Tel Aviv* 27 (2000): 75–90. https://doi.org/10.1179/tav.2000.2000.1.75

Knoppers, Gary N. "Sex, Religion, and Politics: The Deuteronomist on Intermarriage." *Hebrew Annual Review* 14 (1994): 121–41.

———. "The Vanishing Solomon: The Disappearance of the United Monarchy from Recent Histories of Ancient Israel." *Journal of Biblical Literature* 116, no. 1 (1997): 19–44. https://doi.org/10.2307/3266744

———. *Two Nations Under God: The Deuteronomistic History of Solomon and the Dual Monarchies*. 2 volumes. Harvard Semitic Monographs 52–53. Atlanta: Scholars Press, 1993.

Koch, Ido. "On Philistines and Early Israelite Kings: Memories and Perceptions." In *Saul, Benjamin, and the Emergence of Monarchy in Israel: Biblical and Archaeological Perspectives*, edited by Joachim J. Krause, Omer Sergi, and Kristin Weingart, 7–32. Atlanta: SBL Press, 2020.

Kochavi, Moshe. "Hadar, Tel." In *The New Encyclopedia of Archaeological Excavations in the Holy Land*, edited by Ephraim Stern, 551–52. Jerusalem: Israel Exploration Society & Carta, 1993.

———. "The Eleventh Century BCE Tripartite Pillar Building at Tel Hadar." In *Mediterranean Peoples in Transition: Thirteenth to Early Tenth Centuries BCE*, 468–78. Jerusalem: Israel Exploration Society, 1998.

———. "The History and Archeology of Aphek-Antipatris: A Biblical City in the Sharon Plain." *The Biblical Archaeologist* 44, no. 2 (1981): 75–86. https://doi.org/10.2307/3209863

Kochavi, Moshe, and Miriam Tadmor. *Aphek in Canaan: The Egyptian Governor's Residence and Its Finds*. Jerusalem: Israel Museum, 1990.

Koehler, Ludwig, and Walter Baumgartner. *The Hebrew and Aramaic Lexicon of the Old Testament*. 2 volumes. Revised edition. Leiden, Boston: Brill, 2001.

Kopcke, Günter. "1000 B.C.E.? 900 B.C.E.? A Greek Vase from Lake Galilee." In *Leaving No Stones Unturned: Essays on the Ancient Near East and Egypt in Honor of Donald P. Hansen*, edited by Erica Ehrenberg, 109–17. Winona Lake: Eisenbrauns, 2002.

Kourou, Nota. "Phoenicia, Cyprus and the Aegean in the Early Iron Age: J. N. Coldstream's Contribution and the Current State of Research." In *Cyprus and the Aegean in the Early Iron Age: The Legacy of Nicolas Coldstream*, edited by Maria Iacovou, 33–51. Nicosia: Bank of Cyprus Cultural Foundation, 2012.

———. "The Aegean and the Levant in the Early Iron Age: Recent Developments." *Bulletin d'Archéologie et d'Architecture Libanaises* 6 (2008): 361–74.
Kroll, John H. "Early Iron Age Balance Weights at Lefkandi, Euboea." *Oxford Journal of Archaeology* 27 (2008): 37–48. https://doi.org/10.1111/j.1468-0092.2007.00294.x
LaBianca, Oystein. S, and Randall W. Younker. "The Kingdoms of Ammon, Moab and Edom: The Archaeology of Society in Late Bronze/Iron Age Transjordan (ca. 1400–500 BCE)." In *The Archaeology of Society in the Holy Land*, edited by Thomas E. Levy, 399–415. 2nd ed.. New Approaches in Anthropological Archaeology. London: Leicester University Press, 1998.
Lamon, Robert S., and Geoffrey M. Shipton. *Megiddo I: Seasons of 1925-1934, Strata I-V*. Oriental Institute Communications 42. Chicago: University of Chicago Press, 1939.
Larson, Kara, Elizabeth Arnold, and James W. Hardin. "Resource Allocation and Rising Complexity during the Iron Age IIA: An Isotopic Case Study from Khirbet Summeily, Israel." *Quaternary International* (2022). https://doi.org/10.1016/j.quaint.2022.03.022
Leahy, M. Anthony. "The Libyan Period in Egypt: An Essay in Interpretation." *Libyan Studies* 16 (1985): 51–65. https://doi.org/10.1017/S0263718900007287
Lehmann, Gunnar. "The Emergence of Early Phoenicia." *Jerusalem Journal of Archaeology* 1 (2021): 272–324. https://doi.org/10.52486/01.00001.11
Lehmann, Gunnar, and Hermann Michael Niemann, "When Did the Shephelah Become Judahite?" *Tel Aviv* 41, no. 1 (2014): 77–94.
Lemaire, André. "Edom and the Edomites." In *The Books of Kings: Sources, Composition, Historiography and Reception*, edited by André Lemaire, Baruch Halpern, and Matthew Joel Adams, 225–44. Supplements to Vetus Testamentum 129. Leiden: Brill, 2010.
———. "From the Origin of the Alphabet to the Tenth Century B.C.E.: New Documents and New Directions." In *New Inscriptions and Seals Relating to the Biblical World*, edited by Meir Lubetski and Edith Lubetski, 1–20. Atlanta: Society of Biblical Literature, 2012).
———. "Les Premiers Rois Araméens Dans La Tradition Biblique." In *The World of the Aramaeans I: Biblical Studies in Honour of Paul Eugène Dion*, edited by P. M. Michèle Daviau, John William Wevers, Michael Weigl, and Paul-Eugène Dion, 113–43. Journal for the Study of the Old Testament Supplement Series 324. Sheffield: Sheffield Academic Press, 2001.
———. "Levantine Literacy ca. 1000–750 BCE." In *Contextualizing Israel's Sacred Writing: Ancient Literacy, Orality, and Literary Production*, edited by Brian B. Schmidt, 11–46. Atlanta: SBL Press, 2015.
Lemche, Niels Peter. *The Israelites in History and Tradition*. London; Louisville: Westminster John Knox Press, 1998.
Lemos, Irene S. "Lefkandi in Euboea: Amongst the Heroes of the Early Iron Age." *Minerva* (2008): 30–32.
Lemos, Tracy Maria. *Marriage Gifts and Social Change in Ancient Palestine: 1200 BCE to 200 CE*. Cambridge: Cambridge University Press, 2010.
Leonard-Fleckman, Mahri. *The House of David: Between Political Formation and Literary Revision*. Minneapolis: Fortress Press, 2016.
Lev-Tov, Justin. "A Preliminary Report on the Late Bronze and Iron Age Faurnal Assemblages from Tell Es-Safi/Gath." In *Tell Es-Safi/Gath: The 1996-2005 Seasons*, edited by Aren M. Maeir, 589–612. 2 volumes. Ägypten und Altes Testament 69. Wiesbaden: Harrassowitz, 2012.
Levenson, Jon D., and Baruch Halpern. "The Political Import of David's Marriages." *Journal of Biblical Literature* 99, no. 4 (1980): 507–18. https://doi.org/10.2307/3265190
Levy, Thomas E. "Ethnic Identity in Biblical Edom, Israel, and Midian: Some Insights from Mortuary Contexts in the Lowlands of Edom." In *Exploring the Longue Durée: Essays in Honor of Lawrence E. Stager*, edited by J. David Schloen, 251–61. Winona Lake: Eisenbrauns, 2009.
———. "Pastoral Nomads and Iron Age Metal Production in Ancient Edom." In *Nomads, Tribes, and the State in the Ancient Near East, Cross-Disciplinary Perspectives*, 147–77. Oriental Institute Seminars 5. Chicago: Oriental Institute of the University of Chicago, 2009.

Levy, Thomas E., Erez Ben-Yosef, and Mohammad Najjar. "The Iron Age Edomite Lowlands Regional Archaeological Project: Research, Design, and Methodology." In *New Insights into the Iron Age Archaeology of Edom, Southern Jordan: Surveys, Excavations and Research from the University of California, San Diego & Department of Antiquities of Jordan, Edom Lowlands Regional Archaeology Project (ELRAP)*, edited by Thomas E. Levy, Mohammad Najjar, Erez Ben-Yosef, and Neil G. Smith, 1–87. 2 volumes. Monumenta Archaeologica 35. Los Angeles: The Cotsen Institute of Archaeology Press, 2014.

Levy, Thomas E., Mohammad Najjar, and Erez Ben-Yosef. "Conclusion." In *New Insights into the Iron Age Archaeology of Edom, Southern Jordan: Surveys, Excavations and Research from the University of California, San Diego & Department of Antiquities of Jordan, Edom Lowlands Regional Archaeology Project (ELRAP)*, edited by Thomas E. Levy, Mohammad Najjar, Erez Ben-Yosef, and Neil G. Smith, 977–1001. 2 volumes. Monumenta Archaeologica 35. Los Angeles: The Cotsen Institute of Archaeology Press, 2014.

Levy, Thomas E., Mohammad Najjar, Erez Ben-Yosef, and Neil G. Smith, eds. *New Insights into the Iron Age Archaeology of Edom, Southern Jordan: Surveys, Excavations, and Research from the University of California, San Diego & Department of Antiquities of Jordan, Edom Lowlands Regional Archaeology Project (ELRAP)*. 2 volumes. Monumenta Archaeologica 35. Los Angeles: The Cotsen Institute of Archaeology Press, 2014.

Levy, Thomas E., Mohammad Najjar, Thomas Higham, Yoav Arbel, Adolfo Muniz, Erez Ben-Yosef, Neil G. Smith, Marc Beherec, Aaron Gidding, Ian W. Jones, Daniel Frese, Craig Smitheram, and Mark Robinson. "Excavations at Khirbat En-Nahas, 2002–2009: An Iron Age Copper Production Center in the Lowlands of Edom." In *New Insights into the Iron Age Archaeology of Edom, Southern Jordan: Surveys, Excavations and Research from the University of California, San Diego & Department of Antiquities of Jordan, Edom Lowlands Regional Archaeology Project (ELRAP)*, edited by Thomas E. Levy, Mohammad Najjar, Erez Ben-Yosef, and Neil G. Smith, 88–245. 2 volumes. Monumenta Archaeologica 35. Los Angeles: The Cotsen Institute of Archaeology Press, 2014.

L'Heureux, Conrad. "The Ugaritic and Biblical Rephaim." *The Harvard Theological Review* 67, no. 3 (1974): 265–74. https://doi.org/10.1017/S0017816000016813

———. "The Yelîdê Hārāpā': A Cultic Association of Warriors." *Bulletin of the American Schools of Oriental Research*, 221 (1976): 83–85. https://doi.org/10.2307/1356087

Lichtheim, Miriam (translator). "The Report of Wenamun." In *Ancient Egyptian Literature: A Book of Readings: Volume II: The New Kingdom*, edited by Miriam Lichtheim, 224–29. Berkeley: University of California Press, 1973.

———(ed.). *Ancient Egyptian Literature: A Book of Readings: Volume III: The Late Period*. Berkeley: University of California Press, 2006.

Lipiński, Edward. *Itineraria Phoenicia*. Orientalia Lovaniensia Analecta 127. Studia Phoenicia 18. Leuven; Dudley: Uitgeverij Peeters en Departement Oosterse Studies, 2004.

Liverani, Mario. *Israel's History and the History of Israel*. London; Oakville: Equinox Publishing, 2005.

Luciani, Marta. "Pottery from the 'Midianite Heartland?' On Tell Kheleifeh and Qurayyah Painted Ware. New Evidence from the Harvard Semitic Museum." In *To the Madbar and Back Again: Studies in the Languages, Archaeology, and Cultures of Arabia Dedicated to Michael C.A. Macdonald*, edited by Laïla Nehmé and Ahmad Al-Jallad, 392–438. Leiden: Brill, 2017.

———. "Qurayyah." In *Roads of Arabia: Archaeological Treasures from Saudi Arabia*, edited by Alessandra Capodiferro and Sara Colantonio, 140–55. Milan: Electa, 2019.

Luciani, Marta, and Abdullah S. Alsaud. "Qurayyah 2015: Report on the First Season of the Joint Saudi Arabian-Austrian Archaeological Project." *ATLAL, Journal of Saudi Arabian Archaeology* 28 (2020): 47–78.

Lundberg, Marilyn J. "Editor's Notes: The Aḥiram Inscription." *Maarav* 11, no. 1 (2004): 81–93. https://doi.org/10.1086/MAR200411105

Luke, Joanna. *Ports of Trade, Al Mina and Geometric Greek Pottery in the Levant*. British Archaeological Reports International Series 1100. Oxford: Publishers of the British Archaeological Reports, 2003.

Maeir, Aren M., "A 'Repertoire of Otherness'? Identities in Early Iron Age Philistia." In *Proceedings of the 5th "Broadening Horizons" Conference (Udine 5-8 June 2017): Volume 1. From the Prehistory of Upper Mesopotamia to the Bronze and Iron Age Societies of the Levant*, edited by M. Iamoni, 161–70. Trieste: University of Trieste, 2020.

———. "Chapter 1: Introduction and Overview." In *Tell es-Safi/Gath II: Excavation and Studies*, edited by A. M. Maeir and J. Uziel, 3–52. Ägypten und Altes Testament 105. Münster: Zaphon, 2020.

———. "On Defining Israel: Or, Let's Do the *Kulturkreislehre* Again!," *Hebrew Bible and Ancient Israel* 10, no. 2 (2021): 106–48. https://doi.org/10.1628/hebai-2021-0010

———. "Philistine and Israelite Identities: Some Comparative Thoughts." *Die Welt Des Orients* 49, no. 2 (2019): 151–60. https://doi.org/10.13109/wdor.2019.49.2.151

———, ed. *Tell Es-Safi/Gath: The 1996–2005 Seasons*. 2 volumes. Ägypten und Altes Testament 69. Wiesbaden: Harrassowitz, 2012.

———. "The Tell Es-Safi/Gath Archaeological Project 1996–2010: Introduction, Overview and Synopsis of Results." In *Tell Es-Safi/Gath: The 1996–2005 Seasons*, edited by Aren M. Maeir, 1–88. 2 volumes. Ägypten und Altes Testament 69. Wiesbaden: Harrassowitz, 2012.

———. "The Tell Eṣ-Ṣâfi/Gath Archaeological Project: Overview." *Near Eastern Archaeology* 80, no. 4 (2017): 212–31.

Maeir, Aren M., Alexander Fantalkin, and Alexander Zuckerman. "The Earliest Greek Import in the Iron Age Levant." *Ancient West & East* 8 (2009): 57–80. https://doi.org/10.2143/AWE.8.0.2045838

Maeir, Aren M. and Itzhaq Shai. "Reassessing the Character of the Judahite Kingdom: Archaeological Evidence for Non-Centralized, Kinship-Based Components." In *From Sha'ar Hagolan to Shaaraim: Essays in Honor of Prof. Yosef Garfinkel*, edited by Saar Ganor, Igor Kreimerman, Katharina Streit, and Madeleine Mumcuoglu, 232–40. Jerusalem: Israel Exploration Society, 2016.

Maeir, Aren M., Stefan J. Wimmer, Alexander Zukerman, and Aaron Demsky. "A Late Iron Age I/Early Iron Age II Old Canaanite Inscription from Tell Eṣ-Ṣâfi/Gath, Israel: Palaeography, Dating, and Historical-Cultural Significance." *Bulletin of the American Schools of Oriental Research* 351 (2008): 39–71. https://doi.org/10.1086/BASOR25609285

Maisler [Mazar], Benjamin. "Two Hebrew Ostraca from Tell Qasile." *Journal of Near Eastern Studies* 10 (1951): 265–87. https://doi.org/10.1086/371052

Malena, Sarah. "A Woman's Place(s): Pharaoh's Daughter, Jerusalem's Landscape, and Layers of Meaning." Paper presented at the Society of Biblical Literature annual meeting, San Diego, 2019.

———. "History without Texts: Interdisciplinary Interpretive Methods for Understanding the Early Iron Age." In *"And in Length of Days Understanding" (Job 12:12): Essays on Archaeology in the Eastern Mediterranean and Beyond in Honor of Thomas E. Levy*, edited by Erez Ben-Yosef and Ian W. N. Jones, 535–54. Interdisciplinary Contributions to Archaeology. Cham: Springer, 2023.

———. "Influential Inscriptions: Resituating Scribal Activity during the Iron I–IIA Transition." In *Scribes and Scribalism*, edited by Mark Leuchter, 13–27. The Hebrew Bible in Social Perspective. London; New York: Bloomsbury Publishing, 2020.

———. "Spice Roots in the Song of Songs." In *Milk and Honey: Essays on Ancient Israel and the Bible in Appreciation of the Judaic Studies Program at the University of California, San Diego*, edited by Sarah Malena and David Miano, 165–84. Winona Lake: Eisenbrauns, 2007.

Marom, Nimrud, Amihai Mazar, Noa Raban-Gerstel, and Guy Bar-Oz. "Backbone of Society: Evidence for Social and Economic Status of the Iron Age Population of Tel Rehov, Beth-Shean Valley, Israel." *Bulletin of the American Schools of Oriental Research* 354 (2009): 1–21. https://doi.org/10.1086/BASOR25609315

Martin, Mario A. S., Adi Eliyahu-Behar, Michael Anenburg, Yuval Goren, and Israel Finkelstein. "Iron IIA Slag-Tempered Pottery in the Negev Highlands, Israel." *Journal of Archaeological Science* 40 (2014): 3777–92. https://doi.org/10.1016/j.jas.2013.04.024

Martin, Susan Rebecca. "'Hellenization' and Southern Phoenicia: Reconsidering the Impact of Greece Before Alexander." Ph.D. dissertation. University of California, Berkeley, 2007.

Master, Daniel M. "State Formation Theory and the Kingdom of Ancient Israel." *Journal of Near Eastern Studies* 60, no. 2 (2001): 117–31. https://doi.org/10.1086/468899

Matthews, Victor H. "Back to Bethel: Geographical Reiteration in Biblical Narrative." *Journal of Biblical Literature* 128 (2009): 149–65. https://doi.org/10.2307/25610172

———. "The Unwanted Gift: Implications of Obligatory Gift Giving in Ancient Israel." *Semeia* 87 (1999): 91–104.

Mazar, Amihai. "An Ivory Statuette Depicting an Enthroned Figure from Tel Reḥov." In *Bilder Als Quellen, Images as Sources: Studies on Ancient Near Eastern Artefacts and the Bible Inspired by the Work of Othmar Keel*, edited by Susanne Bickel, Silvia Schroer, René Schurte, and Christoph Uehlinger, 101–10. Orbis Biblicus et Orientalis. Fribourg; Göttingen: Academic Press; Vandenhoeck & Ruprecht, 2007.

———. "Archaeology and the Biblical Narrative: The Case of the United Monarchy." In *One God – One Cult – One Nation. Archaeological and Biblical Perspectives*, edited by Reinhard G. Kratz and Hermann Spieckermann, 29–58. Beihefte zur Zeitschrift für die alttestamentliche Wissenschaft 405. Berlin; New York: De Gruyter, 2010.

———. *Excavations at Tell Qasile*. Qedem 12, 20. Jerusalem: Institute of Archaeology; Hebrew University of Jerusalem, 1980.

———. "Reḥob." In *The Oxford Encyclopedia of Bible and Archaeology*. Edited by Daniel M. Master, Beth Alpert Nakhai, Avraham Faust, L. M. White, and J. K. Zangeberg, 221–30. New York: Oxford University Press, 2013.

———. "Reḥov, Tel." In *The New Encyclopedia of Archaeological Excavations in the Holy Land*, edited by Ephraim Stern, Ayelet Lewinson-Gilboa, and Joseph Aviram. Jerusalem; New York: Israel Exploration Society & Carta; Simon and Schuster, 2008.

———. "The Beth Shean Valley and its Vicinity in the 10th Century BCE." *Jerusalem Journal of Archaeology* 1 (2021): 241–271. https://doi.org/10.52486/01.00001.10

———. "The Debate over the Chronology of the Iron Age in the Southern Levant: Its History, the Current Situation and a Suggested Resolution." In *The Bible and Radiocarbon Dating: Archaeology, Text and Science*, edited by Thomas E. Levy and Thomas Higham, 15–30. London; Oakville: Equinox Publishing, 2005.

———. "The Iron Age Chronology Debate: Is the Gap Narrowing? Another Viewpoint." *Near Eastern Archaeology* 74, no. 2 (2011): 105–11. https://doi.org/10.5615/neareastarch.74.2.0105

———. "The Northern Shephelah in the Iron Age: Some Issues in Biblical History and Archaeology." In *Scripture and Other Artifacts: Essays on the Bible and Archaeology in Honor of Philip J. King*, edited by Michael David Coogan, J. Cheryl Exum, and Lawrence E. Stager, 247–67. Louisville: Westminster John Knox Press, 1994.

———. "Three 10th-9th Century B.C.E. Inscriptions From Tel Reḥov." In *Saxa Loquentur: Studien Zur Archäologie Palästinas/Israels. Festschrift Für Volkmar Fritz Zum 65. Geburtstag*, edited by Cornelius G. Den Hertog, Ulrich Hübner, and Stefan Münger, 171–84. Alter Orient und Altes Testament 302. Münster: Ugarit-Verlag, 2003.

Mazar, Amihai, and Christopher Bronk Ramsey. "14C Dates and the Iron Age Chronology of Israel: A Response." *Radiocarbon* 50, no. 2 (2008): 159–80. https://doi.org/10.1017/S0033822200033506

———. "A Response to Finkelstein and Piasetzky's Criticism and 'New Perspective.'" *Radiocarbon* 52, no. 4 (2010): 1681–88. https://doi.org/10.1017/S0033822200056411

Mazar, Amihai, and Nota Kourou. "Greece and the Levant in the 10th-9th Centuries BC: A View from Tel Reḥov." *Opuscula* (2019).

Mazar, Amihai, and Nava Panitz-Cohen. "It Is the Land of Honey: Beekeeping at Tel Reḥov." *Near Eastern Archaeology* 70, no. 4 (2007): 202–19. https://doi.org/10.1086/NEA20361335

Mazar, Benjamin. "The Aramean Empire and Its Relations with Israel." *The Biblical Archaeologist* 25, no. 4 (1962): 98–120. https://doi.org/10.2307/3210938

Mazar, Eilat. "Did I Find King David's Palace?" *Biblical Archaeology Review* 32, no. 1 (2006): 16–27, 70.

———. *Discovering the Solomonic Wall in Jerusalem: A Remarkable Archaeological Adventure*. Jerusalem: Shoham Academic Research and Publication, 2011.

———. "Excavate King David's Palace!" *Biblical Archaeology Review* 23, no. 1 (1997): 50–57, 70.

———. *Preliminary Report on the City of David Excavations 2005 at the Visitors Center Area*. Jerusalem; New York: Shalem Press, 2007.

———. *The Palace of King David: Excavations at the Summit of the City of David, Preliminary Report of Seasons 2005-2007*. Jerusalem; New York: Shoham Academic Research and Publication, 2009.

Mazar, Eilat, David Ben-Shlomo, and Shmuel Aḥituv. "An Inscribed Pithos from the Ophel, Jerusalem." *Israel Exploration Journal* 63 (2013): 39–49.

Mazar, Eilat, Wayne Horowitz, Takayoshi Oshima, and Yuval Goren. "A Cuneiform Tablet from the Ophel in Jerusalem." *IEJ* 60, no. 1 (2010): 4–21.

Mazar, Eilat, and Benjamin Mazar. *Excavations in the South of the Temple Mount*. Qedem 29. Jerusalem: Institute of Archaeology, the Hebrew University of Jerusalem, 1989.

McCarter, P. Kyle. *I Samuel: A New Translation with Introduction, Notes, and Commentary*. Anchor Bible 8. Garden City: Doubleday, 1980.

———. *II Samuel: A New Translation with Introduction, Notes, and Commentary*. Anchor Bible 9. Garden City: Doubleday, 1984.

McCarthy, Dennis J. "II Samuel 7 and the Structure of the Deuteronomistic History." *Journal of Biblical Literature* 84, no. 2 (1965): 131–38. https://doi.org/10.2307/3264134

McKenzie, Steven L. *The Trouble with Kings: The Composition of the Book of Kings in the Deuteronomistic History*. Supplements to Vetus Testamentum 42. Leiden; New York: Brill, 1991.

Mendenhall, George E. *The Tenth Generation: The Origins of the Biblical Tradition*. Baltimore: Johns Hopkins University Press, 1973.

Mettinger, Tryggve N. D. *Solomonic State Officials: A Study of the Civil Government Officials of the Israelite Monarchy*. Coniectanea Biblica Old Testament Series 5. Lund: Gleerup, 1971.

Meyers, Carol. "Basemath 2." In *Women in Scripture: A Dictionary of Named and Unnamed Women in the Hebrew Bible, the Apocryphal/Deuterocanonical Books, and the New Testaement*, edited by Carol Meyers, 57. Grand Rapids: Eerdmans, 2001.

Miano, David. *Shadow on the Steps: Time Measurement in Ancient Israel*. Atlanta: Society of Biblical Literature, 2010.

Mieroop, Marc Van De. *A History of Ancient Egypt*. 2nd ed. Hoboken: Wiley Blackwell, 2021.

Millard, Alan R. "Does the Bible Exaggerate King Solomon's Golden Wealth." *Biblical Archaeology Review* 15, no. 3 (1989): 20–29, 31, 34.

———. "The Ostracon from the Days of David Found at Khirbet Qeiyafa." *Tyndale Bulletin* 62, no. 1 (2011). https://doi.org/10.53751/001c.29303

Millek, Jesse M. *Exchange, Destruction, and a Transitioning Society: Interregional Exchange in the Southern Levant from the Late Bronze Age to the Iron I*. Tübingen: Tübingen University Press, 2019.

Miller, James C. "Ethnicity and the Hebrew Bible: Problems and Prospects." *Currents in Biblical Research* 6, no. 2 (2008): 170–213. https://doi.org/10.1177/1476993X07083627

Miller, J. Maxwell. "Geba/Gibeah of Benjamin." *Vetus Testamentum* 25, no. 2 (1975): 145–66. https://doi.org/10.2307/1517263

———. "Saul's Rise to Power: Some Observations Concerning 1 Sam 9:1–10:16; 10:26–11:15 and 13.2–14:46." *Catholic Biblical Quarterly* 36 (1974): 157–74.

Miller, J. Maxwell, and John Haralson Hayes. *A History of Ancient Israel and Judah*. 1st ed. Philadelphia: Westminster Press, 1986.

———. *A History of Ancient Israel and Judah*. 2nd ed. Louisville: Westminster John Knox Press, 2006.

Miller Jr., Patrick D., and J. J. M. Roberts. *The Hand of the Lord: A Reassessment of the "Ark Narrative" of 1 Samuel*. Atlanta: Society of Biblical Literature, 2008.

Misgav, Haggai, Yosef Garfinkel, and Saar Ganor. "The Ostracon." In *Khirbet Qeiyafa Vol. 1, Excavation Report 2007-2008*, edited by Yosef Garfinkel and Saar Ganor, 243–57. Jerusalem: Israel Exploration Society; Institute of Archaeology, Hebrew University of Jerusalem, 2009.

Mobley, Gregory. "Glimpses of the Heroic Saul." In *Saul in Story and Tradition*, edited by Marsha C. White and Carl S. Ehrlich, 80–87. Forschungen zum Alten Testament 47. Tübingen: Mohr Siebeck, 2006.

Monroe, Lauren and Daniel E. Fleming, eds. *Hebrew Bible and Ancient Israel. Israel before the Omrides* 10, no. 2 (2021). https://doi.org/10.1628/hebai-2021-0009

Monson, John. "The New ʿAin Dara Temple: Closest Solomonic Parallel." *Biblical Archaeology Review* 26, no. 3 (2000): 20–30, 32–35, 67.

Montet, Pierre. *La Nécropole Royale de Tanis, Volume 1: Les Constructions et le Tombeau d'Osorkon II à Tanis*. Paris, 1947.

———. *Les Constructions et le Tombeau de Psousennès á Tanis*. Volume 2 of *La Nécropole Royale de Tanis*. Paris: s.n., 1951.

Montgomery, James A. "Archival Data in the Book of Kings." *Journal of Biblical Literature* 53, no. 1 (1934): 46–52. https://doi.org/10.2307/3259339

Moore, Megan Bishop. *Philosophy and Practice in Writing a History of Ancient Israel*. New York: T&T Clark, 2006.

Moore, Megan Bishop, and Brad E. Kelle. *Biblical History and Israel's Past: The Changing Study of the Bible and History*. Grand Rapids: Eerdmans Publishing, 2011.

Moran, William L. "The Ancient Near Eastern Background of the Love of God in Deuteronomy." *Catholic Biblical Quarterly* 25 (1963): 77–87.

Moran, William L. "The Syrian Scribe of the Jerusalem Amarna Letters." In *Amarna Studies: Collected Writings*, 249–74. Harvard Semitic Studies 54; Leiden: Brill, 2003.

Münger, Stefan, and Thomas E. Levy. "The Iron Age Egyptian Amulet Assemblage." In *New Insights into the Iron Age Archaeology of Edom, Southern Jordan: Surveys, Excavations and Research from the University of California, San Diego & Department of Antiquities of Jordan, Edom Lowlands Regional Archaeology Project (ELRAP)*, edited by Thomas E. Levy, Mohammad Najjar, Erez Ben-Yosef, and Neil G. Smith, 741–65. 2 volumes. Monumenta Archaeologica 35. Los Angeles: The Cotsen Institute of Archaeology Press, 2014.

Murray, Sarah C. *The Collapse of the Mycenaean Economy*. Cambridge: Cambridge University Press, 2017.

Naʾaman, Nadav. "Azariah of Judah and Jeroboam II of Israel." *Vetus Testamentum* 43 (1993): 227–34. https://doi.org/10.1163/156853393X00061

———. *Borders and Districts in Biblical Historiography: Seven Studies in Biblical Geographic Lists*. Jerusalem Biblical Studies 4. Jerusalem: Simor, 1986.

———. "Cow Town or Royal Capital? Evidence for Iron Age Jerusalem." *Biblical Archaeology Review* 23, no. 4 (1997): 43–47, 67.

———. "David's Sojourn in Keilah in Light of the Amarna Letters." *Vetus Testamentum* 60 (2010): 87–97. https://doi.org/10.1163/004249310X12585232748145

———. "Egyptian Centres and the Distribution of the Alphabet in the Levant." *Tel Aviv* 47, no. 1 (2020): 29–54. https://doi.org/10.1080/03344355.2020.1707449

———. "Hiram of Tyre in the Book of Kings and in the Tyrian Records." *Journal of Near Eastern Studies* 78, no. 1 (2019): 75–85. https://doi.org/10.1086/701707

———. "Israel, Edom and Egypt in the 10th Century B.C.E." *Tel Aviv* 19 (1992): 71–93. https://doi.org/10.1179/tav.1992.1992.1.71

———. "Judah and Edom in the Book of Kings and in Historical Reality." In *New Perspectives on Old Testament Prophecy and History. Essays in Honour of Hans M. Barstad*, edited by Rannfrid I. Thelle, Terje Stordalen, and Mervyn E. J. Richardson, 197–211. Vetus Testamentum Supplements 168. Leiden; Boston: Brill, 2015.

———. "Solomon's District List (1 Kings 4, 7–19) and the Assyrian Province System in Palestine." *Ugarit-Forschungen* 33 (2001): 419–36.

———. "Sources and Composition in the History of Solomon." In *The Age of Solomon: Scholarship at the Turn of the Millennium*, edited by Lowell K. Handy, 57–80. Studies in the History and Culture of the Ancient Near East 11. Leiden; New York: Brill, 1997.

———. "The Contribution of the Amarna Letters to the Debate on Jerusalem's Political Position in the Tenth Century B.C.E." *Bulletin of the American Schools of Oriental Research* 304 (1996): 17–27. https://doi.org/10.2307/1357438

———. "The Contribution of the Suḫu Inscriptions to the Historical Research of the Kingdoms of Israel and Judah." *Journal of Near Eastern Studies* 66 (2007): 107–22. https://doi.org/10.1086/519031

Nam, Roger S. *Portrayals of Economic Exchange in the Book of Kings*. Biblical Interpretation Series 112. Leiden; Boston: Brill, 2012.

Namdar, Dvory, Ayelet Gilboa, Ronny Neumann, Israel Finkelstein, and Steve Weiner. "Cinnamaldehyde in Early Iron Age Phoenician Flasks Raises the Possibility of Levantine Trade with South East Asia." *Mediterranean Archaeology and Archaeometry* 12, no. 3 (2013): 1–19.

Naveh, Joseph. "Achish-Ikausu in the Light of the Ekron Dedication." *Bulletin of the American Schools of Oriental Research* 310 (1998): 35–37. https://doi.org/10.2307/1357576

———. "Nameless People." *Israel Exploration Journal* 40 (1990): 108–23.

Negbi, Ora. *The Hoards of Goldwork from Tell El-'Ajjul*. Studies in Mediterranean Archaeology 25. Göteborg: Studies in Mediterranean Archaeology, 1970.

Niemann, Hermann Michael. "The Socio-Political Shadow Cast by the Biblical Solomon." In *The Age of Solomon: Scholarship at the Turn of the Millennium*, edited by Lowell K. Handy, 252–99. Studies in the History and Culture of the Ancient Near East 11. Leiden; New York: Brill, 1997.

Nightingale, Georg. "Lefkandi: An Important Node in the International Exchange Network of Jewellery and Personal Adornment." In *Between the Aegean and Baltic Seas: Prehistory across Borders: Proceedings of the International Conference Bronze and Early Iron Age Interconnections and Contemporary Developments between the Aegean and the Regions of the Balkan Peninsula, Central and Northern Europe, University of Zagreb, 11-14 April 2005*, edited by Ioanna Galanaki, Helena Tomas, Yannis Galanakis, and Robert Laffineur, 421–430. Aegaeum (Annales d'archéologie égéenne de l'Université de Liège et UT-PASP) 27. Liège, Belgique; Austin, TX: Universitè de Liège, Histoire de l'art et archéologie de la Grèce antique; University of Texas at Austin, Program in Aegean Scripts and Prehistory, 2007.

Noth, Martin. *The Deuteronomistic History*. Translated by David J. A. Clines. Journal for the Study of the Old Testament Supplement Series 15. Sheffield: JSOT Press, 1981.

Oblath, Michael D. "Of Pharaohs and Kings – Whence the Exodus?" *Journal for the Study of the Old Testament* 87 (2000): 23–42. https://doi.org/10.1177/030908920002508702

Oded, R. A. "Taxation in Biblical Israel." *Journal of Religious Ethics* 12, no. 2 (1984): 162–82.

Olley, John W. "Pharaoh's Daughter, Solomon's Palace, and the Temple: Another Look at the Structure of 1 Kings 1–11." *Journal for the Study of the Old Testament* 27, no. 3 (2003): 355–69. https://doi.org/10.1177/030908920302700305

Olyan, Saul M. "Honor, Shame, and Covenant Relations in Ancient Israel and Its Environment." *Journal of Biblical Literature* 115 (1996): 201–18. https://doi.org/10.2307/3266852

Oren, Eliezer D., ed. *The Sea Peoples and Their World: A Reassessment*. Philadelphia: University of Pennsylvania Press, 2013.

Papadopoulos, John K. "Phantom Euboians." *Journal of Mediterranean Archaeology* 10, no. 2 (1997): 191–219. https://doi.org/10.1558/jmea.v10i2.191

Park, Kim Ian. "The Limits to Solomon's Reign: A Response to Amos Frisch." *Journal for the Study of the Old Testament* 16, no. 51 (1991): 15–21. https://doi.org/10.1177/030908929101605102

Parr, Peter J. "Contacts between North West Arabia and Jordan in the Late Bronze and Iron Ages." In *Studies in the History and Archaeology of Jordan*, edited by A. Hadidi, 127–133. Amman: Hashemite Kingdom of Jordan, Department of Antiquities, 1982.

———. "Pottery of the Late Second Millennium B.C. From North West Arabia and Its Historical Implications." In *Araby the Blest: Studies in Arabian Archaeology*, edited by Daniel T. Potts, 73–90. Copenhagen: Museum Tusculanum Press, University of Copenhagen, 1988.

———. "Pottery, People and Politics." In *Archaeology in the Levant: Essays for Kathleen Kenyon*, edited by Roger Moorey and Peter J. Parr, 203–9. Warminster: Aris & Phillips, 1978.

Parr, Peter J., G. Lankester Harding, and John E. Dayton. *Preliminary Survey in N.W. Arabia, 1968*. London: Institute of Archaeology, 1970.
Pearce, R. A. "Shiloh and Jer. VII 12, 14 & 15." *Vetus Testamentum* 23, no. 1 (1973): 105–8. https://doi.org/10.1163/156853373X00252
Pioske, Daniel. "David's Jerusalem: A Sense of Place." *Near Eastern Archaeology* 76, no. 1 (2013): 4–15. https://doi.org/10.5615/neareastarch.76.1.0004
———. *David's Jerusalem: Between Memory and History*. New York; London: Taylor & Francis, 2015.
———. *Memory in a Time of Prose: Studies in Epistemology, Hebrew Scribalism, and the Biblical Past*. Oxford; New York: Oxford University Press, 2018.
———. "Placing the Past: On Writing a History of 'David's Jerusalem.'" *The Bible and Interpretation*, October 2014. http://www.bibleinterp.com/articles/2014/11/pio388012.shtml
Podany, Amanda H. *Brotherhood of Kings: How International Relations Shaped the Ancient Near East*. Oxford; New York: Oxford University Press, 2010.
Polanyi, Karl. "Ports of Trade in Early Societies." In *Primitive, Archaic, and Modern Economies: Essays of Karl Polanyi*, edited by G. Dalton, 238–60. Boston: Beacon Press, 1971.
———. *Primitive, Archaic, and Modern Economies; Essays of Karl Polanyi*. Edited by G. Dalton. Boston: Beacon Press, 1971.
———. *The Great Transformation*. Boston: Beacon Press, 1962.
Popham, Mervyn R. ed., *Lefkandi III: The Toumba Cemetery: The Excavations of 1981, 1984, 1986 and 1992-4*. British School at Athens Supplementary Volume 29. London: British School of Athens, 1996.
Popham, Mervyn R., P. G. Calligas, Leyland Hugh Sackett, eds. *Lefkandi II: The Protogeometric Building at Toumba*. British School at Athens Supplementary Volume 22–23. London: British School of Archaeology at Athens, 1993.
Popham, Mervyn R., and Irene S. Lemos. "A Euboean Warrior Trader." *Oxford Journal of Archaeology* 14, no. 2 (1995): 151–57. https://doi.org/10.1111/j.1468-0092.1995.tb00391.x
Popham, Mervyn R., Leyland Hugh Sackett, Petros G. Themelis, eds. *Lefkandi I, the Iron Age*. British School at Athens Supplementary Volume 11. London: Thames and Hudson, 1979.
Porter, Benjamin W. *Complex Communities: The Archaeology of Early Iron Age West-Central Jordan*. Tucson: University of Arizona Press, 2013.
Prag, Kay. "Jerusalem in the Third and Second Millennia BC: The Archaeological Evidence." In *Jerusalem before Islam*, edited by Zeidan Abdel-Kafi Kafafi and Robert Schick, 54–68. BAR International Series 1699. Oxford: Archaeopress, 2007.
———. *Re-Excavating Jerusalem: Archival Archaeology*. Oxford: Oxford University Press, 2018.
Pratico, Gary D. "Nelson Glueck's 1938–1940 Excavations at Tell El-Kheleifeh: A Reappraisal." *Bulletin of the American Schools of Oriental Research* 259 (1985): 1–32. https://doi.org/10.2307/1356795
———. *Nelson Glueck's 1938-1940 Excavations at Tell El-Kheleifeh - A Reappraisal*. Atlanta: Scholars Press, 1993.
Priest, John. "The Covenant of Brothers." *Journal of Biblical Literature* 84 (1965): 400–406. https://doi.org/10.2307/3264866
Rainey, Anson F. "Compulsory Labour Gangs in Ancient Israel." *Israel Exploration Journal* 20 (1970): 191–202.
———. "Looking for Bethel: An Exercise in Historical Geography." In *Confronting the Past: Archaeological and Historical Essays on Ancient Israel in Honor of William G. Dever*, edited by Seymour Gitin, J. Edward Wright, and J. P. Dessel, 269–73. Winona Lake: Eisenbrauns, 2006.
———. "Possible Involvement of Tell Eṣ-Ṣâfî (Tel Ẓafit) in the Amarna Correspondence." In *Tell Es-Safi/Gath: The 1996-2005 Seasons*, edited by Aren M. Maeir, 133–40. 2 volumes. Ägypten und Altes Testament 69. Wiesbaden: Harrassowitz, 2012.
Rainey, Anson F. *The El-Amarna Correspondence: A New Edition of the Cuneiform Letters from the Site of El-Amarna Based on Collations of All Extant Tablets*, edited by William M. Schniedewind. Leiden; Boston: Brill, 2014.

Rainey, Anson F., and R. Steven Notley. *The Sacred Bridge: Carta's Atlas of the Biblical World.* Jerusalem: Carta, 2006.

Regev, Johanna, Yuval Gadot, Helena Roth, Joe Uziel, Ortal Chalaf, Doron Ben-Ami, Eugenia Mintz, Lior Regev, and Elisabetta Boaretto. "Middle Bronze Age Jerusalem: Recalculating Its Character and Chronology." *Radiocarbon* 63, no. 3 (2021): 853–83.

Regev, Johanna, Yuval Gadot, Joe Uziel, Ortal Chalaf, Yiftah Shalev, Helena Roth, Nitsan Shalom, et al. "Radiocarbon Chronology of Iron Age Jerusalem Reveals Calibration Offsets and Architectural Developments." *Proceedings of the National Academy of Sciences* 121, no. 19 (May 7, 2024): e2321024121. https://doi.org/10.1073/pnas.2321024121

Reich, Ronny, and Eli Shukron. "A New Segment of the Middle Bronze Fortification in the City of David." *Tel Aviv* 37 (2010): 141–53.

———. *Excavations in the City of David, Jerusalem (1995-2010).* University Park: Penn State University Press, 2021.

———. "The Middle Bronze Age II Water System in Jerusalem." In *Jérusalem Antique et Médiévale. Mélanges En l'honneur d'Ernest-Marie Laperrousaz*, edited by C Arnould-Béhar and André Lemaire, 17–29. Paris: Peeters, 2011.

Reinhartz, Adele. "Anonymous Women and the Collapse of the Monarchy: A Study in Narrative Technique." In *The Feminist Companion to Samuel and Kings*, edited by Athalya Brenner, 43–65. Feminist Companion to the Bible 5. Sheffield: Sheffield Academic, 1994.

Reis, Pamela Tamarkin. "Unspeakable Names: Solomon's Tax Collectors." *Zeitschrift für die alttestamentliche Wissenschaft* 120 (2008): 261–66. https://doi.org/10.1515/ZAW.2008.016

Renfrew, Colin. "Introduction: Peer Polity Interaction and Socio-Political Change." In *Peer Polity Interaction and Socio-Political Change*, edited by Colin Renfrew and John F. Cherry, 1–18. New Directions in Archaeology. Cambridge; New York: Cambridge University Press, 1986.

———. *The Emergence of Civilisation: The Cyclades and the Aegean in the Third Millennium B.C.* London: Methuen, 1972.

———. "Trade as Action at a Distance: Questions of Integration and Communication." In *Ancient Civilization and Trade*, edited by Jeremy A. Sabloff and C. C. Lamberg-Karlovsky, 3–59. Albuquerque: University of New Mexico Press, 1975.

Revere, Robert B. "'No Man's Coast': Ports of Trade in the Eastern Mediterranean." In *Trade and Market in the Early Empires: Economies in History and Theory*, edited by Karl Polanyi, Conrad M. Arensberg, and Harry W. Pearson, 38–63. Glencoe: Free Press, 1957.

Richelle, Matthieu. "Elusive Scrolls: Could Any Hebrew Literature Have Been Written Prior to the Eight Century BCE?" *Vetus Testamentum* 66 (2016): 1–39. https://doi.org/10.1163/15685330-12341250

———. "Quelques Nouvelles Lectures Sur L'ostracon de Khirbet Qeiyafa." *Semitica* 57 (2015): 147–62.

Robin, Simone Burger. "Analysis, Interpretation and Dating of a Problematic Egyptian Statuary Fragment Discovered in Jerusalem." In *Solomon and Shishak: Current Perspectives from Archaeology, Epigraphy, History and Chronology: Proceedings of the Third BICANE Colloquium Held at Sidney Sussex College, Cambridge 26-27 March, 2011*, edited by Peter James and Peter van der Veen, 258–63. BAR International Series, 2732; Oxford: Archaeopress, 2015.

Rollston, Christopher A. "The Dating of the Early Royal Byblian Phoenician Inscriptions: A Response to Benjamin Sass." *Maarav* 15, no. 1 (2008): 57–93.

———. "The Phoenician Script of the Tel Zayit Abecedary and Putative Evidence for Israelite Literacy." In *Literate Culture and Tenth-Century Canaan: The Tel Zayit Abecedary in Context*, edited by Ron E. Tappy and P. Kyle McCarter, 61–96. Winona Lake: Eisenbrauns, 2008.

———. *Writing and Literacy in the World of Ancient Israel: Epigraphic Evidence from the Iron Age.* Atlanta: Society of Biblical Literature, 2010.

Rollston, Christopher, Yosef Garfinkel, Kyle H. Keimer, Gillan Davis, and Saar Ganor. "The Jerubbaʻal Inscription from Khirbat Al-Raʻi: A Proto-Canaanite (Early Alphabetic) Inscription." *Jerusalem Journal of Archaeology* 2 (2021): 1–15.

Rost, Leonhard. *The Succession to the Throne of David*. Translated by Michael D. Rutter and David M. Gunn. Sheffield: Almond Press, 1982.
Rothenberg, Beno. *Timna: Valley of the Biblical Copper Mines*. London: Thames and Hudson, 1972.
Rothenberg, Beno, and Jonathan Glass. "The Midianite Pottery." In *Midian, Moab, and Edom: The History and Archaeology of Late Bronze and Iron Age Jordan and North-West Arabia*, edited by John F. A. Sawyer and David J. A. Clines, 65–124. Journal for the Study of the Old Testament Supplemental Series 24. Sheffield: Journal for the Study of the Old Testament Press, 1983.
Routledge, Bruce E. "Is There an Iron Age Levant?" *Revista Del Instituto de Historia Antigua Oriental* 18 (2017), 49–76.
———. *Moab in the Iron Age: Hegemony, Polity, Archaeology*. Philadelphia: University of Pennsylvania Press, 2004.
Rowlands, M. J. "The Archaeological Interpretation of Prehistoric Metalworking." *World Archaeology* 3, no. 2 (1971): 210–24. https://doi.org/10.1080/00438243.1969.9979502
Russell, Stephen C. *Space, Land, Territory, and the Study of the Bible*. Leiden: Brill, 2017.
———. *The King and the Land: A Geography of Royal Power in the Biblical World*. Oxford: Oxford University Press, 2016.
Sabloff, Jeremy A., and C. C. Lamberg-Karlovsky, eds. *Ancient Civilization and Trade*. Albuquerque: University of New Mexico Press, 1975.
Sagrillo, Troy L. "Shoshenq I and Biblical Šîšaq: A Philological Defense of Their Traditional Equation." In *Solomon and Shishak: Current Perspectives from Archaeology, Epigraphy, History and Chronology; Proceedings of the Third BICANE Colloquium Held at Sidney Sussex College, Cambridge 26-27 March, 2011*. BAR International Series 2732. Oxford: Archaeopress, 2015.
———. "The Geographic Origins of the 'Bubastite' Dynasty and Possible Locations for the Royal Residence and Burial Place of Shoshenq I." In *The Libyan Period in Egypt: Historical and Cultural Studies into the 21st-24th Dynasties: Proceedings of a Conference at Leiden University, 25-27 October 2007*, edited by Gerard P. F. Broekman, Robert Johannes Demarée, and Olaf E. Kaper, 341–60. Leiden: Peeters, 2009.
Sanders, Seth L. "From People to Public in the Iron Age Levant." In *Organization, Representation, and Symbols of Power in the Ancient Near East: Proceedings of the 54th Rencontre Assyriologique Internationale at Würzburg 20-25 July 2008*, edited by Gernot Wilhelm, 191–211. Winona Lake: Eisenbrauns, 2012.
———. *The Invention of Hebrew*. Urbana: University of Illinois Press, 2009.
———. "What Was the Alphabet For? The Rise of Written Vernaculars and the Making of Israelite National Literature." *Maarav* 11, no. 1 (2004): 25–56. https://doi.org/10.1086/MAR200411103
———. "Writing and Early Iron Age Israel: Before National Scripts, Beyond Nations and States." In *Literate Culture and Tenth-Century Canaan: The Tel Zayit Abecedary in Context*, edited by Ron E. Tappy and P. Kyle McCarter, 97–112. Winona Lake: Eisenbrauns, 2008.
Sapir-Hen, Lidar, and Erez Ben-Yosef. "The Emergence of a Nomadic Desert Polity: An Archaeozoological Perspective." *Archaeological and Anthropological Sciences* 14, no. 12 (2022): 232. https://doi.org/10.1007/s12520-022-01694-0
Sass, Benjamin. *The Alphabet at the Turn of the Millennium: The West Semitic Alphabet ca. 1150-850 BCE: The Antiquity of the Arabian, Greek and Phrygian Alphabets*. Tel Aviv: Emery and Claire Yass Publications in Archaeology, 2005.
———. "The Emergence of Monumental West Semitic Alphabetic Writing, with an Emphasis on Byblos." *Semitica* 59 (2017): 109–41.
———. "Wenamun and His Levant – 1075 B.C. or 925 B.C.?" *Egypt and the Levant* 12 (2002): 247–55.
Sass, Benjamin and Israel Finkelstein. "The Swan-Song of Proto-Canaanite in the Ninth Century BCE in Light of an Alphabetic Inscription from Megiddo." *Semitica et Classica* 9 (2016): 19–42. https://doi.org/10.1484/J.SEC.5.112723
Schade, Aaron. "The Syntax and Literary Structure of the Phoenician Inscription of Yeḥimilk." *Maarav* 13, no. 1 (2006): 119–22. https://doi.org/10.1086/MAR200613106

Schipper, Bernd U. "Egypt and Israel: The Ways of Cultural Contacts in the Late Bronze Age and Iron Age (20th–26th Dynasty)." *Journal of Ancient Egyptian Interconnections* 4, no. 3 (2012): 30–47. https://doi.org/10.2458/azu_jaei_v04i3_schipper

———. "Nocheinmal zur Pharaonentochter – ein Gespräch mit Karl Jansen-Winkeln." *Biblische Notizen* 111 (2002): 90–98.

———. "Salomo und die Pharaonentochter – zum historischen Kern von 1 Kön 7,8." *Biblische Notizen* 102 (2000): 84–94.

Schley, Donald G. *Shiloh: A Biblical City in Tradition and History*. Journal for the Study of the Old Testament Supplement Series 63. Sheffield: Journal for the Study of the Old Testament Press, 1989.

Schloen, J. David. "Caravans, Kenites, and Casus Belli: Enmity and Alliance in the Song of Deborah." *Catholic Biblical Quarterly* 55, no. 1 (1993): 18–38.

———. *The House of the Father as Fact and Symbol: Patrimonialism in Ugarit and the Ancient Near East*. Studies in the Archaeology and History of the Levant 2. Winona Lake: Eisenbrauns, 2001.

Schniedewind, William M. "Excavating the Text of 1 Kings 9: In Search of the Gates of Solomon." In *Historical Biblical Archaeology and the Future: The New Pragmatism*, edited by Thomas E. Levy, 241–49. London; Oakville: Equinox Publishing, 2010.

———. *Society and the Promise to David: The Reception History of 2 Samuel 7:1-17*. New York: Oxford University Press, 1999.

———. "The Search for Gibeah: Notes on the Historical Geography of Central Benjamin." In *"I Will Speak the Riddles of Ancient Times": Archaeological and Historical Studies in Honor of Amihai Mazar on the Occasion of His Sixtieth Birthday*, edited by Aren M. Maeir and Pierre de Miroschedji, 711–22. Winona Lake: Eisenbrauns, 2006.

Schortman, Edward M. "Interregional Interaction in Prehistory: The Need for a New Perspective." *American Antiquity* 54, no. 1 (1989): 52–65. https://doi.org/10.2307/281331

Schortman, Edward M., and Patricia A. Urban. "Modeling Interregional Interaction in Prehistory." *Advances in Archaeological Method and Theory* 11 (1987): 37–95. https://doi.org/10.1016/B978-0-12-003111-5.50005-1

Schrader, Sarah A., Stuart Tyson Smith, Sandra Olsen, and Michele Buzon. "Symbolic Equids and Kushite State Formation: A Horse Burial at Tombos." *Antiquity* 92, no. 362 (2018): 383–97. https://doi.org/10.15184/aqy.2017.239

Schreiber, Nicola. *The Cypro-Phoenician Pottery of the Iron Age*. Culture and History of the Ancient Near East 13. Leiden; Boston: Brill, 2003.

Schulman, Alan R. "Diplomatic Marriage in the Egyptian New Kingdom." *Journal of Near Eastern Studies* 38, no. 3 (1979): 177–93. https://doi.org/10.1086/372739

Schuster, Ruth. "In First, Ivory Panels Mentioned in Bible Found in Jerusalem – Archaeology." *Ha'aretz*, September 8, 2022. https://www.haaretz.com/archaeology/2022-09-08/ty-article/.premium/in-first-ivory-panels-mentioned-in-bible-found-in-jerusalem/00000183-0c93-d968-abc7-4cf315aa0000

Scott, R. B. Y. "Solomon and the Beginnings of Wisdom in Israel." In *Wisdom in Israel and in the Ancient Near East Presented to Professor Harold Henry Rowley*, edited by Martin Noth and D. Winston Thomas, 262–79. Supplements to Vetus Testamentum 3. Leiden: Brill, 1960.

Sergi, Omer. "Saul, David, and the Formation of the Israelite Monarchy: Revisiting the Historical and Literary Context of 1 Samuel 9–2 Samuel 5." In *Saul, Benjamin, and the Emergence of Monarchy in Israel: Biblical and Archaeological Perspectives*, edited by Joachim J. Krause, Omer Sergi, and Kristin Weingart, 57–91. Atlanta: SBL Press, 2020.

Sergi, Omer, Hannes Bezzel, Yoav Tsur, and Karen Covello-Paran. "Ḥorvat Ṭevet in the Jezreel Valley: A Royal Israelite Estate." In *New Studies in the Archaeology of Northern Israel*, edited by Karen Covello-Paran, Adi Erlich, and Ron Beeri, 31*–48*. Jerusalem: Israel Antiquities Authority, 2021.

Service, Elman. *Primitive Social Organization*. 2nd ed. New York: Random House, 1971.

Sharon, Ilan, Ayelet Gilboa, A. J. Timothy Jull, and Elisabetta Boaretto. "Report on the First Stage of the Iron Age Dating Project in Israel: Supporting a Low Chronology." *Radiocarbon* 49, no. 1 (2007): 1–46. https://doi.org/10.1017/S0033822200041886

Shectman, Sarah. "Back to the Past: An Overview of Feminist Historical Criticism." In *Feminist Interpretation of the Bible in Retrospect*, edited by Susanne Scholz, 55–73. Volume 3. Sheffield: Sheffield Phoenix Press, 2016.

Sherratt, Andrew, and Susan Sherratt. "The Growth of the Mediterranean Economy in the Early First Millennium BC." *World Archaeology* 24, no. 3 (1993): 361–78. https://doi.org/10.1080/00438243.1993.9980214

Sherratt, Susan. "Greeks and Phoenicians: Perceptions of Trade and Traders in the Early First Millennium BC." In *Social Archaeologies of Trade and Exchange: Exploring Relationships among People, Places, and Things*, edited by Alexander A. Bauer and Anna S. Agbe-Davies, 119–42. Walnut Creek: Left Coast Press, 2010.

———. "Phoenicians in the Aegean and Aegean Silver, 11th–9th Centuries BC." In *Les Phéniciens, Les Puniques et Les Autres: Échanges et Identités En Méditerranée Ancienne*, edited by Luisa Bonadies, Iva Chirpanlieva, and Élodie Guillon. Orient & Méditerranée 31. Paris: Éditions de Boccard, 2019.

———. "'Sea Peoples' and the Economic Structure of the Late Second Millennium in the Eastern Mediterranean." In *Mediterranean Peoples in Transition: Thirteenth to Early Tenth Centuries BCE*, edited by Seymour Gitin, Amihai Mazar, and Ephraim Stern, 292–313. Jerusalem: Israel Exploration Society, 1998.

———. "The Mediterranean Economy: 'Globalization' at the End of the Second Millennium B.C.E." In *Symbiosis, Symbolism, and the Power of the Past: Canaan, Ancient Israel, and Their Neighbors from the Late Bronze Age through Roman Palaestina*, edited by William G. Dever and Seymour Gitin, 37–62. Winona Lake: Eisenbrauns, 2003.

Shortland, Andrew. "Shishak, King of Egypt: The Challenges of Egyptian Calendrical Chronology in the Iron Age." In *The Bible and Radiocarbon Dating: Archaeology, Text and Science*, edited by Thomas E. Levy and Thomas Higham, 43–54. London; Oakville: Equinox Publishing, 2005.

Silver, Morris. *Prophets and Markets: The Political Economy of Ancient Israel*. Boston; Hingham: Kluwer-Nijhoff, 1983.

Simkins, Ronald A. "Family in the Political Economy of Monarchic Judah." *The Bible and Critical Theory* 1, no. 1 (2004): 1–17. https://doi.org/10.2104/bc040006

———. "Patronage and the Political Economy of Monarchic Israel." *Semeia* 87 (1999): 123–44.

Singer, Itamar. "Egyptians, Canaanites, and Philistines in the Period of the Emergence of Israel." In *From Nomadism to Monarchy: Archaeological and Historical Aspects of Early Israel*, edited by Israel Finkelstein and Nadav Na'aman, 282–338. Jerusalem: Israel Exploration Society, 1994.

Singer-Avitz, Lily. "Epilogue: The Dating of Qurayyah Painted Ware in the Southern Levant." In *The Ancient Pottery of Israel and Its Neighbors from the Middle Bronze Age Through the Late Bronze Age (Volume 3)*, edited by S. Gitin, 388–389. Jerusalem: Israel Exploration Society, 2019.

———. "The Earliest Settlement at Kadesh Barnea." *Tel Aviv* 35, no. 1 (2008): 73–81. https://doi.org/10.1179/tav.2008.2008.1.73

———. "The Qurayyah Painted Ware." In *The Renewed Archaeological Excavations at Lachish (1973–1994)*, edited by David Ussishkin, 1280–87. Tel Aviv: Emery and Claire Yass Publications in Archaeology, 2004.

Smend, Rudolf. "The Law and the Nations: A Contribution to Deuteronomistic Tradition History." In *Reconsidering Israel and Judah: Recent Studies on the Deuteronomistic History*, translated by P. T. Daniels; edited by Gary N. Knoppers and J. Gordon McConville, 494–509. Winona Lake: Eisenbrauns, 2000.

Smith, Neil G., Yuval Goren, and Thomas E. Levy. "The Petrography of Iron Age Edom: From the Lowlands to the Highlands." In *New Insights into the Iron Age Archaeology of Edom, Southern Jordan: Surveys, Excavations and Research from the University of California, San Diego & Department of Antiquities of Jordan, Edom Lowlands Regional Archaeology Project (ELRAP)*, edited by Thomas E. Levy, Mohammad

Najjar, Erez Ben-Yosef, and Neil G. Smith, 460–91. 2 volumes. Monumenta Archaeologica 35. Los Angeles: The Cotsen Institute of Archaeology Press, 2014.

Smith, Neil G., and Thomas E. Levy. "Iron Age Ceramics from Edom: A New Typology." In *New Insights into the Iron Age Archaeology of Edom, Southern Jordan: Surveys, Excavations and Research from the University of California, San Diego & Department of Antiquities of Jordan, Edom Lowlands Regional Archaeology Project (ELRAP)*, edited by Thomas E. Levy, Mohammad Najjar, Erez Ben-Yosef, and Neil G. Smith, 296–459. 2 volumes. Monumenta Archaeologica 35. Los Angeles: The Cotsen Institute of Archaeology Press, 2014.

Smith, Neil G., Mohammad Najjar, and Thomas E. Levy. "New Perspectives on the Iron Age Edom Steppe and Highlands: Khirbat Al-Malayqtah, Khirbat Al-Kur, Khirbat Al-Iraq Shmaliya, and Tawilan." In *New Insights into the Iron Age Archaeology of Edom, Southern Jordan: Surveys, Excavations and Research from the University of California, San Diego & Department of Antiquities of Jordan, Edom Lowlands Regional Archaeology Project (ELRAP)*, edited by Thomas E. Levy, Mohammad Najjar, Erez Ben-Yosef, and Neil G. Smith, 246–95. 2 volumes. Monumenta Archaeologica 35. Los Angeles: The Cotsen Institute of Archaeology Press, 2014.

Sogas, Judith Muñoz. "Was Knossos a Home for Phoenician Traders?" In *Greek Art in Motion: Studies in Honour of Sir John Boardman on the Occasion of His 90th Birthday*, edited by Rui Morais et al., 408–416. Oxford: Archaeopress, 2019.

Stager, Lawrence E. "The Archaeology of the Family in Ancient Israel." *Bulletin of the American Schools of Oriental Research* 260 (1985): 1–35. https://doi.org/10.2307/1356862

———. "The Patrimonial Kingdom of Solomon." In *Symbiosis, Symbolism, and the Power of the Past: Canaan, Ancient Israel, and Their Neighbors from the Late Bronze Age through Roman Palaestina*, edited by William G. Dever and Seymour Gitin, 63–74. Winona Lake: Eisenbrauns, 2003.

Stager, Lawrence E., and Philip J. King. *Life in Biblical Israel*. Library of Ancient Israel. Louisville: Westminster John Knox Press, 2001.

Stager, Lawrence E., Daniel M. Master, and Adam J. Aja, editors. *Ashkelon 7: The Iron Age I*. University Park: Eisenbrauns, 2020.

Stansell, Gary. "The Gift in Ancient Israel." *Semeia* 87 (1999): 65–90.

Stein, Gil J. "From Passive Periphery to Active Agents: Emerging Perspectives in the Archaeology of Interregional Interaction." *American Anthropologist* 104, no. 3 (2002): 903–16. https://doi.org/10.1525/aa.2002.104.3.903

———. "Local Identities and Interaction Spheres: Modeling Regional Variation in the Ubaid Horizon." In *Beyond the Ubaid: Transformation and Integration in the Late Prehistoric Societies of the Middle East*, edited by Robert A. Carter and Graham Philip, 23–44. Studies in Ancient Oriental Civilization 63. Chicago: Oriental Institute of the University of Chicago, 2010.

———. "Rethinking World Systems: Power, Distance, and Diasporas in the Dynamics of Inter-Regional Interaction." In *World Systems Theory in Practice: Leadership, Production, and Exchange*, edited by P. Nicholas Kardulias, 153–77. Lanham: Rowman and Littlefield, 1999.

Steindorff, Georg. "The Statuette of an Egyptian Commissioner in Syria." *Journal of Egyptian Archaeology* 25, no. 1 (1939): 30–33, plate VII. https://doi.org/10.1177/030751333902500104

Steiner, Margreet L. "Jerusalem in the Late Bronze and Iron Ages. Archaeological Versus Literary Sources?," In *Jerusalem before Islam*, edited by Zeidan Abdel-Kafi Kafafi and Robert Schick, 69–74. BAR International Series 1699. Oxford: Archaeopress, 2007.

———. "Re-Dating the Terraces of Jerusalem." *Israel Exploration Journal* 44, no. 1 (1994): 13–20.

———. "The 'Palace of David' Reconsidered in the Light of Earlier Excavations." *Bible and Interpretation*, September 2009. http://www.bibleinterp.com/articles/palace_2468.shtml

Stone, Bryan Jack. "The Philistines and Acculturation: Culture Change and Ethnic Continuity in the Iron Age." *Bulletin of the American Schools of Oriental Research* 298 (1995): 7–32. https://doi.org/10.2307/1357082

Streit, Katharina. "A Maximalist Interpretation of the Execration Texts – Archaeological and Historical Implications of a High Chronology." *Journal of Ancient Egyptian Interconnections* 13 (2017): 59–69.

Struever, Stuart. "The Hopewell Interaction Sphere in Riverine – Western Great Lakes Culture History." In *Hopewellian Studies*, edited by Joseph R. Caldwell and Robert L. Hall, 85–106. Illinois State Museum Scientific Papers 12. Springfield: Illinois State Museum, 1964.

Sukenik, Naama, David Iluz, Zohar Amar, Alexander Varvak, Orit Shamir, and Erez Ben-Yosef. "Early Evidence of Royal Purple Dyed Textile from Timna Valley (Israel)." *PLOS ONE* 16, no. 1 (2021): e0245897. https://doi.org/10.1371/journal.pone.0245897

Suriano, Matthew James. "The Formulaic Epilogue for a King in the Book of Kings in Light of Royal Funerary Rites in Ancient Israel and the Levant." Ph.D. dissertation. University of California, Los Angeles: 2008.

Sweeney, Marvin A. "A Reassessment of the Masoretic and Septuagint Versions of the Jeroboam Narratives in 1 Kings/3 Kingdoms 11–14." *Journal for the Study of Judaism in the Persian, Hellenistic, and Roman Period* 38, no. 2 (2007): 165–95. https://doi.org/10.1163/157006307X180174

———. "The Critique of Solomon in the Josianic Edition of the Deuteronomistic History." *Journal of Biblical Literature* 114, no. 4 (1995): 607–22. https://doi.org/10.2307/3266477

Tadmor, Hayim. "Que and Muṣri." *Israel Exploration Journal* 11, no. 3 (1961): 143–50.

Tappy, Ron E., P. Kyle McCarter, Marilyn J. Lundberg, and Bruce Zuckerman. "An Abecedary of the Mid-Tenth Century B.C.E. from the Judaean Shephelah." *Bulletin of the American Schools of Oriental Research* 344 (2006): 5–46. https://doi.org/10.1086/BASOR25066976

Taylor, John. "The Third Intermediate Period (1069–664 BCE)." In *The Oxford History of Ancient Egypt*, edited by Ian Shaw, 330–68. Oxford: Oxford University Press, 2002.

Tebes, Juan Manuel. "A New Analysis of the Iron Age I 'Chiefdom' of Tel Masos (Beersheba Valley)." *Aula Orientalis* 21 (2003): 63–78.

———. "Pottery Makers and Premodern Exchange in the Fringes of Egypt: An Approximation to the Distribution of Iron Age Midianite Pottery." *Buried History* 43 (2007): 11–26.

Theis, Christoffer. "Θεκεμείνας Und תַּחְפְּנֵיס in 1 Könige 11,19," *Journal of Septuagint and Cognate Studies* 49 (2016): 50–60.

Thomas, Zachary. "On the Archaeology of the 10th Century BCE Israel and the Idea of the 'State,'" *Palestine Exploration Quarterly* 153, no. 3 (2021): 244–57. https://doi.org/10.1080/00310328.2021.1886488

Thomas, Zachary, Kyle H. Keimer, and Yosef Garfinkel. "The Early Iron Age IIA Ceramic Assemblage from Khirbet al-Raʿi." *Jerusalem Journal of Archaeology* 1 (2021): 375–449.

Thompson, Christine M., and Sheldon Skaggs. "King Solomon's Silver? Southern Phoenician Hacksilber Hoards and the Location of Tarshish." *Internet Archaeology* 35 (2013). https://doi.org/10.11141/ia.35.6

Thompson, Thomas L. *Early History of the Israelite People: From the Written and Archaeological Sources*. Leiden; New York: Brill, 1992.

———. *The Historicity of the Patriarchal Narratives: The Quest for the Historical Abraham*. Beihefte zur Zeitschrift für die alttestamentliche Wissenschaft 133. Berlin; New York: Walter de Gruyter, 1974.

Torijano, Pablo A. *Solomon the Esoteric King: From King to Magus*. Supplements to the Journal for the Study of Judaism 73. Leiden; Boston: Brill, 2002.

Turkanik, Andrzej S. *Of Kings and Reigns: A Study of Translation Technique in the Gamma/Gamma Section of 3 Reigns (1 Kings)*. Tübingen: Mohr Siebeck, 2008.

Vaelske, Veit, Michael Bode, and Christian E. Loeben. "Early Iron Age Copper Trail between Wadi Arabah and Egypt during the 21st Dynasty: First Results from Tanis, ca. 1000 BC." *Zeitschrift Für Orient-Archäologie* 12 (2019), 184–203.

Vaknin, Yoav, Ron Shaar, Oded Lipschits, Amihai Mazar, Aren M. Maeir, Yosef Garfinkel, Liora Freud, Avraham Faust, Ron E. Tappy, Igor Kreimerman, Saar Ganor, Karen Covello-Paran, Omer Sergi, Ze'ev Herzog, Rami Arav, Zvi Lederman, Stefan Münger, Alexander Fantalkin, Seymour Gitin, and Erez Ben-Yosef. "Reconstructing Biblical Military Campaigns Using Geomagnetic Field Data." *Proceedings of the National Academy of Sciences* 119, no. 44 (2022): e2209117119. https://doi.org/10.1073/pnas.2209117119

Van Bekkum, Koert. "'The Situation Is More Complicated': Archaeology and Text in the Historical Reconstruction of the Iron Age IIA Southern Levant." In *Exploring the Narrative: Jerusalem and Jordan in the Bronze and Iron Ages: Papers in Honour of Margreet Steiner*, edited by Noor Mulder-Hymans, Jeannette Boertien, and Eveline van der Steen. Library of Hebrew Bible/Old Testament Studies 583. London; New York: Bloomsbury T&T Clark, 2014.

Van der Veen, Peter. "When Pharaohs Ruled Jerusalem." *Biblical Archaeology Review* 39, no. 2 (2013): 42–48, 67.

Van der Veen, Peter, and David Ellis, "'He Placed His Name in Jerusalem': Ramesside Finds from Judah's Capital." In *Solomon and Shishak: Current Perspectives from Archaeology, Epigraphy, History and Chronology: Proceedings of the Third BICANE Colloquium Held at Sidney Sussex College, Cambridge 26-27 March, 2011*, edited by Peter James and Peter van der Veen, 264–73. BAR International Series, 2732; Oxford: Archaeopress, 2015.

Van Seters, John. *Abraham in History and Tradition*. New Haven: Yale University Press, 1975.

Veldhuijzen, H. Alexander, and Thilo Rehren. "Slags and the City: Early Iron Production at Tell Hammeh, Jordan and Tel Beth-Shemesh, Israel." In *Metals and Mines – Studies in Archaeometallurgy*, 189–201. London: Archetype, British Museum, 2007.

Von Rad, Gerhard. "Die Deuteronomistische Geschichtstheologie in Den Königsbüchern." In *Gesammelte Studien Zum Alten Testament*, edited by Gerhard von Rad. Theologische Bücherei 8. München: Chr. Kaiser, 1958.

Waldbaum, Jane C. "Early Greek Contacts with the Southern Levant, Ca. 1000–600 B.C.: The Eastern Perspective." *Bulletin of the American Schools of Oriental Research* 293 (1994): 53–66. https://doi.org/10.2307/1357277

———. "Greeks in the East or Greeks and the East? Problems in the Definition and Recognition of Presence." *Bulletin of the American Schools of Oriental Research* 305 (1997): 1–17. https://doi.org/10.2307/1357743

Waldbaum, Jane C., and Jodi Magness. "The Chronology of Early Greek Pottery: New Evidence from Seventh-Century B. C. Destruction Levels in Israel." *American Journal of Archaeology* 101, no. 1 (1997): 23–40. https://doi.org/10.2307/506248

Wallenfels, Ronald. "Shishak and Shoshenq: A Disambiguation." *Journal of the American Oriental Society* 139, no. 2 (2019): 487–500. https://doi.org/10.7817/jameroriesoci.139.2.0487

Wallerstein, Immanuel. *The Modern World System: Capitalist Agriculture and the Origins of the European World-Economy in the Sixteenth Century*. New York: Academic Press, 1974.

Walsh, Jerome T. "Symmetry and the Sin of Solomon." *Shofar* 12 (1993): 11–27. https://doi.org/10.1353/sho.1993.0102

———. "The Characterization of Solomon in First Kings 1–5." *Catholic Biblical Quarterly* 57 (1995): 471–93.

Walter's Art Gallery. "Statue of a Vizier, Usurped by Pa-di-iset." http://art.thewalters.org/viewwoa.aspx?id=33246

Weber, Max. *Ancient Judaism*. Translated by Hans H. Gerth and Don Martindale. Glencoe: Free Press, 1952.

———. *Economy and Society: An Outline of Interpretive Sociology*. Edited by Guenther Roth and Claus Wittich. Translated by Ephraim Fischoff. New York: Bedminster Press, 1968.

———. *The Protestant Ethic and the Spirit of Capitalism*. Translated by Talcott Parsons. New York: Scribner, 1958.

Weeks, Lloyd. "Metallurgy." In *A Companion to the Archaeology of the Ancient Near East*, edited by Daniel T. Potts, 295–316. Malden: Wiley-Blackwell, 2012.

Weitzman, Steven. *Solomon, the Lure of Wisdom*. Jewish Lives. New Haven: Yale University Press, 2011.

Wente Jr., Edward F. "The Report of Wenamun." In *The Literature of Ancient Egypt: An Anthology of Stories, Instructions, Stelae, Autobiographies, and Poetry*, edited by William Kelly Simpson, 116–124. New Haven; London: Yale University Press, 2003.

Westbrook, R. "Patronage in the Ancient Near East." *Journal of the Economic and Social History of the Orient* 48 (2005): 210–33. https://doi.org/10.1163/1568520054127121

White, Marsha. "'History of Saul's Rise': Saulide Propaganda in 1 Samuel 1–14." In *"A Wise and Discerning Mind": Essays in Honor of Burke O. Long*, edited by Saul M. Olyan and Robert C. Culley, 271–92. Brown Judaic Studies 325. Providence: Brown University, 2000.

———. "Saul and Jonathan in 1 Samuel 1 and 14." In *Saul in Story and Tradition*, edited by Marsha C. White and Carl S. Ehrlich, 119–38. Forschungen zum Alten Testament 47. Tübingen: Mohr Siebeck, 2006.

———. "Searching for Saul." *Bible Review* 17, no. 2 (2001): 22–29, 52–53.

Whitelam, Keith W. *The Invention of Ancient Israel: The Silencing of Palestinian History*. New York: Routledge, 1996.

Willesen, F. "The Philistine Corps of the Scimitar from Gath." *Journal of Semitic Studies* 3 (1958): 327–35. https://doi.org/10.1093/jss/3.4.327

Williams, David S. "Once Again: The Structure of the Narrative of Solomon's Reign." *Journal for the Study of the Old Testament* 86 (1999): 49–66. https://doi.org/10.1177/030908929902408603

Wilson, Ian Douglas. *Kingship and Memory in Ancient Judah*. New York: Oxford University Press, 2017.

Wright, G. Ernest. "The Provinces of Solomon." *Eretz-Israel* 8 (1967): 58*–68*.

Yadin, Azzan. "Goliath's Armor and Israelite Collective Memory." *Vetus Testamentum* 54, no. 3 (2004): 373–95. https://doi.org/10.1163/1568533041694573

Yadin, Yigael. "New Light on Solomon's Megiddo." *Biblical Archaeologist* 23, no. 2 (1960): 62–68. https://doi.org/10.2307/3209161

———. "Solomon's City Wall and Gate at Gezer." *Israel Exploration Journal* 8 (1958): 80–86.

Yahalom-Mack, Naama, and Adi Eliyahu-Behar. "The Transition from Bronze to Iron in Canaan: Chronology, Technology, and Context." *Radiocarbon* 57, no. 2 (2015): 285–305. https://doi.org/10.2458/azu_rc.57.18563

Yannai, Eli. "A Stratigraphic and Chronological Reappraisal of the 'Governor's Residence' at Tell El-Farʿah (South)." In *Studies in Archaeology and Related Disciplines*, edited by Eliezer D. Oren and Shmuel Aḥituv, 368–76. Aharon Kempinski Memorial Volume, Beer Sheba XV. Beersheba: Ben-Gurion University of the Negev Press, 2002.

Yardeni, Ada. "Further Observations on the Ostracon." In *Khirbet Qeiyafa Vol. 1, Excavation Report 2007–2008*, edited by Yosef Garfinkel and Saar Ganor, 259–60. Jerusalem: Israel Exploration Society; Institute of Archaeology, Hebrew University of Jerusalem, 2009.

Yasur-Landau, Assaf. *The Philistines and Aegean Migration at the End of the Late Bronze Age*. Cambridge: Cambridge University Press, 2014.

Yeivin, Shmuel. "Did the Kingdoms of Israel Have a Maritime Policy?" *Jewish Quarterly Review* 50 (1960): 193–228. https://doi.org/10.2307/1452922

Yoffee, Norman. "Mesopotamian Interaction Spheres." In *Early Stages in the Evolution of Mesopotamian Civilization: Soviet Excavations in Northern Iraq*, edited by Norman Yoffee and Jeffrey J. Clark, 257–70. Tucson: University of Arizona Press, 1994.

Zorn, Jeffrey. "An Inner and Outer Gate Complex at Tell En-Nasbeh." *Bulletin of the American Schools of Oriental Research* 307 (1997): 53. https://doi.org/10.2307/1357703

———. "A Note on the Date of the 'Great Wall' of Tell En-Naṣbeh: A Rejoinder." *Tel Aviv* 26 (1999): 146–50. https://doi.org/10.1179/tav.1999.1999.1.146

———. "New Insights from Old Wine Presses." *Palestine Exploration Quarterly* 130 (1998): 154–61. https://doi.org/10.1179/peq.1998.130.2.154

———. "Reconsidering Goliath: An Iron Age I Philistine Chariot Warrior." *Bulletin of the American Schools of Oriental Research* 360 (2010): 1–22. https://doi.org/10.1086/BASOR41104416

———. "The Dating of an Early Iron Age Kiln from Tell Al-Nasbah." *Levant* 30 (1998): 199–202. https://doi.org/10.1179/lev.1998.30.1.199

Index of Subjects

page number in *italics* refers to figure; page number in **bold** refers to table; n after page number refers to note

ʿAbdi-Ḥeba 45, 122, 123
abecedary of Tel Zayit 137, **137**, 140
Achish of Ekron 50–1, 64n96, 64n97
Achish of Gath 50–1, 194, 204
    alliance between David and 42, 45, 46, 47, 49–55, 125, 200
    before alliance with David 47, 48
Achziv 139, **168**, *169*, 170, *171*, 180
Adullam 45–9, 52, 165, 199
Aegean, the 78, 89
    ceramic imports from 142–3, 153, 159–61, 175–82, *175–6*, **177**, 196, 200
    chronology of ceramic sequences of 156–7
    relationship between Philistia and 26, 51, 180
    silver from 82, 90, 155
    trade between the southern Levant and 1, 7, 52, 82, 90, 202
Ahimaaz of Naphtali 98, 197
Aḥiram sarcophagus 144
Akko (region) 170, 172, 201
Al Mina 177, 188n87
almug-wood 83–4
alphabet *see* writing, alphabetic
Amarna letters 77, 108n39, 131n33
    from ʿAbdi-Ḥeba of Urusalim/Jerusalem 21n37, 45, 121–3, 129
    from Shuwardata of Gath 21n37, 45

Amathus 166, *167*, 178
Amenhotep III 77, 122
Amman 158, 159, *162*, 163–4, **163**, 166, *164*, 198
Amun 78, 145
Aphek 27, 29–30, 39, 53, 198
apiary, Tel Reḥov **137**, 140, 141, 143, 196, 204, 206
Aqaba *see* Eilat/Aqaba
Arabah Valley
    copper from 80, 88, 89–92, 155, 165
    Cypriot imports 166
    David's control of trade routes from 52–3, 55, 200
    dyed textiles in the 154–5
    part of copper exchange network 89–90, 155, 161–6, 181, 200, 208
    Qurayyah Painted Ware (QPW) 153, 158–65, *162*, **163**, 181, 200
    shared cultural practices with the Hejaz (Ḥijāz) 160–1
    Shoshenq I interest in 79
    Solomon's smelting operations 90–2, 201
    trade routes 35–6, 85, 103, 161
    see also Faynan region; Jordan; Timna
Arabia 1
    Hejaz (Ḥijāz) 158, 160–1, 162, 163, 185n47
    northwest 17, 87–8, 158–60, 166, 181, 196, 200
    part of copper exchange network 153, 155

INDEX OF SUBJECTS

possible location of Ophir 84
queens from north 88
routes connecting the Levant to 161, 163, 165, 181, 200, 201, 202
Solomon's trade with 72, 84, 86–8, 92, 156
source of gold 84, 91
spice trade and 107n29, 154, 155
see also Ophir; Qurayyah Painted Ware (QPW)
Aram 73, 85, 86, 98, 103, 197
Arameans 4, 16, 113n96
king(s) of 72, 73
Argolid, the 51, **177**, 177, 190n126, 194, 200
Ark Narrative 26, 27–32, *28*, *29*, 53, 198–200, 207
arrowheads, inscribed 135, **137**, 140, 143, 146, 199, 205
artisans 90, 91, 99, 101
Hiram 61n57, 114n115
Phoenician 81, 99, 101, 104, 127
Ashdod
Abimelech (Ahimelech), king of 49
ark's journey from 30, 31
Cypriot imports **168**, 168–9, **170**, *171*, 172, *173*, 200
Yamani, king of 51
Ayalon
city of 48
Valley road 58n25, 58n27, 207

Baʿalat Gebal 144
Baalath 100, 101, 103, 119n166, 199
banqueting 77, 165, 196
Barqa al-Hatiya *162*, **163**, 164, *164*
Basemath 98, 197
Bashan 94, 95, 191n144
beekeeping industry *see* apiary
Beersheba 48, **168**, *169*, 170, **170**, 172, *173*, 200
Beersheba Valley 65n115
Arabah-Beersheba route 161, 162, 164–5
highway between Benjamin and 48
route along the 30, 110n68, 132n38, 172, 181, 199
Shoshenq's campaign and the 187n68, 200, 207

Ben-Abinadab 98, 196
Benjamin territory *42*, 59n29, 131n33, 194
Ark Narrative and 29, *29*, 199
David's control of 52–5, 125, 199
fertile plateau of 121
power base of Saul 5, 33–4, 42, 47, 49, 52–3, 204
roads through 36, 48, 52–3, 55, 125, 199
Beqaʿ Valley 39, 172
Besor River 165, **170**, 180
Bethel 30
Beth-Horon
Lower 48, 100, 101, 103, 199
road 35, 207
Upper 101, 103
Bethlehem
Philistine presence near 44, 46, 47–8, 52, 125, 199
Ridge Road between Hebron and 121, 165
route to Transjordan via 48, 52
Bethsaida 170
Beth-Shean 62n69, 96, 123
Cypriot imports at **168**, 169, 170, 180
(cross)roads near 30, 39, *40*, 172, 180, 197
Beth-Shemesh 124, 139
Ark Narrative 31, 32, 52
Cypriot imports at **168**, 172, 181, 199
game board with inscription from 137, **137**, 140–1, 143, 205, 209n12
iron and copper production at 36, 38, 140, 208
Beth-zur 48, **168**, 170, 172, 174, 199
biblical archaeology 2–3, 8, 10, 66, 156–7
biblical criticism 2–3, 10, 16, 66, 120, 147n6
Bichrome wares
Cypriot 159, 166, 168, **168**, *169*, 174
Levantine 58n19, 159, 161, 178
Bir el-ʿAbd *162*, **163**, *164*, 165
black burnished juglets 88, 127, 161, 174
Black-on-Red (BoR) pottery
in burial deposits 139
distribution of 168–74, **168**, *169*, *171*, *173*, 180, 198, 206
from the Faynan 160–1, 174
from Jerusalem 127, 129

source and chronology of 166–8, *167*, 178
bowls
    from the Argolid 51, **177**, 177
    inscribed bronze 80, **137**, 139, 140, 146, 197
    inscribed sherds of **137**, 140
    Qurayyah Painted Ware (QPW) 159
Braudel, Fernand 12
bullae, clay 128, 135–6, 149n29
burial practices 14, 73, 109n57, 160
Byblos
    craftsmen from 99
    epigraphic evidence from 17, 81, 135, 143–4, 145, 207
    in Report of Wenamun 145, 179, 203
    statues of Shoshenq and Osorkon I 79, 144

Cabul 82–3, 98, 112n84, 196
Canaanites 1, 56n4, 75, 76, 97, 100
Carmel 52
    /Akko region 178, 179, 201
    Cypriot imports at **168**, *169*, 170–2, *171*
Chief of Meshwesh 78, 79, 208
chronology **7**, 8–9
    based on ceramic analyses 5–6, 157
    of Black-on-Red (BoR) pottery 166
    Low (LC) 4–5, 20n28, 148n9, 190n128
    Modified Conventional (MCC) 5, 189n124, 190n128
    of Protogeometric pottery 175–8, 189n123
    of Qurayyah Painted Ware (QPW) 158–9, 165
    of Shoshenq I 8, 79, 193
    traditional biblical 4, 7–8, *8*, 156, 194
cinnamon 86, 107n29, 113n92, 154, 200
consumption, conspicuous 142, 153–5, 196, 200, 203, 207 *see also* display, conspicuous
copper
    Arabah 36–7, *37*, 80, 89–92, 145, 155, 200
    exchange network 88, 91, 178, 181, 187n69, 201
    Faynan 36–7, *37*, 41, 139
    ingots 36
    and iron workshops 36, 38, 140, 208
    production and Qurayyah Painted Ware (QPW) 87–9, 153, 158, 159–66, 200
    route (trade) 37, 139, 149n38, 155, 182, 200, 201
    Solomon and his involvement in the production of 89–92, 114n102
core-periphery 12–13, 14
craftsmen *see* artisans
crossroads
    near Bethlehem 48, 121
    near Beth-Shean 39, 172, 197
    of east-west routes with north-south routes 121, 139, 165, 181
    fortifications situated near *102*, 103
    of Jezreel corridor with the Jordan Valley 39, 139, 180, 197–8
    near Megiddo 178–9, 197
    of the Ridge Road 30, 48, 125, 165
    sites that guarded over 139, 153, 165–6, 172, 174, 178–82, 197, 202–4
    near Tel ʿAmal 139
    near Tel Masos 161, 165, 181, 204
    near Tel Reḥov 139, 172, 178–9, 180, 181, 204
    wadi between Michmash and Geba/Gibeah 35, 48
Cyprus
    (ceramic) chronology of 156–7
    gateways to exchange with 172, 179, 180, 196, 198, 202–3
    Jerusalem's LBA tombs contain imports from 123
    maritime network and pottery from *167*, 170, 172, 178, 180
    PG Euboean vases found in 178
    Philistia's kinship with Greeks on 51
    southern Levantine trade with 82, 153, 178, 179, 180
    see also Bichrome wares, Cypriot; Black-on-Red (BoR) pottery; White Painted (WP) ware

Damascus 73, 98, 124, 189n108, 197
Dan *see* Tel Dan
Darb el-Ghazza (road) 85, 164, 165, 181
David *42*, 66, 146

INDEX OF SUBJECTS

Adullam, stronghold of 45–9, 52
alliance with Achish of Gath 42, 45, 46, 47, 49–55, 125, 200
chronology of 7–9, *8*
conquests of 156, 193, 195, 197, 200, 201, 209n1
diplomatic relations with Tyre 81, 111n78
Hebron, powerbase of 45–6, 52, 53, 124–5, 199
interactions with Philistines 25, 27, 42–50, 54, 194, 199–200
international/intercultural marriages for 75
Jerusalem, powerbase of 45, 46, 53, 124–9, 199
mas policy of 99
member of elite class 142, 194–5, 204, 206, 207, 208
and Saul 8, 32, 43–50, 52, 55
united Israelite kingdom under 4, 5, 27, 120, 142, 206
Delphi 89
Delta (Lower Egypt) 78, 155, 165
diffusion 11, 206
display, conspicuous
 of luxury goods 88–90, 91, 180, 207
 of inscriptions 145–6, 196
 see also consumption, conspicuous
district officials 95, 97, 98
Dor *see* Tel Dor
dye, purple 154–5, 182n2

Eben-ezer, battles at 26–32, *28*, *29*, 35, 41, 53, 55, 199
Edom 197
 and Arabah copper sites 21n37, 114n117, 160, 185n52
 competing for trade routes 74
 Ezion-geber in the land of 83, 85–6, 114n102, 163
 Hadad, member of royal family of 73–4, 75, 108n44
 Solomon foreign wife from 76
 see also Qurayyah Painted Ware (QPW)
Edomite Lowlands Regional Archaeology Project (ELRAP) 160, 183n18

Egypt 9, 12, 72, 84, 90
 administrative presence in southern Levant 4, 14, 35, 45, 121–2, 142, 165
 and copper from Arabah Valley 89, 92, 155, 158, 160–2, 165–6, 198
 Cypriot imports 168
 imports from 128–9, 159, 160, 161, 182n1, 202
 Jerusalem's interaction with 104, 109n50, 121–3, 126, 129
 miṣrym (biblical *miṣrayim*) 72
 muṣri (in Assyrian texts) 72
 Ramesside Dynasties 121–3
 routes connecting with 139, 165, 181, 201
 Solomon's interaction with 16, 71–80, 104, 125–6, 156, 195, 199
 and 10th century BCE monumental inscriptions 79, 91, 121, 144–6, 195, 197, 204, 207
 see also Report of Wenamun; Shoshenq I; Wendjebauendjed, tomb of
Eilat/Aqaba 164
 Gulf of 85, 86, 153, 159, 163, 181
Ekron (Tel Miqne) 30–1, 50, 53, 58n25, 58n27, 64n96
Elah Valley 47, 52, 58n25, 165, 201
Elath (Eloth) 85–6
elites and elite culture
 Egyptian 21st and 22nd Dynasties 80
 horses and chariotry 71, 72–3, 80, 87, 90, 92, 104
 during Iron I–IIA transition 73, 92, 178–80, 196
 of Jerusalem 104, 109n50, 123, 126, 129
 of Megiddo 178–9
 Nubian 72–3, 80
 scribal activity as part of 17, 139–46
 of Tel Hadar 179
 of Tel Masos 200
 of Tel Reḥov 140, 179, 204
 of Tell eṣ-Ṣafi (Gath) 178–9, 204
 writing as part of 17, 143
emulation 1
 of Egypt by Solomon 109n51
 of Egypt by Jerusalem's vassal rulers 123

of New Kingdom model by 11th and 10th
century BCE pharaohs 78–9, 144,
146, 208
    peer polity interaction and 13, 15, 205–8
    of predecessors by Levantine Iron Age
elites 9, 132n46, 142, 146, 161, 180
En Gev **168**, 170, 172, 180, 197
En Haseva 119n166, 165, 201
Ephraim hills 95, 100, 198
ethnicity 13, 88, 109n57
    an Aegean(-oriented) 51, 78
    notions of 9–10, 55n2, 58n28, 117n147,
134n66, 156
Euboea 175, **177**, 177–80, 197, 198
exile, the 27, 56n4, 83
Exodus 3, 20n31, 31, 109n51, 119n160,
209n4
exotica 9, 83–4, 178, 179, 194, 200 *see also*
luxury goods; prestige
Ezion-geber 83, 85–6, 114n102, 163 *see also*
Tell el-Kheleifeh

Faynan region (biblical Punon) 35–6,
108n38, 182n8
    copper from the 139, 161, 165, 201
    Qurayyah Painted Ware (QPW) from
113n98, 158–61, **163**, 163–4, *164*
    shared metallurgical technology with
Timna 206, 208
    Shoshenq I's campaign 145, 187n68, 200
    see also Arabah Valley
folk sayings 3, 43, 45, 49, 50
fortifications
    in Hazor 4, 100, 101, 103, 105n2, 197
    in Jerusalem 122, 125–8
    in the Ophel 127, 128, 129
    Solomon's 66, 99, *102*, 100–4, 125–9, 199,
200, 201
    in Tell eṣ-Ṣafi (Gath) 140

Galilee 93, 179, 189n117, 197
Galilee, Sea of (Lake Kinneret) 86, 154, 179,
197
game board (Beth-Shemesh) **137**, 140, 146,
205, 209n12
Gath *see* Tell eṣ-Ṣafi
Geba *see* Gibeah

Gezer 100, 103, 129
    Cypriot imports **168**, *169*, 170, *171*, 172,
173, 181, 199
    gift of pharaoh to Solomon 71, 75, 76,
77, 126
    part of elite cultural sphere 166
    Qurayyah Painted Ware (QPW) 158, *162*,
163, *164*, 165–6, 181, 199
    Siamun's Tanis relief and battle at 78
    Solomon's building project at 4, 100,
101, 199
    tablet (calendar) 17, 137, **137**, 140
Ghrareh *162*, **163**, 163, *164*
Gibeah
Geba, modern Jaba 33, 35, 125, 199
Gibeath-ha-Elohim 33
    Saul's capital 33, 59n37, 60n38, 69, 125
Gibeonites 101
gifts 88, 123, 155, 191n152
    of gold 31, 91
    reciprocal, between Solomon and
Hiram 81–2
    reciprocal, between Solomon and
Queen of Sheba 86–7
    temple, recorded by Shoshenq I and
Osorkon I 91, 144
    see also tribute
Gilboa, Mount 39
Gilead 34, 94, 95
gold 89, 91, 154
    currency of diplomacy and commercial
exchange 155
    gifts of 31, 91
    Hiram paying Solomon talents of 82, 90
    from Ophir 83, 84, 87, 91, 92
    Solomon's throne of ivory and 126
    vessels 90, 139
Goliath 43, 47, 204, 207

Hadad 73–4, 75, 108n44
harbors 81, 170 *see also* ports
Harod River Valley 39, 139
Hazael 85
Hazor
    Cypriot imports **168**, *169*, 170, *171*, 172,
180, 197
    iron production 36

Solomon's building projects 4, 100, 101, 103, 105n2, 197
Hebron
    David's base at 45–6, 52, 53, 124–5, 199
    Qurayyah Painted Ware (QPW) near 162
    routes between Judahite hill country and 30, 48, 165, 201
heirlooms 73, 91, 140, 160, 161, 190n138
Hejaz (Ḥijāz) 158, 160–1, 162, 163, 185n47
Hezekiah 92, 95, 111n79
Hiram, king of Tyre 91
    control of territory in the north (Cabul) 82, 104, 112n81, 195, 196
    diplomatic relations with David 81
    8th century BCE ruler 81, 112n91
    exchange relationship with Solomon 78, 80–3, 86, 90, 91, 98–100
    maritime partnership with Solomon 80, 83, 86, 87, 112n81
horse trade 71, 72–3, 80, 87, 90, 92, 104

identity 111n80, 156
    Arabah and Hejaz (Ḥijāz) cultural 185n47, 185n52, 186n53
    early Iron Age 6, 9–10, 25, 26, 154, 174, 193–4
    elite 18, 181, 208
    formation and cultural interaction 156
    interaction sphere model and 14–15, 203–4, 206, 208
    of Israelites 56n4, 134n66
    Libyan 78
    name formulae and elite 140–1
    peer polity interaction and formation of 14, 18
    Philistine Aegean 26, 51, 180
    salient 13, 15
Ikausu, king of Ekron 50–1, 64n96, 64n97
India 83, 84, 86
Indian Ocean 107n29, 154
inequality 11–12, 141–3
interaction spheres 13, 14–15, 18, 88, 191n143, 202–5, 208
International Coastal Highway *see* Via Maris
iron production 36, 37, 61n58, 90, 198, 206, 208

Ishbaal 125
ivory 83
    carved object of 143, 161, 195
    inlays 127, 128, 129
    Solomon's throne of gold and 126
Jeroboam 71, 73, 74, 75, 106n15, 119n160
Jerusalem
    ʿAbdi-Ḫeba, ruler of (Amarna letters) 21n37, 45, 121–3, 129
    black burnished juglets from 88, 127, 161
    Cypriot Black-on Red (BoR) jug 127, 129, **168**, 170, 172, *173*, 174, 199
    David's conquest of 42, 46, 53, 120, 124, 129
    early Iron Age inscriptions from Ophel 137, **137**, 139, 140–1, 199
    Egyptian influence on architecture of 104, 109n50, 123, 126
    excavations of 127–8, 129, 195
    Jebusite 120–5, 127
    march of Shishaq (Shoshenq I) to 121
    Ophel excavations 88, 127, 128–9, 131n18
    Solomonic 75, 76, 121, 125–7, 129, 199
Jezreel *see* Tel Jezreel
Jezreel Valley
    battle between Saul and Philistines at 26, 34, 38–42, 47, 53, 182, 194, 197
    David's role in battle of the 49, 52, 55, 125
    distribution of Cypriot imports in 170, 172, 180, 197–8
    Ridge Road connection to 30
    routes along and into 103–4, 139, 178, 180, 182, 197, 201
    Shoshenq I campaign into 39, 198, 207
    Solomon's fifth district 95–7, 104, 197
Jonathan 44
    armed conflict with Philistines 33, 34, 35, 38, 125, 194, 199
    warrior-hero 59n36, 194
    weaponry attributed to 61n55, 205, 207
Jordan River 26, 36, 127, 203
    fords across 39, 41, 47, 164
Jordan Valley 26
    Aegean imports 153, 178–9, 180

Cypriot imports 153, 166, 170, 172, 180, 198
metal production and trade in 89–90, 198, 200
occurrence of name (*nmš*) in northern 141, 196
Philistine interest in routes to 30, 35, 38–42, 46–9, 52–5, 125, 198, 207
road systems of the 139, 198, 201
Shoshenq I targeting commercial route of the 79, 198, 199, 207
Solomon's (metallurgical) interest in 92, 93, 95–7, 104, 197, 198
Jordan 87–8, 158, 162, 163–4, *164*, 198 *see also* Arabah Valley; Faynan region
Josiah 27, 79, 86
Judah 4, 85
border tensions between Philistia and 31, 194
and David 47, 54, 55
elites and Cypriot imports in 173–4
Ezion-geber and Eloth under control of 85–6
kings and kingdom of 3, 20n34, 68, 76, 77, 86
northwest Arabian (copper) trade and 87–8, 201
roads crossing 48, 58n22, 187n79, 201
Solomon's administrative systems and 94–5
jugs and juglets
black-burnished 88, 174
Black-on-Red (BoR) 127, 129
Cypriot barrel 166, 168
Iron IIA black 127, 128, 129, 133n61
Phoenician bichrome 178

Kadashman-Enlil's daughter 77
Kadesh Barnea *see* Tell el-Qudeirat
Karib-il, king of Saba 88
Karnak relief (Bubastite portal) 15, 79, 91, 107n16, 121, 197, 207
Kefar Veradim burial deposit 80, 137, **137**, 139–40, 197, 205
Khirbat en-Nahas (KEN) 6, 129
copper production site 36, 160, 206

Cypriot imports **168**, *169*, 170, 172, *173*, 174, 181
imported black burnished juglets (Jerusalem) 88, 174
part of an elite cultural sphere 161, 166, 181, 200
part of southern exchange network 181, 201
Qurayyah Painted Ware (QPW) 88, 158–61, *162*, **163**, 164, *164*, 174, 181, 186n62
Khirbet Duwar 163, *164*
Khirbet esh-Shedeiyid *162*, 163, **163**, *164*
Khirbet Qeiyafa 6, 124, 128, 129, 139
Cypriot imports 168, **168**, 169, 172, *173*, 181, 199
inscriptions 17, 137, *137*, 140, 199
ostracon 137, *137*, 140, 150n53
King's Highway 163, 165, 178
kingship
Delta 78
Jerusalem and the history/memory of 124
Solomon's 69, 92, 106n7, 106n8
Kinneret, Lake (Sea of Galilee) 86, 154, 179, 197
Kiriath-jearim 31, 32, 53, 57n13, 59n29, 199
Kourion 166, *167*

labor, forced (*mas*) 99–103, 195
Lachish 199
Cypriot imports at **168**, 169, **170**, 172, *173*, 181
Qurayyah Painted Ware at *162*, **163**, *164*, 165, 181
Lefkandi 168, 178, 180
literacy 141–2, 146, 147n6, 204, 209n6 *see also* scribes
Low Chronology (LC) 4–5, 190n127
luxury goods 147n6
Aegean imports as 178, 179–80
Amarna period Levantine rulers and access to 122
at Beth-Shemesh 31, 205
biblical Sheba as source of 87
Cypriot imported found in association with 174, 175

early Iron Age Jerusalem's access to 129
exchange between Philistia and Israel of 32
from far off lands 83–4, 86–7, 146, 178
inscription on (portable) 143, 146, 195–6
interaction spheres and 14, 18, 205–7
Iron I and IIA elites collected and conspicuous displayed 180, 196, 207
Kefar Veradim burial contained 139–40, 205
at Khirbat en-Nahas (KEN) 174
Osorkon I's record temples in Egypt received 91
Qurayyah Painted Ware (QPW) as 158, 159–60, 165
Wendjebauendjed's tomb contained 80, 139
see also exotica; prestige

marriages
Deuteronomic laws and ideology on inter- 77, 106n8
diplomatic 71, 75–9, 98, 126, 180, 195
of Solomon with pharaoh's daughter 71, 75–80, 104, 126, 195, 199
of Solomon's daughters to district officials 98, 104, 195, 196, 197
mas (forced labor policy) 99–103, 195
Megiddo 39, 96, 129, 157
Aegean imports at 175, 177, 178–9, 190n126, 191n144
alphabetic inscription from 148n11
Cypriot imports at **168**, 169, 170, *171*, 172, 188n89, 188n96, 189n107
destructions of 6, 179
iron production at 36
Shoshenq I's victory stele at 79, 144–5, 197, 207
Solomon's building projects at 4, 100, 101, 103, 105n2, 197
Merneptah stele 9
Mesad Gozal *164*, 165
Meshwesh *see* Chief of Meshwesh
Mesopotamia 1, 88, 98, 139, 156, 159
metallurgy 37
Arabah and Jordan Valleys and 89–90, 158, 198, 201, 206, 208

at Beth-Shemesh 36, 38, 140, 208
Philistine and 33, 35–6, 38, 41, 53, 194, 201
prestige and 203
Qurayyah Painted Ware (QPW) correlation with 158–66, 174
roads and trade in 36, 38, 41, 53, 139, 160
shared technology in 36, 89, 160, 208
Shoshenq I targeted areas active in (trade of) 79, 198, 207
Solomon's involvement in 89–92, 104, 158, 198, 201
at Tell el-Hammeh 36, 61n58, 90, 198, 206, 208
at Tell eṣ-Ṣafi (Gath) 36, 38, 140
Michal 43, 44
Michmash Pass (modern Mukhmas)
battle at 26, 32–8, *37*, 41–2, 55, 194, 199
outpost at the 33, 35, 36, 48, 53, 125, 198
Midian *see* Arabia, northwest
Midianite pottery *see* Qurayyah Painted Ware (QPW)
minimalist versus maximalist debate 3, 19n11, 23n61, 66, 120, 147n6
Mizpah 27, *29*, 30, 53, 58n26, 199 *see also* Tell en-Nasbeh
Modified Conventional Chronology (MCC) 5–7, *7*, 20n28, 189n124, 190n128

Nahal Besor 165, **170**, 180
Nahal Yarkon 29, 30, **170**, 180
name formula 17, 136–7, **137**, 146
Naphath-Dor, Solomon's fourth district 95, 97, 98, 196
Naphtali, Solomon's eighth district 98, 127
Negev 48
Cypriot imports 153, 166, *169*, 200
imports from 161, 174, 186n61
Qurayyah Painted Ware (QPW) 162, *162*, **163**, *164*, 164, 200
routes 52, 55, 74, 164, 181, 195, 200
Shoshenq I targets the 74, 200, 201
Neo-Assyrian Empire 7
Arabian queens in royal inscriptions of 88

capture of Levantine coastal cities by 154
control of routes and commerce 86
control of the southern Levant 4, 14, 35, 68, 72, 75
destruction of sites in the southern Levant by 4, 77, 82, 112n90
Elath and Ezion-geber controlled by 85, 86
Jerusalem and 92
records of the 10, 50, 72, 81
Solomon's districts and the influence of the later 95, 114n105, 117n142
Neo-Babylonian Empire 3, 77, 120
networks, exchange
Arabian 88, 155, 200
associated with Black-on-Red (BoR) ware 170–4, 181
David and Saul's participation in 38, 44, 52–3, 55
early Iron Age long-distance 17, 36, 62, 157, 178–82, 194–6, 200, 209
elite 15, 86, 135, 139, 156, 166, 179–82, 202–9
interregional 14, 129, 204
Jerusalem's role in 88, 104, 125–7, 129, 195
Late Bronze Age 1, 153, 160, 166, 181, 202
local 14, 141
maritime 160, 178, 180, 189n102
Phoenician (long-distance) 86, 154
southern copper (long-distance) 36, 88, 114n102, 153, 161–6, 181, 187n69, 201
Nile river 72, 78
Delta (Lower Egypt) 78, 155, 165
shells from the 160
northern kingdom of Israel 4, 5, 69, 73
Nubia
gold from 84, 91
horses and elite culture of 72–3, 80
possible location of Ophir 84

oils 86, 129, 166, 168, 174, 196
Olympia 89, 200
Omrides 4, 5, 85

Ophel
early Iron Age inscriptions from 131n18, 137, **137**, 140–1, 199
excavations 88, 127, 128–9, 131n18
Ophir 83, 84, 87, 91, 92
Osorkon I 144
Osorkon IV 72
ostraca 15, 84, 135, 137, **137**, 140

patrimonial structure, Weber's 11–13
patronage, elite 140, 143
peer polity interaction model 13–15, 18, 67, 98, 104, 195, 205–8
Pella **168**, *169*, 170, *171*, 172, 180, 198
Persian period 24n77, 83, 105n1, 114n105
Philistia 127, 173
Aegean imports in *175*, *176*, **177**, 178, 200
ark's journey from 31, 53
battles with Saul and David 31–5, 39, 44–9, 53, 125
control of roads and key passages 16, 36, 47–9, 53, 195, 200
Cypriot imports in **168**, *169*, *173*, 178, 200
David's interaction with 42, 49–55, 125, 200
inscriptions from **137**, 139, 200
nonlocal (Aegean) origins of culture of 26, 51, 180
pottery from 5, 58n19, 161, 189n118
Qurayyah Painted Ware (QPW) 164, 200
Siamun and 78
Shoshenq I campaign passed southern 200, 207
Phoenicia
artisans from 61n57, 81, 99, 101, 104, 127, 114n115
ceramic imports in 153, 166, **168**, 168, 173
control of territory in the north (Cabul) 82, 104, 112n81, 195, 196
early Iron Age chronology of 151n 67, 156–7
Jerusalem's integration into exchange network of 125–7, 129
Jezebel from 75
Khirbat en-Nahas (KEN) and pottery from 174

Lefkandi and pottery from 178
maritime trade of 84–6
purple dye from 154
silver trade and 91
Solomon's exchange relationship with 16, 78, 80–3, 86, 90, 98–100
Solomon's maritime partnership with 80, 83, 86–7, 112n81
Tel Hadar and pottery from 191
Tel Masos and pottery from 161
Tell el-Farʿah (S), Tomb 542 contained pottery from 160
use of script from 139
Piankhi/Piye 72–3
ports 81
   Acco 139
   Achziv 139, 180
   Byblos 81, 203
   control over traffic from 95, 97, 98, 104, 163
   Ezion-geber 85–6, 163
   in Joppa region 172, 198
   northern Levantine 180, 182, 207
   Shiqmona 180
   Tel Ashdod **170**
   Tel Dor 168, 178–9, 180, 196–7, 201, 203–4
   Tell Abu Hawam 170, **170**, 178–9, 180, 197
   Tell Qasile 30, 170, **170**, 172, 198
   Tyre 81, 168, 178–9, 180, 197, 203–4
prestige
   control of access and production of metal to gain 90, 200
   Cypriot ceramic as item of 174, 197, 199
   inscribed objects 140, 144, 146, 197, 199, 208
   interaction spheres and items of 161, 180, 196, 202–5
   Late Bronze Age exchange network and items of 202
   marriage to an Egyptian princess 77
   Qurayyah Painted Ware (QPW) as item of 158, 161, 165, 174, 196, 199, 200
   see also exotica; luxury goods
Protogeometric pottery 175, *175*, *176*, **177**, 177–8, 198

Psusennes I 80, 110n59
Psusennes II 79, 110n60

Qeʿilah (Qiltu) 44–5, 48–9, 52, 108n39, 199
Que (*qwh*; kingdom of Hiyawa) 72
Qurayyah 87, 158, 159, **163**
Qurayyah Painted Ware (QPW; Midianite ware) 113n98
   Amman, 'Airport structure' 158, 159, *162*, **163**, 163, *164*, 198
   in burial contexts 159–60, 199, 200
   chronological range of 158–60, 165, 184n36, 184n39, 186n59, 186n62
   distribution of copper and 159, 160–6, *162*, **163**, *164*, 181, 200
   items of prestige 158, 161, 165, 174, 196, 199, 200
   Khirbat en-Nahas (KEN) 88, 158–61, *162*, **163**, 164, *164*, 174, 181, 186n62
   production site 158, 159
   Timna 158, 160–1, *162*, **163**, 165, 184n36

Red Sea 74, 80, 83–6, 93, 163
Rehoboam 8, 75, 99, 106n15, 121, 132n35
Renfrew, Colin 13–14, 205–6, 207
Rephaim Valley 44, 45–6, 48, 52, 199
Rezin, king of Aram 85
Rezon, ruler of Damascus 73, 197
Ridge Road 199
   Ark Narrative and the 30, 35, 53
   Jerusalem situated on the 121
   Saul, David and Philistines fight to control the 48–9, 125
   Tel Masos guarded crossroad between east-west valley route and 165

Samaria 30, 86, 187n79
Samuel 43, 194
   Ark Narrative 27–8, 32, 58n26
   career of 8, 16, 25, 34
   interaction with Philistines 27, 35
Sarepta 169, *169*, *171*
Sargon II 72
šarratu 88
Saul ben Kish of Benjamin 3, 16, 27, *54*
   battle in the Jezreel Valley and death of 8, 38–42, *40*, 44, 53, 182, 197, 199

battle at Michmash 26, 32-8, 37, 53
Benjamin, power base of 5, 42, 204
chronology of regnal years of 7-9, *8*
David in service of 43, 46-7, 55
descendants of 9, 125-6
member of elite class 32, 34, 146, 194, 204-5, 207-8
rivalry with David 8, 32, 44-50, 52, 55, 194-4, 199

scribes
Assyrian 88
Egypt and the use of 145-6, 152n78, 195, 204
implements used by 135
Jerusalem and the employment of 129, 111n79, 121
practices of 135-6
as privilege of elites 17, 51, 135, 139-46, 195-6, 204-7
statehood and 9, 116n139, 136, 142-3, 202
writing exercises for 82, 95, 137, *137*, 140

seals 135-6, 141
Sennacherib 88
shabti figurines 80, 89, 200
Shalmaneser V 72
Sharon Plain 171, 179, 198
Sheba, Queen of 83, 86-8
Shechem, 30, 123
Shephelah 26, 36
Ark Narrative and 27-31, *28*, *29*, 41, 199
Cypriot imports 166, 172, 180-1, 199
David and the 47, 51-2, 55, 199
early Iron Age inscriptions found in the *138*, 139, 140-1, 196, 199, 208
Qurayyah Painted Ware (QPW) 162, 165, 180-1, 199
region of intense interactions 38, 182, 199, 201, 204
Saul battles with Philistines 36-8, *37*, 41, 47, 182, 194
Shoshenq I campaign through 199

Shiloh 27, 30, 32, 53, 198
Shiqmona **168**, 170, 171, *171*, 180
Shishaq *see* Shoshenq I
Shoshenq I (biblical Shishaq) 107n16, 110n64-5
campaign in southern Levant of 72, 74, 79, 104, 182, 193, 198-201, 207-8
'Chief of the Meshwesh' title and Libyan background of 78, 79, 208
chronological anchor 4, 8
Faynan region and scarab of 145
Karnak relief (Bubastite portal) 15, 79, 91, 107n16, 121, 197, 199, 207
marriage alliances of 78-80, 98
pillage of Jerusalem (Rehoboam's reign) 8, 71, 106n15, 107n16, 121
Sousakim in the Septuagint 75-6
statue of 144
stele fragment in Megiddo bears name of 144-5, 197, 207
support of Jeroboam 71, 74, 75-6, 106n15

Shunem 39, 61n59
Siamun 78, 79, 110n66, 144
silver
Arabah copper used to debase 89, 91, 155, 200
collection/hoarding in temples of 90-1
currency of diplomacy and commercial exchange 72, 155
import of 82, 89, 90-2, 155, 208
'Tarshish' and trade in 85
tribute of 182n2
Wendjebauendjed's vessels of gold, electrum and 139

Sinai 162, **163**, 164, 200
Socoh 48, 52
Solomon Narrative
book of 1 Kings and the extent of 68-9
critical reading of the 66-7, 69, 92, 104
international horse trading in the 71, 72-3, 80, 87, 90, 92, 104
Jerusalem in the 125-7
long-distance exchange in the 69-71, *70*
Rezon, ruler of Damascus in the 197
Solomon's acquisition of metals 89-92
Solomon's administrative system in the 93-9, *96*, 104
Solomon's forced labor (*mas*) policy 99-103, 195

Solomon's marriage with pharaoh's daughter in 71, 75–80, 104, 126, 195, 199
Solomon's interactions with Arabia 86-8, 92
Solomon's interactions with Hiram, king of Tyre 78, 80–6, 90, 91, 99–100, 104
Song of Songs 1, 76, 105n1
Soreq Valley (highway) 31, 53, 58n25, 140–1
Sousakim *see* Shoshenq I (biblical Shishaq)
spice trade 86, 88, 107n29, 154, 155, 200–1
statehood 9, 19n12, 136
Succession Narrative 62n72, 68–9
Succoth 89–90

Taanach *see* Tel Taanach
Tamar, fortification of 100, 101, *102*, 103, 119n166, 200, 201
Tanis 110n66, 124
    exchange relations between southern Levant and 104
    Siamun's relief 78
    tomb of Wendjebauendjed 80, 89, 139, 149n35
Taphath 98, 196
Tarshish ships 83, 85
Tawilan *162*, **163**, 163, *164*, 187n76
Tayma 87, 158, *162*, **163**, 184n39
Tel ʿAmal
    Cypriot ceramic imports at 149n37, **168**, 170, *171*
    inscriptions from 137, **137**, 139, 141, 150n55, 197, 205
Tel Azor **168**, *169*, *171*, 172, 198
Tel Batash (Timnah) 137, **137**, 140–1, 150n55
Tel Dan
    Cypriot imports **168**, *169*, 170, *171*, 172, 180, 197
    stele 9, 108n36, 136
Tel Dor
    Aegean imports 175, **177**, 177–8, 180, 181
    cinnamon residue in Phoenician flasks 86, 154

Cypriot imports **168**, 169, *169*, 170, 171, *171*, 180, 181
gateway for Mediterranean trade 178, 180, 181, 197, 201
part of Solomon's fourth district (Naphath-Dor) 95, 98, 196
in Report of Wenamun 118n150, 145, 179, 196–7, 203–4
Sea peoples and Aegean heritage 98, 180
Tel Gerisa **168**, *169*, *171*, *173*, 198
Tel Hadar
    Aegean imports 175, *177*, 177, 178–9, 180, 197
    destruction marking end of Iron I 6, 179, 191n144
    Phoenician imports 191n144
Tel Halif 65n114, **168**, *169*, 170, 172, *173*, 199
Tel Jedur (biblical Gedor) 159, *162*, **163**, *164*, 165, 185n49, 199
Tel Jezreel 39, **168**, *169*, 170, *171*
Tel Keisan 6, **168**, *169*, *171*, 188n96
Tel Masos 65n114
    Cypriot imports **168**, *169*, 170, 172, *173*, 181, 200
    elite culture of 161, 166, 181, 200, 201, 204
    part of southern copper exchange network 166, 181, 201
    Qurayyah Painted Ware (QPW) at 161, *162*, **163**, *164*, 181, 186n62, 200
    situated on east-west and north-south crossroads 161, 165, 181, 204
Tel Mevorakh **168**, *169*, 170, **170**, 171, *171*, 198
Tel Michal **168**, *169*, 170, *171*, 172, 198
Tel Miqne *see* Ekron
Tel Qiri **168**, *169*, 170, 171, *171*
Tel Reḥov 6, 62n69, 124, 129, 191n146
    Aegean imports 140, 142, 175, **177**, 177–8, 180, 198
    apiary at 140, 143, 196, 204, 206
    Cypriot imports 140, **168**, *169*, 170, *171*, 172, 180
    destroyed in mid to late 9th century BCE 179
    elite culture of 140, 142–3, 180, 201, 204
    feasting 140, 143, 180, 196, 204, 209n12

inscriptions from 137, **137**, 140, 141, 142–3, 197, 204
iron production 36
situated on crossroads of interregional routes 139, 172, 178–9, 180, 181, 204
Tel Taanach **168**, 170, **170**, *171*
Tel Zayit 114n65, 137, **137**, 140, 143
Tel Zeror **168**, *169*, **170**, 171, *171*, 198
Tell Abu al-Kharaz **168**, 170, 198
Tell Abu Hawam 6
Aegean imports 175, **177**, 177–8
    Cypriot imports **168**, *169*, 170, **170**, 171, *171*, 180, 188n96
    port 170, 178–9, 180
Tell Beit Mirsim **168**, *169*, 172, *173*, 199
Tell el-Ajjul 166, **168**, *169*, **170**, 172, *173*, 180, 200
Tell el-Farʿah (N) (biblical Tirzah) 124, *169*, 170, *171*, 172, 174, 180, 198
Tell el-Farʿah (S)
    Cypriot imports 166, *167*, *169*, **170**, *173*, 181, 200
    participated in the southern copper exchange network 172
    Qurayyah Painted Ware (QPW) 160, *162*, **163**, *164*, 165, 181, 185n51, 200
    Tomb 542 160, 161
Tell el-Ful 59n37, 60n38
    Cypriot imports **168**, 169, 172, *173*, 174, 199
    located near the Ridge Road 180
Tell el-Hammeh
    Cypriot imports **168**, *169*, 170, *171*, 180
    iron production at 36, *37*, 61n58, 90, 198
    shared metallurgical technology 206, 208
Tell el-Kheleifeh 158, *162*, **163**, *164*, 165 *see also* Ezion-geber
Tell el-Qudeirat (Kadesh Barnea)
    Cypriot imports **168**, *169*, 170, 172, *173*, 181, 200
    participated in southern copper exchange network 161, 181
    Qurayyah Painted Ware (QPW) at 161, *162*, **163**, *164*, 181, 186n62, 200
Tell en-Nasbeh

    Cypriot imports **168**, *169*, 170, *171*, 172, *173*, 174, 199
    located near the Ridge Road 180
    possible biblical Mizpah 58n19
Tell eṣ-Ṣafi (Gath) 125, 129, 199, 204
    Aegean imports at 175, *175–6*, **177**, 177–80
    ark's journey passed 30–1, 53
    cultural and ethnic identity of 50–1, 56n2, 56n5–6, 139, 143, 181
    Cypriot pottery imports at 168–9, **168**, *169*, 172, *173*, 181, 200
    David flees to 50
    feasting at 140
    inscriptions from 136–7, **137**, 140, 148n13
    iron production activity 36, 38, 140
    routes from 47–8, 52
    Shuwardata of 45
    see also Achish of Gath
Tell Hammeh
    Cypriot imports **168**, *169*, 170, *171*, 180
    iron smelting production site 36, 61n58, 90, 198, 206, 208
Tell Jemmeh **168**, **170**, 172, 200
Tell Qasile 6, 30
    cinnamon residue in Phoenician flasks from 86, 154
    Cypriot imports **168**, *169*, 170, **170**, *171*, 172, *173*, 180, 198
    ostracon from 84
Tell Summeily 136, 149n29
Tell Yoqneam 6, **168**, 170, **170**, 171
temple, Solomon's 7, 20n31, 82, 106n13, 121
    collecting/hoarding of metals and luxury goods in 90–1
    Egyptian and Syro-Phoenician style influences on 61n57, 77, 126
    Shishaq (Shoshenq I) pillaged 121
    Solomon's *mas* (forced labor) policy and 99–100
textiles 154, 155, 182n2, 183n13
Thebes 78, 79, 110n60, 179
Tiglath-Pilesar III 72, 88, 154
Timna Valley
    copper production at 35–6, 89, 158, 163, 206, 208

INDEX OF SUBJECTS

Iron I and II transition at 6
participated in southern copper exchange network 201
purple dyed textiles at (Site 34) 154–5
Qurayyah Painted Ware (QPW) at 158, 160–1, *162*, **163**, 165, 184n36
Timnah *see* Tel Batash
Tombos burial 73
Transjordan 48, 94, 125, 165, 195
tribute 88, 135
  of ʿAbdi-Ḫeba to the king of Egypt 123
  the Ark Narrative 31–2
  horses and chariotry as 72
  Shoshenq I and Osorkon I recorded 144
  Solomon's wealth from trade and 83, 87, 89, 90, 91
  see also gifts
Tukulti-Ninurta II 88
Tyre 98, 124, 129, 191n146
  Aegean and Cypriot ceramic imports at 153, **168**, 169, *169*, 170, 175, **177**, 177–8
  artisan from 61n57, 114n115
  Phoenician (long-distance) trade via 85, 86, 91, 179, 180
  in Report of Wenamun 203–4
  transition of Iron I to Iron II 6, 81, 86, 92, 104
  see also Hiram, king of Tyre

Um Guweah *162*, **163**, 163, *164*
United Monarchy 5, 6, 67, 97, 206

Via Maris (International Coastal Highway) 48
  Arabah-Beersheba route connected to the 165
  at Ashdod 31
  course of the 29–30, 39
  distribution of Cypriot imports and travel along the 171–2
  at Kadesh Barnea, the Darb el Ghazza met the 164
  at Megiddo 103, 178, 197
  Tell eṣ-Ṣafi (Gath) close to southern portion of the 177

warrior(-heroes) 43, 44, 46, 47, 194, 204
weaponry
  in burial cave at Tel Jedur 160
  Goliath's 63n74, 207
  inscribed arrowheads 135, **137**, 140, 143, 146, 199, 205
  Jonathan and Saul's 61n55, 205, 207
  as prestige items 61n55, 140, 143, 146, 160, 203–5, 207
Weber, Max 11–12
Wenamun, Report of 207, 209n4
  Byblos in 145, 179, 203
  Dor in 118n150, 145, 179, 196–7, 203–4
  Egypt's relation with the Levant 16, 71–2, 143–4, 145, 151n72, 203
  Tyre in 203–4
  use of metals in trade 90, 155
Wendjebauendjed, tomb of 80, 89, 139, 149n35
White Painted (WP) ware 166, **168**, 168–9, *169*, *171*, 172, 174
World Systems Analysis 12–14
writing, alphabetic **137**, 147n2
  name formula 136–7
  statehood and 136
  as status statement 141–3, 206–7, 208
  Tell eṣ-Ṣafi (Gath) 51, 136–7, 200

Yarkon River 29, 30, **170**, 180
Yoqneam *see* Tell Yoqneam
Yotvata **163**, *164*, 165, 184n27

Zarethan 90–1
Zarqa River (biblical Jabbok) 36, 90
Ziklag 49, 52, 61n59

Index Locorum

n after page number refers to note

Genesis 2	64n94
Genesis 4:17-22	61n57
Genesis 20	49
Genesis 26	49
Genesis 26:34	118n149
Genesis 36:1-17	118n149
Exodus 1:11	119n160
Exodus 3:8	118n156
Exodus 3:17	118n156
Exodus 23:23	118n156
Deuteronomy 3:1-17	116n132
Deuteronomy 7:1	118n156
Deuteronomy 15:2	119n165
Deuteronomy 16:16	101
Deuteronomy 17	106n12
Deuteronomy 17:14-20	106n13
Deuteronomy 17:14-17	208
Deuteronomy 19:4	119n165
Deuteronomy 20:10-11	100–1
Deuteronomy 20:17	118n156
Joshua 3:10	118n156
Joshua 9:27	100–1
Joshua 10:1-27	124
Joshua 12:8	118n156
Joshua 15:10	58n28
Joshua 16:10	100
Joshua 19:22	58n28
Joshua 19:24-31	82
Joshua 21:16	58n28
Joshua 24:11	118n156
Judges 1:33	58n28
Judges 3:5	118n156
Judges 13-16	34
1 Samuel	51, 59n34, 194
1 Samuel 4 – 7	26, 27, 55
1 Samuel 4:1-2	27, 29
1 Samuel 4:1	29, 58n21
1 Samuel 4:1b – 7:1	27
1 Samuel 4:10	28
1 Samuel 5:6 – 7:2	30–1
1 Samuel 7	28, 58n26
1 Samuel 7:2-14	27, 29
1 Samuel 7:12-17	3
1 Samuel 7:12	57n12
1 Samuel 7:13	34
1 Samuel 8	106n12
1 Samuel 8:4–18	208
1 Samuel 9:1-2	204
1 Samuel 9:1	34, 61n55
1 Samuel 9:16	32, 34
1 Samuel 10:5	33, 60n41
1 Samuel 10:5	33
1 Samuel 11	34
1 Samuel 11:2	116n130
1 Samuel 13 – 14	26, 33, 60n39
1 Samuel 13:1	*8*
1 Samuel 13:2 – 14:23	33
1 Samuel 13:2-6	59n36
1 Samuel 13:3-4	33, 60n41

INDEX LOCORUM

1 Samuel 13:7b-15a	59n36	1 Samuel 28:4	38, 39, 61n59
1 Samuel 13:19-21	36	1 Samuel 29: 1-11	49
1 Samuel 13:19b	36	1 Samuel 29:1	38, 39, 61n59
1 Samuel 13:20	38	1 Samuel 29:6-10	64n95
1 Samuel 13:23	34, 60n41	1 Samuel 31	32, 38, 47, 61n59
1 Samuel 14:1-23	59n36	1 Samuel 31:1-3	39
1 Samuel 14:1	60n41	1 Samuel 31:1-7	39
1 Samuel 14:4	60n41		
1 Samuel 14:6	60n41	2 Samuel	93, 194
1 Samuel 14:11	60n41	2 Samuel 1:1-10	38
1 Samuel 14:21	36, 38	2 Samuel 1:17-27	8
1 Samuel 13:22	36, 204	2 Samuel 1:19-27	38
1 Samuel 16	43, 64n99	2 Samuel 2 – 9	62n72
1 Samuel 16 – 2 Samuel 5	43	2 Samuel 2 – 4	125
1 Samuel 16 – 18	43	2 Samuel 8	107n31
1 Samuel 16:12	204	2 Samuel 3:3	75
1 Samuel 16:18	43, 204	2 Samuel 5	43, 45, 124, 131n34, 133n58
1 Samuel 17 – 2 Samuel 8	26		
1 Samuel 17	43, 47, 62n74	2 Samuel 5:4	8
1 Samuel 17:1	44, 47, 48	2 Samuel 5:5	116n130
1 Samuel 18 – 20	44	2 Samuel 5:6-16	45
1 Samuel 18	43–4	2 Samuel 5:6-9	121
1 Samuel 18:7	3, 43, 44, 45	2 Samuel 5:6	131n32
1 Samuel 18:20-27	43	2 Samuel 5:7	124, 133n58
1 Samuel 18:30	63n75	2 Samuel 5:9	45
1 Samuel 21	64n99	2 Samuel 5:10	45
1 Samuel 21:9-10	63n74	2 Samuel 5:11-16	45
1 Samuel 21:11-15	49, 50	2 Samuel 5:11	81, 111n78, 127
1 Samuel 22:7-13	48	2 Samuel 5:17-25	44, 45, 46, 63n82
1 Samuel 23:1-13	44	2 Samuel 6	58n26
1 Samuel 23:1	63n78	2 Samuel 7	62n71
1 Samuel 23:5	48, 63n78	2 Samuel 8	197
1 Samuel 23:7-13	48	2 Samuel 8:1	44, 63n76
1 Samuel 23:27-28	52	2 Samuel 8:16-18	141
1 Samuel 24	64n84	2 Samuel 9 – 20	62n72
1 Samuel 25	146	2 Samuel 9	125
1 Samuel 26	64n84	2 Samuel 10	63n81
1 Samuel 26:12	64n84	2 Samuel 16	125
1 Samuel 27 – 31	50	2 Samuel 19	146
1 Samuel 27 – 29	49	2 Samuel 20:24	99
1 Samuel 27:1 – 28:2	49	2 Samuel 20:23-26	141
1 Samuel 27:5-6	45, 52	2 Samuel 21	26, 46, 47
1 Samuel 27:5	64n95	2 Samuel 21:15-22	44, 47
1 Samuel 27:6	64n95	2 Samuel 21:16	63n82
1 Samuel 28 – 31	26, 39	2 Samuel 21:18	63n82
1 Samuel 28	61n59	2 Samuel 21:19	62n74
1 Samuel 28:3-25	49	2 Samuel 21:20	62n82

2 Samuel 21:22	62n82	1 Kings 5:10-13	126
2 Samuel 23	26, 46, 47, 64n86	1 Kings 5:15-25	80, 81, 101, 111n78
2 Samuel 23:1-17	46		
2 Samuel 23:8-12	44	1 Kings 5:16 – 6:38	118n152
2 Samuel 23:9-10	47	1 Kings 5:16-32	118n153
2 Samuel 23:13-17	44, 46	1 Kings 5:17-19	82
2 Samuel 23:13	45, 64n84	1 Kings 5:21	82
2 Samuel 23:18-23	44	1 Kings 5:27-32	99–101, 103, 119n162
2 Samuel 30:24	99		
		1 Kings 6 – 7	99–100, 118n154
1 Kings 1 – 2	62n72	1 Kings 6	90
1 Kings 2:3-40	51	1 Kings 7 – 19	115n129
1 Kings 2:11	*8*	1 Kings 7:1-51	118n152
1 Kings 2:39-46	49	1 Kings 7:8-12	132n42
1 Kings 3 – 11	25, 68–9, 70, 76, 92, 94, 98, 104, 194	1 Kings 7:8	71, 75, 76
		1 Kings 7:13-47	89, 61n57
		1 Kings 7:13-14	114n115, 118n153
1 Kings 3	98, 109n49		
1 Kings 3:1	70, 71, 75	1 Kings 7:45-46	118n153
1 Kings 3:1-2	132n42	1 Kings 7:46	89, 158
1 Kings 3:2	3	1 Kings 7:48-50	90
1 Kings 3:4-28	106	1 Kings 7:51	90
1 Kings 3:4-15	69	1 Kings 8:1 – 9:9	106n13
1 Kings 4 – 5	70, 118n154	1 Kings 8:8	3
1 Kings 4	94–5, 115n129, 136	1 Kings 9 – 10	70
		1 Kings 9	98, 99, 19n9, 98, 118n154
1 Kings 4:1-6	119n162		
1 Kings 4:1	116n130	1 Kings 9:1-9	101
1 Kings 4:2-6	99	1 Kings 9:10-28	118n153
1 Kings 4:6	99, 100, 103	1 Kings 9:10-25	118n152, 132n42
1 Kings 4:7	95, 116n130, 117n145	1 Kings 9:10-14	80, 81, 82, 83, 90, 100, 111n78
1 Kings 4:7-19	117n142	1 Kings 9:13	81, 82
1 Kings 4:7-8a	93	1 Kings 9:15-18	*102*
1 Kings 4:8-19	93, 94, 95, 101, 116n136	1 Kings 9:15-19	100, 101
		1 Kings 9:15-25	99–100
1 Kings 4:9-18	103	1 Kings 9:15	4, 66, 100, 101, 103, 105n2, 128
1 Kings 4:9	58n28, 140		
1 Kings 4:11	98	1 Kings 9:16	71, 75, 76, 78, 101, 126
1 Kings 4:13	98		
1 Kings 4:15	98	1 Kings 9:17-18	101, 103
1 Kings 4:20	94	1 Kings 9:19	101, 119n160
1 Kings 5 – 10	99	1 Kings 9:20-25	100, 101, 103, 118n156
1 Kings 5	99, 100, 114n104, 118n160		
		1 Kings 9:24	75, 76
1 Kings 5:1-12	78	1 Kings 9:26 – 10:29	83
1 Kings 5:7	95, 117n145	1 Kings 9:26-28	80, 83, 84, 87

INDEX LOCORUM 257

1 Kings 9:26	85, 163	1 Kings 12:20	116n130
1 Kings 9:27-28	90	1 Kings 14:21	75
1 Kings 10	72, 86, 91	1 Kings 14:25	8, 110n67, 193
1 Kings 10:1-15	86–7	1 Kings 14:25-26	104, 106n15, 121
1 Kings 10:1-10	83, 87, 108n45	1 Kings 15	98
1 Kings 10:6-9	87, 114n104	1 Kings 15:33	116n130
1 Kings 10:11-12	80, 83–4, 87, 90, 112n88	1 Kings 16	141
		1 Kings 16:31	75
1 Kings 10:12	84, 118n152	1 Kings 20	98
1 Kings 10:13	83, 87	1 Kings 22:48-50	113n95
1 Kings 10:14-15	83, 87	1 Kings 22:49	85, 163
1 Kings 10:16-20	118n152	1 Kings 22:50	113n97
1 Kings 10:16-21	83, 90	1 Kings 24	75
1 Kings 10:18-20	126		
1 Kings 10:22	80, 81, 83–4, 85, 90, 112n89	2 Kings 3	193
		2 Kings 9	141
1 Kings 10:23-27	83	2 Kings 14	113n95
1 Kings 10:23-25	126	2 Kings 14:1-12	58n28
1 Kings 10:25	90	2 Kings 14:22	85
1 Kings 10:26-29	72	2 Kings 16:1	113n97
1 Kings 10:27	90	2 Kings 16:6	85, 113n97
1 Kings 10:28-29	71, 72, 73, 107n22	2 Kings 23:13-14	76
1 Kings 10:29	87, 90	Isaiah 13:12	84
1 Kings 11	74, 98, 100, 108n36, 109n49	Isaiah 23	85
1 Kings 11:1-13	77	Jeremiah 28	141
1 Kings 11:1-8	132n42	Jeremiah 36	135
1 Kings 11:1-6	75		
1 Kings 11:1	75, 76, 77	Ezekiel 27	85
1 Kings 11:2-13	76		
1 Kings 11:7-8	108, 126	Psalm 34:1	49
1 Kings 11:9-13	106n13		
1 Kings 11:14-40	74–5, 80	1 Chronicles 10:1-12	62n61
1 Kings 11:14-25	71	1 Chronicles 11:12-14	47
1 Kings 11:19	74, 75, 108n44	1 Chronicles 11:13	47, 64n85
1 Kings 11:26 – 14:20	108n44	1 Chronicles 11:15-19	46
1 Kings 11:40	70, 71, 74		
1 Kings 11:41	3, 106n11, 106n14, 116n138	2 Chronicles 1:16	107n17
		2 Chronicles 8:5	119n163
1 Kings 11:42	8, 116n130	2 Chronicles 8:7	118n156
1 Kings 12	118n149	2 Chronicles 9:10–11	112n88
1 Kings 12:18	99	2 Chronicles 9:21	83